Mr. Madison's
WAR

Mr. Madison's
WAR

POLITICS, DIPLOMACY, AND WARFARE IN THE EARLY AMERICAN REPUBLIC, 1783-1830

by

J.C.A. STAGG

PRINCETON UNIVERSITY PRESS
PRINCETON, NEW JERSEY

LIBRARY OF CONGRESS CATALOGING IN PUBLICATION DATA WILL BE
FOUND ON THE LAST PRINTED PAGE OF THIS BOOK

THIS BOOK HAS BEEN COMPOSED IN LINOTRON MONTICELLO

CLOTHBOUND EDITIONS OF PRINCETON UNIVERSITY PRESS BOOKS
ARE PRINTED ON ACID-FREE PAPER, AND BINDING MATERIALS ARE
CHOSEN FOR STRENGTH AND DURABILITY. PAPERBACKS, WHILE SATISFACTORY
FOR PERSONAL COLLECTIONS, ARE NOT USUALLY SUITABLE
FOR LIBRARY REBINDING

PRINTED IN THE UNITED STATES OF AMERICA BY PRINCETON
UNIVERSITY PRESS, PRINCETON, NEW JERSEY

Designed by Laury A. Egan

for

ROSEMARY

CONTENTS

★

PREFACE	IX
ACKNOWLEDGMENTS	XV
ABBREVIATIONS	XVII
CHAPTER I THE ROAD TO CANADA, 1783-1812	3
CHAPTER II THE POLITICS OF WAR, 1808-1812	48
CHAPTER III ORGANIZING THE REPUBLIC FOR WAR, 1783-1812	120
CHAPTER IV THE WAR IN THE WEST, 1812-1813	177
CHAPTER V THE WAR IN THE EAST, 1812	227
CHAPTER VI MEN, MONEY, AND MEDIATION, 1812-1813	270
CHAPTER VII POLITICS AND WAR, 1813	304
CHAPTER VIII A WINTER OF DISCONTENT, 1813-1814	348
CHAPTER IX THE CAMPAIGNS OF 1814 AND THE FALL OF WASHINGTON	387
CHAPTER X THE ADMINISTRATION AND CONGRESS, 1814-1815	419
CHAPTER XI THE FINAL CRISES: HARTFORD AND NEW ORLEANS	469
EPILOGUE 1815-1830	501
APPENDIX THREE *National Intelligencer* EDITORIALS ON CANADA	519
INDEX	525

PREFACE

★

THE HISTORICAL LITERATURE on the War of 1812 can be divided into two broad categories. It consists for the most part of a lengthy and inconclusive debate on the causes of the war, and a more diffuse body of writings devoted largely to the operational histories of its various military and naval campaigns. Initially, this study was intended principally as an addition to the second of these categories, the first having become so preoccupied with conflicting theories of causation that it seemed impossible to say anything that had not already been said. The war years seemed more inviting precisely because historical controversy about them was less well developed, and because research on the problems of conducting the war was less detailed. But eventually, I had to deal with the tangled matter of causation as well, since it proved to be impossible to understand the problems of waging the war without having some clearer sense of why the conflict had occurred in the first place. This accounts, in part, for the first two chapters of the study, though it is not my purpose there to weigh the merits of the various historiographical approaches that have been taken to the causes of the war. I have dealt briefly with historiographical issues in other places, but, throughout Chapters I and II, I have sought to concentrate on two questions that need further discussion. The first is why James Madison believed he could win a war against Great Britain, and win it, moreover, by seizing Canada. The second deals with why the war occurred when it did. Much of the narrative relating to this second problem has been told before, but the story requires retelling in order to make more intelligible the dynamics behind the events leading up to the declaration of war.

The remainder of the study is devoted to examining, in the widest sense, the politics of the War of 1812. I have tried here to synthesize several fields of inquiry which relate to the conduct of the war, namely, Anglo-American diplomacy, party politics and ideology, American-Indian relations, federal-state relations, financial policy, internal dissent, and the methods employed to mobilize early American society for waging war. Some, if not all, of these issues have been discussed in previous writings, though not always as fully as they might be. But at the risk of oversimplification, I think it fair to say that, ever since the appearance in the 1890's of Henry Adams's classic history of the Jefferson and Madison administrations, the dominant feature of almost all the literature on the war years has been its emphasis on the sheer ineptitude of the American war effort between 1812 and 1815. That the United States failed to win the war because of bad strategy, inadequate supply, and political and military incompetence has always seemed so obvious to historians as to preclude the need for further discussion. There can, of course, be no denying that evidence of incompetence in many forms is more than abundant for the War of 1812, but an overemphasis on the subject risks making the conflict seem incomprehensible. Indeed, many accounts of the War of 1812, especially those which concentrate only on the period of fighting itself, emerge as narratives of apparently disconnected military disasters. They lack any visible pattern and make no particular sense.

To stress ineptitude as the theme of the War of 1812, however, is to neglect an important, albeit obvious, point about its history—which is that no administration could have actually intended what happened to have occurred. It seemed, therefore, plausible to assume that somewhere there must have existed another conception of what the war was supposed to be about, very different from any notions we might derive on this subject from our reading. Any sense of this conception, however, is almost completely absent from much of the historical literature on the war. Even Henry Adams—whose treatment is often more detailed than that found in many recent works—is usually more intent on insinuating what the Madison administration might have done than he is on presenting its own understanding of its situation with any degree of sympathy. As Madison himself complained in 1827, his war policies were always criticized "more on account of a mismanaged execution than of a mismanaged formation," and the historical balance has still to be redressed. Consequently, it became my purpose to develop a detailed study of what the Madison administration intended to happen in the War of 1812, of how it translated this intention into specific policies, and only then to consider what happened to those policies as they were carried out.

This task proved to be less straightforward than I had anticipated, especially since the administration's conception of the war had to be wrung from documentary materials which themselves seemed to take it for granted rather than make it explicit. And the explanation of many concealed assumptions here eventually required a rather broader approach to the problems of the war than was originally intended. This broader approach, though, provided better insights into the confusion of the war, while it also made it possible to comprehend the conflict as a more significant and integral part of the history of the early American Republic. The incompetence that seemed all-pervasive during the war years was more than simply the failings of so many individuals; rather it was symptomatic of political and administrative problems deeply rooted in the government of American society. Yet the Founding Fathers, including Madison himself, had justified the introduction of a new Constitution in 1789 very much on the grounds that it would provide the United States with a more efficient system of government and prevent a recurrence of the disorder that had characterized the War for Independence. On the face of it, therefore, the experiences of the War of 1812 suggested that some of the constitutional reforms of the 1780's were less successful than their proponents would have wished. Why this was so is still a puzzle, and it cannot be dealt with by arguing—as Henry Adams did—that Madison and his associates had to abandon the inadequate principles of Republicanism in favor of the more realistic policies of Federalism. The much discussed "principles of '98" were only one variant of the principles of Republicanism and by no means a dominant one at that, and even when the Madison administration did emulate some of the measures of Federalism the result was usually no more satisfactory. In short, the War of 1812 was more than merely the crisis of Jeffersonian Republicanism; it was a demanding trial of all the issues and assumptions that were at the heart of post-independence American politics.

For this reason, the study of the War of 1812 must embrace a larger time scale than the one adopted by either Henry Adams or most other historians. The starting point of the inquiry cannot be the advent of the Republican party to power in 1801, but the period following the Peace of Paris in 1783. The problems confronting the United States then—as well as the responses to them by American statesmen at the time—dominated the history of the nation for the next thirty years. Indeed, the War of 1812 might be best understood as the sum total of the difficulties experienced by Americans after 1783 as they labored to establish their experiment in republican government on secure foundations. Despite the many fluctuations of American politics in the thirty years after independence, the continuities of the period are also significant and impressive, and they need to be more strongly emphasized than they have been. Moreover, the War of 1812 did not solve many of the problems confronting the post-revolutionary generation, nor did these same problems just disappear with the Treaty of Ghent and the ending of the Napoleonic wars in Europe. Madison himself realized as much when he lamented in 1819 that the Treaty of Ghent was not "a final adjustment" of all the questions that had so troubled the United States, and he predicted that another war in Europe would see the Republic again added to the number of Great Britain's enemies. Eventually, the passage of time removed the root causes of the War of 1812, and this gave the United States further opportunities for remedying the organizational problems experienced in that conflict. What was most important in this development was not the sudden rise of Anglo-American "friendship" after 1815 but the final dismantling of the colonial world of the eighteenth century as it affected the United States. This can be said to have substantially occurred by 1830 with the emancipation of Latin America and the British decision to throw open the previously protected West Indian trades that had always been the cause of so much Anglo-American conflict.

It is, of course, impossible for one person and one study to do full justice to all the themes outlined here. It has been necessary to oversimplify complex issues, rely heavily on the works of other scholars, and resort to many devices to achieve my purpose. It has also been necessary at times to treat some issues in more than one context. While this may seem to create some overlap in the development of the argument, it is, I feel, essential to separate on occasions the diplomatic, political, and administrative consequences of many policy measures in order to achieve greater analytical clarity. Consequently, some readers may find some problems to be overstudied, while others have been less comprehensively covered than they might have liked. I have, however, tried to devote more space to army administration than is normally the case with works on the War of 1812, though even here the study is still very far from complete. The War Department and the Office of the Adjutant General were, nonetheless, the critical agencies involved in mobilizing the nation for war, and greater knowledge of their workings is essential to further our still limited understanding of the relationship between government and society in the early Republic.

More generally, the difficulties of understanding the broader politics of the war are compounded by the requirement that, ideally, American historians should be equally competent in both state and national affairs. The War of 1812 was not so much one war as a series of conflicts, and the problems they raised were perceived quite differently by Americans according to the level and the location of their involvement. The ideal of equal competence in both local and national history to create a total or a "seamless" conception of America's past can probably never be realized, but I have attempted to integrate the most readily available materials about the politics and the societies of the states most closely involved in the conduct of the War of 1812 in order to relate them to the wider course of events. Finally, too, I have chosen to discuss some of the major problems of the years between 1783 and 1812 by focusing almost wholly on Madison's understanding of them. This tactic, I think, can be justified by Madison's constant involvement in the national politics of the period, as well as by his reputation as one of the more thoughtful and analytic spokesmen of an entire generation of statesmen who were intent on consolidating American independence. In any event, I believe it is possible, within these limitations, to use a study of "Mr. Madison's War" as a means of gaining some broader perspectives on the history of the early American Republic.

ACKNOWLEDGMENTS

★

WHILE PREPARING THIS MANUSCRIPT over the past few years, I have become indebted to many organizations and individuals. For their assistance and permission to examine and use their collections, I am grateful to the staffs of the following institutions: the Maine Historical Society; the Massachusetts Historical Society; the Essex Institute; the Peabody Museum; the Museum of the City of New York; the New-York Historical Society; the New York Public Library; the New York State Library; the Butler Library of Columbia University; the Firestone Library of Princeton University; the Historical Society of Pennsylvania; the Library of Congress; the National Archives of the United States; the Alderman Library of the University of Virginia; the Perkins Library at Duke University; the Southern Historical Collection at the University of North Carolina; and the National Library of Scotland. In New Zealand, the assistance of the University of Auckland Library in obtaining interloan requests is also gratefully acknowledged.

Special thanks are due to the Research and Leave committees of the University of Auckland for research funds and a period of study leave; and for the invaluable support and assistance furnished through the J. Franklin Jameson Fellowship in 1978-1979 I am deeply indebted to the staffs of the American Historical Association and the Library of Congress, particularly Mack Thompson, Eileen Gaylard, Paul Sifton, and Evelyn Sinclair. For the right to examine and use the Legislative Records of the House of Representatives in the National Archives, the permission of the Clerk of the House, Mr. Edmund Henshaw, Jr., is gratefully acknowledged, and I also greatly appreciated the willingness of Roger H. Brown to make available some material he gathered from the Thomas Worthington Papers in the Ross County Historical Society, Chillicothe, Ohio—a collection to which I was otherwise unable to obtain access. In a similar vein, Ronald Hatzenbuehler has shared with me the results of his research over the past few years, and his cooperation has constituted a valuable contact with other scholarship in the field of the early Republic.

Parts of the manuscript have already appeared in two articles in the *William and Mary Quarterly*: "James Madison and the 'Malcontents':

The Political Origins of the War of 1812," 3d Ser., 33 (1976), 557-585; and "James Madison and the Coercion of Great Britain: Canada, the West Indies, and the War of 1812," 3d Ser., 38 (1981), 3-34. I am grateful to the *Quarterly* for permission to incorporate material from these articles into the present work. In typing the manuscript Barbara Batt, Freda Christie, Margaret Spicer, and Sisilia Tonga all provided me with cheerful and efficient service, while at Princeton University Press Gail Filion and William Hively have expertly smoothed its path into publication.

On a more personal note, I have incurred a deep obligation to James M. Banner, Jr., for his interest in this manuscript as it progressed from its origins as a doctoral dissertation at Princeton University. His belief that the War of 1812 would repay fresh and intensive study has sustained me over the years, and he has given freely of his time and energy in reading drafts, making suggestions for improvements, and generally offering his encouragement. Without his efforts, the manuscript could not have been completed. While at Princeton I also benefited greatly from the advice and judgment of Wesley Frank Craven. The assistance and stimulation he gave to students working in early American history was a privilege for which I shall always be grateful. In Auckland, two of my students, Allan Henderson and Murray McLauchlan, have shared my interest in the War of 1812, and they have contributed greatly to those apects of the manuscript bearing on army recruitment and administration. Personal friends, too, have assisted me in various ways over the years, and it is with gratitude that I recall the contributions of Margot and Bob Dewar, Michael and Gill Green, Elizabeth and Barry Vercoe, and Vernon Burton.

To my wife Rosemary, who will, I hope, forgive the indignity of being neglected until the end, I can hardly express my gratitude adequately. For her, the War of 1812 has lasted far longer than it did for James Madison or any of his contemporaries. And that is no small feat of endurance.

ABBREVIATIONS

★

AC   Joseph Gales, comp., [Annals of Congress] *Debates and Proceedings in the Congress of the United States* (Washington, D.C., 1834-1856).

AG   Adjutant General.

ASP   Walter Lowrie et al., eds., *American State Papers: Documents, Legislative and Executive of the Congress of the United States* (Washington, D.C., 1832-1861).

BEHS   Buffalo and Erie County Historical Society.

CHR   Canadian Historical Review.

CULS   Confidential and Unofficial Letters Sent by the Secretary of War (M-7), Records of the Office of the Secretary of War (RG 107), NA.

F.O. 5   (Public Record Office, Great Britain) *Foreign Office*, Series 5 (photostats in LC).

HSP   Historical Society of Pennsylvania.

JM Papers   Robert A. Rutland et al., eds., *The Papers of James Madison* (Chicago and Charlottesville, 1962-).

LC   Library of Congress.

LRAG   Letters Received by the Office of the Adjutant General (M-566), Records of the Adjutant General's Office (RG 94), NA.

LRHR   Legislative Records of the House of Representatives (RG 233), NA.

LRRS   Letters Received by the Secretary of War, Registered Series (M-221), Records of the Office of the Secretary of War (RG 107), NA.

LRUS   Letters Received by the Secretary of War, Unregistered Series (M-222), Records of the Office of the Secretary of War (RG 107), NA.

LSAG   Letters Sent by the Office of the Adjutant General (M-565), Records of the Adjutant General's Office (RG 94), NA.

LSIA   Letters Sent by the Secretary of War Relating to Indian Affairs (M-15), Records of the Bureau of Indian Affairs (RG 75), NA.

LSMA   Letters Sent by the Secretary of War Relating to Military Affairs (M-6), Records of the Office of the Secretary of War (RG 107), NA.

MCNY   Museum of the City of New York.
MeHS   Maine Historical Society.
MHS   Massachusetts Historical Society.
MLDS   Miscellaneous Letters of the Department of State (M-179),
   Records of the Department of State (RG 59), NA.
MVHR   Mississippi Valley Historical Review.
NA   National Archives.
Natl Intelligencer (Washington, D.C.) *National Intelligencer and
   Washington Advertiser.*
NLS   National Library of Scotland.
NYHS   New-York Historical Society.
NYPL   New York Public Library.
NYSL   New York State Library.
OSL   Ohio State Library.
RCHS   Ross County Historical Society.
RCSW   Reports to Congress from the Secretary of War (M-220),
   Records of the Office of the Secretary of War (RG 107), NA.
SHSW   State Historical Society of Wisconsin.
UNC   University of North Carolina.
UVa   University of Virginia.
WMQ   William and Mary Quarterly.

Mr. Madison's
WAR

CHAPTER I

★

THE ROAD TO CANADA,

1783-1812

ON JUNE 19, 1812, President James Madison issued a proclamation announcing that the Congress of the United States had declared war the previous day on the "United Kingdom of Great Britain and Ireland and the dependencies thereof."[1] This declaration was the climax of nearly three decades of troubled relations between the two countries, yet it caught the government of Great Britain unawares and was seen by many Americans as a step of very doubtful expediency. These sentiments arose not from the fact that there was no cause for war but from surprise that the United States, after so deliberately having avoided war in the past, should now abandon that policy and attempt to settle its grievances against Great Britain by force. The risks involved in discarding the cautious neutrality pursued by successive American administrations since 1789 were undeniably very great. The United States was a barely stable republic, untested by the strains of war. Its government, at the time of the declaration, could command little more than six thousand regular troops and a naval force consisting of sixteen vessels of all sizes. Yet with such limited forces the Madison administration had chosen to challenge an enemy that could maintain a navy of over six hundred vessels in active service while also supporting a regular army at home and abroad that totaled nearly one quarter of a million men.[2]

Still, as he proclaimed a state of war, President Madison did not seem unduly daunted by the task that Congress had entrusted to him. As Commander in Chief he donned "a little round hat [with] a huge

[1] See *Natl Intelligencer*, June 20, 1812.
[2] See Harry L. Coles, *The War of 1812* (Chicago, 1965), 43, 71-73; Correlli Barnett, *Britain and Her Army, 1509-1970: A Military, Political and Social Survey* (London, 1970), 258; and Russell F. Weigley, *History of the United States Army* (New York, 1967), 115-116.

cockade" and visited the Navy and War Departments in Washington, exhorting their officials and the public at large to support "all measures which may be adopted ... for obtaining a speedy, a just, and an honorable peace."[3] Just how Madison thought he could obtain such a peace was unclear to many of his contemporaries, but the President, in fact, had often reflected on the problems of making Great Britain respect the international standing of the new Republic. As a delegate from Virginia he had entered the Continental Congress in the difficult days of the Revolution in 1779, and a good portion of his subsequent career in public service had been devoted to the issues of Anglo-American relations. As the future President remarked in 1790, the injuries the United States received from Great Britain formed a "copious subject" which led him to "serious and important considerations," and in the years after the 1783 Peace of Paris he was in the front rank of those statesmen who advocated commercial restrictions as a diplomatic weapon against the former mother country.[4] By 1812, however, the diplomacy of commercial restriction had been tried and found wanting. In its place Madison sought, and Congress agreed to adopt, a policy of waging war. The goal was to invade and occupy Great Britain's Canadian possessions, and for a period of thirty months after June 1812 the United States tried consistently, albeit unsuccessfully, to realize that ambition.

The motives behind this Canadian policy were the subject of much speculation. Contemporaries, particularly if they opposed the Madison administration, hinted at unworthy desires for territorial aggrandizement—motives which the President and his colleagues always denied. Canada would be invaded, asserted Secretary of State James Monroe, "not as an object of the war but as a means to bring it to a satisfactory conclusion."[5] Yet there can be little doubt that, had the War 1812 been a successful military venture, the Madison administration would have been reluctant to have returned occupied Canadian territory to the enemy. At the same time that Monroe was denying that the United States sought to annex Canada, he was also instructing the American chargé d'affaires in London, Jonathan Russell, to inform the British government that once American forces had entered the British provinces it would be very "difficult to relinquish territory which had been conquered." A successful war in Canada, Monroe pointed out, would for a variety of reasons "present very serious obstacles to an accom-

[3] Richard Rush to Benjamin Rush, June 20, 1812, Benjamin Rush Papers, Library Company of Philadelphia Papers, HSP. *Natl Intelligencer*, June 20, 1812.

[4] AC, 1st Cong., 1st sess., 213.

[5] James Monroe to John Taylor, June 13, 1812, James Monroe Papers, LC.

modation" with Great Britain.[6] Behind such ambiguous, if not contradictory, statements about the objects of the war, however, lay a body of important assumptions.

Americans, of course, had always been interested in the fate of Canada, especially when that region was held by a hostile power. In 1812, as had been the case in the earlier colonial wars on the North American continent, they were drawn to the strategy of invading enemy territory to the north by considerations arising both from the right of retaliation under the law of nations and from the obvious fact of geographical proximity.[7] Moreover, Canada was undoubtedly vulnerable. With a total population of barely half a million, the various provinces of Canada seemed to be the weakest links in the chain of British imperial power, and many Americans assumed that they could be easily seized by the United States, with its vastly superior population of nearly seven and one half million.[8] Yet Canada did not seem in itself to be the source of the most important grievances that the United States wished to settle by war. The purpose of the War of 1812 was to break various manifestations of the British navigation system—the Orders in Council, impressment on the high seas, illegal blockades, the "rule of '56"—as they oppressed Americans during Britain's long struggle with Napoleonic France, and a war for Canada seemed to bear little direct relationship to this goal. Although many Americans declared that the seizure of Canada would enable the United States to wrest a pledge of good behavior from the Royal Navy, such statements by no means made it clear why Britain would abandon the belligerent measures it had adopted for the defense of its navigation system on account of the loss of some, or even all, of its Canadian territories. For this reason, most opponents of the war never ceased to point out that the conquest of Canada promised neither to guarantee respect for American maritime rights nor even to reimburse the nation for the expense of the effort. As John Randolph of Roanoke put it with his customary exaggeration: "What is Canada toward the enforcement of our commercial rights? No more than a *Froggy Man's* mountains."[9] Similar doubts, though,

[6] Monroe to Jonathan Russell, June 26, 1812, Diplomatic Instructions: All Countries (M-77), Records of the Department of State (RG 59), NA.

[7] For a brief discussion of these points see Alfred T. Mahan, *Sea Power in its Relations to the War of 1812* (Boston, 1905), I, 292-296. See also *Natl Intelligencer*, February 4, 1812.

[8] Coles, *The War of 1812*, 38. The best-known statement of American optimism about the ease of seizing Canada was Thomas Jefferson's claim that "the acquisition of Canada . . . as far as the neighborhood of Quebec will be a mere matter of marching." To William Duane, August 4, 1812, Thomas Jefferson Papers, LC.

[9] John Randolph to Richard K. Randolph, February 7, 1812, John Randolph Papers, LC. See also John Taylor to Monroe, May 10, June 18, 1812, Monroe Papers, LC, and

were shared by some of the war's supporters, including Senator Jesse Franklin of North Carolina, who confessed that he too could not see how taking Canada would "settle the issue about which we are now like to get to war, that is our *Commercial Rights*. . . ." As for territory, he added, "God knows we [have] enough already."[10]

Madison was untroubled by these criticisms and seldom bothered to comment on them in detail, either in his public statements or in his private correspondence. In the period between his decision to prepare the Republic for war and the end of the conflict in February 1815, the President was more preoccupied with denouncing the malignant consequences of the British policies he wanted to resist than he was in explaining the strategic role of Canada.[11] Consequently, the motives behind Madison's policy of trying to seize Canada remained obscure for many of his contemporaries, the more so as they became increasingly disenchanted with his mismanagement of a war effort that seemed hardly likely to jeopardize Britain's possession of Canada at all. Yet it cannot be seriously imagined that Madison, a statesman with a deserved reputation as a systematic thinker, gave no thought to how a Canadian war might relieve the United States from the burdens of the British navigation system, especially when he had spent much of his public life studying how that system harmed the interests of his country.[12] Indeed, one reason why Madison may have neglected to explain his Canadian policy was the simple fact that it was quite obvious to him, a close observer of British affairs, what role Canada played in the minds of his British adversaries. It was against these adversaries, especially the most determined defenders of the navigation system, that Madison's Canadian war was waged, and, had the war been successful, Madison had good reason to believe that the British government would have been extremely alarmed by the loss of Canada and would have been compelled to pay greater respect to American maritime rights.

---

the protest of the Massachusetts legislature against the war, June 5, 1812, *ASP: Miscellaneous*, II, 186-187.

[10] Jesse Franklin to William Lenoir, February 15, 1812, Lenoir Family Papers, UNC. See also Burwell Bassett to Josiah Bartlett, January 13, 1813, Josiah Bartlett Papers, LC.

[11] For a classic example of Madison's way of justifying war see his letter to the South Carolina House of Representatives, January 8, 1812, James Madison Papers, LC.

[12] For a brief discussion of this point see Richard Glover, "The French Fleet, 1807-1814; Britain's Problem, and Madison's Opportunity," *Journal of Modern History* 39 (1967), esp. 249-252. Glover raises the problem of Canada in relation to Madison's weighing the chances for success in a war with Britain. His argument—that Madison was probably aware that the strength of the Royal Navy by 1812 was less formidable than it seemed and that he counted on France defeating Britain in the European war—is sound enough, but it neglects to explore the importance that Canada itself might have had in the President's calculations.

The basis for this assumption depends not on anything the President wrote or said during the War of 1812—as opposed to what he tried to do—so much as it rests on the view that the attempt to conquer Canada was both a logical sequel to Madison's entire mode of thinking about Anglo-American relations after 1783 and a natural reaction to the problems he encountered in trying to translate that thinking into working policy. Once the problem of Canada has been placed in this broader perspective, though, it is apparent that there was a very considerable degree of continuity in the assumptions underlying *all* the policies Madison pursued toward Britain throughout his long public career. And, paradoxical though it may seem, Madison's decision to wage war for Canada was not basically inconsistent with the diplomacy of peaceful commercial restriction he had advocated prior to 1812, a policy he hoped would enable the United States to avoid hostilities with Britain. In fact, given the circumstances Madison had to confront by 1812, the policy of a Canadian war followed logically from his previous diplomatic strategies. All along, Madison assumed that the British empire needed the raw materials of North America. Thus, he believed that efforts to restrict British access to those resources would be instrumental in coercing Britain to accept American definitions of its rights as a neutral nation. For by 1812 Canada had become an integral part of the British trade in American resources, and it was for this reason that the United States made the attempt to deprive Britain of its remaining North American colonies.

★

WHILE THE ELEMENTS of economic theory that went into Madison's diplomacy of commercial restriction can, to some extent, be understood through reference to the writings of the European Enlightenment as well as the Scottish school of political economy, it is necessary to stress here that their development as policies was governed by the commercial relationships between Great Britain and the United States after 1783 and, more importantly, by the British justification for those relationships.[13] Of great significance in this respect was the British decision— embodied in the Order in Council of July 2, 1783—to deny the United States any of their former commercial privileges in the trade of the empire, particularly the West Indian trade, and the arguments put forward in support of that decision by John Baker Holroyd, first Earl of Sheffield, in his pamphlet *Observations on the Commerce of the Amer-*

[13] See Drew R. McCoy, *The Elusive Republic: Political Economy in Jeffersonian America* (Chapel Hill, 1980); and Ralph Ketcham, "The Mind of James Madison," (Ph.D. diss., Syracuse University, 1956).

ican States.[14] The outline of Sheffield's ideas is well known, especially his assertions that the United States were by definition not a nation and that America had no future, and therefore its independence had been for Britain a blessing in disguise. But the distinctive impact of Sheffield's lifelong defense of the British navigation system and his vision of a reconstructed British empire on an entire generation of quarreling Englishmen and Americans after 1783 has perhaps been less clearly understood. This impact, however, was central to Madison's study and understanding of the problems of Anglo-American relations, and his own policies of commercial restriction were conceived very much in response to it.

Sheffield developed his case for keeping the United States in a subordinate position by analyzing the commerce between the two nations under four headings: British exports to America; American exports to Britain; and American exports to and imports from the West Indies. Most of the goods, Sheffield believed, that Britain had traditionally sent to the United States, notably its manufactures, would continue to be brought by Americans because they had no alternative source of supply, and could not, for various reasons, manufacture locally. Even where Americans could establish manufactures, the Englishman dismissed them as expensive and shoddy, which thus obtained for their British counterparts a continuing market based on lower cost and superior quality. American exports to Britain, largely bulky raw materials, posed rather more difficulty, but among them Sheffield claimed that tobacco alone was of any real value, and then only as an item in Britain's entrepôt trade. Most of the other commodities could be obtained either from the rest of the empire or from the Baltic region. The American trades with the West Indies were dealt with in a similar manner; Britain itself and its other colonies, principally Canada and Ireland, could supply the West Indies equally as well as the United States. Even where there might be difficulties, as with the furnishing of lumber, the transition could be eased by compensating West Indian planters with lower duties on their exports to the mother country.[15]

The purpose of this analysis was to justify the treatment of Americans as foreigners and, as such, make them subject to the British navigation laws.[16] Since these laws were widely regarded as the foundation of

[14] 2d ed. (London, 1784).

[15] Sheffield, *Observations*, 9-129. For a brief discussion of Sheffield's views and their background see Gerald S. Graham, *British Policy and Canada, 1774-1791: A Study in Eighteenth Century Trade Policy* (London, 1930), 33, 35, 36, 56-72.

[16] For a more detailed discussion of the subject of allegiance in relation to trade privileges see George Chalmers, *Opinions on Interesting Questions of Public Law and Commercial Policy*

British commercial and naval supremacy, Sheffield believed that to relax them for the benefit of Americans would be to tolerate a ruinous competition for trade which would ultimately destroy Britain as a major power. His demonstration that it was possible to reconstitute the British empire as a self-sufficient economic unit was made all the more attractive by his prediction that Britain could continue enjoying the advantages both of dominating the American market and of carrying its own trade there. With "prudent management," he wrote, Britain "will have as much of [America's] trade as it will be in her interest to wish for."[17] Nor did Sheffield expect any serious American reaction to this state of affairs, mainly because the Articles of Confederation provided for a government no more effective than that of the Diet of Germany. He conceded that some Americans would indulge themselves in "puerile insolence," but that they might close their markets or withhold their products in protest he dismissed as a "possibility too ridiculous to be insisted on."[18]

The restrictive policies of Britain as well as the offensive arguments of Sheffield—some of which he repeated in a pamphlet on Irish trade in 1785—provoked strong reactions on both sides of the Atlantic, including a sizable polemical literature not unlike that which had surrounded the controversy over annexing Canada or Guadeloupe to the British empire after 1760.[19] Among the best-known pamphlets published in Britain were those by Edward Long and Bryan Edwards, both writing as spokesmen for the West Indian planters, while the most comprehensive assault on all Sheffield's positions was written by Richard Champion, a Bristol china manufacturer of liberal opinions who had been Deputy Paymaster of the Forces in the early 1780's before resigning his office in disgust at the Treaty of Paris to settle in South Carolina in 1784.[20] In the United States, Tench Coxe's seven

---

arising from American Independence (London, 1784), 3-19. Chalmers was a Maryland Loyalist whose thinking on trade problems was similar to that of Lord Sheffield. See Grace Amelia Cockroft, The Public Life of George Chalmers (New York, 1939).

[17] Sheffield, Observations, 135.

[18] Ibid., 185, 198.

[19] Sheffield's pamphlet on Ireland was Observations on the Manufactures, Trade and Present State of Ireland (London, 1785), see 88-91. For the Canada-Guadeloupe debate see William L. Grant, "Canada versus Guadeloupe, An Episode of the Seven Years War," American Historical Review 17 (1912), 735-743.

[20] Edward Long, A Free and Candid Review of a Tract Entitled 'Observations on the Commerce of the American States': Shewing the Pernicious Consequences both to Great Britain and to the Sugar Islands of the Systems recommended in that Tract (London, 1784). Bryan Edwards, Thoughts on the Late Proceedings of Government Respecting the Trade of the West India Islands with the United States of North America (London, 1784). Richard Champion,

critical essays, which were assembled under the title of *A Brief Inquiry into the Observations of Lord Sheffield*, were the most extended American response.[21] Madison too had been in the forefront of the protests against the British decision to subject the American states to the navigation laws with his sponsorship of the retaliatory Virginia Port Bill of 1784; he also greatly admired Coxe's pamphlet and may have even sent a copy of it, in vain, to Lord Sheffield for his instruction.[22] And there is, furthermore, no doubt that Madison was thoroughly familiar with almost all of the writings of Lord Sheffield as well as those of his opponents, for he noted on one occasion that the issues they raised were "coeval with our political birth and [have] at all times exercized the thought of reflecting citizens."[23] Madison drew on these writings

---

Considerations on the Present Situation of Great Britain and the United States of America with a View to their Future Commercial Connections, Containing Remarks upon the Pamphlet published by Lord Sheffield, entitled 'Observations on the Commerce of the American States with some Observations upon the State of Canada, Nova Scotia, and the Fisheries; and upon the Connexions of the West Indies with America: Together with various accounts, necessary to shew the State of Trade and Shipping of both Countries (London, 1784). The pamphlet by Champion was a second, enlarged edition of a similarly titled work, also published in 1784, which attacked the first edition of Lord Sheffield's *Observations* and drew unfavorable comments from Sheffield in the second edition of his pamphlet. See C. H. Guttridge, ed., *The American Correspondence of a Bristol Merchant, 1766-1776; Letters of Richard Champion* (Berkeley, 1934), 8.

[21] (Philadelphia, 1791). Some other pamphlets to appear were James Allen, *Considerations on the Present State of the Intercourse between His Majesty's Sugar Colonies and the Dominions of the United States of America* (London, 1784); (William Bingham), *A Letter from an American Now Resident in London to a Member of Parliament on the Subject of the Restraining Proclamation and Containing Strictures on Lord Sheffield's Pamphlet on the Commerce of the American States* (London, 1784); [Anon., but attributed to a Mr. Ruston], *Remarks on Lord Sheffield's Observations on the Commerce of the American States; by an American* (London, 1784). In the controversy, Sheffield received support from Arthur Young, "Considerations on the Connection between the Agriculture of England and the Commercial Policy of Her Sugar Islands, Particularly Respecting a Free Trade with North America," *Annals of Agriculture* 1 (1784), 437ff; and John Stevenson, *An Address to Bryan Edwards Esq., Containing Remarks on his Pamphlet . . . Also Observations on some parts of a Pamphlet, lately published by the West India Planters entitled "Considerations on the Present State of the Intercourse etc. etc."* (London, 1784).

[22] On the Virginia Port Bill see Robert Bittner, "Economic Independence and the Virginia Port Bill of 1784," Richard A. Rutyna and Peter C. Stewart, eds., *Virginia in the American Revolution* (Norfolk, Va., 1977), 73-92; and Drew R. McCoy, "The Virginia Port Bill of 1784," *Virginia Magazine of History and Biography* 83 (1975), 288-303. For Madison's sending Coxe's pamphlet to Sheffield see Jacob Cooke, *Tench Coxe and the Early Republic* (Chapel Hill, 1978), 206. Sheffield certainly received a copy of Coxe's pamphlet from an American in the early 1790's and, Coxe later learned, was most annoyed at the criticisms of his work. See Cooke, *Tench Coxe*, 208.

[23] AC, 3d Cong., 1st sess., 210. Madison to Edmund Randolph, May 20, 1783, *JM Papers*, VII, 61. See also Madison to Jefferson, July 31, 1791, Madison Papers, LC.

freely—especially those by Champion, Coxe, and Edwards—to the point where he occasionally even lifted key words and phrases, blending them with his own thoughts and feelings derived from his wider reading and active role in public affairs. As he did so, his policies toward Britain became part of a transatlantic debate on the future development of the political economies of the United States and the British empire.[24]

Madison rejected all of Lord Sheffield's arguments save one—the Englishman's derogatory comparison between the Continental Congress and the Diet of Germany. The truth behind the slur, though, only encouraged the Virginian in his efforts to bring about constitutional reform in the 1780's. Because Madison believed that the United States had yet to reap the full benefits of the changes set in motion by the American Revolution—which he told Lafayette in 1785 should lead to a "further revolution in the commerce between the old and the new world"—he was one of the earliest advocates of a broad national power over commerce, including the avowed aim of passing an American navigation act for the purpose of retaliating against Britain.[25] Since Sheffield's views still held sway in the British government as the new federal government came into existence in America, Madison introduced in Congress between 1790 and 1794, as an accompaniment to

[24] Madison became acquainted with Sheffield's *Observations* while in the Continental Congress. See Madison to Randolph, August 30, 1783, *JM Papers*, VII, 295-296. Jefferson read Edwards's attack on Sheffield in 1784 and appears to have been influenced by it in drawing up some notes on Sheffield's views in 1784. Jefferson then sent Edwards's pamphlet to Madison—see Jefferson to Madison, July 1, 1784, Julian P. Boyd, ed., *The Papers of Thomas Jefferson* (Princeton, 1950–), VII, 356-357. Jefferson also lent Madison his notes on Lord Sheffield in 1790-1791, and a copy of them may be found in the Madison Papers, LC, under the heading "Notes on Exports and Navigations." Jefferson, Madison, and Coxe obviously reread much of this polemical literature between 1790 and 1794, drawing on it in preparing their speeches and reports for Congress. See Boyd, *Papers of Jefferson*, XIX, 121-139. At this time Madison also read Champion's pamphlet—in the second 1784 edition, to judge by the pagination he cited—as well as rereading the one by Edwards. He relied on them both extensively in compiling data on British imports, insurance rates in wartime, and on the costs of supplying the West Indies. In Madison's "Notes on Trade and Shipping for a Speech in Congress," May 14, 1790, both Sheffield and Champion are cited several times. The notes also contain a rhetorical question asking how the West Indies fared during the American Revolution, to which the answer was "very badly"; the islands had to divert labor "to less profitable cultivation to avoid starving." If Madison did not paraphrase these remarks from Champion's *Considerations*, 160-161, he certainly took them from some other pamphlet, for this was a problem every critic of Sheffield raised, usually in exactly the same form and language.

[25] See Madison's "Ancient and Modern Confederacies" (1786), *JM Papers*, IX, 4-24; Madison to Lafayette, March 20, 1785, *JM Papers*, VIII, 252; and Madison to George Washington, August 24, 1788, *JM Papers*, XI, 241.

Thomas Jefferson's reports on the state of American fisheries and commerce, a series of discriminatory tariff and tonnage duties against nations refusing to trade with the United States on reciprocal terms.[26] The details of Madison's proposals by 1790 were not especially original—the duties being similar to those discussed in the Continental Congress in 1783, while Madison added to them the tonnage clauses of the Virginia Port Bill—but collectively their purpose was to weaken British commercial power while strengthening that of the United States.

By proposing discriminatory tariff duties against Britain, Madison intended to undermine Lord Sheffield's system as it operated on the patterns of Anglo-American trade. Tonnage duties levied in favor of American navigation would encourage its expansion, thereby enabling it to carry a greater volume of American produce to the markets of the world while at the same time furnishing the human and material resources for naval power and self-defense in the event of war. The discrimination in tariffs was designed to encourage foreign goods and merchants to compete with the British, for the ascendancy of the latter rested, Madison believed, on the lack of competition together with the habitual American acceptance of outmoded colonial practices.

If foreign trade and navigation thus won a larger share of the American market, the United States would be progressively released from British commercial control. The drain of specie from America to pay for British goods imported in British bottoms would also be stemmed, and the United States could begin building up a favorable balance of trade. Furthermore, tariff duties might encourage Americans to supply some of their own manufacturing needs, or, more simply, to do without such goods altogether. Even if the economy was not stimulated by such abstinence, the republican virtue of the people would be; for Madison had long feared the "corrupting" influence of British imports and capital.[27] In all these ways, therefore, the policies of commercial discrimination would complete and consolidate the work of the Revolution.

In defense of these policies, Madison declared that he wished to begin making the commercial relationship between Britain and the

[26] Madison to Jefferson, June 30, 1789, Madison Papers, LC. Of interest here is the official British document, written by Lord Hawkesbury, in Jefferson's Papers, LC, entitled *Report of a Committee of the Privy Council on the Trade of Great Britain with the United States*, January 1791. Jefferson no doubt showed this to Madison, and it is to this same report that Madison is probably referring in his *Political Observations*, April 20, 1795. See Congressional Edition, *Letters and Other Writings of James Madison* (Philadelphia, 1865), IV, 489, 503.

[27] AC, 1st Cong., 1st sess., 190, 192, 209; AC, 3d Cong., 1st sess., 214-213, 222, 391. See also Madison to Randolph, April 8, 1783, *JM Papers*, VI, 439.

United States more nearly equal. Yet to call for greater reciprocity between the two nations was also to desire a significant reduction in Britain's present status, and, as this process occurred, Madison believed that his discriminatory policies would operate in ways to make Britain amenable to the demands of American foreign policy. This expectation was based on a number of considerations. Madison knew from his reading of history that England had used its own navigation acts in the seventeenth century to challenge the power of Holland, but probably more important, he knew how senseless were Lord Sheffield's assertions that Britain could control American commerce without making concessions in return.[28] There had been a growing awareness among British political economists in the eighteenth century that the American colonies had been making a vital contribution to British power, especially in the wars with France, and in that sense it had already been argued that Britain was bound to become increasingly dependent on America rather than less so. Since all commerce was assumed to originate in apprehended or actual wants, it was illogical for Sheffield to argue that Britain no longer needed American trade to the extent that it had needed it before independence.[29] If America had made Britain great, its greatness could hardly continue without America, and Madison on more than one occasion specifically attacked Lord Sheffield for his claim that the old colonial system could bring prosperity to a greatly shrunken British empire without taking into consideration the contribution of the United States.[30]

The past and present manifestations of Britain's impressive commercial and naval strength were, then, in Madison's eyes, likely to become the very sources of its future weakness. The British empire, Lord Sheffield's optimistic predictions about its self-sufficiency notwithstanding, still needed to import raw materials to help manufacture

[28] See Madison's "Notes on Trade and Shipping," May 14, 1790, Madison Papers, LC.

[29] The influence of Adam Smith on Madison is often detected in this line of thought, but Madison could have become acquainted with these ideas in the works of any number of Smith's contemporaries, including Benjamin Franklin. See, for example, Joshua Gee, *The Trade and Navigation of Great Britain Considered* (5th ed., London, 1750); and Josiah Tucker, *A Brief Essay on the Advantages and Disadvantages which Respectively Attend France and Great Britain with Regard to Trade* (2d ed., London, 1750). Particularly important in stressing the American contribution to British power was a work often used by Madison: Adam Anderson, *An Historical and Chronological Deduction of the Origin of Commerce from the Earliest Accounts Containing an History of the Commercial Interests of the British Empire* (2 vols., London, 1764), esp. I, xxx-xliii. All these titles were on a 1783 list of books Madison recommended for purchase by the Continental Congress. For a discussion of Franklin's thought see Gerald Stourzh, *Benjamin Franklin and American Foreign Policy* (2d ed., Chicago, 1969), 66-104; and McCoy, *The Elusive Republic*, 48-75.

[30] AC, 3d Cong., 1st sess., 233, 379.

or process its exports, and a nation which thus relied on exports had, Madison believed, a vulnerable economy. This vulnerability was heightened by those exports being, so Madison declared, "luxuries" or "superfluities" which most nations might do without, while American exports were "necessaries" which no nation, least of all Britain and its West Indian colonies, could forgo.[31] Because the United States was both a large market for British exports as well as a provider of British imports, Madison felt that the operation of commercial restrictions—ranging from discriminatory duties through bans on imports and embargoes to complete nonintercourse—could place the United States in an advantageous position.[32] In the last analysis, British power depended on the credit of the nation, which, in turn, rested on commerce; and by damaging British commerce the United States could strike at the very heart of the British system of government.[33] This situation could be exploited for diplomatic purposes, especially if Congress should delegate control of the restrictions to the President. This would enable the American executive, as Madison put it, "to speak a language proper for the occasion" in dealing with the ministers of the Crown, who had the advantage of being able to regulate British trade through Orders in Council.[34]

The single most important diplomatic goal Madison wanted to attain in the 1790's was American entry into the carrying trade of the British West Indies. The need for this was all the more urgent since Britain, as a result of the 1783 exclusion, was successfully encouraging this trade as a new branch of its navigation at the expense of American merchants.[35] In this matter Madison believed he acted as a representative not only for Virginia, whose planters eagerly sought to sell surplus wheat to the Caribbean, but also for the New England merchants, whose interests too had been harmed by the British exclusion.[36] Since Madison well understood that the West Indies had throughout the

[31] AC, 1st Cong., 1st sess., 256; 3d Cong., 1st sess., 216.

[32] AC, 1st Cong., 1st sess., 248; 3d Cong., 1st sess., 156-157, 605, 682. See also Madison to Jefferson, March 2 and 9, 1794, Madison Papers, LC.

[33] *Political Observations*, Cong. Ed., *Writings*, IV, 487-502.

[34] AC, 1st Cong. 1st sess., 248; 1st Cong., 2d sess., 163.

[35] Madison to Monroe, August 9, 1789, Madison Papers, LC. AC, 1st Cong., 2d sess., 1626. For discussions of the background to this issue see F. Lee Benns, *The American Struggle for the British West India Carrying Trade, 1815-1830* (Bloomington, 1923), chap. 1; and Frederick W. Marks III, *Independence on Trial: Foreign Affairs and the Making of the Constitution* (Baton Rouge, 1973), 70-77.

[36] Madison to Richard Henry Lee, July 7, 1785, *JM Papers*, VIII, 315. For the effectiveness of British restrictions in reducing American participation in the West India carrying trade see Curtis P. Nettels, *The Emergence of a National Economy, 1775-1815* (New York, 1962), 55-56.

1780's suffered extensive famine from war and hurricanes, he believed that discriminating against British trade would compound the difficulties of supplying the islands. A further demand that American produce could only be taken to the West Indies in American bottoms, he declared, would soon lead to "very different language" from Britain about the terms of American trade, and he also claimed that the brief embargo imposed by Congress in 1794 had been instrumental in moderating Britain's anti-American policies because of the "known effect of that measure in the West Indies."[37] Alternatively, the United States could strike at the prosperity of Britain itself by restricting its own imports from that country, and Madison spent some mental energy in calculating how many people across the Atlantic would be "driven to poverty and despair" by such actions.[38] While political opponents argued that Madison exaggerated the power of the United States to accomplish its diplomatic goals in this way, Madison believed he was justified, both by the fears of many British economists that the growth of population was outstripping resources and by the problems of "scarcity" in Britain resulting from bad harvests throughout the 1790's. All through his life, Madison was convinced that "in proportion as a nation manufactures luxuries" it would always be "at a disadvantage with its customers."[39]

As he explored these sources of British weakness, Madison concluded that Britain could only remain prosperous so long as its navigation could constantly enlarge its markets, monopolize the trade routes of the world, and then rely on the Royal Navy for protection. To this need for commerce Madison thus attributed Britain's frequent involve-

[37] AC, 1st Cong., 1st sess., 248-249; 1st Cong., 2d sess., 1626; 3d Cong., 1st sess., 216, 274, 392. Madison to Jefferson, May 25, 1794, Madison Papers, LC; and see also *Political Observations*, Cong. Ed., *Writings*, IV, 500. For discussions of West Indian hardship see Lowell J. Ragatz, *The Fall of the Planter Class in the British Caribbean, 1763-1833* (New York, 1928), 142-173; and Richard B. Sheridan, "The Crisis of Slave Subsistence in the British West Indies during and after the American Revolution," *WMQ* 3d Ser., 33 (1976), 615-641.

[38] AC, 1st Cong., 2d sess., 1626; 3d Cong., 1st sess., 215. On material taken from Anderson's *Historical Deduction*, Madison calculated that nonimportation could put 300,000 people out of work in Great Britain. See as well his observations in January 1791 on how to reduce Great Britain's share of American imports to one-seventh of its existing level. "Notes on Exports and Navigations," Madison Papers, LC.

[39] AC, 3d Cong., 1st sess., 174, 216. Madison to Edmund Pendleton, December 6, 1792; to Jefferson, December 27, 1795; and to James Madison, Sr., January 17, 1796, Madison Papers, LC. The elements of "Malthusian" population theory were available to students of political economy long before the appearance of Thomas Malthus's celebrated pamphlet in 1798. Madison very probably became familiar with them while reading the works of Sir William Petty, Benjamin Franklin, David Hume, and Sir James Steuart. For a brief discussion see Kenneth Smith, *The Malthusian Controversy* (London, 1951), 3-32.

ment in war throughout the eighteenth century, but he believed that by the mid-1790's the reliance of her trade on her military and naval prowess was becoming a disadvantage. The cost of the British war establishments required burdensome taxes and excises which robbed the people of the rewards of their labor, while the servicing of the massive national debt had increasingly corrupted her once "republican" political system by conferring power on interests which were tempted to pursue still greater power and prosperity through selfish means in conflict with the public good.[40] Moreover, the purposes and methods of British war-making offended many European nations, particularly in the resource-rich Baltic region, on which the Royal Navy had become heavily dependent for ship timber and naval stores. Britain thus seemed to be vulnerable to the risks of diplomatic isolation, while the social strains created by war threatened upheaval at home. Indeed, Madison did not entirely dismiss the possibility that Britain would suffer the loss of its trade from a combination of rival European powers and undergo internal revolution as a consequence, which would bring in its aftermath another republic in the concert of nations.[41] Thus, in a period when Madison believed that the progression of events was toward freer trade and freer governments, Britain would, as he understood its situation, be hard pressed to maintain its "monopolizing" practices of the past. On this basis, he was confident that despite the failure of his commercial resolutions to pass into law in the 1790's, the Republic could still risk a trial of economic strength with its greatest rival. Britain *was* "more vulnerable in her commerce than her armies," and if the United States had the disposition for waging a commercial war, it could, Madison claimed, surely "vindicate [its] cause."[42]

★

THE CONCLUSIONS which Madison reached during the 1780's and the 1790's about the usefulness of commercial restriction remained unaltered after he became Secretary of State in 1801, as did his attitudes

[40] See Madison's "Notes made for Mr. Jefferson," December 16, 1793, Madison Papers, LC. AC, 3d Cong., 1st sess., 217. See also Madison's essays on "British Government," January 28, 1792, and "Universal Peace," February 2, 1792, in Cong. Ed., *Writings*, IV, 469-472; and *Political Observations*, Cong. Ed., *Writings*, IV, 501.

[41] Madison to Pendleton, September 12, 1780, November 7, 1780, *JM Papers*, II, 82, 165; to Jefferson, May 1, 1781, *JM Papers*, III, 97; to Arthur Lee, May 28, 1782, *JM Papers*, IV, 293; to Madison Sr., July 2, 1790, Madison Papers, LC; to Horatio Gates, March 24, 1794, Gaillard Hunt ed., *The Writings of James Madison* (New York, 1900-1910), VI, 208-209; to Jefferson, November 16, 1794, Madison Papers, LC; to Monroe, December 4, 1794, Madison Papers, LC; to [Alexander James Dallas?], August 23, 1795, James Madison Papers, NYPL; to Jefferson, February 7 and May 22, 1796, and January 10, 1801, Madison Papers, LC. See also AC, 3d Cong., 1st sess., 384.

[42] AC 1st Cong., 1st sess. 214; *Political Observations*, Cong. Ed., *Writings*, IV, 492.

toward Britain.[43] The application of these ideas in specific situations, however, was no simple matter, and here Madison was to experience many difficulties. In dealing with Britain he could theoretically draw on a variety of responses, depending on the seriousness of a particular problem, but despite the steady worsening of Anglo-American relations after 1803, the administration of Thomas Jefferson made no real attempt to coerce Britain before the embargo crisis of 1807 to 1809. This belated response to harmful British maritime policies might be explained in a number of ways. Retaliatory duties, for example—which had been designed to encourage the growth of American navigation—were ruled out by the terms of Jay's Treaty, complicated by American sectional rivalries, and then rendered largely irrelevant by the enormous increase in American tonnage during the Napoleonic wars.[44] Of more importance, though, was Jefferson's willingness to allow the coercive potential of American commercial policy to be subordinated to other considerations which required him to maintain reasonably good relations with Britain. This was particularly true for American territorial ambitions in the south involving difficulties with Spain. Jefferson also hoped, the more so as his retirement approached, that the restoration of peace in Europe would spare him the necessity of finding a permanent solution for problems with Britain. As he admitted to the British minister, David Erskine, in November 1808, he had always thought that the United States and Britain could have "shoved along" and made some reasonable compromises, leaving time to take care of their more fundamental differences.[45]

[43] Many of Madison's views became standard fare in the columns of the *National Intelligencer*, where it became something of a ritual to reprint his speeches in Congress between 1790 and 1794. These reprintings were often accompanied by essays which re-argued, almost to the point of plagiarism, Madison's ideas about the effect of commercial restrictions on the British economy. While it would do little violence to Madison's thought to identify him as the author of these pieces, it is very difficult to do so with certainty on more than only a few occasions. Madison undoubtedly contributed personally to the administration newspaper, but on many occasions he may have done little more than suggest the outlines of an argument and left the editor to fill in the details. Some of the relevant editorials here are those dated December 2, 1801; November 8, 13, 18, 20, 22, and 25, 1805; January 31, 1806; February 3 and 17, 1806; November 28, 1806; July 22, 29, and 31, 1807; August 3, 7, 12, 14, and 19, 1807; December 21, 23, and 28, 1807; January 4, 1808; April 26, 1809; May 1, 1809; July 30, 1809; August 8 and 13, 1810; October 15, 19, and 22, 1810; November 15, 1810; April 16, 1811; and October 8, 1811.

[44] See William Thornton's dispatches to the British Foreign Office of December 18, 1801; January 2, 1802; May 1, 1802; February 1 and 25, 1803; and October 3, 1803, F.O. 5, vols. 32, 35, and 38. See also Vernon G. Setser, *The Commercial Reciprocity Policy of the United States, 1774-1829* (Philadelphia, 1937), 149-161.

[45] See Jefferson's "Conversation with Mr. Erskine," November 9, 1808, Jefferson Papers, LC.

This attitude did not necessarily imply Jefferson's abandonment of the principles that he and Madison had championed in the 1790's, and his administration never failed to protest British offenses against American maritime rights. But since Jefferson believed that time and delay would always work in favor of the United States, he attempted little more between 1803 and 1806 than to try to persuade Britain to accept a convention governing the most contentious issues between the two nations for the duration of the European war. Madison—who was rather more skeptical about the chances for success here than the President and who probably would have preferred taking a firmer line— drew up instructions for these negotiations, which, had they been adopted in a convention, would have been extremely favorable to American commercial interests. There was, however, no attempt to back up the diplomacy of persuasion with policies that exerted any pressure on the British economy, and Madison made it clear to the American minister in London, James Monroe, that he had a degree of latitude to define the shape of the various articles of a convention in ways which "may find a balance in the general bargain."[46] Negotiations consequently dragged on for years, interrupted by ministerial crises in Britain and Monroe's frequent departures for Paris and Madrid for discussions on Spanish problems. As one British Foreign Secretary, Lord Harrowby, pointed out to Monroe when the latter requested a delay in talks, there was indeed reason to believe that the difficulties of Anglo-American relations "were not of an urgent nature on either side."[47]

Throughout 1805, though, Madison, along with many other Republicans, became alarmed at the rising rate of British impressment of American seamen and the seizure of merchantmen in the West Indies under the "rule of '56," and these problems came to dominate the Secretary of State's interest while that of the President remained fixed on Spanish affairs. In Madison's opinion, the growing severity of British policies toward neutrals that began in 1805 and culminated in the Orders in Council of November 1807 had very little to do with making war on France, but was instead designed to serve the purposes of the West India interest in Great Britain. This alliance of bankers, merchants, and factors became greatly agitated about the rapid growth of American shipping in the colonial trades, which was not only depriving British shipping of cargoes but also harming the West Indies by en-

[46] Madison to Monroe, December 20, 1803, Madison Papers, LC; Anthony Merry to Lord Hawkesbury, December 31, 1803, F.O. 5, vol. 41. See also Madison to Monroe, January 16 and 18 and March 8, 1804, Madison Papers, LC.

[47] Monroe to William Pinkney, May 18, 1804, William Pinkney Papers, Princeton University Library.

abling Americans to dump sugar and coffee on European markets. Many of the notoriously anti-American pamphlets which began to appear in great numbers after 1804—such as James Stephen's *War in Disguise* and Joseph Marryat's *Concessions to America the Bane of Britain*—originated, often with the blessing of the ministry, with this interest group.[48] These writings catalogued the many economic ills of the British West Indies in the early nineteenth century, occasionally suggesting such remedies as cutbacks in production or alternative uses for sugar and molasses, but more commonly they advocated driving American shipping out of almost all the colonial trades. Under the pressure of this sustained lobbying, and feeling a need to encourage the growth of shipping as well, the British government gradually adopted these suggestions, first by a vigorous enforcement of the "rule of '56" to control vessels in the colonial trades and ultimately by the Orders in Council of November 1807, which enabled Britain to regulate the disposal of the cargoes carried by those vessels.[49]

This perception of the motives governing British policies became firmly fixed in Madison's mind during the summer of 1805 as he began research into the historical origins of the "rule of '56," which, even before he started work, he denounced for threatening "more loss and vexation to neutrals than all the other belligerent claims put together."[50] His conclusions that the rule had no standing in international law and that the British manipulated it for their own convenience were temperately expressed in a bulky pamphlet released late in 1805.[51] Privately, though, Madison's views were a good deal less restrained. Shortly before his pamphlet appeared, he bluntly informed the British minister

[48] See Reginald Horsman, *The Causes of the War of 1812* (Philadelphia, 1962), 33-43, 112-117, 119, 129. On the West India interest see Lillian M. Penson, "The London West India Interest in the Eighteenth Century," *English Historical Review* 36 (1921), 373-392; and Barry W. Higman, "The West India 'Interest' in Parliament, 1807-1833," *Historical Studies* 13 (1967), 1-19.

[49] These motives for British policy were openly avowed. See Earl Bathurst's remarks in Parliament on March 22, 1808, in *Cobbett's Parliamentary Debates* (London, 1806-1820), X, 1239-1240. See also Alexander Baring, *An Inquiry into the Causes and Consequences of the Orders in Council; and an Examination of the Conduct of Great Britain towards the Neutral Commerce of America* (London, 1808). Madison accepted Baring's analysis (Madison to Pinkney, May 1, 1808, Pinkney Papers) as it reinforced a viewpoint he himself had reached before 1808. For conditions in the West Indies see Ragatz, *Fall of the Planter Class*, 286-330.

[50] Madison to Coxe, June 11, 1805; to Monroe, September 24, 1805, Madison Papers, LC. Madison to Jefferson, September 14 and October 5, 1805, Jefferson Papers, LC. Anthony Merry to Lord Mulgrave, November 3, 1805, F.O. 5, vol. 45.

[51] [James Madison], *An Examination of the British Doctrine which subjects to Capture a Neutral Trade Not Open in Time of Peace* (Philadelphia, 1805).

in Washington, Anthony Merry, that the "rule of '56" could not be justified as legitimate warfare against France but was a fraudulent legalism to gain "a pure and manifest commercial monopoly" for British shippers.[52] In time, Madison came to work up a very considerable animosity against the West India interest—the "partisans of colonial monopoly" and the "London smugglers of sugar and coffee"—which he regarded as the source of all America's difficulties; and his anger finally found release in the outburst that West India merchants belonged to a lower moral order than African slave traders.[53] He had, however, less difficulty in prescribing the remedy, which was to strike at the heart of the problem in the British West Indies. As early as March 1805 he suggested that the United States demand complete reciprocity with Britain in its West Indian trade as a way of compounding the severe difficulties of that sector of the imperial economy, but by the middle of the year he realized that an embargo on trade to the islands was a much more effective policy, and he urged the measure on Jefferson thereafter.[54] "The efficacy of an embargo," Madison argued, "cannot be doubted. If indeed a commercial weapon can be properly shaped for the executive hand, it is more and more apparent to me that it can force all nations having colonies in this quarter of the globe to respect our rights."[55]

The American response to the crisis of 1805, however, was the Nonimportation Law of April 1806, a measure of minimal coercive potential which was immediately further reduced by Jefferson's suspension of it in an attempt to bring negotiations in London to an amicable agreement. While Madison would never have denied that commercial restrictions might operate on Britain in a number of ways, it is difficult to avoid the conclusion that he thought the Nonimportation Law was the wrong remedy for the wrong problem, not simply

[52] Merry to Mulgrave, December 2, 1805, F.O. 5, vol. 45. For other unfavorable remarks on the rulings of British Admiralty courts see Madison's "Notes on Orders in Council etc." [1805], Madison Papers, LC.

[53] Madison to Monroe and Pinkney, May 20, 1807, Diplomatic Instructions: All Countries, NA. Madison to Albert Gallatin, July 28, 1809, Carl Prince and Helen Fineman, eds., *The Papers of Albert Gallatin* (microfilm ed.). Madison to Jefferson, August 16, 1809, Madison Papers, LC; Madison to Pinkney, October 23, 1809, Pinkney Papers.

[54] Madison to Monroe, March 6, 1805, and to John Armstrong, June 6, 1805, Diplomatic Instructions: All Countries, NA; Madison to Jefferson, August 20, 1805, Jefferson Papers, LC.

[55] Madison to Jefferson, September 14, 1805, Jefferson Papers, LC. For the volume of American trade to the West Indies in this period see John H. Coatsworth, "American Trade with European Colonies in the Caribbean and South America, 1790-1812," *WMQ* 3d Ser., 24 (1967), 243-266.

because it was weak but also because it did not go to the root of America's difficulties. He complained in 1806 that there were too many "discordant opinions and projects" in Congress, and when the British minister taunted him with the observation that the Nonimportation Law would not work, Madison, obviously angered by its truth, gave him a "very short answer" in return.[56] To his kinsman, Richard Cutts, he remarked that there was no reason to suppose that an attempt at nonimportation "would otherwise affect the negotiation [in London] than by slackening it," and this prediction was reinforced by his realization that the passage of the so-called Two Million Act during the same session of Congress could be used by Britain to require explanations, if not concessions, from the United States.[57] Admittedly, the administration tried to link the repeal of the unenforced Nonimportation Law to concessions on impressment and American interests in the colonial trades, but when its diplomats in London—James Monroe and William Pinkney—traded off the first two issues for some lesser concessions on the last, the futility of the policy was clearly exposed. Throughout 1806 and for much of 1807, then, the diplomacy of commercial restriction was undermined by the American attempt to pursue too many objects simultaneously at the cost of achieving none of them.

Madison, though, remained constant in his wish for a "radical cure" of Anglo-American difficulties, and he continued to regard the problems of the West Indies as the source of British weakness that should be exploited. While issuing fresh instructions for Monroe and Pinkney in May 1807, he noted that it was within the power of the United States to destroy the value of the West Indies to the British empire, since it could, he claimed, be no longer unknown even "to the most sanguine partisan of the colonial monopoly that the necessaries of life and of cultivation can be furnished to those Islands from no other source than the United States, and that immediate ruin would ensue if this source were shut. . . ."[58] The *Chesapeake* incident of June 1807 only heightened his anger, and Madison finally accomplished his desire to punish Britain with the adoption of the embargo in December of

[56] Madison to Monroe, March 11, 1806, Madison Papers, LC. Merry to Charles James Fox, May 4, 1806, F.O. 5, vol. 49.

[57] Madison to Richard Cutts, July 11, 1806, Cutts Collection of the Papers of James and Dolley Madison, University of Chicago (microfilm in LC). The Two Million Act could be described as a thinly disguised bribe to Napoleon to assist the United States in advancing its territorial ambitions in Florida at Spanish expense. Since Great Britain allied with the Spanish monarchy against Napoleon in 1806, the British government resented American encroachments on its ally's possessions.

[58] Madison to Monroe and Pinkney, May 20, 1807, Diplomatic Instructions: All Countries, NA.

that year. As early as October 1807 it had become known to the administration—with the receipt of some parliamentary reports on the deplorable conditions in the West Indies—that Britain was contemplating drastic measures against neutral trade, and when the Orders in Council of November came into effect, along with the Berlin and Milan decrees of France, Madison was able to carry the day in cabinet with his advocacy of an embargo as the American response.[59] His cabinet colleagues, particularly Jefferson, seem to have valued the measure for its precautionary aspects and for the appearance of impartiality that it presented to the simultaneous aggressions of Britain and France, but Madison's emphasis from the outset was different.[60] Although no admirer of Napoleon, he had never believed that French violations of neutral rights were as serious as those by Britain, and it was his hope, as the *National Intelligencer* darkly declared, that the embargo would "coerce the settlement of longstanding and complicated accounts."[61] When the often suspended Nonimportation Law finally came into force at the end of 1807, Madison bluntly told the British minister that neither it nor the embargo would be lifted until his government had given satisfaction on the Orders in Council, impressment, and the reparations for the *Chesapeake* affair.[62]

Throughout 1808, therefore, Madison waited for the embargo to accomplish its purpose, though, as he did so, he seriously miscalculated both the unpopularity of the measure in the northern states and the problems of enforcing it. Beginning with the Treasury Department's

[59] For discussions of West Indian affairs reaching Madison in this period see George Joy to Madison, August 25, 1807, and Pinkney to Madison, December 31, 1807, Madison Papers, LC. Also see Madison to Pinkney, October 2, 1807, Pinkney Papers. For Madison's role in the imposition of the embargo see Dumas Malone, *Jefferson the President: Second Term, 1805-1809* (Boston, 1974) 475-489.

[60] For a discussion of the embargo from Jefferson's point of view, which perhaps overemphasizes the precautionary aspects of the measure to the exclusion of its coercive nature, see Burton Spivak, *Jefferson's English Crisis: Commerce, Embargo, and the Republican Revolution* (Charlottesville, 1979), 102-111. The *National Intelligencer* on December 21, 1807, stressed the value of the embargo in preserving American resources but also noted that it would have the "collateral effect" of compelling nations hostile to the United States to change their policies. Great Britain, the editorial argued, could be expected to suffer the loss of raw materials for manufacturing, the loss of naval stores, and the loss of supplies for the West Indies. See also *Natl Intelligencer*, December 28, 1807.

[61] *Natl Intelligencer*, December 25, 1807.

[62] David M. Erskine to George Canning, December 23, 1807, F.O. 5, vol. 52. In conveying these demands, Madison was well aware that Britain could not at this time draw on the Baltic for grain or naval supplies, because of Alexander I's adherence to the Treaty of Tilsit in July 1807. See *Natl Intelligencer*, August 7 and 19, September 9, 11, and 16, and December 7, 1807.

attempts to cut off exports by land in March 1808, there developed along the Great Lakes and the St. Lawrence and Richelieu rivers a massive clandestine trade, principally in lumber, provisions, and potash, much of which ultimately found its way through Canada to the West Indies.[63] To stop this traffic, Albert Gallatin first demanded a "little army on the lakes," but by August he believed that the embargo had failed in this area and should be ended.[64] The issues raised by this regional protest could not be postponed indefinitely, and between Madison's election as President and his inauguration he and Gallatin met with congressional leaders on several occasions to consider alternatives to the embargo. There was little political support for immediate war, partly because of the difficulty of justifying a choice between Britain and France as enemies, and partly because of a lack of military preparations. The War Department had neither recruited nor disciplined the Additional Military Force voted by Congress in 1808, while Jefferson had, in fact, divided the few troops that had been raised between garrison duties and policing the embargo on the St. Lawrence and Savannah rivers.[65] There was not, furthermore, even a Secretary of War on duty in the last weeks of Jefferson's administration, Henry Dearborn having retired early to the collectorship at Boston.[66] Despite Jefferson's insistence, which became marked after March 1808, that the embargo would have to be followed by war if the belligerent edicts were not lifted, he ended his Presidency in the tragic situation of being more afraid that Britain would invade the United States than being able instead to threaten Britain with an invasion of Canada.[67]

Madison did not want the embargo to give way to war. He did not think war was necessary, nor did he ever attempt to conceal from the British minister that the United States was in no position to commence

---

[63] Louis M. Sears, *Jefferson and the Embargo* (Durham, N.C., 1927), 90, 93, 95, 201. H. N. Muller III, "Smuggling into Canada: How the Champlain Valley Defied Jefferson's Embargo," *Vermont History* 38 (1970), 5-21. Israel I. Rubin, "New York State and the Long Embargo," (Ph.D. diss., New York University, 1961), 107-140.

[64] Gallatin to Jefferson, July 29, 1808, Jefferson Papers, LC; same to same, August 6, 1808, *Gallatin Papers*. The best study of Treasury problems in enforcing the embargo is Richard J. Mannix, "The Embargo: Its Administration, Impact, and Enforcement" (Ph.D. diss., New York University, 1975), esp. 155-298.

[65] Jefferson to James Wilkinson, August 30, 1808, Jefferson Papers, LC; and Gallatin to Henry Dearborn, December 19, 1808, *Gallatin Papers*.

[66] Dearborn to Jefferson, December 19, 1807; and Jefferson to John Smith, February 17, 1809, Jefferson Papers, LC.

[67] Jefferson to Gallatin, September 2, 1808, *Gallatin Papers*. Cabinet Notes, December 1, 1808, in Franklin B. Sawvel, ed., *The Anas of Thomas Jefferson* (New York, 1903), 272.

hostilities.[68] Throughout the transition period between November 1808 and March 1809, he hoped for the adoption of such measures as "an invigoration of the embargo, a prohibition of imports, *permanent* duties for encouraging manufactures, and a *permanent* navigation act: with an extension of preparations and arrangements for the event of war." These measures, he informed William Pinkney in London, "would give a severity to the contest of privation . . . for which the British government would seem to be very little prepared in any sense of the word. . . ."[69] In truth, there was even less chance for the acceptance of Madison's preferences than there was for a declaration of war, since Congress was insisting on some modification of the embargo; in its place the members talked either of nonintercourse with the offending belligerents—while opening trade with other nations—or of issuing letters of marque and reprisal to assume the risks of an armed trade. Madison disliked these alternatives, regarding neither as sufficiently coercive of Britain, and the second removed the choice of peace and war from the authorities constitutionally entrusted with it. No matter in what form the embargo was relaxed, the resumption of American trade, Madison believed, would favor Britain, since that nation, even if only by circuitous routes, would be able to gain access to American supplies. And should the Royal Navy make massive seizures of American vessels, Madison would then be compelled to consider fighting a war with an inadequate military establishment.[70]

The decision of the Tenth Congress to replace the embargo with the Nonintercourse Law and to summon an early session of the Eleventh Congress in May 1809 to consider future policies therefore left Madison at a loss. He strongly disapproved of nonintercourse and could only hope either that Britain would repeal the Orders in Council before May 1809 or that public opinion would inspire the Eleventh Congress to make a more determined stand against belligerent aggressions after that date.[71] The best he could do with the Nonintercourse Law was to use it not to coerce Britain but to offer it as a diplomatic concession. The British minister had complained throughout 1808 that the imposition of the Nonimportation Law against his country and not against France was unjustified, and the shift to nonintercourse with both bel-

[68] Erskine to Canning, December 3, 4, and 7, 1808, F.O. 5, vol. 58. See also Spivak, *Jefferson's English Crisis*, 189.

[69] Madison to Pinkney, November 9, 1808, Madison Papers, LC; same to same, November 10, 1808, Pinkney Papers.

[70] Madison to (Wilson Cary Nicholas), February 1809, Madison Papers, LC; Madison to Pinkney, January 3 and February 11, 1809, Pinkney Papers. Same to same, February 10, 1809, Diplomatic Instructions: All Countries, NA.

[71] Madison to Pinkney, March 17, 1809, Pinkney Papers.

ligerents, in effect, removed this inequality. It could therefore have
been an occasion, had the British government been seeking one, to
negotiate a simultaneous removal of the Orders in Council and the
embargo. The new administration hinted at these possibilities, but in
fact Madison did not really expect that the British Foreign Secretary,
George Canning, would seize them, dismissing the British leader on
one occasion as being not so much a statesman as a "Belle Esprit" with
too much of the "upstart arrogance" in him.[72]

Madison's difficulties in coercing Britain with a law whose workings
actually favored that nation were unexpectedly removed, albeit briefly,
by the restoration of Anglo-American trade which the British minister,
Erskine, negotiated with the administration in April 1809. The President regarded Erskine's agreement as a last-minute vindication of the
embargo, and he even became confident that Britain, after the experience of "adversity," could be talked into a fair commercial treaty.
Canning's prompt disavowal of his minister's diplomacy, however,
coupled with new British Orders in Council in April 1809, suddenly
placed Madison in a far more difficult position.[73] The seeming bad
faith of the British government required a strong response, but Madison doubted he had the freedom to act without inconveniently calling
Congress into session again.[74] A return to the embargo was politically
impossible and war even more so, especially as the army in the summer
of 1809 was in no condition for combat, while a reimposition of nonintercourse under the circumstances, Madison believed, was extremely
dangerous.[75] Here the root of the problem was again the West India
interest, whose hand Madison detected in Canning's conduct, above
all in the impossible British demand that in return for the repeal of
the new Orders in Council the United States acknowledge the "rule
of '56" and let Britain enforce it as she saw fit.[76] All the evidence from
Britain as Madison understood it in the middle of 1809, including the

[72] Erskine to Canning, February 10 and 13 and March 9, 16, and 17, 1809, F.O. 5, vols.
62 and 63. For Madison's remarks about Canning see his letter to Pinkney, November 25,
1808, Pinkney Papers.

[73] Madison to Jefferson, April 9 and 24 and May 1, 1809, Madison Papers, LC.

[74] Madison to Jefferson, August 3, 1809, ibid.

[75] Madison to Gallatin, July 30, 1809, *Gallatin Papers*. Gallatin to Madison, July 24,
1809, Madison Papers, LC. The army was unprepared for war, largely because General
Wilkinson had displayed poor judgment in encamping detachments under his command at
Terre aux Boeufs, Mississippi Territory, in 1809, thus leading to a large number of deaths
and casualties from disease. To all intents and purposes, this left New Orleans defenseless,
and it had always been assumed that the city would be a primary British objective in the
event of war. See Weigley, *History of the United States Army*, 113-114.

[76] Madison to Gallatin, July 28 and 30, 1809, *Gallatin Papers*. *Natl Intelligencer*, August
18 and 21, 1809, Madison to Pinkney, October 23, 1809, Pinkney Papers.

appointment of the notorious Francis James Jackson as British minister to Washington, suggested that the ministry was about to embark on even more extreme antineutral policies, for which a sudden return to nonintercourse—while virtually all of America's mercantile property was afloat on the high seas—might provide a pretext. Yet if Madison made no response at all, he would have submitted to a gross humiliation from Britain as well as run the risk of war with France at the same time, since Napoleon would be bound to resent an American policy of inaction. Madison hoped to escape the dilemma by a subterfuge that was worthy of the French Emperor himself—issuing a circular authorizing customs officers to seize British imports without openly proclaiming it as official American policy—but Gallatin insisted that the President come to Washington and restore nonintercourse by proclamation.[77] In August 1809, Madison, after some reflection, did so; the measure at least avoided the risk of war with France and indicated a disposition to resist the conduct of Britain.

A continuation of nonintercourse, however, was undesirable for a number of reasons. It had never been intended as a permanent policy, and its effects were not only harming the revenue but also being evaded by Britain in a rapidly growing entrepôt trade which it opened to American merchants in Halifax, Nova Scotia; Amelia Island, off the coast of Georgia; and even in Montreal.[78] A desire to escape from the Nonintercourse Law as decently as possible led Madison to open negotiations with Jackson, but he soon learned that the British minister had no powers to discuss anything, and he finally decided to dismiss him in November 1809 for his overbearing arrogance.[79] Toward the end of 1809 the ministry dominated by Canning fell in Britain, but its replacement, headed by Spencer Perceval, held out no prospects of change for the United States. Perceval, in Madison's view, was even worse than Canning, since under his authority the abuse of the license system—whereby British shippers could take West Indian produce to the Continent in a trade that was denied to American merchants—was

[77] The customs-circular solution was hinted at in Madison to Gallatin, July 28, 1809, *Gallatin Papers*.

[78] See Eli F. Heckscher, *The Continental System: An Economic Interpretation* (Oxford, 1922), 137-138.

[79] This was the reason for one of Robert Smith's many indiscretions as Madison's Secretary of State when he remarked to Jackson: "Then Sir, you have no proposal to make to us? No explanation to give? How then shall we be able to get rid of the Non-Intercourse Act?" Jackson to Canning, October 17, 1809, F.O. 5, vol. 64. The announcement of Jackson's dismissal appeared in the *National Intelligencer* on November 13, 1809.

carried to a hitherto unprecedented height.[80] The President was appalled by such "quackeries and corruptions," and the *National Intelligencer* during this period indulged in some strong language about
the need for the "restoration and purification of the British monarchy."[81] After thus indicating its opinions, the administration then
decided to wait for the death of George III or his replacement by the
Prince Regent before trying to resume any purposeful negotiations
with Britain.[82]

In the interval, Madison hoped that public opinion might swing
back to favoring an embargo once the public understood how British
policies operated to restrict American commerce, but his more immediate problem was to find some way to deal with that very matter.[83]
At no time after 1807 did Madison ever consider "free trade" to be a
solution for the problems of American neutrality, but by the end of
1809 the realities of domestic politics as well as complications abroad
had greatly reduced his stock of commercial weapons. In particular,
the resumption of American trade to the West Indies during the operation of the Erskine agreement and the advantages this had conferred
on Great Britain annoyed Madison. To coerce Britain through nonimportation as an alternative, however, was ruled out because of Gallatin's insistence that the Treasury needed revenue if it was to avoid
taxation and borrowing, and this left Madison with no choice but to
abandon most of the more drastic methods for restricting the flow of
trade between Great Britain and the United States.[84] In their place,
he fell back to the old idea of a navigation act, which, if it did not

[80] See Bradford Perkins, *Prologue to War: England and the United States, 1805-1812*
(Berkeley and Los Angeles, 1961), 305.

[81] Madison to Jefferson, November 6, 1809, Madison Papers, LC. *Natl Intelligencer*,
October 4 and November 27, 1809. Madison was always outraged by Britain's trading with
its enemy while it denied the United States the right to do the same as a neutral. As the
War of 1812 approached, he remarked sarcastically to the British minister that it seemed
necessary for the United States to become a belligerent in order to enjoy the legitimate fruits
of commerce. See Augustus J. Foster, Journal entry, January 30, 1812, Augustus J. Foster
Papers, LC.

[82] Toward the end of 1809 the administration received a report from Pinkney that the
Prince of Wales had deplored the conduct of his father's ministers toward America. See
Pinkney to Robert Smith, October 18, 1809, Dispatches from United States Ministers to
Great Britain (M-30), Records of the Department of State (RG 59), NA. For the admin-
istration's reaction see Ezekiel Bacon to Joseph Story, December 19, 1809, Joseph Story
Papers, LC.

[83] *Natl Intelligencer*, October 6, 1809; Madison to Pinkney, October 23, 1809, Pinkney
Papers.

[84] Madison to Pinkney, October 23, 1809, Pinkney Papers; Gallatin to Madison, November 29, 1809, Madison Papers, LC.

deprive Britain of exports and imports, at least gave most of the benefits of trade between the two nations to American navigation, while also repairing some of the damage inflicted on American revenues by the policies pursued since 1807. This essentially was the purpose of Macon's Bill Number 1, which, much to Madison's annoyance, was defeated by a misalliance of Republican and Federalist Congressmen who declared it too weak to coerce Britain and yet strong enough to provoke that country into retaliating against it as well.[85] With the failure of this scheme, Madison, in March 1810, tried to obtain a bill which would re-enact nonintercourse at some specified future date, thus giving each of the European belligerents, France and Great Britain, the option to avoid its effects by repealing its edicts first; if one belligerent should do so, the President would be empowered to enforce restrictions on the other before the law was due to come into effect.[86] Congress, however, would not tolerate any more executive experiments with cutting off commerce, and eventually settled for the misnamed substitute of Macon's Bill Number 2, which released American trade from all restrictions and gave the President authority to impose nonintercourse only after one of the European belligerents had first revoked its edicts against neutrals.[87]

Madison was appalled at this weak result and at the political factionalism producing it, the more so since the episode exposed a serious rift within the Republican party between those who advocated commercial restrictions as the main instrument of American foreign policy and those who were inclining to free trade, without restrictions, while resisting by armed force any belligerent aggressions on this freedom.[88] The removal of all restraints on American trade, furthermore, created a situation extremely favorable for Britain, and Madison could only hope that the disadvantages which Macon's Bill Number 2 worked on

[85] Madison to Pinkney, January 20, 1810, Hunt, ed., *Writings of Madison*, VIII, 91-92. For the Congressional debate see AC, 11th Cong., 2d sess., 577, 602-610, 1160-1354, 1635-1701. See also Chapter II below.

[86] The draft of this proposal in Madison's hand is in *Gallatin Papers*, March 1810, and it is probably to this same proposal that Nathaniel Macon was referring when he said it was modified in the House foreign relations committee by John Taylor of South Carolina. See Macon to Joseph H. Nicholson, April 6, 1810, Joseph H. Nicholson Papers, LC.

[87] Macon to Nicholson, April 10 and 21, 1810, Nicholson Papers, LC. AC, 11th Cong., 2d sess., 1772-1930.

[88] Madison to Jefferson, April 23, 1810, Madison Papers, LC. The quarrel among Republicans over the means of retaliation can be seen in the conference committee reports for March 15 and May 1, 1810, Legislative Records of the House of Representatives and the Senate (RG 233 and 46), NA. The reports are in HR 11 A-B1 and Sen 11 A-C2 respectively. For the political consequences of the disagreement see Chapter II below.

France would inspire Napoleon to accept its terms as a way of equalizing his position.[89] Throughout the summer of 1810 both Madison and the *National Intelligencer* lamented the loss of the embargo and berated Congress for its inability to follow a consistent course.[90] Nonetheless, Madison was prepared to give the nonintercourse provisions of Macon's Bill Number 2 a chance to coerce Great Britain through the damage it would cause its manufacturing interests, and he seized his chance by accepting in October 1810 the Cadore letter as proof of repeal of the Berlin and Milan decrees.[91] The effects of the policy, though, would be slow, since it would take time for the relatively disorganized and isolated British manufacturing interests to organize a protest campaign against the better-represented shipping and West India interests, which supported the Orders in Council.[92] Aided by the distress and protests resulting from a severe depression in Britain, nonintercourse, ironically, did finally bring down the Orders in Council in June 1812, but long before that date the Madison administration, for a variety of reasons, perceived the policy to be insufficiently coercive.[93] And, as was the case with the embargo, the roots of its ineffectiveness could be traced back to Canada.

The difficulties of enforcing nonintercourse became apparent throughout 1811 in two areas: the first was in the trade from Passamaquoddy through Eastport and from there to other major American ports; and the second lay in the region between Lakes Ontario and Champlain. It would seem that a growing number of American merchants sailed to Eastport to import British merchandise under fraudulent bills of lading for local plaster of paris, while British West Indian rum was widely passed off as Spanish produce in New England in the sudden absence of any experts to testify to the contrary in the courts.[94]

[89] Madison to Jefferson, April 23, May 7 and 25, 1810; to Pinkney, May 23, 1810, Madison Papers, LC.

[90] *Natl Intelligencer*, June 1 and 4, August 27, October 19, 22 and 31, and November 7, 1810.

[91] Madison to Armstrong, July 5, 1810; to Pinkney, October 30, 1810, Madison Papers, LC. See also *Natl Intelligencer*, October 26 and 31, 1810. For a more detailed discussion of the French decrees and the Cadore letter see Chapter II below.

[92] This point was made by Baring, *Inquiry into the Causes and Consequences of the Orders in Council*, 7. The *National Intelligencer*, June 2, 1812, also noted that, by maintaining the Orders in Council at the risk of suffering nonintercourse, the British government had chosen to sacrifice the manufactures of its people to the interests of West India merchants.

[93] See Chapter II below.

[94] Dearborn to Gallatin, August 31, 1811; Gallatin to James McCulloch and Larkin Smith, September 6, 1811, all in *Gallatin Papers*. See also Gerald S. Graham, "The Gypsum Trade of the Maritime Provinces: Its Relation to American Diplomacy and Agriculture in the Early Nineteenth Century," *Agricultural History* 12 (1938), 212-218; and Herbert

Equally as serious was the smuggling of British manufactures from Montreal through the lakes region, a business which, the Treasury reported, gave all the indications of having a determined and large-scale organization.[95] Nor was the Treasury equipped to cope with the problem. Only one collector, Peter Sailly at Champlain, showed any zeal to enforce the law; the others either lacked the will or the means to stop the smuggling.[96] By October 1811, Gallatin felt compelled to report to Madison, as he had done to Jefferson three years previously, that nonintercourse could not be enforced without a considerable expansion in the numbers and powers of customs officers, including the right to search private houses on suspicion for smuggled goods.[97] The Attorney General, Caesar A. Rodney, also urged the adoption of this course, calling for the creation of a "perfect system" to "bring England to her senses."[98]

Madison did not oppose these suggestions, though he may have doubted their effectiveness. He was certainly aware of the enforcement problems, regretting as early as May 1811 that Congress had not banned American exports to Nova Scotia so as to lessen the inducements for British merchants to come there with imports, and by the end of the year he knew that Britain had decided to assist further the efforts of smugglers of both British manufactures and West Indian produce by throwing open more free ports in Canada to American shipping.[99] Moreover, these problems would get worse over the winter of 1811-1812 as the freezing of rivers and roads would multiply op-

Heaton, "Non-Importation, 1806-1812," *Journal of Economic History* 1 (1941), 193-198. The significance of Canadian smuggling is also noted by François Crouzet, *L'Économie Britannique et Le Blocus Continental, 1806-1813* (Paris, 1958), II, 703-704

[95] In some documents sent to Congress in November 1811, Gallatin included a report "from an intelligent agent sent to Montreal" which contained descriptions of disguised American merchants purchasing British goods and arranging for their movement to the United States. See Sen 12A-D1, Legislative Records of the Senate, NA.

[96] Nathan Sage to Gabriel Duvall, August 10, 1811; Peter Sailly to Gallatin, August 24, September 10, October 8 and 15, 1811; Samuel Buell to Gallatin, September 13, 1811, all in *Gallatin Papers*.

[97] Gallatin sent Madison an annotated copy of a Treasury circular, October 7, 1811, describing and warning about the infractions of the law. See also Gallatin to Thomas Newton and Samuel Smith, November 28, 1811, *Gallatin Papers*.

[98] Caesar A. Rodney to Gallatin, October 20, 1811, ibid.

[99] Madison to Cutts, May 23, 1811, Cutts Collection; *Natl Intelligencer*, May 23, 1811; Joy to Madison, October 18, 1811, Madison Papers, LC. In this last letter Joy described applications by British merchants to the Board of Trade to open the ports of St. Andrews and St. John in New Brunswick and Halifax in Nova Scotia to allow American merchants to receive British manufactures and West Indian produce in exchange for American supplies. On the use of free ports to subvert American commercial restrictions see Gerald S. Graham, "The Origins of Free Ports in British North America," *CHR* 21 (1941), 25-34.

portunities to evade customs officers, and it would be a nice question as to how those officers were going to stop land traffic without running the risk of being shot as highwaymen by Americans who were obviously determined to smuggle.[100] Apart from the economic consequences of these violations, which could not be truly calculated anyway, there was also the undesirability of tolerating a situation in which Britain could encourage American citizens to flout their own laws. Not only did this undermine the republican virtue of the people but it also led Britain to resist American demands longer than Madison felt it might otherwise have done. As Madison told the Twelfth Congress in November 1811, "the practice of smuggling is odious," especially "when it blends with a pursuit of ignominious gain a treacherous subserviency in the transgressors to a foreign policy adverse to that of their own country."[101] In pondering the solution to these questions, the President accepted the case for tighter restrictions on illicit trade with Britain, but he could hardly have escaped the conclusion that belligerency too was another way of transcending the difficulties of enforcing a system of trade restraint. Indeed, he may have concluded after the experiences of 1808 and 1811 that war was the only way to seal off the North American continent from British trade, for, as he confessed to Monroe after the War of 1812, Canada was of some importance to Great Britain "as a channel for evading and crippling our commercial laws."[102] Even Gallatin, who was no advocate of war, could accept this much, pointing out to Madison, as the cabinet made its recommendations to Congress in November 1811 for raising troops, that such measures would not "interfere with the attentions which the defects of our restrictive laws render necessary."[103]

★

WHILE the practical problems of enforcing commercial restrictions were undoubtedly important in leading Madison toward his decision to prepare for war with Britain, they do not, in the final analysis, fully explain his understanding of the coercive impact an invasion of Canada

[100] Sailly to Gallatin, November 12, 1811; Hart Massey to Gallatin, November 8 and 12, 1811, *Gallatin Papers.*

[101] James D. Richardson, comp., *A Compilation of the Messages and Papers of the Presidents, 1789-1902* (New York, 1897-1914), II, 480.

[102] Madison to Monroe, November 28, 1818, Madison Papers, LC. Throughout the first session of the Twelfth Congress the *National Intelligencer* deplored all talk of repealing nonintercourse after the declaration of war, remarking that commercial restrictions were essential to wage war "with energy." "Nothing will be more grateful to the British," the administration paper remarked, "if we will in any manner, direct or indirect, admit her manufactures or supply her with provisions." *Natl Intelligencer*, July 2, 1812.

[103] See Gallatin's "Sketch on the Militia" for Madison, November 1811, *Gallatin Papers.*

would have on his enemy. What that impact might be was first suggested by Lord Sheffield, whose observations on the United States had also included some controversial predictions about the contribution Canada would make to the imperial economy. Sheffield was, in fact, the first important promoter of the new Canada that arose from the remnants of British power in North America after 1783, and many of his writings to 1809 constituted a fulsome assertion of its economic potential. Indeed, the very basis for his claim that Britain could successfully apply its navigation laws against the United States was a fervent belief that Canada possessed the resources to occupy the role that had been filled by the American colonies before independence.[104] On this subject, as his critics unkindly noticed, Sheffield was sometimes a little ambivalent; his arguments hovered awkwardly between asserting that Canada was *already* capable of matching the economic performance of America and demonstrating that with proper encouragement it would *soon* be in a position to do so.[105] These contradictions in Sheffield's writings notwithstanding, successive British governments after 1783—caught as they were between the conflicting pressures of resentment toward the United States, the need to discharge obligations to Loyalists who resettled in Canada, and the concern to maintain the navigation system—accepted his views as a justification for their policies, and then tried to live with the consequences as best they could.[106] The royal governors of the Canadian provinces in the 1790's often painted similarly bright pictures of Canadian prosperity, and two of them in particular, Lord Dorchester and John Graves Simcoe, also believed that Canada, by virtue of its control of the Great Lakes and the St. Lawrence, could command much of the trade of the American interior.[107]

Yet such optimistic arguments and the policies they justified ran directly counter to many firmly held opinions about the relative economic worth of Canada and the United States to the British economy. The notion that Canada could ever be as valuable a plantation for Britain as America had already been rejected—even before independence—by many political economists, and no group was quicker to

[104] Sheffield, *Observations*, 134-201; Chalmers, *Opinions*, 63-123.

[105] Sheffield, *Observations*, 118, 145. And cf. Coxe, *Brief Examination*, 17-19; Champion, *Considerations*, 23, 124, 259; Edwards, *Thoughts*, 21, 35; [Bingham], *A Letter from an American* . . . , 7, 17; and Allen, *Considerations on the Present State*, 22.

[106] Vincent T. Harlow, *The Founding of the Second British Empire, 1763-1793* (London, 1952), I, 448-492; D. G. Creighton, *The Commercial Empire of the St. Lawrence, 1760-1850* (Toronto, 1937), 106.

[107] See Gerald S. Graham, *Sea Power and British North America, 1783-1820: A Study in British Colonial Policy* (Cambridge, Mass., 1941), 77, 78, 88-89.

reassert this point of view after 1783 than the West Indian planters. The planters, as opposed to the merchants who carried their produce, did not believe that Canada could provide them with lumber and provisions as readily and as cheaply as the United States. Moreover, after the hardships brought to them by the American Revolution, they were not prepared to risk making the experiment.[108] Their demands that the United States be exempted from the navigation laws were thus presented as a sustained assault on the political economy of Lord Sheffield and his vision of Canada. In this endlessly repetitive polemic, Canada was depicted as an ice-bound, snow-covered, windy, foggy, sterile desert where crops simply froze in the ground.[109] Indeed, so outraged were the West Indian planters at being asked, as they believed, to risk starvation and ruin for the Canadian fantasies of a man who understood nothing of their situation that, led by Bryan Edwards, they continued their attacks on Sheffield and the navigation laws well into the early nineteenth century. In successive editions of his history of the West Indies, Edwards, with pious outrage, offered the bodies of thousands of dead slaves as martyrs to the folly of Lord Sheffield's attempts to promote Canada.[110] Even Richard Champion, who did not

[108] See the works cited in notes 20, 21, and 29 above.

[109] See Long, *A Free and Candid Review*, 10-89; Allen, *Considerations on the Present State*, 26-39; and Edwards, *Thoughts*, 15-21.

[110] Bryan Edwards, *The History Civil and Commercial of the British Colonies in the West Indies* (London, 1794), II, 393-500. In the preface Edwards warned that the consequences of Sheffield's policies would "haunt administration in a thousand hideous shapes. . . ." The *History* was reissued in 1798, 1801, 1806, 1810, and 1818, and it was but one of a major body of literature on the West Indies to appear in this period, much of it also attacking Lord Sheffield. See, for example, Simon Cock, *An Answer to Lord Sheffield's Pamphlet on the Subject of the Navigation System Proving that the Acts Deviating therefrom which His Lordship Censures were Beneficial to Our Trade and Navy in the Last War and ought to be Renewed in the Present* (London, 1804); Gibbes W. Jordan, *The Claim of the West India Colonists to the Right of Obtaining Necessary Supplies from America and Employing the Necessary Means of Effectually Obtaining these Supplies Under a Limited and Duly Regulated Intercourse, Stated and Vindicated in Answer to Lord Sheffield's Strictures* (London, 1804); Joseph Lowe, *An Inquiry into the State of the British West Indies* (London, 1808). Macall Medford, *Oil Without Vinegar and Dignity Without Pride; Or British, American and West Indian Interests Considered* (London, 1807); and William Spence, *The Radical Cause of the Present Distresses of the West India Planters Pointed Out, and the Inefficiency of the Measures which have been Proposed for Relieving them Demonstrated* (London, 1808). Madison was familiar with most of these works, having requested Pinkney to forward copies of them for deposit in the State Department library. See Madison to Pinkney, March 21 and April 4, 1808, and April 21, 1809, Pinkney Papers. Madison's personal copy of Medford's pamphlet is in the collection of Madison pamphlets in the Alderman Library, University of Virginia. Even if it is not clear that Madison owned copies of particular works, he would have been familiar with their contents from his reading of the *Edinburgh Review*, a periodical which devoted much space to the problems of neutral rights and the West Indies.

have quite the personal concern of the planters, agreed that Sheffield's Canadian visions were both "extravagant" and "mischievous," and concluded that Canada was "a subject of which no pleasant picture can be drawn. Till we can force Nature to make," he wrote, "a free and open navigation and to soften the climate, we will not derive any advantage from Canada or Nova Scotia in any degree equal to the hopes that are held out to us."[111]

American critics of Sheffield, notably Madison, Jefferson, and Coxe, of course, had their own grounds for rejecting the Englishman's observations, but they were for that very reason all the more inclined to accept the unfavorable picture of Canada that was presented in these polemical controversies. As they did so, they explicitly premised their belief in the effectiveness of American commercial restrictions on the assumption that Canada could make no worthwhile contribution to the imperial economy. Here Madison also singled out for attack in the 1790's William Knox, the British official responsible for incorporating Lord Sheffield's views into law in the Order in Council of July 2, 1783, and charged him with an egregious error.[112] It would only be a matter of time, Madison believed, before the American policies of commercial discrimination exposed the fact that the theories of the British navigation acts did not fit the new economic realities of the North Atlantic and Caribbean regions. This confidence was increased by Madison's knowledge that in the years immediately after 1783 there was no sudden growth in the trade between Canada and the West Indies, and that to cope with this situation the British government, especially during wartime, constantly had to exempt the West Indies from the navigation laws to allow them to receive supplies in American bottoms. Indeed, at times the situation in the Canadian provinces themselves seemed so unpromising, even in the Newfoundland fishery, that Canadians occasionally had to import food from the United States.[113] The fact of Canadian underdevelopment was prominent among the considerations that led Madison to oppose the Federalists and their military preparations during the crisis in Anglo-American relations of 1793-1794, since that course, he wrote, amounted to saying no more

[111] Champion, *Considerations*, 123.

[112] AC, 3d Cong, 1st sess., 223. For the background on William Knox see Leland J. Bellot, *William Knox: The Life and Thought of an Eighteenth Century Imperialist* (Austin, Tex., 1977), esp. 189-194.

[113] Coxe, *Brief Examination*, 21-22. For the exemptions in the West India trade see Alice B. Keith, "Relaxations in the British Restrictions on the American Trade with the British West Indies, 1783-1802," *Journal of Modern History* 20 (1948), 1-19. See also Lowell J. Ragatz, *Statistics for the Study of British Caribbean Economic History, 1763-1833* (London, 1928), 6; and Graham, *British Policy and Canada*, 72-76.

to Britain than "do us justice or we will seize on Canada, though the loss will be trifling to you, while the cost will be immense to us."[114] A decade later, as Secretary of State, his views on Canada had not changed. He declared to Monroe in 1805 that Britain could only escape the pressure of American commercial restriction as it would operate on the West Indies by "forcing the growth of the Continental provinces of Nova Scotia etc." This, he believed, would be a "preposterous" policy for Britain to adopt, since the West Indies were unquestioningly a "source of wealth and power" and contributed greatly to "the revenue, commerce, and navigation of the parent state," while Canada he dismissed as a benighted series of "unproductive establishments . . . rather expensive than profitable" to the empire.[115]

These convictions on the subject of Canada were strengthened by Madison's research into the history of the "rule of '56" and its effects on the West Indian economies, and it was clearly this same body of knowledge that gave him his supreme confidence in the effectiveness of the embargo to bring Britain to terms.[116] Any British policies that did not take into consideration these fundamental realities—as Madison believed them to be—only worsened the plight of the West Indies, and he could scarcely believe that Britain would adhere to the Orders in Council at such risk. As early as May 1808 Madison declared that Great Britain would be forced to repeal the Orders in Council because of distress in the West Indies, and he noted again in July that "on the whole, connecting the embargo with the Orders in Council, the West India interest has no reason to exult in the policy of the latter."[117] It

[114] *Political Observations*, Cong. Ed., *Writings*, IV, 498.

[115] Madison to Monroe, March 6, 1805, Diplomatic Instructions: All Countries, NA. Madison gave the same message to the British minister in Washington. See Merry to Lord Mulgrave, June 2, 1805, F.O. 5, vol. 45, while the *National Intelligencer*, on November 20, 22, and 25, 1805, printed some old attacks on Lord Sheffield written by James McHenry in 1784.

[116] During the summer of 1805 Madison also read Edward Long's *The History of Jamaica: Or General Survey of the Antient and Modern State of that Island* (3 vols., London, 1774). See his "Extracts from Long's Hist. Jamaica," Madison Papers, LC. Shortly after this he received a report on American trade from Jacob Crowninshield which stated that "the British provinces in America can by no means in their present state furnish important supplies to the British West Indies." See John H. Reinoehl, "Some Remarks on the American Trade by Jacob Crowninshield to James Madison, 1806," *WMQ* 3d Ser., 16 (1959), 83-118. Medford, in his *Oil without Vinegar*, 66, also argued that to bring Britain to terms, America "has nothing to do *but not to let a barrel of provisions go out of her ports for eighteen months*, and the West India islands will declare themselves independent."

[117] Madison to Pinkney, May 1, 1808, Madison Papers, LC; same to same, July 21, 1808, Pinkney Papers. As early as 1790 Madison believed that if Britain should be forced to supply the West Indies at wartime costs without American aid, "she could not afford to keep them."

was for these reasons that he regarded the evasions of the embargo as so serious, pointing out to Jefferson that but for such lawlessness "there must have been an uproar in the West Indies far more operative (on the British government) than the disturbance among the weavers."[118] For these same reasons, he could not approve of the repeal of the embargo, and to the end of his life always maintained that the crisis it should have caused in the West Indies would have eventually brought Britain to terms.[119] How far Jefferson accepted these ideas is not wholly clear. Very probably throughout the embargo Jefferson placed a greater emphasis on British difficulties in Europe as the factor that might persuade the ministry to cease its violation of neutral rights, but it is possible to suggest that one reason, among many to be sure, why he never seriously prepared for an invasion of Canada to follow a repeal of the embargo was a lingering belief shared with Madison that Canada was not a sufficiently valuable possession to Britain to justify the difficulties of a war.[120]

Yet the ideas of Lord Sheffield and other promoters of Canada did not disappear over the years simply because they seemed grossly unrealistic or were not immediately fulfilled—and Madison knew it.[121] Sheffield continued to assert his claims, and he was one of the earliest pamphleteers after 1803 to warn of the dangers to British navigation in making concessions to Americans in the West Indian trades.[122] In

See "Notes on Trade and Shipping," May 14, 1790, Madison Papers, LC. Similar views were also expressed in *The Monitor*, May 31, 1808, a Washington journal edited in Madison's interest by John Colvin.

[118] Madison to Jefferson, August 14, 1808, Jefferson Papers, LC. The opposition to the ministry in Parliament argued in a similar way. Lord Holland, while noting claims that the Orders in Council were designed to benefit the West India interest, asked "how this was to arise if a war took place with the U. States, which, he contended, the Orders in Council were calculated to produce, when it was clearly ascertained that the West Indian islands depended on the U. States for a large proportion of their provisions." See *Cobbett's Parliamentary Debates*, X, 1275.

[119] Madison to Henry Wheaton, July 11, 1824, Madison Papers, LC. As the problems of embargo enforcement grew throughout 1808, *The Monitor*, on September 17 and December 15, 1808, advocated the conquest of Canada as the solution.

[120] On Jefferson's hopes for peace in Europe see Jefferson to James Steptoe, February 7, 1808, Worthington C. Ford, ed., *Thomas Jefferson Correspondence: From the Collection of William Keeney Bixby* (Boston, 1916), 160; Jefferson to John Strode, April 3, 1808; to Charles Pinckney, March 30, 1808; and to B. Smith, May 20, 1808, Jefferson Papers, LC.

[121] When Madison was inaugurated as President, George Joy reported to him that the British government was still attracted by the notion that the West Indies could receive "nourishment from the British colonies in America." Joy to Madison, March 8, 1809, Madison Papers, LC.

[122] John Baker Holroyd, Earl of Sheffield, *Strictures on the Necessity of Inviolably Maintaining the Navigation and Colonial System of Great Britain* (London, 1804).

fact, Sheffield was quick to appreciate that in the West India interest—for which his previous feelings had been rather ambivalent—he could find some important allies in his campaign to uphold the navigation acts.[123] Accordingly, he warmly endorsed in 1806 James Stephen's *War in Disguise*, while many of the pamphleteers for the West India interest, particularly merchants, adopted in return Sheffield's enthusiasm for Canada, thus hoping to strengthen their case for driving neutral commerce out of the colonial trades.[124] One result of this alliance united by the shibboleth of the "maritime rights of Great Britain" was the parliamentary investigation into the state of the West Indies in 1807, during which an assortment of West India merchants, Canadian traders, and the governor of New Brunswick produced testimony leading to a report which summarized the message of *War in Disguise* and added to it the conclusion that the United States should no longer be regarded as "essential" to the supply of the West Indies.[125] This report, received in Washington in October 1807, drew from Madison his sharpest statement ever about the "infatuating prejudices" which led Britain to overvalue Canada. "Nothing is known with more certainty

[123] In the 1780's Sheffield had been so incensed by the planters' attempts to exempt the United States from the navigation laws that he declared it would be better for Great Britain to lose the West Indies altogether than to take such a step. *Observations*, 152. The situation was, in fact, more complex. Sheffield really feared that if the planters succeeded in their campaign to get American supplies, they would then seek the chance to join the United States, thus destroying the empire. See Sheffield to Knox, July 3, 1783, and Lord Sackville to Knox, September 20, 1783, both in Great Britain, Historical Manuscripts Commission, Knox MSS, *Various Collections 55* (London, 1909), VI, 191, 192.

[124] See Sheffield, *Strictures* (2d ed., London, 1806), 105. Joseph Marryat, *Concessions to America the Bane of Britain, or the Cause of the Present Distressed Situation of the British Colonial and Shipping Interests Explained and the Proper Remedy Suggested* (London, 1807), 46; and also his *Hints to Both Parties: Or Observations on the Proceedings in Parliament upon the Petitions against the Orders in Council* (London, 1808). Supporting Sheffield here were also Jerome Alley, *A Vindication of the Principles and Statements advanced in the Strictures of the Right Hon. Lord Sheffield on the Necessity of Inviolably Maintaining the Navigation and Colonial System of Great Britain* (London, 1806). See also Nathaniel Atcheson, *Collection of Interesting and Important Reports and Papers on the Navigation and Trade of Great Britain, Ireland, and the British Colonies in the West Indies and North America* (London, 1807); and his *American Encroachments on British Rights: Or Observations on the Importance of the British North American Colonies. And on the Late Treaties with the United States: With Remarks on Mr. Baring's Examination; and a Defence of the Shipping Interest from the Charge of having attempted to Impose on Parliament, and of factious conduct in their Opposition to the American Intercourse Bill* (London, 1808). Atcheson, a Canadian merchant, was later appointed by the merchants of Montreal and Quebec to lobby in London against concessions to the United States. Most of his pamphlets were dedicated to Lord Sheffield.

[125] British Parliamentary Papers, *Report from the Committee on the Commercial State of the West India Colonies* (July 1807). The report is on pp. 3-7, while the testimony is on pp. 9-85.

here," he reminded William Pinkney in London, "than the impossibility of drawing supplies for the West Indies from the British colonies in our neighbourhood." Only the United States, Madison stressed, could provide the supplies the empire so badly needed.[126] But about a year later, toward the end of 1808, Madison began to sense that this "infatuating prejudice" was far more dangerous to the United States than he had at first realized, and from that time onward he never again made any remarks suggesting that he still felt Canada was of little or no value to the British empire.

Sheffield, in his continuing advocacy of Canada—while also indulging in some fairly free remarks about the "childishness" of the early American attempts at commercial restriction—had challenged, indeed almost begged, the United States to resort to an embargo in order to obtain for Canada the full benefits of the navigation laws.[127] This point was taken up in 1808 by the influential West India merchant Joseph Marryat in his anonymous pamphlet *Hints to Both Parties*, which, too, spoke of the need to raise "our much neglected provinces in North America to that prosperity and importance of which they are capable of attaining" in order to render the West Indies "independent of the caprice of any foreign power." Marryat, though, took the argument one stage further by suggesting that this would enable Britain to enforce her maritime rights so stringently that it could totally subordinate all neutral commerce to its wartime needs. For this purpose, he specifically advocated that Britain adhere to the Orders in Council for the duration of the war with France, regardless of whether France repealed its decrees against neutral commerce and despite the fact that the Orders in Council had to that point been publicly justified as no more than fair retaliation against the French decrees.[128] In London, Pinkney seized on Marryat's pamphlet and sent Madison a copy in September 1808, pointing out that its author had been instrumental in shaping Britain's antineutral policies. The Secretary of State abstracted Marryat's arguments in the *National Intelligencer* in November—with special reference to the sections on Canada, the West Indies, and the Orders in Council. The administration newspaper concluded its summary with the observation that if a perpetual enforcement of the Orders in Council and the development of Canada should prove to be "the real object of

[126] Madison to Pinkney, October 2, 1807, Pinkney Papers. Madison received two copies of the West India report, one from Pinkney and one from Joy, who also enclosed notes from Marryat's *Concessions to America*. On the same subject of the underdevelopment of Canada see Joy to Madison, March 12, 1808, Madison Papers, LC.

[127] Sheffield, *Strictures* (2d ed.), 155, 191, 197, 200.

[128] [Joseph Marryat], *Hints to Both Parties*, 37-38.

the British ministry . . . it is important that the American people should know it . . . as in that case very different measures might be required than those called for by a *temporary* restriction or suspension of neutral trade."[129] The implication, though unspoken, seemed clear. The United States might under these circumstances have to consider depriving Britain of its Canadian possessions.

In the fullness of time, a British minister, Augustus J. Foster, did declare to Madison, in July 1811, that his government would refuse to repeal the Orders in Council almost regardless of what Napoleon said was the status of the French decrees, but long before that occurred Britain had taken the decision to force the economic growth of Canada.[130] This was not done in accordance with the dictates of either the West India interest or on behalf of Lord Sheffield's enthusiasm for Canada, but resulted simply from a more desperate need to obtain lumber and naval stores for the Royal Navy after Napoleon had induced Russia in 1807 to close the Baltic to British trade.[131] Nor was this new British interest in Canada merely a temporary one for the duration of the war, since British timber companies demanded a long-term commitment in return for their willingness to invest in what would otherwise have been regarded as a difficult enterprise.[132] The British government gave this commitment in 1809 and 1810 by doubling the duties on lumber imports from the Baltic into Britain and increasing them again in 1811 and 1812.[133] Under this stimulus the Canadian economy, and the Canadian lumber trade in particular, began to grow far more rapidly than it had in any period since 1783. The increase in Canadian lumber production and exports between 1808 and 1812

[129] Pinkney to Madison, September 7, 1808, Reverend William Pinkney, *The Life of William Pinkney* (New York, 1853), 213; *Natl Intelligencer*, November 23 and 25, 1808. Madison would have recognized Marryat as the author of important testimony in the 1807 report on the West Indies concerning the volume of colonial sugar and coffee carried by Americans into Amsterdam. Hence Madison's outraged remarks on the "London smugglers of sugar and coffee" as the interest group responsible for the Orders in Council. See Madison to Gallatin, July 28, 1809, *Gallatin Papers*.

[130] See Chapter II below.

[131] Gerald S. Graham, "Napoleon's Baltic Blockade and the Birth of the Canadian Timber Trade," *Baltic and Scandinavian Countries* 5 (1939), 28-30. See also John Quincy Adams to Robert Smith, May 19 and 26, 1811, pointing out that with the closure of the Baltic, Canada became Britain's only source of timber. Worthington C. Ford, ed., *The Writings of John Quincy Adams* (New York, 1914-1917), IV, 83, 87.

[132] Robert G. Albion, *Forests and Sea Power: The Timber Problem of the Royal Navy, 1652-1862* (Cambridge, Mass., 1926), 353-355. See also *Natl Intelligencer*, August 10, 1810.

[133] Arthur R. M. Lower, *Great Britain's Woodyard: British America and the Timber Trade, 1763-1867* (Montreal, 1973), 53-56.

was simply astronomical, and it is no exaggeration to say that Canada sustained the Royal Navy for the duration of the war against France.[134] The impact of this development shifted much of Britain's commercial interest in Canada away from the Maritime Provinces toward Quebec, Montreal, and the hitherto undeveloped region of Upper Canada, which became the center of the supply of great and middling masts for the Royal Navy. But even in the Maritimes, the demands of the new trade soon led to the production of food surpluses for export. It was, in short, an almost classic case of a discriminatory trading system multiplying the benefits of colonies to the mother country, and the point could hardly have been lost on Madison.[135]

Even worse from the American point of view was that the growth of Canada was also stimulated by, and in turn contributed to, the growth of the United States itself. The volume of oak cut in Vermont after 1808 for shipment down the Richelieu and St. Lawrence rivers actually increased as Anglo-American tensions rose, and the settlers in this northeastern region were as likely to cross into Canada in search of new prosperity as they were to remain in the United States.[136] Americans who had neither the means nor the wish to obtain land from the landlords of upstate New York moved into the southwest corner of Lower Canada and into Upper Canada in steadily increasing numbers. Land was, in fact, far cheaper and far easier to obtain in many parts of Canada than it was in the United States, and by 1812 around the northern shore of Lake Ontario there existed an unbroken chain of settlements where there had been almost none at all in 1800. These new settlements were in most respects remarkably like their American counterparts and quickly began to produce surpluses of

[134] Albion, *Forests and Sea Power*, 346, 356. Figures on the timber trade can be seen in British Parliamentary Papers, *An Account of the Quantity of Timber Imported into Great Britain from British North America in each year from 1800 to 1818* (June, 1819). Between 1807 and 1811, the volume of Canadian exports of oak and plank timber rose 549%, of great and middling masts 519%, and of fir and pine timber 556%. In each case, the volume taken from Canada by 1811 exceeded British timber imports from the Baltic in any year before 1807. See also Crouzet, *L'Économie Britannique*, I, 91-96, 400.

[135] W. T. Easterbrook and Hugh G. J. Aitken, *Canadian Economic History* (Toronto, 1956), chaps. 7 and 9. See also John Bartlett Brebner, *North Atlantic Triangle: The Interplay of Canada, the United States and Great Britain* (New Haven, 1941), 81; W. S. MacNutt, *The Atlantic Provinces: The Emergence of Colonial Society, 1712-1857* (Toronto, 1965), 129-144; and Michael S. Cross, "The Dark Druidical Groves: The Lumber Community and the Commercial Frontier in British North America to 1854" (Ph.D. diss., University of Toronto, 1968), 82-88, 91, 105, 131.

[136] H. N. Muller III, "The Commercial History of the Lake Champlain–Richelieu River Route, 1760-1815," (Ph.D. diss., University of Rochester, 1969), 218-292. See also John Lambert, *Travels through Lower Canada and the United States of North America in the years 1806, 1807, and 1808* (2d ed., London, 1813), I, 244-255.

timber, staves, flour, wheat, meat, and potash, all of which could contribute significantly to the economies of both Britain and the West Indies.[137] Furthermore, the trade in these products in both Canada and the United States was conducted across the Great Lakes and down the St. Lawrence to Montreal and Quebec, where it was ultimately Canada rather than the United States that derived the most benefit from it. As the discredited British minister, Francis James Jackson, reported after a visit to Canada in 1810, the number of vessels clearing from Quebec increased fivefold between 1805 and 1810 and yet could still not cope with the volume of timber and agricultural produce that was coming down the St. Lawrence.[138] It did not escape Jackson's attention that the growth of Upper Canada was a significant step toward freeing the British empire from the effects of American economic restrictions, but the development, ironically, alarmed William Knox. The old Georgia Loyalist, now colonial agent for New Brunswick, feared that Upper Canada, by virtue of its prosperity and vulnerability, was simply being prepared to tempt the United States into attacking it in the event of an Anglo-American war.[139]

As Madison himself recalled some years later, there had quickly developed in the years after 1807 "in the portion of the United States connected with the [St. Lawrence] and the inland seas . . . a world of itself," where patterns of trade and personal allegiances cut across the established political boundaries.[140] And it was in this "world of itself" that his policies of embargo and nonintercourse had come to failure.

[137] Marcus Lee Hansen and John Bartlett Brebner, *The Mingling of the Canadian and American Peoples* (New Haven, 1940), 70, 73, 81, 86; and Gerald M. Craig, *Upper Canada: The Formative Years, 1784-1841* (Toronto, 1963), 43-54. See also the works cited in note 135 above.

[138] Francis James Jackson to Earl Bathurst, January 23, 1810, and to Lord Wellesley, September 15, 1810, F.O. 5, vol. 69. The papers of Francis James Jackson—Foreign Office, Ser. 353, vols. 30, 57-61—contain much material on the economic potential of Canada. See, for example, "Memoranda of the Points wherein Canada has an interest which may come into discussion in the approaching negotiation with the United States of America" and "Notes Respecting Upper Canada," F.O. 353, vol. 57 (photostats in LC).

[139] Knox to the Clerk of the Council, July 5, 1804, and to E. Cooke, January 27, 1808, Knox MSS, 220, 221, 227, 228.

[140] Madison to Richard Rush, November 13, 1823, Madison Papers, LC. As the *Annual Register* reported: "Canada has . . . risen to a degree of importance and prosperity altogether unexampled. In 1810, upward of 600 sail of ships arrived at Quebec for timber; and sawmills everywhere sprung up. . . . Our navy is supplied with her timber; our West India islands with her lumber; large and every year increasing quantities of corn, the growth of both the Upper Province, and of the States bordering upon the Lakes and the river St Lawrence, supply the deficiency of what had before been obtained from New York, Philadelphia, and the towns situated within the Virginian Cape." *Annual Register* 52 (1810), 260-261. See also W. A. Mackintosh, "Canada and Vermont: A Study in Historical Geography," *CHR* 8 (1927), 9-30.

If anything, the American restrictive policies, with the enormous premium they placed on smuggling, stimulated rather than retarded the Canadian economy. Canadian officials and merchants boasted to British companies that it would be business as usual during the nonintercourse period, while the withdrawal of American vessels from the seas during the embargo gave Canadian merchants a very real incentive to develop a trade with the West Indies. And despite the heavy demands made on Canadian shipping to carry lumber to Britain, Canadian navigation to the West Indies did increase significantly, albeit with some fluctuations, in the years after 1807, and the British North American provinces began to supply the islands to a greater degree than before.[141] The president of the Board of Trade, Earl Bathurst, produced figures in Parliament in February 1809 demonstrating that the commerce between British North America and the West Indies "was in a rapid state of increase," and both Lord Sheffield and William Knox, who so aroused Madison's ire in the 1780's and 1790's, at last had the satisfaction of seeing events begin to move toward the realization to their lifelong dreams.[142] As Knox wrote in 1808: "I applaud Jefferson very much as an Englishman and especially as a New Brunswick agent and planter for the measure of the embargo as it . . . raises our continental colonies at the expense of the American states. I hope it will continue during the war with France. . . ."[143] Lord Sheffield, it hardly need be pointed out, was equally delighted.[144]

[141] Figures for Canadian trade in the early nineteenth century are not wholly reliable, but all the available estimates reflect sizable increases for the years after 1807. The most comprehensive estimates of the trade of Quebec up to 1810 are by Gilles Paquet and Jean-Pierre Wallot, "International Circumstances of Lower Canada, 1786-1810: Prolegomenon," *CHR* 53 (1972), 371-401, and "Aperçu sur le commerce international et les prix domestiques dans le Bas-Canada (1793-1812), *Revue d'Histoire de l'Amérique Française* 12 (1967), 447-473. For the trade of Halifax see David Sutherland, "Halifax Merchants and the Pursuit of Development," *CHR* 49 (1978), 1-17. See also the figures in the appendices of Graham's *Sea Power and British North America* and the discussions by J. Holland Rose, "British West India Commerce as a Factor in the Napoleonic War," *Cambridge Historical Journal* 3 (1929), 42-43, and Ferdnand Ouellet, *Histoire économique et sociale du Québec, 1760-1850: Structure et conjuncture* (Montreal, 1966), 181.

[142] *Cobbett's Parliamentary Debates*, XI, 786. Bathurst's figures showed an increase from 120 to 259 vessels leaving Canada for the West Indies in the first nine months of 1808, and an increase in loads of timber from 16,269 to 40,123 over the same period. The diary of Augustus Foster recorded an increase in vessels annually clearing the St. Lawrence from 70 in 1804 to 400 in 1809. Journal entry for April 20, 1812, Augustus Foster Papers, LC.

[143] Knox to Edward Winslow, May 4, 1808, W. O. Raymond, ed., *Winslow Papers, A.D. 1776-1826* (St. John, 1901), 622.

[144] John Baker Holroyd, Earl of Sheffield, *The Orders in Council and the American Embargo Beneficial to the Political and Commercial Interests of Great Britain* (London, 1809). As Sheffield pointed out, "these are opinions I offered to the attention of the public twenty five

The beginning of Canada's transition from "a few acres of snow" to a collection of "respectable" colonies was a development of considerable significance for the future course of Anglo-American relations, and Madison in the years after 1815 explicitly stated his belief that it encouraged Britain to resist the recognition of more liberal maritime rights for neutral nations.[145] At first Madison was probably skeptical about the claims made for a newly developed Canadian–West Indian trade after 1808, but the dispatches sent to the State Department by the American consul in Kingston, Jamaica, at the beginning of 1809 left little doubt that a major change in the commercial relationships between Canada and the Caribbean was taking place.[146] The consul, William Savage, reported that the operation of the embargo, as Madison predicted, had caused the West Indian planters much hardship, but he also added that "the Canadas had furnished through the navy of Quebec flour to a greater magnitude than anticipated as also the article of lumber which comprises the implement of conveyance of the produce of the colonies to the mother country."[147] Admittedly, many of these new Canadian exports would have been American rather than Canadian in origin, but Madison would have derived no comfort from that fact. He had long been aware that even if Canada itself seemed to lack resources for development, the waterway of the Great Lakes and the St. Lawrence possessed the potential to command much of the trade of the American interior. As early as 1780 he had predicted that should events ever channel the commerce of the American hinterland down the St. Lawrence, the commercial benefit to Britain would be enormous. "So fair a prospect," he then wrote, "could not escape the commercial sagacity of that nation [and] she would embrace it with avidity [and] cherish it with the most studious care." If Britain ever succeeded in fixing America's inland commerce "in that channel," Madison added, "the loss of her exclusive possession of the trade of the United States might prove a much less decisive blow to her maritime pre-eminence and tyranny than has been calculated."[148] The failure of

---

years ago and everything that has happened since proves that they were well founded" (p. 45).

[145] H. A. Innes and Arthur R. M. Lower, eds., *Select Documents in Canadian Economic History, 1783-1885* (Toronto, 1933), 3-4; Madison to Coxe, March 20, 1820, Madison Papers, LC.

[146] Spivak, *Jefferson's English Crisis*, 168-169. See also Pinkney to Madison, June 22, 1808, Dispatches from United States Ministers to Great Britain, NA.

[147] William Savage to Madison, January 20, 1809; and see also Savage to Robert Smith, June 17, 1809, Dispatches from United States Consuls in Kingston, Jamaica (T-31), Records of the Department of State (RG 59), NA.

[148] Madison to [John Jay], October 17, 1780, *JM Papers*, II, 134. Here Madison was

the embargo and its consequences turned this prediction into a growing reality. After 1808 Gallatin began to collect statistics on the trade of Quebec, and these confirmed other reports of rising exports in lumber and provisions as well as a steady growth in Canadian tonnage and seamen. In fact, the figures on Canadian trade compiled by John Jacob Astor in 1810 for the Treasury Department were higher than those reported to the British Foreign Office by Francis James Jackson.[149]

Further news about the rising prosperity of Canada, moreover, was readily available in the United States, and it is inconceivable that Madison was not familiar with this information as well. Several American newspapers, including the administration's *National Intelligencer* in Washington, published throughout 1811 and 1812 accounts of developments in Canada, speculated on their importance for Britain, and hinted that the United States should lose no time in depriving that nation of such a vital resource for her commercial and naval power. The editor of the Anglophobe *Aurora General Advertiser* in Philadelphia, William Duane, in October 1811 predicted that Britain would never voluntarily renounce its anti-American policies and suggested that his readers consult the pamphlets of Lord Sheffield and James Stephen for the reason why.[150] At the same time, the *Virginia Argus* claimed that "many of the effects of a successful naval warfare would result to us from the conquest of the British provinces adjacent to us," though the editor hastened to add that this did not mean that the United States would have any territorial ambitions in a war with Britain.[151] In Washington, the *National Intelligencer* reported that some of the assemblies of the West Indian islands—which had usually been as skeptical as Madison about claims made for Canada's economic potential—were finally considering resolutions that they should rely on Canadian rather than American lumber.[152] Moreover, it had become ap-

comparing and contrasting the merits of the Mississippi and the St. Lawrence as river systems, noting that the former was "manifestly the most natural and by far the most advantageous." The latter, though, he wrote, "will be found far from . . . impracticable." Forty years later Madison made the same point again in his letter to Rush, November 13, 1823 (see note 140 above).

[149] John Jacob Astor to Gallatin, January 14, 1810, *Gallatin Papers.*

[150] (Philadelphia) *Aurora General Advertiser*, October 26, 1811. See also September 25, October 21, November 4, 1811, and July 8, 1812.

[151] (Richmond) *Virginia Argus*, November 11, 1811.

[152] *Natl Intelligencer*, September 14, October 22 and 29, November 2 and 12, December 9, 1811, and February 22, 1812. For similar statements see also (Philadelphia) *Democratic Press*, May 27, July 6, and November 18, 1812; (Baltimore) *Baltimore Whig*, December 14, 1811; (Baltimore) *The Weekly Register*, May 30, 1812; (Albany, N.Y.) *Albany Republican*, May 27, 1812; and (Canandaigua, N.Y.) *Ontario Repository*, January 15, 1811, and January 21, 1812.

parent that the British government was far less disposed than it had been before 1808 to grant West Indian governors the power to exempt American shipping from the navigation laws, and one sign of this determination had been the decisions in 1809 to authorize all West Indian assemblies to adopt discriminatory duties against American produce and to institute an enlarged convoy system to protect the Canadian–West Indian trade from French privateers.[153] Consequently, the growing number of Royal Navy ships on the North American station became in itself, as the *Little Belt* affair of May 1811 demonstrated, an additional irritant to Anglo-American relations.[154] Finally, in an Order in Council dated September 6, 1811, Great Britain excluded American salt fish from the West Indies altogether and imposed heavy duties on all other articles imported into the islands from the United States. As the *National Intelligencer* observed, this measure could only have been designed to promote the Canadian–West Indian trade while injuring that of the United States.[155]

Discussing the Order in Council of September 6, the administration newspaper, on November 2, 1811, argued that the West Indies could only be supplied from the United States, but the significance of the growth in Canada after 1808 for a policy predicated on the underdevelopment of Britain's North American possessions was not to be mistaken, and the *National Intelligencer* admitted as much very shortly afterward. In a series of articles in late November and early December 1811, the *Intelligencer* commented at length on the problem of Canada. To remove any impression among the members of the Twelfth Congress—who were on the point of considering a report from the House foreign relations committee on preparations for war—that the comments were merely occasional pieces, the editor stated that they came from a "valuable correspondent whose sources of information are unquestioningly correct and whose statements may therefore be relied on." More significantly, that correspondent, after providing detailed discussions of the economy, soils, waterways, and population of Canada, noted that his information about the Canadians was "the more necessary as it is intimately connected with their reduction and affiliation with the United States." Admitting that former ideas about Can-

---

[153] For a copy of the Order in Council of August 16, 1809, authorizing West Indian assemblies to impose discriminatory duties see Jackson Papers, F.O. 353, vol. 59. See also Gerald S. Graham, *Empire of the North Atlantic: The Maritime Struggle for North America* (Toronto, 1950), 234-235.

[154] For the *Little Belt* affair see Mahan, *Sea Power in its Relations to the War of 1812*, I, 257-259.

[155] *Natl Intelligencer*, November 2, 1811.

ada as a "sterile" region had been proved "erroneous" by Canada's rise to "wealth and importance," the author declared that "in the present state of the world Canada was "of more vital importance to Great Britain than one half her West India colonies." This rapid rise in Canada's value he attributed to recent changes "effected by settlements, by commerce, and by war," particularly the growing needs of Britain's West Indian colonies; to the exclusion of that nation's trade from the "north of Europe" by France and Russia; to the operation of "our embargo and other restrictive laws"; and, above all, to the expansion of American settlements, especially in New York, "to those places which naturally communicate with Canada." This last cause, he feared, "will continue to increase the trade down the St. Lawrence till it will be equalled only by that of the Mississippi," and he added the warning that should the growth of Canada go unchecked and should "Great Britain be allowed to retain possession of [it] she may laugh at any attempts to distress her West Indies or exclude her from the Baltic, for she will have more than a Baltic of her own."[156]

These editorials were the closest that Madison's administration ever came to admitting by word, as distinct from deed, that the growth of Canada had the potential to destroy the very basis of Madison's diplomacy of commercial restriction: his assumption that the British empire was dependent on the United States for "necessaries." Without such dependence between the two nations, the United States, as Madison understood its position, would have few means of bringing effective pressure on Britain other than by trying to build up its own naval and military forces to match those of the enemy. This would not have been an attractive proposition for Madison, and, given the considerations that he knew had justified British policies toward the United States since 1783, it was entirely logical for him to conclude by 1812 that the time had come to deprive Britain of Canada. As he recalled on more than one occasion after the War of 1812, a developing Canada presented "serious difficulties . . . in self-denying contests with Great

---

[156] Ibid., November 23 and 28, December 3, 1811. For the full text of these editorials see below, Appendix. For a similar report on Canada, taken from the *Boston Patriot*, see *Natl Intelligencer*, February 8, 1812. For a slightly later argument stressing the economic importance of the region between Montreal and Quebec see David Anderson, *Canada: Or a View of the Importance of the British American Colonies; shewing their Extensive and Improveable Resources and Pointing Out the Unprecedented Advantages which have been allowed to the Americans over our own colonists; Together with the Great Sacrifices which have been made by our late Commercial Regulations of the Commerce and Carrying Trade to the United States; Also Exhibiting the Points Necessary to be Kept in View for the Future encouragement of British Shipping and the Protection and Support of the Commercial Interests of Great Britain and her North American Colonies* (London, 1814).

Britain for commercial objects," especially since "the supplies attainable *from* Canada and from the contiguous parts of the United States, now become so productive *through* Canada, may render the contest[s] more obstinate than might have happened . . . when the dependence of the [West Indian] Islands on our exports was more acutely felt."[157]

As it took steps to foster the growth of Canada after 1808, the British government also counted on drawing increasing amounts of grain, timber, and naval stores from the Baltic region as nations there struggled to break away from Napoleon's Continental System, but it was the belief of many Americans, including Madison and his minister to Russia, John Quincy Adams, that Napoleon would probably succeed in 1812 in excluding British commerce altogether from the north of Europe.[158] This development promised to leave Britain almost wholly dependent on Canada for the resources it would need to maintain its navigation system, and for this reason Madison believed that a Canadian war could compel Britain to respect the shipping rights of neutrals. An American victory in Canada would leave Britain little alternative but to accept American terms for trade if its ministry wished to preserve the remnants of its empire from further damage. The defenders of the navigation system could have presented the critics of that system, both in America and in Britain, with no answer to their argument that the empire, without Canada, would be unquestionably dependent on the United States. As James Monroe declared while justifying the recourse to war, "Britain . . . wants and must have [provisions] as do her Islands." He was confident therefore that the American decision for war would "at an early day rid the British nation of its present ministry and that an accommodation [would] soon follow the change."[159]

[157] Madison to Churchill C. Cambreleng, March 8, 1827; to Coxe, March 20, 1820, Madison Papers, LC.

[158] John Quincy Adams to Monroe, June 22, August 16, 1811, and May 9, 1812, Ford, ed., *Writings of John Quincy Adams*, IV, 115, 117, 179, 325. For Madison's view see his letter to Henry Wheaton, February 26, 1827, Madison Papers, LC. For a more general discussion see Lawrence S. Kaplan, "France and Madison's Decision for War, 1812," *MVHR* 50 (1964), 652-671.

[159] Monroe to John Taylor, June 13, 1812, Monroe Papers, LC.

CHAPTER II

THE POLITICS OF WAR,
1808-1812

WHILE THE GROWING IMPORTANCE of Canada to the British empire after 1808 undermined a critical assumption in the diplomacy of Republicanism, political events within the United States also weakened American attempts to apply policies of economic coercion against Britain. These latter developments originated in Jefferson's decision to retire and in the fact that Madison was by no means the unanimous choice of the Republican party as his heir. Many Republicans in the northern states believed that Jefferson's second Vice President, George Clinton of New York, was a more logical successor than his Secretary of State, and Clinton himself certainly believed that this was the case.[1] He was older than Madison, could claim a more prominent record of public service during the Revolution, and his native state was rapidly growing in both wealth and population to challenge Virginia as the pre-eminent state of the union.[2] Madison's claims to the Presidency, furthermore, were also questioned by the vocal faction of "Old Republicans" in the southeastern states led by John Randolph of Roanoke. The "Old Republicans" had steadily deplored the tendency of Jefferson's administrations to depart from their conception of pure Republicanism, and for this they held Madison—partly on the basis of his Federalism during the 1780's—to be largely responsible.[3] As an al-

[1] Josiah Masters to Edmond Genet, March 29, 1808, Edmond Genet Papers, LC; Michael Leib to Caesar A. Rodney, May 19, 1808, Simon Gratz Autograph Collection, HSP. See also E. Wilder Spaulding, *His Excellency George Clinton: Critic of the Constitution* (2d ed., New York, 1964), 287-288.

[2] Between 1790 and 1810 the population of New York rose by nearly 182%—from 340, 120 to 959,049—making it the largest state in the Union. The population of Virginia, the largest state in 1790, increased by only 26% in the same period—from 691,737 to 877,683. In the electoral college between 1789 and 1812 New York's share of the electoral vote increased from 8% to 13%, while that of Virginia fell from 15% to 11%.

[3] Norman K. Risjord, *The Old Republicans: Southern Conservatism in the Age of Jefferson* (New York, 1965), 32-38, 40-71.

ternative, the "Old Republicans" in 1808 promoted the candidacy of James Monroe of Virginia, and Monroe—since he was seeking vindication against Jefferson and Madison for their rejection of the treaty he and William Pinkney of Maryland had negotiated with Britain in 1806—was prepared to let them use his name for this purpose.[4]

Madison's candidacy prevailed over these challenges, but the problems they had raised were not removed by his electoral success. The Clintonian campaign failed, partly because of doubts among Republicans about the New Yorker's age and declining abilities and partly because of its sectional nature, but the Vice President's nephew, DeWitt Clinton, finessed these problems to some extent by simultaneously leaving his uncle in the second spot on the Madisonian ticket while also seeking an alliance with Monroe's followers in Virginia.[5] Monroe, rather surprisingly, ignored the electoral possibilities presented by Clinton's tactics, but both men remained estranged from Madison after 1809, and the President could do little to reconcile them to his administration. With Clinton, Madison assumed there was, in fact, nothing that could be done to win him over, and he continued the practice, already well-developed by preceding Presidents, of ignoring his Vice President throughout his first term.[6] With Monroe, Madison attempted a gesture of reconciliation by sounding out the chances of his accepting nomination as territorial governor of Louisiana, but Monroe rebuffed the approach with the remark—which surprised Madison—that he would not consider an appointment below the level of the cabinet or a high military command.[7] Compounding the President's problems after 1809, though, was the development of opposition to his administration among Republicans who had previously supported him, especially during the election of 1808. The most important defectors here were, first, Wilson Cary Nicholas and William Branch Giles of Virginia, then William Duane of Pennsylvania, and finally Robert and Samuel Smith of Maryland. The two Virginians had been essential to Madison's success in outmaneuvering Monroe for the electoral vote of

[4] Harry Ammon, "James Monroe and the Election of 1808 in Virginia," *WMQ* 3d Ser., 20 (1963), 33-56.

[5] Irving Brant, "The Election of 1808," in Arthur M. Schlesinger, Jr., and Fred L. Israel, eds., *History of American Presidential Elections, 1789-1968* (New York, 1971), I, 202. Clinton was sixty-eight years old in 1808.

[6] Spaulding, *George Clinton*, 297. In their treatment of the Vice President, John Quincy Adams felt that Madison and his friends should recollect the "peculiar situation in which Mr. C. has been placed and make allowances for the feelings of human nature." To Orchard Cook, December 8, 1808, Worthington C. Ford, ed., *The Writings of John Quincy Adams* (New York, 1913-1917), III, 261.

[7] Thomas Jefferson to James Madison, November 30, 1809, Thomas Jefferson Papers, LC; Madison to Jefferson, December 11, 1809, James Madison Papers, LC.

his native state, while the other Republican leaders had been prominent in staving off the Clintonian challenge in their states.[8]

The precise motives of these Republicans—often referred to as the "Invisibles" or the "malcontents"—for their opposition to Madison were mixed, though they were in most cases sincerely held. Often they were personal and sometimes even rather petty in their origin. The Smith brothers, Duane, and Giles simply could not tolerate Albert Gallatin's presence in the administration as Treasury Secretary and Madison's most trusted adviser, and Giles and the Smiths had, in fact, been instrumental in frustrating Madison's original intention to name Gallatin as his Secretary of State. To preserve harmony within the Republican party Madison appointed Robert Smith to the State Department, but relations between the Smiths and Gallatin were always tense thereafter.[9] From the Treasury, Gallatin waged intermittent political warfare on the Smiths; he accused the family firm of Smith and Buchanan of mishandling government funds, intrigued unsuccessfully to prevent Samuel Smith's re-election to the United States Senate, and occasionally even snubbed the Secretary of State socially.[10] He justified this behavior not simply because he was resentful but because he believed that the Smiths were plotting to oust him from office and place Robert Smith in the Presidency in 1812.[11] Duane, together with the Clintonian Senator from Pennsylvania, Michael Leib, led the "Philadelphia Junto" of the Pennsylvania Republican party, and their long-standing dislike of Gallatin was rooted in the highly factionalized politics of the Keystone State. In return for supporting Madison in 1808, however, Duane expected to receive government printing contracts to

[8] Brant, "The Election of 1808," 191-194. Frank A. Cassell, *Merchant Congressman in the Young Republic: Samuel Smith of Maryland, 1752-1839* (Madison, Wis., 1971), 144-147; Sanford W. Higginbotham, *The Keystone in the Democratic Arch: Pennsylvania Politics, 1800-1816* (Harrisburg, 1952), 151-161.

[9] William Branch Giles to Madison, February 1809, February 27, 1809; Wilson Cary Nicholas to Madison, March 1809, Madison Papers, LC. See also Dice R. Anderson, *William Branch Giles: A Study in the Politics of Virginia and the Nation from 1790 to 1830* (Menasha, Wis., 1914), 147-159.

[10] Cassell, *Merchant Congressman*, 147-153; [Joseph Gales], "Recollections of the Civil History of the War of 1812 by A Contemporary," (Washington, D.C.) *Daily Natl Intelligencer*, September 12, 1857; Louis Marie Turreau to duc de Cadore, December 31, 1810, Archives du Ministère des Affaires Étrangères: Correspondance Politique, États Unis, vol. LXIII (photostats in LC).

[11] Albert Gallatin to Jefferson, November 8, 1809, Henry Adams, ed., *The Writings of Albert Gallatin* (Philadelphia, 1879), I, 465. See also Henry Dearborn to Gallatin, March 15, 1810, Carl Prince and Helen Fineman, eds., *The Papers of Albert Gallatin* (microfilm ed.); and Nathaniel Macon to Thomas Worthington, April 9, 1810, Miscellaneous MSS, Alderman Library, UVa.

ease his financial problems, and when he failed to get them he invariably vented his spleen against Gallatin, to whom he attributed Machiavellian powers of political manipulation.[12]

Yet regardless of the personal motives of those Republicans who opposed Madison, the target for their criticism was increasingly the President's handling of foreign policy problems, especially British violations of American maritime rights. Indeed, many Republicans disliked Madison's attempts after 1809 to continue the diplomacy of economic coercion rather than simply preparing the nation for war. It was this line of diplomacy, along with problems of illness, that led Wilson Cary Nicholas to withdraw his support from the President by retiring from Congress.[13] In Pennsylvania, Duane and Leib were equally disenchanted with administration policies, particularly after the former had learned of Gallatin's unofficial role in negotiations with the British minister, David Erskine, in 1808, which included, in Duane's opinion, some near-treasonous remarks on Jefferson's foreign policy.[14] With this development Duane's dislike of Gallatin hardened into implacable hatred, and he became convinced that the "Genevan Secretary" had misled Madison into adopting a policy of "base submission" to Britain in order to replenish the Treasury from the flow of customs receipts. Thereafter he called for both the dismissal of Gallatin and the adoption of a policy of armed neutrality and retaliation against Britain.[15] On this subject Duane was often carried away by the excesses of his own rhetoric, but his intense Anglophobia was understandable enough in Pennsylvania,

[12] See Higginbotham, *Keystone in the Democratic Arch*, 72, 73, 158, 159. For a typical example of Duane's invective against Gallatin see his letter of June 16, 1811, where he declared: "I consider Gallatin as the evil genius of this nation, more pernicious and corrupt than Hamilton was and much more dangerous because insidious, frigid, and profound in artifice. . . ." To Joseph Carrington Cabell, Cabell Papers, UVa.

[13] Nicholas to Samuel Smith, December 3, 1808; to Jefferson, December 22, 1809, Smith-Carter Papers, UVa. To the latter Nicholas wrote that he could not support "any kind of commercial warfare" since any "expedient short of war [was] submission . . . and . . . will only tend to our embarrassment and disgrace."

[14] The remarks that so offended Duane were Gallatin's suggestions that Jefferson had never viewed the respective policies of Britain and France in a "fair light" and that Madison, unlike Jefferson, could not be accused of bias toward France, since he often spoke approvingly of British "institutions, energy, and spirit." These were reported by David Erskine to George Canning, December 4, 1808, F.O. 5, vol. 58 (photostats in LC). The remarks became public knowledge after the publication of Erskine's diplomatic correspondence, and for an example of Duane's unforgiving resentment see (Philadelphia) *Aurora General Advertiser*, July 8, 1811 (cited henceforth as *Aurora*).

[15] William Duane to Madison, December 1 and 8, 1809; and to Jefferson, July 16, 1810, Worthington C. Ford, ed., "Letters of William Duane," *Proceedings of the Massachusetts Historical Society* 20 (1907), 325-328, 331, 338-339. See also Duane to Dearborn, July 3, 1810, Miscellaneous MSS, LC.

where many Republican voters were of non-English stock and many of the party's leaders were, in fact, Irish.[16] Duane, moreover, was a very effective publicist, the more so since his newspaper, the *Aurora General Advertiser*, was, as a rival editor conceded, "the oldest and most influential newspaper in Pennsylvania, and probably had as much, or more, influence with that party in the Union than any other paper."[17]

Madison's other Republican critics pursued a more ambiguous course on the issue of foreign policy. At the outset Giles and the Smith brothers supported the President, but it was Samuel Smith who was responsible for defeating Macon's Bill Number 1 in the Senate over the winter of 1809-1810. Smith opposed the bill as dishonorable "submission" to the Orders in Council, but there was good reason to suspect that his real motive was the fear that merchants would suffer should the British retaliate against the measure by excluding American vessels from their ports. The failure of Macon's Bill Number 1 resulted in the passage of Macon's Bill Number 2, which almost all Republicans, including both Smith and Madison, regarded as more shameful than its predecessor, and Smith thereafter proposed to uphold the Republic's honor by arming merchantmen and strengthening the navy to do convoy duty.[18] This last proposal could never win Gallatin's approval while he remained in the cabinet, but in advocating it Smith was joined by Giles, who also came to fear that Britain and France could reduce the United States to a "makeweight" unless the administration asserted its independence and repelled belligerent aggressions on the rights of neutrals more vigorously.[19] In the cabinet Robert Smith assented to all Madison's foreign policy initiatives but did little to win support for them in Congress, thereby arousing suspicions, especially with Gallatin, that some ulterior motive governed his conduct. The behavior of the Smiths here was partly responsible for the political paralysis that characterized Madison's first two years in the Presidency, and it left the administration in the difficult position of bearing the responsibility for ineffective foreign policies that were not of its own making.

These confused developments, however, suited the Clintonians very

---

[16] For the background see Kim T. Phillips, "William Duane: Revolutionary Editor" (Ph.D. diss., University of California at Berkeley, 1968), 204-286; and Martin Kaufman, "War Sentiment in Western Pennsylvania: 1812," *Pennsylvania History* 31 (1964), 436-448. See also Robert Kelley, *The Cultural Pattern in American Politics: The First Century* (New York, 1979), 128-129.

[17] John Binns, *Recollections of the Life of John Binns* (Philadelphia, 1854), 191.

[18] AC, 11th Cong., 2d sess., 577, 602-610. See also Cassell, *Merchant Congressman*, 157.

[19] Samuel Smith to Nicholas, January 13, 1810, Randolph Family Papers, UVa; William H. Crawford to James Hamilton, January 8, 1810, William H. Crawford Papers, LC. See also AC, 11th Cong., 2d sess., 573-580.

well. They had considered a variety of grounds on which to oppose Madison, and initially had concentrated on exploiting sectional resentment at the attempts of Virginia to monopolize the Presidency. To this charge they added, especially after the embargo had caused considerable disruption to the trade of New York and other northern states, the claim that Virginians were hostile to commerce, but their spokesmen did not pursue this line of argument consistently, largely because as Republicans they, like the Virginians, felt the need to make some sort of protest against British seizures of American shipping.[20] George Clinton, however, had always suspected that the diplomacy of Jefferson and Madison was based on "too much theory" and "too little practical knowledge," and, like Nicholas, Samuel Smith, Duane, and Giles, he grasped at the solution of upholding the nation's honor by forcible resistance.[21] This policy necessarily implied increased defense expenditures, especially on the navy, and the Vice President's son-in-law, Edmond Genet, duly developed this argument into a full-scale justification for a program of American armed neutrality. The Clintonians, like most Republicans at this time, shrank from fully accepting the realities of war, but they presented themselves as advocates of an "energetic" neutrality as opposed to the "passive" neutrality of commercial restriction. If the Republic was ready for war, the Clintonians believed, the belligerent nations of Europe would respect its rights.[22]

Toward this growing Republican disunity and rising criticism of his foreign policy, Madison was outwardly tolerant. He was no stranger to factional politics and had long anticipated that "schisms" would occur among Republicans as they "lost the cement given to their union by the rivalship of the Federal party." He was even prepared to regard such "breaches" in the party as permissible, provided that the Republic was confronted with no serious threats to its stability, but in the event of "dangers" arising from abroad Madison anticipated that Republicans

[20] Spaulding, *George Clinton*, 286-291; Brant, "The Election of 1808," 191, 209, 210. See also Morgan Lewis to Madison, June 20, 1808, Madison Papers, LC.

[21] George Clinton to Pierre Van Cortlandt, Jr., February 5, 1808, Pierre Van Cortlandt, Jr., Papers, NYPL.

[22] See Harry Ammon, *The Genet Mission* (New York, 1973), 177-178; and Spaulding, *George Clinton*, 291, 296. For some of Genet's editorials on armed neutrality see (Albany, N.Y.) *Albany Register*, September 6 and 27, October 8 and 25, 1811. See also George Clinton to Van Cortlandt, December 21, 1809, and January 3 and 24, 1810, Van Cortlandt Papers, NYPL; Obadiah German to Pierre Van Cortlandt, Jr., January 27, 1810, Jacob Judd, ed., *Correspondence of the Van Cortlandt Family of Cortlandt Manor, 1800-1814* (Tarrytown, N.Y., 1978), 315-316; and Nicholas Gilman to Josiah Bartlett, March 18, 1810, Josiah Bartlett Papers, LC.

would close ranks to carry the nation through the crisis.[23] Unfortunately for the President, though, the failure of the embargo, combined with the divisions created by the election of 1808, invalidated this prediction by destroying the reasonably harmonious relationships that had existed between the administration and the party's regional and factional components during Jefferson's term in office. In fact, the state-by-state coalition of Republican interests that had elected Madison to the Presidency began to disintegrate, and in the critical states between New York and Virginia there emerged an array of dissidents demanding a more aggressive foreign policy.[24] Their spokesmen in the Senate, moreover, especially when they cast their votes with Federalists, enjoyed throughout the sessions of the Eleventh Congress a virtual veto power over administration actions.[25] Only Monroe and the "Old Republicans" stood aloof from this call for tougher diplomatic measures, but Monroe remained constant in the belief he had formed in 1806 that the United States could come to some sort of accommodation with Britain which would do away with the need for commercial retaliation.[26] Yet, as was the case with the President's other Republican critics, foreign policy differences were central to this disagreement, and this fact made it unlikely that the administration would be able to cope with the Republic's external problems without attempting a resolution of its domestic disputes at the same time.

While Madison chafed under these domestic constrictions on his freedom of action, his problems in dealing with Britain after 1810 were also gravely complicated by the behavior of France. Napoleon, in response to the failure of the United States to replace the Nonintercourse Law of 1809 with some other form of protest against the Orders in Council, retaliated in March 1810 by seizing, under the decree of Rambouillet, large numbers of American vessels that had entered the ports of the French empire and its satellites. So serious was this development that French seizures of American vessels soon began to outnumber those made by the Royal Navy, and their combined impact

[23] Madison to Monroe, May 17, 1806, and July 6, 1807, Madison Papers, LC.

[24] See Duane to Dearborn, July 3, 1810, Miscellaneous MSS, LC; Nicholas to Giles, December 10, 1810, Edgehill-Randolph Papers, UVa; Macon to Joseph H. Nicholson, February 9, 1811, and John Randolph to Nicholson, February 14, 1811, Joseph H. Nicholson Papers, LC.

[25] For a study of the Senate see Ronald L. Hatzenbuehler, "Foreign Policy Voting in the United States Congress, 1808-1812," (Ph.D diss., Kent State University, 1972), 313, 317, 346, 354, 373-387. The "malcontent" Republicans in the Senate included, in addition to Smith and Giles, John Smith and Obadiah German of New York, Elisha Matthewson of Rhode Island, Nicholas Gilman of New Hampshire, and Michael Leib of Pennsylvania.

[26] Monroe to William Short, February 16, 1811, William Short Papers, LC.

on American trade vividly underlined the ineffectiveness of the administration's diplomacy.[27] In response to this worsening situation, Madison, in October 1810, clutched at the offer Napoleon had made in the Cadore letter of the previous August that he would withdraw his decrees against neutral shipping by November 1810 on the condition that either Britain had lifted its Orders in Council or the United States had forced that nation to respect its rights. Although the wording of this letter did not meet Madison's ideal for a settlement of the difficulties with France—it did not, for example, address the question of restoring American commerce already seized under the decree of Rambouillet— he chose, nonetheless, to accept it as evidence of an actual change in French policy. In the hope that Napoleon would not give him any reason to insist on a further clarification of these matters, Madison, under the powers conferred on him by Macon's Bill Number 2, proclaimed nonintercourse against Britain on November 2, 1810.[28]

This decision was one of the most controversial of Madison's career, and his reasons for it were the subject of much speculation. Madison was not, as his opponents later argued, duped by Napoleon so much as he was eager, perhaps even desperate, to give Britain the opportunity to live up to its claim that the Orders in Council were no more than justifiable retaliation on Napoleon's Berlin and Milan decrees and that they would be lifted as soon as these French decrees had disappeared. The President did not really expect that Britain would give up its efforts to control the flow of American trade to Europe, but he did anticipate that the policy might be continued in a series of more limited blockades rather than in the blanket blockades imposed by the Orders in Council. Such a development would have amounted, though, to a fair diplomatic triumph for the United States; it might have spared American shipping from the worst of the belligerent seizures while leaving Madison free to contend with Britain over the legality of specific blockades, which would have been a far more manageable subject than the Orders in Council. Indeed, Madison hoped that it would be possible for Britain to conduct its policies so as to "irritate France against our non-resistance without irritating this country to the resisting point."[29] On the domestic front, too, accepting the Cadore letter promised to have its uses; the anticipated concessions belatedly vindicated the Pres-

[27] For a discussion of the number of vessels seized by the respective belligerents see Bradford Perkins, *Prologue to War: England and the United States, 1805-1812* (Berkeley and Los Angeles, 1961), 71-72.

[28] Ibid., 245-250.

[29] Madison to Rodney, September 30, 1810, Rodney Family Papers, LC. Madison to Jefferson, October 19, 1810; to John Armstrong, October 29, 1810, Madison Papers, LC.

ident's diplomacy and could have a favorable effect on the congressional elections to be held in eight states later in the year.[30]

Subsequent events, however, failed to live up to Madison's expectations. France did not, as the President had hoped, "do what she [was] understood to be pledged for," and French officials not only did not release previously seized American vessels but continued their old policies, citing "municipal regulations" as justification.[31] Napoleon's conduct here, as John Quincy Adams pointed out from St. Petersburg, was so obviously deceptive as "to give sight to the blind," and this news caused Madison no little embarrassment throughout the third session of the Eleventh Congress.[32] The bill to give legislative sanction to the President's imposition of nonintercourse against Britain passed, as House Republican leader John Wayles Eppes of Virginia predicted, with "groans at every step" as the legislators voiced doubts about the sincerity of Napoleon's conduct, and finally the law was even amended to prevent the courts from considering evidence which contradicted the contents of the presidential proclamation of November 1810.[33] Even more serious, though, was the behavior of Robert Smith. The Secretary of State, so far, had been a fairly passive member of the administration, and his initial reaction to the offer of the Cadore letter had been that the President "must take the declaration [of French repeal] for the fact."[34] However, in the absence of further information explaining what Napoleon really meant in the hypothetical wording of the letter, Smith changed his mind, and probably wanted to wait for news on the status of American shipping in the French empire before deciding his response. Smith, in fact, could see no commercial advantage for the United States in accepting the Cadore letter, while the move would not necessarily solve the more serious problem of compelling Britain to repeal the Orders in Council. The British gov-

[30] [Gales], "Recollections of the Civil History of the War of 1812" for September 27, 1810, *Daily Natl Intelligencer*, July 30, 1857.

[31] Madison to Armstrong, October 29, 1810, Madison Papers, LC. On the same day as Cadore's letter to Armstrong announcing the conditional repeal of the Berlin and Milan decrees, Napoleon in fact signed the secret Decree of Trianon condemning and selling American vessels still held under earlier decrees.

[32] John Quincy Adams to William Eustis, August 24, 1811, Ford, ed., *Writings of John Quincy Adams*, IV, 188.

[33] John Wayles Eppes to Madison, [undated 1810], Madison Papers, LC. AC, 11th Cong., 3d sess., 547, 863-1094.

[34] [Gales], "Recollections of the Civil History of the War of 1812" for September 27, 1810, *Daily Natl Intelligencer*, July 30, 1857. Ezekiel Bacon to Joseph Story, September 19, 1810, Joseph Story Papers, LC.

ernment, Smith believed, would also want further evidence of French intentions before responding.[35]

Consequently, Smith argued that the Cadore letter did not furnish a firm basis for another questionable experiment with commercial restriction, and he thus placed himself squarely in opposition to the President. Stronger, more dignified policies against the European belligerents, he believed, were necessary, and, according to the retiring French minister in Washington, Louis Marie Turreau, this opinion was shared by two of his cabinet colleagues, Navy Secretary Paul Hamilton and War Secretary William Eustis.[36] To justify this stand Smith intended to prod Turreau's replacement, Louis Sérurier, when he arrived in the capital, into admitting that there had been no change in French policy at all, and his chances of obtaining such a statement were by no means unreasonable. It was thought in Washington at the time that Sérurier had left France before the offer in the Cadore letter was made, and that the minister would therefore be in no position to confirm that Napoleon had repealed his decrees. For this reason Madison tried to deter Smith from raising the issue, and the President, as Joseph Gales of the *National Intelligencer* noted, also appeared "to be afraid to think that France would not fulfill her engagement."[37] Sérurier, though, had not left Paris until November 19, 1810, so Smith decided to continue with his plan, and he duly learned that the minister had nothing to convey to the administration about either the repeal of the French decrees or the restoration of previously seized vessels. Disgusted by the fact that Madison had seemingly made yet another blunder because of his attachment to commercial restrictions, Smith became so indiscreet in his comments as to inform the British chargé d'affaires, John Philip Morier, that Madison had indeed committed a diplomatic error. The result, the Secretary of State predicted, would be that Congress would repudiate the President's policies by doing away with "the whole of their restrictive commercial systems."[38]

Robert Smith's decision to oppose the President over the Cadore letter coincided with the return to the United States of John Armstrong

[35] John Philip Morier to Lord Wellesley, October 29, 1810, F.O. 5, vol. 70. Samuel Smith to Madison, October 22, 1810, Madison Papers, LC.

[36] Turreau to Cadore, December 31, 1810, Correspondance Politique, vol. LXIII.

[37] Morier to Wellesley, October 26, December 28, 1810, F.O. 5, vol. 70. [Gales], "Recollections of the Civil History of the War of 1812" for January 30, 1811, *Daily Natl Intelligencer*, August 8, 1857.

[38] Sérurier to Cadore, February 11, 1811, Correspondance Politique, vol. LXV; Morier to Wellesley, February 4 and 14, 1811, F.O. 5, vol. 74. See also James Mercer Garnett to Randolph, February 19 and 26, 1811, Randolph-Garnett Letterbook, LC.

of New York, the minister to France, who had first received and conveyed the contents of that document. Armstrong had been contemplating his return home for some time, since he had long been tired of the difficulties of coping with Napoleon's seizures of American vessels. He was, as John Quincy Adams noted, a man of "morose, captious, and petulant" moods, and his reaction to the administration's inability to defend American rights was, like that of most of the President's Republican critics, instinctively bellicose.[39] While in France, Armstrong had been disgusted with Madison's policies, fearing that they would reduce the Republic to a "proverb of weakness and irresolution." He felt that there could be advantages—as he suggested to Samuel Smith—in resisting French and British conduct by maritime war, and on more than one occasion he had even exceeded his instructions by claiming that war would result if France did not redress American grievances.[40] In fact, his endorsement of a rumor in July 1810 that Madison had called Congress to declare war on France had led, in Armstrong's opinion—albeit erroneous—to the offer of the Cadore letter.[41] Having acted in such a dubious way, Armstrong may have decided to terminate his diplomatic career on a high note by departing immediately for home, but he always worried thereafter that the administration would disgrace both him and itself by revealing his position to be one of "mere gasconade."[42]

Madison was well aware of Armstrong's views on foreign policy, but he was surprised by the minister's sudden return, not expecting him home before the summer of 1811.[43] Gallatin, however, suspected

[39] John Quincy Adams to Robert Smith, April 13, 1811, Ford, ed., *Writings of John Quincy Adams*, IV, 51.

[40] Armstrong to Madison, September 18, 1809, Madison Papers, LC; to Samuel Smith, September 1809 and January 17, 1810, Ferdinand Dreer Autograph Collection, HSP.

[41] Armstrong to Madison, August 5, 1810, Madison Papers, LC.

[42] Armstrong had good reason to be worried here. At the time of his return he was involved in a bitter quarrel with David Baillie Warden—a consular officer in Paris and Armstrong's secretary—because Armstrong had not named Warden as chargé d'affaires. Warden returned home and, as Morier put it, was threatening "to make disclosures not to the credit of the general [Armstrong], criminating his conduct in the late negotiation in France, which he [Warden] says was a mere trick [between Armstrong and Cadore] to embroil this country with England." Morier to Wellesley, November 21, 1810, F.O. 5, vol. 70. Another consular officer in France, William Lee, also returned home at the end of 1810 and made allegations that Armstrong had presidential ambitions. Armstrong accordingly attempted to sue Lee for defamation, claiming $10,000 in damages, but Gallatin and Joel Barlow—who believed Lee's charges—sheltered Lee from the efforts of the marshall of the District of Columbia to serve the writ; then they placed him on an American warship returning to France. See Lee's Memorandum Book, July 25, 1811, Lee-Palfrey Family Collections, LC.

[43] Madison to Armstrong, October 29, 1810, Madison Papers, LC.

deeper motives in Armstrong's resignation and stated that the New York was "returning on the invitation of a party, probably the Vice President," to assist in organizing dissident middle-state Republicans against Madison in the 1812 election. Clinton's age and declining faculties were supposed to have put paid to the Vice President's political ambitions, but Gallatin believed that Clinton "seemed to increase in ambition the older he grew."[44] Also circulating in Washington at the end of 1810 were rumors that Armstrong, especially if he took up residence not in New York but in his native state of Pennsylvania, might even be seeking the Vice Presidency himself. The minister's reception in the Middle Atlantic states on his return from France did nothing to remove this impression. While traveling to Washington to settle his accounts and report to the President, he was honored with public dinners in New York City, Philadelphia, and Baltimore, and, according to William Lee, there was on these occasions much talk of him "for Governor of Pennsylvania, Secretary of State, and even for President."[45]

Armstrong was almost certainly approached by some "malcontent" Republicans, probably the Clintonians, about the election of 1812, but he appears to have shown little immediate interest in his political future.[46] While still in France he had considered settling in Philadelphia, but, in truth, he was not greatly disposed to become a schismatic, having realized long ago that it was politically unwise to defy the sentiments of the majority as they were expressed in the Republican party.[47] Moreover, he was immediately preoccupied with the problems of settling his family in America and he did not take up residence in Pennsylvania, retiring instead to his wife's estates in New York. Although he was somewhat disappointed that Madison had not been more openly enthusiastic about his performance in France, Armstrong remained in New York until the end of 1812, content by and large to observe the increasing diplomatic and political problems of the administration and to dabble occasionally in politics.[48] War, he was convinced, was the best remedy for the nation's ills, though he felt that the "spirit" to attempt it was lacking in the administration. "We are,"

[44] [Gales], "Recollections of the Civil History of the War of 1812" for November 13, 1810, *Daily Natl Intelligencer*, July 30, 1857.

[45] William Lee to Susan Lee, December 10, 1810, Lee-Palfrey Family Collections, LC.

[46] John Smith to [Nicholas], March 3, 1811, Randolph Family Papers, UVa. William Burwell to Nicholas, February 14, 1811, Wilson Cary Nicholas Papers, LC.

[47] Armstrong to Short, May 2, 1810, Short Papers, LC. Also see Armstrong to Ambrose Spencer, June 8, 1807, Miscellaneous MSS, NYHS.

[48] Armstrong to Madison, December 10, 1810, Madison Papers, LC.

he lamented, "a nation of quakers without either their morals or their motives."[49]

By early 1811, however, Madison had come to share Gallatin's belief that Armstrong would help organize and possibly even head an anti-administration ticket in 1812.[50] The President may have been driven to this conclusion by reports of statements attributed to Armstrong after his departure from Washington at the end of 1810. In Baltimore on his return home Armstrong was quoted as having stated that all his diplomatic correspondence with the French government should be made public because it would prove that "he, at least, was influenced by a just regard for the honor, dignity, and independence of our country." The implication was that the administration was not motivated by similar considerations, and Madison resented the statement, since he took the trouble to preserve it in his personal papers.[51] While the belief that there would be an anti-administration ticket in 1812 credited the "malcontent" Republicans with far more unity of purpose than they then, or ever, possessed, the potential for such a development undeniably existed. Armstrong, thanks to his authorship of the Newburgh letters in 1783 inciting the Continental Army to mutiny, was notorious both as an intriguer and as a polemicist of great ability, and he had, furthermore, important political and family ties with some of the leading Republicans of New York—notably the Clintons, the Livingstons, the Lewises, and the Spencers.

Nor would any future anti-administration ticket be short of important allies or issues to use against the President. Duane, as he moved toward open revolt against Madison as both his financial difficulties and his dislike of administration policies increased, was inclining more and more to support the Clintonians, while Robert Smith, in another incautious conversation with the French minister in early March 1811, declared that Clinton would have made a far better President than

---

[49] Armstrong to Spencer, February 15, 1811, William Astor Chanler Collection of John Armstrong Photostats, NYHS.

[50] Duane to Jefferson, January 25, 1811, Ford, ed., "Letters of Duane," 344. Here the editor related that George W. Erving, about to become minister to Denmark, had warned him that Jefferson's "nearest friends" in Washington (i.e., Madison and Gallatin) were "persuaded that he [Duane] had entered into some arrangements with General Armstrong to promote him to the Presidency." Duane denied personal involvement but admitted that rumors of schemes to "blow up" the administration "were not without foundation." For similar reports see Morier to Wellesley, February 22, 1811, F.O. 5, vol. 74; Erving to John Quincy Adams, July 13, 1811, Adams Family Papers, MHS, and William Lee to Susan Lee, September 9, 1811, Lee-Palfrey Family Collections, LC.

[51] The Madison Papers contain an extract from the (Baltimore) *Federal Republican*, filed under the date March 31, 1812, which contains the remarks attributed to Armstrong. The filing date, however, seems to be incorrect.

Madison. The Secretary of State justified this preference on the grounds that the New Yorker would not have lacked the nerve to go to war with Britain, while his brother, Samuel, began denouncing the President for neglecting to nominate him to replace Armstrong in Paris.[52] Moreover, the capacity of the Smith family to indulge in political intrigue certainly equaled that of the Clintonians. The Smith and Nicholas families were united by three marriages, and their friends and relatives were politically influential in New York, Maryland, and Virginia. Jefferson, in retirement at Monticello, quickly sensed the drift of events: he feared that Madison's Republican critics would coalesce and oppose the administration by advocating policies of military preparedness and war. So alarmed was the former President by the possibility that the Republican party would "break into squads, every one pursuing the path he thinks most direct," that he wrote to Duane imploring him not to quarrel with Madison under any circumstances. The nation required, Jefferson argued, "the union of all its friends to resist its enemies within and without. If we schismatize on men and measures, if we do not act in phalanx," he continued, "I will not say our *party*, the term is false and degrading, but our *nation* will be undone. For the Republicans are the nation."[53]

Administration suspicions about Armstrong and the other "malcontents" soon became Washington gossip, spreading among Republicans generally. So too did the news that Robert Smith and Madison had disagreed over how to respond to the Cadore letter, with Gales noting at the time that Smith did "not seem sorry that such a *report* had got abroad."[54] And it was these developments, combined with the Senate rejection of the bill to recharter the Bank of the United States in

[52] Duane to David Baillie Warden, March 21, 1811, David Baillie Warden Papers, LC; *Aurora*, March 1, 5, 16, and 29, 1811. See also Morier to Wellesley, March 3, 1811, F.O. 5, vol. 74; Smith to [Nicholas], March 3, 1811, Randolph Family Papers, UVa; and Sérurier to Cadore, March 5, 1811, Correspondance Politique, vol. LXV. Among the reasons for Samuel Smith wanting the appointment to Paris was to persuade Napoleon to accept the marriage of his brother, Jerome, to Smith's niece, Elizabeth Patterson. Napoleon had opposed the marriage and no doubt would have refused to accept Smith as minister at his court.

[53] Jefferson to Duane, March 28, April 30, 1811, Jefferson Papers, LC. The network of alliances among the Jefferson, Nicholas, Smith, Clinton, Livingston, Lewis, and Armstrong families provided the Republican party with much of its informal and organized support. Jefferson realized that the quarrel between Madison and the Smiths was fraught with immense personal and political consequences, and he begged all concerned to consider him as neutral. Jefferson to Robert Smith, April 30, 1811, Robert and Samuel Smith Papers, Maryland Historical Society.

[54] [Gales], "Recollections of the Civil History of the War of 1812" for February 18, 1811, *Daily Natl Intelligencer*, August 8, 1857. See also Charles Cutts to William Plumer, February 25, 1811, William Plumer Papers, LC; Dearborn to Jefferson, April 14, 1811, Jefferson Papers, LC.

February 1811, that drove Gallatin to the conclusion that his enemies were now finally uniting to force him out of the cabinet. The bank recharter bill failed because the Vice President as well as the Republican Senators from New York, New Jersey, Pennsylvania, Maryland, and Virginia all voted against it, and thus against the known wishes of the Secretary of the Treasury. Gallatin, who had often contemplated withdrawing from the cabinet, decided to stand no more. Complaining of the growing strength of "personal factions" within the Republican party, he sent the President a letter of resignation in the first week of March, and waited for the reaction.[55]

As the third session of the Eleventh Congress ended, its members were well aware that personal and political relationships within the administration were strained to the breaking point. As John Randolph remarked: "Things as they are cannot go on much longer. The administration are now, in fact, aground [and] nothing remains but to lighten the ship"; therefore the President would have to make some critical decisions about separating his friends from his enemies.[56] This view was reinforced by a group of Republican Congressmen—whose number included Senator William H. Crawford of Georgia and Representative Nathaniel Macon of North Carolina—who called on the President early in March to urge him to unify his supporters. Madison admitted he was aware of the intrigues against the administration, but, according to Macon, he seemed disinclined to take any action, on the grounds that his Republican opponents would ultimately be unable to agree among themselves.[57] However, as he reflected on his position, the President could hardly have avoided the conclusion that the rising opposition within the party boded ill for the future, and the resignation of Gallatin finally forced him to act. Should the Treasury Secretary insist that his resignation be accepted, the President would be left almost entirely dependent on the Smith brothers and their connections for advice and political support.[58] And since Madison had never been

[55] Irving Brant, *James Madison: The President, 1809-1812* (Indianapolis, 1956), 265-270. Gallatin probably talked with Madison after submitting his resignation. His kinsman Joseph H. Nicholson urged him to do so and to point out that Gallatin's opponents were also foes of the President. "The cabal," Nicholson declared, was "just beginning their attack more openly on Mr. Madison by holding up Clinton." Nicholson to Gallatin, March 6, 1811, *Gallatin Papers.*

[56] Randolph to Nicholson, February 17, 1811, Nicholson Papers, LC.

[57] Macon to Nicholson, February 9, 11, and 15, 1811; Crawford to Macon, March 1, 1811, ibid.

[58] As Randolph observed to Nicholson, March 10, 1811, ibid.: "I do . . . doubt whether Madison will be able to meet the shock of the 'Aurora,' 'Whig,' 'Enquirer,' 'Boston Patriot' etc etc; and it is highly probable that, beaten in detail by the superior activity and vigor of

enthusiastic about having Robert Smith in the cabinet in the first place, he made a crucial decision. He offered James Monroe, recently elected as governor of Virginia, the position of Secretary of State.[59]

This action promised to relieve some of Madison's problems, though only at the expense of aggravating others. There was little point in making a change in the State Department if Madison wanted to continue the foreign policies that Smith and many other Republicans disliked. In this respect, the invitation to Monroe indicated that the President might wish to make a new attempt to settle American grievances with Britain. Indeed, as rumors of the cabinet change spread, many Republicans believed that such a change in policy was imminent.[60] Monroe's appointment might also help in restoring the support of the "Old Republicans" to the administration, but there Monroe's political usefulness would probably end. The schisms in the Middle Atlantic states posed the more serious threat to Republican unity, and in this context Monroe, as a Virginian, was a distinct liability. In fact, the reports that Monroe would succeed Smith jolted Armstrong out of his retirement, drawing him back into presidential politics.

The prospect of a cabinet change annoyed Armstrong. Not only had he always questioned Monroe's talents as a diplomat, but he now feared that the Virginian would be placed in a favorable position to seek the Presidency after Madison. Such a development, he complained to Justice Ambrose Spencer of New York, would do more to disrupt the Republican party and the union than "anything else that has yet occurred." The union of the states, Armstrong declared, was still no stronger than a mere "bundle of twigs," and he predicted that if Monroe should attempt to succeed Madison, the ascendency of the Republicans "must and will go." "Neither western, middle, nor northern states," he felt, would "consent to take a third president in succession from Virginia." Armstrong hoped that Monroe and his Virginian supporters "would steer us clear of this rock" by turning down Madison's offer.[61]

Monroe had no desire to refuse the post, but he was aware that his appointment would raise a problem of credibility. Since he was known

---

the Smiths, he may sink ultimately into their arms, and unquestionably will . . . receive the law from them."

[59] Madison to Monroe, March 20, 1811, Madison Papers, LC.

[60] Littleton Tazewell to Monroe, March 24, 1811, James Monroe Papers, LC. Philip Norbonne Nicholas to Samuel Smith, April 3, 1811, Samuel Smith Papers, LC. Randolph to Garnett, March 25, 1811, Randolph-Garnett Letterbook, LC. J. G. Jackson to Madison, April 1, 1811, Madison Papers, LC. Henry St. George Tucker to Garnett, May 25, 1811, James Mercer Garnett Papers, Duke University Library. (Richmond, Va.) *The Enquirer*, May 10, 1811.

[61] Armstrong to Spencer, March 19, 1811, Chanler Collection, NYHS.

publicly as a critic of Madison's policies, he was somewhat surprised by the President's move, realizing as well that the "near connections" of Robert Smith would "naturally feel some sensibility and would be apt to indulge in some portion of resentment." Even worse, he feared that his acceptance of office under such circumstances could lead to a political crisis that would threaten "the overthrow of the whole Republican party."[62] Accordingly, Monroe sought assurances from Madison about the role he would play in making foreign policy, wishing to know to what extent that policy had been fixed by actions already taken. Believing privately that the Cadore letter was not an honest repeal of Napoleon's decrees and that commercial restrictions were ineffective, Monroe clearly stated to the President that he favored a settlement with Britain "even on moderate terms rather than hazard war or any other alternative."[63] He also requested from the President a written answer which he could lay before the Virginia Council of State to justify his resignation from the governor's office. In other words, Monroe was tentatively asking whether the President was prepared to concede that the acceptance of the Cadore letter and his subsequent actions toward Britain had been mistaken.

Madison did not wish to be drawn out on these questions. He already had enough trouble without admitting that Napoleon might have deceived him. At the time, though, the President did believe—on the basis of the recently arrived news that in Britain the Prince of Wales had just assumed the Regency as George III succumbed to his latest bout of insanity—that there was a chance for "a material change" in British maritime policies.[64] The Regent and his Whig friends had always stated that they favored a more lenient policy toward America than the Tories in Spencer Perceval's ministry, and to exploit this possibility Monroe had the advantage of a personal acquaintance with many of these Whig leaders.[65] For these reasons Madison indulged

[62] Monroe to Charles Everett, April 23, 1811, *Tyler's Quarterly Historical and Genealogical Magazine* 4 (1922), 101; Monroe to Richard Brent, March 18, 1811, *Gallatin Papers. Aurora*, April 8, 1811.

[63] Monroe to Madison, March 23, 1811, Madison Papers, LC.

[64] Madison to Jefferson, March 18, 1811, ibid. The American minister in London, William Pinkney, had predicted the Regency, hoping that it would bring a change in the British cabinet as well. He warned the President, though, that if the Regent did *not* change ministers, British policy toward the United States would be "permanent and irretrievable." To Madison, December 17, 1810, ibid. See also Pinkney's reports to Robert Smith, November 6 and 7, 1810, Dispatches from United States Ministers to Great Britain (M-30), Records of the Department of State (RG 59) NA. The *National Intelligencer*, on March 19, 1811, reported there had been a change of ministry in Britain.

[65] Sérurier to duc de Bassano, May 24, 1811, Correspondance Politique, vol. LXV.

himself in the hope that the Orders in Council might soon be repealed, but he concealed this optimism in a vague reply to Monroe which merely expressed his desire for an honorable arrangement with the British government. Monroe's previous differences with the Jefferson administration, Madison added, would not be an obstacle to this goal.[66] This reply did not commit the President to accepting Monroe's views on foreign policy, but Monroe was prepared to enter the State Department on this basis, believing that a successful venture in Anglo-American diplomacy would also help reunite the Republican party.

Madison then rid himself of Robert Smith. He held two final meetings with the Secretary at the end of March 1811 to review their differences, especially those concerning the wisdom of the "restrictive system." The President reproved Smith for consenting to decisions taken in the cabinet and then organizing opposition to them "out of doors." Evidence of such activity, he noted, had been brought to his attention "from so many sources and with so many corroborations that it was impossible to shut [his] mind against them." To smooth Smith's departure and to avoid offending his many friends and relatives, Madison offered him the position of minister to Russia. Smith at first agreed to consider the offer but then refused it, imprudently admitting that he had done so on the advice of his "friends in Baltimore, Pennsylvania and New York." The *Aurora*, in the interval, had declared that Smith "owed it to his friends" not to accept the Russian mission and warned Madison to abandon Gallatin or risk being abandoned by the voters in 1812. At the end of the second interview Smith broke off relations with Madison, remarking as he did so that his dismissal would seriously injure "the Republican cause." Smith also mentioned that he would be "supported by a body of friends and that he knew he could stand on good ground in justifying himself to his country."[67]

Madison could only have understood this last statement by Smith as a barely concealed threat to disrupt the Republican party by making public their differences over foreign policy. Shortly afterward Jefferson warned the President against the "secret workings of an *insatiable* family" and their allies, who would "sound the tocsin against the *antient* dominion" in the election of 1812.[68] This warning was scarcely nec-

---

[66] Madison to Jefferson, March 18, 1811; to Monroe, March 26 and 31, 1811, Madison Papers, LC. The Smith brothers, on the other hand, did not expect the Regency to bring any change in British policy. Samuel Smith to John Spear Smith, March 24, 1811, Smith Papers, LC.

[67] "Memorandum as to R. Smith," April 1811, Madison Papers, LC. *Aurora*, March 25, 1811.

[68] Jefferson to Madison, April 7 and 24, 1811, Madison Papers, LC.

essary, since signs of intrigue against the administration were widely apparent by April 1811. Duane attributed Smith's dismissal to the machinations of Gallatin, then spread rumors that Madison would get rid of his Navy and War Secretaries in order to divide his New York opponents by offering the War Department to Armstrong. Armstrong's brother-in-law, Morgan Lewis of New York, informed the President however that his former minister to France had been in contact with the Smith brothers and was now working with DeWitt Clinton on electoral strategy for 1812. And in April 1811, Armstrong and the Clintonians were indeed brought together by Ambrose Spencer in Albany to discuss ways in which the "weight" of New York might "be felt in the national scale."[69]

These discussions in Albany, centering on the scheme that Armstrong should move to Pennsylvania to run as Vice President on a Clintonian ticket, were inconclusive. Although Spencer argued that Armstrong's "personal interests" and those of the Clintonians were "not in opposition," Armstrong seems to have preferred to watch developments from New York without committing himself too openly. Madison, however, was aware of the meetings and, already deeply upset by Robert Smith's conduct, expected both Armstrong and the Smiths to declare "open warfare" on the administration any day. He made ready for battle by gathering all the information he could about his adversaries, including the preparation of a memorandum on Robert Smith with a view to releasing it to the public should events make such a course necessary. The President also suspected that Armstrong might have had some influence on Smith's decision not to accept the Russian mission.[70]

The developments in New York had their counterparts in Philadelphia and Baltimore. The *Aurora* offered an "authorized" version of the dismissal of Smith which Madison believed had been provided by none other than the former Secretary himself. Duane denied this charge but, by doing so, only further exasperated Madison, who concluded that the editor showed a regrettable "want of candor" in his politics. Gallatin then received a warning that the "Philadelphia Junto" of

[69] *Aurora*, April 14, 1811. John Smith to Gallatin, April 15, 1811, *Gallatin Papers*; Lewis to Madison, April 8, May 2, 1811, Madison Papers, LC: Armstrong to Spencer, [March 1811?]; Spencer to Armstrong, March 20, 1811, Chanler Collection, NYHS; Sérurier to Bassano, April 26, 1811, Correspondance Politique, vol. LXV. There were also rumors that Eustis would be sent to London to replace Pinkney. Morier to Wellesley, March 26, 1811, F.O. 5, vol. 74.

[70] Spencer to Armstrong, March 20, 1811, Chanler Collection, NYHS. Madison to Jefferson, April 11 and 19, 1811, Madison Papers, LC. [Gales], "Recollections of the Civil History of the War of 1812," *Daily Natl Intelligencer*, August 8, 1857.

Duane and Leib was planning to deprive Madison of Pennsylvania's electoral votes in 1812 by exploiting the bad relations that had always existed between the administration and the supporters of Governor Simon Snyder over the longstanding Olmstead affair.[71] Madison undertook to forestall this possibility by promoting the "pro-Smith" Comptroller of the Treasury, Gabriel Duvall of Maryland, to the Supreme Court and replacing him with a "Snyderite," Richard Rush of Pennsylvania, while Gallatin acted to prevent Leib from securing control of important patronage positions in Philadelphia.[72]

These moves, amounting to the formation of an alliance between the administration and the majority Republican faction in Pennsylvania, promised to bring Madison some badly needed political support. Yet changing the personnel of the cabinet and paying greater attention to the political uses of federal patronage in the states would not necessarily stem the rising tide of criticism of Madison's foreign policies. The administration's troubles with the "malcontents" had always involved disputes over "measures" as well as "men." As John Wayles Eppes had observed to Jefferson at the time of Smith's dismissal, "only a change in our foreign relations would enable Mr. Madison to ride triumphant, put down his opponents in Congress, and silence the growlings of those who ought to possess his entire confidence."[73]

Duane, for example, was still calling for stronger measures against Britain, convinced that the appointment of Monroe signified that the administration would continue the policy of attempting to negotiate agreements peacefully. The *Baltimore Whig*, a paper edited by Baptist Irvine on behalf of the Smith interest in the city, indirectly took up the same theme with a series of criticisms of the abortive Monroe-Pinkney treaty of 1806, arguing that it was a more shameful agreement than the detested Jay Treaty of 1794. The *Baltimore Whig* also began to adopt freely the anti-Gallatin rhetoric of the *Aurora*, claiming that Gallatin and Madison had made a "corrupt" bargain with Monroe to "sustain themselves in that power which their tergiversation ought to have forfeited."[74] Both papers then published laudatory articles about

[71] *Aurora*, April 5, 1811. Madison to Jefferson, May 3, 1811, Madison Papers, LC; John Binns to Gallatin, April 27, 1811, *Gallatin Papers*. The Olmstead affair involved a dispute between federal and state courts in Pennsylvania over claims to a prize captured in 1778. For the background and for how the affair contributed to Madison's unpopularity and Republican disunity in Pennsylvania see Higginbotham, *Keystone in the Democratic Arch*, 182-204.

[72] John H. Powell, *Richard Rush: Republican Diplomat* (Philadelphia, 1942), 13-16.

[73] Eppes to Jefferson, March 20, 1811, Edgehill-Randolph Papers, UVa.

[74] *Aurora*, March 29, April 13 and 30, 1811. (Baltimore) *Baltimore Whig*, March 22 and 23, April 3, 1811. There is some question about the authorship of the anti-administration

the Clinton family and deplored the administration's hostility to all such "true Republicans."

As the "malcontents" warmed to the business of accusing Madison of being too soft on Britain, the President received in the second week of April some news that destroyed his recent hopes for a settlement with that nation. He learned not only that the American minister in London, William Pinkney of Maryland, was returning home because he felt it was a waste of time attempting to gain any further concessions from the Perceval ministry but also that the Prince Regent had been unable to make room for his Whig friends in that ministry. Even worse was the report, albeit incorrect, that George III—whom the *National Intelligencer* had confidently declared on March 19, 1811, to be permanently ill—was now recovering.[75] This development, as Madison noted, reduced the Regent to a "cypher" while also guaranteeing that Perceval's ministry would remain "inflexible in its folly and depravity" toward the United States.[76] Admittedly, among the Regent's first acts had been to announce that he was sending a new minister to Washington—Augustus Foster—to replace the long departed Francis James Jackson, but, as the *National Intelligencer* pointed out, once the Regent had been reduced to "a mere ministerial agent" for his father's appointees, there was no reason to believe that Foster would bring to Monroe concessions that Lord Wellesley, Perceval's Foreign Secretary, had just refused to Pinkney.[77] In short, Madison came to the conclusion that the Foster mission would almost certainly fail, and this belief also compelled him to consider what he might have to do should this prediction be confirmed.

Indications of the President's thinking were not long in appearing. On April 13, 1811—while the *Aurora* was lamenting that Madison would succumb to British "duplicity" and "insults" instead of firmly upholding American rights—the President invited the editor of the *National Intelligencer* to a private dinner, during which a lengthy dis-

---

editorials in the *Aurora* at this time. Duane denied he was responsible for the material relating to Robert Smith. See Duane to Warden, May 29, 1811, Warden Papers, LC. Kim T. Phillips suggests that Irvine of the *Baltimore Whig* supplied the *Aurora* editorials—see Phillips, "William Duane: Revolutionary Editor," 343—but Madison later received a report attributing them to George Stevenson, a nephew of the Smiths in the employ of Smith and Buchanan. Stevenson was also the son-in-law of Peter Carr, a nephew of Jefferson. See Edward Coles to Dolley Madison, June 10, 1811, James Madison Papers, NYPL.

[75] *Natl Intelligencer*, April 9, 1811.

[76] Madison to Jefferson, April 19, 1811, Madison Papers, LC.

[77] *Natl Intelligencer*, April 16, 1811. Joel Barlow reported at this time that he did not believe British policy would change either. Barlow to Dearborn, April 11, 1811, Henry Dearborn Papers, MHS.

cussion of foreign policy took place. Three days later Gales presented a summary of this discussion in the administration newspaper, and its tone suggested that Madison had considerably hardened his attitude to British infringements of American maritime rights. The editorial stated that any talks with Foster would fail, and Madison's purpose, Gales recalled, was "to prepare the public mind" for that event. The President also defined his conditions for a settlement with Britain, declaring that that nation would have to meet American demands for the abandonment of the Orders in Council, that its system of blockades would have to be altered to conform to American notions of the rights of belligerents, and that the practice of impressment should be ended. In his correspondence in March with Monroe, Madison had implied that this last item might not necessarily be a bar to a settlement, but now the President seemed to be suggesting that none of these matters could be successfully negotiated at all, to say nothing of any "minor points of difference." The editorial therefore concluded with the warning that later in the year the Twelfth Congress would either have to "nerve the executive arm to enforce rigorously the present non-importation [i.e., nonintercourse] or substitute for it some measure more consonant with the feelings of the nation."[78]

The editorial of April 16 was, as Gales recalled, "the first indication from any source approaching to official authority of a disposition to resort to any more effective measures than embargoes and non-importation acts" in the disputes with Britain. Its contents, however, caught both Duane and Monroe by surprise, and they suspected that the editorial had been written by Robert Smith's departmental clerk as a way of embarrassing the administration's quest for a negotiated settlement. Monroe, in particular, was upset by the uncompromising tone of the editorial, and he upbraided Gales angrily for publishing it.[79] The new Secretary of State had commenced his duties in April 1811 under the impression that he had a free hand to make a settlement with Britain, and later in the month he accepted in principle a plan for that purpose outlined to him by his son-in-law, George Hay. Hay, who had never greatly admired the policies of either Jefferson or Madison, claimed that the Republican party schisms in the middle states could be ended only by some decisive stroke of foreign policy. That

[78] *Aurora*, April 13, 1811. [Gales], "Recollections of the Civil History of the War of 1812" for April 13 and 16, 1811, *Daily Natl Intelligencer*, August 8, 1857.

[79] [Gales], "Recollections," *Daily Natl Intelligencer*, August 8, 1857. See also *Natl Intelligencer*, April 25, 1811. Morier did not believe that Monroe's appointment would improve Anglo-American relations, and he cited the editorial of April 16 as proof. Morier to Wellesley, May 9, 1811, F.O. 5, vol. 74.

stroke, he argued, should be an agreement with Britain in the summer of 1811, even if it meant risking war with France.[80]

In pursuit of this goal, Monroe first attempted to bring the supporters of his 1808 presidential candidacy to unite with the administration by claiming that he could moderate Madison's attitudes toward Britain. A settlement with that nation, he argued, would help unify the party while also keeping "a certain Yorker [Armstrong] from the presidency." This last prospect, James Mercer Garnett told John Randolph, was seriously troubling the Secretary of State. Most of the "Old Republicans," though, were not convinced by Monroe's optimism, for they could see little evidence that Madison favored their Anglophile way of thinking. John Randolph—who regarded Monroe's joining the administration as a personal betrayal—simply dismissed all talk of a peaceful settlement with the remark that either Monroe was trying to dupe his friends or Madison was duping his new colleague.[81] Thereafter Monroe and the "Old Republicans" came increasingly to differ on foreign policy issues, and a revival of their bid for the Presidency in 1812 became an impossibility.[82]

Nonetheless, between April and July 1811 Monroe met on several occasions with the French minister and closely questioned him on the repeal of Napoleon's decrees. At times the Secretary's manner seemed so abrupt that Sérurier reported to his superiors that the administration did indeed seem to be contemplating a breach with France.[83] The President's thoughts, however, were moving in the opposite direction, and he could hardly have failed to notice the widespread approval among Republicans of Commodore John Rodgers' vindication of American honor in his brief naval encounter with H.M.S. *Little Belt* off Cape Henry on May 16, 1811.[84] Furthermore, the President realized he needed to define his stand against the Orders in Council more clearly and in ways that removed the confusion in the public mind over whether France or Britain was the more serious violator of American maritime rights.[85] But there could be no point in attempting this

[80] George Hay to Monroe, April 22, 1811, Monroe Papers, LC; same to same, January 23, 1812, James Monroe Papers, NYPL. Monroe to Short, June 4, 1811, Short Papers, LC.

[81] Randolph to Garnett, March 25 and 28, April 11, and May 27, 1811; Garnett to Randolph, April 15 and 30, May 21, 1811, Randolph-Garnett Letterbook, LC. Randolph to John Taylor, September 22, 1811, John Randolph Papers, UVa.

[82] Risjord, *The Old Republicans*, 118-119.

[83] Sérurier to Bassano, June 30, July 10, 1811, Correspondance Politique, vol. LXV.

[84] Perkins, *Prologue to War*, 272-273. Samuel Smith to John Spear Smith, May 23, 1811, Smith Papers, LC.

[85] Madison to Richard Cutts, May 23, 1811, Cutts Collection of the Papers of James and Dolley Madison, University of Chicago (microfilm in LC).

before the scope of Foster's instructions was fully known in Washington and before Monroe had had a proper opportunity to exercise his negotiating skills. In the meantime, though, Madison's critics kept up their attacks on his foreign policy. Duane, who had continued to editorialize on the dismissal of Smith, finally reduced the episode to one issue. The Secretary had been removed, he cried, for his opposition to the *"feeble, faithless, dishonest, degrading* and *temporizing* system pursued since the repeal of the embargo," and the President, the editor warned, should no longer postpone the inevitable and necessary decision to go to war with Britain. If he continued to hesitate, Duane predicted political disaster both for the administration and for the nation.[86]

Much as he disliked Duane's tendency to confuse the issues with the rhetoric of indignant patriotism, Madison would not have disagreed with the editor's assessment of his choices. Vocal and influential factions of Republicans were demanding more positive action to uphold American rights, and Madison had every reason to believe that Britain would offer him no concessions here at all.[87] Moreover, Madison also learned from his private secretary, Edward Coles, that the "little clan" of the Smiths, believing that they could "make and unmake any administration," intended to "spur on their friends and relations to attack the President and Colonel Monroe."[88] By June 1811, therefore, on the eve of Foster's arrival, Madison knew that he had to obtain a settlement of American grievances. If this did not take place there could be, he predicted to Jefferson, "new shapes" in American diplomacy, including the possibility of an "open rupture" with Britain.[89]

★

THE CLIMAX to the diplomatic and political events set in motion by Madison's acceptance of the Cadore letter and his dismissal of Robert Smith came in July 1811. In the first week of that month the new British minister finally arrived in Washington for fresh negotiations, while Smith, by releasing his pamphlet, *Address to the People of the United States*, openly attacked the administration. Republicans

[86] *Aurora*, May 2, 3, and 11, 1811.

[87] All the news Madison received from Britain after April could only have confirmed his suspicion that Foster's mission would fail. In one of his final dispatches Pinkney reported that he had been informed of Foster's powers for his mission and he declared that the administration would find them unsatisfactory. The Perceval ministry, Pinkney concluded, "is scarcely yet capable of authorizing such an arrangement as ought to content us. . . ." The American chargé d'affaires in London, John Spear Smith, later confirmed this pessimism. See Pinkney to Robert Smith, March 13, 1811; Smith to Monroe, May 25, 1811, Dispatches from United States Ministers to Britain, NA.

[88] Coles to Dolley Madison, June 10, 1811, Madison Papers, NYPL.

[89] Madison to Jefferson, June 7, 1811, Madison Papers, LC.

throughout the nation were horrified by the evidence which Smith provided of the disunity that had prevailed in the cabinet. His administration colleagues, William Eustis and Paul Hamilton, who had both sympathized with Smith in the past, quickly repudiated the pamphlet, while there was much speculation about the motives behind Smith's action.[90] Madison, though, was not taken by surprise. For some time he had been expecting Smith to protest his dismissal, and the publication of the *Address* was nicely timed to coincide with Foster's arrival in Washington and the Independence Day celebrations.[91] At the same time, the administration also worried that Armstrong was about to publish a book exposing the "errors" of Madison's diplomacy as a prelude to seeking the Presidency in 1812. Monroe, after reading Smith's *Address*, remarked that "Armstrong will probably follow him and the sooner the better."[92]

The *Address* re-argued the differences between Smith and Madison with embellishments to make the circumstances seem more favorable to the former. The pamphlet included arguments which were neither wholly consistent nor very honest, but which collectively were intended to convey the impression that Madison was averse to preparing the nation for war, that Smith had always supported such a policy, and that Madison had been wrong both in his belief that the French decrees had been repealed and in his subsequent policy toward Britain. Coming as it did on the eve of discussions with a new British minister, the publication of the *Address* was as serious as Smith's earlier sabotage of Madison's diplomacy. The President described it as "a wicked act which could not be allowed to escape with impunity."[93] Equally as serious was the political threat contained in the *Address*. Although the former Secretary of State denied that he and Armstrong were engaged in organizing opposition to Madison's re-election, he concluded his observations with the suggestion that the continued ascendancy of the Republican party required a President of stronger views than Madison in maintaining "the rights of our much-injured and insulted country."

[90] Dolley Madison to Anna Cutts, July 13, 1811, Cutts Collection, LC. Monroe later recorded that Eustis, who had been brought into the War Department at the suggestion of Robert Smith, expected to be dismissed after Smith left the administration. To Duane, September 4, 1812, Monroe Papers, LC.

[91] Robert Smith appears to have completed writing the *Address* by June 7, 1811, and it was published toward the end of the month. It received wider publicity when it appeared in the *National Intelligencer* on July 2, 1811.

[92] Monroe to Hay, July 3, 1811, Monroe Papers, NYPL. Samuel Smith to John Spear Smith, June 13 and 18, 1811, Smith Papers, LC. Augustus Foster to Wellesley, July 18, 1811, F.O. 5, vol. 76. See also *Natl Intelligencer*, July 25, 1811.

[93] Madison to Jefferson, July 8, 1811, Madison Papers, LC.

Privately, however, Smith confessed that his object was indeed Madison's overthrow, and he vowed that he would accomplish it.[94]

The *Address* was immediately attacked in the *National Intelligencer* by Joel Barlow, friend of the President and minister-designate to France, who asserted that Smith *was* organizing an opposition party to work himself "at the next presidential election into a higher station than he did at the last" and that this was the real reason for Smith's refusal of the Russian mission. "We needed not," Barlow continued, "the publication of [Smith's] pamphlet to enable us to understand this project. *The parties concerned and the manner in which they have distributed the characters for the new administration are distinctly known*; and it is evident that this machinery could not be so well put in motion from the bottom of the Gulph of Finland as (Smith) thought it could from Baltimore." Ignoring the comments that this observation might provoke about Madison's motives in offering Smith the Russian mission, Barlow then refuted in detail the pamphlet's major claims against the administration, ridiculing as he did so the dishonesty of the former Secretary's arguments.[95] The State Department also contributed to the cause by producing the testimony of a clerk who swore that he had written many of the "manly" diplomatic dispatches that Smith had claimed as his own.[96] Since Barlow also demonstrated that Smith, for as long as he had been in the cabinet, had advocated no alternative policies to uphold American maritime rights, he dismissed his adversary's belated concern with this issue as "inflated verbiage" and pointed out correctly that Madison had often recommended measures of military preparation which Congress had declined to adopt, thanks in no small part to Samuel Smith and "his little phalanx."

Barlow's response destroyed the personal credibility of Robert Smith, but this did not wholly refute the charge of the administration's weak-

[94] Robert to Samuel Smith, March 26, 1811, Smith Papers, LC. Samuel Smith had doubts about the wisdom of the *Address*, but he supported his brother out of loyalty and his dislike for the President. Smith to John Spear Smith, June 13, 1811, Smith Papers, LC.

[95] *Natl Intelligencer*, July 4, 6, and 9, August 13 and 15, 1811. William Lee collaborated with Barlow in drawing up the administration's response, though Lee preferred to think that "the answer is my work, corrected by Barlow." To Susan Lee, September 9, 1811, Lee-Palfrey Family Collections, LC.

[96] *Natl Intelligencer*, August 8, 1811; [Gales], "Recollections of the Civil History of the War of 1812," *Daily Natl Intelligencer*, August 15, 1857. The clerk was John B. Colvin, an importunate editor, who in 1808 had owned *The Monitor*, a pro-Madison journal in Washington. In 1810 Colvin went bankrupt but was saved from hardship when Robert Smith gave him a State Department clerkship, which he retained until John Quincy Adams became President. See Charles Francis Adams, ed., *Memoirs of John Quincy Adams* (Philadelphia, 1874-1877), VI, 288.

ness that he and other "malcontents" were seeking to advertise. As the *Aurora* pointed out, even if the administration's case against Smith was valid—which Duane did not concede—there was still no reason for the public to feel confident about the abilities of a President who managed his affairs in so unsatisfactory a manner.[97] Privately Duane believed that the administration was now too weak to defend the Republic, which, he added, "nothing can save but true foreign aggression such as will unite all men by annihilating the horrid spirit of intrigue which has destroyed the public virtue of this country." In Virginia, Giles, like Duane, defended Smith's *Address*, circulated it among his friends, and informed them that "republicanism was not safe in [Madison's] hands."[98] Both the *Aurora* and the *Baltimore Whig* then followed the *Address* with accusations that Monroe would make a humiliating arrangement with Britain, though the editor of the latter paper, Baptist Irvine, wrote privately to a State Department clerk expressing his hope that Madison would do no such thing. Surely, Irvine thought, the President "has too many warnings before him to allow him to swerve from the right track. Should he deviate, however, it is not in the power . . . of *coalitions* between *Virginia* and *Massachusetts* or of bargains in *Pennsylvania* to re-elect him." Duane reinforced this threat by promising to republish all the diplomatic correspondence from the Erskine affair of 1808-1809, which would emphasize the folly of attempting to negotiate with Britain as well as deeply embarrass the administration.[99]

To publicize their aggressively nationalistic views, the "malcontent" Republicans also made use of the Independence Day celebrations. On July 4, Samuel Smith's Baltimore militia company not only pointedly omitted to toast the President's health but drank toasts with cheers to Robert Smith, Armstrong, George and DeWitt Clinton, and the *Aurora*. A few days later, the *Baltimore Whig* bluntly stated that Madison was not entitled to re-election because of his "pusillanimous" conduct

[97] *Aurora*, July 11, 1811. As Samuel Smith had pointed out to his brother: "whether you succeed or not in your attack [on Madison] will depend on our foreign relations. If France completes her engagement, the President's measures will be eulogized; if a Regency should take place and the Orders in Council be repealed with the blockade, his conduct and wisdom will be immortalized. If none of these should happen, your attack will have some weight. . . ." To Robert Smith, March 27, 1811, Smith Papers, LC.

[98] Duane to Warden, July 11, 1811, Warden Papers, LC. Giles to Robert Smith, July 5, 1811, Dreer Collection, HSP.

[99] *Aurora*, July 3, 8, 12, and 13, August 24, 1811; *Baltimore Whig*, July 6, 10, 13, 19, and 31, 1811. The letter from Irvine to Colvin was written on July 17, 1811, and appeared in the *National Intelligencer*, August 8, 1811.

of the nation's diplomacy.[100] In Pennsylvania, the "Philadelphia Junto" celebrated Independence Day in an identical fashion, as did John Armstrong and Chancellor Robert Livingston at a public dinner in Rhinebeck, New York. On the latter occasion the toast list also included some volunteered remarks about "unfettered commerce" and a vigorous defense of American rights. An embarrassed Swedish consul at the Rhinebeck dinner proposed a toast to the President only to find that the name of Madison drew no cheers from the guests. Whether Armstrong on this occasion was actually doing much more than indulging his vanity is perhaps unlikely, but Morgan Lewis reported to the President that the "Old Soldier" was now considered to be "in the field" for 1812.[101]

Against this background, Monroe met Foster for what would prove to be the final round of negotiations on Anglo-American problems. That the administration was sensitive to the political context of the talks was revealed in Barlow's prediction that the conduct of Robert Smith had virtually crippled the prospects for a settlement. Indeed, Monroe constantly fretted over how to deal with the distorted accounts of his motives and conduct that were appearing in the *Aurora* and the *Baltimore Whig*.[102] The administration even discounted the possibility of sending a new American minister to London, on the grounds that any nominee might be rejected by the "malcontent" Republicans in the Senate.[103] Shortly after Madison formally received Foster on July 6, he learned that the British minister was empowered only to settle the four year old *Chesapeake* affair and to state that some agreement on the legality of specific blockades might be reached after the removal of the Orders in Council. On this last issue, however, Foster offered no concessions. Pointing to the continuing French seizure of American vessels after the supposed repeal of Napoleon's decrees restricting the

[100] *Baltimore Whig*, July 6, 12, and 18, 1811. On the politicization of militia companies and Independence Day celebrations see Whitman H. Ridgway, *Community Leadership in Maryland, 1790-1840* (Chapel Hill, 1979), 76-79.

[101] *Aurora*, July 10, 1811. Lewis to Madison, July 15, 1811, Madison Papers, LC. On August 13, 1811, the *National Intelligencer* called on Armstrong to deny the charge that he had allied with the Smiths. Armstrong saw the call and wrote to Madison accordingly. Armstrong to Madison, September 2, 1811, Madison Papers, LC.

[102] James Woodress, *A Yankee's Odyssey: The Life of Joel Barlow* (Philadelphia, 1958), 280-281. Monroe to Madison, August 11, 1811, Madison Papers, LC.

[103] Foster to Wellesley, July 18, August 5, and November 12, 1811, F.O. 5, vols. 76 and 77. In his final conversations with Robert Smith in March 1811 Madison had implied that the United States would continue to maintain a minister in London, but after Pinkney returned home he was not replaced. See "Memorandum as to R. Smith," Madison Papers, LC, and note 69 above.

rights of neutral shipping, he declared that Madison's imposition of nonintercourse against Britain was unjustified. His government would be convinced that France was in fact respecting the rights of neutrals only when American merchants could carry British goods as neutral property into European ports and when France had restored neutral commerce to the condition in which it stood prior to the operation of the Berlin and Milan decrees. If the United States did not provide such proof or rescind the policy of nonintercourse followed since November 1810, Foster warned that the British government would be justified in retaliating on American commerce.[104]

As Madison had predicted in April, Britain had failed to meet the American demands. He summoned the cabinet for July 9, 1811, undoubtedly for the purpose of considering the response to be made to Foster.[105] Three days later Foster reported that the Secretaries of State, War, and the Treasury were opposed to any step that might worsen relations with Britain, while Madison had not immediately committed himself to any decision. The minister did record, though, that Madison was showing considerable "asperity" in his remarks about British policy.[106] The President was, in fact, extremely angry with the contents of Foster's diplomatic notes, and with good reason. Madison was not so much concerned about threats of British retaliation as he was alarmed by the stated conditions for the repeal of the Orders in Council. The most significant of these was the claim that the Orders could only be lifted when France had restored neutral commerce to its condition prior to the operation of the Berlin and Milan decrees. Given the enormous political changes that had occurred in Europe with the expansion of the French empire since 1806, Foster's position could be understood as a suggestion that the Orders in Council might remain in force for as long as it took Britain to defeat Napoleon. If so, it was manifestly impossible for the United States to fulfill the British demand, nor could it accept the practical consequences of such a definition of its rights as a neutral nation.[107]

[104] Foster to Wellesley, July 7, 1811, F.O. 5, vol. 76. What was involved in the British threat of retaliation was never made clear. Possibly Britain might have imposed discriminatory duties on American imports and excluded American merchants from the East Indies, but rumors in Washington centered on the dispatch of a fleet to American waters and the exclusion of Americans from the West Indies. See above, Chapter I.

[105] Madison to Gallatin, July 8, 1811, *Gallatin Papers*.

[106] Foster to Wellesley, July 12, 1811, F.O. 5, vol. 76.

[107] As long ago as October 26, 1810, the *National Intelligencer* had predicted Britain might demand the "*status quo ante* 1806" as a condition for the repeal of the Orders in Council and had noted that there was some ambiguity as to whether this referred simply to the state that neutral commerce would be left in after repeal or whether it involved the reversal of

The contents of Foster's notes, moreover, represented a significant shift away from past British justifications of the Orders in Council. Previously, British ministries had defended the Orders as no more than fair retaliation on similar French decrees, but now the Perceval ministry was suggesting that British policies were not necessarily contingent on specific acts of the enemy and that a far-reaching regulation of neutral commerce under Orders in Council might be fairly considered as part of Britain's customary "maritime rights." Foster's avowal of such a position only confirmed suspicions long held by both Jefferson and Madison that the real motive for Britain's maritime policies was to claim an absolute dominion of the seas at the expense of its commercial rivals.[108] Just as serious for the President were Foster's reasons for refusing to accept the American case for the removal of the Orders in Council. Here Foster, like Robert Smith, questioned the President's word on the critical issue of whether the French decrees had been repealed, and the British minister reported to the Foreign Office that his notes to Monroe were indeed designed to throw onto the United States the burden of proof that "even any part of the decrees had ceased to operate."[109] The President, of course, resented having his word questioned, and he suspected that Foster might be able to exploit the differences within the Republican party on this subject for British advantage. Also, Madison, in order to have responded positively to Foster's demands, would have had either to acknowledge that Napoleon's decrees were still in force or to have begun challenging the legality of French "municipal regulations." In both cases the President would have been admitting the charges in Smith's *Address* that he had been tricked by Napoleon and that his attempts to use the Cadore letter to extract concessions from Britain were futile and mistaken.[110]

As the negotiations between Foster and Monroe continued fruitlessly

---

both the political and commercial changes that had occurred since that date. Before 1806 Prussia, Russia, Holland, Spain, Portugal, and Denmark were all, to varying degrees, less constrained by French influence or control than they had been subsequently. If Britain insisted on the latter as a condition for repeal, she would, in effect, be seeking the advantages of peacetime trade in war as well as requiring the United States to challenge the "municipal laws" that excluded British produce from the French empire and its satellites.

[108] See Jefferson to Madison, April 19, 1809, June 27, 1810, October 15, 1810; and Madison to Jefferson, July 23, 1809, Madison Papers, LC. See also *Natl Intelligencer*, November 25, 1808, March 17, 1809, and June 10, 1810; and Chapter I above.

[109] Foster to Wellesley, July 18, 1811, F.O. 5, vol. 76.

[110] Madison to Monroe, [August] 2, 1811, Monroe Papers, LC. (The letter is misdated July 2.) Here Madison pointed out that Foster's demands, "though not very skilfully made up," were "evidently calculated for the public here, as well as for his own [government]." "In this view," the President warned, "his evasion and sophistical efforts may deserve attention."

throughout July 1811, Madison found himself in an absolutely impossible position. British maritime pretensions, far from moderating, were increasing to a "preposterous" level, while Madison's "malcontent" critics were demanding action in belligerent tones.[111] The President's immediate response, probably decided by the third week of July, was to issue a proclamation on July 24 calling the Twelfth Congress into an early session on November 4.[112] This proclamation, rather than the acceptance of the Cadore letter in October 1810, was the most critical act of Madison's first term, for it amounted to no less than a decision to prepare the United States for war with Britain. This course now remained the only honorable one for the President. If Britain were to adhere to the Orders in Council for the duration of the war in Europe—to which no one predicted an end in the foreseeable future—an American response limited to economic retaliation no longer seemed adequate, the more so since Madison now knew that the federal government could neither enforce an effective restriction of trade nor command its continuing acceptance by large numbers of influential Republican leaders.[113] Repeated experience had revealed that sealing off the frontier with Canada was all but impossible, and the one thing that Madison could not do was release to a new session of Congress and the newspapers later in the year the correspondence between Foster and Monroe, then simply continue with the policies of the past three years. Such conduct would only have given substance to the charges of the "malcontents" that Madison was so weak he would submit to anything, including deceit from France and insults from Britain at the same time.

The President, no doubt, carefully considered all these matters in Virginia on his summer vacation during August and September, but he could have found no prospect of relief from his painful dilemma. The continuation of peace under the existing circumstances would be both dishonorable to the Republic and politically dangerous for the President. There was still the remote possibility that the Prince Regent would assert himself to replace his father's ministers, but for as long as Perceval and his colleagues remained in power there was no chance

[111] For the administration's rejection of Foster's demands see Monroe to Foster, July 23 and 26, October 1 and 29, 1811, F.O. 5, vol. 77.

[112] *Natl Intelligencer*, July 25, 1811. See also Madison to Dearborn, [July 1811], Charles Roberts Autograph Collection, Haverford College Library.

[113] Napoleon was only forty-two years of age in 1811, and most Americans, including Madison, did not predict any sudden end to his so far largely successful career. Previously, Madison had also considered the possibility that Britain would adhere to the Orders in Council permanently and had hinted that economic coercion was not the proper response. See Chapter I above.

of obtaining any concessions substantial enough to justify prolonging American neutrality. Madison also believed that the criticisms of Robert Smith and other "malcontents" would "be renewed in every shape that deadly hatred could prompt," and they would presumably intensify as the presidential election of 1812 drew near.[114] Republican disunity on foreign policy, furthermore, would only reinforce British stubbornness. As the *National Intelligencer* pointed out on several occasions during the summer, Britain could hardly be expected to make concessions while Robert Smith was not simply exposing differences of opinion within the cabinet but openly proclaiming them "from the housetops" of the nation.[115] And Foster did report to Lord Wellesley at this time that precisely because Madison did not stand on "high ground" in the Republican party, he believed that he could ultimately force the President to make some concessions for the sake of preserving peace.[116] Preparations for war, though, would unite both the supporters and the critics of the President as well as bring more pressure on Britain, even to the extent of enabling the United States to seize Canada.[117] All these considerations pushed Madison toward a policy of war, and, although he disliked espousing so drastic a measure, he did not shrink from the demands of the nation's situation, as he understood it. Consequently, Madison returned to Washington in October 1811 and began work on a "war message" for Congress.

This message, delivered to an expectant Congress on November 5, briefly outlined the failure of the summer negotiations, with Madison criticizing Britain for putting its Orders in Council "into more rigorous execution." In response, the President informed the legislators that "the time had now arrived for them to put the United States into an armor and an attitude demanded by the crisis," and he accordingly recommended that they expand the regular army, raise volunteer corps, attend to the organization of the militia and the navy, and increase the supply of munitions.[118] The tone of this message and the scope of some of its recommendations were not quite as decisive as Madison had originally intended, since it would seem that the members of his cabinet, especially Gallatin, were less convinced of the need for preparations than the President. The Treasury Secretary was alarmed at the contents of the "war paragraphs" in earlier drafts of the message—

[114] Madison to Cutts, August 24, 1811, Cutts Collection.

[115] *Natl Intelligencer*, September 17 and October 29, 1811.

[116] Foster to Wellesley, August 5, 1811, F.O. 5, vol. 76.

[117] For a similar prediction see Sérurier to Bassano, August 31, 1811, Correspondance Politique, vol. LXVI.

[118] For a fuller discussion of the provisions of the message see below, Chapter III.

especially Madison's hints of "authorizing reprisals" to the "direct and undisguised hostility" of Britain—and he advised the president against prejudging the issue in ways that both encroached on the prerogatives of Congress and possibly gave the Royal Navy the pretext for a pre-emptive "sweep" of American commerce from the seas. In fact, Gallatin doubted the effectiveness of war policies under any circumstances, preferring instead to rely on nonintercourse with all its "evils" and difficulties, and he warned Madison that war measures would be necessarily "unpopular." Possibly too, he argued, they could lead to a "change of men . . . , a disgraceful peace, and to absolute subserviency thereafter to G.B."[119] Monroe was also disappointed that he could not achieve more by means of diplomacy, and perhaps in deference to his colleagues Madison decided to tone down parts of his message, especially by omitting a recommendation for Congress to authorize the arming of merchantmen.[120] Since this last measure would have precipitated armed conflicts at sea, it could have "scarcely failed," as Madison noted, "to bring on war in its full extent," but in its place he was prepared to convey to Congress the impression that war should be the "final though not immediate" consequence of Britain's adherence to the Orders in Council.[121]

As a broad statement designed to accommodate a wide variety of opinions in the Republican party while also announcing a major change in foreign policy, the President's message was reasonably successful. Some Congressmen, according to William A. Burwell of Virginia, were confused by the "equivocal import" of the message for recommending military preparations without making any clear commitment to their use, but generally the reaction was favorable to Madison.[122] Most of the Republican-dominated state legislatures throughout the nation passed resolutions approving the call for preparations, and, among Madison's

[119] For the text see James D. Richardson, comp., *A Compilation of the Messages and Papers of the Presidents* (New York, 1897-1914), II, 476-481. For Gallatin's comments see his "Notes on the President's Message," [November 1811], Madison Papers, LC.

[120] For Monroe's disappointment see his letter to "Some Person of High Influence in England" [undated, but late 1811], Monroe Papers, LC. There is in Madison's hand a draft, dated November 5, 1811, recommending the arming of merchantmen. Madison Papers, LC. Isaac Coles, the President's kinsman, observed that the arming of merchantmen was "problematical" and desirable only "as it may be the means of bringing on the crisis which (Congress) is preparing to meet." Coles to Cabell, December 9, 1811, Cabell Papers, UVa. See also Sérurier to Bassano, September 29 and November 10, 1811, Correspondance Politique, vol. LXVI.

[121] Madison to John Quincy Adams, November 15, 1811, Madison Papers, LC.

[122] Burwell to Nicholas, November 28, 1811, Wilson Cary Nicholas Papers, UVa. See also Edward Coles to John Coles, November 22, 1811, Coles Collection, HSP.

Republican opponents, both Duane and Armstrong applauded the move toward war. Neither the *Aurora* nor the Clintonian *Albany Register* made any serious criticism of the administration for several weeks after the beginning of November, and even the *Baltimore Whig* gave its grudging approval, though it could not resist the observation that Madison had vindicated the views of Robert Smith by "taking a hint."[123] Some "malcontent" Republicans, notably Samuel Smith and Nicholas Gilman of New Hampshire, privately believed that the administration did not seriously intend to prepare for, let alone wage, war—thus dismissing the message as a mere tactic either to "soothe the noisy" or to "answer electioneering purposes"—but they too refrained from public criticism in the meantime.[124] Madison's "Old Republican" opponents in Virginia liked war preparations even less than commercial restriction, but, as Creed Taylor put it, "lacking the *spartan* independence of John Randolph," they also generally chose to remain silent rather than risking "the gulph . . . ready for their reception" should they decide to "come out for Robert Smith" or stay as "honest minority men."[125] Temporarily, at least, Madison seemed to be invulnerable to criticism within the Republican party, and he enjoyed a brief, but rare, period of widespread public approval.

Yet the President's political problems, not to mention his diplomatic ones, had by no means disappeared. Early in November the administration learned that two members of the New York State Canal Commission, DeWitt Clinton and Gouverneur Morris, wanted to come to Washington to discuss the prospects of obtaining congressional aid for constructing a canal connecting Lake Erie with the Hudson River. The merits of this scheme—as opposed to a less ambitious canal plan extending to the eastern end of Lake Ontario—had been publicly debated since 1807, and the main arguments in favor of a canal to Lake Erie included the belief that it would free the frontier of western New York from its increasing dependence on the Lake Ontario–St. Lawrence River route to the markets of Montreal as well as reduce the attractions to New Yorkers of smuggling with the British in Canada.[126]

[123] For the resolutions see *ASP: Miscellaneous*, II, 167-174. See also *Baltimore Whig*, November 6, 1811; *Albany Register*, November 12, 15, and 23, 1811; *Aurora*, November 7, 11, and 15, 1811; Armstrong to Alexander Phoenix, December 17, 1811, Miscellaneous MSS, NYSL; and George Logan to Nicholas Gilman, November 10, 1811, Logan Papers, HSP.

[124] Smith to Nicholas, November 20, 1811, Nicholas Papers, UVa; Gilman to Logan, January 28, 1812, Logan Papers, HSP.

[125] Creed Taylor to Benjamin Botts, November 24, 1811, Creed Taylor Papers, UVa.

[126] The idea behind the Erie Canal is generally credited to Jesse Hawley, who publicized it in fourteen essays written under the pseudonym "Hercules" in the *Ontario Messenger* in

The administration, particularly Gallatin, was not inclined to accept these claims for an Erie canal, nor did Madison particularly want to see Clinton and Morris in the capital while he was trying to obtain preparedness legislation from Congress. Through their intermediary, Congressman Peter B. Porter from New York, the President tried to persuade the New York commissioners to defer their visit until the following year, but they chose not to do so and arrived in mid-December, remaining through the first week of January 1812.[127] Madison accordingly tried to expedite their business with an oblique message to Congress that it should consider the advantages of canal schemes in conjunction with "the arrangements and exertions for the general security." Since the Clintonians, their criticisms of Madison's foreign policy notwithstanding, did *not* advocate the conquest of Canada, the President was perhaps trying to suggest that his preparedness policies promised a quicker solution than a canal to some of the problems of which the New Yorkers were complaining.[128]

Such a hint, however, was probably unnecessary, since most Congressmen were instinctively hostile to a costly scheme which promised to benefit only New York and Ohio, and Gallatin duly submitted a report pointing out that the United States could not afford to subsidize expensive internal improvements and that a canal to Lake Erie would not significantly "arrest the illicit trade from Canada." The House committee investigating the subject endorsed this verdict, thus killing the New York scheme.[129] Many southern Republicans, though, suspected that Clinton was far more interested in lobbying for the Presidency than he was in building a canal, and indeed the task of prom-

1807. DeWitt Clinton was certainly familiar with Hawley's essays, and both he and the other members of the New York State Canal Commission were very mindful of the problem that Montreal stood to capture much of the trade of western New York because of poor communications between the eastern and western sections of the state. See David Hosack, *Memoir of DeWitt Clinton* (New York, 1829), 390-422. Clinton's "Canal Journal" for 1810 is in William W. Campbell, *The Life and Writings of DeWitt Clinton* (New York, 1849), 27-205. See also Ronald E. Shaw, *Erie Water West: A History of the Erie Canal, 1792-1854* (Lexington, 1966), 40, 80.

[127] In his report on internal improvements in 1808, Gallatin had advocated for New York a canal system that extended only to the eastern end of Lake Ontario. See *ASP: Miscellaneous*, I, 724-921. See also Peter B. Porter to DeWitt Clinton, November 14, 1811, DeWitt Clinton Papers, Columbia University Library; Gouverneur Morris to Clinton, November 20, 1811, Gouverneur Morris Papers, LC.

[128] Richardson, *Messages and Papers*, II, 482. For the Clintonian view of Canada see *Albany Register*, October 25, 1811, where Edmond Genet wrote: "We may, it is true, threaten England to take the Canadas and realize it . . . but having gratified our just vengeance and obtained satisfaction for past depredations, how shall our rights be secured against future excesses and future robberies?"

[129] Gallatin to Henry M. Ridgely, January 6, 1812, *ASP: Miscellaneous*, II, 179.

oting the canal seemed to fall mainly on Morris, while Clinton spent a great deal of time in wide-ranging discussions with the legislators.[130] According to the French minister, Clinton sounded out the Federalists with promises of a "vigorous" administration, including the strengthening of both the army and the navy, and Jonathan Roberts of Pennsylvania reported that the New Yorker had approached him and others on the prospects of a Clintonian nomination in the congressional caucus.[131] From most of the Republicans this last idea appears to have met with a flat refusal, though many may have been willing to consider DeWitt Clinton as a replacement for his uncle in the vice-presidential position.

Clinton's visit to Washington thus failed in both its objectives, but it did make an impact on the capital's society, since the New Yorker clearly impressed many as an able and formidable man.[132] Where the Vice President stood in regard to all this politicking was not easy to say, but George Clinton—in his seventy-third year—was now definitely regarded by all observers as too old to remain active in politics. Even the aging "malcontent" himself admitted that he gave little thought to the issues of the day, and consequently the rumor that his nephew would become his political heir by challenging Madison for the Presidency in 1812, with either Samuel Smith or Governor Simon Snyder of Pennsylvania as his running mate, became accepted as a fact in Washington.[133] Clinton's friends noted that the administration was "discomforted" by this possibility, and one of Madison's supporters, Hugh Nelson of Virginia, did indeed confess that he had "fears for our worthy little James."[134]

[130] Felix Grundy to Andrew Jackson, February 12, 1812, Andrew Jackson Papers, LC; James A. Bayard to Rodney, December 22, 1811, "James Ashton Bayard Letters, 1802-1814," *Bulletin of the New York Public Library* 4 (1900), 232.

[131] Sérurier to Bassano, January 12, 1812, Correspondance Politique, vol. LXVII; Foster to Wellesley, December 21, 1811, F.O. 5, vol. 77. See also Philip S. Klein, ed., "Memoirs of a Senator from Pennsylvania: Jonathan Roberts, 1771-1854," *Pennsylvania Magazine of History and Biography* 62 (1938), 227.

[132] Sylvanus Miller to Pierre Van Cortlandt, Jr., December 22, 1811, Judd, ed., *Correspondence of the Van Cortlandt Family*, 414.

[133] George Clinton to John McKesson, January 19, 1812, George Clinton Papers, NYSL. Augustus Foster, Journal entry April 26, 1812, Augustus John Foster Papers, LC; Randolph to Garnett, April 29, 1812, Randolph-Garnett Letterbook, LC. See also Dolley Madison to Anna Cutts, January 14, 1812, Cutts Collection; Samuel Taggart to John Taylor, December 28, 1811, George H. Haynes, ed., "Letters of Samuel Taggart," *Proceedings of the American Antiquarian Society* 33 (1923), 370-371.

[134] Gordon Mumford to George Clinton, January 1, 1812; Mattias B. Tallmadge to same, February 4, 1812, George Clinton Papers, NYSL. Hugh Nelson to Cabell, December 28, 1811, Cabell Papers, UVa.

While Clinton, as Nelson vividly put it, was preparing to work "in all the filth, muck, and mire of intrigue," Peter B. Porter, as chairman of the House foreign relations committee, brought forward for debate on November 29, 1811, a report on the President's message calling for war preparations. In the course of writing the report, the committee—as was standard practice with the framing of much important legislation—had consulted with Monroe on the precise intentions behind the President's message.[135] According to committee member Felix Grundy of Tennessee, both he and his colleagues, while quite sympathetic to the call for stronger measures, wanted to be sure that the administration meant to resort to war should British policies remain unchanged. Monroe unequivocally gave them this assurance. The committee and the Secretary of State then reached an understanding that the preparedness legislation could proceed and that the issues of war and peace would definitely be settled before the session ended.[136] Porter accordingly presented to the House the committee's report, which stated the case for war against Britain in the strongest terms and culminated with six resolutions giving the substance of the preparations sought by the administration. The most important of these embraced plans to raise an additional regular force of 10,000 men for three years, to create a volunteer force 50,000 strong, and also to arm merchantmen, the proposal Madison had earlier discarded. One week later, on December 6, Porter again took the lead in justifying war in defense of American maritime rights, and this time he argued as well that Canada, given its growing importance to Britain as a source of naval supplies since Napoleon's closure of the Baltic, was the proper object for an American war effort. He then informed Congressmen that "ulterior measures"—that is, a declaration of war—would be brought forward later in the session after the preparations were more advanced and after the dispatch vessel U.S.S. *Hornet* had returned from Europe with the latest information. In the meantime he urged his fellow legislators to

[135] Porter to Monroe, November 19, 1811, MLDS. On the subject of executive-legislature relations generally see Joseph Cooper, "Jeffersonian Attitudes Toward Executive Leadership and Committee Development in the House of Representatives, 1789-1829," *Western Political Quarterly* 18 (1965), 45-63; and for the Twelfth Congress specifically see Ronald L. Hatzenbuehler, "The War Hawks and the Question of Congressional Leadership in 1812," *Pacific Historical Review* 14 (1976), 1-22

[136] Grundy to Jackson, November 28, 1811, Jackson Papers, LC. See also Burwell to Nicholas, November 28, 1811, Nicholas Papers, UVa; William Lowndes to Elizabeth Lowndes, December 7, 1811, William Lowndes Papers, UNC; John Harper to Plumer, December 2, 1811, Plumer Papers, LC; Richard M. Johnson to James Barbour, December 9, 1811, James Barbour Papers, NYPL.

consider seriously their responsibilities and to give only "honest votes" when finally deciding the question of peace or war.[137]

This announcement effectively postponed a declaration of war until about March 1812 at the earliest, and, as Senator George Bibb of Kentucky reported, many Congressmen allowed themselves the "sickly hope" that Britain would change its policies by the time the *Hornet* returned.[138] This hope, as well as the delay, however, convinced some of Madison's Republican critics that the administration was not at all sincere in its new-found belligerence. The *Baltimore Whig* therefore reverted to its previous tactics on December 11 by calling for an immediate declaration of war, and its editor accused Gallatin and Madison of plotting "submission" when the *Hornet* returned with a suitable pretext.[139] Both Armstrong and Samuel Smith shared this suspicion, with the latter informing his Nicholas family connections in Virginia that the administration's lack of serious purpose about war notwithstanding, Congress would "adopt such measures as will force the Executive into war. . . ."[140] However, it was Giles, not Smith, who devised the means to make this threat a reality. The Virginia Senator dismissed the preparations recommended in the House foreign relations committee report as the "most ridiculous pop gun of paper wadding" to be fired at Britian since the two Macon bills, and his hostility to the administration had recently been sharpened by Monroe's rather devious efforts to have him simultaneously censured in the Virgina legislature and removed from his chairmanship of key Senate committees.[141] Determined not to be outflanked in "the chase of patriotism," as John Randolph put it, Giles retaliated by launching an investigation of Monroe's past diplomatic accounts as a condition for confirmation of his nomination to the State Department and by attacking the administration bill to raise an additional regular force. On the question of Monroe's accounts, Giles found nothing discreditable to the Secretary

[137] AC, 12th Cong., 1st sess. 374, 377, 413-418. Porter told the House that he had been "credibly informed" that Quebec exports in 1811 amounted to $6 million, "most of these too in articles of the first necessity—in ship timber and in provisions for the support of [British] fleets and armies." A similar point had been made in the *National Intelligencer* on December 3, 1811. See below, Appendix.

[138] George Bibb to Charles Scott, December 29, 1811 (Lexington) *Kentucky Gazette*, January 14, 1812.

[139] *Baltimore Whig*, December, 2, 6, 9, 27, and 28, 1811.

[140] Armstrong to Spencer, January 12, 1812, Chanler Collection, NYHS; Samuel Smith to Philip Norbonne Nicholas, December 13, 1811, Nicholas Papers, LC.

[141] Giles to Nicholas, December 26, 1811, Randolph Family Papers, UVa. Throughout this period Giles was frequently in conflict with the Virginia legislature over the propriety of the legislature's issuing instructions to bind Senators' votes.

of State—and he had to endure the humiliation of endorsing a unanimous vote to confirm him in office—but on the army bill the Senator
had a field day, using the occasion to accuse the administration of
promoting "scarecrow" measures in pursuit of policies of "protracted
moderation" governed by an unpatriotic obsession with economy.[142]

These allegations, made in a lengthy speech on December 17, shocked
many of his fellow Senators, since Giles was patently more concerned
with attacking Gallatin than he was in discussing the problems of a
war, though he did openly encourage the Senate to defy the administration's military policies as well. Administration supporters, led by
Joseph Anderson and George Washington Campbell of Tennessee,
protested that Giles's remarks were irrelevant and designed for "some
other purpose" which decency forbade them to discuss.[143] Yet because
Giles was chairman of the Senate foreign relations committee, which
included three other Republican Senators—Andrew Gregg of Pennsylvania, John Pope of Kentucky, and Stephen Bradley of Vermont—
who were also not well disposed toward Madison, he had little trouble
in setting aside the administration's army bill and replacing it with his
own laboriously drafted measure to enlist 25,000 regulars for five
years.[144] The Senate then passed the Giles army bill on December 20
and rejected the House's attempts to restore the original figure of
10,000 men. This the administration's supporters in the House tried
to do in a number of ways, mainly by amendments introduced by
Speaker Henry Clay of Kentucky and William Burwell of Virginia
limiting the number of regiments to be raised and the officers to be
appointed under Giles's bill. The House foreign relations committee
in conference suggested the compromise figure of an army 15,000
strong, but the Senate would not accept this either, and the House
finally gave way on January 9, 1812, from fear of losing the army bill
altogether.[145] Yet all Republicans agreed that it was quite impossible
to raise, equip, and train 25,000 men in a few months, and years later

[142] Randolph to Nicholson, January 17, 1812, Nicholson Papers, LC. *Journal of Executive
Proceedings of the Senate of the United States, 1805-1815* (Washington, D.C., 1828), II,
188, 192.

[143] Campbell predicted that many in Congress who voted for the 25,000-man army would
not vote for war. "Time alone," he added, "will develop their views." To Jackson, December
24, 1811, Jackson Papers, LC.

[144] AC, 12th Cong., 1st sess., 34-85. Giles's draft of his army bill, dated December 9,
1811, may be found in Sen 12A-B.1, Legislative Records of the United States Senate (RG
46), NA. Like Giles, the *Baltimore Whig*—on December 18, 19, and 21—criticized the
administration's preparations as inadequate.

[145] AC, 12th Cong., 1st sess., 585, 596-609, 611-619, 700-717. See also Campbell to
Willie Blount, February 24, 1812, George Washington Campbell Letterbook, LC.

Madison recalled with some bitterness that the terms of Giles's bill had been made deliberately "repulsive" to recruits.[146] The British minister, however, could report with some truth and considerable satisfaction that the purpose of Giles's actions was not to promote war on Britain, but war "as a means to overthrow Mr. Madison and his administration."[147]

The "malcontent" Republicans pressed home the advantage won on the army bill in the debates on the second major administration measure of preparations—the bill to allow the President to commission 50,000 volunteers for short-term service. In some respects, this proposal was more controversial than increasing the regular army, since the President would be most likely to draw the desired volunteers and their officers from units of the state militias. Past Congresses had always been unwilling to sanction any measure that threatened state control over the militias, and there was no reason to think that the Twelfth Congress would react differently.[148] That this was the case was suggested by Peter B. Porter's action on January 10, 1812, of reporting from the House foreign relations committee a volunteer bill which entrusted the organization of this force to the state governments but which also allowed the President to make use of it. The House then became bogged down in a long debate on the constitutional aspects of the bill before Madison tried to interrupt these proceedings on January 16 by releasing further correspondence between Monroe and Foster. These letters, the President declared, provided fresh evidence of "the hostile policy of the British Government against our national rights," and he urged Congress to get on with "the preparation of adequate means for maintaining them."[149] The next day Speaker Clay pressed the House to make a decision, and the volunteer bill passed the House in the form desired by the administration. The Senate, however, again thwarted the President when Nicholas Gilman of New Hampshire successfully carried an amendment on January 31 authorizing the state governments to organize the volunteers and commission their officers.[150] But, as Foster correctly reported to the Foreign Office, the

[146] Madison to Henry Wheaton, February 26, 1827, Madison Papers, LC. Monroe also complained that Giles's bill, "by enlisting the whole for five years, a difficult thing in this country, put the means of making war . . . at a distance." To John Taylor, June 13, 1812, Monroe Papers, LC.
[147] Foster to Wellesley, December 18, 1811, and January 12, 1812, F.O. 5, vols. 77, 84.
[148] See below, Chapter III.
[149] AC, 12th Cong., 1st sess., 728-793.
[150] Ibid., 796-803. For the Senate, ibid., 107-110, 112, 1694-1701.

administration considered such volunteers to be quite "useless as an invading force."[151]

Madison was greatly irritated by the behavior of the Senate, but he could hardly afford to repudiate its legislation openly if his intention to resort to war was still to carry any conviction. When a group of Congressmen asked the Secretary of State whether he approved of Giles's army bill, Monroe, no doubt with a touch of irony, replied that the Senate's conduct was "proof of further confidence" on the part of Congress in the abilities of the administration.[152] Madison signed Giles's army bill, while the *National Intelligencer* proclaimed it as the "first *war measure*," though the administration newspaper on January 18 also pointed out that the President still assumed that a smaller force could be more easily raised and would provide the "celerity of movement" essential to the invasion of Canada.[153] The administration then began to consider ways in which it still might realize its original legislative goals. One tactic used here was to press Congress to vote the taxes needed to conduct a war on the scale contemplated by Senator Giles, and on January 28 the *National Intelligencer* asked the advocates of war, especially those who had attacked Gallatin, whether they seriously expected "a bloodless war to be waged by a nerveless force."[154] The House Ways and Means Committee had requested an estimate of war costs on December 9, 1811, but Gallatin, it would seem, deliberately delayed his reply until January 10, 1812, the day after the passage of Giles's army bill. The administration could probably have killed the army bill before its passage by stressing the expense it would impose, but there were also advantages in not debating the costs of war before a majority of Republicans had agreed to prepare for the event in the first place. As John Randolph rather cynically remarked, Gallatin was "too cunning to open his budget before he had them [the Senate malcontents] fixed." Having done this, Gallatin then recommended to Congress on January 10 a comprehensive financial program of double duties, loans, and direct and indirect taxes, and rumors about the high costs of his demands began to spread ripples of alarm throughout the Republican ranks.[155]

[151] Foster to Wellesley, January 17, 1812, F.O. 5, vol. 84. After the Senate's amendment of the Volunteer Bill, Samuel Smith dismissed the notion of war "as a farce." Randolph to Garnett, February 1, 1812, Randolph-Garnett Letterbook, LC.

[152] See Charles Tait to (David B. Mitchell), January 10, 1812, Gratz Autograph Collection, HSP.

[153] *Natl Intelligencer*, January 7 and 18, 1812.

[154] Ibid., January 28, 1812.

[155] Ezekiel Bacon to Gallatin, December 9, 1811; Gallatin to Bacon, January 10, 1812,

Another administration tactic against the army bill was to nominate on January 20 Henry Dearborn of Massachusetts as the first major general in the additional army, and for Eustis to summon him to Washington immediately to persuade Congressmen of the utter impracticality of trying to recruit 25,000 men. Dearborn's presence in the capital, the Secretary of War declared, was necessary to determine "what can be effected in what time" and to convince "some of our friends (as they are called) what cannot be done." Eustis admitted too that the war preparations would have made better progress had Congress voted an army of 10,000 men, but he believed that the legislators, "now that their means are bro't to view, would be glad of an opportunity . . . for treading back their steps" by considering another bill to raise a smaller force to serve for a year.[156] Unfortunately for the administration, Congress showed a greater regard for its own sense of consistency than these predictions allowed for. A week after the passage of the volunteer bill at the end of January, the House foreign relations committee decided to request a written statement from the administration whether the legislation passed to date, particularly the volunteer bill, was "adequate for national defense and other purposes contemplated by the executive." Madison declined to give a written statement in response, but he allowed Monroe to suggest to the committee that both the size and the period of enlistment of the additional army should be halved. The committee, though, on February 11 refused to consider any modifications to Giles's army bill, nor would it even support a motion then suggested by Porter that the volunteer bill be superseded by allowing the President discretion to organize for any military service a "provisional army" of 20,000 men.[157]

The use of the tax issue to modify the military legislation was no more successful, and in fact it badly complicated the administration's program of preparations. Gallatin had never attempted to deny that the Treasury would require taxation in 1812, but most Congressmen probably took comfort in the Secretary's financial reports made in November 1811, which merely suggested that some additional duties, loans, and "a proper selection of moderate internal taxes" would suffice in the event of war.[158] Extensive taxation, however, was quite another

---

Gallatin Papers. See also Randolph to Garnett, January 20, 1812, Randolph-Garnett Letterbook, LC; Foster to Wellesley, January 11, 1812, F.O. 5, vol. 84.

[156] Eustis to Dearborn, January 28, 1812, Dearborn Papers, MHS.

[157] "Minutes of the Committee on Foreign Relations," February 6 and 11, 1811, Peter B. Porter Papers, BEHS. Porter to Monroe, February 6, 1812, MLDS. See also Randolph to Garnett, February 11 and 13, 1812, Randolph-Garnett Letterbook, LC.

[158] For Gallatin's financial report of November 25, 1811, see *ASP: Finance*, II, 495-497.

matter, and all Congressmen became familiar with the details of Gallatin's plans when the Ways and Means chairman, Ezekiel Bacon of Massachusetts, released them on January 20.[159] This development focused attention again on Gallatin's influence over policy—which had long been a grievance with most of the "malcontent" Republicans. Anticipating some outcry on the subject, the *National Intelligencer* began republishing in the last week of January some of the *Aurora* editorials Duane had written in 1808 and 1809 when he supported Madison for the Presidency. This move stung Duane to retaliate on January 30 by printing a long and abusive rejoinder entitled "The Rat in the Treasury," in which he predictably accused Gallatin of exploiting his control of the finances to frustrate war policies which he was widely believed to oppose. In fact, Duane even alleged that Gallatin was calculating his budget with the cooperation of the British minister, and by the time the Ways and Means Committee finally reported his proposals to the floor of the House on February 17, such was the reaction that some credence was given by many Republicans to the *Aurora*'s claims.[160] As Eustis observed, "the budget has had its influence," but Congressmen were now greatly alarmed, both by the amount of taxation required—$5 million—and by its incidence, including direct taxes as well as indirect levies on spirits, stills, sugar, salt, auction sales, retailers' licenses, carriages, and stamped paper.[161]

Briefly, Gallatin tried to divert attention from his letter of January 10 by arguing that it was not intended for publication, yet this statement hardly helped matters.[162] The Treasury did need taxation; the only question was how much. But this, in turn, depended on the extent of the military preparations, which, as far as the administration was concerned, was still the point to be settled. The result was that the Republicans in the House sanctioned the loans and double duties required by the Treasury with little difficulty, but balked at the taxes. The situation here was complicated by the behavior of the Federalists, who to date had supported the military preparations, though not with any serious expectation that the administration would actually use

[159] AC, 12th Cong., 1st sess., 846.

[160] *Natl Intelligencer*, January 23, 1812; *Aurora*, January 25 and 30, 1812; (Philadelphia) *Democratic Press*, January 30, 1812. Pierre Van Cortlandt, Jr., to Philip Van Cortlandt, March 4, 1812, Judd, ed., *Correspondence to the Van Cortlandt Family*, 467; Harper to Plumer, February 17, 1812, Plumer Papers, LC.

[161] Eustis to Dearborn, January 28, 1812, Dearborn Papers, MHS; Abner Lacock to Charles Jared Ingersoll, February 12, 1812, Charles Jared Ingersoll Papers, HSP; George Troup to David B. Mitchell, February 12, 1812, Edward J. Harden, *The Life of George Troup* (Savannah, 1859), 107.

[162] Harper to Plumer, February 17, 1812, Plumer Papers, LC.

them, but who now began to oppose any further drift toward war. In fact, thanks to Federalist cohesion and Republican abstensions, the first taxation vote, on salt on February 28, resulted in a serious defeat for the administration.[163] It was only after the administration brought some "out of doors" influence to bear, and the *National Intelligencer* pleaded time and again for Republican unity, that Congress reconsidered and passed the tax on salt. Thereafter, a Republican majority, albeit a reduced one from that which had supported the military legislation, approved by March 4 resolutions to support the remainder of the taxes, but even then they displayed a lingering distrust of the Treasury and a prudent concern for their own popularity by stipulating that the levies were to go into effect only after the commencement of war "against a European nation."[164] Throughout the debate, as Federalist Senator James A. Bayard of Delaware recalled, it was an open question whether "the war (would) float the taxes or the taxes sink the war."[165]

Consequently, as the session of Congress entered its fifth month— and the thoughts of the legislators began to turn toward the return of the *Hornet* and adjournment—the administration and its supporters were placed in a peculiarly difficult position. With the exception of a small handful of John Randolph's "Old Republicans," Madison had succeeded in obtaining broad Republican support for war preparations if the Orders in Council were not promptly repealed, only to discover in the process that the Republicans were anything but united over the means to give effect to that decision. As Richard Rush reported, Madison was "above them all in spirit and tone," but "he has not the support he should have."[166] Nor was it at all clear that the preparations actually gave the administration the ability to wage war, for as Madison himself informed Jefferson, Congress, "with a view to enable the executive to step at once into Canada . . . have provided after two months delay a regular force requiring twelve to raise it and after three months a volunteer force on terms not likely to raise it at all for that object." The mixture of motives both "disguised and avowed" of the legislators who had been responsible for this outcome the President declined to

---

[163] AC, 12th Cong., 1st sess., 1050-1056, 1086, 1087, 1089-1105, 1106-1115. For an analysis of the decline in Republican cohesion and the behavior of the Federalists see Hatzenbuehler, "Foreign Policy Voting," 442-445, 447, 449-451. See also Donald R. Hickey, "The Federalists and the Coming of the War of 1812," *Indiana Magazine of History* 75 (1979), 79.

[164] *Natl Intelligencer*, February 29, March 3, 1812. Pierre to Philip Van Cortlandt, March 4, 1812, Judd, ed., *Correspondence of the Van Cortlandt Family*, 467. AC, 12th Cong., 1st sess., 1118-1155.

[165] Bayard to Rodney, March 9, 1812, "Bayard Letters," 236.

[166] Richard Rush to Ingersoll, February 26, 1812, Ingersoll Papers, HSP.

discuss in a letter, even to his closest friend, but his political position might have been fairly regarded as rather like that of John Adams during his ill-fated administration.[167] To proceed to a declaration of war without effective means of waging it would obviously be dangerous, yet to make a last-minute bid for peace, as Adams himself had done with France in 1800, would shatter the tenuous unity of the Republican coalition. As one Republican newspaper, the *Virginia Argus*, observed, whether the recent acts of Congress had been intended as "scarecrows" or not they had been passed, and "to recede from this position under the present irritation of the American spirit would turn the present party out of power and would place one in office that would make war."[168] DeWitt Clinton fully agreed with this sentiment, pointing out from Albany that if Congress rose "without doing anything, somebody [i.e., Madison] will have an awful account to settle with the sovereign people."[169] The unspoken testimony about the extent to which the President had still failed to solve all his difficulties was the fact that the congressional caucus—which in 1804 and 1808 had nominated the Republican presidential candidate by February of the election year—had not yet assembled, nor was there any serious discussion of when it would do so.[170]

★

DESPITE THE ABSENCE of any lead from Washington about the nomination of the Republican presidential candidate, Republican state legislators began to caucus to express their preferences and in some cases to choose their slates of presidential electors. By the first week in March the Republicans of Virginia and Pennsylvania, both critical states, had pledged themselves to electors committed to Madison, and the governor of Pennsylvania, his past differences with Madison notwithstanding, had endorsed his re-election as well.[171] No formal challenge to Madison's renomination had yet emerged, though there were rumors that the Clintonians were laying the groundwork for a New York

[167] Madison to Jefferson, February 7, 1812, Madison Papers, LC. As Madison later recalled, "it was not the suddenness of war as an executive policy but the tardiness of the legislative provisions" that left the United States so badly prepared for conflict. To Henry Wheaton, February 26, 1827, Madison Papers, LC.

[168] (Richmond, Va.) *Virginia Argus*, February 3, 1812.

[169] DeWitt Clinton to Pierre Van Cortlandt, Jr., February 24, 1812, Judd, ed., *Correspondence of the Van Cortlandt Family*, 458.

[170] On January 23, 1812, the *National Intelligencer* noted that Madison's conduct had increased his claims "to the approbation of his country," but added that the time was not yet ripe for "a review of the principles of his administration."

[171] *The Enquirer*, February 8, 1812. Binns to Roberts, March 9, 1812, Jonathan Roberts Papers, HSP; Alexander James Dallas to Gallatin, March 2, 1812, *Gallatin Papers*.

Republican caucus in Albany, where the result would presumably be unfavorable to the President.[172] Madison was no doubt heartened by the developments in Virginia and Pennsylvania, and he also chose to regard the recent decision of Congress to impose taxes in the event of war as evidence that the legislature would not "flinch from the contest" should he continue to pursue the policies outlined in November 1811.[173] Republican unity, though—somewhat eroded in the taxation debates— needed to be consolidated for the remaining decisions which could lead to war, and this was one of the reasons for Madison's release, on March 9, 1812, of the letters of John Henry. The administration had acquired these controversial documents earlier in the year, and Henry, in turning them over to the State Department, had suggested that they would be useful in the accomplishment of some "great object," such as obtaining a declaration of war from Congress. Their contents, he predicted, would "confuse the opposition, arouse the spirit of the public, and unite all people against the enemy."[174]

The letters of John Henry revealed that he had been sent as an agent into the United States by the governor of Lower Canada during the embargo crisis of 1808-1809 to assess the possibility of the New England states seceding from the union. Henry's disclosures on this subject were in no way remarkable, but there can be little doubt that by sending the letters to Congress at this time Madison deliberately intended to bring Anglo-American relations to the point of rupture, and most observers believed, as John Taylor of Caroline put it, that the act would "wind up the mob to take the war plunge."[175] Apart from uniting Republicans in a burst of patriotic indignation, the administration also anticipated a number of other advantages from publicizing this evidence of British espionage. The conduct of the governor of Lower Canada—supported as it was by the British ministry—highlighted

[172] *Natl Intelligencer*, March 26, 1812. On March 13, 1812, the *Albany Register* declared that it was time for New York "to advance a column of its strength and an irridation of its genius into the national cabinet to vindicate its neglected interests, to maintain its augmenting force, and to place upon an imperishable base her power, her dignity, and her splendor." On March 24 the *Register* predicted there would be no congressional caucus at all in 1812, only a series of state nominations of presidential candidates.

[173] Madison to Jefferson, March 6, 1812, Madison Papers, LC.

[174] John Henry to Monroe, February 13, 1812, E. A. Cruikshank, *The Political Adventures of John Henry: The Record of an International Imbroglio* (Toronto, 1936), 87-88 (for the background see 1-85); and Samuel E. Morison, "The Henry-Crillon Affair of 1812," *Proceedings of the Massachusetts Historical Society* 69 (1950), 207-231.

[175] John Taylor to Monroe, March 12, 1812, Monroe Papers, LC. Sérurier to Bassano, March 2 and 22, 1812, Correspondance Politique, vol. LXVII. See also *Virginia Argus*, March 12, 1812.

Madison's belief that Britain's possession of Canada was not only injurious in its effects on American foreign policy but also a danger to the integrity of the Republic. Such considerations reinforced his other reasons for wanting to deprive Britain of Canada, and these included, as the *National Intelligencer* reiterated, the fact that Canada over the past few years had become of far greater importance in sustaining British maritime pretensions than most Americans seemed to realize.[176] Moreover, the President and the administration newspaper both noted the coincidence of Henry's mission with Madison's efforts in the winter of 1808-1809 to arrange a solution to the problem of the Orders in Council with the British minister in Washington, and suggested that British diplomacy was governed by motives of insidious hypocrisy which rendered futile any sincere American attempts at negotiation. To remain at peace with such a nation, the *National Intelligencer* argued, was like drinking from a "poisoned chalice."[177] Among the more narrowly partisan benefits from "the discoveries made by Henry," as Gallatin pointed out, was the prospect of "a salutary effect in annihilating the spirit of the Essex Junto, and even . . . the new focus of opposition in Albany."[178] To allow Republican Governor Elbridge Gerry of Massachusetts to make whatever use of the episode he chose in the forthcoming state elections in April, the President's private secretary forwarded to him copies of the material that Madison sent to Congress.[179]

Throughout the second week of March, the reaction to the Henry letters was everything the administration desired. The outcry, Richard Rush wrote, led to a "visible increase of the war tone" among Republicans, while the Federalists feared that some of their leaders might stand convicted of treason.[180] The British minister, deeply embar-

[176] Monroe to John Quincy Adams, February 22, 1812, Adams Family Papers, MHS. On March 23 the *National Intelligencer* argued that Canada, with its resources, had become "a plume of no ordinary splendor to [Britain's] magnificence." See also Chapter I above.

[177] For Madison's remarks see Richardson, *Messages and Papers*, II, 483. (The President also mentioned the episode again in his war message on June 1, 1812; see p. 488.) See also *Natl Intelligencer*, March 21, 1812.

[178] Gallatin to Jefferson, March 19, 1812, *Gallatin Papers*. See also Dearborn to Jefferson, March 10, 1812, Jefferson Papers, LC; Rush to Ingersoll, March 12, 1812, Ingersoll Papers, HSP. Rush reported Washington rumors that New York was about to nominate DeWitt Clinton for the Presidency, "but the Henry business topples it down. . . ."

[179] Elbridge Gerry to Edward Coles, March 17, 1812, acknowledged receipt of Henry's letters from Coles. The discovery of the plot, Gerry noted, "must be attended with vast advantages." Coles Family Papers, Princeton University Library.

[180] Rush to Ingersoll, March 12, 1812, Ingersoll Papers, HSP; Charles Turner to William Bentley, April 3, 1812, William Bentley Letters, Essex Institute; Harper to Plumer, March 11, 1812, Plumer Papers, LC.

rassed, remained silent, since he could think of no way in which to defend the conduct of his government.[181] With the exception of Giles, who continued to advocate war, many of the "malcontent" Republicans were caught at a disadvantage as well. It was becoming difficult for them to reap any political advantage from trying to oppose the administration by advocating a different program of military preparation, and an immediate rupture with Britain as a result of the Henry letters only promised to increase these tactical problems.[182] Vice President George Clinton—who according to John Randolph was beginning to shift toward an antiwar position anyway—was severely critical of Madison's release of the letters, which he likened to "putting pepper under a horse's tail."[183] Even Duane, who normally could not restrain his Anglophobia, was cautious, at first doubting whether the Henry letters were genuine and then remaining silent about the entire business. And Samuel Smith and his friends were reported after March 9 to be "in higher dudgeon than the feds. . . ."[184]

In the midst of these developments, Monroe met with Speaker Clay on the morning of March 15 to discuss arrangements for the remainder of the congressional session. That evening Clay, accompanied by his mess mate, Langdon Cheves of South Carolina, visited Senator Bayard, who reported that both men had assured him that "war was inevitable and would be declared in a short time."[185] At this time Clay also wrote a letter to Monroe, recapitulating, very probably, the essence of their conversation in the morning. The Speaker suggested that the President recommend a thirty-day embargo which would be followed by war, and that he also request Congress to allow him to organize a volunteer force of 10,000 men for a short period of service. The embargo was intended to notify the public, particularly merchants, of the approach of war and to advise them to secure property at risk from hostilities, while the new volunteer force would allow the administration to commence the war more easily than it could by trying to implement the existing preparedness legislation.[186] The meeting between the Speaker

---

[181] Foster to Wellesley, March 9 and 10, 1812, F.O. 5, vol. 84; Sérurier to Bassano, March 12, 1812, Correspondance Politique, vol. LXVII.

[182] See Foster, Journal entry, March 25, 1812, Foster Papers, LC.

[183] Quoted by John Binns to Roberts, March 18, 1812, Roberts Papers, HSP. See also Randolph to Garnett, February 13, 1812, Randolph-Garnett Letterbook, LC, where Randolph predicted that the Vice President would be antiwar.

[184] *Aurora*, March 13 and 15, 1812; Macon to Nicholson, March 23 and 27, 1812, Nicholson Papers, LC.

[185] Bayard to Rodney, March 16, 1812, "Bayard Letters," 236.

[186] Henry Clay to Monroe, March 15, 1812, James F. Hopkins et al., eds., *The Papers of Henry Clay* (Lexington, 1959–), I, 637.

and the Secretary of State, as well as Clay's letter with its recommendation of formal executive messages, suggested neither administration
reluctance to wage war nor congressional pressure on the President
to do so. Instead, the exchange was indicative of a genuine Republican
doubt in the absence of relevant precedents about how a state of war
could be created according to the provisions of the Constitution. Madison was sufficiently scrupulous not to want to impose a policy of war
on the legislature, while Clay was probably hinting that Congress, for
its part, had reservations about declaring war without some clear indication that the President was prepared to exercise his functions as
Commander in Chief.[187]

In addition to the events of March 15, several other facts indicated
that the administration was now looking forward to the end of the
session and a declaration of war. The Secretary of War—rashly—assured members of the House foreign relations committee that regular
army recruiting and the business of army supply would be well advanced within the next six weeks, while the *National Intelligencer*
announced on March 24 that there was no point in waiting for any
further news from Britain before deciding the questions of peace and
war.[188] The nation's honor, the editorial added, could now only be
saved by an "appeal to arms." Admittedly, the U.S.S. *Hornet*—which
was supposed to return with news of the British reaction to American
preparations—had not yet arrived, and Clay's suggested thirty-day
embargo assumed that the vessel would do so shortly; but Madison
did not expect this event to change the situation. A British dispatch
vessel had already reached Washington on March 20, and its news
revealed not only that was there no change in Foster's instructions but
also that the Prince of Wales, after a year in power and freed from the
restrictions of the Regency bill, had taken no steps toward removing
his father's ministers whom Madison found so obnoxious.[189] Instead,

[187] For discussions of Madison's concern with the need to observe constitutional forms see
Abbott Smith, "Mr. Madison's War: An Unsuccessful Experiment in the Conduct of National
Policy," *Political Science Quarterly* 57 (1942), 299-246; and Ralph Ketcham, "James Mad-
ison: The Unimperial President," *Virginia Quarterly Review* 54 (1978), 116-136. See also
Navy Secretary Paul Hamilton's remark of March 8, 1812, that "if war were determined
on tomorrow, it would have [Madison's] ready concurrence." Quoted in Reginald Horsman,
The Causes of the War of 1812 (Philadelphia, 1962), 242.

[188] John C. Calhoun to James McBride, March 16, 1812, Robert L. Meriwether et al.,
eds., *The Papers of John C. Calhoun* (Columbia, S.C., 1959–), I, 93. Eustis also ordered
all army contractors to have rations for the regular army ready within thirty days. See his
circular letter, March 14, 1812, LSMA. On March 22, Sérurier reported to Bassano that
he expected a declaration of war by May 10. Correspondance Politique, vol. LXVII.

[189] See Perkins, *Prologue to War*, 378, See also Madison to Cutts, February 25, 1812,
Cutts Collection.

he had replaced Lord Wellesley as Foreign Secretary in the cabinet with Lord Castlereagh, whom the *National Intelligencer* described as a "decided enemy" to the United States.[190] As the President remarked to Foster shortly afterward, Spencer Perceval seemed "as fixed in his place as [he was] in his purposes."[191] Accordingly, when the administration newspaper called for an "appeal to arms" on March 24, the House foreign relations committee met to appoint a deputation consisting of Porter, John Calhoun of South Carolina, and John Smilie of Pennsylvania to confer with Monroe about the remaining steps required to produce and give effect to a state of war. The committee wanted to know what measures to recommend to Congress.[192]

The House foreign relations committee repeated this request six days later, but the administration delayed its response because a rapid succession of events after the third week of March had begun to retard the momentum created by the release of the Henry letters.[193] Collectively, the effect of these events conspired both to weaken Madison's case against Britain and to give new life to the barely contained factionalism in the Republican party. The result was that Madison delayed any recommendation of war to Congress for a further two months while waiting for the restoration of more propitious circumstances. The first development in this chain of events originated in the congressional investigations of the Henry letters, which disclosed that there was both more and less to those documents than Madison had led the legislature to believe. Not only had John Henry not provided any proof that New England Federalist leaders had engaged in subversive activities, but it also became public knowledge that the administration had paid $50,000 for information that was no more than commonplace gossip. Furthermore, the Republican governor of Massachusetts, a French swindler posing as a Count Edouard de Crillon, the French minister in Washington, and the alcoholic Senator Richard Brent of Virginia were all exposed as intermediaries in a very questionable transaction. As the details emerged, the President began to look both very dishonest and incredibly stupid.[194]

---

[190] *Natl Intelligencer*, April 2, 1812. See also *The Enquirer*, April 7, 1812; and *Virginia Argus*, April 9, 1812.

[191] Foster, Journal entry, April 8, 1812, Foster Papers, LC.

[192] "Minutes of the Committee on Foreign Relations," March 24, 1812, Porter Papers, BEHS. Porter, Calhoun, and Smilie to Monroe, March 24, 1812, Monroe Papers, NYPL.

[193] Porter to Monroe, March 30, 1812, Monroe Papers, NYPL.

[194] See the "Reports of the Committee of Foreign Relations on the Henry Documents," March 9, 12, and 13, 1812, Porter Papers, BEHS; and a more extensive report on the meeting of March 13 in Sen 12 A-E.3, Legislative Records of the United States Senate, NA. See also Randolph to Richard K. Randolph, March, 19, 1812, John Randolph Papers,

This news shocked and delighted the Federalists as well as the "malcontent" Republicans. For the former, these new revelations released them from the imputation of treason while seeming to give fresh substance to their standard charge that the French government had tricked the President into pursuing anti-British policies. For the latter, the devious aspects of the Henry affair seemed typical of an administration whose members they had long charged with pusillanimity, and Giles remarked with considerable relish that the President seemed unable to practice "the force of diplomacy in its highest *gusto*."[195] Rather more serious, though, was the distraught reaction of Republicans who normally supported the administration. The President had been caught doing a "wicked thing" complained Ezekiel Bacon of Massachusetts, while his fellow Congressman, John Clopton of Virginia—appalled at the waste of public money in the affair—confessed that he simply did "not know how [he could] vote for Mr. Madison's re-election" under such circumstances.[196] Madison had not been tricked by France, but he could not refute that charge without seeming to confirm a far worse one—that he had, in Senator Bayard's words, made "a fearful prostitution of the first office in our country" to influence state elections for partisan purposes.[197] Belatedly, Madison made a desperate effort to obtain positive proof that Federalist leaders had been engaged in subversion with Henry in 1808, but his only real lead here, Jonathan Dayton of New Jersey, failed to provide him with the necessary evidence.[198]

This unsatisfactory aftermath, however, was by no means the end of the Henry affair, for by a cruel and ironic twist of fate it combined with events in East Florida to deliver the President a truly mortifying setback. At the end of March the news reached Washington that an American agent, General George Mathews, was openly organizing a

LC; Taggart to Taylor, March 13 and 21, 1812, Haynes, "Taggart Letters," 388-391; Abijah Bigelow to his wife, March 25, 1812, Clarence S. Brigham, ed., "Letters of Abijah Bigelow to his Wife, 1810-1815," *Proceedings of the American Antiquarian Society* 40 (1930), 333.

[195] Giles to Nicholas, March 19, 1812, Nicholas Papers UVa.

[196] Bacon to Gallatin, March 15, 1812, *Gallatin Papers*; John Clopton to Sarah Clopton, March 30, 1812, John Clopton Papers, Duke University Library.

[197] Bayard to Rodney, March 22, 1812, "Bayard Letters," 237.

[198] Madison to Jonathan Dayton, March 17, 1812, Madison Papers, LC; Dayton to Madison, March 25, 1812, Dayton-Madison Letters, Princeton University Library. Madison contacted Dayton because he had received anonymous letters from New Jersey in 1808-1809 under the pseudonym of Cyrus which related information about the secessionist aims of New England Federalists. In 1812, Dayton denied that he was Cyrus, though it would seem that he almost certainly was. The Cyrus letters are included in the Dayton-Madison Letters in Princeton University Library.

revolution in that Spanish territory as a prelude to American annexation. Mathews had long had oral, though not written, authorization for his activities, but the real problem was one of timing, since the United States was now caught committing the very offense for which Madison had attempted to convict Britain with the Henry letters.[199] To enable Monroe to deal with any protest from the British minister— whose government was allied with Spain and had already protested similar American activities in West Florida—the administration immediately disavowed Mathews's activities.[200] This action was necessary, but it annoyed many southern Republicans, who had expected that Madison would be able to realize their ambitions to acquire Spanish territory. The disavowal also infuriated Mathews, so much so that he threatened to come to Washington and, like Henry, tell all.[201] Foster, perhaps reckoning that the activities of Henry and Mathews canceled each other out, decided to grant the President the charity of his silence on the affair, but it was unlikely that in future the British minister could so easily be embarrassed into silence.[202]

Madison bitterly lamented his misfortune in finding himself in such a "distressing" position, but these difficulties were nothing compared with the report, reaching Washington on March 23, that French frigates had recently burned at sea two American merchantmen bound for Spain.[203] This event, in fact, promised to destroy almost entirely the basis of Madison's case against Britain—that France had repealed her edicts against neutral commerce while her enemy had not. The issue of French repeal, as Madison privately admitted, had continued to be a subject of "malignant cavil" in Washington, and Samuel Smith had recently commenced a Senate investigation of seizures of American vessels in the Baltic by French and Danish privateers.[204] Now, as Monroe bluntly informed the French minister, "the Clinton party, the Smith party and the Republican malcontents will rise up en masse and ask why we insist on making war on England over her maintenance

---

[199] For the background see Isaac J. Cox, "The Border Missions of General George Mathews," *MVHR* 12 (1925), 309-333; and Rufus K. Wyllys, "The East Florida Revolution of 1812-1814," *Hispanic American Historical Review* 9 (1929), 439. See also Rembert W. Patrick, *Florida Fiasco: Rampant Rebels on the Georgia-Florida Border, 1810-1815* (Athens, Ga., 1954), 120-122.

[200] Monroe to Mathews, April 4, 1812, copy in LRUS.

[201] See Cox, "Border Missions," 333. See also Crawford to Monroe, August 6, 1812, Monroe Papers, LC.

[202] Foster to Wellesley, April 2, 1812, F.O. 5, vol. 85.

[203] Madison to Jefferson, April 24, 1812, Madison Papers, LC.

[204] Madison to Cutts, February 25, 1812, Cutts Collection. AC, 12th Cong., 1st sess., 161-162.

of the Orders in Council when we have such a terrible and recent proof that the French decrees are not withdrawn."[205] Sérurier's response— that France was entitled to retaliate on nations that supplied British forces in Spain and that French antineutral decrees would be repealed when the United States had forced Great Britain to respect its rights— could have afforded the Secretary of State no satisfaction whatsoever, nor did Madison obtain any better answer when he later summoned the minister to complain personally about French policy.[206] Foster then predictably seized the opportunity to demand from Monroe formal proof of the repeal of the Berlin and Milan decrees. Meanwhile, in Philadelphia, Duane, after repeatedly claiming throughout March that the administration had no intention of waging war, finally declared himself for a Clintonian candidacy on the grounds that men of greater ability and energy were needed in the executive branch of government.[207] The consequences of all these developments for Republican unity and the administration's policy of pushing on to a declaration of war were clear; as Monroe told Sérurier, if the question of war should be put to Congress in such circumstances, the administration would not get a majority.[208]

Of all these complicated problems, that posed by the British minister was perhaps the easiest to deal with. Madison labored briefly over a note arguing that the British government was not entitled to ask the United States for proof of the repeal of the French decrees, but then he decided on the simpler course of instructing Monroe to tell Foster that the administration declined to discuss the matter any further.[209] A similar step, however, was not open to the President in dealing with critics on the domestic scene. Madison could still convince himself that the "malcontents'" suspicions of France were "erroneous," but he was clearsighted enough to admit that they were also "unavoidable . . . and [that] the fault did not lie with those who entertained them"[210] For this reason, when Monroe finally responded to the House foreign re-

---

[205] Sérurier to Bassano, March 23, 1812, Correspondance Politique, vol. LXVII.

[206] Ibid., April 24, 1812.

[207] Foster to Wellesley, April 1, 1812, F.O. 5, vol. 85. *Aurora*, March 9, 27, and 28, April 14, 1812. At this time Duane began to attack Eustis as well as Gallatin, claiming that the Secretary of War was incompetent and that the army, supposedly being raised for war, was "dead of the doctor."

[208] Sérurier to Bassano, March 23, 1812, Correspondance Politique, vol. LXVII. See also Foster to Wellesley, March 22, 1812, F.O. 5, vol. 85. Foster estimated there were seventy-five votes for war in the House, but twenty against it in the Senate.

[209] Draft note in Madison's hand [March 1812], Madison Papers, LC. Foster to Wellesley, April 1, 1812, F.O. 5, vol. 85.

[210] See Madison to Barlow, February 24, 1812, Madison Papers, LC.

lations committee's request for information on "ulterior measures" at the end of March, he now argued for a delay to allow for the return of the *Hornet* with news from France which would clarify the situation with respect to the French decrees. He further bolstered the case for this delay by repeating to the committee the administration's previous complaints about defects in the preparedness legislation, particularly the army bill, and he asked for an amendment to Giles's measure to permit the War Department to enlist only 15,000 regulars for the shorter period of eighteen months. Since an embargo of thirty days duration—which Monroe had agreed on with Speaker Clay two weeks earlier—might not be sufficient to accomplish these new purposes, the Secretary of State asked that its period of operation be doubled to sixty days, and, if the administration did not get all that it wanted, Monroe added a very strong hint to the committee that the President would be unwilling to assume the responsibility for waging war.[211]

In meeting with the House foreign relations committee on March 31 to seek the delay, Monroe also asserted that the administration had *not* altered the position it had taken in November 1811 about the need for a declaration of war by the end of the session, but to many his claims were not convincing.[212] No Congressman welcomed the prospect of prolonging an already arduous session into the beginning of summer, and, during the meeting with the Secretary of State, Porter openly expressed the view that the way in which the nation was preparing for war could only bring disaster. Other committee members, such as Calhoun, stressed the need to give the preparedness legislation the "tone" it so obviously lacked, while John Randolph, as part of his campaign against war, took the unusual step of reading some of the details of the meeting between Monroe and the foreign relations committee to the whole House.[213] As he did so Randolph emphasized the recent difficulties with France as one of the reasons for the administration's delays, but he announced as well that Monroe had said that should France deny the United States justice, the embargo sought by the administration would "leave the policy as respects France, and indeed both countries, in our hands." The implication of this remark was that the administration might ultimately leave Congress to consider

[211] Notes on the meeting between Monroe and the House foreign relations committee, including some caustic comments, can be found in Samuel Smith Papers, LC, dated March 30 and 31, 1812. Smith could not have attended the meeting, but he may have been present in the House when John Randolph later recounted his version of the meeting to his fellow Representatives.

[212] See Macon to Nicholson, March 31, 1812, Nicholson Papers, LC.

[213] See source cited in note 211.

war against France as well as Britain, although other foreign relations committee members present, notably Calhoun and Grundy, promptly denied that Monroe had intended any such thing.[214]

More immediately, though, the conclusion that many of the "malcontents" drew from Monroe's performance was that the President's nerve in the game of bluff he had embarked on last November was beginning to falter. The request for a delay at this late stage in the proceedings, Samuel Smith felt, could only mean that the administration sought "a fair occasion to sneak out of war."[215] Nonetheless, the House foreign relations committee agreed to report the sixty-day embargo, and probably the changes in the military legislation as well, provided that the President committed himself publicly to the policies by sending a formal message to Congress. Madison sent in the request for the embargo on April 1, and the *National Intelligencer* stressed shortly after that the administration did *not* regard the measure as "an engine to be wielded in negotiation" with Britain. The House duly passed both the embargo and the amendments to Giles's army bill on April 2, while the Senate followed suit the next day, though on the motion of Michael Leib of Pennsylvania the duration of the embargo was extended from sixty to ninety days. Instead of expiring on June 4, it would now run to July 4, 1812.[216]

The Senators had many reasons for extending the embargo, principally the hope that the crisis with Britain might yet be negotiated and the belief that American vessels abroad would need a longer period to return home.[217] Their votes on the issue fell into no coherent pattern—with six Republican "malcontents" voting against the prolongation of the embargo—but that Leib, another "malcontent," should have led the majority struck some observers as rather odd. As Richard Rush later pointed out, Leib had long favored war with Britain, and, as a Clintonian, it was unlikely that he had been belatedly convinced of the desirability of commercial restrictions.[218] A more probable cause of Leib's "total change of conduct" here, surmised Congressman Samuel Shaw of Vermont, was "some strange management" by the Clin-

[214] AC, 12th Cong., 1st sess., 1593-1594.

[215] See note 211.

[216] AC, 12th Cong., 1st sess., 187-189, 193, 1587-1589. *Natl Intelligencer*, April 9, 1812. Monroe's draft for this editorial can be found in James Monroe Papers, NYHS. On the changes in the military legislation see below, Chapter III.

[217] Bibb to Scott, April 5, 1812, *Kentucky Gazette*, April 21, 1812.

[218] Richard to Benjamin Rush, June 13, 1812, Benjamin Rush Papers, Library Company of Philadelphia Papers, HSP. See also Campbell to Jackson, April 14, 1812, Jackson Papers, LC; Roberts to Matthew Roberts, May 7, 1812, Roberts Papers, HSP.

tonians with regard to nominating a presidential candidate.[219] The supporters of DeWitt Clinton in New York had been preparing since mid-March to nominate their man in a state legislative caucus, and they had also formed a committee to obtain information from Congress and other states about the likely extent of support for Clinton. These plans were badly upset by the decision of New York Governor Daniel D. Tompkins on March 27 to prorogue the state legislature for sixty days. The governor took this step to prevent the local Federalists, with the aid of a few Republicans as well as much bribery and corruption, from passing a bank bill, but his action also made it impossible for Clinton to receive a presidential nomination before the end of May.[220] News of the New York developments had reached Washington by April 2, and Leib may have wished to postpone a congressional decision on war and peace until the arrangements for Clinton's nomination were more advanced. The nomination of a schismatic Republican presidential candidate *after* a declaration of war was a tactic that the Clintonians would have preferred to avoid, for, as a New York newspaper pointed out, once war had been declared, "the importance of the presidential election [would] be lost in the permanent interests of national character and independence."[221]

Yet if it was Leib's intention to aid Clinton with the ninety-day embargo, he failed. Even worse, from the "malcontents' " point of view, Clinton's standing as a northern Republican candidate received another serious blow in April 1812, when he fell out with some important New Yorkers who had hitherto been included among his fellow partisans. Clinton's failure to support Tompkins wholeheartedly over the bank issue cost him some of his popularity as Republicans throughout the state gathered in meetings to praise the governor for his stand.[222] This development helped convince Ambrose Spencer and John Armstrong that Clinton's determination to oppose Madison at all costs was dangerous, since it promised to divide Republicans both in New York

[219] Samuel Shaw to Daniel D. Tompkins, April 2, 1812; William K. Paulding to Tompkins, May 5, 1812, Daniel D. Tompkins Papers, NYSL. Madison, too, noted that the temper of the Senate was "equivocal" and predicted that the embargo would give fuel to "interested clamor." To Jefferson, April 3, 1812, Madison Papers, LC.

[220] Charles Cooper to Van Cortlandt, March 20, 1812, Judd, ed., *Correspondence of the Van Cortlandt Family*, 483; *Albany Register*, March 31, 1812. See also Ray W. Irwin, *Daniel D. Tompkins* (New York, 1968), 111-127.

[221] (Albany, N.Y.) *Albany Republican*, April 13, 1812. Sérurier also believed the Republican "malcontents" were playing for time by extending the embargo to ninety days. To Bassano, April 9, 1812, Correspondance Politique, vol. LXVII.

[222] *Albany Register*, April 3, 10, 14, 21, and 24, 1812. [Robert Macomb] to Tompkins, April [3], 1812, Tompkins Papers, NYSL.

and throughout the nation without necessarily placing a New Yorker in the Presidency.[223] Consequently, Spencer decided to support both Tompkins's stand on the bank bill and the administration's preparations for war, pointing out publicly that the prorogation of the state legislature effectively obstructed the "anti-republican, anti-patriotic, and anti-virtuous ambition" of Clinton.[224] Spencer went even further in his opposition to Clinton. In order to counteract the dominating influence of the Clintonian *Albany Register*, he founded a short-lived newspaper in upstate New York, the *Albany Republican*, which he used to advocate war with Britain and to suggest that Madison divide the "malcontent" Republicans by dismissing Secretary of War Eustis and appointing Armstrong in his place. The "Old Soldier" and ex-diplomat was, Spencer declared, a man with "great acquisitions in military tactics," familiar with all the "modern improvements in the art of war." But Madison chose to ignore this overture for as long as he could.[225] The President did not trust either Spencer or Armstrong, and he would hardly have forgotten that in the 1808 election Spencer had opposed the embargo, belatedly declared himself for Madison in order to get a place on the electoral ticket, and then voted for George Clinton. Nor would Madison have overlooked the remarks and ambitions that had been attributed to Armstrong since his return from France. The President's reluctance to invite him into the cabinet, however, only confirmed Spencer in his long-held belief that "policy at Washington [was] governed by mean and paltry motives," principally jealously of Armstrong.[226]

As his rival's prospects dwindled, Madison waited for a suitable occasion to seek a congressional decision about war with Britain, since he remained as firm as ever in his conviction that concessions from that nation would not be forthcoming.[227] The first opportunity seemed to be the arrival of news from Paris that the American minister there, Joel Barlow, was about to make a commercial treaty with France. Madison did not really want such a treaty, suspecting that France might use the negotiations as a pretext for avoiding the redress of past American grievances, and for this reason alone he would have been

[223] Spencer to Armstrong, April 9, 1812; Armstrong to Spencer, May 18 and 23, 1812, Chanler Collection, NYHS.

[224] *Albany Republican*, April 22, 1812.

[225] Ibid., May 6 and 8, 1812.

[226] See Lewis to Madison, September 7, November 14, 1808; Mathew Tillotson to Madison, November 15, 1808, Madison Papers, LC. Spencer to Armstrong, April 9, 1812, Chanler Collection, NYHS.

[227] Madison to Jefferson, April 3, 1812, Madison Papers, LC; Rush to Ingersoll, April 12, 1812, Ingersoll Papers, HSP.

reluctant to submit the document to the mercies of the Federalists and the "malcontent" Republicans in the Senate.[228] But the news did seem sufficiently promising to counter the bad impression created in Congress by the recent burning of American merchantmen bound for Spain, and it was always possible to assume that Barlow would not accept a treaty that did not finally provide for a settlement of all American disputes with France. On this basis therefore Monroe, on April 14, instructed the *National Intelligencer* to resume its editorials calling for war with Britain. To convince the doubtful and to reassure the hesitant members of the legislature, the administration newspaper declared that nothing could be expected from Britain, that the military preparations were "adequate to every essential object," and that war—with British power being overextended in the vast hemisphere between the West Indies and India—involved no real military hazard to the United States.[229]

Congress, however, chose to ignore this lead, and responded by debating motions for a recess and for the repeal of the nonintercourse policy as well as considering petitions against the ninety-day embargo. These proposals commanded a fair degree of support in the legislature, and they were promoted with particular vigor in the Senate as delaying tactics by Republican "malcontents" Bradley, Leib, and Pope. The motion for recess was popular, since many Congressmen were weary at the extreme length of the session, and even administration supporters assumed that little would be decided before the embargo expired. They wished in the interval to return home, both to visit their families and to sound out their constituents on the question of war.[230] For repealing nonintercourse, the case could be made, even by supporters of war, that an influx of British goods would aid in financing the war by filling the Treasury with customs receipts. Yet had either motion passed, the conclusion would have been inescapable that Congress was not really considering war with Britain. The recess would have belittled the seriousness of the earlier measures of preparation, and repealing nonintercourse would have relieved distress in Britain while also promising to create further complications with France. But because some thirty

[228] For the background to the treaty see Barlow to Monroe, January 28, February 8, and March 3 and 15, 1812, Dispatches from United States Ministers to France (M-34), Records of the Department of State (RG 59), NA. For the administration's caution see Monroe to Barlow, February 23, April 23, 1812, Diplomatic Instructions: All Counties (M-77), NA. See also Madison to Barlow, February 24, 1812, Madison Papers, LC.

[229] *Natl Intelligencer*, April 14, 1812. See also Brant, *Madison: The President*, 434-436.

[230] Foster reported Rhode Island Senator William Hunter as saying he felt "brutalized and stupified" by continual "confinement" in Washington. Journal entry, April 26, 1812, Foster Papers, LC. See also Turner to Bentley, April 27, 1812, Bentley Letters, Essex Institute.

to forty Congressmen had already taken unofficial leaves of absence anyway, the fate of both motions was problematical, and the size of the Republican majority on the many roll calls taken before the proposals were defeated was quite small.[231] On the motion to repeal nonintercourse, the administration, according to Sérurier, felt it necessary to warn the House foreign relations committee of the harmful consequences of such an action, while the petitions against the embargo, flooding in from the grain-selling areas of New York and Pennsylvania, were not finally rejected in the House until May 11.[232] Slowly, if reluctantly, the majority of congressional Republicans resigned themselves to the hard fact that war and a system of commercial restrictions were not, as their past speeches had implied, alternative measures of coercion against Britain but that they were mutually reinforcing methods of bringing maximum pressure on the enemy.

Two days after disposing the petitions against the embargo, the House voted to recall its absent members "forthwith" with the intention that they should all be back in the capital by June 1.[233] After this vote was taken, John Harper of the House foreign relations committee reported that the question of war would be put before Congress in early June, probably by "an important and very argumentative message" from the President.[234] And as the absent members began returning to await the final news from Europe that was still anticipated on the *Hornet*, the circumstances seemed to be as favorable as they ever would for holding the congressional caucus. Since George Clinton had died on April 20, Madison was now, as Henry Clay pointed out, indisputably the only candidate who could command a majority in this caucus. His only other rival, DeWitt Clinton, was still in no position to present himself to the electorate through a different nominating agency.[235] Consequently, the call for the congressional caucus was issued on May 16, and two days later Madison received a unanimous

[231] AC, 12th Cong., 1st sess., 211-215, 225, 235, 237, 239, 1279, 1280, 1281-1314, 1334, 1342. See also Macon to Nicholson, April 10, 1812, Nicholson Papers, LC; Harper to Plumer, May 11, 1812, Plumer Papers, LC.

[232] Sérurier to Bassano, April 24, 1812, Correspondance Politique, vol. LXVII. Randolph to Garnett, April 14, 1812, Randolph-Garnett Letterbook, LC. AC, 12th Cong., 1st sess., 1379-1419. The petitions against nonintercourse and the embargo can be found in the Legislative Records of the House and the Senate, particularly HR 12A-G1.2 and Sen 12A-G2, NA. See also Chapter V below.

[233] AC, 12th Cong., 1st sess., 1424, 1427.

[234] Harper to Plumer, May 13, 1812, Plumer Papers, LC; Lowndes to Elizabeth Lowndes, May 10, 1812, Lowndes Papers, UNC.

[235] Clay to James Taylor, May 17, 1812, Letters Received by the Secretary of War, Registered Series (M-221), Records of the Office of the Secretary of War (RG 107), NA.

nomination from those Republicans present, although these constituted barely two-thirds of the party's strength in both branches of the legislature. With the notable exceptions of Senators Leib and Pope—who appear to have been coerced into attending by the other members of their state delegations—most of Madison's Republican opponents simply boycotted the event.[236]

For the Vice Presidency, in the absence of a trustworthy New Yorker, the caucus sought a New Englander to balance the ticket and to strengthen the party in a region where the spring elections had displayed an unwelcome swing toward Federalism.[237] These considerations narrowed the choice to one between John Langdon and Elbridge Gerry, the former Republican governors of New Hampshire and Massachusetts respectively. The administration's preference was for Langdon. He was a more popular hero of the American Revolution than was Gerry, and the career of the latter, furthermore, had been characterized by several marked changes in political conduct which could only have struck more orthodox Republicans as disturbing. As Gallatin remarked, Gerry in the Vice Presidency "would give us as much trouble" as the late George Clinton had done.[238] Indeed, there were even rumors in Washington that Gerry had already been approached as a vice-presidential candidate by DeWitt Clinton in an effort to unite the voters of the northern states against the administration.[239] Langdon, however, declined the nomination, thus leaving Madison's supporters in the caucus with little alternative but to select Gerry.[240]

Five days after Madison's renomination for the Presidency, the long-awaited news from Europe conveyed by the *Hornet* arrived in Washington. Unfortunately for the administration, Barlow's dispatches were not as favorable as many Republicans felt they needed to be in order

[236] *Natl Intelligencer*, May 16 and 19, 1812. On May 18, 82 Republicans voted for Madison's nomination and another 10 endorsed it after the passage of the war bill in the House on June 4. *Natl Intelligencer*, June 9, 1812. There were 134 Republicans in both houses of Congress; thus the nomination gave Madison, ultimately, the support of 68% of the congressional wing of the Republican party. Since a total of 98 Republican Representatives and Senators duly voted for war—about 73% of the party—it would seem that war policies commanded rather more support among Republicans than Madison did personally. On the "malcontents" at the caucus see Roberts to Matthew Roberts, May 20, 1812, Roberts Papers, HSP.

[237] Gallatin to Nicholson, May 21, 1812, *Gallatin Papers*. See also Chapter V below.

[238] Ibid., May 21, 1812; Harper to Plumer, May 5, 1812, Plumer Papers, LC.

[239] See Gerry's denial that he had been approached by Clinton in his letter to Richard Cutts, June 15, 1812, Elbridge Gerry Papers, LC.

[240] John Langdon to Gallatin, May 30, 1812, *Gallatin Papers*. *Natl Intelligencer*, June 6, 9, and 11, 1812.

to simplify a decison about war.[241] The minister to France could only report that he was still negotiating a treaty of commerce, while the status of American shipping seized under Napoleon's decrees remained as ambiguous as it had been since November 1810.[242] To be set against this inconclusive news, however, was the fact that there was no change in the position of Britain either. Admittedly, the American chargé d'affaires in London, Jonathan Russell, reported that the Orders in Council were now under heavy attack from British manufacturing interests, but he held out no hope for their repeal, nor did Foster receive instructions to offer any. The very most that the British minister was authorized to offer the United States to prevent a rupture was the possibility of Americans obtaining a share of the British license trade to Europe, but Madison, deploring this trade as he did, would have regarded this as no concession at all.[243] In short, Britain's adherence to and defense of the Orders in Council was no different from what it had been when Foster commenced his mission in July 1811.

Yet this news seems to have disappointed many Republicans rather than encouraged them to move on to declare war against Britain, and it may have even opened up divisions within the cabinet itself. Gallatin was no keener on war than he had ever been, Eustis had become totally confused by his inability to manage the administrative problems of preparedness, and Monroe, according to Foster, had from time to time shown himself to be very depressed about his failure to negotiate a settlement.[244] The President, on the other hand, Foster reported to be as "unvarying" as ever in his hostility to Britain, but even he seems to have been affected, at least temporarily, by the lack of enthusiasm for war that prevailed in the capital.[245] One expression of this mood was the revival of the idea, earlier promoted by John Randolph and the Federalists, that war could only be justified if it was declared against

[241] Burwell to Nicholas, May 23, 1812, Nicholas Papers, UVa; Rush to Ingersoll, May 24, 1812, Ingersoll Papers, HSP; Randolph to Garnett, May 26, 1812, Randolph-Garnett Letterbook, LC; John Sevier to George Washington Sevier, May 31, 1812, Miscellaneous MSS, LC. See also Sérurier to Bassano, May 27, 1812, Correspondance Politique, vol. LXVII; and *Virginia Argus*, May 25 and 28, 1812.

[242] Barlow to Monroe, April 22, 1812, Dispatches from United States Ministers to France, NA.

[243] Jonathan Russell to Monroe, March 20 and April 9, 1812, Dispatches from United States Ministers to Britain, NA. See Lord Castlereagh's four sets of instuctions to Foster, April 10, 1812, Bernard Mayo, ed., *Instructions to the British Ministers to the United States, 1791-1812* (Washington, D.C., 1941), 353-371.

[244] Rush to Dallas, May 26, 1812, George Mifflin Dallas Collection, HSP; Foster to Lord Castlereagh, May 3, 1812, F.O. 5, vol. 85; Foster, Journal entry, April 7, 1812, Foster Papers, LC.

[245] Foster to Castlereagh, May 23, 1812, F.O. 5, vol. 86.

both France and Britain. Madison confessed that he found French policy "puzzling" and realized that war with Britain alone risked dividing his supporters, but he could not at the same time take the notion of a "triangular war," as it was called, very seriously. The project presented, as the President said, "a thousand difficulties," and its essential absurdity had already provoked jokes in Washington about the possibility of the French and British ministers meeting to coordinate their self-defense against a common American enemy. Nor would a "triangular war" solve Madison's political problems. He was not convinced that his opponents advocating the scheme were sincere in their professions of an impartial dislike of both European belligerents, and they could try instead to turn all the practical difficulties of such a war against the administration.[246]

If Madison hesitated, though, it was not for long. Shortly after the arrival of the news from the *Hornet*, the President was visited between May 25 and 29 by a deputation of congressional Republicans headed by Speaker Clay. What they discussed can only be conjectured, but it seems likely that they resumed the earlier discussions that Clay had held with Monroe about the responsibilities of the executive and the legislature in initiating a declaration of war. Both the President and the legislators, moreover, must have realized that a decision for either peace or war could now no longer be postponed, and according to Joseph Gales's recollection many years later, Clay informed Madison that a majority of Congressmen would support war if the President recommended it.[247] On May 30, the *National Intelligencer* stated that Congress was bound to carry the measures of preparation against Britain to their logical conclusion and pointed out that the period of the sixty-day embargo Madison had sought in April was now about to expire. There were, undeniably, many practical difficulties still to be overcome in order to wage war effectively, but, as Madison later admitted, "it had become impossible to avoid or even delay war at a moment when we were not prepared for it and when it was certain that effective preparations would not take place whilst the question of war was undecided." The President therefore felt, as Richard Rush put it, that he had little choice but to "put the machine of power in motion" in the hope that "thousands will run after its wheels." "While

---

[246] Madison to Jefferson, May 25, 1812, Madison Papers, LC. Foster to the Duchess of Devonshire, April 19, 1812; Journal entry, April 16, 1812, Foster Papers, LC.

[247] "Joseph Gales on the War Manifesto of 1812," *American Historical Review* 13 (1908), 309-310. See also Theodore C. Smith, "War Guilt in 1812," *Proceedings of the Massachusetts Historical Society* 64 (1931), 342-345.

still," Rush added, "everybody is pulling it to pieces."[248] Rush also suggested that Madison and his cabinet appear in person before Congress to deliver a request for war, but the President rejected the idea, probably because it smacked of trying to influence the congressional deliberations too openly.[249] Instead Madison finally took on June 1 the step that had been implicit in his conduct since his decision to summon the Twelfth Congress into an early session. He sent its members a message asking them to consider a declaration of war.

★

MADISON'S MESSAGE of June 1 presented to Congress four major grievances to justify a declaration of war against Britain: impressment, illegal blockades, the Orders in Council, and an allegation that British agents had been responsible for the renewal of Indian warfare on the northwestern frontier over the winter of 1811-1812. The President's purpose here was not so much to explain the causes of the war he now sought as it was to expose British behavior concerning those grievances in ways which suggested to the legislators that the continuation of peace only allowed the enemy to pursue policies that were hostile to the interests and the sovereignty of the Republic behind hypocritical professions of amity. Britain was, Madison stressed, already in a "state of war with the United States," and hence there could be no justification for Congress to tolerate the wrongs which the preservation of peace would entail. The President thus concluded his case by asking Congress to reach a decision "worthy of the enlightened and patriotic councils of a virtuous, a free, and a powerful nation."[250] Similarly, the question which the message posed to Congress was not really whether the American grievances justified war—for most Republicans had long agreed that they did—but whether President Madison should be granted the support of the representatives of the people in the months to come. Given the predominantly partisan context of politics in this period, the expediency of supporting or opposing war was transformed into a party decision, and, as Foster reported to the Foreign Office, the war was also a "question on which depended the election of the next Presidency."[251] Indeed, the proceedings of Congress throughout June sug-

[248] Madison to John Nicholas, April 2, 1813, Madison Papers, LC; Rush to Ingersoll, May 10, 1812, Ingersoll Papers, HSP.

[249] Rush to Ingersoll, May 24, 1812, Ingersoll Papers, HSP.

[250] For the war message see Richardson, *Messages and Papers*, II, 484-490. For a discussion of the rhetorical devices in the message see Robert L. Ivie, "The Republican Dramatization of War" (Paper delivered at the Western Speech Association Meeting, San Francisco, November 1976).

[251] Foster to Castlereagh, June 9, 1812, F.O. 5, vol. 86; Sérurier to Bassano, June 7, 1812, Correspondance Politique, vol. LXVII.

gested that its response to war was determined, with a few exceptions, more by partisan and political considerations than by any individual or sectional attitudes toward the issues which had produced the crisis.[252]

In the House the administration had throughout the session normally been able to muster a majority in support of its measures, though at times that majority had constituted barely half the total membership—hardly an ideal basis of support for the commencement of a war. However, after receiving a report from the foreign relations committee on June 3 which amplified the themes of the President's message, the Republican majority quickly rallied and voted for a declaration of war the next day by seventy-nine to forty-nine.[253] The vote was an adequate, if not overwhelming, endorsement of the President's policies, and it reflected the opinions of a Republican majority drawn from all parts of the nation. Of the votes against war, thirty-three were cast by Federalists and eleven by Republicans from New York and New Jersey, nearly all of whom were supporters of DeWitt Clinton.[254] The remaining five Republican votes against war came from John Randolph of Virginia, Richard Stanford of North Carolina, William Rodman of Pennsylvania, Josiah Bartlett of New Hampshire, and Peleg Tallman

[252] For two studies that measure party cohesion as a factor in congressional voting see Ronald L. Hatzenbuehler, "Party Unity and the Decision for War in the House of Representatives, 1812," *WMQ* 3d Ser., 29 (1972), 367-390; and Randolph M. Bell, "Mr. Madison's War and Long-Term Congressional Voting Behavior," ibid., 36 (1979), 373-395. See also Roger H. Brown, *The Republic in Peril: 1812* (New York, 1964), 45.

[253] AC, 12th Cong., 1st sess., 1624-1629, 1630-1632, 1633-1637. The draft of the House foreign relations committee report of June 3 can be found in HR 12A-C5.1, LRHR. It bears the title "Report or Manifesto of the Causes and Reasons of War with Great Britain" and is largely in the hand of John Graham, chief clerk of the State Department. The concluding paragraphs, however, are in a different hand, possibly that of either Calhoun or Grundy of the committee.

[254] Of the eleven New York and New Jersey Republicans against war, eight boycotted the caucus of May 18 which renominated Madison. Of the other three, Thomas Sammons of New York attended the caucus but cast no vote, while Samuel Mitchill of New York and Adam Boyd of New Jersey both supported Madison but seem to have opposed war in order to conform with the majority sentiment in their state delegations. Many Clintonians had supported war preparations earlier in the session—assuming probably that such a course would not conflict with an anti-administration position—but then changed to an antiwar stance in order to avoid supporting the President. The *National Intelligencer*, October 3, 1812, complained about his inconsistency, as did many other Republican newspapers. See *Virginia Argus*, June 18, 1812, and also the (Albany, N.Y.) *Albany Argus*, April 6, 1813, for a scathing attack on the antiwar vote of Pierre Van Cortlandt, Jr., of New York. Such inconsistency probably helps explain why practitioners of legislative roll call analysis have been compelled to omit many of the Clintonians from their calculations. See Hatzenbuehler, "Party Unity and the Decision for War," 374.

of Massachusetts. Randolph and Stanford were "Old Republicans," in opposition to the administration since 1805, and their votes were entirely predictable.[255] Pennsylvania Republicans had likewise written off Rodman as a latent convert to Federalism; his voting record throughout the session revealed a consistent aversion to war measures as well as a reluctance to cooperate with the sixteen other members of the Pennsylvania Republican delegation.[256] Josiah Bartlett, who supported Madison for President, opposed the House declaration of war as "too hasty," but after the Senate had voted for war, he reversed his opinion and declared his support for the measure.[257] Peleg Tallman was thus left as the only other House Republican who openly defied the sentiments of his party; he was, though, absent for much of the session, tending to business interests which he felt would be harmed by war.[258]

The Senate, unlike the House, nearly defeated the declaration of war. It had long been clear in this faction-ridden body that the President could not safely rely on more than twelve to fifteen votes, while the strength of his opponents, both Federalist and "malcontent" Republican, was estimated at times to number twenty out of a total membership of thirty-four. Indeed, as the President sent in his war message on June 1, members of his cabinet freely admitted that the upper branch might well vote for something less than "unqualified war," and it was probably the fear of sustaining a humiliating defeat in the Senate that tempted Monroe and Gallatin to flirt with the idea of trying to persuade the House to support "at present . . . maritime war only" as the lowest common denominator of Republican thinking.[259] These fears proved to be only too well justified. After the Senate began debating the war bill on June 9, both the Federalists and the "malcontents" made a last-ditch stand to defeat the administration; they proposed, though not with any great consistency, three other

[255] Risjord, *The Old Republicans*, 142-143.

[256] Thomas Rogers to Roberts, May 10, June 7, 1812; Roberts to Matthew Roberts, May 20, 1812, Roberts Papers, HSP. See also Victor A. Sapio, *Pennsylvania and the War of 1812* (Lexington, 1970), 128-166.

[257] Josiah Bartlett to Ezra Bartlett, May 30, June 18, 1812, Bartlett Papers, LC.

[258] The letters of Tallman to William King reveal a strong fear that war would be bad for business. See those written on November 21, December 22, 1811, William King Papers, MeHS. See also Brown, *The Republic in Peril*, 139-140. Even Madison's kinsman Richard Cutts, who also represented a Maine district, felt war would be harmful. See Cutts to Thomas Cutts, June 11, 17, and 29, 1812, Henry S. Burrage, ed., "Some Letters of Richard Cutts," *Collections and Proceedings of the Maine Historical Society* 2d Ser., 9 (1898), 39-41.

[259] Eustis to Dearborn, June 4, 1812, J. S. Fogg Autograph Collection, MeHS; Monroe to Gallatin, June 1, 1812, *Gallatin Papers*. See also Andrew Gregg to Mr. Logue, June 4, 1812, *Democratic Press*, December 3, 1812; and Roberts to Matthew Roberts, June 7, 1812, Roberts Papers, HSP.

courses of action. Some of the Clintonians, notably Obadiah German of New York and Nicholas Gilman of New Hampshire, favored postponing war until the fall pending further military preparations. The Federalists declared that there should be no war at all or only war with both France and Britain, while the remaining "malcontent" Republicans, especially Samuel Smith and Leib, felt—as Monroe had sensed—that a decision to confine hostilities to the high seas would be more appropriate.[260]

By advocating maritime war alone, some of the "malcontent" Republicans, particularly the Clintonians, argued that they were doing no more than adhering to their long-held belief about the need to strengthen the navy, and they could also reinforce their point by claiming that the Republic was by no means ready to commence offensive operations against Canada.[261] But, as Senator Bayard and several other observers noted, all the alternatives to the "direct question" proposed by the "malcontent" Republicans also provided a "good cover" for those among them who were "disposed to retreat" and yet left them some latitude to come out for "stronger measures" later, should they be able to defeat the present House war bill.[262] All the alternatives to the House bill were eventually voted down by narrow margins, and this left the Senators with no choice but to decide between full-scale war or the continuation of peace. At this advanced stage in the congressional proceedings the most plausible argument for remaining at peace was that the nation was not yet ready for war, but as William Crawford of Georgia pointed out, if the Senate rejected war for this reason, it invited the President to keep Congress in session until the preparations for war were adequate.[263] This prospect was probably too much for any Republican to contemplate. Even the "malcontents" may have concluded that it was now preferable to declare war and leave Madison

[260] AC, 12th Cong., 1st sess., 252-254, 263-296. See also Gilman to Logan, June 14, 1812, Logan Papers, HSP. For another analysis see Leland R. Johnson, "The Suspense was Hell: The Senate Vote for War in 1812," *Indiana Magazine of History* 65 (1969), 247-267.

[261] Brown, *The Republic in Peril*, 141-147. See also *Albany Register*, May 1 and 29, 1812.

[262] Bayard to Andrew Bayard, June 4 1812, Elizabeth Donnan, ed., *The Papers of James A. Bayard, 1796-1815* (Washington D.C., 1915), 198. Edward Fox told Roberts, June 24, 1812, that he feared Leib and Gregg would oppose war "so that the Clinton faction might have room to come out with the remainder. . . ." Roberts Papers, HSP. See also Binns to Roberts, June 6, 1812, Roberts Papers, HSP.

[263] Crawford's argument was not reported in the *Annals of Congress*, but it was recorded by Thomas Worthington in his "Notes on the Answers to Proposals for Letters of Marque," June 1812, Thomas Worthington Papers, RCHS. (I am grateful to Roger Brown for making copies of this document available to me.)

to get on with its prosecution rather than suspend the Republic's affairs in an intolerably indecisive state. Finally, therefore, the Senate passed on June 17 a declaration of war against Britain by nineteen votes to thirteen.[264]

As was the case with the House, all the votes for war came from Republicans representing all sections of the nation. The six Federalist Senators predictably rejected war, and they were joined by a core of four Clintonians—German of New York, Gilman of New Hampshire, John Lambert of New Jersey, and Pope of Kentucky.[265] Throughout the session one Republican Senator, Philip Reed of Maryland, had voted fairly consistently with the Federalists in opposing war measures; his motives for doing so were not at all clear, though he may have been the only Republican in the Senate who openly shared the anti-administration attitude of the "Old Republicans" in the House.[266] On the final vote, these consistently anti-administration Senators were joined by two colleagues who normally supported the President but whose nerve failed them at the last moment. Jeremiah Howell of Rhode Island had supported measures of preparation for most of the session as well as endorsing Madison's renomination in the congressional caucus, but in the final crisis after June 1 his party regularity suddenly collapsed, perhaps because his home state was reported to be overwhelmingly opposed to war.[267] The final antiwar Senator, Thomas Worthington of Ohio, would doubtless have preferred to support the administration, but on June 14 he sought an interview with Madison to explain that he could not vote for war, partly because his home state was vulnerable to Indian attacks and partly because he felt that the nation as a whole was not adequately prepared for hostilities. The President accepted Worthington's views as a sincere and isolated difference of opinion, then named the Senator as a commissioner to negotiate with the northwestern Indians in the fall of 1812.[268]

[264] AC, 12th Cong., 1st sess., 297.

[265] For evidence of Pope's support of Clinton see *Albany Register*, November 6, 1812; *Kentucky Gazette*, May 29, October 27, and December 8, 1812.

[266] Macon once described Reed as an "old-fashioned republican." To Nicholson, April 11, 1808, Nicholson Papers, LC. See also Reed to Macon, April 1, 1811, Nicholson Papers, LC. Later in 1812, Reed supported DeWitt Clinton for the Presidency. See John Comegys to Van Cortlandt, October 29, 1812, Judd, ed., *Correspondence of the Van Cortlandt Family*, 568.

[267] Perkins, *Prologue to War*, 412. David Howell to Madison, October 22, 1812, Madison Papers, LC.

[268] Thomas Worthington, Diary entry, June 14, 1812, Thomas Worthington Papers, LC; Worthington's "Notes on Answers etc," June 1812; and Worthington to ——, November 1812, Worthington Papers, RCHS.

The declaration of war passed in the Senate only because some of the most prominent "malcontent" Republicans—notably Giles, Gregg, Leib and Samuel Smith—rejoined the pro-administration group to provide a majority. They had called for military preparations in some form to uphold the nation's honor long before Madison had been prepared to espouse the cause, but there was now no further political advantage in their stand.[269] Yet if the declaration of war were to fail, it could only be by their votes, and they could not therefore easily reject the logical conclusion to policies which they had urged on the President without revealing that motives other than patriotism had governed their conduct.[270] Samuel Smith, in particular, agonized over the decision he was required to make, and he was quoted by observers as being on all sides of the issue. Gallatin's kinsman, Joseph H. Nicholson of Baltimore, rejoiced that the Senator was "broken down," suspecting that he would eventually endorse commercial restrictions in order to maintain his stance of opposition to the President, but Foster, who had deliberately cultivated the Maryland Republican, more accurately predicted that Smith would vote for war to save his property in France while hoping that the President's mismanagement of the conflict would eventually lead to his downfall.[271] For those "malcontents" whose conduct had been inspired largely by personal contempt for Madison, there was, in truth, little alternative but to vote for war, and, as Charles Jared Ingersoll put it, they could "not withstand the impulses propelling them over the shoals of faction and, after floundering there rather long indeed, ultimately floated in the old and customary channels."[272]

The declaration of war on June 18, 1812, can thus be best understood as Madison's response to the long-term diplomatic and political problems that had beset his administration since 1809. Confronted

[269] Monroe to Taylor, June 13, 1812, Monroe Papers, LC. Monroe here wrote at length on the problems created for the administration by the "habitual opponents of the government" in the Senate—by whom he did *not* mean the Federalists—who had "unceasingly circulated the report that the Executive did not intend to make war." "These men," he continued, were now being "brought to the issue by the proposition for war," and Monroe had no doubt "that the measure will finally pass, perhaps by the votes of those very men who, finding that their inconsistency and improper views are seen thro' . . . , will join in to mask their real conduct and views from the public eye."

[270] Rush to Ingersoll, June 15, 1812, Ingersoll Papers, HSP; Randolph to Edward Cunningham, June 24, 1812, Randolph Papers, LC. See also *The Enquirer*, June 15, 1812; and *Albany Republican*, July 14, 1812.

[271] Nicholson to Gallatin, June 30, 1812, *Gallatin Papers*; Foster, Journal entry, May 30, 1812, Foster Papers, LC.

[272] Ingersoll to Dallas, June 25, 1812, Ingersoll Papers, HSP.

with obduracy from Britain over the issues of American maritime rights and facing rising pressures from his own Republican supporters and critics for effective action, Madison decided to prepare for war. He pressed the issue on Congress as far as he thought was constitutionally and politically advisable and he persisted in his course, though at times his leadership seemed neither clear nor skillful. His private secretary, Edward Coles, recalled years later that the President was "less rampant in the onset" than some of "the noisy politicians of the day" who found him "too tolerant and forebearing," but he was also "less crouching under difficulties and disasters than some of them were."[273] And the decision to resist Britain by force did bring the President some political benefits which he might not have otherwise enjoyed. In order to carry the nation through the ordeal of war, most Republicans felt they had no choice but to support the administration, and by the end of 1812 many of Madison's former critics, including Wilson Cary Nicholas, Duane, Giles, Spencer, and Armstrong, were all supporting the war, albeit with varying degrees of enthusiasm.[274]

Here the most significant development was the emergence of Armstrong as a public advocate of the war. On July 4, 1812—in marked contrast to his behavior on the same day in the previous year—he offered in Rhinebeck a toast to the President, coupling it with a denunciation of "ambitious demagogues and interested intrigues."[275] This was an unmistakable reference to DeWitt Clinton's refusal to support the administration, and in the months leading up to the presidential election Armstrong attacked the Clintonians in articles and pamphlets, which, as Martin Van Buren wrote, showed that the "pen that had indited the Newburgh Letters . . . had lost none of its pungency or venom." His best-known effort here perhaps was a pamphlet entitled *The Coalition*, in which he accused Clinton of becoming a Federalist and sarcastically described his supporters as a forlorn "brotherhood of hope" who sang "hymns of praise to describe the wonderful endowments . . . and unparalleled services of their Chief!"[276] Armstrong, too, was instrumental in persuading Duane to retract his earlier endorsement of Clinton, warning the editor that he must reject "dis-

[273] Coles to William Cabell Rives, January 21, 1856, "Letters of Edward Coles: Third Installment," *WMQ* 2d Ser., 7 (1927), 162-164.

[274] Nicholas to [Samuel Smith], October 27, 1812, Nicholas Papers, LC. Nicholas declared he still found Madison to be "childish and impractical," but he preferred him to DeWitt Clinton as President.

[275] *Albany Register*, July 14, 1812.

[276] John C. Fitzpatrick, ed., *The Autobiography of Martin Van Buren* (Washington, D.C., 1920), 42.

affection" and "take the field in support of principles which are . . . common to us both."[277] Rather reluctantly, Duane announced in October 1812 that the war had to have the support of all Republicans. He thus tacitly admitted that his approval of war against Britain outweighed his personal reservations about Madison as President.[278]

Consequently, DeWitt Clinton's campaign for the Presidency was both overshadowed by the commencement of the war and frustrated by the closing of Republican ranks behind the administration. The impact of his nomination by a Republican caucus in Albany on May 31 was obscured by the congressional deliberations on war for the first three weeks of June, while he also found himself desperately short of influential political allies in his bid to cast the "Virginia Dynasty" from power. The New York Republican party was split, and his attempts to undermine Madison's strength in the southern and western states by seeking a vice-presidential candidate in Kentucky came to nothing.[279] Only the Smith family in Maryland, still piqued by Madison's conduct, and Michael Leib offered him any significant Republican support. Electoral necessities thus forced him in the second half of 1812 to solicit Federalist votes to augment his limited Republican base.[280] The resulting coalition, as Duane and Armstrong noted, was "a group more oddly consorted than the assemblage in the ark," and Clinton's platform was no better. To win over the Federalists he promised to oppose the war, while to attract Republicans he claimed that he could prosecute it more vigorously than Madison.[281] Yet Clinton's candidacy was flawed by more than inconsistency on the great national issue of the war. His real difficulty arose from his having begun to organize his challenge to the administration too late for it to have had any chance of success. When seeking support in areas south of New York in the last months of 1812, Clinton found that local Republican

[277] Armstrong to Duane, August 20, 1812, "Selections from the Duane Papers," *Historical Magazine* 2d Ser., 4 (1868), 60-61.

[278] Duane to Jefferson, September 20, 1812, Ford, "Letters of Duane," 353; *Aurora*, October 24, 1812.

[279] *Kentucky Gazette*, May 5, 1812; Maturin Livingston to Gallatin, May 30, 1812, *Gallatin Papers*.

[280] Robert Smith to ——, [July 1812], Charles E. French Collection, MHS. For Smith's attempts to organize Federalist votes against Madison see Albert J. Beveridge, *The Life of John Marshall* (Boston, 1919), IV, 35. See also *Albany Register*, September 29 and November 24, 1812. For Clinton's overtures to the Federalists see the "Statement in R. King's Handwriting," Charles R. King, ed., *The Life and Correspondence of Rufus King* (New York, 1894-1900), V, 265-272.

[281] *Aurora*, October 24, 1812; *Albany Register*, May 1, July 10, August 28 and September 8, 1812. For an account of the 1812 election see Risjord, "The Election of 1812," Schlesinger and Israel, eds., *History of American Presidential Elections*, I, 249-296.

leaders had, by and large, already committed themselves to voting for Madison.[282] The resulting resentment, particularly in the critical state of Pennsylvania, at the attempt of an outsider to meddle with a consensus that had already been arrived at made Clinton far more enemies among Republicans than did his ambivalent stand on the war.[283]

For these reasons the likelihood of Clinton triumphing over Madison at the polls in November 1812 seemed remote after the declaration of war, and the campaigns against Canada became the focus of the administration's attention. Despite the difficulties experienced in preparing for the conflict, events immediately after the declaration of war augered well for the President. The day after the declaration, June 19, news reached Washington of the assassination of Spencer Perceval, along with reports of considerable social unrest in Britain and a sustained campaign against the Orders in Council. That this campaign was successful in removing the Orders on June 16 was confirmed in Washington by mid-August. Madison must have viewed these developments with mixed feelings. All that he had most desired since 1809—the removal of the Orders in Council and the departure of Perceval—had suddenly been achieved, and, to that extent, the diplomacy of commercial restriction had been vindicated, though the President would have regretted that these occurrences had not come slightly earlier.[284] But a closer examination of events in Britain, especially the lifting of the Orders in Council, only confirmed Madison in his decision to prosecute the war until all American grievances with the enemy had been settled. The death of Perceval did not lead to the formation of a ministry in Britain more sympathetic to American views on maritime rights, and the Orders in Council were removed in a way that allowed the cabinet of Lord Liverpool to adhere to the assumptions that had led to their imposition in the first place. The new ministry still regarded

[282] The Clintonian campaign in Pennsylvania was not organized before the last week in August 1812. See Higginbotham, *Keystone in the Democratic Arch*, 259-260. In Kentucky the Clintonian newspaper in Lexington, the *American Statesman*, did not begin promoting its candidate until mid-September. See John Pope to Van Cortlandt, September 17, 1812, Judd, ed., *Correspondence of the Van Cortlandt Family*, 558. In North Carolina, contacts between the Federalists and the Clintonians appear to date from the end of August. See John Steele to Joseph Pearson, August 31, 1812, Henry M. Wagstaff, ed., *The Papers of John Steele* (Raleigh, N.C., 1914), II, 645.

[283] *Democratic Press*, August 1, September 14, and October 2, 1812. The *Press* complained bitterly that Pennsylvania's citizens had been "beset by gangs of hungry expectants, needy adventurers and impertinent impostates . . . laying hold of them by the skirts and interrupting their daily business—coaxing, cozzing, promising, whispering, swaggering, and bothering." See also (Northumberland, Pa.) *Der Republicaner*, October 3 and 24, 1812.

[284] Foster to Rear Admiral Sawyer, June 23, 1812, F.O. 5, vol. 86.

the Orders as an integral part of British maritime rights, declaring, in effect, that they had been no more than suspended and could be restored if circumstances required.[285] For this reason, the case for war remained almost as strong as it had ever been, and with growing unrest and political instability in Britain it was not improbable that the enemy would be increasingly vulnerable to the pressures of an American war. The only question remaining, therefore, was whether the Madison administration could organize the government and society of the Republic for a successful war.

[285] For brief summaries of these developments see Perkins, *Prologue to War*, 300-341; and Brant, *James Madison: Commander-in-Chief, 1812-1836* (Indianapolis, 1961), 33-34, 55-66.

CHAPTER III

★

ORGANIZING THE REPUBLIC
FOR WAR, 1783-1812

WITHOUT EXCEPTION the Founding Fathers in the 1780's believed that constitutional reform would make the United States a more efficient military power. Their reasons for this belief were clear, and arose from their experiences as army officers and legislators during the Revolution. Throughout the first war against Great Britain, the Continental Congress, compelled to requisition men and money from the state governments, had to contend unceasingly with indifferent compliance and conflicting jurisdictions. In practical military terms, these problems became manifest in the constant short-term enlistment of raw recruits, in a demoralized officer corps whose members felt that their duties were often inconsistent with their honor and self-interest, and in an inefficient supply system which was both cause and consequence of an inflationary financial policy. The creation of a new national government with the broadly defined authority to act directly on all citizens for the purposes of organizing the armed forces, coupled with power to finance such activities by taxation, would, it was believed, remove many of the difficulties of war-making that had been experienced under the Articles of Confederation.[1] The movement for constitutional reform also promised great improvements in matters of administration, not only by overcoming the political and economic obstacles to policy enforcement but also by eliminating the series of committees and boards that had flourished under Congress and replacing them with departments controlled by single administrative heads, all of whom would be united in their responsibility to a new Chief Executive.[2]

The desire for military reform, though, preceded by several years

[1] For a brief discussion of the problems of the Confederation period see Andrew C. McLaughlin, *The Confederation and Constitution, 1783-1789* (New York, 1905).

[2] Lloyd M. Short, *The Development of National Administrative Organization in the United States* (Urbana, 1924), 36, 37, 42, 43, 54, 55, 74, 78, 100.

the movement for constitutional change which culminated in the Philadelphia convention of 1787. No sooner had independence been won when George Washington and the officers of the Continental Army submitted to Congress in May 1783 a report calling for the establishment of a national peacetime army and a thorough overhaul of the state militias. Although the authority of Congress to take such action was doubtful, Washington recommended the creation of a small, permanent frontier force of 2,600 officers and men as well as a select militia whose members, serving from three to seven years, were to be obtained by a uniform classification of young militiamen between eighteen and twenty-five years of age. Here Washington advised, so far as was practicable, the amalgamation of Continental and state troops "to remove as much as possible all ideas of state distinction," and he clearly regarded military reform not simply as an end in itself but also as a means of consolidating the Union.[3] A committee of Congress, which included men of widely differing military experience such as Hamilton and Madison, unanimously endorsed and expanded Washington's report. Madison favored a peace establishment of four regiments and a corps of engineers, while Hamilton, who had been instrumental in obtaining the report, further advocated placing the new forces completely under congressional control and creating an elite force of volunteers, trained on a monthly basis, to serve as a long-term reserve. The formation of special volunteer forces had many precedents in the colonial years, but Hamilton failed to carry any of his recommendations into law. The reasons for the failure were complex, but the mutiny of dissatisfied troops in Philadelphia demanding back pay in 1783 undoubtedly reminded many Congressmen of the dangers of establishing a regular army in the new nation.[4]

The proposals of 1783, nonetheless, provided the basis for all subsequent discussion about the organization of the armed forces in the early Republic, and, as the inadequacies of the Articles of Confederation became increasingly apparent, the Federalists desired to incorporate these proposals into a wholly new constitutional structure. In the Philadelphia convention, the delegates readily agreed to give Congress the

---

[3] Lawrence D. Cress, "The Standing Army, the Militia, and the New Republic: Changing Attitudes toward the Military in American Society, 1768-1820" (Ph.D. diss., UVa, 1976), 204-222. See also Richard Kohn, *Eagle and Sword: The Federalists and the Creation of the Military Establishment, 1783-1802* (New York, 1975), 42-48; and Russell F. Weigley, *History of the United States Army* (New York, 1967), 74-80.

[4] Cress, "The Standing Army," 222-227; Kohn, *Eagle and Sword*, 48-53. For the colonial precedents see John Shy, "A New Look at Colonial Militia," *WMQ* 3d Ser., 20 (1963), 175-185.

unquestioned power to "raise and support" armies and navies while entrusting their employment to the President in his capacity as Commander in Chief. Only permanent national forces controlled by a national government, they believed, could effectively defend the Republic while British, French, Spanish, and Indian forces were present on its borders. Some Federalists, notably Hamilton, also felt that American society had reached the point where its diverse interests required the establishment of a profession of arms for their protection; most, however, were not prepared to go so far, probably regarding this argument as too closely approximating the traditional justification for the "standing armies" of European nations. Instead, they preferred to legitimate a regular army by claiming that a force raised by the representatives of the people and dependent upon them for its existence would not constitute a threat to public liberty.[5]

The issue of militia reform in 1787 was more problematical. To wage future wars with unreformed militias seemed to risk either a repetition of the problems of the Revolution or an overreliance on a large regular army. The delegates therefore generally conceded the inadequacies of the existing militias, wishing to give the national government some degree of power to remedy them in order to provide supplementary forces for the regular army while also avoiding the possible proliferation of armies within the states. The problem thus became part of the larger debate over how far the new government would encroach on the powers of the states. Here the more dedicated nationalists, including Madison, wanted to establish a congressional veto over the states, along with a similar authority to organize and command their militias.[6] Eventually the matter was compromised by omitting the veto and dividing control of the militias between the states and the national government; Congress gained the authority to use state militia units in "the service of the United States," while the organization of the militias and the right to appoint their officers remained with the states. Many Federalists, however, regretted these compromises, maintaining that the power of the states in the new government, including their control over the militias, was still too great. Madison, in particular, was uneasy, and bluntly informed Jefferson that the new Constitution would not "effectually answer its national object."[7]

[5] Cress, "The Standing Army," 254-263.

[6] Max Farrand, ed., *The Records of the Federal Convention of 1787* (New Haven, 1911), II, 332, 387, 388.

[7] Madison to Jefferson, September 6, 1787, William T. Hutchinson et al., eds., *The Papers of James Madison* (Chicago and Charlottesville, 1962–), X, 163-164. See also Charles F.

Despite this setback, the Federalists worked to ratify and implement the military clauses of the Constitution. Suppressing their reservations, they defended a regular army as well as militia reorganization and permanent naval forces with the claim that these measures were essential to make the United States militarily "respectable" to the powers of Europe. Such respectability in itself, they believed, together with the distance between the Old and New Worlds, constituted a form of defense, although their arguments also recognized the probability of American involvement in war in the foreseeable future.[8] Expanding on these themes of necessity and possible danger, the supporters of the Washington and Adams administrations throughout the 1790's used successive diplomatic and military crises with the Indians, the Algerians, the British, and the French to build up the regular forces, including artillery, infantry, dragoons, engineers, and even some naval forces. The climax of these efforts was the Quasi-War with France between 1797 and 1800, during which Congress provided for the creation of two armies of regular troops, which were to be supplemented with three provisional forces of short-term volunteers, and a new naval force of thirteen frigates, all to be supported by taxes.[9] Equally as important as the establishment of these forces were the Federalists' attempts to provide them with an appropriate administrative apparatus. Starting with only a Secretary of War and a handful of clerks in 1790, Congress steadily created inspectors, quartermasters, adjutants, paymasters, and accountants. The purchase of matériel was entrusted to the Purveyor of Public Supplies, established in 1792, and its distribution, in 1794, to the Superintendent of Military Stores, though here the administrative efficiency of the War Department was impaired somewhat by the 1795 decision to lodge the Purveyor's office in the Treasury Department. Offsetting this defect, on the other hand, were the separation of army and navy affairs by the creation of the Navy Department in 1798 and the increasing centralization of the administration of the armed forces at the seat of government in Philadelphia.[10]

The question of militia reorganization, however, did not receive so

Hobson, "The Negative on State Laws; James Madison, the Constitution and the Crisis of Republican Government," *WMQ* 3d Ser., 36 (1979), 215-235.

[8] See, for example, Madison's arguments in the Virginia ratifying convention in Jonathan Elliot, ed., *Debates in the Several State Conventions on the Adoption of the Federal Constitution* (Philadelphia, 1836), III, 90-97, 249-252, 381-383.

[9] Kohn, *Eagle and Sword*, 91-127, 174-189, 219-238.

[10] Short, *Administrative Organization*, 119-122. See also Harry M. Ward, *The Department of War, 1781-1795* (Pittsburgh, 1962); and Leonard D. White, *The Federalists: An Administrative History* (New York, 1948), 253-255.

comprehensive a solution. In 1790, Washington, drawing on schemes discussed in the previous decade, requested Congress to classify the state militias into three groups according to age. His purpose was to create a select force of about 30,000 young men who were to receive special annual training for immediate mobilization to assist regulars in times of crisis; the older classes, with less training, were to form a reserve pool of manpower which might be called on for defense in a long war or during an invasion.[11] The plan, which required considerable reorganization at the state and local levels, won little support. Congress put off a decision until forced into action after the defeat of General Arthur St. Clair by the northwestern Indians in 1792, and even then it continued to ignore Washington's suggestions. The Uniform Militia Act of May 8, 1792, simply required, with certain exceptions, all adult white males between eighteen and forty-five years of age to arm themselves and belong to a militia unit. Their organization and training were left almost entirely to the state governments; there was little in the law to ensure national uniformity, and it did not enable the War Department to call up readily identifiable bodies of troops in an emergency.[12] In truth, Congress had done no more than re-enact the deadlock that had arisen in the 1787 convention, and later legislation on the militia, such as the laws of February 28 and May 2, 1795, specifying the circumstances under which state militias could be used in national service, did nothing to alter the situation. Accordingly, the Federalists during the Quasi-War fell back on variations of colonial precedents to raise special volunteer corps in order to bypass the administrative obstacles to mobilizing militiamen that were now established in law. The ability of the national government to organize troops in this manner was not put to the test at the time, with the result that by 1800 the overall organization of the nation's military resources was still far from satisfactory to those who had been urging change since 1783. The need for an effective military force tended to make the regular army too large and too costly, while the militias remained an uncertain, if not inefficient, supplement. Nevertheless, the growth of military organization throughout the 1790's, like the growth of the national government itself, was still remarkable compared with the rudimentary beginnings of the 1780's.[13]

During the period of the ratification of the Constitution, however, some Federalists had been deeply impressed by the political strength,

[11] AC, 1st Cong., 3d sess., 2142-2158.
[12] Kohn, *Eagle and Sword*, 128-138.
[13] White, *The Federalists*, 253-255.

if not the cogency, of the Anti-Federalist arguments against the new government. Among them was Madison, who felt that the extent of this opposition would impose limits to the exercise of national power; these could not be disregarded without jeopardizing public acceptance of the regime. This adjustment of his priorities was reflected in his contribution to the *Federalist* papers as well as in all his future thinking about the nature of the American system of government. After 1788, Madison accepted what he had previously rejected—the notion that the union of states could survive as "a feudal system of republics" rather than as either a "mere confederation" or, as he had hoped, a "consolidated national government." The essence of the compromises of the new Constitution, as Madison now understood them, had been to create a "federal" government which was supposedly independent in the operation of its powers but which, by virtue of its construction, was in fact dependent on the other sources of political power in the nation, the people of the states and the state governments. The most likely source of difficulty here, Madison felt, was continuing competition between the state and federal governments, and to have to solve any conflicts between the two by resorting to federal coercion would probably defeat the purpose of what constitutional reform had been achieved, since he was not confident that the balance of forces would always favor the federal government. To avoid difficulties here, Madison anticipated the development of a mutually advantageous, quasi-voluntaristic relationship in matters of policy enforcement between the federal and state governments. His arguments on this subject were necessarily vague, but they implied that the agenda for national politics after ratification was to produce "a sympathy of interests" between the federal and state governments and the people. This, Madison believed, could be achieved through the representative mechanisms of the Constitution, which, he thought, would elect to power an enlightened elite of rulers capable of defining and communicating a broad conception of the national good that would be neither dependent on nor antagonistic to the interests of any particular group or region.[14]

Working from these redefined assumptions, the future President played a prominent part in establishing the federal government, including introducing bills to set up both the Department of War and some naval forces, and up until about mid-1794 he generally supported

[14] See *The Federalist*, Nos. 19, 44, 45, 46; Elliot, *Debates*, III, 255-260; and Madison to Jefferson, October 24, 1787, *JM Papers*, X, 205-214. See also Hobson, "The Negative on State Laws," 233-235; and Robert J. Morgan, "Madison's Theory of Representation in the Tenth Federalist," *Journal of Politics* 36 (1974), 852-885.

measures to increase the regular army and reform the militias.[15] At the same time, the Anti-Federalists, who usually opposed the military buildup, warned at length of the dangers of a "standing army," with the intensity of their protest increasing as the Federalists added to the armed forces. Madison, who had by 1791 expressed some concern about Hamilton's financial program and its implications for American foreign policy, gradually came to share some of this anxiety about the growth of the army, especially after its use in the suppression of the Whiskey Rebellion in 1794 and the decision of the Washington administration not to reduce its size after the resolution of the crises with the British and the northwestern Indians in 1795. Since he did not believe that the United States could yet compel European powers to respect American interests by armed force alone, he became intensely suspicious of those who acted as if it could do so, fearing that many of his Federalist associates were playing the "old game of turning every contingency into a resource for accumulating force in the government."[16] This opposition to the administration's policies did not mean, however, that Madison had abandoned his earlier support for national control of a regular army; instead, he simply wished to limit the size of that army as much for financial reasons as any others, and insisted that the laws for its support should clearly specify its limited, defensive functions.[17] His attitude toward naval forces, on the other hand, did change more significantly, though again it was not that Madison ceased to believe that the United States should have a modest naval program or that a small navy could deal with such problems as the Algerian pirates. Rather, he came to suspect in 1794 that these pirates—whose actions provided the occasion for the attempt to expand the navy— were acting as agents of British naval power, and this larger problem of the Royal Navy, Madison had always believed, could best be dealt with through commercial restrictions to undercut the very basis of Great Britain's naval resources. A premature program of naval expansion at a time when Great Britain was attacking American commerce seemed only to promise a more likely involvement in war rather than advancing the true interests of the nation.[18]

[15] AC, 1st Cong., 3d sess., 1842-1843, 1856, 1860, 1864; 2d Cong., 1st sess., 354, 552, 1577; and 2d Cong., 2d sess., 792.

[16] Madison to Jefferson, March 14, 1794, James Madison Papers, LC.

[17] AC, 3d Cong., 1st sess., 709; 3d Cong., 2d sess., 1164, 1168, 1222; and 4th Cong., 1st sess., 1418. What Madison found objectionable in Federalist policies was not that they raised armies but that they delegated discretionary power to the President in ways that effectively reduced the role of Congress over military policy.

[18] AC, 3d Cong., 1st sess., 433-437; and 4th Cong., 1st sess., 877.

Yet the emerging Republican critique of Federalist military policy, which owed much to Madison's leadership, was molded by more than his tactical disagreements with the Federalists over specific issues. Many of his supporters did subscribe to the long-established belief that a "standing army" endangered a free state, and regarded the navy, in particular, as a totally unnecessary item of expense. Indeed, the expansion of the army and the navy in the 1790's was extremely costly. The armed forces quickly became the largest single cause of non debt-related expenditure in the national budget; between 1790 and 1794 annual military expenditures rose from about $700,000 to over $2.5 million, the latter figure amounting to nearly 40 percent of all expenditures.[19] From the outset, the Republicans were concerned about the large debt that Hamilton's financial program had funded, and they feared that constantly rising military expenditures, possibly leading to war, would either prevent the retirement of the debt or increase it still further. Certainly, Federalists and Republicans accepted direct and indirect taxation as a way of increasing federal revenues, but the public dislike of taxes, as demonstrated by the Whiskey Rebellion, inclined men of both persuasions to regard borrowing as a politically safer method of financing the national government's expenditures. The prospect of an evergrowing debt, though, especially to maintain military establishments, was not attractive to the Republicans. In fact, it was possible for them to interpret such a development as an attempt to produce in the United States the patterns of political and economic growth that had characterized English history after 1689. And few Americans could deny that the government of England, once free and happy, had become "corrupt" and "tyrannical."[20]

Such fears for the future of the Republic underlay the rising opposition to Federalism in the 1790's, though the opponents of the administration often lacked the leadership and the numbers for effective political action. Nor could they, from a position of opposition, always formulate alternative policies to deal with the defense of the nation. The magnitude of the crisis of the Quasi-War, however, required the Republicans to consider the matter of national defense as a whole rather than piecemeal, and in shaping their response the appearance of Albert Gallatin in Congress was as significant as the earlier contributions of Jefferson and Madison had been. Gallatin's main interest lay in finance, but his ideas carried profound implications for matters of defense and

[19] Kohn, *Eagle and Sword*, 175.
[20] See the discussions in Lance Banning, *The Jeffersonian Persuasion: Evolution of a Party Ideology* (Ithaca, 1978), 92-270; and Richard Buel, Jr., *Securing the Revolution: Ideology in American Politics, 1789-1815* (Ithaca, 1972), 1-261.

foreign policy which became generally accepted by most Republicans. By providing in debate and in two major pamphlets, *Sketch of the Finances of the United States* (1796) and *Views of the Public Debt* (1800), a straightforward description of the revenues and expenditures of the federal government as well as the way in which they were administered by the Treasury, Gallatin furnished Republicans with information that enabled them not only to attack Federalist financial management but also to comprehend more vividly the prominent role of military spending in the political economy of Federalism.[21] Personally, Gallatin did not have any fear that the armed forces were a threat to liberty; rather, he detested the waste of human resources involved in the careless administration of large sums of money, especially in war, and he demonstrated in detail that Hamilton had padded the funded debt, that the debt was rising to finance the expenditures of the Quasi-War, and that the Treasury and War Departments were somewhat cavalier in their spending of congressional appropriations.[22] Military spending was thus excessively high, and Gallatin, moreover, believed it was basically unnecessary, since he argued that the state of Franco-American relations, no matter how bad, did not require the United States to maintain armed forces for offensive operations. Even in the unlikely event of an invasion, Gallatin believed that the extent of the American population was sufficient guarantee against conquest, and thus the problem of defense became the efficient administration of existing resources rather than the costly creation of new ones.[23] Since there could, however, be no repudiation of Hamilton's settlement of the debt and since there were limits to economies in the civil list, the clear implication of Gallatin's analysis was to isolate military expenditures as the proper item for reduction if the nation was to avoid the undesirable political and economic consequences of long-term indebtedness.[24]

These arguments received their fullest expression in the opposition to the military preparations for the Quasi-War, and they suggest that Republicanism was too complex a body of thought to be described as merely the negative image of Federalism, least of all in matters of

[21] The best discussion of Gallatin's career in the 1790's is Edwin G. Burrows, "Albert Gallatin and the Political Economy of Republicanism" (Ph.D. diss., Columbia University, 1974), 274-506.

[22] AC, 4th Cong., 1st sess., 883, 909, 1475, 1499; 4th Cong., 2d sess., 2321; and 5th Cong., 2d sess., 835, 1263, 1540.

[23] AC, 4th Cong., 2d sess., 2128-2130, 2138-2148; 5th Cong., 1st sess., 244, 278-380; and 6th Cong., 1st sess., 350-360.

[24] AC, 4th Cong., 2d sess., 1979, 2067; 5th Cong., 2d sess., 1129-1142; and 5th Cong., 3d sess., 2860-2870.

military policy. Throughout the crisis of the late 1790's the leading Republicans in Congress, notably Gallatin and Henry Dearborn, argued that they were *not* opposed in principle to the exercise of federal powers nor to the existence of national establishments such as the army and the navy.[25] Indeed, Gallatin explicitly stated in 1797 in the debates on the army that "had it not been for the depressed state of our revenues, he should have been for increasing rather than diminishing the present establishment."[26] In opposition to the Federalist program, the Republican leaders offered to support coastal fortifications and a small peacetime regular army, to be expanded for an efficient war effort in the event of hostilities being declared against France. In the place of the volunteer forces, they offered to give the President authority to call out 80,000 militiamen for national service.[27] These proposals were basically in harmony with most of the suggestions for military reform that had been made since 1783, and were not incompatible with Madison's revised conceptions of how the 1787 Constitution might provide a framework for administering effective national policies. If these policies had a uniquely Republican element, it was not so much an ideological hostility toward military establishments but the degree to which they were influenced by broader financial considerations.

Consequently, the military policies of the Republican administrations after 1801 did not represent a new departure so much as they did an attempt to administer a synthesis of the policies that had already been practiced and debated in the 1780's and the 1790's. The attitudes of those Republican leaders who held executive power after 1801 had, in most cases, never been predicated on the extreme anti-army prejudices of the Anti-Federalists, though those prejudices, especially as they were articulated by the "Old Republican" faction, remained an influential part of the Republican movement and were employed, especially after 1805, somewhat unjustly to reproach administration members for abandoning principles that they had never held.[28] This division of opinion within the party was apparent before the Jefferson administration took office, although it was largely concealed by the united front that the Republicans presented in opposing the policies

[25] AC, 4th Cong., 2d sess., 1957, 1962; and 5th Cong., 2d sess., 1592, 1633, 1659. For Dearborn's belief that in the event of war with France the United States should raise a regular army of 64,000 men and that its command should be given Alexander Hamilton see Richard A. Erney, "The Life of Henry Dearborn" (Ph.D. diss., Columbia University, 1957), 36.

[26] AC, 4th Cong., 2d sess., 1957.

[27] AC, 5th Cong., 2d sess., 1385, 1631, 1725-1752.

[28] Banning, *Jeffersonian Persuasion*, 283-284. See also Norman K. Risjord, *The Old Republicans: Southern Conservatism in the Age of Jefferson* (New York, 1965).

of the Adams administration. As Gallatin remarked in January 1800, he assumed that his recommendations on military policy would "have no weight with gentlemen who supposed the liberty and independence of the country were concerned in the reduction of a Military Establishment," since to him "it was only a question of economy."[29] The reorganization of the Peace Establishment, the basic standing army deemed sufficient for peacetime duty, was thus quite in keeping with the support that most leading Republicans could give to the national institutions created by their predecessors. The workings of the law of March 1802 which created the Peace Establishment, in fact, had little effect on the real strength of the army, and it could be fairly regarded as an effort to organize a military system comparable to that attained and supported by most Congressmen of both parties prior to the Quasi-War.[30] The bitter quarrels over foreign policy in the 1790's, inflamed as they were by a number of specific disagreements over a wide range of issues, tended to obscure the fact that there was still a fair degree of consensus over how the military forces of the Republic should be organized, if not over the uses that might be made of them.

★

IN THE YEARS between Jefferson's inauguration and the outbreak of the War of 1812, Gallatin's financial program continued to be the most important factor shaping Republican military policy. Although his goals were in harmony with the overall aim of successive Republican administrations to retire the Federalist debt of $82 million within sixteen years, Gallatin throughout these years had to operate under greater constraints than he anticipated or wished, with the result that the management of neither the finances nor the armed forces was as successful as he had hoped. After Jefferson had decided, against Gallatin's better judgment, to repeal the taxes that had sustained the military programs of the Federalists, and later the salt tax in 1807, the Treasury had to plan on receiving an estimated annual revenue, drawn mainly from customs receipts, of about $10 million, nearly three-quarters of which was to be committed to debt repayment. This left little more than $2.7 million annually for all other items in a budget in which the navy alone by 1801 had required over $2 million, and the army more than $1.75 million. The Louisiana Purchase of 1803 added a further $11 million to the debt, and, in turn, required an additional

[29] AC, 6th Cong., 1st sess., 360.
[30] Kohn, *Eagle and Sword*, 300-303; and Erney, "Dearborn," 66-68. The size of the regular army during the Quasi-War was well under its authorized strength, amounting in 1801 to only 4,410 men. To accomplish the figure of 3,350 set by the law of March 1802, Dearborn had to discharge only about 1,000 men.

annual allocation of $700,000 for its repayment. Since the civil list together with miscellaneous and diplomatic expenses could not be reduced much below $1 million, Gallatin was required to set all military spending as far below $2 million per year as possible.[31] Despite his conviction of the wastefulness of such expenditure, Gallatin did not relish his task, knowing well that his margin for flexibility was slight and that the United States lived in an imperfect world where circumstances might require it to increase defense spending at almost any time. Nor would the Republicans, their desire for peace notwithstanding, avoid war at all costs; they simply wished to be spared the consequences of anticipating its occurrence. War would, therefore, be part of Republican policy, but preferably, as Jefferson remarked in 1805, as "a suspension of useful works" only.[32]

In this respect the army caused few problems in Jefferson's early years in office. Secretary of War Henry Dearborn, although a veteran of the Revolution, had served in Congress with Madison and Gallatin in the 1790's, and he accepted the Treasury Secretary's assumption that the United States required only a small regular force which could be expanded in times of hostilities. For the most part, Dearborn was content to preside over the routine administration of the Peace Establishment of 1802 while also supervising the construction of coastal fortifications and the conduct of Indian affairs. These took up much of his time, since he received little assistance from the senior army officer, Brigadier General James Wilkinson, whose various careers as governor of Louisiana Territory, Indian negotiator, and conspirator, to say nothing of frequent illnesses, left him no freedom for any professional duties. Occasionally, Dearborn attempted to make changes, such as the standardization of arms manufacture, improvements in the quality and supply of rifles, gunpowder, cannons, and gun carriages, the study of recent European developments in strategy and tactics, and the abolition of corporal punishment, all of which, if pursued to a successful conclusion, might have significantly improved the army. Almost invariably, though, the Secretary lacked both the will and the ability to effect change, and he would have been happy to have left the army as he found it. Encouraged by the return of peace in Europe after 1801, he even allowed the army to drop below its authorized strength; by 1803 its numbers included only 2,579 officers and men,

[31] Alexander Balinky, *Albert Gallatin: Fiscal Theories and Policies* (New Brunswick, 1958), 90, 103, 118, 123.

[32] James D. Richardson, comp., *A Compilation of the Messages and Papers of the Presidents* (New York, 1897-1914), I, 367.

thus enabling Gallatin for some years to bring army costs to under $1 million annually.[33]

Nonetheless, Dearborn realized that the organization of the Peace Establishment made the implementation of militia reform all the more urgent. His experience during the Revolution left him with no desire ever to meet an invading force of regulars with mere militiamen, and Jefferson, in all his annual messages save that of 1803, likewise pointed out to Congress the necessity for changing "the laws regulating the militia until they [were] sufficiently perfect" for effective defense.[34] Republican Congresses after 1801, however, proved to be little different from their Federalist predecessors, and they rejected the assumption that any administration could reorganize the state militias for national purposes. Early in 1803, a committee of the House of Representatives reported that the unworkable militia law of 1792 had made the only possible provision for a militia system that was within the powers of Congress, adding that the law allowed for "a complete national defence, if carried into effect by the state governments."[35] The House therefore would go no further than passing a supplementary law requiring state governments to make annual returns of their militias and approving a resolution urging the President to write to the state governors to request them to put the 1792 law into effect. The administration did not take these proposals seriously, submitting to Congress in March 1804 a report on the condition of the militia which showed that the law of 1792 had failed to produce uniform militia systems. The report revealed wide variations in brigade structures, ratios of officers to men, size of regiments, and distribution of arms; indeed, there were few points at which any two militias were similar, thus making impossible the interchangeability of units which was regarded as the essence of any national reserve force.[36]

The next year, 1805, the administration, concerned about deteriorating relations with Spain and England, made a determined effort to obtain militia reform. Gallatin and Dearborn drew up detailed plans for a naval militia for coastal defense and the reorganization of the state militias into four classes, the main purpose being to create a junior class of about 190,000 men between twenty-one and twenty-five years of age to be specially trained for action anywhere within and beyond the United States for a period of one year. The men in this class were to be listed numerically in battalions and, in the event of war, called

[33] Erney, "Dearborn," 61, 62, 64, 68, 78-84.
[34] Richardson, *Messages and Papers*, I, 311, 317, 333, 360, 373, 398, 416, 443.
[35] AC, 7th Cong., 2d sess., 521.
[36] *ASP: Military Affairs* I, 168-172.

out for service by number; the remaining minor, middle, and senior classes were to be employed solely in defense, either of their own states or, in the case of the middle class, the defense of an adjoining state as well. Before submitting the schemes to Congress, Jefferson deleted the provisions for training the junior class under federal supervision, preferring to persuade the legislature to accept first the principle of classification, after which greater changes could be achieved.[37] A bill framed along these lines was defeated in the Senate and failed to reach the floor of the House, where some of the President's most prominent supporters, notably Barnabas Bidwell and Joseph Varnum of Massachusetts, led the opposition. Their objections involved matters of principle as well as detail; Bidwell argued that the discrimination by age involved in the classification was inherently unjust, while other Congressmen pointed out that the establishment of the junior class would deprive the states of a sufficient number of officers to meet their own organizational needs.[38] While the President was disappointed with the decision, Congress eventually passed in February 1807 a substitute measure permitting him to accept for service up to 30,000 state-organized volunteer troops. This bill at least opened to the administration the potential to tap the increasing number of elite volunteer companies which were splitting off from the state militias, a development inspired by the desire to attain better military discipline and a more exclusive sense of social solidarity than was possible under the traditional communal muster.[39]

The future of the navy also caused the Republicans more problems than they anticipated. Gallatin had long regarded the navy as the largest single source of financial savings, and only once, in 1806, did he concede the need for naval expansion; yet it proved impossible to reduce expenditure here very significantly. Eight of the thirteen frigates authorized during the Quasi-War had already been canceled when the Republicans took office, but both Jefferson and Madison, much to Gallatin's distress, insisted on retaining the rest as a modest force to bring the pirates of Tripoli to terms rather than paying the ransoms they demanded. Although this decision for a limited war created a short-term conflict with the need to reduce expenditure, it was not inconsistent with the administration's larger aim of freeing American

[37] Jefferson to Gallatin (November 1805), Henry Adams, ed., *The Writings of Albert Gallatin* (Philadelphia, 1879), I, 267-275.

[38] AC, 9th Cong., 1st sess., 69, 110, 141, 1069. See also Dumas Malone, *Jefferson the President: Second Term, 1805-1809* (Boston, 1974), 513.

[39] For the development of elite volunteer corps in the states see John K. Mahon, *The American Militia: Decade of Decision, 1789-1800* (Gainesville, 1960), 56-61.

commerce from foreign restrictions.[40] The Tripolitanian War required Gallatin to levy additional duties—the Mediterranean Fund—to cover its costs, but he tried, nonetheless, to make cuts in naval expenditures, convincing himself that the apparent inability of the Secretary of the Navy, Robert Smith of Maryland, to control his budget was evidence of incompetence.

While the subject of naval administration needs more detailed research than it has received, it is likely that here Gallatin was being less than fair to his colleague, since it would seem that the organization of the Navy Department, particularly in the procurement of supplies for vessels and naval yards, did not allow the Secretary or the chief clerk to control costs effectively; instead they had to pay accounts as they fell due, and their total frequently exceeded the sum Gallatin believed he could afford.[41] Neither Gallatin nor Smith appear to have perceived this aspect of the problem, and the Treasury Secretary only complicated matters by wrongly assuming that naval and army business could be managed in comparable ways. The subject of naval appropriations thus became an annual contest between Gallatin and Smith with Jefferson acting as mediator. Smith felt that the Treasury was using the power of the purse to regulate naval affairs, an intention which Gallatin denied, but he did insist that on the subject of costs alone he was right.[42] Ultimately, the President was responsible for much of the tension that developed, since he desired both cost-cutting and the maintenance of a naval force, while at the same time he tried to introduce new schemes involving gunboats. The Republicans, in truth, did not have a naval policy; they had several policies which so tempered their avowed disapproval of navies that it became impossible for the administration to follow a wholly consistent course of action.

It is not altogether clear when Jefferson conceived the idea of building a navy of gunboats and smaller vessels rather than oceangoing frigates, but his enthusiasm for the former type of force certainly increased as a result of the Mediterranean war. During its course gunboats had proved to be an effective defense force in shallow coastal waters, and Jefferson noted that they had been equally successful in a

---

[40] Alexander Balinky, "Albert Gallatin, Naval Foe," *Pennsylvania Magazine of History and Biography* 82 (1958), 303; and Julia H. MacLeod, "Jefferson and the Navy: A Defense," *Huntington Library Quarterly* 8 (1945), 153-184.

[41] See Gallatin's memorandum on naval administration, dated July 21 1802, Madison Papers, LC. That navy captains and agents had a great deal of freedom from departmental control in the early nineteenth century is strongly suggested by Edward Eckert, *The Navy Department in the War of 1812* (Gainesville, 1973), 42, 52, 53, 74.

[42] Balinky, "Albert Gallatin, Naval Foe," 293-304.

number of previous wars defending Gibraltar and on the Black Sea. Moreover, their low cost—which Jefferson estimated at about $10,000 as opposed to $250,000 for a frigate—provided a seemingly irresistible argument against Federalist claims that fleets of frigates were the best form of coastal security, while they also reflected a concept of local defense that complemented the administration's plans for militia reform and coastal fortifications. Basically, Jefferson, as with the army, was seeking ways to involve the navy more with coastal defense at skeleton levels of organization which could be expanded in time of war. As a step toward this goal he recommended to Congress in 1802 the construction of dry docks and extensive storage facilities for naval property. With a temporary cessation in the Mediterranean war in 1806, he finally felt able to call for the construction of large numbers of gunboats as well. Congress readily accepted gunboats as a cheaper alternative to frigates but generally refused to follow the President's suggestions for dry docks and storage areas.[43]

As a result of these various elements in the Republican naval program little money was saved, while there were few long-term benefits from the money that was spent. The victories won in the Mediterranean were not sufficient to bring a permanent halt to the piracy, and of the 176 gunboats eventually built by the Republicans too few were ever adequately maintained for active service. In only one year of Jefferson's administrations—1802—did naval expenditures fall below $1 million, and by the end of his second term they had again risen to nearly $2 million per year. And in the long run, the problems arising from the contradictory elements of Republican naval policy were not merely self-defeating but often unnecessary and harmful. Until 1807 the annual revenues from customs receipts exceeded by $3 million to $6 million the sum allowed by the administration in 1801, but the surplus was invariably applied to debt retirement instead of financing some of the military expenditures that administration members felt were necessary.[44] In time, the conflict between the Navy and Treasury Secretaries became so bitter that it was instrumental in driving Jefferson's successor to a decision for war, which economy was supposed to help avoid.

By the middle of Jefferson's second term, therefore, the Republicans had met with only limited success in realizing their military goals, when the attack on the *Chesapeake* in 1807, followed by the embargo

---

[43] Harold and Margaret Sprout, *The Rise of American Naval Power, 1776-1918* (2d ed., Princeton, 1967), 53-62; and Craig L. Symonds, *Navalists and Antinavalists: The Naval Policy Debate in the United States, 1785-1827* (Newark, 1980) 105-133.

[44] Balinky, "Albert Gallatin, Naval Foe," 304.

provided something of a test of the policies that had been established. While there were some differences of opinion among administration members over the degree to which the embargo was a coercive or merely defensive measure, all were aware that Jefferson's diplomacy after the summer of 1807 might have to be reinforced by military operations. In dealing with this possibility, Gallatin took the lead. Assuming that the attack on the *Chesapeake* indicated that Great Britain might soon invade the United States, he drew up in July 1807 a series of proposals for improving the existing coastal defenses and for taking the offensive against Upper and Lower Canada. His plans required the raising of 30,000 troops, 12,000 of which were to be stationed on the coasts and the frontiers while the remainder were to attack Canada at selected points between Detroit and Nova Scotia. The purpose of these offensive operations, however, was clearly to assist the defensive preparations, and Gallatin believed that the American war effort would be "in a great degree passive." By preparing to take positions in Canada, he hoped to be able to draw away from the United States the Royal Navy and landing forces he anticipated arriving in American waters by the end of 1807. Here the British naval base at Halifax was of the first importance; its seizure, Gallatin suggested, would save the principal seaports, particularly New York, Philadelphia, and Charleston, from blockade, as well as enable the United States "to draw some advantage from our small navy on our own coast."

Given the failure to accomplish militia reform, however, the mobilization of such a large number of men posed problems. In accordance with the outlines laid down in Jefferson's first inaugural address, Gallatin was willing to expand the regular forces to the strength required for offensive operations while employing both regulars and militiamen in garrison duty. If, on the other hand, the War Department could not recruit large numbers of men at short notice, he preferred to use the volunteer law of February 1807 to embody militiamen for twelve months of special service rather than rely on the state governments to organize militia detachments for national service under the law of 1792. In this respect, volunteering would accomplish some of the benefits of militia classification without the federal intervention that Congress had always found so objectionable. Much of the initial organization would necessarily occur on the local level, though Gallatin wished to introduce a degree of federal control into the process by changing the volunteer law to allow the President to commission the officers, and he advised Jefferson to consult in advance with the state governors to ensure that state and federal efforts were in harmony. Gallatin believed that Jefferson should have the details of these plans worked out before any meeting of Congress in order to avoid criticism that the administration had neglected to follow the laws for calling out the militias. The cost of the plans the Treasury Secretary estimated at $18 million, over half of which, because of an inevitable decline in customs receipts in war, would have to come from loans, additional duties, and taxes. These last measures were "evils" indeed in Gallatin's eyes, but they could not as such be "put in competition with the independence and honor of the nation."[45]

Shortly after, Dearborn also presented plans for military preparations to the President. The details of his scheme differed from Gallatin's, but its underlying assumptions were very similar. Like Gallatin, Dearborn appears to have doubted the ability of the War Department to raise large forces quickly; finding officers who were suitably qualified and willing to serve had always been a problem for the army, and the pay for enlisted men had remained unaltered since 1798 at the unattractive rate of $5.00 per month. Accordingly, the Secretary of War suggested a force containing fewer regulars—only 15,000—with a larger number of 32,000 volunteers, who would be called into special training camps for three months of the year under federal inspectors. Dearborn claimed that his plan would give the United States up to 47,000 troops to call on at a cost which he believed to be less than Gallatin's estimate for 30,000 men.[46] Jefferson accepted Dearborn's plan, possibly because of its provision for special training, and submitted it for congressional consideration in October 1807, along with greatly increased appropriations for coastal defense.[47] But Congress became preoccupied with enacting the embargo in December in response to the crisis over maritime rights in Europe, and the scheme languished in committee. In February 1808, after the failure of negotiations with George Rose to produce a solution to the *Chesapeake* affair, Jefferson again raised the subject of increasing the army. He recommended a revised plan by Dearborn for 6,000 regulars and 24,000 volunteers, the reduction of the August 1807 plans being more in line with the Treasury's resources and the War Department's organizational abilities.[48] After much debate, Congress consented to the 6,000 regulars as an Additional Military Force but ignored the call for volunteers, no doubt regarding the law of February 1807 as meeting this need.

---

[45] Gallatin to Jefferson, July 25, 1807, Thomas Jefferson Papers, LC.

[46] Dearborn to Jefferson, August 7, 1807, ibid.

[47] Jefferson to Madison, August 9, 1807, Madison Papers, LC; and Malone, *Jefferson the President: Second Term*, 463, 501.

[48] See the memorandum dated February 18, 1808, Jefferson Papers, LC. See also Jefferson's message of February 25, 1808, Richardson, *Messages and Papers*, I, 429.

Alternatively, Congress authorized the President to call out 100,000 militia for national service and passed a law to improve the militias by allowing the War Department to distribute arms among them. This last piece of legislation satisfied a longstanding congressional complaint that the supply of arms was insufficient for the states' needs, particularly in the southern and western regions.

The legislation of 1808 increased the regular army to 10,000 men, while the provision for volunteers and militia, on paper, furnished the nation with formidable manpower reserves. This expansion, however, exposed serious weaknesses in the Republican military organization. Dearborn concentrated on trying to fill the ranks of the regular army but became distracted by the problems of selecting officers, with the result that little effective recruiting was done. By August 1808 only an additional 869 men had been enlisted, and at the time of Jefferson's retirement neither the Peace Establishment nor the Additional Military Force was at full strength; the former had just under 3,000 officers and men and the latter numbered only about 3,700. Thereafter the overall effective strength of the regular army fluctuated between 5,500 and 7,000, while its staff and support arrangements remained fairly rudimentary, consisting of little more than a handful of adjutants, in-spectors, paymasters, and surgeons. The most important needs of the army, most notably supply, had to be supervised by the Secretary of War and his clerks, and here Dearborn found the burdens of his office to be too great. He complained that departmental business was beyond the capacity of a single Secretary, and his task was undeniably made more difficult by the separation of army administration and supply that had arisen from the shift of the War Department to Washington while the supply officers remained in Philadelphia. Under such circum-stances, even the making and distribution of uniforms to new recruits became an extremely difficult task.[49]

The experiment with volunteering as a method of mobilization, as had been the case in 1798, remained largely untested. Jefferson re-ceived many enthusiastic offers of volunteer forces immediately after the *Chesapeake* affair and in some cases these did furnish local defense patrols, but Congress declined to make them as efficient a force as the administration would have liked. This result reflected the continuing failure of the federal and state governments to find mutually satisfactory ways of organizing the militias for national service, and the dimensions of the problem became fully apparent during Jefferson's final year in

[49] Erney, "Dearborn," 230. For the details on the strength of the regular army see William Eustis to Roger Nelson, June 1, 1809, RCSW.

office. To help enforce the embargo throughout 1808, the President called out quotas of militia and volunteers, first in April in New York and Vermont, then in all states in October and November. These forces were active in suppressing smuggling in New York and Vermont, but elsewhere the response was almost nonexistent: fully half the states failed to provide the War Department with inspection returns of any militia mobilized; five governors made no acknowledgment of any communication from Washington throughout the entire exercise; and only one state, New Hampshire, furnished a report and a quota according to law. Most governors sent partial reports pleading the difficulty of compliance and mentioning that they could not guarantee the condition of their troops or their arms.[50] It is hardly surprising, therefore, that Dearborn sickened of his duties in the War Department; by the middle of 1808 he longed to withdraw to the collectorship at Boston and he finally left office in January 1809.

The retirement of Jefferson in 1809, together with the end of the embargo, resulted in the lapse of most of the military preparations of 1808, with the exception of the Additional Military Force. This policy of relaxation was further encouraged by the apparent settlement of Anglo-American differences with the Erskine agreement in April 1809, and the first session of the Eleventh Congress lost no time in repealing the legislation for calling out the militia and reducing the appropriations for recruiting and fortifications. However, Madison was no less mindful of the need for an efficient defense establishment than his predecessor, and he did not neglect to pursue that goal. In fact, as Madison gradually assumed the duties of the Presidency after the election of 1808, it had been his wish to replace the embargo with stronger forms of commercial restriction while also increasing the nation's preparedness for war with Great Britain. The President revived this intention after the British repudiated the Erskine agreement in the summer of 1809, and he hoped to make the second session of the Eleventh Congress the occasion for a thorough appraisal of the nation's military policies.

In his annual message at the end of 1809, Madison made only a brief allusion to the need to give the militias an "organization . . . best adapted to eventual situations for which the United States ought to be prepared." Soon after, in January 1810, the President supported his case with a lengthy War Department report on the noncompliance with administration militia requisitions throughout 1808.[51] In similar

---

[50] A full report on the extent of state compliance with the militia quotas of 1808 was sent by the War Department to the Speaker of the House on January 17, 1810, see ibid.

[51] Richardson, *Messages and Papers*, I, 461. See also the report cited in note 50.

reports to Congress, however, the new Secretary of War, William Eustis of Massachusetts, requested more comprehensive changes. In the regular army, he attempted to improve the conditions of service by abolishing corporal punishment as well as such humiliating practices as making deserters wear dresses. As a sequel to Madison's call for militia reform, Eustis, on the basis of earlier plans by Gallatin and Dearborn, advocated the creation of a force of 50,000 volunteers, equipped and armed at public expense and trained, inspected, and commanded by officers appointed by the President. Noting the preponderance of infantry units in the state militias and the relative shortage of artillery and riflemen, Eustis required 6,000 troops of these latter descriptions in the new force, and all were to be organized in regiments and companies in the manner prescibed for the regular army. Finally, the Secretary pointed to the need for change in the War Department itself, including the construction of better office facilities and the establishment of a Superintendent of Ordnance and a Quartermaster General's Department, and he argued that the existing system of attaching agents and brigade quartermasters to the regiments made coordination and accountability impossible, while they also compelled the Secretary to perform the "laborious" duties of a Quartermaster himself. He concluded with the claim that the Quartermaster's Department was "the right hand of an army" and that for the United States to fight a war without one "would expose to hazard and defeat every military operation."[52]

The new Secretary of the Navy also had some recommendations for Congress. Although Paul Hamilton of South Carolina had no knowledge of naval affairs and may have owed his appointment to Madison's expectation that he would be unable to continue the feuding between the Navy and the Treasury Departments, he was for those very reasons quite dependent on the advice of his professional officers. For their part, the navy officers were concerned about the expansion of gunboat-building at the expense of maintaining frigates during the embargo, and they accordingly pointed out the high costs of letting the five ships of the line fall into disrepair. They even went so far as to argue that the expense of using gunboats as a method of coastal defense could be greater than keeping the frigates in service. Hamilton transmitted this information to Congress along with a recommendation that the frigates be maintained.[53] And no sooner had Congress begun to consider these

[52] Eustis to John Dawson, December 19, 1809, and to William B. Giles, January 1, 1810, both in RCSW.

[53] Thomas Tingey to John Rodgers, November 21 and December 4, 1809, Rodgers Family Papers, LC. *ASP: Naval Affairs*, I, 193-200.

matters when Madison, prompted by a crisis in relations with Spain over West Florida, called on January 3, 1810, for the renewal of the act authorizing the President to call out 100,000 militia, for filling up the regular army to its authorized strength, for the establishment of a further force of 20,000 volunteers to serve "at the shortest warning," and for funds to put "into actual service any part of the naval armament not now employed." It was, without doubt, the largest military program suggested to date by a Republican President.[54]

The effect of all these proposals was to expose some awkward contradictions in the political economy of Republicanism that had developed since 1807. Galatin's financial program, like that of Hamilton, depended on the continuation of peace, especially with Great Britain, whose trade with the United States still provided much of the customs revenue. Under the combined impact of the Orders in Council, the Berlin and Milan decrees, and the embargo, the customs receipts dropped from their record level of $16 million in 1807 to $6.5 million at the end of 1809, and Gallatin believed he could avoid future budget deficits only by holding army and navy expenditures at $3 million for 1810, then reducing them by a further $500,000 thereafter. The cost of the administration's military measures for 1810, however, totaled a record peacetime sum of $6,037,000, which could only be financed by falling back on loans, additional duties, and taxes. Gallatin was not prepared to adopt such policies; he was, moreover, weary of his duties, especially after Robert Smith had thwarted his ambitions to become Secretary of State, and he refused, as he told Jefferson, to become "a mere financier, a contriver of taxes, a dealer of loans, a seeker of resources for the purposes of supporting useless baubles, of increasing the number of idle and dissipated members of the community, of fattening contractors, pursers and agents, and of introducing in all its ramifications that system of patronage, corruption and rottenness. . . ."[55] As a concession to Madison, Gallatin was prepared to manage the debt indefinitely at its existing level of $57 million and settle for a balanced budget, although he realized that even this goal would be difficult in a period of great fluctuations in the revenues. The President, on the other hand, wanted both increased military spending and Gallatin's services as an administrator; Madison was, it would seem, less concerned about the future of the debt, and he hinted to Congress that

[54] Richardson, *Messages and Papers*, I, 463-464.
[55] Gallatin to Jefferson, November 8, 1809, Adams, ed., *Writings of Gallatin*, I, 465-466; and *ASP: Finance*, II, 373-384. See also Balinky, *Albert Gallatin: Fiscal Theories and Policies*, 137, 159.

he would tolerate loans to finance his plans.[56] Nonetheless, he could only balance the contradictory elements in his situation by agreeing to let Gallatin submit his proposals for a balanced budget to Congress.

Congressmen were not unnaturally bewildered by the incompatible policies coming from the cabinet. Led by John Randolph of Roanoke, the House considered drastic cuts in the armed forces—reducing the navy to three frigates and the army to three regiments—before eventually voting to perpetuate the situation that emerged after the repeal of the embargo. The appropriation to repair the frigates was defeated—though not before Hamilton had authorized expenditures in anticipation of its passage—as were all the other proposals for raising volunteers, filling the ranks, and reforming army discipline. A small loan of $2.75 million was authorized to help Gallatin balance the budget, and Congress further supported Treasury priorities by restoring all trade with the European belligerents in Macon's Bill Number 2.[57] The President did receive authority to call for militia quotas but was otherwise left defending the Republic in a period of international crisis with mere diplomacy, with defense arrangements that were known to be unsatisfactory in many respects, and with a budget where military spending would be predicated on levels achieved during the tranquil years of Jefferson's first term.

For the sake of preserving the appearance of unity among his supporters, Madison was willing to accept this difficult situation for the meantime. The financial situation remained precarious, though less so than Gallatin had feared. At the end of 1810, he declared that a limited borrowing of only $1 million was needed to balance the budget as well as continue the program of annual debt reduction. Congress authorized a loan of $5 million, thus giving the Treasury some reserve funds in case the customs receipts should fall in 1811. Although army and navy costs remained at over $2 million, the loan was not needed and not taken up. Accordingly, the Navy and War Secretaries made a few new recommendations to Congress for the armed forces, and for the most part requested appropriations only to maintain the status quo.[58] Eustis, however, did repeat his request for a Quartermaster General's Department, taking pains to demonstrate that reorganization here would not require an increase in salaried staff but might even effect savings

[56] Richardson, *Messages and Papers*, I, 461. See also Irving Brant, *James Madison: The President* (Indianapolis, 1956), 124-125; and Gallatin to Madison, May 18, 1809, Madison Papers, LC.

[57] Brant, *Madison: The President*, 131-136.

[58] Ibid., 225; *ASP: Finance*, II, 439-449.

amounting to $674.50.[59] Such parsimony was now *de rigueur*, but Congress denied the request and voted to continue the defense establishments at their existing levels.

The President, though, was still clearly troubled by the inadequacy of the arrangements for mobilizing the nation's reserves of manpower, and he continued to suggest changes for greater efficiency. Since extensive militia reform and the public funding of volunteer forces seemed immediately unattainable, Madison requested in his message of December 1810 that Congress consider a more limited program for training selected militia officers. In this way he foresaw a degree of uniformity in discipline being diffused throughout the state militias, thereby making the 1792 law a somewhat more workable measure than previous administrations had allowed. This emphasis on training was reinforced by a further request for the establishment of a second military academy in Washington, to be devoted, unlike the one at West Point, largely to the "scientific" study of military operations. In the President's opinion, this step would "assist the public defence . . . at little expense," and it presented no threat to public liberty.[60] One week later, Eustis expanded on this interest in training by claiming that the "Blue Book," drawn up in 1779 by Baron Steuben for military drill, should now be replaced by "the system of organization and tactics of the French Armies." While the Secretary hastened to add that he was not seeking the "entire reorganization" that this change would entail—he knew full well that few militia officers "would bestow gratuitously the time and attention necessary for their own . . . instruction in new and additional duties"—he did urge Congress to prescribe a new national system of militia instruction based on revisions of Steuben and including "some more modern tactics."[61] The Senate tabled the report and, as was the case with previous suggestions for reform, took no further action.

Yet even if these proposals had become law, it seems unlikely that they would have contributed significantly toward solving the administration's dilemma of balancing the need for increased military strength against the limitations on its freedom to spend money. By the beginning of 1811 the difficulties inherent in such a situation were felt by almost all Republicans to be intolerable, and Madison was increasingly pressed to overcome them. He did so by deciding by the end of July 1811 to prepare for war against Great Britain in order to settle permanently

[59] Eustis to Michael Leib, January 2 and 15, 1811, and to John Wayles Eppes, January 15 and 17, 1811, both in RCSW.

[60] Richardson, *Messages and Papers*, II, 471-472.

[61] Eustis to President of the Senate, December 13, 1810, RCSW.

143

the disputes over maritime rights.[62] Once this decison was taken, though, there was little sign of increased activity on the part of the administration. Both the Navy and the War Secretaries took the rather unusual step of remaining in Washington over the summer of 1811, with Eustis examining the productivity of the national armories on the assumption that the next year would require a large increase in output, while Hamilton concentrated on completing coastal fortifications and commissioning gunboats.[63] Their presence in Washington, however, reflected less an interest in long-term planning than it did a more immediate concern with the problems arising out of the court-martial of James Wilkinson and the possibility that the vessels of the Royal Navy off the American coast might be tempted to make a retaliatory gesture after the *Little Belt* episode, which had occurred earlier in the year. Extensive military preparations could not be made before the meeting of Congress in November, and the *National Intelligencer* provided no clues as to the future direction of policy beyond pointing out that the coming session would require hard decisions about the size and the role of the armed forces.[64]

★

IN MAKING recommendations to the Twelfth Congress for the conquest of Canada, the administration was guided largely by policies that had been attempted or contemplated in the past. There was, in fact, little that was unusual or original about the preparations for war in 1812, except possibly the uses for which the mobilization was intended and the hope that it would be more successful than previous experience suggested. Madison's third annual message sketched the outlines of his thinking on preparedness by calling for the filling up of the ranks, the creation of an auxiliary regular force, provision for the navy, volunteers and detachments of militia, and an increase in the production of arms and other war matériel.[65] The contents of the message were then amplified through letters and informal discussions between cabinet members and select congressional committees until, on November 29, 1811, the House committee on foreign relations produced its report. Specifically, the committee asked the House, sitting as a committee of the whole, to approve legislation to bring the existing army up to full strength, establish a second regular army of 10,000 men to

[62] See above, Chapter II.

[63] Eustis to Madison, August 13 and September 2, 1811; Paul Hamilton to Madison, August 27 and September 17, 1811, all in Madison Papers, LC. See also Eustis to Captain Swett, September 5, 1811, LSMA.

[64] *Natl Intelligencer*, October 17, 1811.

[65] Richardson, *Messages and Papers*, II, 479.

be enlisted for three years, enable the President to organize 50,000 volunteers for immediate service, repair and commission the naval forces, provide for the detachment of militia units for national service, and allow American merchantmen to arm for self-defense on the high seas. The proposals differed slightly from previous defense schemes only insofar as they did not clearly call upon Congress to reform the militia. Madison had hinted that he would welcome "such a preparation of the great body (of militia) as will proportion its usefulness to its intrinsic capacities," but he may have considered it impolitic to press the issue when he was also hoping to draw from that source the select volunteer units whose "patriotic ardor may court a participation in urgent services."[66]

The shaping of these proposals owed much to Gallatin's continuing influence. Indeed, the claim made by the chairman of the House foreign relations committee, Peter B. Porter, that they provided for a "public war on land and a war by individual enterprise at sea" described Gallatin's thinking almost exactly.[67] Although personally opposed to war, the Treasury Secretary accepted the decision to prepare for it, while never ceasing to stress the organizational difficulties it would involve. "The resources of the country," he told Madison, "both in men and money can be drawn but with great difficulty and will be found much less than a view of its population and wealth would lead us [at] first to believe." The 10,000 additional regulars intended for offensive operations was a far smaller number than Gallatin had advocated in 1807, but in early November he thought it necessary to supplement them by only 30,000 volunteers. For the militia Gallatin suggested no more than the renewal of the 1808 law authorizing the President to call up to 100,000 militiamen into national service. More importantly, he claimed that these army forces could not be adequately organized if the administration also wished to use the navy in the war. Referring to the navy as a "substantial evil," he argued against any war effort on the seas other than privateering, on the grounds that the United States Navy could not match the Royal Navy and that it was necessary to free as much money as possible for financing the invasion of Canada.[68] Although Gallatin had not yet begun to work out the details of financing Madison's increased military spending, his annual report to Congress, submitted at the end of November, glanced at the difficulties by revealing that it would be impossible both to continue the defense

[66] Ibid. For the report see *ASP: Foreign Relations*, III, 537-538.
[67] AC, 12th Cong., 1st sess., 414.
[68] See Gallatin's "Notes—suggested as to 'war message' to Congress," November 1811, Madison Papers, LC.

establishments at even their peacetime levels and to maintain the program of debt repayment without increasing duties and resorting to further borrowing.[69] The financial outlook for 1812 was poor, and it was hardly surprising that Gallatin felt that any sort of war effort, regardless of its nature, would lead to further debt, thereby retarding the nation's progress.

The Secretary of the Navy was caught unawares by this attack on his department. Hamilton had suggested no new policies for the President to include in his message to Congress, and it took him some time to consult with his officers to find a way of involving the navy more actively in the war.[70] Prompted by a congressional request of November 19 for a statement on the condition and future of the navy, Hamilton seized the opportunity to call for a very sizable increase, with the building of twelve ships of the line carrying seventy-four guns and twenty frigates of thirty-eight guns. He justified his position with the argument that the existing naval forces were inadequate to protect either harbors or the coastal trade against Royal Navy vessels that were likely to appear in American waters, while the proposed vessels would be ample to accomplish these goals as well as annoy enemy commerce. This ambitious policy, costing at least $4.5 million, was submitted to Congress on December 3, and it conflicted not only with Treasury priorities but also those of the War Department.[71] Eustis, reporting to congressional committees at the same time on the subject of coastal defense, claimed that an appropriation of $1 million would be adequate to complete the programs already commenced and that it was not necessary to provide forces "fully efficient to man all fortifications on the coast." Local defense, the War Department believed, required preparations to meet "probable emergencies" only at "important and exposed points" such as New York City and Newport, Rhode Island.[72] Clearly, the administration was still divided over defense policy, though less bitterly than had been the case before Robert Smith's dismissal. But, as in the past, Madison preserved harmony within his administration by allowing his colleagues to submit their own reports, and he left Congress to make the final decision.

The adequacy of the administration's plans for a war against Canada

[69] See Gallatin's report of November 22, 1811, *ASP: Finance*, II, 495-497.

[70] Hamilton to Gallatin, October 28, 1811, Carl Prince and Helen Fineman, eds., *The Papers of Albert Gallatin* (microfilm ed.); see also Symonds, *Navalists and Antinavalists*, 150.

[71] *ASP: Naval Affairs*, I, 247-252.

[72] Eustis to Langdon Cheves, December 3, 1811; to David R. Williams, December 5, 1811, both in RCSW.

were no less controversial. Most Republicans in the House were not convinced by the view of Congressman Porter and his fellow committeeman, John Smilie of Pennsylvania, that the combination of regulars and volunteers proposed in the foreign relations committee report would be sufficient for offensive purposes while still furnishing enough regulars to assist the militias in their defensive role. In this connection, Speaker Henry Clay later briefly entered the debate to observe that the War Department had estimated that it would require over 12,000 troops to garrison fully all the posts on the coasts and the frontier, and that if such a disposition of forces should be necessary, it would scarcely leave enough regulars for operations in Canada, especially if these included an attempt to besiege Quebec.[73] This concern, it would seem, contributed to the decisions of the House in December 1811 to support the regular forces suggested in the report of November 29, and then in January 1812 to accept the very different Senate bill to raise 25,000 additional regulars for five years. The motives of the Senators for more than doubling the size of the proposed auxiliary force were mixed, but the author of the bill, William B. Giles, spoke at length on the need for a regular force to provide for *all* offensive and defensive needs, despite the fact that this stand violated his previous position on the "republican" way to organize the armed forces.[74] The administration supporters in the Senate, led by Anderson and Campbell of Tennessee, declared that a total of some 17,000 regulars, aided by volunteers, represented the only troops that could be raised for action by the spring of 1812, and that such forces were all that the occasion demanded. Their concluding argument that the Canadian war did not "require the utmost exertions of the nation," however, did not carry much conviction.[75] Republicans in both houses of Congress, having ignored repeated administration requests for a more flexible organization of the military forces, thus voted by mid-January 1812 to raise a regular army of 35,000 men.

The bill to raise 50,000 volunteers—who would have been subject to the allowances, bounties, and discipline prescribed for regular troops—was reported to the House by Porter on January 10, 1812. According to Monroe, it was intended by the administration not as a "revival of Mr. Adams's measure, but [as] a regular body under a popular name for short enlistment," and it was a critically important force for the

---

[73] AC, 12th Cong., 1st sess., 597.

[74] Ibid., 38-50. See also (Philadelphia) *Democratic Press*, January 20, 1812; and Chapter II above.

[75] AC, 12th Cong., 1st sess. 55-66, 76, 84. See also Samuel Mitchill to Daniel D. Tompkins, December 19, 1811 Daniel D. Tompkins Papers, NYSL.

invasion of Canada. Although the evidence is scanty, it would seem that the administration intended to raise the force by selecting as officers "prominent men" who, by their "virtuous conduct," had acquired "the confidence of their fellow citizens." These men "would go to their homes, look around the country where they [were] known," and seek volunteers who would step forward in response to the pressures of patriotism and social conformity. The several corps, as Monroe put it, would thus "consist of neighbours, friends and brothers. . . . Generous motives would be excited, patriotism aroused, and the ties of kindred would unite with love of country, and of free government, to call [our] young men to the field."[76] However, since most of the volunteers would have to be drawn out of the state militias, Porter felt compelled to introduce the bill with some remarks on the constitutional question of whether militia in any form could be used beyond the United States.[77] The ensuing debate, centering on the issue of whether the President should commission volunteer officers, was long and confused. Most Congressmen did not want to deny the administration's request for volunteers—which they had already approved in principle in the form of a resolution—yet many Republicans clearly disapproved of the bill. To some it seemed doubtful whether volunteers were necessary after the passage of the 25,000-man army bill, especially as the President stood to gain enormous patronage and influence from his control over 85,000 regular or near-regular troops, and all feared that the bill would give the administration the potential power to subvert the fundamentally defensive purposes of the militias and their organization.[78]

Rather reluctantly, the House voted on January 17 to let the President commission volunteer officers, while also trying to protect the militias by stipulating that volunteers were not to be exempt from militia duty until actually called into service by the President.[79] At the end of January, though, the Senate, following the pattern of previous volunteer bills, voted with almost no debate to confer the power to commission volunteer officers on the state governments.[80] This version of the bill, as Giles pointed out in his argument for its rejection, was almost totally unworkable, since several states either made no provision for or actually prohibited the commissioning of volunteer officers by

[76] Monroe made these remarks, specifically addressing the problem of volunteering in 1812, to George Washington Campbell and David R. Williams on December 23, 1812. See RCSW.

[77] AC, 12th Cong., 1st sess., 728-730.

[78] Ibid., 733-793.

[79] Ibid., 800-801.

[80] Ibid., 112.

state authorities.[81] The House accepted the Senate amendment with relatively little opposition and refused to consider a plea by Porter on February 18 to accept a compromise which would instead authorize the President to raise a "provisional military force" of 20,000 men.[82] This provisional army bill, Porter claimed, was absolutely essential for the administration to realize its plan of having an invasion force ready by June of 1812, and its failure, he declared, was an extremely serious setback for the President.[83] The foreign relations committee chairman then spoke at length on the defects of all the military legislation passed to date and criticized his fellow legislators' indifference to the practical problems of mobilization by remarking that "we have made a parade in passing laws . . . but, in truth, and in fact we have not given [the President] a single man. . . ."[84]

The remaining resolutions of the report of November 29, with the exception of the arming of merchantmen, eventually became law, though their passage was far from straightforward. The way in which the federal government might employ the militias in the war, in particular, caused some difficulty. At the end of January, the chairman of the House committee on the armed services, David R. Williams of South Carolina, reported two bills to classify the militia and to allow the federal government to present each militiaman with a stand of arms on his eighteenth birthday. The changes were not to take effect until April 1813—thus the reform would not necessarily disrupt the war preparations for the coming year—but it was not wholly clear whether Williams was acting in accordance with administration wishes; the report of November 29 had not called for classification, and no correspondence appears to have passed between the committee and the War Department on the subject. At some point too, by February 1, the two bills seem to have been combined into one, which led to the House rejecting it three days later because of its classification clauses.[85] Williams responded to this defeat by reintroducing on February 13 as a separate bill the plan to arm militiamen on their eighteenth birthday, a practice which might have given the federal government, by virtue of its ownership of the arms, some degree of control over the militiamen. The House passed this bill on February 21, but the Senate failed to

[81] Ibid., 107-110, 1694-1705. Giles pointed out that neither Massachusetts nor Vermont allowed for the commissioning of volunteer officers by state authority.

[82] Ibid., 1058.

[83] Ibid., 1060-1068.

[84] Ibid., 1069. Madison agreed with Porter. See Madison to Jefferson, February 7, 1812, Madison Papers, LC.

[85] AC, 12th Cong., 1st sess., 1010-1014, 1014-1018, 1021-1022.

report it from committee.[86] The immediate consequence, therefore, was to leave the administration without provision of any sort for mobilizing the militias for the coming war, and the matter was not taken up again until April 1812.[87]

The debate on naval policy, however, was far less complex and settled far more quickly. Initially, Secretary Hamilton's report of December 3 on expanding the navy horrified most Republicans, but at the same time its arguments about a naval role in coastal defense were not wholly unattractive to them. The chairman of the House committee on naval affairs, Langdon Cheves of South Carolina, stressed on December 17 the desirability of the United States having undisputed control of its territorial waters, while also pointing out that the Republicans so far had failed to adopt a naval policy which met the needs of "the just economy of our republican institutions" and was yet calculated "to enlarge itself gradually with the progress of the nation's growth . . . or expand with an energy proportioned to a crisis of particular danger." Considerations of cost made the immediate adoption of Hamilton's report unrealistic, but Cheves urged Congress to support a policy of gradual naval expansion by reporting a bill to stockpile timber, build a dry dock, and construct ten new frigates with an average firepower of thirty-eight guns.[88] In the debate on this report in January 1812, Cheves went further by justifying frigates as a cheaper and more effective form of coastal defense than fortifications and gunboats, which he dismissed as virtually useless for this purpose. Gunboats, he added, had no proper connection with the navy, and his bill proposed their separation from that department with no further appropriation for their construction. These remarks provoked many Republicans into denouncing Cheves's report as an insult to the principles of Jefferson's administrations, and, after repeating time-honored remarks about the costs and dangers of naval establishments, they voted for repairing the existing naval forces and for stockpiling timber, but against the ten extra frigates and the dry dock.[89]

In these ways Congress, by mid-February 1812, had disposed of the war preparations recommended by the administration and the House foreign relations committee in November 1811. The legislature was next required to consider the problem of war finance. The House Ways and Means Committee had requested Gallatin's views on the matter

[86] Ibid., 1084-1085.
[87] Eventually, Congress approved on April 10, 1812, a bill authorizing the President to call out detachments from the state militias totaling 100,000 men.
[88] AC, 12th Cong., 1st sess., 553-554.
[89] Ibid., 803-843, 859-869, 875-896, 901-1061.

on December 9, 1811, and the Treasury Secretary sent them his reply one month later. Gallatin had already reflected on this subject in the past, and it was his belief that the United States should meet the costs of military operations through loans, provided that government revenues during wartime remained equal to its ordinary, nonwar expenditures plus the cost of servicing the total debt. Had war occurred during the embargo crisis, Gallatin believed that the revenue surpluses of earlier years, together with the lending facilities provided by the Bank of the United States, would have enabled him to finance military operations without having to impose taxes, but the same conditions no longer existed in 1812. By that date government revenues were barely sufficient to meet ordinary expenses, while the schedule of debt repayments was already requiring additional small loans. To continue such a system of finance even in peacetime would require, as Gallatin noted in November 1811, an increase in duties as well as "a proper selection of moderate internal taxes," and these measures would become even more necessary if further loans had to be raised for waging a war.

Moreover, with the closing of the Bank of the United States in March 1811, the Treasury would have to borrow in a competitive market, thus making it imperative in Gallatin's mind for him to be able to service the interest charges on all the new loans in order to maintain public confidence in the government's credit. These considerations led Gallatin to request Congress to double all duties, reimpose the old duty on imported salt, levy direct and indirect taxes to the amount of $5 million, and authorize a loan of $10 million, giving the Treasury the discretion to set the interest rate. In making these recommendations, Gallatin was uncertain what the total size of the budget in 1812 would be.[90]

The House Ways and Means Committee reported on February 17 ten resolutions in line with Gallatin's thinking, varying from it only in their decision to fix the loan at $11 million with an interest rate set by law at 6 percent. Between February 27 and March 4, the House, in a committee of the whole, readily adopted resolutions for the loan and the double duties, but initially rejected that for the salt duty and balked at the prospect of taxes.[91] To make taxation both politically acceptable and easy to administer, Gallatin had suggested that the taxes be imposed on a selection of items already taxed by the state governments, and he hoped that a Republican majority would vote for all the taxes rather than allow a series of legislative coalitions to defeat

[90] Ezekiel Bacon to Gallatin, December 9, 1811, and Gallatin to Bacon, January 10, 1812, both in *Gallatin Papers*.
[91] AC, 12th Cong., 1st sess., 1092-1105, 1108-1111, 1114-1126.

specific levies in a piecemeal fashion. With some difficulty, the administration persuaded the committee of the whole to reverse its decision on the salt duty, and then obtained resolutions approving taxes on a variety of items ranging from stills to bank notes and carriages.[92] In the long run, though, the administration suffered a defeat when the committee also voted for resolutions authorizing a deduction of 15 percent if the state governments assumed the direct taxes and, finally, postponing all taxes and duties until after war had been declared.[93] The result of this decision was to leave the administration to raise a loan at interest rates which Gallatin suspected would not be attractive to money-lenders, who had no guarantee that Congress would vote the funds to provide them with their return. Nevertheless, Gallatin had no choice but to go ahead and organize the loan, seeking funds mainly from state and local banks where the Treasury had placed public money after the Bank of the United States had ceased its operations.[94] The loan was opened to the public in the first week of April 1812, with the *National Intelligencer* predicting that it would be oversubscribed by local "monied men" who would want to invest in local defense.[95] In fact, just over $6 million was subscribed, mostly by banks already holding government funds, and very little by local "monied men," of whom so much had been expected. Gallatin philosophically accepted this as the best that could be achieved under the circumstances and waited for a more favorable moment to press Congress for the balance of the funds required.[96]

With this decision to postpone taxation until after the war had commenced, many Congressmen felt that the preparations for war were complete and that they should now settle the question of war or peace, then adjourn. The administration did not share this view, believing that the financial and military measures passed so far by Congress were either inadequate or unworkable. The President was, in fact, greatly upset by the treatment of his legislative program, and he observed angrily to his administration colleagues in March 1812 that if Congress "will continue to procrastinate the means of military equipment, it

[92] *Natl Intelligencer*, February 29 and March 3, 1812.

[93] AC, 12th Cong., 1st sess., 1128-1155.

[94] See Gallatin to Alexander J. Dallas, March 19, 1812; Thomas Francis to Dallas, March 22, 1812; and Thomas Law to Gallatin, March 24, 1812, all in *Gallatin Papers*.

[95] See the bank circulars of March 31, April 7, and May 11, 1812, ibid. See also *Natl Intelligencer*, April 12, 1812.

[96] Gallatin to Cheves, May 14, 1812, *Gallatin Papers*; and Richard Rush to Benjamin Rush, May 18, 1812, Benjamin Rush Papers, Library Company of Philadelphia Papers in HSP.

[will] be in vain to expect or hope for any good" in the war.[97] This complaint tacitly conceded that much of the time needed to realize the administration's goals had already been lost, but Madison was still unwilling to attempt to wage war in any other way. His problem was, therefore, to persuade Congress to grant him the substance of his original proposals in the time remaining before a declaration of war. Here Monroe took the first step by informing the House foreign relations committee at the end of March that the executive "was not prepared to take upon itself the responsibility of stating that we are prepared for war," while Eustis suggested that the President try to obtain significant modifications to the army bill of January 1812.[98] Specifically, he recommended that the size of the regiments, set by the law at 2,000, be cut to 1,200 and that the enlistment period be reduced from five years to nine months, with special allowances for a bounty and three months pay upon discharge. The Secretary also felt that the state militias should be called into service at once and that the President should be enabled to appoint two additional major generals and three brigadier generals for the regular army. These measures had the appearance of an attempt to dramatize the urgency of the situation and thus to attract into a hastily reorganized regular army some of the men who, the administration hoped, might have served as volunteers.[99]

Monroe's warning to the foreign relations committee had some effect, and its members offered a compromise by reporting a bill to authorize the President to enlist up to 15,000 men for eighteen months service. The House passed this amendment on April 2, and the Senate accepted it without question five days later.[100] Equally promptly both houses of Congress reported and passed a bill to detach quotas of state militiamen totaling 100,000, but the bill for additional army generals failed by one vote in the House at the end of April.[101] Still, the administration regarded these concessions as inadequate for its purposes and continued to press for a bill for additional generals and for changes to the volunteer law of February 1812. Congress resisted this pressure until the end of the session, the House even rejecting the bill for additional generals on July 3 before grudgingly agreeing the next day to create two more

[97] Richard Rush to Charles Jared Ingersoll, March 21, 1812, Charles Jared Ingersoll Papers, HSP.

[98] For Monroe's remarks see "Notes," March 31, 1812, Samuel Smith Papers, LC.

[99] See the undated notes from Eustis to Madison, filed at the end of 1812, Madison Papers, LC. Their contents suggest that they were written early in April 1812. See also Eustis to Felix Grundy, April 9, 1812, LRUS.

[100] AC, 12th Cong., 1st sess., 193, 1598-1599.

[101] Ibid., 1334.

brigadier generals.[102] On June 10, Congress agreed to reduce the size of the regiments in the 25,000-man army to 1,000 men, and in the last days of the session, between July 3 and 6, it also agreed to amend the volunteer law by allowing the President to commission volunteer officers.[103] According to the *National Intelligencer*, this change made volunteers an "efficient" body instead of merely a "nominal" one, and provided "a force more congenial to the nature of our government and [to] the patriotic war in which we are engaged" than did the regular army.[104] The administration victory, though, was a pyrrhic one, and the War Department made no attempt to raise a separate force of volunteers at this late stage. The Secretary of War instead suggested that army officers and state governors should encourage those disposed to volunteer to enter the army as eighteen-month enlistments.[105]

The Secretary of the Treasury had rather less success in persuading Congress to reconsider the matter of war finance before its adjournment. Within a week of the declaration of war on June 18, Gallatin sent the House Ways and Means Committee a financial statement which showed that only some $16.6 million of the total expenditure for 1812—which he now estimated at $26 million—had been obtained. Since he was not sure whether the military establishments would actually spend the amounts allocated to them, he left it to the committee's discretion to decide "whether any additional provision ought to be made during this session."[106] The committee responded by reporting a bill to levy double import duties and thirteen separate tax bills. Both House and Senate passed the double duties bill by June 30, but the House, taking Gallatin at his word that the war might not cost as much as he had estimated and by now desperate to adjourn, postponed consideration of the taxes until the next session.[107] The only concession made to the Treasury's difficulties was the passage of a bill to allow the anticipation of revenue through the issue of Treasury notes, a fiscal device which Gallatin in principle deplored. The problems of preparing for war had indeed stretched many of the contradictory elements in the political economy of Republicanism beyond breaking point, but for Gallatin perhaps the most ironic twist of fate was reserved for the end. The declaration of war on June 18, 1812, preceded as it was by

---

[102] Ibid., 1581-1582.

[103] Ibid., 318, 1584-1586.

[104] *Natl Intelligencer*, July 4, 1812.

[105] Monroe to the President of the Senate, January 26, 1813, Sen 12B-D2, Legislative Records of the Senate (RG 46), NA.

[106] Gallatin to Bacon, June 24, 1812, *Gallatin Papers*.

[107] AC, 12th Cong., 1st sess., 311, 1531, 1555-1558.

a precautionary embargo of two months duration, promised the Treasury some windfall revenues from customs duties as American merchants in Europe returned home with fresh imports. To protect this commerce and to ease the financing of the war against Canada, Gallatin at last acquiesced in sending American frigates to sea to attack the Royal Navy.[108]

★

THE DIFFICULTY in obtaining suitable war legislation was only one aspect of the problems of preparation. Equally as important was the task of implementing these laws through the creation of appropriate administrative structures for organizing the war effort. All the executive departments were subjected to an increasing workload with the coming of war and most of them seemed capable of adapting, but the Department of War, as the agency of government most responsible for preparing for hostilities, undeniably had special problems. Here Eustis was the first to admit his inadequacies as an administrator, and most of his contemporaries had little hesitation in condemning him as a military tinker, a man who, in the words of Senator William Crawford, spent all his time "reading the advertizements of petty retailing merchants to find where he [might] purchase one hundred shoes or two hundred hats."[109] This verdict was perhaps less than just, especially when Eustis himself had previously pointed out to Congress that the very organization of his office forced such time-consuming and trivial duties on the Secretary. The need to operate in such a manner had always created problems, which now, as the war approached, became completely unmanageable. It was Eustis's misfortune to try to prepare for war under a system which he knew did not function adequately, while also trying to introduce a better one. This goal, given the behavior of Congress alone, was difficult, but in some respects Eustis made the situation worse than it might have been. The organization of the war preparations consequently bordered on the chaotic, yet Eustis stuck grimly to his duties, supported only by Madison, who realized that few men in the Republican party were willing to accept such an intolerable burden.

The most essential features of war administration involved the purchase and distribution of supplies. Here the least difficult function was the provision of subsistence for the army. This had long been performed by contractors at the direction of the Secretary of War, and no significant changes to this system were considered in 1812. Contractors

[108] Gallatin to Madison, June 20, 1812, Madison Papers, LC.
[109] William H. Crawford to Monroe, September 9, 1812, James Monroe Papers, LC.

made competitive bids to the War Department to provide the army on an annual basis with a specified number of rations, consisting basically of bread, which could be either wheat or corn, meat in the form of beef or pork, and liquor, usually whiskey and rum. The mixture of the ingredients and the price of each ration were laid down in the contract, though the contents of the rations often varied according to region; cornbread and pork tended to be most common in the southern states, while beef and wheat were preferred in the northern. Any other items of food, such as vegetables, chocolate, or coffee, had to be obtained by the soldiers themselves from sutlers, who were normally controlled by the army officers.[110] For the invasion of Lower Canada, Eustis in January 1812 called to Washington two of the army's established contractors, Elbert Anderson of New York and James Byers of Massachusetts, and asked them if they could meet the country's needs.[111] Both claimed they could, and spent the next three months organizing the purchase and deposit of rations at army posts as well as along the routes to Lower Canada running through New England and New York.[112] Byers had difficulty in purchasing food, especially beef, in the Connecticut Valley and in Vermont, finding that the farmers in both areas had already sold their supplies either to towns in New York or to Montreal.[113] He fulfilled his contract by substituting pork for beef, and purchased supplies for the Lake Champlain region in the Middle Atlantic states; these he concentrated at Troy, New York, to await further shipment.[114] By May the business was complete, and the contractors provided the War Department with the names and location of their numerous agents and subcontractors upon whom troops on the march could call for provisions.[115] Thereafter, the efficiency of the system depended not on the War Department but on the integrity of the contractors and their employees.

More complex than the feeding of the army was its equipment, especially clothing. In a series of letters beginning in October 1811, Eustis instructed the Purveyor of Public Supplies in Philadelphia, Tench Coxe, to find out how far the needs of the army could be supplied

[110] Erna Risch, *Quartermaster Support of the Army: A History of the Corps, 1775-1939* (Washington, D.C., 1962), 119; Marguerite M. McKee, "Service of Supply in the War of 1812," *The Quartermaster Review* 6 (1927), 45-49.

[111] Eustis to Messrs Byers and Anderson, January 8, 1812; to Byers, February 22, 1812; to Anderson, February 25 and March 18, 1812, all in LSMA.

[112] Byers to Eustis, February 29, 1812; Anderson to Eustis, February 25, March 4, 12, 14, and 20, 1812, all in LRRS.

[113] Byers to Eustis, March 12, 30, 1812, LRRS.

[114] Byers to Eustis, April 9, 15, 1812, LRRS.

[115] Anderson to Eustis, May 22, 1812, LRRS.

by domestic manufacturing and, where there were likely to be deficiencies, to buy as discreetly as possible large quantities of vital items such as clothing, camp equipage, and saltpeter.[116] The emphasis on discretion probably reflected a concern not to drive up prices rather than a desire to preserve secrecy about the administration's intentions, and Eustis appears to have assumed that the Purveyor could readily provide the necessary information, since Coxe had long advocated that the United States should be better prepared for war. Coxe also believed, wrongly as it proved, that the nation could be self-sufficient in matters of supply, but he had no idea how to deal with Eustis's request beyond distributing, on December 5, 200 copies of a handbill to members of Congress calling upon "all public-spirited men" to forward him information about the state of local manufacturing, which he would then compile in a report for the War Department.[117] This procedure was too slow and unreliable for the Secretary's needs, and the Purveyor also showed an irrelevant interest in such projects as arming the people for self-defense with pikes, claiming that the weapon would affect the British "as does the Irish axe."[118] Unimpressed, Eustis summoned Coxe to Washington for a discussion of the clothing problem, but the meeting seems to have had little effect.[119] The War Department wanted Coxe to purchase cloth for 20,000 men regardless of its color and texture, and suggested he establish Purveyor's agents throughout the northern states to obtain and deliver clothing to the troops.[120] Coxe's knowledge, however, did not extend much beyond Philadelphia, and he relied instead on manufacturers to send him supplies in response to handbills and newspaper advertisements, realizing that most of the material purchased would have to come to Philadelphia for processing and distribution anyway.[121]

After such experiences, Eustis came to appreciate even more the need to streamline most aspects of army administration by establishing an entire staff of general officers, the most important of them being a Quartermaster General. The Senate in late December 1811 had already reported and passed a bill for a Quartermaster's Department which, with some minor modifications, Eustis strongly recommended to the

[116] Eustis to Coxe, October 16 and November 23, 1811, LSMA.
[117] Coxe to Eustis, December 11, 1811, LRRS.
[118] Coxe to Eustis, November 21, 1811, LRRS.
[119] Eustis to Coxe, December 10, 1811, LSMA.
[120] Eustis to Coxe, January 15, 18, and 23, and February 19, 1812, LSMA.
[121] Eustis to Coxe, March 12, 1812, LSMA. Coxe to Eustis, February 21 and March 8, 1812, LRRS. For an example of Coxe's advertisements see *Democratic Press*, April 18, 1812. See also Jacob Cooke, *Tench Coxe and the Early Republic* (Chapel Hill, 1978), 423.

House committee on the armed services.[122] The establishment of this new department need not have necessarily encroached on the functions of existing agencies, since the Quartermaster at this time was more concerned with the army on the march than with the whole business of supply. But Coxe had enemies in the Senate who tried to centralize the supply system by giving the Quartermaster additional powers to obtain and issue supplies for the entire army and by replacing the Purveyor with a new official, the Commissary General of Purchases, who would be responsible to the Secretary of War. Eustis did not strenuously oppose these changes, which were embodied in a new bill which was reported to the House in mid-March.[123] Congressmen generally conceded the case for a Quartermaster but delayed the bill by debating the relative merits of the Purveyor as opposed to the Commissary General. In particular, some of the Pennsylvania members, resenting the loss of the Purveyor's office in Philadelphia, tried to strike out the clause establishing the Commissary General; failing that, they reduced the salary of the new office by $500 and imposed what the War Department thought were excessively stringent conditions of financial accountability on the incumbent.[124]

The Senate version of the bill, and Coxe's enemies, finally prevailed. Immediately the bill became law on March 28, Eustis offered the Commissary General's office to William Jones of Philadelphia. He accepted, then hastily declined after reading the conditions of his appointment. The duties were, Jones claimed, underpaid and revolting "to an honest man."[125] Jones predicted that no one would take office, and Eustis did indeed have to establish it with temporary appointees until Samuel Carswell of Philadelphia accepted on July 31, only to resign within the week because of ill-health. The Superintendent of Military Stores, Callender Irvine, finally accepted the position provided that he could remain in Philadelphia.[126] The net administrative change in the purchase of supply after all these transactions was little more than one of name, and throughout the entire preparations for war Eustis was left to work with the redundant Purveyor, who bitterly resented the loss of his office.[127] Irvine later described the supply system as it

[122] John Fenwick to Eustis, January 6, 1812, LRRS; Eustis to Williams, January 9, 1812, RCSW.

[123] Cooke, *Tench Coxe*, 478.

[124] AC, 12th Cong., 1st sess., 1210-1214.

[125] Jones to Eustis, April 11, 1812, LRRS; same to same, April 20, 1812, Uselma Clarke Smith Collection of William Jones Papers, HSP.

[126] Risch, *Quartermaster Support*, 140-142.

[127] Coxe to Eustis, April 1812, LRUS; same to same, May 29, 1812, LRRS.

operated in 1812 as "totally inefficient and so rotten in all its parts as not to admit of being patched."[128]

Under such circumstances, it was perhaps surprising that the supply system functioned at all. With only three clerks for assistance and one cart for transport, Coxe claimed by April 1812 to have 5,000 tailors and seamstresses at work making summer uniforms for the army; these he delivered for distribution to the Superintendent of Military Stores at the Philadelphia Arsenal.[129] The Superintendent was then supposed to dispatch these uniforms to the army at its various recruiting posts throughout the country, but the War Department failed to provide him with the names and locations of the relevant officers before the third week in May.[130] Inevitably, Irvine was swamped with letters from angry recruiting officers demanding the clothing, and he was further alienated when Eustis suggested in early June that he be replaced by a new officer responsible to the Quartermaster General.[131] Eustis did not pursue the idea, but Irvine felt compelled to defend himself. He claimed that by the first week in July he had sent off 9,447 suits of summer clothing and doubted that the army had raised by then an equivalent number of men, thus challenging the Secretary of War to demonstrate whether any of the deficiencies had been his fault.[132] Irvine did admit, however, that many of the uniforms were incomplete, there being a shortage of coats in particular, and that he gave priority to equipping the troops in South Carolina and Georgia, which, for reasons best known to himself, he felt were about to be cut off from seaborne communication with Philadelphia.[133] The result, as he well knew, was that the supply of uniforms to the army in New York was "very inadequate," and he further admitted that there would not be enough summer coats for the army in the northern states before the middle of October.[134]

Comparable delays attended the establishment of the Quartermaster's Department and a new Ordnance Department, the Superintendent of the latter office, Colonel Decius Wadsworth, not commencing his duties until July 15. For Quartermaster General, Madison selected, from among eleven names submitted to him by Eustis, Morgan Lewis, formerly governor of New York and Deputy Quartermaster General

[128] Irvine to AG, December 4, 1812, LRAG.
[129] Coxe to Eustis, April 14, 1812, LRRS.
[130] Irvine to Inspector General, May 15, 1812, LRAG.
[131] Risch, *Quartermaster Support*, 140.
[132] Irvine to AG, July 6, 1812, LRAG.
[133] Ibid., May 28 and July 6, 1812.
[134] Ibid., October 16, 1812.

in the Northern Army during the Revolution.[135] Despite this previous experience Lewis had little enthusiasm for his new job, partly because it gave him no patronage; at the end of May he was still waiting for the nomination of his deputies so he could begin organizing his department.[136] Eustis eventually reappointed most of the military agents of the Peace Establishment as deputy and assistant quartermasters, while Lewis suggested that the country be divided into six districts for the purposes of administration. His division, however, was anything but rational; it required the grouping of Pennsylvania and Ohio as one district and the isolation of New Jersey as another, enabling Lewis to procure gun carriages there and to avoid having to work with his assistant in Philadelphia, William Linnard, whom he disliked.[137] Eustis convinced him to accept a more logical division of the country into eight districts, each with one Deputy Quartermaster General, and even suggested that Lewis work in the first four northern districts while he dealt with the southern and western states.[138] Lewis agreed, basing himself in Albany, New York, to be near the main army, but, after he had provided for its immediate needs, the War Department wanted him back in Washington to organize the Quartermaster's Department on a permanent basis. Lewis had no desire to be in Washington, and at the end of July he requested a command in the army instead.[139] The War Department agreed, relieving him of strict accountability for his finances while requiring his deputies and assistants to post a bond for their good conduct. Unfortunately, the funds appropriated for the Quartermaster's Department were exhausted by October 1812, with the result that the supply of gun carriages and camp equipage was never adequate for the army's needs. Eustis kept the Quartermaster in business by financing him from the army pay funds, and by the time Lewis eventually resigned his position, at the beginning of 1813, the affairs of his department were in hopeless confusion.[140]

The United States at the oubreak of war thus presented, in Eustis's words, the "rare phenonemon" of trying to put an army in the field without a staff department.[141] The Secretary regarded the difficulties of his position as a reasonable explanation, but, in truth, the nature of

[135] Eustis to Madison, April 1, 1812, Madison Papers, LC.

[136] See Augustus Foster, Journal entry April 27, 1812, Augustus Foster Papers, LC.

[137] Lewis to Eustis, May 29, 1812, LRRS.

[138] Risch, *Quartermaster Support*, 140.

[139] Lewis to Eustis, July 29, 1812, LRRS.

[140] Eustis to Madison, October 13, 1812, Madison Papers, LC; and John Armstrong to Robert Swartwout, April 25, 1813, Robert Swartwout Papers, NYPL.

[141] Eustis to Jones, May 3, 1812, Jones Papers, HSP.

the new offices he created did not allow for efficient administration. The broad definition of the powers of the Quartermaster General led to an overlap of functions between that department and all other agencies involved in army administration, and there was a similar overlap between the Ordnance Department and the Superintendent of Military Stores. To prevent duplication of work here would require even greater effort by the Secretary of War than before, and failing that, the Quartermaster's Department was at risk of being dangerously overextended by becoming involved in all aspects of army supply.[142] Consequently, Eustis, who never had more than a dozen clerical assistants throughout 1812, became suddenly overworked by the confusion he had created.[143] In early April he asked the President to relieve the War Department of its traditional responsibility for Indian affairs and military land warrants, then two weeks later requested two assistant secretaries for the War Department and another Adjutant General for the army.[144]

Madison agreed to call on Congress for the assistant secretaries, but the legislature regarded the request as an admission of incompetence on the part of Eustis, and the Senate, prompted by Duane and Leib, voted on May 6 to postpone consideration of the matter indefinitely.[145] Gallatin, fearing a repetition of the chaos of the War for Independence, finally decided to step into the breach. He instructed the Comptroller of the Treasury, Richard Rush, to obtain from the War Department copies of accounts of all its purchases in order to check for duplication. The Treasury Secretary admitted he had no real authority for such action and based his decision on the need for someone to supervise the rapid growth of spending in the military departments; if a basis for his action was needed, he added, it could be found in a section of an old 1792 law which gave the Treasury a vague authority to audit all public accounts.[146] The President, though, did not approve of this move, thus leaving Eustis in his impossible situation. The Secretary's first response appears to have been to offer his resignation of the grounds that he could no longer cope with the burdens of office, but Madison, perhaps unwisely, refused to consider this either. Eustis struggled on as best he could, and, as he complained later to Henry Clay, "when you are told that the movement of the cannon with every other article and

[142] Risch, *Quartermaster Support*, 142; McKee, "Service of Supply," 49-55.
[143] Eustis to Colonel Tallmadge, May 13, 1812, William Eustis Papers, LC.
[144] Eustis to Madison, April 9, 1812, Madison Papers, LC.
[145] AC, 12th Cong., 1st sess., 228, 1354-1376; *Natl Intelligencer*, May 2, 1812. See also George M. Bibb to John Crittenden, April 16, 1812, John J. Crittenden Papers, LC.
[146] Gallatin to Rush, May 21, 1812; Rush to Gallatin, June 6, 1812, *Gallatin Papers*.

implement [of war] is made on [my] table, notwithstanding the provision made by law, you may have some idea of the labour."[147]

Serious as all these deficiencies were, they did not really constitute the principle difficulty in preparing for war—which was the organization of the army itself. Central to the thinking of the Republicans since the late 1790's was the assumption, most clearly expressed in Jefferson's first inaugural address, that the United States could best raise the troops required for war at the time of the crisis itself. But the critical factor in the early months of the war, and throughout its duration as well, was a shortage of effective manpower. Although it is difficult to determine accurately the total number of men who served in the War of 1812, an estimate, made by the Adjutant General in 1836, of the number of enlistments under the various categories of regulars, militia, volunteers, and rangers placed the figure at more than 528,000. This represented a seemingly impressive 47 percent of the white male population of the United States between sixteen and forty-five years of age for the period of the war, yet some 86 percent of those enlistments were in militia and volunteer forces that were not directly under the control of the federal government.[148] The number of men whom the War Department could mobilize for the invasion of Canada, either as regulars or as volunteers, was always small, a situation which deprived the administration of much of its freedom of action and compelled it to rely on forces not of its own creation nor properly under its direction. By November 1812 the War Department believed that only 9,823 men had been enlisted into the additional army of 25,000 authorized by the law of January 1812.[149] These figures suggest that despite a rapidly growing population, greater social stratification, and perhaps increasing hardship for many young adult males, American society in the early nineteenth century still lacked, or was unable to mobilize, the large numbers of impoverished men traditionally regarded as the basis for a regular army.[150] In this sense, the preparations for war seemed to reveal a serious disparity between many of the notions accepted by Americans about the organization of regular forces and the realities of their society.

[147] For Eustis's offering to resign at about this time see Monroe to William Duane, September 4, 1812, Monroe Papers, LC. See also Eustis to Henry Clay, September 29, 1812, Lyman C. Draper Manuscript Collection: Frontier Wars: 9U, SHSW.

[148] See "Troops during the War of 1812," *Tyler's Quarterly Historical and Genealogical Magazine* 12 (1931) 282.

[149] AG to Eustis, November 13, 1812, LSAG.

[150] For a fuller discussion of this problem see Murray A. McLauchlan, "The Army, Society, and the War of 1812," (M.A. research essay, University of Auckland, 1980), 102-105.

The administration was not unaware of this problem, and this aware-ness had contributed to its longstanding preoccupation with militia reform and the need to organize volunteer forces. And even with the failure to obtain legislation for federally controlled volunteers in Feb-ruary 1812, the administration did not immediately give up all hope of raising such troops for service in 1812. Throughout the first session of the Twelfth Congress, the chief clerk of the War Department, Daniel Parker, kept a tally of volunteer tenders of military service made to his department. The results were, however, disappointing. By June 16, 1812, two days before the declaration of war, only twenty-three such tenders had been received, and many of them were far from the Canadian border; three were from New York and two from Ohio, while the remainder came from Pennsylvania, New Jersey, Virginia, South Carolina, and Tennessee.[151] The poor response was hardly sur-prising, since success would have required a significant number of state leaders to have perceived the administration's needs—an unlikely de-velopment—and then to have found effective ways to mobilize local troops for participation in a war whose declaration they were in no position to anticipate. As Monroe later noted, the volunteer law "con-templated a beginning at the wrong end [and] a movement in no particular quarter by no particular person. . . ."[152] Some Congressmen did send copies of the volunteer law back to their constituents, but this had little effect. Senator Thomas Worthington of Ohio was in-formed by one of his correspondents that the inducements for volunteer service—principally 160 acres of land as a bounty—were insufficient for a man to "turn out and get himself killed." His informant continued, in a rather more earthy vein, that "many wished every member of Congress had 160 acres of land stuffed up his xxxx instead of receiving $6.00 per day."[153] State governors appear to have received some offers of service under the volunteer law, but most of these were probably tendered to fill state requirements under the April law for detaching quotas of 100,000 militia.[154]

The failure of volunteering, therefore, left no alternative but to re-cruit as many regulars as possible. An act to bring the Peace Estab-

---

[151] "Memorandum of Volunteer Tenders of Military Service," June 6, 1812, Daniel Parker Papers, HSP.

[152] Monroe to Williams and Campbell, December 23, 1812, RCSW.

[153] J. H. Campbell to Thomas Worthington, June 17, 1812, Thomas Worthington Papers, OSL. See also Clay to Monroe, July 29, 1812, James F. Hopkins, ed., *The Papers of Henry Clay* (Lexington, 1959–), I, 693.

[154] See, for example, the tenders of volunteer service recorded in May and June 1812 in John B. Linn and William H. Egle, eds., *Pennsylvania Archives* (2d ser., Harrisburg, 1880), XII, 538-552. See also (Lexington) *Kentucky Gazette*, May 12, 26, 1812.

lishment and the Additional Military Force of 1808 up to their full strength of 10,000 had been passed on December 24, 1811, and immediately put into effect by the War Department. These regular forces were well under strength at the time, totaling only 5,447 men scattered about the coasts and frontiers in twenty-three posts.[155] The morale of these troops was probably varied, and their effectiveness uncertain. Their commander, Brigadier General James Wilkinson, had just survived the first of many courts-martial in his checkered career, with Madison returning his sword to him with remarks that clearly suggested a lack of confidence in his abilities.[156] The second brigadier general, Wade Hampton of South Carolina, loathed Wilkinson and sulked on his plantation after his acquittal. The younger officers were disgruntled at the apparent lack of prospects in the army, with one of their number, Lieutenant Thomas Jessup, seriously considering resignation as late as February 1812 in order to seek active service in South America.[157] Yet the War Department appears to have made no real effort to reinvigorate these regulars or use them as the nucleus for the forces to attack Canada. The troops remained scattered across the nation, the largest group of barely 1,200 of them staying, as in the past, in the South for the defense of New Orleans. Recruiting for these forces during the first six months of 1812 proceeded at a leisurely pace, averaging little more than 200 men per month, and, on the eve of war, it had increased the old regular establishments to 6,744, still only two-thirds of their authorized strength.[158]

This neglect implied a decision to use the new regular troops, the "additional army," as the core of the invading force. Yet for the first few months of 1812, the additional army had more officers than enlisted men. The administration first considered the problem of who was to command the force, and, according to John Quincy Adams, Madison and Gallatin "designed to place Henry Clay at the head of the army," possibly with the rank of lieutenant general. The other members of the cabinet opposed this idea, arguing that the Kentuckian could not be spared from his role as Speaker of the House.[159] As Monroe later recalled, there was no doubt that such a high military officer, "if he possessed talent of the first order would manage the war with greater

[155] See the return of the army, November 30, 1811, HR 12A-B1, LRHR.

[156] James R. Jacobs, *Tarnished Warrior: Major General James Wilkinson* (New York, 1938), 274.

[157] Thomas S. Jessup to E. A. Taylor, February 17, 1812, Thomas Jessup Papers, LC.

[158] *ASP: Military Affairs*, I, 320.

[159] John Quincy Adams, *The Lives of James Madison and James Monroe* (Boston, 1850), 160.

advantage than it would be managed by several [generals] of equal grade," but there was also a more serious question of the desirability of what amounted to merging the military powers of the President, Secretary of War, and commanding general in the hands of one man. The administration therefore finally decided, in Monroe's words, that it was "more safe and perhaps as eligible to confine the appointments to the grade of major general and to confer it upon several to break the force of the power," and Madison nominated Henry Dearborn on January 20, 1812, as the senior major general of the additional army.[160] Dearborn had little desire for active service, and he was, moreover, very reluctant to relinquish the collector's office at Boston. At Eustis's request he hastened to Washington, where he arranged for his son to deputize for him as collector, but he took few immediate steps to organize the army, being confined to his house for some time after a fall from a horse. Even worse, Dearborn was by now an elderly man of sixty-one years who had grown enormously fat, and he could only move very slowly with great difficulty.[161] His appointment did not impart a sense of purpose to the war effort, and Felix Grundy of Tennessee, in mid-February, voiced the suspicions of many Congressmen by inquiring: "Is there not something rotten in the state of Denmark. . . . If it takes six weeks for one man, how long for 25,000?"[162]

The other generals were not chosen any more quickly. Madison desired to appoint a Federalist as the second major general in a token effort to bridge the nation's partisan divisions in the war, and he offered commissions to both William Polk and Thomas Pinckney of North and South Carolina respectively. Polk was not unwilling to accept, provided he could establish his headquarters in Raleigh, North Carolina, which would enable him to attend to his private affairs as well as to his army duties. He conveyed these conditions to the War Department through Congressmen Nathaniel Macon and James Turner, who gained the impression that Eustis would accept them. When the Secretary of War decided that the headquarters for the Southern Department should be in Columbia, South Carolina, Polk declined the nomination, which was then offered to Pinckney.[163] Pinckney accepted, making his headquarters at Charleston, but he did not begin organizing

[160] Monroe to George Hay, October 16, 1812, James Monroe Papers, NYPL.

[161] Dolley Madison to Anna Cutts, March 20, 1812, Cutts Collection of the Papers of James and Dolley Madison, University of Chicago (microfilm in LC). The British minister in Washington described Dearborn as a "heavy unwieldy-looking man . . . with no great military reputation." Foster to Lord Castlereagh, April 21, F.O. 5, vol. 85.

[162] Grundy to Andrew Jackson, February 12, 1812, Andrew Jackson Papers, LC.

[163] Polk to Eustis, May 22, 1812; to AG, May 26, 1812, both in LRAG.

recruiting and local defense in the southern coastal states until late May 1812.[164] Similar delay was experienced in the selection of a brigadier general to command the invasion of Upper Canada from Detroit before William Hull accepted the assignment, though the remaining brigadier generals—Joseph Bloomfield, James Winchester, Thomas Flournoy, and John Chandler—all accepted readily enough. Winchester, however, did not leave Tennessee to take up his duties until July 1812, with results that were possibly fatal to the administration's strategy.[165]

The lower officers were no less of a problem for the administration than the generals. The War Department simply lacked sufficient information to compile lists of potential officers from all the states and territories, and consequently relied heavily on the advice of congressional delegations; in fact, it seems not unlikely that in most cases the delegations themselves submitted to the War Department the names of the candidates who were eventually nominated.[166] For this reason the nominations tended to reflect political cleavages within the congressional delegations themselves, and, although the administration tried to assess the personal reputation, political background, and military experience of the nominees on the basis of written and oral recommendations, it could not always be certain about some of the men who eventually received commissions. Colonel George Izard, on surveying the officers in the Philadelphia region, remarked that they were sadly lacking in "literary requirements," and "from their habits of life and mechanical pursuits" were "not such men as it is usual to choose for officers in a regular army"; one Irishman among them claimed to have been a lieutenant in the Coldstream Guards—which Izard found "more than improbable"—while another was "a convicted thief" and a surgeon was "said to be a professed swindler who had spent three years in jail in Baltimore."[167] There was, though, as Richard Rush pointed out, "a real dearth of capable military men in the country," especially in the Republican party, and for this reason, as well as the desire to unite as many political opponents as possible behind the war, Madison was willing to nominate Federalists for commissions.[168] This policy was

[164] Pinckney to Eustis, June 6, 1812, LRRS.

[165] James Campbell to AG, July 18, 1812, LRAG. See below, Chapter IV.

[166] For evidence of congressional delegations selecting army officers see William Lowndes to Elizabeth Lowndes, April 23, 1812, William Lowndes Papers, UNC; Clay to Thomas Bodley, May 12, 1812, *Clay Papers*, I, 653; and John Smith to Tompkins, March 3, 1812, Tompkins Papers, NYSL. For confirming appointments the Senate referred all nominations by state to subcommittees consisting of the two Senators of each state.

[167] Izard to AG, May 15, 1812, LRAG.

[168] Rush to Ingersoll, January 25 and February 28, 1812, Ingersoll Papers, HSP.

not universally accepted. Governor Tompkins of New York, for example, reacted strongly to the news that five of the state's most prominent Federalists, including William North, who had been Adjutant General of the army in 1798, were being considered for office, observing that the "Republicans of this state will not relish the appointment of such men. . . ."[169] Even more unpopular was the number of Federalist nominees from the New England states, which by March 1812 had become such a problem that Dearborn warned the President to be more cautious, since the Republicans in the region were feeling "badly" and likely to become "less active in the necessary preparations for war."[170] And by May, the attempt to create a bipartisan officer corps was felt to have been unsuccessful; Richard Rush remarked that the distribution of army commissions had only made "enemies of democrats without turning federalists into friends."[171]

Moreover, the appointment of officers became part of the struggle between the President and Congress over the size of the regular army. Between December 1811 and March 1812, Eustis and Madison pored over the names of hundreds of candidates for army commissions but were unwilling to go to the extent of nominating officers for a force of 25,000, as Congress had mandated. The President did submit nominations for some of the regiments in February but found that the Senate would not consider any of them until they had all been made.[172] This deadlock between the two branches of government was not broken until April 1812, after which most of the commissions were confirmed and issued. A "provisional essay" at drawing up an Army Register was not ready, though, until the end of May.[173] Again, the delay obviously retarded the preparations for war, while the number of refusals and resignations of commissions throughout 1812 was sufficiently high to create further problems. By the end of the year, the President had issued commissions to over 1,100 officers, 15 percent of whom immediately declined them, usually giving personal rather than political reasons for doing so, and a further 8 percent resigned them after only a few months experience in the service. The rate of refusals and resignations was highest in the Middle and South Atlantic

[169] Tompkins to John Smith, February 22, 1812, Hugh Hastings, ed., *The Public Papers of Daniel D. Tompkins* (Albany, 1898-1902), II, 491-492.

[170] Dearborn to Madison, March 21, 1812, Madison Papers, LC.

[171] Richard to Benjamin Rush, May 18, 1812, Rush Papers, Library Company of Philadelphia Papers, HSP.

[172] Samuel Otis to Eustis, February 26, 1812, LRRS.

[173] This was published in the *National Intelligencer*, May 28, 1812.

states, regions from which the Republican party drew its greatest and most important support.[174]

The mere business of nominating officers, though, left untouched the related question of the organization of the additional army into regiments. The army bill of January 1812 set the size of the new regiments at 2,000 officers and men, a figure more than twice as great as that required for the Peace Establishment and the Additional Military Force of 1808. The discrepancy was a serious matter, not only creating administrative problems for the War Department but also making it difficult for recruiting officers to bring regiments to full strength in a short space of time.[175] Yet so busy was Eustis with other issues that he forgot to deal with the formal organization of the army until prompted by a request from the House committee on the armed services on April 28 whether Congress needed to make any futher provision on this matter. Shortly after, Eustis convened a board of officers to report by May 23 on the organization of the army. While the composition and deliberations of this board remain unknown, there was filed in the Adjutant General's office sometime before the declaration of war a "Memorandum" written by Major John B. Walbach. This was a comprehensive fifteen-page report dealing with administration, recruiting, arms, clothing, pay, training, desertion, and discipline, and its contents constituted a critical comment on the failure of successive Republican administrations to realize their own goals for the army; Walbach all too often found that no two sections of the army performed duties or even dressed in a similar manner, thus making the transfer of officers and men a difficult business. More specifically, he recommended the appointment of additional staff and regimental officers, and a standard organization of artillery and infantry companies which would require little alteration "should a momentary increase in the army be necessary." Uniformity could be achieved by dividing the nation into military departments, each under a general officer with his own staff who was to inspect and report to Washington on the condition of his department at least twice a year.

Walbach's "Memorandum," however, was of little use either to the War Department or to Congress. It was far too ambitious to be put into practice on the eve of war, and Walbach himself appears to have assumed that it could be put into effect only in peacetime, to prepare for a future war rather than for the one the United States was about

---

[174] These percentages were calculated by Allan Henderson by tabulating the career information recorded on the folders containing army officers' correspondence preserved in the Adjutant General's office. See Allan J. Henderson, "Ideology, Politics, and the Army of 1812" (M. A. research essay, University of Auckland, 1979), 85.

[175] Eustis to ——, May 1812, LRAG.

to attempt.[176] In the end, the administration and Congress settled for a law, passed on June 10, reducing the size of the regiments of the additional army to 1,000 men. On this basis, the Adjutant General, Alexander Smyth, recommended to Eustis on June 25 a distribution of the additional army which concentrated a main force at Albany, New York, and spread the remainder at the forts and barracks in Detroit, Newport (Kentucky), Nashville, Pittsburgh, Carlisle, New York City, Winchester, Burlington, Portland, Warrenton, Columbia, and Norfolk. Many of the troops had already been ordered to these destinations, and Eustis sometimes increased Smyth's recommendations, particularly in New York, where he wanted 10,000 regulars at Albany and 5,000 in New York City. The total strength of the additional army was thus organized into some sixteen regiments of infantry, two regiments of artillery, and two battalions of cavalry. With the establishment of this organization, the officers and men could be assigned to the regiments in readiness to receive orders for active service.[177]

Unfortunately, the recruits who could give this paper organization any substantial degree of reality simply did not exist. As late as March 19 the *National Intelligencer* admitted that recruiting for the additional army had not yet begun in earnest, and not until March 28 did many of the new officers receive their recruiting instructions. Pending the organization of the army, however, the Adjutant and Inspector General's office divided the country into six recruiting departments, usually consisting of two or three states under a superintending officer; the departments were further divided into forty-eight districts, each with a central recruiting rendezvous, and as many officers as possible were ordered to report to them for duty.[178] To the superintending officers, the War Department forwarded large sums of money to meet the costs of recruiting—up to $20,000 in some cases—copies of forms on which to make out recruiting returns, a manual for drill instructions, and directions on where to obtain provisions for their troops.[179] Sometimes rough quotas for the number of recruits to be raised were also set; the Adjutant General expected Brigadier General Joseph Bloomfield, for example, to raise for the additional army twenty-nine companies in Pennsylvania, two in Delaware, and eight in New Jersey.[180]

---

[176] Walbach, "Memorandum" (1812), LRAG.

[177] AG to Eustis, June 25, 1812, LRAG.

[178] For a publication of the recruiting instructions for 1812 see *Democratic Press*, April 13, 1812.

[179] See, for example, Joseph Bloomfield to AG, April 9, 1812, LRAG.

[180] Ibid., April 4, 1812.

Thereafter, all responsibility for recruiting devolved on the officers in the districts themselves, who were supposed either to man depots in the towns or to take parties into the countryside to induce men to volunteer their services.[181] There were few restrictions on who could be enlisted beyond the broad requirements that the recruits were to be white male citizens between eighteen and forty-five years of age of suitable size and health, the last being usually defined as the absence of "ruptures," "scal'd heads," serious infectious diseases, and such obvious disqualifications for army life as bad legs.[182] For the additional army in 1812, the citizenship requirements were more or less ignored, though not to the point of recruiting blacks, but minors under twenty-one years of age and apprentices were not supposed to be enlisted without the consent of their parents or guardians.[183] Each man had to consent freely to the terms of enlistment before an officer, in return for which he received half of a bounty of $16.00—the other half to be paid when he was mustered into a company—a full set of clothes, pay of $5.00 per month, and a further three months pay and 160 acres of land upon discharge.

To provide the necessary incentive for a recruiting drive, every recruit earned for his enlisting officer a premium of $2.00, and the means of persuasion available to recruiters ranged from delivering patriotic speeches and handbills, preferably to the accompaniment of martial tunes provided by hired musicians, to the use of taverns where men could be plied with liquor.[184] The use of liquor in recruiting frequently caused much personal hardship and complaint—often to wives who found that they and their families had been abandoned—but the Adjutant General refused to ban the practice, remarking that "such an instruction would prevent half the enlistments."[185] Individual officers were supposed to keep weekly and monthly returns of their enlistments and forward them both to the superintending officer of their department and to Washington, where the Inspector General would enter them on a register.[186] The superintending officers were also responsible

[181] Peter P. Schuyler to Eustis, April 6, 1812, LRAG.

[182] Inspector General to Alexander Cummings, November 7, 1811, LSAG.

[183] AG to Messrs Whiting and Ames, June 24, 1812, LSAG.

[184] For examples of both methods of recruiting see (New York) *The Shamrock*, May 9, 16, and 23, June 2, and September 26, 1812.

[185] The Adjutant General received many petitions from women requesting discharges for husbands who had enlisted under the influence of drink. See also AG to George McFeeley, June 29, 1812, LSAG.

[186] The volumes in the National Archives entitled "Records of Men Enlisted in the U.S. Army Prior to the Peace Establishment of May 17, 1815" appear to date from the 1870's or the 1880's. They were compiled from a variety of sources, but the major one was a series

for coordinating the movement of recruits within their departments, their principle aim being to assemble them at the central rendezvous in order to organize them into regiments. The provision of barracks and other accommodations for the troops was usually the duty of the recruiting officers themselves; they had either to construct barracks or to hire an equivalent type of dwelling from the local inhabitants.[187]

The system thus had the appearance of rationality, but in practice it broke down at almost every point. The problems began with the delays in the appointment of the officers and became increasingly apparent as the administration hastened to assemble some sort of force for the opening campaigns of the war. Superintending officers were compelled to organize recruiting with officers whose names they knew, but not their locations, and in the interior regions of the larger states, particularly Pennsylvania and Virginia, it was weeks, sometimes months, before a drive to raise men could be got underway.[188] Farther west, the situation was even worse; in Tennessee, for example, recruiting did not begin until the first week in July, and its difficulties increased as the population became more dispersed.[189] At times, too, the War Department failed to provide officers with the necessary funds for recruiting, and the matter was complicated by a quarrel between the Paymaster and the Adjutant General over who exactly was responsible for sending out the funds.[190] Moreover, the later recruiting was commenced, the less likely it was to be successful. In many parts of the country, the availability of men for recruiting seems to have fluctuated with the rhythm of the agricultural year. At the beginning of spring there were normally large numbers of single, often transient, male agricultural laborers seeking work who could form a pool of potential recruits. By midsummer, though, many such men had contracted for the season, while any surplus had moved on to seek work elsewhere. Officers who sought such men after the onset of summer all too frequently had to report that recruiting was "very dull" or "at a stand,"

---

of 689 volumes kept by the Adjutant General's office covering the years between 1784 and 1821. See Maizie Johnson and Sarah Powell, comps., *Preliminary Inventory of the Records of United States Army Commands, 1784-1821* (RG 98, Washington, D.C., 1966). For a discussion and analysis of the former set of records see McLauchlan, "The Army, Society, and the War of 1812."

[187] David Brearley to Bloomfield, April 25, 1812, LRAG.

[188] Bloomfield to AG, April 3 and June 17, 1812; Eleazer Ripley to Eustis, October 8, 1812; William Winder to AG, April 2 and 16, 1812, all in LRAG.

[189] Evidence on this point is too voluminous to cite conveniently, but see the letters to the AG between June and December 1812 written by the following officers: Nathaniel Adams, David Bissell, Hugh Brady, John Miller, and George Tod, all in LRAG.

[190] Robert Brent to AG, May 29, 1812, LRAG.

and for weeks on end they failed to enlist a single man. Their returns in most cases did not pick up until after the completion of the harvest in the fall.[191]

Even where recruiting was under way by May 1812, mainly in urban areas north of Washington, the army still experienced difficulties. The detachment of state militia quotas under the act of April 1812 created a short-term competition between the regular force and the militias; potential recruits avoided the former service in order to make greater returns from being hired as militia substitutes by those seeking exemption from the latter. This was particularly so in Pennsylvania and New Jersey, where the presence of large Quaker communities put a premium on the hiring of substitutes and drove their price far beyond the level of army pay.[192] Many army officers believed, as did the War Department, that in time the mustering of the militias would provide easy opportunities for regular recruiting, but attempts to enlist militiamen were usually bitterly resented by state authorities. Militia officers frequently refused to allow recruiting officers to approach their men, and even when militiamen were enlisted, it was not difficult to invalidate the engagement through the agency of local courts, against whose decisions the army had no appeal.[193] A similar competition for men, with even more serious consequences for the army, occurred whenever local volunteer forces were organized successfully. This was especially so in the Northwest, where William Henry Harrison's use of volunteers in the late summer and throughout the fall put an almost total stop to all regular recruiting.[194] Recruiting was also hampered by a series of petty obstructions, usually arising from attempts to use writs of *habeas corpus* to get men discharged on a variety of grounds, mainly wrongful enlistment. The practice was most severely felt in the New England states, but it was a nationwide occurrence.[195] As Colonel Richard Dennis of the 16th Infantry in Philadelphia reported: "I am very much harassed by the pettyfogging lawyers and half-vamp'd judges

[191] Evidence here is too voluminous to cite conveniently, but see the letters between July and October 1812 from the following officers, in LRAG: Hugh Brady, James Campbell, Alexander Cumming, George Izard, and Samuel Legat. See also James Burn to Eustis, June 23, 1812, LRRS.

[192] Bloomfield to AG, May 18, 1812, LRAG.

[193] Saterlee Clark to AG, September 7, 1812; William Drayton to AG, July 25, 1812; Constant Freeman to AG, August 13, 1812, all in LRAG.

[194] William Anderson to Eustis, December 18, 1812; James Campbell to AG, July 30, 1812; William McMillan to AG, October 19, 1812, LRAG.

[195] Anderson to AG, October 12, 1812; John Boyd to AG, December 9, 1812; A. Darrington to AG, November 17, 1812; Richard Dennis to AG, September 30, 1812; Henry Grindage to AG, June 2, 1812; John Vail to AG, October 2, 1812, LRAG.

of this place with *habeas corpus.*" Some of his officers, he added, had been imprisoned, which led him to decide to petition the state legislature for the removal of the judge responsible on the grounds of his being a "public nuisance."[196]

More fundamental to the failure of recruiting, though, were shortages of supply. The methods of regular recruiting rested more on the assumption that certain classes of men in the community, particularly single, unattached males, would enlist to satisfy their own needs—be they money, clothes, or the prospect of land—than it did on any belief that large numbers of men would step forward for purely patriotic motives. For this reason alone, the success of recruiting depended heavily on the constant flow of money and supplies to army officers throughout the country, and, as the inadequacy of the staff departments became increasingly manifest, enlistments suffered accordingly. In no aspect was this more true than with clothing. Almost universally, recruiting officers regarded the offer of a uniform as being of the utmost importance; they may have even regarded clothing as being a greater incentive than pay, since army wages lagged well behind rates offered for laborers in all parts of the country.[197] Throughout 1812, officers constantly complained that the shortages of clothing gave the recruits a grievance which, once it became widely known, proved to be an obstacle to continuing enlistments. The spectacle of ragged, barefoot, and destitute soldiers, or soldiers with trousers but no coats, brought the army, the United States government, and ultimately the war into public disrepute.[198]

Sometimes officers would try to provide some of the recruits' basic needs by purchasing such items as shoes out of their own pockets, but

[196] Dennis to AG, November 17, 1812, LRAG. The Guardians of the Poor in Philadelphia repeatedly sought discharges for local men to prevent their families becoming charges on the public purse. See *Democratic Press*, July 10, 1812.

[197] Comprehensive data for wages throughout the nation at this time do not yet exist, but see the material compiled by Carroll D. Wright, *History of Wages and Prices in Massachusetts: 1752-1883* (Boston, 1885), 74-79; and Donald R. Adams, Jr., "Wage Rates in the Early National Period: Philadelphia, 1785-1830," *Journal of Economic History* 28 (1968), 404-426. Rural wage rates for laborers in Pennsylvania were reported as early as 1809 as ranging from $0.67 to $1.00 per day. See Joseph E. Walker, ed., *Pleasure and Business in Western Pennsylvania: The Journal of Joshua Gilpin: 1809* (Harrisburg, 1975), 84-85.

[198] The material here in the Adjutant General's office is too extensive for detailed citation, but it may be sampled in the letters written by the following officers: William Boots, September 1, 1812; Hugh Brady, October 21, 1812; Isaac Coles, June 21, 1812; Constant Freeman, September 21, 1812; Edmund Gaines, September 30, 1812; Thomas Helms, September 1, October 3, 1812; Willoughby Morgan, June 13, 1812; Thomas Pinckney, September 23, 1812; James Preston, October 18, 1812; and James Wellborn, June 5, November 13, December 15, 1812, all in LRAG.

such measures were clearly not an answer to the problem.[199] Even the officers themselves wondered how much honor and glory there was to be won in a war for which the preparations had been so obviously inadequate, and this feeling was a factor in the high resignation rate of officers in the first year of the war.[200] Furthermore, the failure to clothe the troops properly, together with the practice of concentrating them in camps or in barracks to await supplies over the summer, quickly caused health problems, leading to sicknesses which spread rapidly through whole companies of men, thus rendering them unfit for service.[201] The regiment raised in New York by Colonel Zebulon Pike was badly afflicted in this manner by August 1812; the surgeon pronounced the men "curable" but "not competent to the duties of an active campaign."[202] Yet within three days of this verdict, these men— whom Pike described as "the veriest of militia"—were marched northward into active service.

Even after the men were successfully recruited, there were continuing difficulties with their organization. The method of making the returns of the troops was administered in ways which prevented either regimental commanders or the War Department from actually knowing how many men were in the army. While the system of making multiple returns was cumbersome and probably the cause of some confusion, many of the officers suffered from a striking incapacity to fill out the return forms in the prescribed manner. The problem was not one of literacy but rather seems to have been an inability to conceive of the men as an abstract series of numbers to be organized in the most expedient fashion.[203] All too frequently recruiting officers forwarded their returns in a haphazard and incorrect way to their superior officers, who in turn sent them on to the War Department with remarks to the effect that no reliance could be placed on any of the figures in the documents.[204] The Inspector General, Alexander Macomb, tried to obtain a general return of the army in May 1812, but was unable to

[199] Benjamin Forsyth to Eustis, November 21, 1812; Edward Wadsworth to AG, September 7, 1812, LRAG.

[200] See, for example, John Smith to Eustis, April 10, May 10, 1812, LRAG.

[201] William Bailey to Eustis, September 28, 1812; Izard to AG, September 18, October 6, 1812; James Norcum to AG, August 16, 1812, LRAG.

[202] Garrett Prendergast to John Armstrong, August 7, 1812, LRAG.

[203] Anderson to Eustis, July 20, 1812; Coles to AG, May 25, 1812; Drayton to AG, September 29, 1812, LRAG.

[204] Again, the evidence is too voluminous to cite fully, but it can be sampled in the letters to the AG from the following: Thomas Aspinwall, William Beall, E. Beebe, Thomas Biddle, Joseph Bloomfield, Silas Halsey, James Preston, and Peter Schuyler, all in LRAG.

do so for a total want of reliable information.[205] When the Senate asked for the same information in June, however, the seriousness of the problem could no longer be concealed. Eustis drafted several letters to the Senate committee making the request, arguing that "the success which has attended the [recruiting] service has equalled reasonable expectations" before he gave up and sent an officer to explain the "apparent deficits in some of the figures."[206] Eventually, the War Department, apparently on the basis of the number of uniforms dispatched from Philadelphia, guessed that there might be 5,000 recruits in the additional army, a statement which prompted Senator Worthington to observe that if the recruiting service was going so well there was nothing to lose by delaying the declaration of war, since there was not yet "a single regiment on the line of Canada ready to march into it."[207]

Nor did the organization of the recruits into regiments at the end of June make the invasion of Canada any more likely. In some respects, it worsened rather than improved the situation. The army officers had recruited the troops on an individual basis, with both parties tending to regard the act of enlistment as something of a personal contract which implied that recruits would continue to serve with that officer, who in turn would guarantee them the terms of their engagement. The War Department, however, did not share this assumption, and since some officers were more successful at recruiting than others, the division of the army into regiments inevitably separated many men from the officers who had raised them.[208] This development annoyed the officers, particularly those who saw men being transferred to the command of less successful recruiters, and above all it shocked many colonels, who, while supervising recruiting departments and districts, had tended to assume that their own regiments were well on the way to completion.[209] With the assignment of men into regiments, it became apparent, with one or two exceptions, that many companies were only at one-third to two-thirds of their full strength. The reaction of most officers, after voicing their discontent, was to continue recruiting for

[205] Inspector General to Abiel Nicoll, May 4, 1812, LRUS.

[206] Eustis to Anderson, June 6, 1812 (not sent), LRAG; same to same, June 8, 1812, LSMA.

[207] "Notes on Senate Debate," Thomas Worthington Papers, RCHS. (I am grateful to Roger H. Brown for making this information available to me.)

[208] AG to Winder, June 15, 1812, LSAG. Dearborn strongly disapproved of War Department policy here; see Dearborn to Eustis, August 15, 1812, LRRS.

[209] The extensive evidence on this point may be sampled in the letters to the AG from Isaac Coles, July 9, August 7 and 15, 1812; Cornwall Pearce, August 25, 1812; James Ripley, October 19, 1812; Peter Schuyler, June 3 and 23, 1812; Richard Dennis, August 19; and Simon Larned, November 4, 1812, all in LRAG.

perhaps two or three months until the regiments were complete, but the administration's desire to commence the invasion of Canada as quickly as possible allowed for no such delay.[210] The War Department consequently spent the second half of 1812 detaching as many companies as were complete from their regiments and marching them to the northern frontiers to make up an invasion force.[211]

Events were to reveal not only that this hasty improvisation of the invading force was insufficient for victory but also, of equal importance, that it was an administrative disaster for the army. As the regiments were fragmented, their officers found it impossible to complete their organization, let alone attend to their equipment and training. Indeed, most of the recruits received no training at all before being marched into action, and since the campaigns of 1812 brought only defeat, death, sickness, or capture to the American forces, the very structure of many of the regiments was almost completely shattered. The army officers were bitterly disillusioned by this development. Colonel Jonas Simmonds of the 6th Infantry for example, complained that "the principle of reducing one regiment to strengthen another is sensibly felt by the regiment under my command." And, he added, his feelings on the subject were "by no means pleasant."[212] The continuing failure of successive administrations to achieve a workable militia reform thus led the Madison administration, like that of John Adams, to rely in time of war on a large regular army for which the financial and bureaucratic resources of the federal government were still too slender to give proper support. As the army struggled to come into existence, though, the Madison administration, in the cruelest irony of all, was driven by the pressure of events to destroy the very basis of its organization. At the end of 1812 there was no army to speak of, only the remnants of one; and the efforts that had been made in the first year of the war had to be repeated in subsequent years in order to put a force in the field.

[210] Anderson to William Henry Harrison, October 22, 1812; Dennis to AG, August 19, 1812; Pearce to AG, August 25, 1812, all in LRAG.

[211] See, for example, AG to Thomas Parker, August 5 and 25, 1812, LSAG.

[212] Simmonds to AG, December 26, 1812. See also Schuyler to AG, November 13, 1812, LRAG.

CHAPTER IV

★

THE WAR IN THE WEST, 1812-1813

THE COMMENCEMENT of the war was governed by a problem to which the Madison administration, in shaping its preparedness policies, paid relatively little attention: the changing response of the Indian tribes to the American settlers' attempts to occupy the Northwest. At the conclusion of the Indian wars of the 1780's and 1790's with the Battle of Fallen Timbers the dominant tribes of the region, the Miamis and the Delawares, accepted the 1795 Treaty of Greenville as a statement of their territorial rights in the Northwest, and their chiefs, notably Little Turtle, Pacanne, and Anderson, were resigned to abiding by its terms.[1] After 1803, however, both Jefferson and Madison, in order to obtain fresh land for the constant flow of migrants crossing the Appalachian Mountains and to hasten the assimilation of the Indians, sanctioned eight further land cessions culminating in the Treaty of Fort Wayne in 1809. Still badly demoralized by their defeat at Fallen Timbers in 1794 and their tribal way of life increasingly undermined by contact with American culture, the main branches of the Miami and the Delaware seemed neither able nor very concerned to resist these encroachments. The leading American negotiator, Governor William Henry Harrison of Indiana Territory, was a skillful manager of Indian councils, and he obtained the chiefs' signatures for the eight treaties with little resistance.[2] Yet the rate of American advance was still too rapid for some Indians to tolerate. In particular, the 1809 Treaty of Fort Wayne, which completed American control of the lower Wabash Valley, was protested by both the Miami of the upper Wabash Valley and the tribes to the north and the west of Lake Erie.[3]

[1] Bert Anson, *The Miami Indians* (Norman, 1970), 139.
[2] John D. Barnhart and Dorothy L. Riker, *Indiana to 1816: The Colonial Period* (Indianapolis, 1971), 338-340, 377; Reginald Horsman, *Expansion and American Indian Policy, 1783-1812* (East Lansing, 1967), 143-155, 166.
[3] Barnhart and Riker, *Indiana*, 375.

In the past, Indian tribes under pressure from loss of land, disease, and alcoholism had sometimes turned to revival movements and messianic leaders to stem the rate of change. Such movements usually reflected a desperate attempt to combine traditional elements of Indian culture with those aspects of American technology which the Indians realized they needed in order to survive in a changing world.[4] Signs of such revivals in the Northwest were detected by both British and American observers as early as 1805, and when Laulewasikaw assumed the mantle of a dying medicine man and reunited at Greenville, Ohio, some of the dispersed fragments of the Shawnee tribe, the Prophet, as he became known to Americans, emerged as a new spiritual leader of the Indians.[5] Details of the Prophet's early life and religious development remain unclear, but, after apparently undergoing a personal crisis followed by a moral reformation, he claimed to have been sent to the Indians by the Great Spirit, and supernatural powers, such as controlling the moon and making corn and pumpkins grow large, were attributed to him by his followers.[6] Through his preaching he attracted considerable support, much to the alarm of Ohio and United States authorities who did not wish to see so many Indians concentrated within the Greenville treaty lines, and they suggested he move farther away.[7] In 1808, the Prophet established a community on the site of the old Indian town of Kithtippecanuck, near the junction of the Wabash and the Tippecanoe rivers. The location of Prophetstown, as it was called, was of considerable importance. It was little more than a day's journey by river to Vincennes, the capital of Indiana Territory; it was linked by portages with Lakes Erie and Michigan and connected by the Wabash River to other important rivers flowing south and west.

[4] The most convenient general treatment of this phenomenon is Anthony F. C. Wallace, "Revitalization Movements," *American Anthropologist* 58 (1956), 264-281. See also James D. Clifton, *The Prairie People: Continuity and Change in Potawatomie Indian Culture, 1664-1965* (Lawrence, 1977), 179-185.

[5] See the report on the activities of Le Maigouis, an early Indian revivalist, in "Documents Relating to Detroit and Vicinity, 1805-1815," *Michigan Historical Collections* 40 (1929), 127-133. Benjamin Drake, *The Life of Tecumseh and of his Brother the Prophet with a Historical Sketch of the Shawanoe Indians* (Cincinnati, 1852), 86. Drake's account is still one of the best available and is remarkably balanced considering the amount of material he collected that tried to present both Tecumseh and the Prophet in an unfavorable light. Many of the notes Drake made refer to the Prophet as "a liar, a boaster, a coward, but witty, lazy [and] a capital specimen of a modern demagogue." Drake's informants also frequently claimed that the Prophet had about a dozen wives. See Drake's "Notes and Extracts on Tecumseh," Lyman C. Draper Manuscript Collection, 1 and 2 YY, SHSW.

[6] Frederick W. Hodge, ed., *Handbook of the American Indians North of Mexico* (Washington, D.C., 1907-1910), II, 729-730.

[7] Drake, *Life of Tecumseh*, 91.

Delegates from tribes within a six-hundred-mile radius traveled to this region to hear the Prophet's message.[8]

The significance of the Indian revival for continuing American expansion into the Northwest, though not immediately apparent, was very great. The Prophet preached the virtues of the traditional Indian way of life and denounced the evils of trading with the whites. He urged the Indians to forgo alcohol and American clothes and tools— though not the use of guns—as well as the practice of eating the meat of domesticated animals. As the younger warriors of the northwestern tribes absorbed the Prophet's teachings, they became critical of the older chiefs who had accepted the Treaty of Greenville, thus implicitly challenging the system of American-Indian relations that had developed after 1795. This challenge was made explicit when the Prophet's brother, a self-proclaimed maverick Shawnee chief named Tecumseh, began attacking the policy of making land cessions to the Americans; and in particular he encouraged tribes to resist the implementation of the 1809 Fort Wayne treaty.[9] The Shawnee had migrated from the south in the eighteenth century and lacked long-established claims to land of their own in the Northwest; they, along with Wyandots, Kickapoos, Potawatomies, Winnebagos, and Ottawas, who were pressing down from the north, needed the lands of the Wabash Valley for future hunting grounds.[10] To stop the piecemeal alienation of Indian land in this critical area, Tecumseh advocated that the northwestern tribes adopt the doctrine of common property in land and enforce it against future American expansion. Neither the idea of some form of a united Indian front nor the use of religious teaching to support it was wholly new, both having had precedents in Pontiac's rebellion and in the resistance of the Miami to American expansion before 1795, but the rapid rate of American advance after 1800, coupled as it was with increasing violations of the Greenville treaty lines, underlined the need for a more determined response by those Indians alarmed for their future.[11]

Yet the effect of the activities of the Prophet and Tecumseh was not so much to unite the tribes, as many Americans believed, as it was to

[8] Ibid., 105, 138-139.

[9] Ibid., 83, 113, 126. James E. Pallett, "The Indian Menace in the Old Northwest, 1809-1812," *Papers on the War of 1812 in the Northwest* (Columbus, 1959), 4, 7.

[10] Charles Callender, "Shawnee," in William C. Sturtevant, ed., *Handbook of North American Indians: Northeast* (Washington, D.C., 1978), XV, 622-624. See also William Henry Harrison to John Armstrong, March 22, 1814, LRRS.

[11] Anson, *The Miami*, 97, 105; Erminie Wheeler-Voegelin, Emily J. Blasingam, and Dorothy L. Libby, *Miami, Wea and Eel-River Indians of Southern Indiana: An Anthropological Report* (New York, 1974), 78.

fragment them along generational and ideological lines. Most of the Indian peoples of the Northwest, particularly the Miami, were linguistically, though not politically, related, and the Prophet, at the outset, seems to have had no idea of altering the tradition of tribal autonomy.[12] No doubt, he hoped that all Indians would adopt his teachings and their anti-American implications, but his harshly fundamentalistic message met with considerable resistance, especially from the Miami chiefs of the lower Wabash Valley, many of whom had intermarried with French traders and had accepted the need for their people to make some accommodation with American culture. Indeed, even a majority of the Prophet's own Shawnee chiefs, led by Blue Jacket, rejected his preaching. The Prophet responded to such resistance by accusing his opponents of witchcraft and, it would seem, by inciting his supporters to murder them for that reason. This division within the tribes over the Prophet's program tended to coincide with an already existing factionalism over the acceptance of the 1795 treaty, while Tecumseh's efforts to resist land cessions, combined with Harrison's policy of obtaining them, only made the conflicts worse. Most of the Miami in the lower Wabash Valley, moreover, had no wish to acknowledge that other tribes had equal land claims in the region, and it is not altogether impossible that they acceded to many of Harrison's demands as a way of challenging those factions in other tribes who accepted Tecumseh's policy. Like his brother, therefore, Tecumseh, on several occasions, also avowed a wish to see killed those chiefs who had signed treaties with the United States. As the two Indian leaders tried to spread their message, they therefore disrupted tribal harmony in ways that alarmed as many Indians as Americans, and their efforts created not a confederation but rather a growing number of tribal factions of varying strength demanding an end to American expansion.[13]

[12] Ives Goddard, "Central Algonquian Languages," *Handbook of North American Indians*, XV, 583-587.

[13] Most historians have described Tecumseh's efforts as creating an Indian confederation—see, for example, Elmore Barce, "Tecumseh's Confederacy," *Indiana Magazine of History* 12 (1916), 161-174. Apart from the dangers of imposing Anglo-American concepts on Indian political activity, the Prophet and Tecumseh certainly did not establish anything much resembling a confederation, and the divided response of the various Indian peoples, though impossible to measure with any accuracy, is quite clear. See, for example, Arrell M. Gibson, *The Kickapoos: Lords of the Middle Border* (Norman, 1963), 60-62. The emphasis on the rise of an Indian confederation is continued in the most recent study by Herbert C. W. Goltz, "Tecumseh, the Prophet, and the Rise of the Northwestern Indian Confederation" (Ph.D. diss., University of Western Ontario, 1973), although Goltz seems to sense some of the difficulties of explaining the politics of the Indian movement in these terms. See also

Since the rise of the Indian revival movement also coincided with the embargo crisis of 1807 to 1809, both the British and American governments realized that in the event of war the allegiance of the northwestern Indians could be critical. British officials in Upper Canada did not encourage the Indians to make war on the United States, but they did cultivate their good will with gifts in order to strengthen the defenses of Canada against a possible American invasion.[14] The Americans, for their part, realized that Indian hostilities on the frontiers could not only seriously complicate the conduct of a war against the British but also lead to the destruction of recent settlements in areas already ceded to the United States. Consequently, after 1807 Jefferson's Secretary of War, Henry Dearborn, urged American officials to exercise prudence in their relations with the Indians. Rather more belatedly, Madison recognized the risks in continuing to negotiate extensive land cessions from the Miami, and he stopped the policy after the Treaty of Fort Wayne. Thereafter, he too instructed his Secretary of War, William Eustis, to practice caution in dealing with the Indians, stressing as he did so the importance of conciliating them while Anglo-American differences remained unsettled.[15]

While most American officials realized that good relations with the Indians could not always be taken for granted, many tended to underestimate the importance of the Prophet. Jefferson and Madison, for example, were both sufficiently optimistic to believe that the Prophet would make few converts and that American benevolence could prevent the northwestern tribes from allying with the British.[16] In Indiana Territory, however, Harrison took a different view of the matter. Although he always suspected that the activities of the Prophet and the British after 1807 were having a bad effect on the Indians, he felt reasonably confident that by retaining the allegiance of the principle Miami chiefs—miserable, drunken, and starving set he thought they were—he could continue the policy of eventually extinguishing the Indian title to the lands of Indiana.[17] But after 1809, events began to

---

Anson, *The Miami*, 145, 154; Callender, "Shawnee," 631-632; and Drake, *Life of Tecumseh*, 87, 91, 117, 126.

[14] Horsman, "British Indian Policy in the Northwest, 1807-1812," *MVHR* 45 (1958), 51-66.

[15] Eustis to Harrison, April 29, 1809, Logan Esarey, ed., *Messages and Letters of William Henry Harrison* (Indianapolis, 1922), I, 343.

[16] Thomas Jefferson to Thomas Worthington, April 24, 1808, Thomas Jefferson Papers, LC; James Madison to Albert Gallatin, July 26, 1810, Carl Prince and Helen Fineman, eds., *The Papers of Albert Gallatin* (microfilm ed.). See also Bernard W. Sheehan, *Seeds of Extinction: Jeffersonian Philanthropy and the American Indian* (Chapel Hill, 1973), 216-217.

[17] Harrison to Henry Dearborn, July 11, September 5, 1807, and May 9, 1808, Esarey, *Messages of Harrison*, I, 223, 228, 291.

escape his control. The rejection of the Treaty of Fort Wayne by the Miami in the upper Wabash created a series of problems for the governor, starting with the murder of some of the signatory chiefs at the instigation of the Prophet and with Tecumseh's opposition to allowing American surveyors to work in the lower Wabash Valley.[18] In 1810 and 1811 the Prophet and Tecumseh seized the salt annuities intended for many of the tribes friendly to the United States, while Tecumseh also began making extensive journies, both to the British at Fort Malden in search of arms and to various Indian villages to arouse support for his stand against future land cessions.[19] By 1811 he was accompanied on these travels by bands of warriors ranging from 300 to 700 in number, while reports from Prophetstown reaching Harrison estimated its population to be at times as large as 2,000 or 3,000 souls.[20] More generally, the governor regarded the growth of the Prophet's influence as proof of his determined hostility toward the Americans, and his fears on this account seemed justified when, in late 1809, raiding parties began to attack the Indiana frontier, causing panic among the settlers.

Since no part of Indiana was wholly secure from attack, the Indian raids provoked an exodus of settlers, thus retarding the progression of the territory toward statehood.[21] This development alarmed Harrison, who, for personal reasons if no others, desired to hasten the achievement of statehood, though there was little that he could do to end the crisis.[22] He met with Tecumseh in 1810 and 1811 to discuss the problem of land claims, but the talks accomplished nothing, except to convince Harrison further of the danger to the territory. On various occasions he suggested to the War Department that either the Prophet be seized and taken beyond the Mississippi or that he, as governor, be allowed to negotiate a further land cession that would give the United States title to the upper Wabash.[23] Once this cession had been agreed upon with the friendly chiefs, the Prophet and his supporters could be evicted as trespassers, since Harrison did not believe that the Shawnee had any legitimate claims in the area and he had no intention of recognizing Tecumseh's doctrine of common Indian property in the land.[24] Very probably, both suggestions would have required military force to carry

---

[18] Barnhart and Riker, *Indiana*, 378; Drake, *Life of Tecumseh*, 117

[19] Drake, *Life of Tecumseh*, 133.

[20] Pallett, "The Indian Menace," 8.

[21] Harrison to Eustis, April 25, 1810, Esarey, *Messages of Harrison*, I, 418.

[22] Same to same, December 24, 1810, ibid., 498.

[23] Same to Dearborn, May 19, 1808; to Eustis, May 16, 1809, ibid., 291, 346.

[24] Harrison to Eustis, July 4, 1810, ibid., 438-440.

them out, and for this reason the War Department rejected them. The Madison administration, still very much preoccupied throughout 1810 and 1811 with British and Spanish problems, did not want an Indian war in the Northwest.

Despite these setbacks, Harrison had no idea of conceding to the Prophet the control of the upper Wabash Valley, an area the governor described as "one of the most beautiful that can be conceived of."[25] His experience with General Anthony Wayne in the Ohio country during the 1790's led him ideally to prefer dealing with Indian discontent by striking at its sources rather than merely coping with its symptoms. Yet his options here were limited. Federal policy generally restricted the military powers of territorial governors to organizing the local militias for defensive purposes only, and Harrison did not regard the Indiana militia as a particularly effective force anyway. It needed more training and better financing, changes that were ruled out by the precarious state of Indiana's tax system; in 1811, according to one historian, the territorial treasury contained only $3.00.[26] Even if the militia had been in better condition, the wisdom of mobilizing it fully was still questionable. The mustering of militia units throughout the sparsely populated territory would have required most able-bodied males to quit their farms and families, thus leaving them even more exposed to Indian raiding parties. Moreover, Harrison, although an able executive, was far from universally popular in the territory. His policies on slavery and plural officeholding as well as his suspected connections with land speculators had created a sizable body of opposition to his administration, which by 1810 could command a majority in the territorial assembly.[27] The views of these opponents, furthermore, were known in Washington through the agency of Jonathan Jennings, the territorial delegate in Congress, and John Badollet, the collector at the Land Office in Vincennes and lifelong friend of Albert Gallatin.[28] For all these reasons, by the beginning of 1811 Harrison

[25] Same to same, December 10, 1809, ibid., 396.

[26] Harrison to Indiana General Assembly, October 1, 1809; to Charles Scott, March 10, 1810, ibid., 381, 382, 401, 487-496. See also Beverly W. Bond, Jr., *The Civilization of the Old Northwest* (New York, 1934), 172.

[27] John D. Barnhart, *Valley of Democracy: The Frontier versus the Plantation in the Ohio Valley, 1775-1818* (Lincoln, 1970), 167-176. See also David W. Krueger, "Party Development in Indiana, 1800-1832" (Ph.D. diss., University of Kentucky, 1974), 34, 38-46.

[28] For Badollet's constant stream of criticisms of Harrison see Gayle Thornbrough, ed., *The Correspondence of John Badollet and Albert Gallatin, 1804-1836* (Indianapolis, 1963). Writing on September 25, 1810, for example, Badollet gave the definite impression that Harrison's Indian policy was motivated by land speculation, while he presented Tecumseh and the Prophet as enlightened Indian reformers. On several occasions, too, Badollet de-

felt that the developments of the past two years had placed his accomplishments as territorial governor in jeopardy, and he finally concluded that he had no alternative but to try to persuade the federal government to commit regular troops to the Northwest to deal with the Indians.[29]

The Madison administration was reluctant to respond to this request, preferring instead to instruct territorial governors to rely on their own resources in organizing defense. However, as the territorial governors of Michigan, Missouri, and Illinois throughout 1811 also supported Harrison's insistence on the seriousness of the Indian problem, the War Department felt it could no longer safely ignore the matter.[30] In mid-July 1811, Eustis, who was rather more belligerent on the issue than Madison, diverted the 4th Infantry Regiment, en route from Pittsburgh to Newport, Kentucky, to Vincennes and ordered the commander, Lieutenant Colonel John Boyd, to cooperate with Harrison in defending the frontier from attack. Eustis stressed to Harrison, nevertheless, that the President hoped that these troops would not actually be used, and that the preservation of peace with the Indians should still be his goal. Only if the Prophet and his "banditti" did wrong could they be attacked, and even then not unless "absolutely necessary." "Circumstances conspire at this particular juncture," the Secretary wrote, no doubt referring to the negotiations in Washington between Foster and Monroe, "to render it peculiarly desirable that hostilities . . . should be avoided."[31]

Harrison received these orders in Vincennes on August 7, 1811, two days after his second inconclusive meeting with Tecumseh over the surveying of the Fort Wayne tract and the seizure of the salt annuities. Tecumseh, however, had informed the governor that he would be visiting tribes in the south in the next few months, and Harrison immediately realized he had an opportunity to strike a blow against Prophetstown, thus clearing the way for the surveying of the Wabash Valley.[32] Harrison spent the remainder of August organizing and drilling some twelve companies of Indiana militia, dragoons, and riflemen, and making a brief visit to Louisville, Kentucky, where he obtained

scribed Harrison's accounts of Tecumseh's activities as "mere fabrication" (166-175, 182-199).

[29] Harrison to Eustis, August 16, October 5 and 17, and December 24, 1810, Esarey, *Messages of Harrison*, I, 458, 459, 474, 475, 480-481, 497.

[30] See, for example, William Clark to Eustis, July 3, 1811, LRRS; Ninian Edwards to Eustis, July 6, 1811, Clarence E. Carter, ed., *The Territorial Papers of the United States* (Washington, D.C., 1934-1962), XVI, 164-165.

[31] Eustis to Boyd, July 17, 1811, LSMA. Eustis to Harrison, July 17 and 20, 1811, LSIA.

[32] Harrison to Eustis, August 7, 1811, Esarey, *Messages of Harrison*, I, 548.

oral permission from Governor Charles Scott, a veteran of the Indian campaigns of the 1790's, to accept volunteers from that state. Scott had, in fact, burned Kithtippecanuck in 1791 when it was the home of some Potawatomi and Wea Indians who were regarded as pro-British, and he readily sympathized with Harrison's intentions.[33] Kentucky duly furnished about 100 armed riflemen, which, together with some 700 to 800 Indiana militia and just over 400 United States regulars, gave Harrison a total force of about 1,200 men.[34]

Most of these forces assembled at Vincennes in early September and began marching northward on September 26, though Harrison did not finally join them until October 6. His intentions on the campaign are difficult to ascertain precisely, and over the next month his conduct revealed an ambivalence that reflected both doubts and hesitations and the conflicting pressures bearing on him. Previously Harrison had spoken slightingly of the military abilities of the Indians and acted as if the army was expressly intended for attacking and dispersing the settlement at Prophetstown, even though an outright attack would scarcely have accorded with the July instructions from the War Department. As late as September 25, the Prophet sent messengers to Vincennes to protest his peaceful intentions, but Harrison disregarded them and neglected to seize the chance for further discussions. Yet it is not at all clear that Harrison thought an attack would be necessary; he had always believed that many of the Prophet's supporters adhered to him more from fear than from genuine conviction, and the advance of the army on Tippecanoe might encourage some of these supporters to abandon Prophetstown, thus demolishing "part of the fabric" of Tecumseh's influence.[35] In this way, Harrison may have hoped to reconcile the contradictory pressures on him—the need to secure the frontier without at the same time provoking an unwanted Indian war which would have embarrassed the Madison administration.

On October 11, while the army was building Fort Harrison on the Wabash River, there was a minor skirmish between the sentinels and

[33] See Wheeler-Voegelin et al., *Indians of Southern Indiana*, 124.

[34] The size of Harrison's army in the campaign is a matter of some dispute, largely because Harrison himself minimized his numbers during and after the Battle of Tippecanoe in order to magnify his achievement. By November 1811 he claimed he had only about 800 men, but the military rolls show that he started the campaign with a total force of 1,290. See Alfred Pirtle, *The Battle of Tippecanoe* (Louisville, 1900), 71, 111-124.

[35] Harrison to Eustis, August 7 and 13, October 13, 1811, Esarey, *Messages of Harrison*, I, 549, 555, 599. See also Warren M. Hoffnagle, "The Road to Fame: William Henry Harrison and National Policy in the Northwest from Tippecanoe to River Raisin," *Papers on the War of 1812 in the Northwest* (Columbus, 1959), 19-20.

some Indians.[36] Harrison, after receiving a further letter from Eustis dated September 18 authorizing rather stronger measures against the Prophet than he had done earlier, chose to regard the episode as a declaration of war by the Indians, and he pressed on, determined to take "more energetic measures" to "chastize" the Prophet and scatter his followers.[37] But the governor apparently never revealed his intentions to his fellow officers; a month later Colonel Boyd reported that he had no idea of what Harrison was planning and he felt uneasy about the campaign for that reason.[38] Toward the end of October, Harrison tried to isolate his opponent by ordering the Winnebagos, Potawatomies, and Kickapoos to abandon the Prophet and return to their villages, but, after an advance to within two miles of Prophetstown in the next week, his determination seemed to falter.[39] The terrain was difficult and unfamiliar, the exact size and nature of the Indian force against him was unknown, and these considerations, as Harrison later put it, made "the success of an attack upon the town . . . very problematical." On November 6, he decided to go into camp with the intention of trying to persuade the Indians to disperse without resistance the next day, much to the annoyance of most of his officers and a vocal faction of his army, who, led by the Kentucky Volunteer Major Joseph Hamilton Daviess, favored an immediate attack.[40]

Whether Harrison anticipated the night attack that followed is unclear. He admitted afterward that his previous military experience had familiarized him with the Indian tactic of attacking shortly before dawn and that his campsite "afforded great facility to the approach of savages"; but on the night of November 6 extra sentries were not posted, and most of the troops, Harrison included, were caught in a state of partial undress when the Indians attacked.[41] The ensuing Battle of Tippecanoe was therefore fought in and around the American camp, with the Indians initially being aided by light from the campfires. They were driven off with heavy losses only after running out of ammunition, it would seem.[42] When he felt reasonably certain that the Indians would

---

[36] Pirtle, *Battle of Tippecanoe*, 26.

[37] Eustis to Harrison, September 18, 1811, LSIA.

[38] Boyd to Eustis, October 18, 1811, LRRS.

[39] Harrison to Eustis, October 29, 1811, Esarey, *Messages of Harrison*, I, 605.

[40] Harrison to Charles Scott, December 13, 1811, ibid., 667-668.

[41] Harrison to Eustis, November 18, 1811, ibid., 618-630.

[42] (Lexington) *Kentucky Gazette*, November 26, 1811. The Indians seem to have attacked because they were informed by a Negro they seized from the American camp that Harrison intended to attack them. See Matthew Elliott to Isaac Brock, January 12, 1812, E. A. Cruikshank, ed., *Documents Relating to the Invasion of Canada and the Surrender of Detroit* (Ottawa, 1913), 6-7.

not attack again, Harrison entered Prophetstown, found it abandoned, and therefore destroyed it. Then the army quickly withdrew and was disbanded in Vincennes by November 18.[43]

Whether Harrison won a victory was hard to say. He had done better than Arthur St. Clair and Josiah Harmar but not so well as Anthony Wayne, and his reputation as a military hero rested on some very ambiguous circumstances, which created divisions in the American ranks. Those in Harrison's army who had favored an immediate attack on Prophetstown felt vindicated, though their spokesman, Daviess, had been killed in the battle, apparently after a further disagreement with the governor over tactics.[44] The quarrel became an issue in Kentucky politics when Daviess's Federalist kinsmen accused Harrison of incompetence, butchery, and disregard for War Deparment orders.[45] Harrison's opponents in Indiana, headed by Jennings, also tried to turn the episode to their advantage, hoping to "get rid of Harrison by some means or other...."[46] The United States regulars, too, were inclined to blame Harrison for the army being caught at a disadvantage, and Boyd claimed that it was his men alone who had saved the day for the Americans.[47] Harrison, only too well aware that his handling of the army was open to question, smarted under these criticisms. He had, however, no choice but to vindicate himself by claiming Tippecanoe to be a victory that brought peace to the frontier. His lengthy arguments on this score were full of special pleading and frequently contradictory, for, in truth, the impact of the battle on the Indians could not immediately be known. Harrison forwarded to Washington all the evidence he could muster that the Indians were beginning to abandon the Prophet, but the Prophet and many of his followers had clearly escaped to take up residence in the Miami villages along the Mississinewa River.[48] Future American policy toward the Indians, as Eustis pointed out to Harrison, would thus have to depend on "indications of their meditated conduct."[49]

★

[43] Pirtle, *Battle of Tippecanoe*, 76-77.

[44] Ibid., 57.

[45] Harrison to Eustis, December 28, 1811, Esarey, *Messages of Harrison*, I, 687.

[46] Jonathan Jennings to——, March 6, 1812, ibid., II, 28; and Badollet to Gallatin, December 30, 1811, Thornbrough, *Correspondence of Badollet*, 217-225.

[47] Boyd to Eustis, December 11, 1811, LRRS, and also printed in the *Natl Intelligencer*, January 11, 1812.

[48] Harrison to Eustis, December 24, 1811, and March 24, 1812, LRRS. See also Anson, *The Miami*, 158.

[49] Eustis to Harrison, December 25, 1811, LSIA.

ON THE BASIS of Harrison's reports, Madison on December 18, 1811, proclaimed the Battle of Tippecanoe a victory which would restore peace to the northwestern frontier.[50] After reading later accounts from other participants, the President must have realized, though, that the situation was less clear-cut than Harrison had indicated, but, as Eustis informed the governor, no useful purpose could be served by pro-longing public debate over the merits of the contradictory versions circulating in the newspapers.[51] The administration later gave its final verdict on Tippecanoe by ignoring Harrison's request for a commission in the regular army, which the governor claimed in January 1812 on the grounds that no officer in the army could "manoeuvre a battalion with more exactness than [he] could."[52] Congressmen in Washington, too, were generally skeptical about Harrison's achievement; Senator Thomas Worthington of Ohio described Tippecanoe as a "melancholy affair" that need never have occurred.[53] On November 13, 1811, he and the Republican Representatives from Ohio, wishing to spare their state from the "coming storm," called on Madison to suggest an entirely different policy for the Northwest. Their recommendations required the federal government to arm and equip companies of volunteer militia to serve as frontier rangers while the President appointed three com-missioners to meet with the Indians, examine the causes of their dis-content, and settle them "without bloodshed."[54]

At the end of November, Madison decided to accept in principle the advice of the Ohio Congressmen; it was defensive in purpose, economical, and in harmony with his earlier emphasis on the impor-tance of keeping peace with the Indians.[55] The Secretary of War, however, was slow to carry the policy into effect. Eustis did not an-ticipate any serious incidents with the Indians over the winter, and, overburdened with administrative detail, he turned his attention to

[50] James D. Richardson, comp., *A Compilation of the Messages and Papers of the Presidents* (New York, 1897-1914), II, 482-483.

[51] Eustis to Harrison, January 17, 1812, Esarey, *Messages of Harrison*, II, 14.

[52] Harrison to Eustis, January 14, 1812, Carter, *Territorial Papers*, VIII, 159-161. See also Abraham Eustis to William Eustis, December 26, 1811, William Eustis Papers, LC.

[53] Worthington to Richard Anderson, December 7, 1811, Richard Clough Anderson Papers, Virginia State Library. (I am grateful to Roger H. Brown for this source.) See also John Sevier to George Washington Sevier, January 13, 1812, John DeWitt, ed., "Some Unpublished Letters of John Sevier to His Son, George Washington Sevier," *Tennessee Historical Magazine* 6 (1920), 62-63.

[54] Worthington to Return J. Meigs, November 30, 1811, Return Jonathan Meigs Papers, OSL. See also Worthington to Samuel Huntington, December 31, 1811, Elbert J. Benton, ed., "Letters from the Samuel Huntington Correspondence, 1800-1812," *The Western Reserve Historical Society Tract No. 95* (1915), 148.

[55] Worthington added an endorsement to this effect on his letter of November 30 to Meigs.

other matters; Worthington constantly had to remind him of the need to act on Madison's decision.[56] Eventually, the Indian agents and the territorial governors throughout the Northwest were told to meet with the local Indians in the spring of 1812 to impress upon them the President's desire that they remain neutral in the event of war with Great Britain. The agents were instructed to be conciliatory, but they were, at the same time, to threaten the tribes with retribution if they attempted to go over to the British. Harrison was given the unenviable task of inviting the Prophet and Tecumseh to Washington for a meeting with Madison, and he was also authorized to hint to them that the President would raise "a large force in the spring of the year to drive beyond the great waters all those who have been or shall be found in arms."[57] Force, though, was not what Madison wished; the threat was intended to encourage the factions in the tribes that had joined the Prophet to abandon him and return to their own villages.

Implementing this policy was not without its difficulties. Tecumseh and the Prophet were unlikely to accept Madison's invitation, while securing the good will of the Indians would require a lavish distribution of presents and generous terms of trade, including possibly the right for Indians to continue their commerce with Canada.[58] Both courses of action threatened to overstrain the resources of the American Indian Department and also contradicted Madison's policy of enforcing trade restrictions against Great Britain. Eustis recognized the problems and asked Congress to modify the nonintercourse policy to allow for the entry of British blankets, even though the apparent inconsistency created here exposed the administration to some ridicule.[59] Nor did these measures, even in combination with the use of frontier rangers, seem to be enough to remove the anxieties of settlers and officials in the Northwest, for whom the battle of Tippecanoe had only underlined the vulnerability of the vast frontier stretching below the western Great Lakes. The United States garrisoned this region in 1811 with six isolated forts containing only 625 regular soldiers.[60] The northwestern governors and many of the settlers, particularly in the more isolated areas, desired in the main peace, but their letters and petitions to Washington repeatedly asserted the need to have adequate defensive

[56] Worthington to Meigs, January 8, 1812, Thomas Worthington Papers, RCHS. (I am indebted to Roger H. Brown for this source.)

[57] Eustis to Harrison, March 7, 1812, LSIA.

[58] Harrison to Eustis, February 19, 1812, Esarey, *Messages of Harrison*, II, 25.

[59] (Philadelphia) *Aurora General Advertiser*, February 4, 1812; *Natl Intelligencer*, January 30 and February 4, 1812.

[60] Bond, *The Old Northwest*, 267.

arrangements—troops, arms, and blockhouses—in reserve.[61] Even the governor of Ohio, Return Jonathan Meigs, who was more hopeful of peace than many in the Northwest, insisted on the need for the United States to raise an army for its defense. "It ought *never* to be forgotten," Meigs warned, "that *fear alone* keeps the Indian quiet."[62]

In this respect, the territory of Michigan seemed especially vulnerable. Remote from Washington, Michigan had, since 1805, scarcely been settled by Americans and had still to be connected by road to the principal towns in Ohio. There were, in fact, more settlers of French-Canadian origin in the region than there were Americans, and the governor, William Hull, seemed either unable to obtain, or was not interested in winning, their support for his administration. A small clique of quarreling, ineffectual officials from New England governed the territory on behalf of a few hundred Americans, almost all of whom were gathered within the stockaded town of Detroit. Yet Detroit itself was dangerously exposed to attack from both the British in Upper Canada and the Indians in the Michigan Peninsula. The British were better able than the Americans to exploit Lake Erie for ease of communication, and their main settlements, Amherstburg and Fort Malden, lying to the south of Detroit, had become focal points for hundreds of dissatisfied Indians seeking food, weapons, and support against the United States.[63] Hull had long been aware of the weakness of his position, his service at Detroit instilling into him a deeply pessimistic and defensive attitude to military problems, and he urged the Secretary of War to improve the defenses of Michigan. He had also requested permission to make special military arrangements with the governor of Ohio in case of an emergency and occasionally indulged in flights of fantasy about the "reduction of the Canadas" as a permanent solution to his security problems.[64] The administration and Congress, however, ignored all these suggestions, thus failing to provide for the special needs of the territory.

Yet when Congress began debating preparations for war with Great

[61] See, for example, the following letters to Eustis from Ninian Edwards, January 25, February 19, 16, and 18, 1812; William Clark, February 13, 1812; Stanley Griswold, March 5, 1812; Jonathan Jennings, March 11, 1812; and Return J. Meigs, February 19, 1812, all in LRRS.

[62] Meigs to Worthington, January 23 and February 5, 1812, Thomas Worthington Papers, OSL.

[63] For the background to events in Michigan see Bond, *The Old Northwest*, 207-240; and Timothy F. Sherer, "The Rule of the Governor and Judges in Michigan Territory, 1805-1823," (Ph.D. diss., Michigan State University, 1976), 43-133.

[64] William Hull to Dearborn, July 25, August 13, and November 8, 1807, "Documents Relating to Detroit," 159-161, 179-180, 214.

Britain, Hull seemed untroubled. He felt "some concern" over the Battle of Tippecanoe but hoped that the Michigan Indians would not make "common cause" with those in Ohio and Indiana. While visiting his family in Massachusetts at the end of 1811 he offered his military experience and services to the administration, but probably more with the hope that Madison would appoint him Secretary of War than from any sense that he might be urgently needed in the Northwest.[65] Partly because Hull's relations with the War Department had become somewhat strained and partly because Eustis felt Detroit was in no danger, the offer was ignored. But Hull's lieutenant governor, Reuben Attwater, and the leading citizens of Detroit felt that they were in extreme peril, and they petitioned Congress, the President, and the Secretaries of War and State for assistance.[66] In response, Eustis reluctantly agreed to send extra cannon and a company of regular soldiers to Detroit, but he repeated as he did so his opinion that Great Britain would commit no hostile act in the Northwest.[67] Hull, after traveling to Washington in early 1812, read this correspondence and finally decided he could not agree with Eustis. On March 6 he pointed out to the Secretary of War that both the existing defense arrangements and the additional measures planned were inadequate to prevent the British and the Indians from occupying Michigan, then carrying the war into the northwestern part of Ohio. His recommendations for dealing with the situation, however, were ambiguous, possibly reflecting the governor's desire to provide both for the defense of his territory and to win for himself some military glory.

In fact, Hull's wishes proved to be contradictory, and put into practice, they eventually led to his downfall. The administration had begun military preparations in November 1811 for a war effort to be directed principally against Montreal, presuming that the fall of that city would also entail the fall of the British positions in Upper Canada.[68] Hull attacked this assumption in order to counter the possibility that the

[65] Hull to Eustis, November 17 and December 11, 1811, ibid., 355-357. Madison had wished to appoint Hull as Secretary of War in 1809 but named Eustis instead when he found that Hull's nomination would be controversial because of his reputation as a "Yazoo man." There were rumors, however, that Eustis would retire after the dismissal of Robert Smith and that a new Secretary of War would therefore be needed. See Augustus Foster to Lord Castlereagh, April 21, 1812, E. A. Cruikshank, ed., *Documentary History of the Campaign on the Niagara Frontier* (Welland, Ontario, 1898-1902), III, 54.

[66] Memorial to Congress by Michigan citizens, December 10, 1811; Attwater to Eustis, December 15, 1811, and February 11, 1812; to Monroe, February 11, 1812, all in "Documents Relating to Detroit," 346-353, 355, 356, 359, 360-365.

[67] Eustis to Attwater, March 6, 1812, LSMA.

[68] See below, Chapter V.

administration's concern with Lower Canada would induce it to risk leaving Michigan to its fate should hostilities occur there. He therefore argued at some length to demonstrate that even a remnant of a British force near Detroit would still be sufficiently strong for the seizure of much of the American Northwest. Hull also declared that he had always believed that the United States "ought to have built as many armed vessels on the lakes as would have commanded them," but, failing that, he stressed the need to maintain an army at Detroit large enough to defend the inhabitants and control the Indians. But to persuade Madison to his point of view and to create a more active role in the war for himself, Hull then proceeded to reverse the thrust of his argument by suggesting that an army based at Detroit might also be used to occupy Upper Canada. In fact, he went so far as to claim that a sizable force at Detroit would "probably induce the Enimy [*sic*] to abandon the province of Upper Canada without opposition. The [British] naval force on the Lakes, would in that event, fall into our possession, and we should obtain command of the waters, without the expense of building such a force."[69]

Hull's letter had some impact, and the administration discussed its ideas with him throughout March 1812, consulting as well Senator Worthington and Peter B. Porter from the House committee on foreign relations.[70] A decision to strengthen considerably the defenses of Detroit appears to have been reached with little difficulty, probably because it could be carried out in conjunction with the existing policy of securing the neutrality of the Indians in the spring. In March, the War Department further decided to summon two special Indian councils in the Northwest in addition to those already planned, one at Piqua in Ohio and the other at either Kaskaskia in Illinois Territory or St. Louis in Missouri Territory. At these councils the Indians could be safely gathered beyond the reach of British influence while also being assured that the army advancing to Detroit intended them no harm.[71] About the ultimate purpose of the army at Detroit, though, there was less certainty. Hull was probably more interested in building up the defenses of Michigan, even though parts of his arguments were open to quite a different construction, and the matter was not clarified in his further talks with the administration.

According to Peter B. Porter, he, Madison, and Hull agreed that it was inexpedient to build a naval force on Lake Erie for either offense

---

[69] Hull to Eustis, March 6, 1812, "Documents Relating to Detroit," 362-368.

[70] See James G. Forbes, *Report of the Trial of Brigadier General William Hull* (New York, 1814), 126.

[71] See John Johnston to Eustis, March 21, 1812; to John Mason, April 2, 1812, LRRS.

or defense, and they also discussed the operations of the Detroit army in the event of war. Madison appears to have offered Hull the rank of brigadier general to command an army of 2,000 men to strengthen the defenses of Detroit, with the possibility of invading Upper Canada to be decided according to circumstances. Hull refused the offer, arguing that the projected force was too small for both offensive and defensive operations without the addition of a naval force on Lake Erie. Probably exasperated with this apparent inconsistency, Madison then made the same offer to Lieutenant Colonel Jacob Kingsbury, commander of the garrison at Detroit, but Kingsbury, who was at this time unwell and trying to avoid further service in the Northwest, also refused. Madison therefore returned to Hull and finally prevailed upon him to accept the command of 2,000 men, but without, it would seem, deciding on the ultimate destination of the army in case of war.[72] Hull left Washington on April 9 with orders to take command of the troops intended for Detroit and to adopt whatever measures with the Indians that "may be best calculated to secure the peace of the country. . . ."[73] The reluctant general thereafter always maintained that these forces and orders were understood by both himself and the administration to be inadequate for offensive operations—though he must have known that before he left Henry Dearborn had submitted plans to the President calling for invasions of both Upper and Lower Canada—while Madison stated that it was Hull who had held out the prospect of conquering Upper Canada without the aid of a fleet on Lake Erie.[74] This was not the first occasion on which the President had used ambiguity as a way of advancing his goals, and he probably hoped that once war was declared Hull would respond to orders to enter Upper Canada. The subsequent problems and ultimate failure of the northwestern campaign, however, all originated in the misunderstandings thus created.

To provide Hull with the nucleus of an army, Eustis assigned to him the 4th Infantry Regiment augmented by one company since the Battle of Tippecanoe. Since recruiting for the new army was not sufficiently advanced to provide additional regiments, the War Department was compelled to call on the state government of Ohio for as-

[72] Forbes, *Trial of Hull*, 127. See also Abiel Nicoll to Jacob Kingsbury, March 7, 1812, Jacob Kingsbury Papers, LC.

[73] Eustis to Hull, April 9, 1812, LSIA.

[74] William Hull, *Memoirs of the Campaign of the Northwestern Army of the United States, A.D. 1812. In a Series of Letters Addressed to the Citizens of the United States* (Boston, 1824), 19, 22, 24. Cf Madison to Dearborn, October 7, 1812, and to John Nicholas, April 2, 1813, James Madison Papers, LC.

sistance. On March 26 the Secretary of War requested Governor Meigs to raise 1,200 volunteer troops to serve at Detroit.[75] That the President could not, under the terms of the Volunteer Law of February 1812, commission their officers was too slight an objection to delay action on Hull's claim for the need to have an army at Detroit by the time war was declared. The War Department therefore gave the governor a free hand to raise and organize the troops in whatever way he thought fit. At first sight, the governor's prospects for success were not good. A recruiting drive would inevitably interrupt the routine of farmers and laborers who needed to plant the spring crops, and, in the north-western part of Ohio, he would have to overcome the widespread fear that the Indians would shortly attack the more isolated settlements.[76] These problems notwithstanding, Meigs quickly and easily mobilized the force required by the administration.

The administration's supporters in Ohio consisted of a loose asso-ciation of county- and township-based political juntas that merged into two larger factions. Each faction was differentiated by nativity, resi-dence, and religion as well as by sharply conflicting attitudes on the issue of judicial review. Senator Worthington was generally acknowl-edged to be the leader of the "radical" Republicans or Tammany men, a political group dominated by settlers from the old Virginia Military District, often Methodist in religion, who denied that the courts could pass on the constitutionality of legislation. Governor Meigs led the "conservative" faction of New England-born Congregationalists resid-ing mainly in the old Ohio Purchase and the Western Reserve, who argued for an expanded and independent role for the judiciary.[77] Al-though this dispute was central to local Republican politics, by 1812 it was losing much of its urgency. Meigs and the "conservatives" had carried their point of view decisively, and the leaders of both factions tended to think alike on the problems of foreign policy and defense.[78] Worthington himself conceded as much when he suggested to Meigs at the end of 1811 that they unite their efforts "to manage the public affairs to the best advantage."[79]

[75] Eustis to Meigs, March 26, 1812, LSMA.

[76] Worthington to Eustis, March 24, 1812, LRRS. Worthington to Meigs, March 28, 1812, and Edward Tiffin to Worthington, April 12, 1812, Worthington Papers, RCHS. Jessup N. Couch to Worthington, April 17, 1812, Worthington Papers, OSL.

[77] William T. Utter, "Judicial Review in Early Ohio," *MVHR* 14 (1927), 3-24; and Utter, "St. Tammany in Ohio: A Study in Frontier Politics," *MVHR* 15 (1928), 321-340. See also Donald J. Ratcliffe, "The Experience of Revolution and the Beginnings of Party Politics in Ohio, 1776-1816," *Ohio History* 85 (1976), 204-211.

[78] Jeffrey P. Brown, "Frontier Politics: The Evolution of a Political Society in Ohio, 1788-1814" (Ph.D. diss., University of Illinois, 1979), 392.

[79] Worthington to Meigs, November 30, 1811, Meigs Papers, OSL.

Meigs could easily appreciate the importance of Detroit to the security of Ohio as well as the need for decisive action to neutralize, if not destroy, the potential alliance between the British in Canada and the Indian tribes of the Northwest.[80] Even isolated Indian raids would be serious, and, as Meigs pointed out, the future growth of Ohio could be retarded if "population should be deterred and the present frontiers retreat."[81] Consequently, the governor responded quickly to the administration's request for troops, and in the early months of 1812 most of the local leaders of the two Republican factions sank their past differences in an uneasy alliance, where rivalry was transformed into a heightened form of patriotism which gave priority to the defense of the state.[82] In fact, Meigs was probably able to exploit any remaining sense of rivalry as he toured the major areas of settlement, notably Chillicothe, Cincinnati, Lancaster, and Zanesville, to raise troops for Hull. In each community, Meigs issued quotas to the militia officers, while consulting informally with the local political leadership about the chances to obtain volunteers, and he was usually able to gain their cooperation by persuasion, appeals to patriotism, and the suggestion of a commission should the recruiting efforts prove successful.[83] The governor and the local leaders then mustered the militia, and to the accompaniment of martial music they called upon the rank and file to take up arms against the "proud and tyrannical nation whose injustice prior to 1776 aroused the honest indignation of our fathers to manly resistance."[84]

The society of the early Republic greatly esteemed the virtuous citizen who willingly assumed public duties in a selfless, disinterested manner. In the newer western states in particular, as one contemporary historian observed, where the creation of communities was frequently linked with war against the Indians, "great merit was ascribed to volunteer service and by consequence demerit was reflected on those who did not turn out."[85] When Ohio's "citizens of the first respectability" stepped forward for service in response to Meigs's call, the

[80] Meigs to John Gano, April 6, 1812, L. B. Hamlin, ed., "Selections from the Gano Papers," in *Quarterly Publication of the Historical and Philosophical Society of Ohio* 15 (1920), 53-54.

[81] Meigs to Eustis, April 5, 1812, LRRS.

[82] See the prediction by Elijah Van Horne to Worthington, December 19, 1811, Worthington Papers, OSL.

[83] See the circular issued by Meigs, April 10, 1812, in "Selections from the Gano Papers," 52-53.

[84] See an undated address, 1812, ibid., 48-49.

[85] Humphrey Marshall, *The History of Kentucky* (Frankfort, 1824), II, 459. See also Stephen M. Millett, "Bellicose Nationalism in Ohio: An Origin of the War of 1812," *Canadian Review of Studies in Nationalism* I (1974), 233-236.

militiamen, stimulated by their example, the patriotic rhetoric, and fear of the Indians, also volunteered for Hull's army.[86] Few citizens seemed interested in Edward Tiffin's more searching question of whether the volunteers for Detroit were intended for "offensive or defensive purposes," and the cumulative emotional nature of the response was well illustrated in Cincinnati in May 1812 when a "great concourse" turned out to hear a minister preach to the troops a sermon based on the text, "Prepare war, wake up the mighty men."[87] The communal aspects of recruiting were well emphasized by Meigs when he enjoined the officers to be to the men "as parents to children" and the men to regard their officers "as fathers."[88] In little more than a month, the War Department quota of 1,200 men was reached, with Lewis Cass observing that "ten times the number" could have been raised. The governor's efforts, Cass added, had obliterated the "artificial distinctions of party" in the "general name of Americans."[89]

Early in May, Hull arrived in Cincinnati, where he stayed for two weeks waiting for the arrival of the regulars from Vincennes and for Meigs to complete the organization of the Ohio volunteers. The 4th Infantry, however, was delayed, and it did not join Hull until June 10. In the interval, Meigs handed over to Hull on May 25 the command of the Ohio forces at Dayton, and the general began his advance shortly after, sending small detachments ahead of the main body of the army to clear a road and build blockhouses. In April, Eustis and Worthington had agreed that to make speed Hull should march up the Auglaize River from Dayton to Fort Defiance, then travel down the Maumee to Miami of the Rapids, but Hull, learning that the routes along the rivers would be difficult, chose instead to cut a new road through central Ohio to Detroit.[90] Hull had seen the need for such a road since 1808, and he may have believed that its construction now was even more essential if the United States were to go to war with Great Britain without having a naval force on Lake Erie. If this was the reason for his action, it cast serious doubt on his later claim that he was expecting

[86] An Ohio Volunteer (James Foster), *The Capitulation or A History of the Expedition Conducted by William Hull* (Chillicothe, 1812), 185. See also Robert B. McAfee, *History of the Late War in the Western Country* (Lexington, 1816), 49.

[87] Tiffin to Worthington, April 12, 1812, Worthington Papers, RCHS. See also Bond, *The Old Northwest*, 478; and Utter, "Ohio Politics and Politicians, 1802-1815," (Ph.D. diss., University of Chicago, 1929), 145.

[88] Meigs to Ohio Volunteers, May 25, 1812, "Documents Relating to Detroit," 381.

[89] Lewis Cass to Worthington, April 13, 1812, Worthington Papers, OSL.

[90] Worthington to Eustis, April 6, 1812, LRRS; Hull to Eustis, June 3, 1812, "Documents Relating to Detroit," 382-383; and Cass to ——, June 8, 1812, in H. S. Knapp, *History of the Maumee Valley* (Toledo, 1872), 134-135.

the administration to take steps to put a force on the lake in 1812, and it suggested that his primary concern was not the invasion of Upper Canada but simply the defense of Michigan.[91] The march to Detroit, though, was no easy matter; and, while Hull could have claimed with some justice that he advanced as rapidly as he could under the circumstances, the cutting of the road undoubtedly delayed his progress. It also led him to reduce the size of his regular force by some 300 men as he advanced, by placing small groups of sick men and sentries in each of the blockhouses constructed along the way. After crossing the 1795 Greenville treaty line near Solomon's Town on June 18, the army was in Indian territory, and Hull had to negotiate each stage of his march with restless tribes.[92] The Black Swamp, stretching as far westward as Miami of the Rapids, and heavy rain were additional obstacles which further impeded the army, but eventually, on July 5, Hull reached Detroit.[93]

Outwardly, Hull seemed confident and optimistic about his command, but the march to Detroit exposed several difficulties which were to undermine his ability to lead his force. Most of his troops were Ohio militia volunteers who had been haphazardly organized and hastily equipped. They were also quite untrained and undisciplined. Some companies were as small as fifty men, and one mutinied over the details of a clothing allowance even before the army had left Ohio.[94] Since Meigs had been extremely generous in issuing officers' commissions to obtain recruits "in a country where the settlements [were] relatively remote and the population sparse," the force was top-heavy with officers who were excessively sensitive about their rights and privileges.[95] The leading Ohio officers, Colonels Lewis Cass, Duncan McArthur, and James Findlay, quarreled among themselves over precedence and seniority before Meigs, after failing to persuade them to draw lots, finally

[91] Hull, *Memoirs*, 24. Here Hull rested his defense on the facts that he had discussed the issue of a naval force on Lake Erie with Madison, that Madison had appointed a naval agent for Lake Erie, and that the President had offered Navy Captain Charles Stewart a command there. Yet Hull also knew that Madison had concluded that a naval force on Lake Erie was inexpedient and that Stewart had declined the command.

[92] (Chillicothe) *The Supporter*, June 13, 1812. Hull to Eustis, June 26, 1812, "Documents Relating to Detroit," 399-400.

[93] Hull to Eustis, June 24, and July 7, 1812, "Documents Relating to Detroit," 397-398, 402-403. An Ohio Volunteer, *The Capitulation*, 209.

[94] Hull, *Memoirs*, 34-35. For fuller discussions of the organization of the volunteers see James T. Doyle, "The Organization and Operational Administration of the Ohio Militia in the War of 1812," and Perry Le Roy, "The Weakness of Discipline and its Consequent Results in the Northwest during the War of 1812," *Papers on the War of 1812 in the Northwest* (Columbus, 1958).

[95] Meigs to Worthington, April 5, 1812, Worthington Papers, OSL.

had to insist that McArthur be ranked the senior officer by a mere two weeks. The squabbling colonels then united to press the same issue as it affected their relationship with the regular army officers. While in the service of the United States, the senior Ohio officers, according to the federal militia law of 1792, should have been commissioned as lieutenant colonels and given precedence to their counterparts in the regular army. Meigs, however, had commissioned Cass, McArthur, and Findlay as full colonels, and they refused to accept any reduction in rank, threatening to disband the army if this were forced upon them. Hull was almost powerless to resolve the dispute without risking the entire enterprise, so he referred it to the War Department for solution. Eustis requested Meigs to comply with federal law, only to find that the governor insisted that he had acted within his rights according to the state constitution. Then Worthington tried to frame a compromise which depended on the President's dividing the Ohio colonels by raising one of them to the rank of brigadier general, but Madison was unwilling to surrender the principle of federal supremacy, thus leaving Hull stranded in an untenable situation.[96] As the general later complained, the very organization of his army "was peculiarly calculated to create distrust."[97]

These difficulties were compounded by Hull's failure to win the confidence of his men. Despite his age, the general's appearance and revolutionary reputation seemed impressive, but in fact he combined in his character vacillation and stubborn pride to a degree that made his behavior quite unpredictable. These qualities of indecision and inflexibility had possibly been reinforced by a stroke he had suffered about a year before his appointment to the army, after which, as Benjamin Waterhouse later recalled, "he never appeared to be the man he was before."[98] The Ohio colonels were quick to detect these flaws. Regarding their commander as an outsider, they dismissed him as old, indecisive, and irresolute. "Entre nous," Cass told Worthington, "I fear he is not our man," while McArthur predicted that the result of any campaign led by Hull could be "disastrous."[99] The opinions of the officers soon percolated down to the ranks; indeed, the whole army

[96] McArthur to Worthington, May 19, 1812; and Cass to Worthington, June 13, 1812, Worthington Papers, OSL. Hull to Eustis, June 13, 1812; McArthur, Findlay, and Cass to Hull, July 8, and 18, 1812; Worthington to Eustis, July 19, 1812; and to Hull, July 29, 1812, all in LRRS.

[97] Hull's "Defence," March 17, 1814, "Documents Relating to Detroit," 630.

[98] Benjamin Waterhouse to Madison, June 30, 1825, Madison Papers, LC. See also Nicholas Gilman to Pierre Van Cortlandt, Jr., April 3, 1814, Pierre Van Cortlandt, Jr., Papers, NYPL.

[99] Cass to Worthington, May 19, 1812, Worthington Papers, OSL.

saw Hull in great embarrassment when, on parade before leaving for Detroit, the general lost control of his horse, his stirrups, his balance as well as his hat, and frantically clutched the mane of the frightened animal to save himself.[100] No man could survive such ridicule in a society where leadership depended on popular perceptions of the strength and moral character of the commander. The composition of Hull's army, to say nothing of its internal politics, thus made it a poor instrument for the execution of federal policy, if and when the administration should decide to use it to invade Upper Canada.

That decision was late in coming, and the context in which Hull had to implement it was steadily changing to his disadvantage. The important Indian councils of the spring and early summer did not terminate as favorably as the administration had hoped. Indian agents throughout the Northwest reported that most of the Indians attending the councils expressed a wish for peace and neutrality, but the agents doubted their good intentions, and were more troubled by the actions of the Indians who were not present.[101] The supporters of the Prophet and Tecumseh, in fact, seemed to be organizing their own councils in opposition to those arranged by the Americans, and in mid-May delegates from about a dozen tribes met in the Miami villages along the Mississenewa River to hear Tecumseh.[102] The Indian leader still spoke of peace, but American officials in Indiana were convinced that he was only waiting for an opportune time to attack, and the War Department again received letters and petitions pointing out the dangers to the frontier.[103] And American influence in the Northwest did receive a serious setback after the May councils with the death of the Miami chief, Little Turtle, the most prominent defender of the 1795 treaty. His successors, Richardville and François Godfroy, were younger and far less disposed to speak out against the Prophet and Tecumseh.[104]

Harrison, as always, was particularly insistent about the Indian threat, arguing that the reinforcement of Detroit would do little to maintain security in areas farther south; he even predicted that the Indians would

[100] "Autobiography and Correspondence of Allen Trimble," *The Old Northwest Genealogical Society* (n.p., 1909), 82.

[101] Johnston to Meigs, May 8, 1812, printed in *The Supporter*, May 23, 1812. Edwards to Eustis, April 24, 1812; Harrison to Eustis, April 14, 1812, LRRS. See also James Watson's "Report of Council with the Ottawa Chiefs," May 21, 1812, LRRS.

[102] William Claus to Brock, June 16, 1812, Cruikshank, *Surrender of Detroit*, 33. See also Anson, *The Miami*, 159; and Goltz, "Tecumseh," 322-323.

[103] Edwards to Eustis, May 6, 16, and 20, 1812; Jennings to Madison, May 4, 1812; Johnston to Eustis, May 21, 1812; Scott to Eustis, May 3 and 17, 1812, all in LRRS.

[104] Anson, *The Miami*, 160, 161.

be able to surround and capture Hull's army.[105] The War Department disregarded this possibility, hoping to avoid it, in part, by assembling the two Indian councils at Piqua and Kaskaskia during the summer, but the preparations for these meetings, especially the gathering and transport of presents, was proving more costly and time-consuming than had been anticipated. In early June, Eustis therefore postponed the date for the councils until August 1, thus leaving Hull to move through Indian country without extra provision for restraining hostile tribes in his rear.[106] Hull himself hoped to meet and negotiate with Tecumseh and other chiefs from the Wabash area at a council in Brownstown in Michigan Territory, but Tecumseh, accompanied by a large number of supporters, crossed over into Upper Canada at about the same time as Hull reached Detroit.[107] According to the American Indian agent at Fort Wayne, there were already about 1,800 Indians from various tribes at Fort Malden willing to join the British in war against the United States.[108]

Confronted with a deteriorating situation in the Northwest and a faltering war effort in New York and New England, the administration, the risks and the advice of Senator Worthington notwithstanding, felt that it had to take the offensive with Hull.[109] Eustis urged the general to hasten his march to Detroit and, on June 24, instructed him to use his discretion to seize Fort Malden and extend his conquests "as circumstances may justify."[110] The manner in which this decision was communicated to Hull did Eustis no credit, but even less defensible, given Hull's views about offensive operations, was the Secretary's behavior in telling the general he would have to advance into Upper Canada unsupported, while ordering, on June 22, the recruiting officers in Kentucky to dispatch at once a regiment of regulars to reinforce Detroit.[111] The failure to inform Hull about these reinforcements until

[105] Harrison to Eustis, July 7, 1812, Esarey, *Messages of Harrison*, II, 66-67.

[106] See the War Department Circular to Indian agents and Territorial Governors, June 11, 1812, LSIA.

[107] Hull to Eustis, June 3, 1812, "Documents Relating to Detroit," 383. See also John C. Parish, ed., *The Robert Lucas Journal of the War of 1812 during the Campaign under General William Hull* (Iowa City, 1906), 18.

[108] Benjamin F. Stickney to Eustis, May 7, 1812, LRRS.

[109] Worthington to ——, November 1812, Worthington Papers, RCHS. Here Worthington was explaining, probably to a member of the Ohio legislature, his reasons for voting against war in June 1812, and among them he included his lack of confidence in Hull, stating that he had warned the administration of this.

[110] Eustis to Hull, June 24, 1812, "Documents Relating to Detroit," 397.

[111] See Adjutant General to James Winchester, June 22, 1812, and Alexander Macomb to same, July 25, 1812, LSAG.

much later could have significantly influenced the outcome of the campaign, even though Brigadier General James Winchester in Kentucky sent too few reinforcements—only 400—too late to save Hull from surrender. As it was, Hull might fairly have been expected to resent the orders to take the offensive. He curtly acknowledged them on July 9, adding that he doubted whether his forces would be equal to the demand and that the administration "therefore must not be too sanguine."[112] In Hull's mind the success of an offensive was dependent on the nonresistance of the enemy, but the British, on July 3, even before Hull knew of the declaration of war, had already indicated their preparedness by seizing the general's baggage and papers after he had placed them on a boat in the Detroit River.[113]

On July 12 Hull crossed into Upper Canada, though without, it would seem, any serious intention of attacking Fort Malden. If his later claims can be accepted, his motives were simply to prevent the British from taking up positions directly opposite Detroit, to forage for supplies, and to appease the unreasonable desire of his officers and men to take the offensive.[114] He spent two weeks training his troops, controlling traffic on the Detroit River, and going through the motions of preparing artillery for an assault on Fort Malden, hoping thereby to encourage the Canadians to desert the British cause and join that of the Americans. Some of his officers, however, became increasingly suspicious that their commander's concern with these details masked a failure of nerve; not perceiving any dangers in their position, they were eager for quick action, though McArthur, in a letter to Worthington, began to show some awareness that circumstances could easily work against Hull's prospects for success.[115] At the end of the month, the situation of the army changed for the worse, though not quite as dramatically perhaps as Hull believed. On July 29 the general received reports that the small American post of Michilimackinac at the head of Lake Huron had surrendered to a force of more than 1,000 British regulars, Canadian militia, and Indian warriors. These rumors were not confirmed until August 2, but Hull gave them immediate credence. Accordingly, on August 1 he called a council of officers, to whom he proposed that he withdraw the bulk of his army to Detroit in order to open communications with Ohio by establishing further

[112] Hull to Eustis, July 9, 1812, "Documents Relating to Detroit," 405-406.
[113] Hull's "Defence," March 16, 1814, ibid., 591. Hull to Eustis, July 14, 1812, ibid., 413.
[114] Hull, *Memoirs*, 43-44.
[115] Ibid., 53; Parish, *Robert Lucas Journal*, 32; McArthur to Worthington, July 7, 1812, Worthington Papers, OSL.

blockhouses at Brownstown and on the river Raisin.[116] Some of the difficulties that Hull believed justified this step, such as the lack of a supporting invasion of Lower Canada, were real enough, but others, most notably the claim that advancing Indians had already cut off his communications, were then more hypothetical than real and might only materialize the longer the army remained inactive.

Most of the officers at the council, according to Lieutenant Thomas Jessup, expressed "the most decided disapprobation of the measures proposed" and called for an immediate attack on Fort Malden, which Hull, with very bad grace, then consented to lead.[117] Nevertheless, Hull asked the Ohio colonels if they could guarantee the obedience of their men—to which they replied they could not—and some of his remarks about the risks in relying on the bayonet charge of undisciplined militia to storm walls fourteen feet high and protected by twenty-four pieces of cannon had their effect. McArthur and Findlay, even before the council, had concluded that the army did need reinforcements, and a majority of the officers voted with their commander to postpone the attack until some cannon were in position to make a breach in the enemy's walls.[118] Yet the damage had been done, the lack of mutual confidence among the officers fully exposed; and the soldiers, who resented Hull's doubts about their courage, freely described the general in camp as a coward and an "old lady."[119] Some of the officers discussed the possibility of asking Hull to allow the army to attack Fort Malden without him but they concluded that the general's pride in his "revolutionary character" was an insurmountable obstacle.[120] Similar disagreeable scenes, with much the same results, occurred again after a second council of officers held on August 6; Hull agreed to lead an assault, but two days later, on hearing reports that the British were obtaining reinforcements, including "vast numbers of

[116] Thomas Jessup to——, August 2, 1812, Thomas Jessup Papers, LC.

[117] Ibid.

[118] Findlay to Benjamin Whiteman, July 28, 1812, Draper Collection, 8U, SHSW; McArthur to Worthington, July 29, 1812, Worthington Papers, OSL. Interestingly enough, Governor Isaac Shelby of Kentucky, who participated in the Thames campaign of 1813, agreed with Hull's assessment, remarking that Fort Malden was "immensely strong" and that from that position the British could have successfully "defied" American forces. Isaac to Susan Shelby, October 1, 1813, Shelby Family Papers, LC.

[119] Robert C. Vitz, "James Taylor, the War Department and the War of 1812," *Old Northwest* 2 (1976), 117. As one member of the army recalled, "a free and unrestricted confidential intercourse" existed between all branches of the army. "Everything was known to us." See William S. Hatch, *A Chapter in the History of the War of 1812 in the Northwest* (Cincinnati, 1872), 29.

[120] Jessup to ——, August 2, 1812, Jessup Papers, LC.

Indians," he shifted most of his troops back to Detroit without consulting anyone.[121] Between the two councils the artillery engineers had been able to prepare only two cannon for an assault, while Hull had received further confirmation that Dearborn's projected invasion of Lower Canada had been postponed. As a token of his intention to resume the offensive later, the general left a small garrison of 300 men camped in British territory, but he was clearly less than truthful when he asserted to Eustis that the move back to Detroit was "contrary to all his private feelings."[122]

Once in Detroit, Hull began talking of the need to withdraw even farther, to Miami of the Rapids, to maintain his communications with Ohio. He had already requested, on July 29, reinforcements from both the governors of Ohio and Kentucky, and on August 7 he sent a detachment of 200 Ohio volunteers under Major Thomas Van Horne to the river Raisin to see if they could meet up with advance parties of supplies and troops.[123] A mixed force of British, Canadians, and Indians, including Tecumseh, ambushed the Ohioans, but Van Horne, after beating them off, returned to Detroit instead of continuing his mission.[124] Hull therefore argued to his officers that the army was now completely cut off and that to attack Malden under such circumstances would be "useless bloodshed," since it would not reopen communications with any point. He no doubt believed that even with the possession of Malden he would still have been subjected to the same problems of supply and Indian encirclement. The supply problem was undeniably very real, but the argument possibly overlooked the psychological effects on the Indians of an American victory, the more so since the Indians, if their behavior after the Battle of Lake Erie in 1813 is any indication, failed to appreciate the importance of naval control of the lake, which so troubled Hull.[125] The Ohio colonels, though, to prevent any further retreat, responded by again threatening to disband their forces.[126] The Americans remained at Detroit, with their general trapped by his fears of the Indians and the insubordination

[121] Hull to Eustis, August 8, 1812, "Documents Relating to Detroit," 437-438. Hatch, *History of the War*, 35, claimed that on the evening of August 7 Hull declared he would march on Fort Malden the next day but then gave orders to return to Detroit. See also Milo M. Quaife, ed., *War on the Detroit: The Chronicles of Thomas Verchères de Boucherville* (Chicago, 1940), 275-277.

[122] Hull to Eustis, August 8, 1812, "Documents Relating to Detroit," 437.

[123] Hull to Meigs and Scott, July 29, 1812, ibid., 427-428.

[124] Clarence M. Burton, *The City of Detroit, Michigan, 1701-1922* (Detroit, 1922), II, 999.

[125] Hull, *Memoirs*, 63-64.

[126] Forbes, *Trial of Hull*, 54-55.

of his officers, who failed to make any allowance for their deteriorating position. On August 9, Hull ordered Lieutenant Colonel James Miller to take 600 men to make another effort to contact advance parties from Ohio, but again the attempt failed, with the Americans sustaining heavy losses.[127] Hull then abandoned all pretense at an offensive and, preparing for a siege, recalled to Detroit on August 11 the remaining troops from Upper Canada.

This move led to a quarrel between Hull and the army quartermaster, James Taylor, who appears to have informed some of the officers that the general regarded his position as sufficiently desperate to lead him to consider surrender.[128] This probably misrepresented Hull's views at the time, but the report so alarmed Cass and Findlay that they, along with Taylor and Colonel Elijah Brush of the Michigan militia, met on August 12 to discuss whether Hull could be replaced as commander, either by Miller of the regulars or by McArthur, who was not actually present on the occasion. They lacked, however, the nerve for mutiny; instead Cass and Taylor drew up letters for the governors of Ohio and Kentucky informing them of the "crisis" in the army and carefully dissociating themselves from Hull's actions. Probably they hoped that Governor Meigs would lead a force to Detroit and take command of the whole army himself.[129] Hull was only too well aware of these "cabals" against him, and he tried to defuse them by ordering Cass and McArthur the next day to leave Detroit with 400 men and return to the river Raisin to try again to open communications with Ohio.[130] Reluctantly they obeyed, though the thought that Hull might capitulate in their absence must have crossed their minds.

As the Ohio forces left, the British and Indians began to take up positions around Detroit unopposed, while Hull, in dividing and exhausting his army in skirmishes, found that he had greatly restricted his freedom of action. Indeed, once British reinforcements had come up the lake from Niagara, retreat back to Miami of the Rapids along the lakeshore became a very doubtful measure. Moreover, Hull's effective force had been reduced by more than one-third, and, believing that the British had a decisive superiority in numbers, he rejected the possibility of advancing to meet them in a pitched battle. Instead, he

---

[127] Burton, *Detroit*, II, 1004-1009.

[128] Vitz, "James Taylor," 117. Also Parish, *Robert Lucas Journal*, 58-59.

[129] McAfee, *History of the Late War*, 82-84. Cass to Gano, August 12, 1812. L. B. Hamlin, ed., "Selections from the Gano Papers II," *Quarterly Publication of the Historical and Philosophical Society of Ohio* 15 (1920), 85. Knowledge of Cass's letter seems to have been widespread throughout the army. See Quaife, *War on the Detroit*, 289-290.

[130] Forbes, *Trial of Hull*, 49.

concentrated his troops in the fort at Detroit and ordered Cass and McArthur to return. They did not do so immediately, while the British commander, on August 15, called upon the Americans to surrender to avoid a "war of extermination" and the "unnecessary effusion of blood."[131] Hull promptly rejected the demand, but he appears to have been thinking already about the possibility of some sort of truce. He told one of his artillery officers, Captain James Daliba, that he would never fire on the enemy if they did not fire on him, and he added that "people who live in glass houses should take care how they throw stones."[132] Overnight, however, the British threat of an Indian massacre sparing neither women nor children, and Hull's lack of confidence in his army, eventually drained his will to resist. Thereafter, possibly under the influence of both alcohol and narcotics combined with the effects of his earlier stroke, his behavior became increasingly disordered; his speech became indistinct, he dribbled incessantly, and he took to crouching in the corners of the fort. Consulting with no one, and after a final undignified dispute with a captain over whether to use a "very dirty towel" or a "clean sheet," Hull surrendered Detroit on August 16.[133] Cass and McArthur were at the time in the vicinity of the town, though Hull believed they were fifty miles away, and they had received further rumors of surrender; yet they made no attempt to save Hull or even to obey their orders to return. After the event they claimed they could have prevented the surrender by attacking the British in the rear, but McArthur, in fact, halted his men to kill and roast an ox because they were hungry. Hull was thus left alone to stand accused of cowardice, and even treason.[134]

As Hull's campaign collapsed, so too did the administration policy of holding the northwestern Indians to a neutral course during the war. The purpose of the Indian councils here was to strengthen the

[131] Brock to Hull, August 15, 1812, "Documents Relating to Detroit," 451.

[132] See H.A.S. Dearborn, *Defence of General Henry Dearborn against the Attack of General William Hull* (Boston, 1824), 21. There seems to be little foundation for Josiah Snelling's claim, made in 1825, that Hull immediately agreed to surrender on August 15 but that his son, Abraham—whom he deputed to negotiate with Brock—was prevented from doing so by drunkenness and quarrels with other officers. See Snelling, *Remarks on William Hull's Memoirs of the Campaign of the Northwestern Army* (Detroit, 1825).

[133] Dearborn, *Defence*, 23-26. Another territorial official in Michigan, Judge William Witherell, observed that throughout the crisis Hull had been unnerved by old age and "premature mental decay." See "Judge Witherell's Paper upon the Battle of Monguagon," Draper Collection, 8U, SHSW.

[134] C. H. Cramer, "Duncan McArthur: The Military Phase," *Ohio State Archaeological and Historical Society Quarterly* 46 (1937), 128-147; Milo M. Quaife, "General William Hull and His Critics," ibid., 47 (1938), 168-182.

system of American-Indian relations based on the 1795 treaty by "distinctly" explaining to the chiefs that they would be "held accountable for the good conduct of their several tribes," but the slow workings of the War Department were simply overtaken by events.[135] The council at Kaskaskia never met because the governor of Illinois Territory, Ninian Edwards, became convinced that the Indians were so hostile that only armed force could secure his frontiers. At Piqua, the Indian agent, John Johnston, postponed the council there in order to obtain extra food supplies for the large numbers he expected to be present.[136] The council finally began on August 15 with nearly 1,000 Indians in attendance, but by then rumors of Hull's retreat had circulated generally throughout the Northwest. One indication of the changing situation was the decision of the three American commissioners, Worthington, Meigs, and Jeremiah Morrow of Ohio, to travel to the council with a guard, which Worthington had earlier felt would be unnecessary.[137] Under such unfavorable circumstances, the commissioners felt they could do little more than try to hold as many Indian chiefs as possible in one place long enough to limit their opportunites for blocking any reinforcements intended for Detroit.[138] Meigs, in fact, left the council after three days to raise more troops for Hull, though he confessed he was tired of this activity and was beginning to doubt if the general would ever use them.[139]

Worthington and Morrow were left with the almost impossible task of shoring up American prestige, which they did until September 7. They then reported to the War Department that only the Delawares and the Shawnees seemed completely friendly to the United States, that the Wyandots, Potawatomies, and Winnebagos were "decidedly hostile," and that the remaining tribes, especially the Miami, were either doubtful and divided or absent from the council. As American concern for the future of the frontiers mounted, it became difficult to distinguish between friendly and hostile Indians, with many settlers now being unwilling to make the attempt. The fall of Detroit created a panic in the Northwest, especially in Ohio, where the governor was swamped with petitions to defend the state against British invasion

[135] Eustis to Meigs, Worthington, and Morrow, July 1812, LSIA.

[136] Johnston to Eustis, July 2, 1812, LRRS.

[137] Meigs to Sophia Meigs, August 9, 1812, Return Jonathan Meigs Family Papers, LC. See also Benjamin Van Cleve to Meigs, August 22, 1812, Meigs Papers, OSL.

[138] Meigs to Worthington, Morrow, and Johnston, August 19, 1812, Meigs Family Papers, LC; Worthington and Morrow to Eustis, August 20, 1812, and Meigs to Eustis, August 21, 1812, LRRS. See also *The Supporter*, September 5, 1812.

[139] See note 137.

and to punish the Indians.[140] The Indians were thus placed in an awkward position. Even if they had all desired to remain neutral—which they did not—it was becoming increasingly difficult for them to do so, while it was impossible, as Worthington and Morrow pointed out to Eustis, for the United States to treat and fight with the tribes at the same time.[141] A new policy was clearly called for.

★

THE NEWS of the fall of Detroit reached Washington at the end of August, creating a sense of profound shock among those members of the administration who had remained there over the summer. The accounts of the surrender, particularly one written later by Lewis Cass on September 10, were extremely hostile to Hull, and some cabinet members, in order to deflect criticism from themselves, felt inclined to accept them without question. Monroe dismissed Hull as "weak, indecisive, and pusilanimous"; then he and Richard Rush, with Madison's authority, published the criticisms by Cass in the *National Intelligencer* on September 15 as the official account of the northwestern campaign.[142] The fate of the wretched general was reserved for a future court-martial, while the officers who had served under him were all eventually singled out for promotion. Unfortunately, circumstances did not favor the prompt formulation of new policies. Most cabinet members had left for their summer vacations, with Madison resting at Montpelier while Gallatin visited the army in New York. The Secretary of the Treasury, on learning of Hull's difficulties, set out immediately for Washington, but only Eustis and Monroe were in the capital at the time, both of them lacking detailed knowledge about the situation in the western states and territories.[143] Moreover, a series of complicated intrigues, provoked by the crisis at Detroit and intended to alter the composition of both the cabinet and the northwestern army, occupied their immediate attention.

Richard Rush and General John Mason suggested to Monroe that

---

[140] See, for example, the petitions dated August 17 and 24, and Charles Williams to Meigs, August 29, 1812, Meigs Papers, OSL. See also Pallett, "The Indian Menace," 32.

[141] Johnston to Meigs, August 21, 1812, Meigs Papers, OSL; Morrow to Eustis, September 3, 1812; Meigs, Morrow, and Worthington to Eustis, September 10, 1812, LRRS.

[142] Monroe to Jefferson, August 31, 1812, James Monroe Papers, LC; Monroe to Madison, September 2 and 12, 1812, Madison Papers, LC; Madison to Monroe, September 5, 1812, Monroe Papers, LC; Rush to Ingersoll, December 1, 1812, Charles Jared Ingersoll Papers, HSP. Cass, who was not present at the surrender of Detroit, had to rely on others for his account, and he probably drew heavily on the testimony of Robert Lucas. See Parish, *Robert Lucas Journal*, vii.

[143] Huntington to Elijah Wadsworth, September 11, 1812, Benton, "Selections from the Huntington Correspondence," 149.

Thomas Jefferson return to the cabinet as Secretary of State, in the belief that his appointment would strengthen the Republican party for the forthcoming election in the Middle Atlantic states.[144] Monroe agreed. He had for some time been thinking of leaving the cabinet, and both Governor James Barbour of Virginia and Dearborn had rekindled his military ambitions with the proposal that he lead a volunteer army to regain Detroit.[145] His chief clerk, John Graham, who was traveling in Ohio and western Pennsylvania, reported to Washington the frantic efforts being made to raise troops to defend the frontiers and had also suggested that Monroe's presence was needed to bolster the administration's sagging prestige.[146] Failing that, however, Monroe indicated that he was willing to replace Eustis in the War Department; he even hinted to William Duane, again partly to forestall criticism, that his colleague's mind was overwrought by the news from Detroit and that he would shortly retire from office.[147] Gallatin's response to the situation, after arriving in Washington, was more concrete. He argued that the westerners should be encouraged to attack both Michigan and Upper Canada, thereby compelling the British "to keep the savages embodied in that quarter." In this way, it would also be possible to provide some measure of security for the frontier. Gallatin felt that General Winchester would have to be given command of the army for resuming the offensive, but, like Monroe, he doubted whether Eustis would be able to carry these plans into effect.[148] The Secretary of War was indeed distressed by the fate of Hull and begged the President to return to resume the direction of affairs; in the meantime, he sent rather vague letters to both Harrison and Winchester instructing them to raise as many troops as possible, protect the frontier, and continue with the goals of the campaign.[149]

[144] Rush to Monroe and Monroe to Rush, September 4, 1812, Monroe Papers, LC; Rush to Madison, September 4, 1812, Richard Rush Papers, HSP; Alexander J. Dallas to Rush, September 19, 1812, George Mifflin Dallas Collection, HSP.

[145] Rush to Ingersoll, August 29, 1812, Ingersoll Papers, HSP; James Barbour to Monroe, September 1, 1812, Monroe Papers, LC; Dearborn to Monroe, September 4, 1812, James Monroe Papers, NYPL; John Mason to Madison, September 4, 1812, Madison Papers, LC; Monroe to Madison, September 4, 5, and 6, 1812, Madison Papers, LC.

[146] John Graham to Monroe, August 28 and 31, 1812, Monroe Papers, LC.

[147] Monroe to Madison, September 2, 1812, Madison Papers, LC; Monroe to Duane, September 4, 1812, Monroe Papers, LC.

[148] [Gallatin], "Suggestions, Latter end of Campaign of 1812"; Gallatin to Hannah Nicholson Gallatin, August 31, 1812, Gallatin Papers.

[149] Eustis to Madison, September 8, 1812, Madison Papers, LC; Eustis to Harrison, August 30, 1812, and to Winchester, August 31, 1812, LSMA. To Henry Clay, on September 29, 1812, Eustis admitted that he had been "distressed in mind and body" by the failures in the Northwest, Draper Manuscript Collection, 9U, SHSW.

The President liked none of these suggestions. Madison, probably for health reasons, was reluctant to cut short his own vacation, and he was simply not prepared to interrupt Jefferson's retirement. The return of the former President to public life would have been a politically unwise move for the administration. It would have created an almost total Virginian monopoly on the high offices of the Republic during an electoral campaign in which Madison's opponents, both Federalist and Republican, were attacking the preponderant role in the nation's affairs of men from the "Old Dominion."[150] For this reason alone, Madison felt he had to retain Eustis in the War Department; his dismissal and replacement by Monroe risked offending Republicans in the northern states at a time when the administration could ill afford to lose their support. It would also have amounted to an admission that the repeated assertions by Duane and other "malcontent" Republicans of incompetence in high places had been justified all along.[151] Nor was Madison greatly impressed by Eustis's handling of the situation in the Northwest or by Monroe's idea that he should attempt to retake Detroit; he did not reject them out of hand but observed that "the greatness of the distance, the shortness of time, and the uncertainties from these and other causes make it doubtful whether the public advantage would be commensurate to the sacrifice" involved in the schemes.[152]

This response also suggested that the President was still far from sharing the concern of his supporters in the Northwest about the Indian problem. Madison, in fact, believed that all Upper Canada could yet be seized if Dearborn launched a successful invasion across the Niagara Peninsula, thereby capturing the victorious British army as it returned from Detroit.[153] The reinforcements already ordered for Michigan from Kentucky, under Winchester and Lieutenant Colonel Samuel Wells, could then presumably be used to reoccupy the lost American positions. The next day, though, on September 6, the President reconsidered his stand. He had received, principally from Graham, reports of the panic in the Northwest that had followed the fall of Detroit, and he realized the need to capitalize on this feeling by giving it "proper direction" and "reducing [it] to method," especially if Dearborn failed to do anything at Niagara. If something was not done in the Northwest,

[150] George Hay to Monroe, October 9, 1812, Monroe Papers, NYPL.

[151] Same to same, October 16, 1812, ibid.; Rush to [John Binns], October 4, 1812, Simon Gratz Autograph Collection, HSP; Rush to Ingersoll, August 2, 1812, Ingersoll Papers, HSP.

[152] Madison to Monroe, September 5, 1812, Monroe Papers, LC.

[153] Ibid.

Madison sensed there was the risk that "scattered bodies of volunteers may be so multiplied as to exceed the means of employing them," and their subsequent demands on the Treasury for reimbursement for services rendered to the United States would be intolerable.[154] The war in the Northwest therefore required redirection under a single authority, but the choice of a successor to Hull was not easy. The most obvious candidates were Winchester and Harrison, and the President had doubts about them both. Earlier in the year, Madison had regarded Winchester as a man of "acknowledged worth" in the army; now, after learning of the general's delays in reinforcing Hull and of his preference for service at Niagara, he felt he lacked the capacity to command a second northwestern army.[155] Harrison, on the other hand, was more popular in the region and might give the campaign "an impulse," but the President disliked him, regarding his military knowledge as "limited" and his character lacking in the "extensive weight" required for leadership. Madison admitted that he would have preferred to avoid a decision, but he eventually resolved his dilemma by accepting the Secretary of State's offer to go to the Northwest; he instructed Monroe and Eustis to work out the details regarding the commission, and said he would shortly return to Washington to give his final approval.[156]

Events, however, were nullifying these decisions even as they were being made. In the second week of September, the War Department received letters showing that the Republican leadership in the Northwest had rejected the arrangements Eustis had previously made for the defense of the frontier during Hull's campaign. These had involved little more than authorizing territorial governors to use militia to deal with local problems, though Eustis had, under constant pressure from Harrison and Edwards, agreed to give the former a joint command over their two territories and for that purpose had offered him on August 22 a brigadier general's commission in the regular army.[157] Yet even before the British occupation of Michigan was confirmed in Indiana, Harrison was inclined to assume that Hull was lost and that the proper goal of any military activities in the region should not be Detroit but Fort Wayne, which he believed would next be attacked.[158] Harrison, furthermore, declined to say whether he would accept Eustis's offer of a brigadier general's commission, believing that the authority it conferred on him was inadequate for the measures he felt

[154] Madison to Monroe, September 6 and 8, 1812, ibid.
[155] Same to same, September 5, 1812, ibid.
[156] Same to same, September 6, 1812, ibid.
[157] Eustis to Harrison, July 9 and August 22, 1812, LSMA.
[158] Harrison to Eustis, August 12, 1812, Esarey, *Messages of Harrison*, II, 84-86.

were necessary; in fact, the offer deeply offended him and he suspected that the administration was determined to prevent him from resuming a career in the regular army. He had no desire to remain on the fringe of events while more senior army officers, such as Winchester, commanded the regular troops that were being raised.[159] The confusion in the Northwest over how best to deal with the Indian question thus prolonged the sense of crisis, but at the same time it increased the temptation for state and territorial politicians to take unilateral action to solve their local problems.[160]

Indeed, public anxiety about the threat posed by the Indians and the British even extended to secure regions as far south as Kentucky, and it was the state government there that took the decisive steps to deal with the consequences of Hull's surrender. As was the case elsewhere in the West, the early settlement of Kentucky had required a difficult struggle with the Indians, which remained fresh in the memories of many of the state's leaders.[161] As Republicans, these leaders had consistently supported administration policy against Great Britain, partly as an expression of their strong sense of American nationalism and partly as a result of their desire to create a diversified economy based on agriculture, manufacturing, and internal commerce which would help free the Republic forever from its economic dependence on Europe.[162] The declaration of war was genuinely popular in Kentucky, with anti-British sentiment being aroused to fever pitch by the election to the governor's office in July 1812 of Isaac Shelby, the old revolutionary hero of King's Mountain and one of the fathers of Kentucky statehood.[163] The campaign had reopened some old local controversies, the seriousness of which had led Henry Clay to obtain an

[159] Same to same, August 6 and September 3, 1812, ibid., 81-82, 108; Harrison to Scott, July 14, 1812, ibid., 74.

[160] See, for example, Frederick Folley to Eustis, August 31, 1812, LRRS.

[161] Leyland W. Meyer, *The Life and Times of Colonel Richard Johnson of Kentucky* (New York, 1932), 19-20; Richard C. Wade, *The Urban Frontier: The Rise of Western Cities, 1790-1830* (Cambridge, Mass., 1959), 19-26; Patricia Watlington, *The Partisan Spirit: Kentucky Politics, 1779-1792* (New York, 1972), 27-28, 75-77.

[162] Bond, *The Old Northwest*, 406-410; Wade, *The Urban Frontier*, 41-42; Watlington, *The Partisan Spirit*, 106, 136, 195, 227, 229. See also James W. Hammack, "Kentucky and Anglo-American Relations, 1803-1815," (Ph.D. diss., University of Kentucky, 1974), chaps. I to IV.

[163] William Bradford to Isaac Shelby, April 7, 1812, and Robert Wickliffe to same, April 29, 1812, Shelby Family Papers, LC. See also Thomas D. Clark, "Kentucky in the Northwest Campaign," in Philip C. Mason, ed., *After Tippecanoe: Some Aspects of the War of 1812* (Toronto, 1963), 78-95; and Paul W. Beasley, "The Life and Times of Isaac Shelby, 1750-1826," (Ph.D. diss., University of Kentucky, 1968), 182-190.

unprecedented administration endorsement of Shelby's candidacy.[164] Yet, after expressing pleasure at the prospect of seeing the hero of King's Mountain in office again, the administration had failed to allow the state any significant role in the opening of the northwestern campaign, and during the summer frustration and resentment at this neglect surfaced in electioneering addresses and editorials that were increasingly critical of Madison's policies.[165] Clay warned the administration that these sentiments would have to be appeased, while the outgoing governor, Charles Scott, urged the President to employ his friend Harrison in a "strong campaign against the northwestern Indians," and he finally invited the hero of Tippecanoe to Kentucky in early August to discuss how Hull's faltering invasion might be saved.[166]

In a series of meetings held in the second and third weeks of August, Scott, Harrison, Shelby, and an informal caucus of about half a dozen of Kentucky's most prominent Republican leaders, including Henry Clay, agreed that Harrison should be put in charge of a special force of Kentucky volunteers.[167] The caucus reached this decision by August 18, but there appears to have been some disagreement over how the force should be employed.[168] Harrison repeated his opinions that Hull would probably be overwhelmed before he could be reinforced and that the Kentucky troops should concentrate on saving Fort Wayne. In so arguing, he revealed that his main concern was not at all to implement the administration's policy of invading Upper Canada but to try to re-establish American control over the Miami Indians living along the Wabash River and its tributaries. If Tecumseh, with the aid of British military power, could consolidate his influence in this area, the development of Indiana Territory would be set back forever. The Kentucky caucus conceded the force of the argument but still preferred to strike at the source of British power in Upper Canada and probably did not want to act in any way that would create the impression that Hull was being prematurely abandoned to his fate.[169] However, to wait for a decision from Washington to settle this dilemma would mean a

---

[164] Beasley, "Isaac Shelby," 187; and H. Dean Peters, "Isaac Shelby and the Gubernatorial Campaign of 1812," *Register of the Kentucky Historical Society* 72 (1975), 340-345. See also Robert Wickliffe to Clay, May 31, 1812, *Clay Papers*, I, 664.

[165] *Kentucky Gazette*, July 14 and September 15, 1812; Richard M. Johnson to Madison, July 24, 1812, Madison Papers, LC.

[166] Clay to Monroe, July 29 and August 12, 1812; Clay to Eustis, July 31, 1812, *Clay Papers*, I, 697, 698, 703, 713. Scott to Madison, July 30, 1812, Madison Papers, LC.

[167] *Kentucky Gazette*, August 11, 1812; Samuel Hopkins to John J. Crittenden, August 24, 1812, John Jordan Crittenden Papers, LC.

[168] Harrison to Eustis, August 18, 1812, Esarey, *Messages of Harrison*, II, 89-90.

[169] Clay to Eustis, August 22, 1812, *Clay Papers*, I, 717.

delay of at least three weeks, and the sense of the caucus was to take immediate action both to save Hull and to have sufficient time to organize the volunteer force.[170]

Accordingly, on August 20, Governor Scott appointed Harrison as a major general in the Kentucky militia with authority to raise a relief force of 3,000 men for Detroit.[171] The decision was improper insofar as Harrison met neither the nativity nor the residence requirements of the state constitution for officeholding, but for Harrison the main advantage of his commission was its very irregularity; it enabled him to bypass many of the restraints of his territorial governorship while also freeing him from any obligation to make his actions conform to War Department instructions. In accepting his commission, Harrison decided to proceed according to the news from Detroit; if Hull could hold out, he would march to his relief, but if not he would take the offensive against the Indians on the Wabash.[172] The general immediately left for Cincinnati to see if the governor of Ohio could provide him with additional troops, and there, on August 28, he received confirmation of Hull's surrender. Assuming that the Indians would now attack Fort Wayne, Harrison pointed out that "Upper Canada [could not] be conquered this fall and [that] we must of course be subject to all the horrors of Indian war until the next."[173] He decided therefore to set out at once for Fort Wayne. Meigs and the Republican leaders of Ohio did not disagree. After Hull's surrender, the security of Fort Wayne was of prime importance to their state; within one week of the British occupation of Michigan, an observer as far east as Cleveland reported that "the settlements to [the] west are all broken up [and] the poor defenceless inhabitants are arriving here almost every hour." "Our situation," he concluded, "is deplorable."[174]

By the middle of September, therefore, the administration found that there were two armies being formed in the Northwest; one under Harrison, the other under Winchester, who was about to be replaced by Monroe. At first sight, their objectives need not have been mutually exclusive; Harrison's operations on the Wabash could have provided Monroe as he advanced toward Upper Canada with the covering force

[170] See note 168.

[171] Clay to Monroe, August 25, 1812, *Clay Papers*, I, 719.

[172] Harrison to Meigs, August 27, 1812, Draper Collection, 5X7, SHSW.

[173] Harrison to John Gibson, August 28, 1812, Carter, *Territorial Papers*, VIII, 201-202. See also Harrison to Shelby, August 28, 1812, Draper Collection, 5X9, SHSW; same to Eustis, August 28, 1812, Esarey, *Messages of Harrison*, II, 98.

[174] Worthington to Meigs, August 24, 1812, Worthington Papers, OSL. Gaius Pease to Simon Perkins, August 22, 1812, Elbert J. Benton, ed., "Northern Ohio in the War of 1812," *Western Reserve Historical Society Tract No. 91* (Cleveland, 1907), 47.

against the Indians that Hull had so sorely missed.[175] However, Monroe, on learning from Henry Clay of the solid backing that Harrison had from Kentucky's Republican leadership, decided to postpone, at least temporarily, his military ambitions; he informed Madison that Harrison's new appointment would create "difficulties" for his plans, and he immediately left Washington for a brief vacation in Virginia.[176] Monroe's departure and change of plans left in force the orders Eustis had sent to the Northwest at the beginning of September, which now, in effect, implied the merging of the two armies under Winchester's command by virtue of the seniority of his brigadier general's commission. The resulting confusion was inevitable, since one of the reasons for Madison's consenting to Monroe's joining the army was his fear that "jealousies and jars" between Winchester and Harrison might "weaken more than the union of their talents would strengthen their measures."[177] The President, after returning to Washington, hoped to settle this problem by offering Winchester the choice of remaining in the Northwest in command of the forces there or transferring to the Niagara Peninsula, fully expecting him to choose the latter.[178] Surprisingly, however, Winchester chose to stay in the Northwest, and his decision had unfortunate effects on the remainder of the campaign.

Harrison, as Madison well knew, did not respect Winchester, nor did the Kentucky volunteers who made up Harrison's army. The "backwoodsmen of Kentucky," Harrison told Eustis, were "a singular people" who "never did nor never will perform anything brilliant under a stranger."[179] The truth of this remark after the experience with Hull notwithstanding, Harrison feared that Winchester, as the senior regular officer, might try to strengthen his army for the invasion of Upper Canada by demanding the right to command the Kentucky troops and their major general. He tried to deal with this possibility, first by assuming the right to a separate command for his troops destined for Fort Wayne, then by asserting, on the basis of his "personal knowledge of the country," a bolder claim for all the forces that had been intended for the relief of Hull.[180] On the occasion of the first meeting of the two generals in Cincinnati at the end of August, Harrison therefore chal-

[175] Clay to Monroe, September 21, 1812, *Clay Papers*, I, 728-729.

[176] Monroe to Madison, September 10 and 27, 1812, Monroe Papers, LC.

[177] Madison to Monroe, September 6, 1812, ibid.

[178] Alexander Macomb to Winchester, August 27, September 11 and 17, 1812, LSAG.

[179] Harrison to Eustis, September 3, 1812, Esarey, *Messages of Harrison*, II, 110. See also Johnson to Madison, September 3, 1812, LRRS; and same to same, September 18, 1812, Madison Papers, LC; Thomas Smith to William Worsley, September 17, 1812, Draper Collection, 5CC45, SHSW.

[180] Harrison to Eustis, September 3, 1812, Esarey, *Messages of Harrison*, II, 110.

lenged Winchester for command of the forces that would march to Detroit. The latter, rather surprisingly, chose not to make an issue of it; he let Harrison assume control of both his Kentuckians and the regulars on his own responsibility, and returned to Kentucky to continue recruiting.[181]

In this bid for power, Harrison was strongly supported by Governors Meigs and Shelby, who had both been irritated by the series of brief and, in their opinion, inadequate commands issuing from the War Department. In an angry letter to Eustis, Shelby pointed out that it was the state government, not the administration, that had to deal with the consequences of "savage Indian war," and that the President, by his remoteness from "the scene of war," could not possibly "adopt with certainty a line of operations to be observed by any officer appointed to command in this section. . . ." Referring to a precedent established by Washington after Josiah Harmar's defeat by the Miami in 1791, Shelby asked the President to establish a regional board of war consisting of "respectable characters resident in the western country" with the power to organize and direct troops. The present divisions in the command in the Northwest, he argued, rendered the various American forces "unequal to any object of importance." Reminding the administration that its policies could not be implemented without the cooperation of the state governments, the governor also warned that "unless some change of measures is adopted, the objects of the president, as contemplated at present, will be defeated. . . ."[182] Madison took the hint; on September 17 he gave Harrison command of all the troops in the Northwest, instructing him to protect the frontier, then to retake Detroit "with a view to the conquest of Upper Canada which you will penetrate as far as you see fit."[183]

Throughout September, Harrison organized his troops, moving them up the Mary's River toward Fort Wayne with the intention of first relieving the fort, then making a "sweeping blow" against the Indian tribes along the rivers of Indiana.[184] Harrison's forces included six past and present Kentucky Congressmen, and he probably believed that

---

[181] Harrison to Winchester, August 27 and 28, 1812, and Winchester to Harrison, August 27, 1812, William Henry Harrison Papers, LC. Winchester later gave as his motive the belief that the public interest should not suffer because of personal considerations. For Winchester's version of events, see *Natl Intelligencer*, September 16, 1817, and also the narrative written in 1829 by Charles Cassedy, "The Campaign of the Northwestern Army under General James Winchester," Draper Collection, 6U, SHSW.

[182] Shelby to Eustis, September 5, 1812; Meigs to Eustis, September 3, 1812, LRRS. For the 1791 precedent see Meyer, *Johnson*, 30.

[183] Eustis to Harrison, and to Shelby, September 17, 1812, LSMA.

[184] Harrison to Eustis, September 3, 1812, Esarey, *Messages of Harrison*, II, 109.

their presence would assist him in any further dispute with Winchester for the remainder of the campaign.[185] Hoping to strengthen his hand even further, Harrison—unsuccessfully—invited Henry Clay to join his army, reminding the Speaker of the House that he was "pledged" to Harrison's success, and claiming that they should unite to remove reproach from the administration.[186] Harrison advanced to Fort Wayne, only to find that his approach had driven off the parties of besieging Miami and Potawatomi Indians.[187] To prevent future attacks on the fort, he divided his Kentuckians into raiding parties to seek out and punish the Miami and Potawatomi Indians on both the upper and lower branches of the Wabash. By now Harrison was convinced that the Miami were dangerous to the United States. The chiefs, he felt, were still largely friendly, but such had been the influence of Tecumseh and British successes in the war that they could no longer "control the licentious part of their tribe," thus leaving him with no alternative but to "operate on their fears by severe chastizement."[188] The raiding parties usually found the Indian villages deserted, but burned the dwellings and destroyed their accumulations of corn and vegetables. The resulting hardship for the Indians over the winter was intended to reduce their capacity to wage war in the spring of 1813.

In the interim, however, General Winchester had reconsidered his position, and he returned to Fort Wayne on September 18 to discuss with Harrison the command and future operations of their forces. The Kentucky Congressmen appear to have tried to mediate the dispute between the two generals to Harrison's advantage, but Winchester now stood firm on the basis of seniority and orders from the War Department written prior to September 17 which had named him as commander of the forces in the Northwest intended for the relief of Detroit.[189] The next day, September 19, Harrison recognized the Tennessean as commander of the northwestern army and announced that he was returning to Kentucky, thereby provoking "great discontent and murmuring" among the troops.[190] Winchester had acquired a reputation for luxurious living and "aristocratic" habits of command, which his men constantly tried to deflate by submitting him to endless per-

[185] *Kentucky Gazette*, September 29, 1812.

[186] Harrison to Clay, August 30, 1812, *Clay Papers*, I, 724-725.

[187] Harrison to Shelby, September 18, 1812, Esarey, *Messages of Harrison*, II, 138.

[188] Harrison to Eustis, September 21, 1812, ibid., 143-145. See also Martin D. Hardin to Mark Hardin, September 19, 1812, Draper Collection, 7U, SHSW.

[189] Harrison to Eustis, September 21, 1812, Esarey, *Messages of Harrison*, II, 145-147.

[190] Harrison to Winchester, September 19, 1812, ibid., 140.

sonal indignities and cruel tricks.[191] Harrison promptly left the camp, but his departure appears to have been only a temporary move in his attempt to get control of all the forces. He tried first to persuade the officers to sign a paper on behalf of his claims, but when that did not succeed he wrote from St. Mary's to inform Governors Meigs and Shelby that he was planning to upstage Winchester by taking another force of Kentucky volunteers up an old Indian trail on the St. Joseph's River to the river Raisin. From there he would attempt a "coup de main" on Detroit.

The idea was a foolhardy one, conceived in a fit of pique. Harrison wanted the scheme kept a "profound secret"; it involved the same risks which he had deplored in Hull's campaign, and the Kentuckians would have had great difficulty in holding onto Detroit even if they had succeeded in taking it.[192] He dropped the idea when he received on September 24 the letter giving him supreme command in the Northwest, in response to which Winchester retracted his earlier claims, agreeing to accept a divisional command in the army instead. Harrison now had achieved as much as he had dared hope for—authority to protect the frontier and to regain Detroit as well as the discretion to choose his means.[193] The pursuit of these goals under the one command, however, was not possible, and the difficulties Harrison created for himself led to the ultimate failure of the campaign.

The major general fully appreciated the magnitude of the task before him. He called on Meigs and Shelby to forward him additional volunteers to regain Detroit, and appealed to the women of Kentucky and Ohio to donate woolen clothing to enable the volunteers, who normally wore little more than trousers and a linen hunting shirt, to withstand the cold of a winter campaign.[194] For the next three months he based himself in Ohio, mostly at Franklinton, to organize his various forces—the Kentucky volunteers, the regular army, and some 1,500 militia volunteers from Pennsylvania and Virginia accepted by the War Department for six months service in the Northwest. The problems of mobilizing nearly 10,000 men were indeed formidable. The supply system established for Hull's army had broken down, and Eustis se-

[191] See the episodes described in Hammack, "Kentucky and Anglo-American Relations," 261.

[192] Harrison to Shelby, September 22, 1812, cited in Benson J. Lossing, *Pictorial Field Book of the War of 1812* (New York, 1868), 326. Harrison to Eustis, September 21, 1812, Esarey, *Messages of Harrison*, II, 196. See also *Natl Intelligencer*, September 16, 1817.

[193] Harrison to Winchester, September 24, 1812, Esarey, *Messages of Harrison*, II, 152.

[194] Harrison to Meigs, September 27, 1812, Draper Collection 5X16, SHSW. Proclamations by Harrison, September 25 and October 1812, in LRRS and Esarey, *Messages of Harrison*, II, 159, respectively.

lected Ebeneazar Denny and William Piatt to serve as contractor and quartermaster general respectively for the second northwestern army.[195] Harrison, however, preferred to use his own agents, choosing instead James White and John Piatt as special commissaries and James Morrison as his quartermaster.[196] To emphasize even further the personal and regional nature of his command, he again refused to accept the rank of brigadier general in the regular army, thus enabling him to retain his Kentucky commission, while as brigade inspector he chose Nathaniel Hart, the brother-in-law of Henry Clay. The selection of volunteers and not officers of the line as staff officers was contrary to War Department regulations, but Harrison consistently chose his personal staff from the Kentucky forces.[197] To forestall criticism of such actions by the administration, Harrison had warned Eustis that the Kentucky Congressmen accompanying him were prepared to testify in Congress "as to the propriety and necessity of many alterations in the military arrangements.[198] The only federal commission Harrison intended to accept was that of major general, and until he achieved it he used his discretionary powers, backed by state authority, to minimize the degree of War Department control over his conduct.

The material needs of the new army were very great. The sudden demand for clothing, food, timber, wagons, horses, and fodder, to say nothing of the competition between the army's overlapping supply agencies for these necessities, drove up their price sharply, even leading to local shortages.[199] This in turn created shortages of specie, which was never plentiful in the Northwest, and this further complicated the business of supply. For many of his own needs Harrison relied on special credit arrangements with the Miami Exporting Company of Ohio, but most local farmers, and bankers lacked credit facilities and needed to deal in specie.[200] Consequently, Harrison and his supply officers were continually addressing the War Department on the importance of sparing no expense in the prosecution of the war. Quartermaster James Morrison on several occasions revised his cost estimates upward, alternately imploring and threatening Eustis not to embarrass him; by March 1813 he reckoned the cost of Harrison's

[195] Erna Risch, *Quartermaster Support of the Army: A History of the Corps, 1775-1939* (Washington, D.C., 1962), 159.
[196] Ibid., 160-161.
[197] Harrison to Eustis, October 15, 1812, LRRS.
[198] Same to same, September 27, 1812, LRRS.
[199] Risch, *Quartermaster Support*, 160. Marie Dickoré, *General John Kerr* (Oxford, Ohio, 1941), 66, 69.
[200] Bond, *The Old Northwest*, 399-401.

campaign would be over $3 million.[201] Directors of banks throughout Kentucky and Ohio, especially those who were members of the local Republican party, similarly demanded that the Treasury Department deposit in their vaults large sums of specie in order to support the army, and, as one of the directors of a Chillicothe bank put it, "to strengthen the friends of the Government in this quarter. . . ."[202] By complying with these requests, the administration provided tangible benefits to many communities throughout the Northwest, especially the rapidly growing towns located near important communications systems such as Louisville, Lexington, and Cincinnati.[203] Army spending, combined with the need for security against the Indians, created a solid basis of support for the war, which more than compensated for the lack of military success.[204] Many Ohio Republicans were, in fact, irritated by the disappointments of the war, but, as John Kerr told Thomas Worthington, it was not anybody's "place to complain of this. Our state," he added, "will be benefitted by the expense and in proportion to its amount."[205] Harrison's activities therefore probably contributed significantly to Madison's winning the electoral votes of Ohio and Kentucky in the fall presidential election; the campaign preparations, according to Samuel Huntington, "tended to consolidate the friends of Mr. Madison's measures long after they ceased to have any personal attachment to the man."[206]

As he considered the problem of strategy, Harrison never abandoned his notion that it would be difficult, if not impossible, both to control the Indians and to regain Detroit. Although he was committed to doing both, he continued to regard the Indian problem as his first priority, and he made the campaign for Detroit dependent on its success. On September 27 the general informed Eustis that he was postponing his efforts to march directly to Michigan in favor of another sweep against the Indians around the southern and western shores of Lake Erie.[207] To accomplish this, he divided the northwestern, army into three

[201] Morrison to Eustis, October 12, 20 and 28, November 1 and 3, and December 13 and 24, 1812, LRRS. Harrison to Eustis, November 15, 1812, LRRS.

[202] Thomas James to Worthington, November 28, 1812, Worthington Papers, OSL. See also John Woodbridge to Worthington, November 14 and 17, 1812; John Carlisle to Worthington, November 25, 1812; Samuel Findlay to Worthington, November 27, 1812, Worthington Papers, OSL.

[203] Wade, The Urban Frontier, 64-67, 163-164.

[204] John Lanburgh to Worthington, November 25, 1812, Worthington Papers, OSL.

[205] Kerr to Worthington, November 23, 1812, ibid.

[206] Huntington to E. D. Griffin, November 1, 1812, Gratz Autograph Collection, HSP.

[207] Harrison to Eustis, September 27 and October 13, 1812, Esarey, Messages of Harrison, II, 156, 177; same to same, October 22, 1812, LRRS.

sections: one group of 2,000 Kentuckians under Winchester advancing from Fort Wayne down the Maumee River; the second group of regulars and Ohio militia moving from Urbana and Franklinton toward lower Sandusky; and the third group of Virginia and Pennsylvania militia coming across from the east under Brigadier General James Leftwich. The three armies would unite at Miami of the Rapids, then prepare for the advance to Detroit. To deal with the longstanding Indian problem along the Wabash River system, Harrison was now more or less forced to rely on the efforts of Shelby and John Gibson, the acting governor of Indiana, to carry on the punitive expeditions he had started against the tribal villages. He maintained, however, considerable interest in this aspect of the war, even going so far as to divert from Franklinton the 19th Infantry Regiment under Lieutenant Colonel John Campbell to destroy all the Miami settlements on the Mississenewa River.[208] The results of these frontier-style Indian raids, which lasted from September to December, were mixed. Some, like that under General Samuel Hopkins of the Kentucky militia, were fiascoes, resulting largely from inadequate preparation and inexperience, while others, such as that under Campbell, destroyed considerable quantities of Indian corn, though at a cost in deaths, injuries, and frostbite that the regular army could ill afford.[209] The effect of the raids was to end forever the hope held by Madison and many of the Miami chiefs that the Indians could be kept neutral and isolated from the fighting against Upper Canada. The various branches of the Miami were compelled to seek the protection of either the British or the Americans, and in this sense Tecumseh's wish for a united Indian resistance to American expansion also suffered a decisive setback. As John Johnston reported to Harrison, the northwestern Indians had been thrown into the "utmost confusion and distress" by the war.[210]

The advance of the main armies, on the other hand, achieved no comparable results. Winchester made the best progress, reaching Fort Defiance on October 2, but his advance thereafter was halted by discontent among the troops, outbreaks of typhus, shortages of food and clothing, and difficulty in obtaining supplies.[211] The other armies,

[208] Harrison to Eustis, November 15, 1812, LRRS. Same to John B. Campbell, November 25, 1812, Esarey, *Messages of Harrison*, II, 228-231. See also Anderson C. Quisenberry, *Kentucky in the War of 1812* (Lexington, 1915), 32.

[209] Campbell to Harrison, December 25, 1812, Esarey, *Messages of Harrison*, II, 253-265.

[210] Johnston to Harrison, October 23, 1812, ibid., 187.

[211] Elias Darnall, *A Journal Containing an Accurate and Interesting Account of the Hardships, Sufferings, Battles and Defeats of those Heroic Kentucky Volunteers and Regulars Commanded by General Winchester in the Years 1812-1813* (Philadelphia, 1834), 23-33.

particularly that coming from central Ohio, were delayed by bad weather and the Black Swamp. The fall rains made the roads impassable while also flooding the rivers, making them useless for transporting supplies as well. Conditions in the Black Swamp were unbelievably bad; it proved impossible to move men, animals, and heavy artillery through the vast expanses of icy water, two to four feet deep, with the ground underneath full of holes.[212] Harrison exhausted his men and his horses attempting to cross this barrier; in his belief that he needed to deposit one million rations at Miami of the Rapids before advancing northward, he attempted to requisition 3,000 pack horses from the War Department as well as requesting Meigs and Shelby to allow Ohio and Kentucky citizens to fulfill their militia obligations by serving as wagoners.[213] Realizing that his overtaxed quartermaster's department could hardly cope with these demands, the general briefly considered moving his forces to lower Sandusky on the eastern edge of the Black Swamp to attempt to march around the shores of Lake Erie to Miami Bay. Finally, however, he decided to postpone his advance until the swamp was completely frozen over, but this, he informed Eustis, would not occur before January 1813.[214]

Yet such a delay, as Harrison fully realized, was not only unacceptable to the administration, whose members had wanted the speedy recapture of Detroit, but also jeopardized the entire campaign. His army was heavily dependent on the services of short-term militia volunteers, and by February 1813 their period of duty would have expired; if they could not be re-enlisted, Harrison's ambitions, and his army, would simply dissolve.[215] As it was, the general had to hold his troops together by visiting as many of them as possible and making them the unrealistic promise that they would eat Christmas dinner in Fort Malden.[216] He was, moreover, skeptical about the value of Leftwich's troops from Virginia and Pennsylvania, reporting to the War Department that they were "strongly tinctured with that abominable principle that militia under the Constitution was not bound to act out of the precincts

[212] Marguerite M. McKee, "Service of Supply in the War of 1812: Service of Supply in the Northwest," *Quartermaster Review* 6 (1927), 27. See also Risch, *Quartermaster Support*, 162.

[213] Harrison to Eustis, November 15 and 20, 1812, LRRS; same to Meigs, November 21, 1812, Draper Collection, 5X19, SHSW.

[214] Harrison to Eustis, October 26, 1812, LRRS; same to Shelby, December 5, 1812, Draper Collection, 5X20, SHSW.

[215] Harrison to Shelby, January 19, 1813, 5X22, SHSW; see also Clay to Monroe, December 23, 1812, LRRS.

[216] See "The Autobiography of Benjamin Tappan," Benjamin Tappan Papers, Ohio Historical Society (photocopy in LC).

of the United States."[217] And above all, Harrison had still not convinced himself of the wisdom of marching to Detroit while there remained the remotest possibility that the Indians could cut him off, as they had done Hull. He decided therefore to see how far the President would support future campaigning in the Northwest. On December 12 he admitted to Eustis that the immediate recovery of Michigan was unlikely, blaming this on the "villany" of the contractors, and suggested instead that the administration consider postponing future operations until the United States had gained naval supremacy on Lake Erie. Harrison probably doubted whether Madison wanted to wait that long for the chance of a victory in the war, and to maintain a role for the northwestern army he argued that it would be easier for him to attack not Detroit but Fort Malden, by marching across the ice of Lake Erie. Provided the administration was prepared to meet all the expenses, Harrison declared he was willing to "push on."[218]

By now, though, the administration was under few illusions about the chances for success in the Northwest; it had continued to support Harrison this far partly for want of an alternative and partly because the other invasions of Canada at Niagara had been so unsuccessful. Madison, however, was irritated with Harrison, believing that the general's actions did not place the high priority on the reoccupation of Detroit that he had wished; briefly the President may have even flirted with the idea of replacing him as commander with Governor Meigs, but he did not pursue it.[219] Monroe, too, was unimpressed with Harrison's efforts, after having put aside his own hopes for service in the Northwest, while Gallatin was convinced that the campaign would fail, and with enormous political and financial costs to the administration. The Treasury Secretary pointed out that Harrison's force was both larger than was necessary for retaking Detroit and inadequate for holding it, and "its magnitude in the meanwhile," he wrote "[impeded] its own progress from the difficulty of obtaining and supporting supplies." In the winter, Gallatin argued, defense against the Indians was less urgent, and the only effect of Harrison's continuing the campaign would be to "exhaust our resources and the spirit of the people."[220] Support for Harrison in Congress was also low. The Senate refused to confirm his nomination as brigadier general as long as Harrison refused to say whether he would accept it and would not resign his

[217] Harrison to Eustis, November 9, 1812, Esarey, *Messages of Harrison*, II, 204.

[218] Same to same, December 12, 1812, ibid., 242. See also same to same, December 21, 1812, LRRS.

[219] Meigs to Madison, November 24, 1812, Madison Papers, LC.

[220] Gallatin to Monroe, December 26, 1812, *Gallatin Papers*.

territorial governorship. Worthington, who regarded himself as a friend, sharply rebuked the general for the ambitious pride that governed his conduct in this matter.[221] Throughout the Washington community, there circulated rumors that Harrison was ruining the nation by paying $60.00 for a barrel of flour for the army.[222]

The arrival of Harrison's letter of December 12 therefore gave the administration an opportunity to bring the general and his campaign under tighter control. Gallatin advised against an outright order to end the campaign, pointing out that the dissatisfaction created by the "countermanding of an expedition, thought or represented by Harrison to be practicable, would fall exclusively on the administration." Instead, he advocated that Harrison be requested to "state with precision" his plans as well as reminded that the occupation of Detroit and Fort Malden were "important objects, a failure of which, considering specially the extent of the preparation and expense, the President would see with deep regret."[223] Monroe, who had temporarily taken over the War Department from Eustis, accordingly drew up a letter on December 26 embodying these views. He further emphasized the administration's dissatisfaction with the general by declaring that the President had assumed Harrison to be competent to surmount the difficulties of the campaign and stating that his fears about the Indian problem were excessive; the administration still believed that "the plan first conceived," a rapid advance to both Detroit and Upper Canada, would have ended any difficulties with the Indians. Harrison was then instructed to form a campaign plan, to organize his forces accordingly, dismissing those troops that would not be required, and to carry it out without waiting for further orders from the War Department. To ensure that Harrison alone was made responsible for whatever decision he might make, Monroe neglected to inform him of the receipt, on December 25, of his letter of December 12, which had suggested delays and alternative strategies.[224] Since these directions gave Harrison little help in settling his problems, the general wrote to Washington again on receiving them, this time openly admitting his reluctance to go to Detroit and even doubting the success of an attack on Fort Malden. On January 6, 1813, he wrote once more, saying that a suspension of

[221] Worthington to Harrison, November 28, 1812, Harrison Papers, LC. Harrison resigned the territorial governorship of Indiana on December 28, 1812.

[222] McKee, "Service of Supply," 33. Henry Clay also received complaints from officers in the northwestern army that Harrison possessed "more of the Fabius than the Hannibal." John Allen to Clay and George Bibb, December 31, 1812, Draper Collection, 7U, SHSW.

[223] See note 220.

[224] Monroe to Harrison, December 26, 1812, LSMA.

operations would be "prudent."[225] This letter was enough for the administration; Monroe accepted it as a "conclusive" statement that the campaign was over, and agreed with Harrison that it would be unwise for him to take unnecessary risks.[226]

★

By the first week in January 1813, therefore, the northwestern campaign, to all intents and purposes, was finished; it accomplished nothing largely because the administration in Washington and the generals and the governors in the Northwest could not agree on its priorities, above all failing to solve the problems created by the dividing allegiances of the Indians. The final battle in the campaign, though, was fought in the last week of January at the river Raisin, and it was a tragedy born of poor communications and misunderstandings between Harrison and Winchester. The latter had been waiting since October just above Fort Defiance for the former to send supplies, and he had also experienced many of the problems that had impeded his rival's advance. His men were restless, wretchedly cold, and hungry; and, being largely volunteer militia who had already talked of going home, they would almost certainly seek their discharge by February 1813.[227] Yet, shortly before Christmas, Harrison, while contemplating his march to Fort Malden across the ice, had ordered Winchester to advance to Miami of the Rapids to meet him there for that purpose. Winchester left on December 30 and reached his destination on January 10, 1813, where he learned that the settlements near the river Raisin were threatened by a British and Indian force descending from Fort Malden to intercept his advance as well as that by any other American armies. Winchester and his Kentucky officers then agreed, on January 16, that they should advance to the river Raisin to protect the communities there.[228]

Harrison, having since given up all hope of an offensive and believing that Indians from the Wabash would still be able to harass Winchester in the rear, then advised against the advance. Even at lower Sandusky, which he had reached by mid-January, he was still too distant to aid Winchester, and he therefore instructed the Tennessee general instead to try to hold his army together, re-enlisting as many as he could for

[225] Harrison to Monroe, January 4 and 6, 1813, Esarey, *Messages of Harrison*, II, 293, 297, 300.

[226] Monroe to Harrison, January 17, 1813, LSMA.

[227] William Atherton, *Narrative of the Suffering and Defeat of the Northwest Army under General Winchester* (Frankfort, 1842), 9, 18-19.

[228] McAfee, *History of the Late War*, 200-201.

later service.[229] Winchester, however, had already broken camp, and he decided to continue. He suspected Harrison's advice was motivated by a desire to disavow any responsibility for whatever difficulties his army experienced, but even if this had not been the case, Winchester could not have changed his course easily. His badly nourished troops were anticipating plentiful supplies of food at Miami of the Rapids, and, having arrived there, they could hardly have left the communities at Frenchtown to the mercies of an advancing enemy force.[230] Had he retreated, he probably could not have held his own forces together, for as he told Harrison on January 17, only "progressive operations" would retain Kentucky volunteers in the army.[231] On two occasions, therefore, January 18 and 22, he engaged the enemy at Frenchtown, winning the first encounter but losing the second, after which he decided to surrender his army to prevent needless loss of life. On January 23, a party of Wyandot Indians, most of them intoxicated, killed about sixty Kentucky prisoners of war in revenge for atrocities committed by the Kentuckians against Indians taken prisoner in earlier clashes. The massacre outraged Americans throughout the Northwest.[232]

Winchester's defeat, and the highly emotional reaction to it, tended to obscure recognition of the fact that Harrison had failed to accomplish anything. The misfortunes of his rival, though, gave Harrison a last, unexpected opportunity to shore up his prestige. Taking 300 troops and some artillery, he moved from lower Sandusky to Miami of the Rapids, arriving there on January 20. Too late to aid Winchester, he decided to try to turn the predictable reaction to his defeat to advantage by requesting Meigs and Shelby to forward him more volunteers, hoping perhaps to march across the ice to Fort Malden.[233] Both governors, as well as the legislatures of Ohio and Kentucky then in session, were horrified by the Indian atrocities, but they pointed out to Harrison that it was "morally impossible" to expect militia to volunteer for difficult service in the middle of winter; the most they could obtain was special legislation authorizing Harrison to re-enlist for six months his existing volunteers if they agreed to serve.[234] The militia volunteers, however, refused to re-enlist, even with the financial incentive of a

---

[229] Ibid., 202. Harrison to Monroe, January 24, 1813, LRRS.

[230] See *Natl Intelligencer*, December 13 and 17, 1817.

[231] See C. Glenn Clift, *Remember the Raisin* (Frankfort, 1961), 47.

[232] Ibid., 55-87.

[233] Harrison to Shelby, January 19, 1813, Draper Collection, 5X22, SHSW.

[234] Shelby to Harrison, January 30 and February 9, 1813, Harrison Papers, LC. See also *The Supporter*, February 6, 1813, and (Zanesville) *Fredonian*, February 9, 1813.

special bonus. The unrewarding hardship of the service aside, most of the volunteers needed to return home to plant spring corn for their families or risk exposing them to later starvation, and they therefore insisted in early February that their commander discharge them.[235]

This development took Harrison by surprise. He claimed, rather piously, that he had believed his men were too "patriotic" to abandon him in the "country of the enemy."[236] Briefly he toyed with the idea of taking a small party to burn on its stocks a British vessel, the *Queen Charlotte*, being built outside Fort Malden, but he had to abandon it when a six-pound cannon sank through the rotting ice of Lake Erie.[237] Thus he had no choice but to remain with the regulars at Miami of the Rapids, building there a stockade which he named Fort Meigs. This final admission of failure distressed Harrison greatly, and he fully anticipated censure for having cherished his ambitions for too long and for sacrificing "the public interest in a vain pursuit." Quite unfairly, he told his supporters in the Northwest that had it not been for Winchester's defeat, he could have captured Detroit and Fort Malden; but the administration knew better. In the coming year, it tried to avoid the policies that had led to failure in 1812.[238]

[235] E. W. Tupper to Meigs, February 16, 1813, Meigs Papers, OSL. Simon Perkins to Meigs, March 13, 1813, Benton, "Northern Ohio in the War of 1812," 107.

[236] Harrison to Morrison, February 11, 1813, Harrison Papers, LC.

[237] See "Plan for Burning or Destroying the Queen Charlotte," ibid. See also Harrison to Shelby, February 11, 1813, Draper Collection, 5X24, SHSW; to John Armstrong, February 11, 1813, LRRS.

[238] See note 236.

CHAPTER V

★

THE WAR IN THE EAST, 1812

ON DECEMBER 3, 1811, the *National Intelligencer* pointed out that in the event of war with Great Britain it would be the "duty" of the American government to direct about 20,000 troops "to the region of Montreal ... and across the Niagara river" in order to reduce the whole of the enemy's territory above Quebec. This conception of the military operations for 1812 can safely be assumed to have been shared by the President. Madison, although he left few explicit descriptions of his thinking on strategic matters, revealed to some of his correspondents after the war began that it had always been his intention to employ whatever forces could be raised quickly and, relying on the advantages of surprise, to attack Montreal.[1] The President very probably believed that the impressions made by early success in the war would be sufficient to extract concessions from Great Britain or, failing that, would provide a momentum to enable the United States to continue military operations in Lower Canada, culminating presumably in a siege at Quebec. Insofar as the debates of the first session of the Twelfth Congress dealt with the problem of strategy, the arguments of those Republicans who supported the administration's program of military preparations all bore out Madison's assertion. In the House, Peter B. Porter and John Smilie, along with Joseph Anderson and George Washington Campbell in the Senate, urged their colleagues to support legislation to enable the administration to have a large force ready for action by mid-May 1812 and attempt an invasion as soon as the St. Lawrence River was free of ice. Their speeches revealed that they were not so much concerned with the details of training the recruits as they were simply hoping to raise a large body of troops

---

[1] Madison to Jefferson, August 17, 1812; to John Nicholas, April 2, 1813; to William Wirt, September 30, 1813, James Madison Papers, LC.

eager for action who would, by weight of numbers and enthusiasm, be able to overwhelm the most vulnerable points in Canada before Great Britain could move reinforcements down the St. Lawrence and the Great Lakes. The early timing of these operations, as much as anything else, was regarded as the essential element in their success.[2]

This conception of the war, in part, reflected the administration's assessment of Great Britain's military problems in defending Canada. The United States had always collected information, usually from traders, travelers, and revenue officers, on the strength and movements of British forces in Canada, and these sources of information continued to be used in 1811 and 1812. John Jacob Astor sent Gallatin estimates of the British troops in Upper Canada in December 1811, while Gallatin and Eustis, in turn, instructed Treasury and army officials to provide similar information in the regions of Lake Champlain and Nova Scotia. Most of the reports received tended to emphasize the limited number of regular troops Great Britain could draw on for defense and made varying estimates of the effectiveness and loyalty of the local militia. Astor, for example, believed that the French-speaking people of Lower Canada would probably be neutral if not friendly to the United States in the event of war, while the settlers along the St. Lawrence and westward of Kingston he saw as the most likely to resist an invasion.[3] The critical problem, though, was the ability of the British to reinforce weaker areas from Quebec, and, on the size of the garrison there, the administration's informants had no reliable knowledge. Accordingly, in the first week of December 1811, Eustis summoned to Washington Benjamin F. Stickney and instructed him to visit Canada and make a comprehensive report on its defenses.

Reporting back in February, Stickney concentrated on Montreal and Quebec, assessing the British garrison at the latter place to be no more than 4,000 men; and that force, he claimed, was "more nominal than real." With few exceptions, the King's Guard being the most notable, Stickney regarded the British regulars as being of little consequence, dismissing them as men "much debilitated by intemperance" through long years of garrison duty. The troops drawn from the local population he found little better; "the Canadians," he wrote, "appear

[2] AC, 12th Cong., 1st Sess., 57, 58, 67, 418, 701-702. See also Richard Rush to John Binns, February 28, 1812, where Rush quoted Henry Dearborn as saying that the United States would begin the invasion of Canada "a little *clumsily*, but . . . must make up by main *strength*, and the rest will come afterward." Society Collection, HSP.

[3] Gallatin to Madison, December 17, 1811, Madison Papers, LC. J. Harrison to Gallatin, December 19, 1811, and Lemuel Trescott to Gallatin, February 19, 1812, Carl Prince and Helen Fineman, eds., *The Papers of Albert Gallatin* (microfilm ed.).

to be the meanest among the refuse of men." Stickney reckoned the militia of Lower Canada to be 50,000 strong, but, not being armed, they were totally ineffective and were trained only "in drunken frolics on common week days." On the basis of this unflattering opinion, Stickney argued that "it would not be difficult for brave men to penetrate" to Quebec, while the legendary fortifications of the city, he felt, though formidable in parts, were overrated in strength and had been neglected in recent years.[4] In the area between Montreal and Kingston, however, a very different situation existed. Montreal itself had no fortifications, the British having destroyed them after 1760, but the regular troops defending it were, in Stickney's words, "pretty good men," while the Scottish forces guarding the approach through the Trois Rivières region merited a similar description. Moreover, the militia forces were more formidable than their Lower Canadian counterparts, consisting mainly of Scottish settlers "possessed of some information, habituated to personal exposure and abstemious living." Finally, there were a large number of Americans settled in the areas west of Kingston, many of whom were descended from Loyalists, and they would be, Stickney concluded, "very dangerous enemies."[5]

Yet for all its wealth of information, it seems unlikely that Stickney's report had any great impact on administration thinking about how to conquer Canada, except possibly to confirm Madison in his preference for concentrating American forces on Montreal. Of the two major cities in Canada, Montreal still offered the easiest access to an invading army, it controlled the region of Canada that had recently become of great economic value to Great Britain, and Americans had actually occupied the city, albeit briefly, at the outset of the Revolutionary War in 1775.[6] By contrast, Quebec—Stickney's disparagement of the forces there notwithstanding—presented no point of entry which was not protected to some degree either by natural obstacles or by massive numbers of cannon. Nevertheless, it would seem that as the preparations for war advanced Madison was gradually led, probably from considerations of

[4] This assessment of the British position at Quebec agrees closely with that made at about the same time by the governor of Lower Canada, Lieutenant General Sir George Provost. See J. Mackay Hitsman, *Safeguarding Canada, 1763-1871* (Toronto, 1968), 79, 83-85.

[5] This section is based on Benjamin Stickney to Eustis, February 3, 1812, LRAG. This letter is, in fact, a thirteen-page memorandum bearing the subtitle "On Canada, 1812." Stickney was the son-in-law of Madison's friend John Stark of New Hampshire, who had been importuning the President to give him an appointment of some sort for over a year. After Stickney's return from Canada, Eustis appointed him Indian agent at Fort Wayne, Indiana Territory.

[6] These points were emphasized in the *National Intelligencer* editorial on December 3, 1811.

defense as well as offense, to modify his intention of focusing the war effort solely on Montreal. As Gallatin had pointed out in 1807 and subsequently, the British base at Halifax required attention as a place from where the Royal Navy might launch annoying raids on the American coast, although throughout 1812 the administration assumed that the prospects for a British invasion were far fewer than they had been in the period immediately following the *Chesapeake* affair.[7] Still, an attack on New Brunswick and Nova Scotia, even if it did not extend to Halifax, would undeniably strain the enemy's limited forces while also providing an added degree of security for the American coast. Dearborn, as commander of the American forces in 1812 and as the leading Republican in the District of Maine, certainly favored an invasion of New Brunswick, and by April he and Gallatin were considering plans to bring it about.[8] Furthermore, while Madison had assumed that most British possessions west of Montreal would fall into American hands after its capture, he seems to have neglected the possibility, raised by William Hull, that enemy forces in Upper Canada, together with the Indians, might inflict some damage on the American frontier in the Northwest.[9]

Madison duly accepted all these points without assuming, it would seem, that they compromised his original strategy in any way. He accordingly authorized Dearborn to prepare for a more comprehensive attack on Canada than he had at first contemplated, and the general had the plans ready by the first week in April. On the assumption that Great Britain would be unable to reinforce Canada in 1812 or redistribute significantly the existing forces there, Dearborn stated, in accordance with Madison's thinking, that the principal goal of the war would be the conquest of Lower Canada, with Montreal "the first object." A largely "undisciplined" force of 16,000 men, mostly volunteers, would provide "the strong superiority" of numbers required to subdue a force of half that size, after which Dearborn envisaged the Americans advancing toward Quebec. Whether they would actually attack Quebec or only attempt a siege was left to depend on circumstances, though Dearborn, as a survivor of Richard Montgomery's assault on that city in 1775, probably had little inclination for the former tactic. In either event, the American army would require greater

---

[7] Cf. Gallatin to Jefferson, July 25, 1807, Thomas Jefferson Papers, LC. Gallatin systematically collected information about Halifax and New Brunswick, and showed sustained interest in schemes whereby those places might be captured. See, for example, Trescott to Gallatin, January 13, 1811, *Gallatin Papers*.

[8] See "Notes on the Situation at New Brunswick, [April 1812]; Trescott to Gallatin, February 19, 1812, both in *Gallatin Papers*.

[9] See above, Chapter IV.

numbers and discipline far beyond anything the administration hoped to achieve in the summer of 1812. To weaken and divide the British defenses, Dearborn recommended a series of lesser invasions of Upper Canada, to be launched from Detroit, the Niagara Peninsula, and Sacketts Harbor, requiring in all a total of about 8,000 men. Farther east, he advocated "a small expedition" of 3,000 Maine militia, commanded by customs collector Lemuel Trescott of Machias, for the occupation of New Brunswick, which would presumably compel the enemy to concentrate his forces in Halifax. The key to the success of Dearborn's plans, as he admitted, was their speedy execution; once war had been declared, he wrote, it had to be prosecuted to produce peace "in the shortest possible time."[10] Privately, however, the general was not altogether convinced this would happen. He did not doubt that the United States would prevail but expected, as he told Jefferson, "to commence the war clumsily [and] do better and better every year."[11]

Yet Dearborn's record as commander of the American armies was to make even this modest prediction seem excessively optimistic, and for this both Dearborn and the administration must bear much of the responsibility. But contributing very greatly to their failures was the response of the citizens and the state governments in the East to the policies Dearborn was supposed to implement. The Republican parties of the northwestern states and territories, while disagreeing with the administration over strategic priorities, had at least generally, and even enthusiastically, supported the declaration of war. Their eastern counterparts, on the other hand, doubted the wisdom of Madison's policies, and their attitudes to the war could only be described as ambivalent at best. Moreover, the Federalist party, which was few in numbers and powerless in the Northwest, was strong and active in the eastern states. And with few exceptions, the Federalists were bitterly opposed to the war and wished to see it end as soon as possible. In short, the whole context of politics in the eastern states operated to create particular difficulties for the prosecution of a Canadian war. Against the combinations of local politics and local concerns that determined reactions to the war in the East, the administration in Washington, even more so than had been the case in the Northwest, simply lacked the power and influence to prevail.

★

[10] Dearborn to Madison, April 6, 1812, Daniel Parker Papers, HSP. Another copy of these war plans may be found in H.A.S. Dearborn, "The Life of Major General Henry Dearborn" (1824), V, 119-134. The manuscript of this unpublished biography is in the Maine Historical Society.

[11] Dearborn to Jefferson, March 10, 1812, Jefferson Papers, LC.

FOR THE PURPOSE of organizing the American armies for the invasions of both Upper and Lower Canada, several locations in upstate New York were of considerable strategic importance. After some delays in finding a site, the War Department chose the town of Greenbush, just outside Albany, as the main headquarters for the regular army. From this point rivers and roads led directly to the valley of Lake Champlain, to Sackett's Harbor and the eastern end of Lake Ontario, and to the Niagara Peninsula in the west. At Greenbush it would also be convenient to assemble volunteers and regulars from New York and New England before commencing the series of invasions of Canada that Dearborn had recommended in early April. The location, therefore, had its advantages, but it had serious drawbacks as well. Albany, and the region of western New York beyond it, was the most important center of the Clintonian opposition to Madison's re-election, and the problems that the administration encountered in dealing with this opposition as well as with some of the reasons for its existence were to have a decisive and unfortunate effect on the conduct of the war.

The coming of the war with Great Britain created serious problems for many powerful interest groups in New York society. Large numbers of export merchants in New York City and Albany had made massive speculative purchases of wheat in the expectation of selling it at a high price in Europe, and the estimates of the size of the crop on the market by the spring of 1812 ran to over 3 million bushels. Because the rivers took rather longer to thaw in 1812 than usual, the imposition of the embargo in April caught the merchants with much of this crop still on their hands, and they feared either that it would spoil over the summer months or that its price would fall as surpluses accumulated. Consequently, hundreds of merchants and farmers from upstate New York petitioned Congress, protesting against their anticipated ruin; they called for a repeal of the embargo and also for delays in a declaration of war until better defense preparations, and presumably more modest commercial arrangements, had been made.[12] Equally as serious, though, were the problems of the regions of western and northern New York that bordered on Canada. Here the frontiers were dominated by speculators and land companies who had invested in huge tracts of land. Most notable were those areas belonging to the Holland Land Company, which could list as but one of its many holdings the 3.3

---

[12] Petition of Albany Merchants to Congress, April 16, 1812; of Troy merchants, April 23, 1812; of Rensselaer County, June 16, 1812, HR 12A-G1.2, LRHS. See also *Albany Register*, April 14, 1812; (Canandaigua) *Ontario Repository and Messenger*, April 28, 1812.

million acres west of the Genesee River through which ran all the routes to Upper Canada that led across the Niagara Peninsula.[13]

The usual method of land speculation in upstate New York was for individuals or companies to open tracts for settlement, often with improvements such as roads and mills, and to recoup the investment by collecting rents and mortgages from farmers who set up on the land. Success was by no means certain, the less so since the business was highly competitive, and repayments often had to be waived for a period to allow poorer settlers to get started. More generally, the profitability of agriculture in these newer regions was dependent on an expanding export trade to provide the farmer with cash to repay his debts and to produce rising land values.[14] The Republican policies of commercial restriction, especially the embargo, had at first harmed these regions, then inadvertently created the export trade necessary for their survival by forcing the farmers in desperation to seek Canadian outlets. As the agent for the Holland Land Company, Joseph Ellicott, reported in 1810, "had it not been for the Embargo measure, [the Montreal trade] would not have been discovered at so early a date, probably by many years."[15] This trade across Lake Ontario and down the St. Lawrence grew steadily after 1809 because the costs of water transportation were considerably cheaper than those incurred in any overland trade, and the expansion of the frontier economies of New York thus became largely dependent on continuing American access to Canada. This situation was obviously not without its difficulties, but most New Yorkers believed that these were outweighed by the advantages of the trade.[16]

The seizure of Montreal, of course, would disrupt this trade and deprive Great Britain of the advantages she had derived from it, though Madison does not appear to have greatly concerned himself with the

[13] The standard work here is Paul D. Evans, *The Holland Land Company* (Buffalo, 1924).

[14] Ibid., xii, xiii; William D. Chazanof, *Joseph Ellicott and the Holland Land Company* (Syracuse, 1971), 81-91; David M. Ellis, *Landlords and Farmers in the Hudson-Mohawk Region* (Ithaca, 1946), 24-26, 67, 108, 113, 120, 122; William C. Lahey, "The Influence of David Parish on the Development of Trade and Settlement in Northern New York, 1808-1822" (Ph.D. diss., Syracuse University, 1958), 118-119; Neil A. McNall, *An Agricultural History of the Genesee Valley, 1790-1860* (Philadelphia, 1952), 12-16, 25-28, 36-40.

[15] Ellicott to Paul Busti, June 9, 1810, cited by Chazanof, "Joseph Ellicott, the Embargo and the War of 1812," *Niagara Frontier* 10 (1963), 2. Ellicott's reports to Busti provide a comprehensive discussion of the value of the Montreal trade to the Holland Company. See Robert W. Bingham, ed., *Holland Land Company's Papers & Reports of Joseph Ellicott* (Buffalo, 1937-1941), esp. II, 78-88.

[16] *Ontario Repository*, June 11, 1811, and January 21, 1812. See also Chazanof, *Joseph Ellicott*, 114-116; Evans, *Holland Land Company*, 316; and McNall, *Genesee Valley*, 98, 99, 102.

effects of this development on New Yorkers. The President did realize that the embargo of April 1812, followed by a declaration of war, would affect wheat prices, but he believed that with patience New Yorkers could obtain fair returns for their crops.[17] Not unnaturally, however, New Yorkers thought that they could not afford such patience. The frontier settlers were by no means insensitive to American grievances against Great Britain, but they had no conception that the administration's defense of the nation's honor should imperil their livelihoods. Indeed, they appear to have taken the rhetoric justifying a war for maritime rights at face value and assumed that the United States would simply defend its frontier with Canada while forcefully vindicating its interests whenever possible on the high seas.[18] The degree to which they would support the war when its purposes became clear to them was, therefore, uncertain. Most of the large land speculators and land companies, though, did not attempt to conceal their fears that the war would be bad for business.[19] The land agent of the German banker David Parish, who owned most of St. Lawrence County, even took steps to ensure that the editor of the Ogdensburg *Palladium* did not make the mistake of supporting a war that clearly jeopardized his employer's interests, while the Canadian inhabitants of Odletown, opposite Champlain in northeastern New York, reciprocated these sentiments by erecting a large sign depicting an eagle and a lion and bearing the words, "If you don't scratch I won't bite."[20] These economic realities led most of the Congressmen from upstate New York to describe the advocates of war, in the words of Representative Pierre Van Cortlandt, Jr., as "mad." Nothing, he added, could save the state but the election of DeWitt Clinton to the Presidency.[21]

The appeal of Clinton as a presidential candidate throughout the state, however, was probably broadened by the economic disruption the war promised to create. The Republican party drew its largest majorities in the western district of New York, the area that would be

[17] Madison to Jefferson, April 24, 1812, Madison Papers, LC.

[18] J. Hopper to Daniel D. Tompkins, June 24, 1812, Daniel D. Tompkins Papers, NYSL. *Albany Register*, May 29, 1812.

[19] Chazanof, *Joseph Ellicott*, 117, 118, 121; and Lahey, "David Parish," 159.

[20] Harry F. Landon, "British Sympathizers in St. Lawrence County During the War of 1812," *New York History* 35 (1954), 133; Raymond and Phillip G. Walters, "David Parish: New York State Land Promoter," ibid. 26 (1945), 146-159. Parish even renounced ordinance contracts with the United States for fear of provoking a British attack on Ogdensburg. See Lahey, "David Parish," 173-176. For the Odletown sign see (Northumberland, Pa.), *Der Republicaner*, January 23, 1813.

[21] Pierre Van Cortlandt, Jr., to Edmond Genet, June 1, 1812, Edmond Genet Papers, LC.

most affected by the war, and it was required to maintain an ascendancy there in order to retain control of the state government.[22] Moreover, the Clinton family had a long record of championing the interests of small farmers and tenants, and their hostility to the "Virginia Dynasty" for its alleged opposition to the vital interests of New York would find in these groups a ready reception.[23] To these circumstances favoring his campaign DeWitt Clinton added a unique personal combination of reforming benevolence and patrician elitism which defied precise definition as either Republicanism or Federalism. And from the period of the Columbia College riot in August 1811 onward, he seems to have governed his conduct with a view to drawing support from both political parties throughout the state rather than attempting to dominate the factionalized Republican coalition.[24] His position on the war—he would support it if it came, but if he were leading the administration war would not be necessary—was well suited to realize this political strategy in a state where a conflict with Great Britain was regarded as a mixed blessing.[25] For the same reasons, though, the administration was never able to anticipate the local problems and the consequences of waging a war, nor could it, given the increasingly unstable politics of the state, even be sure which New Yorkers could be trusted for appointment to implement its policies.

The preparations for war in New York were thus made in a context of political uncertainty, and the person most affected by the confusion arising from the conflict between Madison and Clinton was the Republican governor, Daniel D. Tompkins. Personally, Tompkins was inclined to support the idea of a war with Great Britain; the nation's

[22] In the statewide elections for lieutenant governor held in May 1811, DeWitt Clinton had a majority over two other candidates of 3,734 votes. A breakdown of the vote by districts revealed, however, that Clinton lost the Southern District to the Federalist candidate by 2,000 votes and shared the vote evenly with him in Eastern and Middle Districts. His victory therefore was dependent on his 5,000 vote majority in the Western District. See *Ontario Repository*, May 21, 1811.

[23] E. Wilder Spaulding, *His Excellency George Clinton: Critic of the Constitution* (2d ed., Port Washington, 1964), 22, 176. See also Ellis, *Landlords and Farmers*, 5, 29. *Albany Register*, April 7, 1812; *Ontario Repository*, August 4 and 25, 1812.

[24] See Robert W. July, *The Essential New Yorker: Gulian Crommelin Verplanck* (Durham, 1951), 33-42. Craig R. Hanyan, "DeWitt Clinton and Partisanship: The Development of Clintonianism from 1811 to 1820," *New-York Historical Society Quarterly* 56 (1972), 111, 114, 124, 125, 130-131. Jabez D. Hammond suggests that by 1811 Clinton's position in the state Republican party was slipping because of rising opposition from the Tammany faction, hence his attempt to create a new constituency for himself. See Hammond, *The History of Political Parties in the State of New York* (4th ed., Cooperstown, 1844-1848), II, 291-292.

[25] Dorothie Bobbé, *DeWitt Clinton* (New York, 1923), 181.

honor required vindication by force, and he felt that both he and the state should play a vital role in the effort. He even offered to assist William Henry Harrison against the northwestern Indians provided that he and his supporters were given warning enough to "muster up our courage, brush our beavers, and grind our swords."[26] Having long believed that New York should not be caught unprepared for war, the governor had, on several occasions in the past, offered the administration full access to and use of the state arsenals in the hope that the federal government would assume some of the costs of the state's military budget.[27] Since the War Department refused to fulfill these hopes, Tompkins, in his annual message to the state legislature on January 28, 1812, recommended that New York prepare itself for war. He suggested that the militia be called into camp for training and that the seacoast and western frontier be garrisoned.[28]

Yet Tompkins also realized that his actions would have to be governed largely by the way in which DeWitt Clinton attempted to realize his political ambitions throughout 1812. Ideally, the governor wanted to avoid political discord in the state during war, preferring to see the Republican party united on "cardinal principles without reference to men."[29] Such unity, however, was beyond his personal power to accomplish. Although he had strong support from the pro-administration Tammany faction of the party in New York City and was popular with Republican voters generally, Tompkins had held office since 1808 mainly because DeWitt Clinton and Judge Ambrose Spencer had agreed to put him forward in the aftermath of the intraparty struggles among the Clinton, Lewis, Livingston, and Burr factions as the least objectionable Republican in the state.[30] Continuing Republican factionalism thus served to remind Tompkins, as one of his correspondents pointed out, that he was, in a sense, only "nominally" governor of the state.[31] His actions up until the declaration of the war therefore reflected a cautious ambivalence that was born of the need not to depart too far from the wishes of the more important Republican leaders.

[26] Tompkins to William K. Paulding, December 3, 1811, Hugh Hastings, ed., *The Public Papers of Daniel D. Tompkins* (Albany, 1898-1903), II, 361-362.

[27] Tompkins to Eustis, November 15, 1809; to Paul Hamilton, January 4, 1810, Daniel D. Tompkins Letterbook, LC. See also Tompkins to Eustis, December 30, 1811, LRRS.

[28] Address to New York legislature, January 28, 1812; and Tompkins to Abraham Van Vechten, February 4, 1812, Hastings, *Papers of Tompkins*, II, 443-457, 459-467.

[29] Tompkins to Robert Macomb, April 6, 1812, ibid., 526. See also Tompkins to William Irving, April 4, 1812; to Henry Rutgers, April 6, 1812; and to Silvanus Miller, April 13, 1812, ibid., 524, 533-535, 547-548.

[30] Hammond, *Political Parties*, II, 238-240.

[31] Jonathan Varnum to Tompkins, April 5, 1811, Tompkins Papers, NYSL.

Consequently, while Tompkins had expressed his disapproval of the Clintonian stand on the Bank of America—finally going to the extent of proroguing the state legislature at the end of March to prevent the bank's charter—he was careful to avoid an open break with Clinton. He argued that Clinton had not shared his supporters' views on the bank issue—which was largely true—and throughout April 1812 representatives of the governor met with the Clintonians for negotiations, hoping that these would "afford an excellent opportunity of reuniting the party" on the basis of pitting "purely republicanism against federalism."[32] These discussions were not successful, and Robert Macomb reported to Tompkins that "the friends of Mr. C" showed no "discernment or discretion"; but even as late as May, when the Republican caucus of the New York legislature nominated Clinton for the Presidency, the governor did not denounce the schismatic candidacy.[33] And, when Clinton and many of the New York Congressmen began to argue for delaying the declaration of war on the grounds that the defenses of the state were "not sufficient to meet it," Tompkins was in full agreement.[34] Since his prorogation of the legislature had ended all chance that the state could complete the defense plans outlined in his annual message, the governor therefore asked the administration to pay greater attention to the problems of defending New York's long frontier with Canada.[35]

The War Department, unable to fathom the political complexities of the state that was to serve as the springboard for two invasions of Canada, reacted by virtually ignoring Tompkins as it went on with its preparations. Admittedly, Eustis asked the governor at the end of March to place 1,600 militia at various points on the frontiers of New York, but Tompkins believed that these troops were only for embargo enforcement. He was surprised to learn on meeting Dearborn in New York City some weeks later that, in the general's opinion, they were for "covering the frontiers of the state against any Indian or any other depredations." Dearborn's definition of the areas these militia had to patrol must also have seemed grossly unrealistic, since he told Tompkins he might consider "the settlements of the St. Lawrence as included

[32] Tompkins to Macomb, April 6, 1812; Macomb to Tompkins, March 31, 1812, ibid. For Clinton's views see DeWitt Clinton to Henry Remsen, March 3, 1812, DeWitt Clinton Papers, NYPL; and *Albany Register*, April 21 and 28, 1812.

[33] Macomb to Tompkins, April 3, 1812, Tompkins Papers, NYSL. See also Maturin Livingston to Gallatin, May 30, 1812, *Gallatin Papers*.

[34] DeWitt to James Clinton, April 19, 1812, Clinton Papers, NYPL. Peter B. Porter to Eustis, April 20, 1812, LRRS.

[35] Tompkins to Porter, May 12, 1812, Tompkins Papers, NYSL.

in the Black river country and the whole distance between the outlet of Lake Erie and the old Niagara for as included in the term Niagara."[36] Moreover, on the role of the state in future offensive operations against Canada, Dearborn simply failed to take Tompkins into his confidence, remarking later that it was pointless to raise the subject until Congress had changed the volunteer laws.[37] Tompkins tried to seek further information on the state's role in the coming war, but often his letters to the War Department were not answered, while the administration, partly by habit and partly by default, continued to bestow most of its patronage on Clintonian Republicans.[38]

Tompkins, only too well aware of the need to build up greater support for a war as well as improve the defenses of the state, could not understand the attitude of the administration. He frequently complained that War Department policy as it related to New York was "very obscurely expressed," and he was quite at a loss to see why the administration continued to grant patronage to men bent only on its overthrow.[39] His confusion here was shared by other New York Republicans who felt that they could not support Clinton in his bid for the Presidency either. Ambrose Spencer, in particular, feared that the behavior of his brother-in-law was a "deleterious influence" which could lead to the "ascendancy of federalism," a possibility which he tried to counter by closing down the Clintonian *Albany Register*. To suppress this source of "the most abominable political heresies ever calculated to mislead the public mind," Spencer first sued the editor, Solomon Southwick, for libel, then pressed false charges of bribery against him, and finally sent his son, John Canfield Spencer, to offer to buy the paper outright for $10,000.[40] He was also a party to the attempt made in October 1812 by William King of Maine and John Taylor of New York to prevail on Clinton to support the war by

---

[36] Eustis to Tompkins, March 24 and April 8, 1812, LSMA; and Dearborn to Eustis, May 10, 1812, Letters Received by the Secretary of War Relating to Indian Affairs (M-271), Records of the Bureau of Indian Affairs (RG 75), NA.

[37] Dearborn to Eustis, May 21, 1812, LRRS.

[38] Tompkins to Eustis, January 19 and March 31, 1812, ibid.; Tompkins to George Fleming, April 2, 1812, Miscellaneous MSS, NYHS. For complaints on the patronage issue see Tompkins to Porter, February 29, 1812, and to Paulding, April 3, 1812, Hastings, *Papers of Tompkins*, II, 510, 522; William Keteltas to Madison, September 12, 1812, and Abraham Lansing to Madison, September 23, 1812, Madison Papers, LC. See also John Smith to Gallatin, October 6, 1812, *Gallatin Papers*.

[39] Tompkins to Porter, May 13, 1812, Peter B. Porter Papers, BEHS. See also John McKinley to Madison, March 27, April 1, and June 1, 1812; and Robert Fulton to Madison, April 30, 1812, Madison Papers, LC.

[40] *Albany Republican*, April 11, 13, 18, and 28, 1812; *Albany Register*, April 14, August 7, October 27 and 29, 1812; *Ontario Repository*, October 29, 1812.

withdrawing his presidential candidacy in return for guarantees of future backing in 1816.[41] The effort was unsuccessful, but Spencer, nonetheless, felt that his work on behalf of the war merited some recognition from the administration, preferably the appointment of John Armstrong to the cabinet. Yet Madison, much to Spencer's disgust, did little more than give the judge's nephew an ensign's commission in the army.[42]

The President, in truth, was as suspicious of the anti-Clintonian Republicans as he was of the Clintonians, believing them to be equally unprincipled and ambitious. Madison revealed these fears at the end of May by appointing the Republican governor of New Jersey, Joseph Bloomfield, as commander of the forces defending New York City. As the *Albany Register* remarked, this appointment of a supporter of Aaron Burr was "no compliment" to the Republicans of New York, and the President's inability to distinguish between his enemies and his friends did nothing at all to help Tompkins prepare the state for war; Bloomfield was already too committed both as governor of New Jersey and as the superintending officer of recruiting there to cope effectively with the defense of the nation's largest port.[43] Nor was Dearborn, whose headquarters for the war were supposed to be at Albany, of any greater assistance. Two days before the declaration of war, the general informed the governor that he would be based in Boston for some time and that, while he had no idea of what measures might be taken for the defense of New York, he was expecting that state to raise a "considerable portion" of the men for the army in accordance with the arrangements made in Washington earlier. What those arrangements were, Dearborn neglected to inform Tompkins, but he concluded with the optimistic remark that New Yorkers were "good hands at managing their affairs" and that he took it for granted that they would "ultimately do well."[44]

The contents of this letter stung Tompkins into action, and he began to prepare New York for war in earnest. Had he not done so, he could possibly have lost the initiative to Clinton. The presidential aspirant, immediately upon hearing of the declaration of war, requested the governor to give him a command in the New York militia so that he

[41] Ambrose Spencer to William King, October 24, 1812, William King Papers, MeHS. *Albany Register*, October 27 and November 6, 1812. See also John C. Fitzpatrick, ed., *The Autobiography of Martin Van Buren* (Washington, D.C., 1920), 41.

[42] See Spencer to Madison, April 18, 1812, Madison Papers, LC. Spencer to Armstrong, April 9, 1812, William Astor Chanler Collection of John Armstrong Photostats, NYHS.

[43] *Albany Register*, August 14, 1812. Bloomfield to Eustis, July 15, 1812, LRRS.

[44] Dearborn to Tompkins, June 16, 1812, Tompkins Papers, NYSL.

might begin organizing the state for war.[45] The New York Council of Appointment, being dominated by Clinton's supporters, promptly commissioned him as a major general, but Tompkins tried to ignore him by declining to assign him a specific command. Instead, he began to call out the militia himself, and he ordered divisions to take up defensive positions on the coasts and the frontiers. He also issued calls for volunteers to join the forces that were starting to gather at the army headquarters in Greenbush. Informing the War Department of his actions, he again requested the administration to indicate clearly its plans for the supply, command, and employment of the troops based in New York.[46]

Dearborn's letter also made Tompkins realize that it was time to break openly with Clinton. In all innocence, the general had asked whether the New Yorker was seriously aiming at the Presidency or whether his nomination was only a "scarecrow to frighten other states into a consent to make Mr. Clinton Vice President."[47] Since the administration shared some of Dearborn's inability to understand the "political management" of New York, it had not sought to weld the anti-Clintonian Republicans—whose number included not only Spencer and Armstrong but also Morgan Lewis, John Tayler, Nathan Sanford, Erastus Root, Elisha Jenkins, Peter B. Porter, Matthew Tillotson, most of the Livingstons, and the Tammany Society—into a political force that would support the war; but Tompkins now attempted to do so. A sufficient degree of Republican unity, he believed, would carry the state through the difficulties of war to victory; if "we maintain the spirit of union, perseverance and patriotism," the governor informed one of his militia generals, "I feel a confidence that we shall make ourselves masters of Canada by militia only. . . ."[48] With the abandonment of Clinton, Spencer became, for Governor Tompkins, the most important Republican leader in the state, and, after consulting with him, Porter, and Jenkins, Tompkins suggested to the administration that it appoint Armstrong as commander of the forces in New York City. The general's "talent and experience," wrote the governor, "ought not to be lost to the country in the approaching crisis. His patriotism

---

[45] Bobbé, *DeWitt Clinton*, 182. Clinton to Madison, June 20, 1812, LRRS. Tompkins to Clinton, June 24, 1812, Hastings, *Papers of Tompkins*, II, 639-640.

[46] Tompkins to Eustis, June 27, 1812, Hastings, *Papers of Tompkins*, I, 653. See also, in the *Papers*, Tompkins's letters to various militia and volunteer officers after the declaration of war, 659-670.

[47] See note 44.

[48] Tompkins to Amos Hall, July 8, 1812, Hastings, *Papers of Tompkins*, III, 22-23.

is awake, and he ... is disposed to do everything in his power to promote the interests of his country."[49]

This intention to create a more cohesive prowar Republican faction in New York, however, was complicated by the long illness, and eventual death on July 2, of Major General Peter Gansevoort, commander of the state militia. His replacement would not only have to command the state forces in war but would also have to be acceptable to a Council of Appointment that consisted of the governor and four Clintonians. The only solution that Tompkins could see to this problem was to suggest that the War Department indicate a preference between either himself or the Federalist politician Stephen Van Rensselaer as commander of the New York forces. Tompkins had hopes that he might be the choice, but, regardless of the administration's preference, he made it clear to Eustis that he regarded the appointment as only a temporary arrangement, until either Dearborn had returned to Albany or some other regular army officer had taken over the command in person.[50] On this occasion, the administration responded quickly to Tompkins's initiatives, approving of his disposition of the militia and hastening to offer Armstrong the command at New York City.[51] Armstrong accepted, subject to the condition that his command was an independent one, which would spare him from the indignity of being subordinate to Dearborn, to whom he had been superior in rank during the Revolution. The current commander in New York City, Bloomfield, suddenly became expendable—the more so since the administration had received reports that Clinton had approached him over the electoral votes of New Jersey—and he was quickly reassigned to Plattsburg. The Clintonians objected to this change of commanders as rank electioneering, but Armstrong defended the administration with the remark that it was not the time "to quarrel about straws."[52]

In regard to the command of the New York forces, though, the administration disappointed Tompkins by indicating a preference for the appointment of Stephen Van Rensselaer, the Patroon landlord of the Hudson Valley. Although Van Rensselaer was a Federalist and his

[49] Tompkins to Porter, June 20, 1812, LRRS. *Albany Register*, August 14, 18, and 25, 1812.

[50] Tompkins to Eustis, June 27, 1812, Hastings, *Papers of Tompkins*, I, 653; to Andrew Sitcher, June 13, 1812, *Papers*, II, 624-625; to Paulding, June 28, 1812, *Papers*, II, 645; to Porter, July 8, 1812, Porter Papers, BEHS.

[51] Eustis to Tompkins, July 6, 1812; to Armstrong, July 20, 1812, LSMA.

[52] Armstrong to Spencer, July 16, 1812, Chanler Collection, NYHS. John Montgomery to Gallatin, July 1 and 3, 1812, *Gallatin Papers*. *Albany Register*, July 14 and August 14, 1812. See also Armstrong to Solomon Southwick, August 17, 1812, Chanler Collection, NYHS.

presence in the army would prove to be a major organizational obstacle, there was a certain logic behind his selection. He had become, on the death of Gansevoort, the ranking senior officer in the New York militia, and as such could not easily be passed over, especially since the War Department, given the failure of volunteering and delays in recruiting, had a greater need of the services of state militia than it had anticipated. Moreover, if Van Rensselaer could rally a signficant number of Federalists behind the war in defense of his state, Clinton's prospects for attaining the Presidency through an alliance of antiwar Republicans and Federalists would inevitably be undermined. Nevertheless, Eustis endorsed Van Rensselaer's appointment only as a temporary measure, and, like Tompkins, he assumed that Dearborn would eventually return to Albany to take full responsibility for the invasions of Canada.[53]

In the meantime, the War Department forwarded as quickly as possible all available recruits to New York. In Washington, the prospects made at least one army officer drunk with optimism; Inspector General Alexander Smyth of Virginia dispatched the troops northward with the vainglorious injunction "to decorate with laurels the tomb of Montgomery and plant the American eagle on the walls of Quebec."[54] The realities, however, were very different, particularly on the Niagara Peninsula. Throughout western New York, there was little enthusiasm at the prospect of invading Upper Canada. Great Britain, not the United States, held naval supremacy on Lake Ontario and had the power, as New Yorkers quickly came to realize, to disrupt their trade and strike at their settlements in retaliation against Madison's policies. British vessels, in fact, sailed the lake at will in the summer and fall of 1812, occasionally entering American harbors and towing off ships without resistance. Also, many houses in Buffalo, including that belonging to Congressman Peter B. Porter, were within range of British cannon in Fort Erie. Since many New Yorkers thus saw their enemy as ready and able to carry the war to them while the United States was barely organized for resistance, let alone attack, it was hardly surprising that they should have felt psychologically on the defensive.[55]

Yet even remaining on the defensive posed almost as many problems as did taking the offensive. Extensive calls on the local militia would diminish the labor force at harvest time, which threatened the Holland Land Company as well as its tenants with a serious loss of income. In

[53] Eustis to Tompkins, July 6, 1812, LSMA.

[54] Alexander Smyth to Isaac Coles, July 9, 1812, LSAG.

[55] Porter to Eustis, June 28, 1812, LRRS. *Ontario Repository*, July 6 and 7, October 6, 1812. See also Orsemus Turner, *History of the Pioneer Settlement of the Phelps and Gorham's Purchase and Morris' Reserve* (Rochester, 1851), 516-517.

fact, the company was already experiencing a loss of business, since the news of the war had provoked a panic and an exodus of refugees who crowded the Buffalo road, where they collided with soldiers and prospective settlers still advancing toward Niagara.[56] Tompkins fully realized the seriousness of the situation, fearing that the "spirit of the yeomanry" was being "broken down," thus impoverishing the state and rendering the war effort "inefficient."[57] Even those settlers who had remained near the peninsula constituted, according to Peter B. Porter, an extremely unreliable militia force for either offense or defense, since they were prepared to do no more than watch the situation by marching and countermarching along the Niagara River.[58] Nor did the groups of raw regular recruits, volunteers, and militia who were beginning to arrive on the frontier seem likely to improve matters. Their officers quarreled without any clear sense of purpose, and almost all the forces lacked arms and basic camp equipment; on one occasion Tompkins almost derived a certain degree of satisfaction from observing that if the New York militia was in a poor condition, the United States regulars were considerably worse.[59]

Since the Niagara Peninsula would almost inevitably be the scene of some fighting, Tompkins, Porter, and the Holland Company agent, Ellicott, all came to the same conclusion—that the anxiety of the inhabitants could be relieved only if the war were brought to a speedy and successful end. Ellicott, in early July, delivered an address to the Holland Company settlers in which he assured them—contrary to his personal judgment—that there was no danger of invasion and that within eight to twelve weeks Canada would "be annexed to the United States."[60] Porter likewise argued to both Eustis and Tompkins that "the policy, interest, and quiet of this state and the United States require that no time be lost in preparing for an invasion of Canada at this place." He suggested an eight-week training period for a force of 5,000 men, half regular and half volunteer, before they crossed over into Upper Canada and seized the British fortifications there.[61] Tompkins agreed, believing that the prompt appearance of an organized American force on the peninsula would end the war, especially if it

[56] Orsemus Turner, *Pioneer History of the Holland Purchase of Western New York* (Buffalo, 1850), 586-587. Chazanof, *Joseph Ellicott*, 122-125.

[57] Tompkins to John Bullus, July 13, 1812, Hastings, *Papers of Tompkins*, III, 30-32.

[58] Porter to Tompkins, July 21, 1812, Tompkins Papers, NYSL.

[59] Louis L. Babcock, *The War of 1812 on the Niagara Frontier* (Buffalo, 1927), 35. Tompkins to Macomb, August 7, 1812, Hastings, *Papers of Tompkins*, III, 60-61; Tompkins to Dearborn, August 26, 1812, Henry Dearborn Papers, MHS.

[60] Turner, *Holland Purchase*, 587-588.

[61] Porter to Tompkins, July 9, 1812, Tompkins Papers, NYSL.

was accompanied by a proclamation extending "the hand of fellowship" to the Canadian militia, which, he felt would then revolt against Great Britain.[62] He reminded General Van Rensselaer that he had the discretion to commence offensive operations, though the governor advised him not to do so until a reasonable number of regular troops had been assembled to accompany the militia.[63]

For its own reasons, the War Department was prepared to fall in with this line of thinking. Since it seemed the best way to relieve pressures on Hull in the Northwest, Eustis ordered Dearborn to leave Boston, return to Albany, and devote some of his attention to the Niagara invasion.[64] To provide more troops for this purpose, the Secretary of War requested Governor Simon Snyder of Pennsylvania to forward to Albany 2,000 volunteers with all speed, and he also sent northward an additional force of 1,650 regulars under Brigadier General Smyth, recently moved from his Inspector's desk in Washington into active service.[65] Thus, under the pressure of events both in the Northwest and in New England, the invasion from western New York was becoming of greater importance than the administration had originally allowed for.[66] Dearborn's priorities, however, were less flexible, and he was reluctant to step into the role Eustis was casting for him. Although at Greenbush he would have control over all the forces raised in New York and New England, the general had never believed that his command would be so extensive as to require him to organize the armies for the attack on Montreal as well as for that across the Niagara.[67] It was to point out the difficulty of performing both these tasks that he wrote an unfortunately phrased letter to Eustis on July 26 inquiring who was to have the command in Upper Canada.[68] By this, Dearborn seems to have meant no more than to ask who was to organize and lead the invading forces across the Niagara Peninsula, but the administration never gave him a clear-cut answer, implying instead in its correspondence with him that his discretion to take over at Niagara

[62] Tompkins to Macomb, July 12, 1812, ibid.

[63] Tompkins to Stephen Van Rensselaer, August 14, 1812, Hastings, *Papers of Tompkins*, III, 78-80.

[64] Eustis to Dearborn, August 1, 1812, LSMA.

[65] Eustis to Simon Snyder, August 13, 1812, LSMA.

[66] See Madison to Dearborn, August 9, 1812; to Jefferson, August 17, 1812, Madison Papers, LC.

[67] As Dearborn wrote on April 6, "the conquest of Upper Canada will not, I presume, be considered as under the direction of the force destined against Lower Canada. . . ." To Madison, Parker Papers, HSP. See also Dearborn to Jefferson, March 10, 1812, Jefferson Papers, LC.

[68] Dearborn to Eustis, July 26, 1812, LRRS.

somehow increased as the prospects for a serious assault on Montreal diminished.[69]

It was with some reluctance, therefore, that Dearborn returned to Albany at the end of July and made arrangements with Tompkins to have his authority recognized by all the troops in New York. He also called another 5,200 militia into the service of the United States, but having asserted his control over these forces he then declined to use it, adhering to the position that his command did not extend to Upper Canada.[70] In fact, he came to believe that the area defined by Niagara, Albany, and Plattsburg included "three distinct commands," and throughout August he was still far too embroiled in New England politics and their effects on the campaign against Montreal to show much interest in New York affairs.[71] These he wished to leave to New Yorkers, while confining his role to giving advice from a distance to Tompkins and Van Rensselaer.[72] Dearborn's only major decision while he was at Albany was to arrange an armistice with the governor of Lower Canada on August 8 in the belief that it would give the Americans more time to prepare for action.[73] Unfortunately, the armistice, while delighting the British, only bewildered the administration and the New Yorkers. Nicholas Gray, Tompkins's private secretary, complained bitterly that "we [were] all knocked on the head in consequence of this news of the armistice. All were preparing to cross over to Canada when this news arrived," he claimed, and "we could now be playing ball on the banks of the Niagara river."[74]

The administration quickly repudiated the armistice on August 15 and ordered Dearborn to proceed with an attack on Upper Canada.[75] The general, in response, duly terminated the armistice on August 25, immersed himself in the details of his staff work, and vaguely told Van Rensselaer, Smyth, and Tompkins to get on with the invasion, coordinating it if at all possible with American movements in the Northwest. He also urged Tompkins to "take the field" at the head of a New

---

[69] See, for example, Eustis to Dearborn, August 15 and 20, September 21, 1812, LSMA.

[70] Dearborn to Tompkins, August 13 and 14, 1812, Henry Dearborn Letterbooks, NYHS. Tompkins to Macomb, August 7, 1812; to Dearborn, August 14, 1812, Hastings, *Papers of Tompkins*, III, 81-82.

[71] Dearborn to Stephen Van Rensselaer, July 29, 1812, Solomon Van Rensselaer, *A Narrative of the Affair at Queenstown* (New York, 1836), 25.

[72] Dearborn to Eustis, August, 10, 1812, LRRS.

[73] Same to same, August 9, 1812, Dearborn Letterbooks, NYHS.

[74] Nicholas Gray to Tompkins, August 19, 1812, E. A. Cruikshank, ed., *Documentary History of the Campaign on the Niagara Frontier* (Welland, Ont. 1898-1902), III, 193. Morgan Lewis to Madison, August 21, 1812, Madison Papers, LC.

[75] Eustis to Dearborn, August 15 and 20, 1812 LSMA.

York army, arguing that the governor's presence at Niagara would "give an additional spirit to the interior country and fresh vigor to the troops in service."[76] No doubt, Dearborn felt that he had been unfairly placed in a difficult position. Even in Greenbush, he was still over 300 miles from the Niagara front, and had he gone there in person to exercise his command, he would have had to abandon all pretense of an advance on Montreal. Dearborn sometimes talked of going to Niagara to take command, though he never told the New Yorkers this. But at the same time, he never gave up the idea of attacking Montreal either, nor did the administration explicitly instruct him to do so.[77] These difficulties notwithstanding, Dearborn's ambivalence and reluctance to take full responsibility for matters which the War Department and the New York Republicans considered properly to belong to him paralyzed the Niagara campaign. At one point, Tompkins, who was constantly trying to raise volunteers, was compelled to confess that an invasion of Canada was "a matter of uncertainty as far as my knowledge goes."[78] The political and military consequences of Dearborn's vacillations, moreover, were fatal. New York Republicans were left with the impression that the administration had abandoned them to carry on the war alone. "For God's sake," Porter raged to Eustis, "arouse and put forth the energies of the nation. The poor but patriotic citizens of . . . the frontiers of New York are . . . alone called out because their march to the frontier is shorter . . . while the rich inhabitants of Pennsylvania are lolling in security and ease."[79]

Just as serious too was Dearborn's failure to clarify the command structure within the army at Niagara. He did nothing to reduce the tensions and confusion inherent in a situation where an army of largely Republican volunteers and militia was commanded by a general and staff officers from the Federalist party. The political effects of Van Rensselaer's appointment thus became precisely the opposite to those that the War Department had intended. "General Van Rensselaer," complained Republican leader John Canfield Spencer, "is openly de-

---

[76] Dearborn to Van Rensselaer, August 25, September 1, 2, 26, and 29, and October 4, 1812; to Tompkins, September 5 and 7, 1812, Dearborn Letterbooks, NYHS. Dearborn to Eustis, September 2, 1812, LRRS.

[77] See, for example, the contradictory stands taken in Dearborn's letters to the following: to Eustis, September 1 and 2, 1812, LRRS; to Bloomfield, September 18, October 1, 11 and 23, 1812. Dearborn Letterbooks NYHS; and to Madison, October 24, 1812, Madison Papers, LC.

[78] Tompkins to I. R. Brown, September 28, 1812, Hastings, *Papers of Tompkins*, III, 152.

[79] Porter to Eustis, August 30, 1812, *Documentary History*, III, 275. See also Porter to Tompkins, August 31, 1812. Tompkins Papers, NYSL.

claring against the war, represents it as undertaken from base, selfish motives, states that General Porter voted for it to make money," while his aides "whisper the same thing and worse. . . ." Spencer hardly needed to add that this partisan behavior irritated the army and that many soldiers lost "confidence in the justice of their cause and that zeal in its support . . . necessary to the successful termination of the war." The army, he concluded, would "never go to Canada under [its] present officers."[80]

The political strife within the army was greatly intensified by the news, reaching Niagara at the end of August, of the surrender of Detroit. Even the rumors of this event, Porter wrote, brought "the public mind to a state of madness," which the British then skillfully exploited by parading Hull and his captured troops before the shocked Americans.[81] The accusations of treachery that were produced on all sides to account for this failure of American arms led Porter and Solomon Van Rensselaer, the general's aide and kinsman, to trade personal insults, culminating in challenges for a duel which was only prevented with the greatest difficulty.[82] With these developments, the rank and file of the army became thoroughly alarmed, especially by the behavior of their superiors. Several militia regiments were on the point of mutiny, and, having neither shoes nor pay as well as no desire to share the fate of Hull's army, they told their commander that they wished to be sent home.[83] Thus the American army began to disintegrate, even as it was still being formed.

Throughout September, Stephen Van Rensselaer, who was never too sure of his abilities as a commander at best, was clearly in an impossible position.[84] He attributed his difficulties to the "weak and despicable" administration in Washington and to the politicking of local Republicans such as Porter and Spencer.[85] Tompkins was a less obvious target; the Federalists could only complain that, by traveling constantly between Albany and New York City, the governor "so managed and economized his time" as to avoid public involvement in

[80] John Canfield Spencer to Tompkins, September 5, 1812, Daniel D. Tompkins Papers, NYHS. (Peter B. Porter was absent from Congress when the vote for war was taken in June 1812.) See also Chazanof, "Ellicott, the Embargo, and the War of 1812," 11.

[81] Porter to Tompkins, August 30, 1812, Tompkins Papers, NYSL.

[82] Stephen Van Rensselaer to Dearborn, September 1, 1812, *Documentary History*, III, 230. Porter to Solomon Van Rensselaer, January 1813, Catherine V. Bonney, *A Legacy of Historical Gleanings* (Albany, 1875), I, 287, and see also 215.

[83] Stephen Van Rensselaer to Tompkins, August 31, 1812, *Gleanings*, I, 223.

[84] Same to Tompkins, September 17, 1812, *Narrative*, 17.

[85] Same to his wife, September 1, 1812, *Documentary History*, III, 231; Solomon Van Rensselaer to Morgan Lewis, September 11, 1812, ibid., 254.

the problems at Niagara.[86] Tompkins had, in fact, hoped that Van Rensselaer would more or less act as governor while at his command, but the political realities of his position made this quite impossible. Both Porter and the Van Rensselaers privately agreed that the only remedy at Niagara was for the War Department to relieve the Federalist commander and replace him with a Republican of equivalent stature, be it Tompkins, Dearborn, Clinton, or Armstrong.[87] Yet Van Rensselaer could hardly request this without exposing himself to imputations of cowardice. He therefore concluded he had no alternative but to remain at his command, taking whatever action was necessary to uphold his reputation and honor, even though he suspected, as one of his aides said, that he might be "Hulled" as a scapegoat for Republican incompetence.[88]

By now, Dearborn was rather more aware of the political turmoil in New York, but he nevertheless heightened Van Rensselaer's suspicions by advising him to retreat if he felt the British forces were too strong or should they attempt to attack American territory.[89] The Patroon's reaction was that he could not think of such a step "until [he had] tried some blustering Democrats who pretend to be full of fighting. . . ."[90] Dearborn then further complicated the politics of the army by devolving his own responsibilities for the Niagara region on Alexander Smyth, and ordering him to cooperate with Van Rensselaer.[91] On September 29, Smyth arrived at Buffalo, where he established his base, announced his presence by letter to Van Rensselaer, and refused thereafter to have any meetings with him. Smyth's action here divided the American forces into two camps—one at Buffalo above, and the other at Lewiston below the Niagara Falls—after which the two generals disputed the best point from which to launch an attack. Their arguments were inconclusive, since the lightly manned British positions opposite Lewiston were safeguarded by the extremely turbulent current of the Niagara River, while their defenses opposite Buffalo, where the river was easier to cross, were considerably stronger.[92]

[86] John Lovett to Abraham Van Vechten, October 25, 1812, *Gleanings*, I, 274.

[87] Porter to Tompkins, August 39, 1812, Tompkins Papers, NYSL; Solomon Van Rensselaer to Lewis, September 11, 1812, *Documentary History*, III, 254.

[88] Lovett to John Alexander, August 26, 1812; and to Van Vechten, September 22, 1812, *Gleanings*, I, 219, 236. Stephen Van Rensselaer to Dearborn, October 8, 1812, *Documentary History*, IV, 40-41; and to Eustis, October 14, 1812, *Narrative*, 64.

[89] Dearborn to Stephen Van Rensselaer, September 2, 1812, *Narrative*, 43.

[90] Stephen Van Rensselaer to Van Vechten, September 5, 1812, *Documentary History*, III, 237.

[91] Dearborn to Eustis, September 14, 1812, LRRS.

[92] See Babcock, *The Niagara Frontier*, 42.

The strategy and organization of an attack therefore required careful consideration and a close understanding between Van Rensselaer and Smyth, which was precluded, however, by the dislike of the latter for associating with Federalists, New Yorkers, and militia.

The aides of the Federalist general thought about coercing Smyth into cooperation, but Van Rensselaer opposed them, deciding instead that he could upstage the Virginia Republican by crossing the Niagara with his own forces, which by October numbered just over 3,000 men, and driving the British off the peninsula.[93] In Washington, Madison had immediately noted the potentially dangerous effects of the division of the American forces between the two generals, but, by relying on Dearborn to overcome them, he really did no more than refer the problem back to its source. Dearborn, too, found the division of the army "regrettable," although later he remarked merely that he disliked the construction Smyth and Van Rensselaer had placed on his advice.[94] Yet even the fragmentation of the American army need not have proved fatal, had the troops had greater confidence in their commanders. After some initial difficulties with obtaining boats and navigating the river, Van Rensselaer did, on October 12, manage to place advance parties in Canadian territory which successfully occupied Queenstown Heights. The majority of the militia in his army, however, refused to leave American soil, fearing that their general might surrender them; so they confirmed Spencer's prediction that Van Rensselaer could never lead an army into Canada. Consequently, the general was compelled to surrender the troops stranded at Queenstown Heights, after which he made a month's truce.[95] He resigned his command in favor of Smyth on October 16, convinced that he had been betrayed.

A remarkably similar tragedy of errors and misunderstanding then followed under Smyth's brief period of command. Dearborn cautioned the Virginia general against taking action unless his senior officers were agreed upon it, and he stressed the need to cultivate harmonious relations between the various bodies of troops in his army.[96] Yet Dearborn, by leaving Albany for Plattsburg on November 8, finally abdicated any responsibility for seeing that these orders were obeyed, and

---

[93] *Narrative*, 19-21.

[94] Madison to Monroe, September 21, 1812, James Monroe Papers, LC. Dearborn to Stephen Van Rensselaer, October 21, 1812, Dearborn Letterbooks, NYHS.

[95] See Babcock, *The Niagara Frontier*, 44-51.

[96] Dearborn to Smyth, October 21, 1812, HR 13A-F4, LRHR. Smyth's papers for the Niagara campaign can be found in this source, since he sent them to the Speaker of the House, Langdon Cheves, on February 8, 1814, to assist the congressional committee that was investigating the conduct of the war.

Smyth, though far more cautious in military matters than his pompous rhetoric suggested, then proceeded to alienate his troops as much as Van Rensselaer had done. The new commander took up his duties promising success where the "imbecility" of others had led to failure.[97] He prevailed upon Porter and other local Republicans to raise additional volunteers from Ontario and Genesee counties but refused to merge this "undisciplined rabble" with his regulars, fearing that the latter would be "corrupted" by the contact.[98] He indulged in indiscreet observations about local politics and even stated that the nearby Seneca Indians could provide more reliable forces than the "degenerated race" of New Yorkers. The volunteers became resentful and mutinous, and several companies announced that they would not follow him into Canada. Thus, as one Buffalo resident reported, the American army was again "demoralized" by "distrust of their leader."[99]

Smyth, no doubt, felt that these developments provided further justification for his contemptuous attitude toward all military forces other than regulars. But when the number of these in his army began to decline from outbreaks of dysentery and measles, the prospects for his winning the military glory he had so boastfully promised were greatly reduced.[100] The inspectors' reports on his army revealed that even before they fell ill the men were in a miserable condition, invariably lacking clothing, arms, ammunition, and training, and for these reasons a majority of Smyth's officers refused to sanction an attack on the enemy.[101] Indeed, Smyth himself was greatly concerned about the condition of his regulars and had no intention of taking the offensive until they were better prepared. Yet the general, who was constantly taunted by Porter to redeem his rash promises, twice went through the motions at the end of November of putting advance parties across the river, embarking the army in boats, and calling on the British commander at Fort Erie to surrender, only to lose face when his officers

[97] Particularly offensive to New Yorkers were Smyth's proclamations to the army of November 10 and 17, 1812. See Frank H. Severance, ed., "The Case of Alexander Smyth," *Publications of the Buffalo Historical Society* 18 (1914), 226-229. See also *Albany Register*, November 20, 1812.

[98] Porter to Stephen Bates, November 12, 1812; Spencer to Bates, November 14, 1812, Porter Papers, BEHS. See also Thomas Parker to Smyth, October 22 and 30, 1812, and J. W. Livingston to Smyth, November 4, 1812, HR 13A-F4, LRHR.

[99] Josiah Robinson to Solomon Van Rensselaer, December 2, 1812, *Gleanings*, I, 283.

[100] Smyth to Dearborn, November 9, 1812, Severance, "Case of Alexander Smyth," 224. *Ontario Repository*, November 17, 1812.

[101] Inspectors' Reports on the 12th and 14th Infantry, October 5, 1812, LRAG. Porter to Smyth, October 22, 1812, HR 13A-F4, LRHR.

refused to alter their opinions.[102] After the second of these false starts on November 29, Smyth ended the campaign and dismissed the volunteers and militia. This time it was the troops who felt betrayed, and the volunteers expressed their resentment in such a dangerous and disorderly way that Smyth felt compelled to maintain a personal guard for his own safety. Local innkeepers then refused him hospitality for fear of provoking the angry troops into destroying their property.[103]

With the end of the campaign the humiliated Americans engaged in bitter recriminations. The War Department censured Smyth's conduct as "highly objectionable," believing that his aspersions about New Yorkers throughout October and November would turn voters against the administration.[104] The Republicans of western New York were even angrier and sent a deputation to Smyth demanding an explanation of his decision to call off the campaign. Unrepentant, the general told them it was not safe to invade Canada "relying on crowds who go to the banks of the Niagara to look on a battle as on a theatrical exhibition."[105] This outburst led the Buffalo papers to accuse Smyth of cowardice and Porter to challenge him to a duel.[106] Smyth accepted, convinced that Porter and his friends had created the outcry against him because they stood to lose money on unfulfilled army contracts.[107] The duel was a harmless affair, with each shot missing its target, and Smyth was thus cleared from imputations of cowardice, but this, as a Federalist sarcastically remarked, no doubt placed the British in Canada in a "desperate" situation. In reality, the very reverse was the case, and Smyth's decision to end the invasion led to the disintegration of the American army. His regulars continued to decline in numbers from sickness and desertion, while, in the first week in December, over half the Pennsylvania militia deserted, leaving their officers "at a loss." The Niagara Peninsula was consequently left in a truly wretched state of defense over the winter, with barely 2,600 troops to guard its entire length.[108]

[102] Smyth to Dearborn, October 30 and November 9, 1812, LRHR. For the refusal of the officers to sanction an invasion see William Winder to Smyth, November 25, 1812, LRHR, See also Smyth to Roger Sheaffe, November 28, 1812, LRHR and Severance, "Case of Alexander Smyth," 230, 231, 241.

[103] *Ontario Repository*, December 8, 1812.

[104] Eustis to Smyth, November 26, 1812, LSMA. *Albany Register*, December 1, 1812.

[105] Severance, "Case of Alexander Smyth," 236-239.

[106] Ibid., 240. Porter to the *Buffalo Gazette*, December 8, 1812, *Documentary History*, IV, 291-292.

[107] For Smyth's version of the campaign see Smyth to Dearborn, December 4, 1812, Dearborn Papers, MHS. *Ontario Repository*, December 13, 1812.

[108] *Ontario Repository*, December 22, 1812, and January 5, 1813. The returns of the 14th

Inevitably, these misfortunes greatly intensified antiwar and antiadministration sentiment in western New York. Madison was exposed to merciless criticism in newspaper accounts of how he plotted to lose American territory in order to claim credit for regaining it, and of how he retained incompetent officers to prove his firmness.[109] Local Republicans who struggled to support the war tried to maintain in response that the nation had been failed by Federalists generals, but the Federalists made it very clear that Smyth was "an arrogant Virginia democrat."[110] In the Congressional and presidential elections in November and December the Federalists and Clintonian Republicans therefore triumphed easily and rendered the "state of parties in New York," in Morgan Lewis's words "useless."[111] John Armstrong, as he reviewed the events some years later, apportioned the blame for these developments among all the individuals involved in the campaign, but the administration came to feel that Dearborn more than anyone else was responsible.[112] Of all the participants in the New York campaign throughout 1812, only Dearborn had sufficient authority to impose some semblance of order on the confusion of events, although, in fairness to him, he could not easily have done so without neglecting matters in New England which he believed to be more important. Nevertheless, his inactivity and preoccupation with affairs outside New York undeniably let the personal and political conflicts among Van Rensselaer, Smyth, and the local Republicans go unchecked, with results that were fatal to the invasions. As Monroe later pointed out, his decision to leave the Niagara campaign in "state hands" allowed administration goals to become "perverted to local and selfish interests."[113] And Monroe's verdict here was given added force by Dearborn's behavior in New England. Despite the general's belief that his efforts in New England justified his conduct with respect to Niagara, his activ-

and 23rd Infantry compiled by Lieutenant Colonel Boerstler show a decline in their effective numbers from 300 to 227 between November 29 and December 1, 1812. On December 5 the 12th and 20th Infantry combined could only muster 221 men fit for duty. See the returns in HR 13A-F4 LRHR. For the desertion of 1,146 Pennsylvania troops see Adamson Tannehill to Smyth, December 7, 1812, *Ontario Repository*. See also Cyrenius Chapin to Solomon Van Rensselaer, December 13, 1812, *Gleanings*, I, 284-285.

[109] See, for example, *Ontario Repository*, November 10, 1812. One Clintonian paper, the *New York Statesman*, even went so far as to encourage the desertion of soldiers who had received no clothing on the grounds that a "naked contract" was not binding. See (Philadelphia) *Democratic Press*, November 27, 1812.

[110] *Ontario Repository*, December 15, 1812.

[111] Lewis to Gallatin, November 10, 1812, *Gallatin Papers*.

[112] John Armstrong, *Notices of the War of 1812* (New York, 1836), I, 116.

[113] Monroe to Jefferson, June 7, 1813, Monroe Papers, LC.

ities in the former area similarly displayed a singular inability and unwillingness to pursue administration goals against conflicting local pressures. For this reason the campaign against Montreal was to fail as well.

★

IF THE MAIN OBJECTIVE of the war in 1812, the occupation of Montreal, was to be accomplished, it was essential that the governments and the citizens of the New England states cooperate with the administration. A secondary objective, the invasion of New Brunswick as a preliminary to an advance on the Royal Navy base at Halifax, also required the participation of New Englanders, even if it was, as Dearborn hoped, only for two or three months over the summer. The administration's supporters in New England, consisting largely of the young, the geographically and upwardly mobile, and the religious dissenters in the region's population, were numerous and well organized in Massachusetts, New Hampshire, Vermont, and Rhode Island, and they had at various times after 1800 held the government of these four states.[114] Only in Connecticut had the Republicans lacked the strength and the organization to win effective political power.[115] Massachusetts, however, by virtue of its size, location, population, wealth, and well-equipped militia, was the critical state for the war effort. If the Republicans there supported the war as energetically as they had organized themselves to challenge the "standing order" of Federalism, the prospects for military success were not unreasonable.

Nevertheless, much would depend on the response to the war by the Massachusetts Federalists, whose political strength—based on the well-established coastal mercantile communities and the older, more static and homogeneous inland counties where opinion was shaped by the leading families and the Congregational clergy—was residually greater than that of the Republicans.[116] Since 1808 the Federalists had argued, with good reason and considerable success, that Republican foreign policy was ruinous for the commercial and agricultural interests of New England, and their opposition to the embargo, much to the distress of Jefferson and Madison, had undermined that measure as well as threatening the very integrity of the Union. Possibly the Mad-

---

[114] William A. Robinson, *Jeffersonian Democracy in New England* (New Haven, 1916), 49, 160-170; Paul Goodman, *The Democratic Republicans of Massachusetts: Politics in a Young Republic* (Cambridge, Mass., 1964), 73-127.

[115] Richard J. Purcell, *Connecticut in Transition, 1775-1818* (New Haven, 1918), 177-194.

[116] James M. Banner, Jr., *To the Hartford Convention: The Federalists and the Origins of Party Politics in Massachusetts, 1789-1815* (New York, 1970), 168-215.

ison administration would not have contemplated war against Great Britain had it believed that its opponents could repeat the tactics used in 1808 and 1809, but the revival of the Republicans in Massachusetts after 1810, leading to their winning total control in both the executive and legislative branches of government in 1811, seemed to make this unlikely.[117] Indeed, the Republican governor Elbridge Gerry and his supporters believed that the victories of 1811 had inaugurated the last phase in the long battle with Federalism, and that a war with Great Britain would materially contribute to the destruction of all organized opposition to the administration. "The lion-like voice of disloyalty," declared the Republicans of the Massachusetts Senate in January 1812, would be "softened" by the conflict "to the sound of the cricket in the wilderness."[118] In preparation for this ultimate struggle for the destiny of the Republic, Gerry embarked on, or consented to, in the period up to April 1812, a series of policies designed to destroy the political influence of the Federalist leadership. These men he hated and feared, describing them as the "antirevolutional federalists . . . who [panted] for monarchy [and were] decidedly for a secession of the Northern states and the erection over them of a Hanoverian monarchy." "If we do not kill them," he warned, "they will kill us."[119]

Such deeply felt emotions were based not only on genuine doubts about the loyalty of some of the Federalists in a war with Great Britain but also on years of resentment at Federalist assumptions of social superiority. These sentiments, in turn, prompted and justified a thoroughly partisan Republican legislative program which included the Religious Freedom Act of 1811 and attacks on the charter of Harvard College; reforms in the courts of common pleas, in the appointment of sheriffs and court officials, and in the taking of legal fees; the creation of a state bank giving Republicans equality with Federalists in the possession of its stock; the threatening of libel suits against newspapers critical of the governor; and the "gerrymandering" of the state's senatorial districts and suffrage reforms on the township level.[120] The Republicans seem to have assumed that these reforms, together with the patriotic appeal of a war, would succeed by detaching many of the

[117] Eustis to Elbridge Gerry, June 20, 1811, Elbridge Gerry Papers, MHS.

[118] For Gerry's address of January 10, 1812, to the legislature, in which he advocated war with Britain, see (Portland, Me.), *Eastern Argus*, January 16, 1812. The Senate's response of January 15, 1812, is in Gerry Papers, MHS.

[119] Gerry to Dearborn, September 2, 1811, J.S.H. Fogg Autograph Collection, MeHS.

[120] Goodman, *Democratic Republicans*, 154-181; Robinson, *Jeffersonian Democracy*, 67-68. See also James T. Austin, *The Life of Elbridge Gerry* (Boston 1829), II, 337-342; and George A. Billias, *Elbridge Gerry: Founding Father and Republican Statesman* (New York, 1976), 319-322.

rank-and-file Federalist voters, who were believed to be basically loyal, from their treacherous leaders. It was in pursuit of this end that Gerry and the Republican press called for a "coalition of parties" in the early months of 1812, much in the same way as Jefferson had declared in 1801 that "we are all republicans, we are all federalists."[121] As Dearborn summed up the hopes of the Massachusetts Republicans for the administration: "There is but one opinion among the Republicans and all moderate men that the opposition will be displaced and support the government as soon as the war shall actually be commenced."[122]

These hopes were not borne out. It was politically impossible for the Massachusetts Republicans to present the issues raised by the war in a way that would both maintain their own numbers and bring them any degree of Federalist support. For this state of affairs their own partisanship was largely responsible. Because the two parties in Massachusetts had been fairly evenly balanced at the polls after 1806, some of Gerry's friends questioned the wisdom of adopting controversial policies that alienated too many powerful enemies.[123] It would not do, wrote Jacob Eustis to his kinsman in the administration, for Republicans "to avow the exclusive principle, for if retaliated by the Federalists, we should suffer the most. . . ."[124] Even the governor himself seems to have had doubts about the grotesquely partisan redistricting law that came to bear his name, while some of his Congregationalist supporters had ambivalent feelings about the Religious Freedom Act.[125] Consequently, as the state elections of April 1812 approached, many Republicans became apprehensive over the "fury of Federalism." Moreover, they found it difficult to denounce convincingly the conduct of their opponents, as Gerry had done, as "mental treason . . . little short of overt acts . . . justified under benefit of clergy," and then to ask all "honest" Federalists to vote for Gerry and the Madison administration.[126]

Nor did the way in which the administration prepared for war make

---

[121] See Gerry's address of January 10, 1812; and *Boston Patriot*, December 28, 1811, and January 22, 1812; *Eastern Argus*, April 2, 1812; and (Boston) *Independent Chronicle*, March 12 and 19, 1812. See also William Plumer to John Harper, April 13, 1812, William Plumer Papers, LC.

[122] Dearborn to Monroe, June 12, 1812, James Monroe Papers, NYPL. See also Isaac Monroe to Daniel Parker, June 29, 1812, Parker Papers, HSP.

[123] Austin, *Gerry*, II, 334.

[124] Jacob to William Eustis, January 3, 1812, William Eustis Papers, LC.

[125] Austin, *Gerry*, II, 347-348. William G. McLoughlin, *New England Dissent, 1630-1833: The Baptists and the Separation of Church and State* (Cambridge, Mass., 1971), 1101, 1104.

[126] *Eastern Argus*, March 12, 1812; *Boston Patriot*, January 18 and March 14, 1812.

the situation any easier. Congress failed to vote for the one measure that would have helped the Republicans of New England—the expansion of the United States Navy—while the news of the April embargo arrived in Massachusetts on the eve of the state elections and was, as Gerry ruefully wrote, "blazoned throughout the state with the utmost rapidity."[127] Before Federalist cries of "Taxes, Embargo, and War," the Republican sense of outrage at the letters of John Henry seemed to pale, especially in the absence of conclusive proof of Federalist treason. Massachusetts Federalists were also able to counter the Henry episode by exploiting the case of Timothy Joy—a man who confessed to having been employed by some Republicans in Haverhill to make false statements implying Timothy Pickering was a traitor—in ways which suggested that Madison's release of Henry's letters was no more than a "wicked measure to which a party resorts to answer [its] purposes."[128] Eventually, the two leading Republican newspapers in Boston became so confused over the problem of reconciling state and national issues in the campaign that they ended up by saying that a vote for Gerry meant a vote for peace instead of a pledge to support war.[129]

Conversely, it was easier for the Federalists, using the Washington Benevolent Society for the first time as an agent of political mobilization, to rouse their supporters by denouncing the Gerry administration, while also appealing to the more pacifically minded groups of dissenting Republicans by opposing the war.[130] The Republicans therefore lost the elections for governor and the lower house, despite the fact that Gerry's services as a revolutionary patriot were infinitely superior to those of his opponent and despite the operation of the gerrymander. In fact, it seems very likely that the gerrymander harmed the Republicans more than it helped them. Admittedly, the law returned a majority of Republican state Senators, but by also increasing the number of towns in the General Court as well as breaking up familiar electoral units it probably distributed Republican votes more

[127] Gerry to Madison, May 19, 1812, Gerry Papers, MHS. See also Amos Binney to Parker, November 8 and December 4, 1811, and March 21, 1812, Parker Papers, HSP. *Boston Patriot*, November 9 and 12, 1811, January 15 and 29, February 18 and 21, 1812; and *Eastern Argus*, February 6, 1812.

[128] "Another Plot! The Heat of Election Hatches a Brood of Plots and Falsehoods," March 21, 1812 Broadside Collection, Essex Institute. [William Bentley], *The Diary of William Bentley, D.D., Pastor of the East Church, Salem, Massachusetts* (Salem, 1905-1914), IV, 91.

[129] *Boston Patriot*, April 1, 1812; *Independent Chronicle*, March 30 and April 2, 1812.

[130] Banner, *To the Hartford Convention*, 264-265, 275, 287. See also William A. Robinson, "The Washington Benevolent Society in New England: A Phase of Politics During the War of 1812, "*Proceedings of the Massachusetts Historical Society* 49 (1916), 276.

thinly across the state, thus making the party vulnerable to even slight shifts of opinion against it.[131] The Republicans were therefore stunned by their defeat; having taken such "high ground," wrote Gerry, "they did not think such a revolution as happened possible."[132] In nearby New Hampshire, where elections were being held at the same time, the Republicans eked out narrow, inconclusive victories in all branches of the state government, but the governor, William Plumer, was well aware that the Federalists in Massachusetts would encourage his opponents to greater lengths of opposition.[133] In short, as the *Boston Patriot* admitted, a "change of opinion very unfriendly to Republicanism [had] occurred," and the political configuration of New England had been suddenly altered very much to the disadvantage of the administration.[134]

The precise course that the Federalist opposition to the war would take in this new situation was difficult for the administration to predict. Nor could it, by May of 1812, seriously reconsider the advisability of a declaration of war for this reason, regardless of the problems that loomed ahead in any attempt to conquer Lower Canada. To retain the loyalties of the Massachusetts Republicans and to prevent possible defections to Clinton, the administration and the congressional caucus in June consented to suggestions from Massachusetts that Gerry be nominated as Madison's Vice President for the November election, while throughout the summer the *National Intelligencer* called upon its supporters in New England to mobilize a majority of the people behind leaders who were "public minded" and "free from ambition," so that "the whole physical force of the country" could be called into service. Every New England Republican, the administration believed, would have to serve both as "a centinal [sic] and as a soldier for the general government," fighting for his country and by his example overawing the opposition at the same time.[135] The party leadership in Massachusetts seemed to accept this definition of its role. Despite the problems and the shock experienced in the April election in Massachusetts, the Federalist margin of victory had been slight, and there seemed to be no reason why the Republicans could not recover lost

[131] Austin, *Gerry*, II, 345-347. Elmer C. Griffith, *The Rise and Development of the Gerrymander* (Chicago, 1907), 65-73. See also L. M. Parker to Daniel Parker, November 4, 1812, Parker Papers, HSP.

[132] Gerry to Madison, May 19, 1812, Gerry Papers, MHS; Madison to Gerry, June 13, 1812, Madison Papers, LC.

[133] Plumer to Harper, May 11, 1812, Plumer Papers, LC.

[134] *Boston Patriot*, May 27, 1812.

[135] *Natl Intelligencer*, May 5 and 14, July 2, 1812. Richard Rush to Benjamin Rush, August 8, 1812, Benjamin Rush Papers, Library Company of Philadelphia Papers, HSP.

ground in a successful war. The strength of the party, Gerry assured Madison, "would rapidly increase in case of war . . . , far exceeds that of our adversaries, [and] will rally in due time." "By war," he concluded, "we shall be purified as by fire."[136]

Given this close balance between the contending parties in Massachusetts, the administration felt fairly confident in ruling out such extreme Federalist responses to the war as secession. For the opposition to attempt this would probably risk a civil war in New England, in which, the *National Intelligencer* warned, the Republicans of other states would not hesitate to intervene.[137] However, since the Federalists now controlled three of the five state executive offices in New England, the War Department felt that these Federalist governors might attempt lesser measures of obstruction, such as refusing to provide requisitions of militia for coastal defense. One of the last acts of Governor Gerry in Massachusetts before he left office had been to increase the number of Republican generals in the militia in preparation for war. His successor, Caleb Strong, had immediately dismissed many of these appointments and assumed direct command of the militia himself.[138] Moreover, on June 2 the lower house of the Massachusetts General Court began debating a resolution to instruct the governor to withhold militia from federal service should the President attempt to call it out.[139]

Accordingly, the Secretary of War advised Dearborn on how to act in such a situation. The administration, Eustis wrote, would "not be arrested in its main object by any opposition which the spirit of party might raise. . . . In case the Govs [*sic*] neglect, refuse or mean to embarrass the means of defense, to leave the responsibility on them and to pursue the principle object," he continued, "is a dictate of duty in the observance of which we shall be borne out by the nation." For operations against Lower Canada, the Secretary specifically instructed Dearborn simply to raise what volunteer forces he could, after the volunteer law of February 1812 had been amended, and he promised that additional forces would be marched to him from states farther south, notably Pennsylvania and Virginia.[140] The administration thus decided to ignore as far as was possible any opposition to the war. Even so, the commencement of hostilities still required a formal test to be made of the intentions of the Federalists, and, on June 22,

---

[136] Gerry to Madison, May 19, 1812, Gerry Papers, MHS.

[137] *Natl Intelligencer*, July 2, 1812.

[138] Gerry to Madison, April 25, May 19, and July 13, 1812, Gerry Papers, MHS; Dearborn to Eustis, July 5, 1812, LRRS.

[139] *Independent Chronicle*, June 8, 1812.

[140] Eustis to Dearborn, June 9, 1812, Dearborn Papers, MHS.

Dearborn requested all the New England governors to place quotas of their militia on the coasts and frontiers for defense.[141] The Republican governors of New Hampshire and Vermont complied, but the Federalist governors of Connecticut, Massachusetts, and Rhode Island did not. All three, after some delay, justified their refusals on the grounds that either the requirements laid down in the 1795 law for calling out the militia had not been met or Dearborn had not observed the proper forms in making his request.[142]

The immediate Federalist response to the war was thus no worse than the administration had allowed for. Supreme Court Justice Joseph Story and Attorney General William Pinkney savored the possibility of reviving the essence of the 1798 Sedition Act for dealing with the Federalist governors and to restore a "holy reverence" for the Constitution, but the other members of the administration failed to see a need for extreme measures.[143] Indeed, in the first month of the war, the situation both at home and abroad, especially with the assassination of the British Prime Minister Spencer Perceval and the repeal of the Orders in Council, was so uncertain that it was not altogether clear whether an immediate invasion of Lower Canada was necessary. In early July, Gallatin drew up for the President a series of agenda which called for no more than the invasion of Upper Canada at Detroit and Niagara, while delaying an attack on Montreal pending the result of further preparations and renewed negotiations with the British government.[144] Furthermore, there were complex legal difficulties in reconciling the federal militia laws with those of some of the states, especially those of Massachusetts, and it seems not unlikely that the administration was unsure on what grounds it might safely assert an unconditional claim to control the calling out and organization of the militias in the absence of state compliance. A forcible solution to this dilemma was neither considered nor was it really possible, and, given the complexity of the issues, a peaceable settlement of the problem by the Supreme Court of John Marshall would not necessarily have been in the administration's interests either.[145]

---

[141] Dearborn to Governors, June 22, 1812, Dearborn Letterbooks, NYHS.

[142] This correspondence is printed in *ASP: Military Affairs*, I, 322-326.

[143] Joseph Story to William Pinkney, June 26, 1812, Madison Papers, LC; same to same, October 8, 1812, William Pinkney Papers, Princeton University Library.

[144] See above, Chapter II. Gallatin, "Agenda," July 12, 1812, Madison Papers, LC.

[145] [Gallatin], "Answers Relating to the Power of the President of the U.S. over Militia," June 1812, *Gallatin Papers*. It was, Gallatin noted, possible to argue that presidential power over the militia did not take effect until a state governor had first called it into federal service. The Attorney General of Massachusetts had pointed this out to Gerry on April 24, 1812, and Gerry, in turn, informed the administration. See LRRS.

For these reasons, then, the administration responded to the defiance of the Federalist governors by simply continuing with its prearranged plans. Eustis informed Dearborn that he was considering measures to enforce the militia laws, but he repeated his earlier advice on the militia by reminding the general that "we must and can do without them."[146] His only action, in fact, was to write a mild letter to Governor Strong urging compliance with Dearborn's request on the grounds that the "danger of invasion" by Great Britain was real and increasing. His argument, however, was unconvincing, and Strong had little difficulty and great pleasure in refuting it in detail; enemy incursions, he wrote, "are not likely to take place in this state."[147] The Federalist governors thus stood their ground, while the administration, unwilling to submit to any further tests of its authority, tried to bypass them. Since the administration had intentionally given Dearborn a considerable degree of latitude in his movements, it assumed that the general would concentrate on raising volunteers, assembling what forces he could at Greenbush before deciding on the details of his invasion of lower Canada.[148] Yet Dearborn was never to reach that final stage of decision, and it was not really because he was prevented from doing so by the behavior of the Federalists. Rather, his goals were undermined by his own inactivity and by the conduct of his fellow Republicans in Massachusetts.

Unlike the administration, the Massachusetts Republicans were profoundly shocked by Governor Strong's actions over the militia, viewing them as the prelude to a British invasion and a Federalist attempt to dismember the Union. The Federalist leaders had announced that they would oppose the war by all means short of forcible resistance, and Strong had quickly sent Warren Dutton and Israel Thorndike to visit the governors of Connecticut and Rhode Island to coordinate the activities of those states for that purpose.[149] To convey to the administration the full extent of their opposition to the war, some Federalist leaders in July called for a state convention, and the scheme, though not implemented, was widely discussed.[150] Very probably, these extensive Federalist activities were intended to produce a large anti-

[146] Eustis to Dearborn, July 1, 1812, LSMA; same to same, July 10, 1812, Fogg Autograph Collection, MeHS.

[147] Eustis to Caleb Strong, July 21, 1812, LSMA; Strong to Eustis, August 5, 1812, *ASP: Military Affairs*, I, 610.

[148] Parker to H.A.S. Dearborn, July 18, 1812, Charles E. French Collection, MHS.

[149] Christopher Ellery to Madison, June 24, 1812, Madison Papers, LC: *Independent Chronicle*, July 9, 1812.

[150] Banner, *To the Hartford Convention*, 263, 294-295, 306-312.

administration vote in the November presidential election, but to the Republicans their "infernal object" could only be to revive the abortive secession schemes of 1804 and 1808.[151] Indeed, so perturbed did Gerry become about "federal wiles" that he never thought of the war as an American offensive against Lower Canada but regarded it instead as a "rebellion" declared by the "Tories" against the United States.[152] Thereafter, he and other Republicans proceeded to take their cues from local traditions of partisanship rather than from what the administration felt were the needs of the nation.

In this context, the lack of coastal defense occasioned by the governor's refusal to call out the militia raised some alarming possibilities, and Gerry, in particular, gave free reign to his darkest suspicions about his opponents. The former governor was convinced that it was Strong's purpose to leave the state defenseless in order to facilitate conquest by a British force descending from Halifax. Conquest would lead to secession, he wrote, thus realizing the "Henry plot," and it would be "necessary to wade knee deep in blood to recover our country." He called for federal legislation to deal with "refractory governors" and vainly suggested a state law to suppress seditious editors, especially Benjamin Parke, who had published a stridently antiwar address in the *Boston Repertory*. The mere thought of a Federalist in office during the war filled him with alarm, and he requested the President to appoint only loyal army officers in Boston and to raise a "commanding force" in other states to hold the "Tories" in check. In the meantime, he and other Republican leaders called for the creation of "minute companies," committees of safety, loyalty lists, and a counterconvention in Massachusetts to watch over the "internal foe" and suppress the impending rebellion.[153]

Initially, Dearborn stood aloof from these frenzied activities of Federalists and Republicans alike. He arrived in Boston at the end of May and confined himself for several weeks to training and organizing recruits for the regular army, grumbling as he did so about the shortage of staff officers. To William Bentley of Salem, however, he seemed to be in "good spirits" and ready to do his duty for his country.[154] Strong's

[151] Charles Warren, *Jacobin and Junto or Early American Politics as Viewed in the Diary of Dr. Nathaniel Ames, 1758-1812* (Cambridge, Mass., 1931), 251, 253-255.

[152] Gerry to Richard Cutts, June 16, 1812; to Samuel Dana, June 27, 1812, Gerry Papers, MHS.

[153] Gerry to Dana, June 27 and July 6, 1812; to Madison, July 6 and 13, 1812, ibid. *Boston Patriot*, July 1, 1812; *Eastern Argus*, July 16, 1812; (Pittsfield) *The Sun*, July 18, 1812.

[154] Dearborn to Eustis, June 3, 1812, LRRS; *Diary of William Bentley*, IV, 99.

refusal of the militia did not greatly alarm him, and he informed the Secretary of State that its presence on the coast, except in the northern part of the District of Maine, was not strictly necessary.[155] Ridiculing the widespread fear of invasion, he expressed surprise that so many in New England were "uneasy as if they contemplated personal danger in the event of war."[156] Yet when the initial outburst of Federalist protest showed no sign of declining, he became alarmed. Along with other "outrageous proceedings," the sight of flags flying at half mast throughout Massachusetts and reports of the President being hanged in effigy distressed him, and he advised the administration to adjust to the fact that the opposition to the war was far greater than it had anticipated.[157]

By July, Dearborn's perceptions of the situation in New England came to coincide with those of Gerry. The general began by thinking there would be no harm in endorsing the former governor's scheme for "minute companies," and by the middle of the month he, too, was talking of the problems of coping with "Tory revolt."[158] In total disregard of the orders he had received from Eustis, Dearborn began to write a series of fruitless complaints to the Federalist governors about the militia, insisting all the while that the administration fine and punish them for their inaction.[159] The alternatives, he told Madison, were either "disgrace" or "strong measures in these refractory states."[160] When Gerry and the general met again in Boston in the third week of July, the former asked what could be done to prevent the British from sacking the city, and the reply he received was "*nothing*." At this prospect Dearborn expressed "great uneasiness," and he agreed to Gerry's request to ask the President to allow United States Senator Joseph B. Varnum to be given command of a special force for the defense of Boston.[161]

Preoccupied with these concerns, Dearborn found little time to organize New England Republicans for an invasion of Lower Canada. Indeed, by July 21 he doubted if any of the troops for Montreal could be raised in New England at all, and he warned the War Department

[155] Dearborn to Monroe, June 12, 1812, Monroe Papers, NYPL.
[156] Dearborn to Tompkins, June 16, 1812, Tompkins Papers, NYSL.
[157] Dearborn to Eustis, June 24, 1812, LRRS.
[158] Dearborn to Madison, June 26, 1812; to Eustis, July 17, 1812, LRRS.
[159] See the letters to Governors Strong, Jones, and Griswold, June 26 and 29, July 3, 14, and 15, 1812, Dearborn Letterbooks, NYHS. Dearborn to Eustis, June 27, 1812, LRRS; and Dearborn to Monroe, July 8 and 30, 1812, Monroe Papers, LC.
[160] Dearborn to Eustis, July 13 and 30, 1812, LRRS.
[161] Ibid. Gerry to Madison, July 22, 1812, Madison Papers, LC.

that they would have to come from states farther south.[162] Still, when he finally received a copy of the amended Volunteer Act of July 6, Dearborn did take some steps to implement it. He circulated handbills, placed notices in newspapers, and wrote to all the Republican governors north of the Potomac, as well as to several prominent Massachusetts Republicans, requesting them to urge "a few popular, influential men" to raise "a considerable body of fine troops . . . very speedily."[163] The results were disappointing. The governor of New Hampshire promised he would do what he could but pointed out that widespread Federalist activity in obstructing militia detachments and army enlistments forbade much hope of success.[164] In the strongly Republican District of Maine, Lemuel Trescott, from whom Dearborn had expected much, declared that his duties as customs collector at Machias had become too burdensome to allow him to take up the assignment. The more energetic Republican leader in the district, William King, was quite willing to step into the breach, but he was not able to start raising volunteers much before the end of August.[165]

By that date, however, Dearborn's actions had departed even further from the administration's intentions. Fully convinced that the Federalist threat in New England required the active presence on the home front of all Republicans, Dearborn consented to the requests of his fellow New Englanders to allow the volunteer forces to be used for local defense in place of the militia that Strong had withheld.[166] Even in Maine, King claimed that volunteers could be obtained only if they understood that they were to serve as militia on the coast and that no one would have to sacrifice his employment by marching off to distant places.[167] In accepting this argument, Dearborn ignored the instructions of the Secretary of War not to "divide, distribute and render inefficient the force authorized by law." This, Eustis had warned, would only "play the game of the enemy within and without." The prediction proved to be only too true.[168] All the volunteers raised by King and his associates in Maine, for example, passed the remainder

[162] Dearborn to Eustis, July 21, 1812, LRRS.

[163] Dearborn to Governors Plumer, Tompkins, Snyder, Bloomfield, and Galusha, and to Lemuel Trescott and William King, July 20, 1812, Dearborn Letterbooks, NYHS. *Independent Chronicle*, July 23, 1812; *Boston Patriot*, July 25, 1812.

[164] Plumer to Dearborn, July 29, 1812, Plumer Papers, LC.

[165] Trescott to Eustis, September 1, 1812, LRRS. King to Eustis, August 6, 1812, LRRS; and same to same, August 24, 1812, King Papers, MeHS.

[166] King to Dearborn, July 27, 1812; Levi Hubbard to King, September 3, 1812; John Chandler to King, July 31, 1812, King Papers, MeHS.

[167] King to Dearborn, July 2, 1812, ibid.

[168] Eustis to Dearborn, June 9, 1812, Dearborn Papers, MHS.

of 1812 seizing livestock and merchandise from Americans who were trying to smuggle these provisions into Lower Canada and waiting for the British to attempt to possess the impounded supplies they needed.[169] Any notion of advancing into New Brunswick simply vanished.

In Washington, the administration viewed these developments with horror. Expecting Dearborn to do little more than take what troops he could raise and give "an impulse to the recruiting business in the Eastern states by passing thro' and making appeals to the patriotism of the people," it saw instead even this modest goal being sacrificed to the needs of local political conflicts.[170] The President, at least before the fall of Detroit, could see no possibility at all of a British invasion of the United States, and, as late as August 12, the War Department was still instructing Dearborn to ignore the activities of the Federalist governors and to "make the most of the means which [had] been pointed out to [him]."[171] In fact, Eustis three times ordered Dearborn to leave Boston for Greenbush, only to see him twice refuse on the grounds that the President had no idea of the seriousness of the situation in New England.[172] And, undeniably, the Federalists did maintain an unceasing opposition to the war. Congregational clergy preached sermons against it, political leaders wrote pamphlets against it, and entire communities interrupted their normal routines to observe fast days in protest. More aggressively, attempts were made to purchase Republican newspapers to silence them, mobs assaulted Republican Congressmen who had voted for war, many Republicans were harassed by loss of employment and threatened with imprisonment for debt, and army recruiters were constantly presented with writs of *habeas corpus* for the purpose of preventing minors and apprentices from entering the ranks.[173]

Gradually, the administration did become aware that the "general chill diffused by Federalism" was undermining the war effort, causing, as Madison admitted, army recruiting "to fall short of the most moderate calculation" and rendering the Volunteer Act "extremely unproductive."[174] But the President had no idea that it was either possible

[169] King to Eustis, December 6, 1812; Joseph Dennison to William Widgery, October 8, 1812, King Papers, MeHS.

[170] Madison to Dearborn, August 9, 1812, Madison Papers, LC.

[171] Eustis to Dearborn, August 12, 1812, Dearborn Papers, NYHS.

[172] Eustis to Dearborn, June 26, July 9 and 26, 1812, LSMA; Dearborn to Eustis, July 1, 5 and 17, 1812, LRRS.

[173] For a general discussion see Samuel E. Morison et al., *Dissent in Three American Wars* (Cambridge, Mass., 1971), 1-14.

[174] Madison to Cutts, August 8, 1812; to Dearborn, August 9, 1812; to Jefferson, August 17, 1812; to Samuel Spring, September 6, 1812, Madison Papers, LC.

or desirable to attempt to do very much about these developments in New England, and it was partly for this reason that he urged Dearborn to pay more attention to the Niagara frontier. While Madison did not completely rule out federal intervention in New England in "an extreme case," he was reluctant, as the *National Intelligencer* made clear, to consider legislation against sedition, and believed that the "wicked project" of his opponents would be defeated, both by its own excesses and by the local countering activities of the "friends of the Union and the General Government."[175] The editorials of the administration newspaper—now largely written by Richard Rush, who considered the "feeble stimulants and vile opiates" of Joseph Gales to be inadequate for the occasion—thus called upon New England Republicans to assume the role of spokesmen for the public interest in their communities and to curb Federalist abuses of free speech in their own way.[176] Yet this attitude failed to allow for the fact that most Republicans, by virtue of their social position, could not easily adopt this role in coping with the organized power of Federalism. Many of the party's leaders, Gerry complained, once out of office were too poor and too busy supporting their families to devote all their energies to politics and war, while a former Republican governor of Rhode Island, John Fenner, likewise pointed out to Dearborn that the administration simply lacked the support and exertions of persons "of very extensive acquaintance" which would be necessary to make the war popular.[177] Not even the Republican clergy, as William Bentley noted, were willing to preach on the obligations of patriots to perform military service, but Bentley, perhaps because he was a Congregationalist, albeit a liberal one, failed to appreciate that dissenting sects were often Republican precisely because the party was supposed to avoid blending its politics too closely with religious concerns.[178]

The New England Republicans were therefore largely incapable of countering the opposition to the war in ways the administration would have desired, though their activities were not always without effect,

[175] *Natl Intelligencer*, August 6, 1812. Madison to Mathew Carey, September 19, 1812, James Madison Papers, NYPL.

[176] *Natl Intelligencer*, May 5 and August 20, 1812. Rush to Charles Jared Ingersoll, August 2 and 16, 1812, Charles Jared Ingersoll Papers, HSP.

[177] Gerry to Madison, August 15, 1812, Madison Papers, LC. Gerry himself was sufficiently embarrassed by his defeat in April to solicit a federal appointment. He sought the collectorship at Boston, recently vacated by Dearborn, but failed to obtain it, since the general had insisted it be kept open for him. See Gerry to Madison, April 16, 1812, Madison Papers, LC. See also J. Fenner to Dearborn, August 12, 1812, Henry Dearborn Papers, MeHS, and Francis Carr to King, September 3, 1812, King Papers, MeHS.

[178] *Diary of William Bentley*, IV, 107, 109. McLoughlin, *New England Dissent*, 1107-1109.

particularly in Vermont, where they controlled the state government. Using the power of the state to exempt soldiers from many forms of Federalist harassment, Vermont Republicans were able to organize a small but respectable effort in support of the war by placing a volunteer force ready for action at the head of Lake Champlain.[179] Elsewhere in New England, though, the political situation made similar measures impossible, and most Republicans felt they could do little more than follow Gerry's advice by assembling in township and county conventions to declare their support for the war, denounce the Federalists, and form armed companies for local defense. Some of these meetings were reported to be attended by as many as 500 people, and their proceedings were, in the words of the *Eastern Argus*, usually "suffused with the glow of patriotism."[180] Madison interpreted the gatherings as evidence of a "better spirit" in New England and hoped that some of his supporters would now feel free to volunteer for a belated march toward Nova Scotia.[181] He was to be disappointed. The psychology of the Republican meetings, no matter how patriotic their resolutions, was deeply defensive; they responded negatively to Federalist activity but not positively to administration directives, which, thanks largely to Dearborn, were only weakly perceived throughout the region anyway.

Throughout these proceedings, Dearborn had continued to go through the motions of preparing for an advance on Montreal. He talked vaguely of "pressing on" to that city, though the tone of his letters became increasingly doubtful, and he was dependent on the governors of New York and Vermont, as well as the War Department, to provide him with the necessary troops.[182] He requested the two governors to station some 4,500 militia or volunteers at the head of Lake Champlain and became very upset when the War Department diverted some of the troops promised from the south to the Niagara frontier.[183] Yet it is impossible to escape the conclusion that Dearborn used his resentment of the administration's increasing interest in the Niagara campaign as an excuse for his own lack of achievement and that he deliberately

[179] See E. P. Walton, ed., *Records of the Governor and Council of the State of Vermont* (Montpelier, 1877-1878), V, 355, 356, 382; VI, 10.

[180] *Boston Patriot*, July 18, 22, and 29, August 1, 12, 19, and 29, September 5, 12, and 26, October 19, 17, 24, and 31, 1812. *Independent Chronicle*, July 23 and 30, August 6, 1812. *Eastern Argus*, July 15, August 5, 13, 20, and 27, September 19, and 17, October 1, 8, and 15, 1812. *The Sun*, July 18 and September 12, 1812.

[181] Madison to Dearborn, October 7, 1812, Madison Papers, LC.

[182] See, for example, Dearborn to Eustis, August 22 and September 7, 1812, LRRS.

[183] Dearborn to Tompkins, August 13, 1812; to Galusha, August 16, 1812; to Madison, September 30, 1812, Dearborn Letterbooks, NYHS.

played off each against the other, the difficulties of attending to the two campaigns at once. On successive days in early September, for example, he told Eustis that he would go to Niagara and enter Upper Canada in triumph, then followed this with the announcement that he would advance on Montreal because he doubted whether anything cold be accomplished on the Niagara Peninsula.[184] To Brigadier General Bloomfield—who waited at Plattsburg throughout the fall for Dearborn to arrive with additional troops—he usually implied that he was going to Niagara and advised him to act with extreme caution, risking nothing more than a mere feint toward Montreal. By the end of October, he confessed, rather more honestly, that he doubted the wisdom of trying to occupy any part of Canada during the remainder of the year.[185] Given such vacillations, it is hardly surprising that even Dearborn, as he put it, found his command "no bed of roses" and that he wished to resign and give way to a younger, more energetic officer.[186]

Late in the fall, though, Dearborn made a last effort to raise volunteers in Massachusetts. This was not done with any intent to invade Lower Canada so much as it was an attempt to embody the Republican party in arms for the presidential election. The appearance of numerous volunteer organizations, the general claimed, would have "a powerful effect on the politics of the state" and would give a "spring and activity to the Republican interest." The operations of the "refractory governors" would thus be countered and the young men who had become apathetic won back to the party, perhaps bringing with them some "moderate" Federalists.[187] Even as an electioneering measure, this hope was baseless. Discouraged by the inability of both Dearborn and the administration to master the situation in Massachusetts, many Republicans became disillusioned with the war and sank into political apathy. With the exception of Vermont, the Federalists carried New England for Clinton in the presidential election with little difficulty.[188] They "strained everything to carry their point," Bentley recorded, while "not

[184] Dearborn to Eustis, September 1 and 2, 1812, LRRS.

[185] Dearborn to Bloomfield, September 18, October 1, 11, and 23, 1812, Dearborn Letterbooks, NYHS. Dearborn to H.A.S. Dearborn, October 14, 1812, Dearborn Papers, MeHS.

[186] Dearborn to Levi Lincoln, September 27, 1812; to King, September 30, 1812, Dearborn Letterbooks, NYHS.

[187] See note 186 and also Dearborn to Benjamin Spurr, September 28, 1812, and to Arthur Buffington, September 30, 1812, ibid.

[188] George Ulmer to King, October 16, 1812, King Papers, MeHS; Plumer to Harper, November 9 and 28, 1812, Plumer Papers, LC; Eastern Argus, November 5, 1812.

while "not a Republican even insinuated to his friends their duty."[189] The Republican turnout at the polls was poor indeed, declining, "mysteriously" Gerry said, by nearly half from the levels recorded in the April election.[190]

After Van Rensselaer's failure at Niagara and the electoral victories of the opposition in New England, Dearborn belatedly realized that he alone could save the nation from total disgrace. Remarking with considerable understatement that the events of the war to date induced "suspicions of a want of foresight, deliberation, or skill," he began to prepare for a winter campaign against Montreal.[191] He left Greenbush on November 8 for Plattsburg, where he anticipated finding about 5,000 regulars and 4,500 militia and volunteers. He discovered, though, that the total force was little more than 5,000 and that many of the militia were reluctant to serve beyond the United States. Furthermore, Bloomfield and some of the troops had fallen ill with an extremely serious throat infection. An attack on Montreal was therefore quite out of the question, and Dearborn decided to settle for a march into Lower Canada to establish a base camp for later operations.[192] On November 19 he crossed the border, attacked a small outpost held by the British and some Indians at La Cole Mill, and withdrew in confusion when he found that his regulars had accidentally fired on the militia and the volunteers. Dearborn then discharged the latter force and sent the regulars into winter camp. His final contribution to the campaigns of 1812 thus ended, as Charles Jared Ingersoll recalled, in a "miscarriage without even the heroism of disaster."[193]

This misfortune notwithstanding, Dearborn was the only general who survived disgrace in 1812 to see further service in the war, but his continuation in command, as Monroe tartly observed, was due to the fact that of all the commanders he had attempted the least and had

[189] *Diary of William Bentley*, IV, 128.

[190] Gerry to Madison, November 8, 1812, Madison Papers, LC. For the election figures and discussions of their meaning see Banner, *To the Hartford Convention*, 274-276, 360-362, and Norman K. Risjord, "Election of 1812," in Arthur M. Schlesinger, Jr., and Fred N. Israel, eds., *History of American Presidential Elections, 1789-1968* (New York, 1971), I, 262-263. Abstention was probably the main reason for the poor Republican performance, though several Republican newspapers believed that many of their supporters had voted for Clinton. See *Boston Patriot*, December 5, 1812, *The Sun*, November 5, 1812, and *Diary of William Bentley*, IV, 131.

[191] Dearborn to Stephen Van Rensselaer, October 31, 1812, Dearborn Letterbooks, NYHS; Dearborn to Eustis, November 10, 1812, LRRS.

[192] Dearborn to Eustis, November 24, 1812, LRRS.

[193] Charles Jared Ingersoll, *Historical Sketch of the Second War with Great Britain* (Philadelphia, 1845), I, 99.

therefore suffered the least in reputation.[194] His reluctance to attempt anything owed something to the administration's failure to provide clearly for the command on the Niagara frontier in relation to its broader strategy against Upper and Lower Canada, but even so it seems undeniable that Dearborn's own actions were seldom logically related to the goals he was supposed to be pursuing. The general, however, made no attempt to justify his inadequacies, expected to receive "a full share of the blame," and begged to be relieved of his command.[195] He had failed not so much because he was a bad soldier— indeed, his fighting skills, whatever they were, were never really tested— but because he was an ineffective politician who could not serve his two constituencies in Washington and in Massachusetts. In trying to help his fellow New Englanders too much, he helped his country not at all.

[194] Monroe to Dearborn, December 18, 1812, LSMA.
[195] Dearborn to Eustis, December 11, 1812, LRRS; Dearborn to Gallatin, December 27, 1812, Dearborn Letterbooks, NYHS.

CHAPTER VI

★

MEN, MONEY, AND MEDIATION, 1812-1813

THE FAILURE of the campaigns of 1812 created serious problems for the Madison administration. Not only was the fact of failure bad enough, but its nature had been so disastrous as to call into question all the assumptions upon which the administration's policies were based. Even Gallatin, who had been by far the most pessimistic cabinet member about the chances for success in the war, reluctantly admitted that the defeats were worse than anything he had anticipated.[1] The administration, it will be recalled, had attempted a series of invasions of the Canadas, believing that the loss of the resources of those colonies would prevent Great Britain from employing its naval power in the ways that had been so distressing to the United States, and that the possession of the strategic points gained in the campaigns of 1812 would be the first stage in driving British power off the North American continent altogether. Since the Canadas were weak and poorly defended and since Great Britain was fully preoccupied with the war against Napoleon, it had been logical to assume that the conquest of Upper and Lower Canada, at least as far as Montreal, would prove to be a relatively easy matter. And even though the administration had not been able to prepare for war in the ways it would have preferred, the President had continued to rely on the possibility of recruiting enough regulars and volunteers in the states adjacent to the Canadian border to accomplish his objectives. On the domestic scene, the administration had also hoped that the crisis of war would contribute to ending the chronic factionalism within the Republican party that had characterized its first term in office.

By November 1812, these hopes were in ruins. One New York Congressman, Samuel L. Mitchill, calmly observed, with much jus-

---

[1] Gallatin to Jefferson, December 18, 1812, Thomas Jefferson Papers, LC.

tification, that "Canadian wars [had] been uniformly disastrous ever since the colonization of these parts of North America, except in the war of 1759 and 1760," but few of his fellow Republicans shared his philosophical sense of detachment.[2] Most felt that the Republic was in a serious state of crisis, and, indeed, at no time since independence had the plight of the nation seemed so desperate. The difficulties of the situation were compounded by the fact that shortly after the declaration of war Great Britain had made significant concessions to the United States on all its demands for peace, with the exception of refusing to abandon the practice of impressment. On this outstanding issue, however, the British showed no sign of relenting, and, given the reports of Napoleon's Russian campaign that began to reach the United States by the end of the year, there was little reason for them to do so.[3] At first, most Republicans were inclined to dismiss the accounts of Napoleon's defeat as grossly exaggerated, if not fabricated, but the administration immediately sensed from the fact that France had plainly not won a clear-cut victory that Great Britain, in alliance with Russia and with access to the resources of the Baltic, was in a far stronger position than it had been at the commencement of the war.[4]

Even worse from the administration's point of view was the humiliation of knowing that the invasions of the Canadas had been frustrated not so much by the superiority of the Canadian resistance as by the inability of the War Department either to assemble or to employ an army successfully. As one Virginian army officer, Major David Campbell, lamented, the nation ran into war *"tail foremost"* by simply trying to march small detachments of untrained and unorganized men from all parts of the country into battle, and the result, as he rightly noted, had "destroyed the recruiting service" and the very organization of the

[2] Samuel L. Mitchill to Elizabeth Mitchill, January 14, 1813, Samuel Mitchill Papers, MCNY.

[3] Madison to Jefferson, January 27, 1813, James Madison Papers, LC.

[4] See, for example (Richmond) *Virginia Argus*, January 18 and 28, 1813; *Boston Patriot*, January 27, 1813; (Boston) *Independent Chronicle*, December 3, 10, 24, and 28, 1812, January 11 and 21, 1813; and (Portland) *Eastern Argus*, November 19, 1812, January 14 and 28, 1813. The Russian minister to the United States, Andrei Dashkov, not unnaturally resented this Republican tendency to belittle the Russian victories. He reported to his government that the administration had counted on a French triumph in 1812 and complained Madison had ignored his suggestions that the United States improve its relations with Russia. Dashkov to Count Nikolai P. Rumiantsev, February 14, 1813, Archives of the Russian Foreign Ministry (microfilm of Arkhiv vneshnei politiki Rossii for 1809-1816, held in LC, henceforth Russian Archives). See also Monroe's reported remark of December 14, 1812, that "the French [were] in a dangerous situation at Mosco [sic]." John Randolph to John Taylor, December 15, 1812, John Randolph Papers, UVa.

regular army itself.[5] Moreover, the abortive invasions had brought the war directly to many Americans in the form of Indian raids in the Northwest and in the threat of invasions on the largely undefended coasts and frontiers. The widespread fears created by these developments had led state and local leaders to press for defensive preparations to a far greater extent than the War Department had allowed for or could afford, and public anxiety had also been among the causes of the military defeats. Nor was such anxiety abating; in November, John Armstrong, the commander in New York City, suggested transforming the volunteer laws into a costly local defense scheme which would certainly have undermined the recruiting of regular forces, while the government of Virginia began debating the possibility of the state's raising its own army to defend the coast and to deter slave revolts. That this latter proposal was in violation of the Constitution was of little concern to Virginia's leaders, who were arguing that local defense should have a higher priority than offensive operations against the Canadas.[6]

The only advantage of the war thus far was the extent to which it had succeeded in containing factionalism within the Republican party. The revolt of DeWitt Clinton and his New York supporters had been singularly unsuccessful in rallying Republican leaders in other states behind an anti-administration presidential candidate. But Clinton, by virtue of his alliance with the Federalist party, had nonetheless still been able to mount a serious challenge to the "Virginia Dynasty" in the most closely contested presidential race since 1800, and the election of 1812 had become not a popular ratification of diplomatic and military triumphs, as the administration had hoped, but a referendum on a mismanaged war.[7] Clinton's tactics made the outcome of the presidential election far more uncertain than most Republicans had predicted, and not until the confirmation of Madison's victories in Pennsylvania, Ohio, and North Carolina in the first week in December was the result beyond doubt. As Mitchill recorded, the month of November

[5] John Campbell to David Campbell, December 16, 1812, Campbell Family Papers, Duke University Library. See above Chapter III.

[6] Armstrong to Gallatin, October 4, and November 6, 1812, Carl Prince and Helen Fineman, ed., *The Papers of Albert Gallatin* (microfilm ed.). Armstrong to Eustis, November 5, 1812, LRRS. James Barbour to Eustis, December 22, 1812, LRRS; and Wilson Cary Nicholas to (William B. Giles), January 3, 1813, Wilson Cary Nicholas Papers, LC.

[7] See Norman K. Risjord, "Election of 1812," in Arthur M. Schlesinger, Jr., and Fred L. Israel, eds., *History of American Presidential Elections, 1789-1968* (New York, 1971), I, 249-291.

was a "dismal and dark" time for the "thin and solemn" gatherings in the President's drawing room, for the news of electoral and military setbacks came in "day after day, like the tidings of Job's disasters."[8] Even re-election only added to Madison's problems, since the Clintonian alliance—by winning four New England states, New York, New Jersey, and Delaware, while also dividing the vote of Maryland— gained control of the most populous and wealthy cities and states nearest the theater of war. Even before the election, George Hay had foretold such an outcome and its consequences; Madison might be narrowly re-elected, he wrote, but would be "unable to get along" with such a victory.[9]

This combination of military defeat and a greatly strengthened opposition to the war created feelings of frustration and helplessness within the administration and among its supporters. Republicans in Congress and throughout the states continued to proclaim their support for the administration and the war, largely out of a sense of party loyalty, but the events of the last months of 1812 seemed to be beyond remedy. Confidence in the abilities of individual cabinet members, particularly the Navy and War Secretaries, had steadily declined throughout the year, and by December the Speaker of the House, Henry Clay, privately declared that even the President himself was "unfit for the storms of war."[10] The usually optimistic Richard Rush likewise detected a "radical impotence" and an "inward shrinking" before the difficulties that lay ahead, but no one could deny that different and more effective policies were required.[11] Above all, the administration needed to find new ways to bring pressure on the enemy, to broaden political support for the war, especially in the northern states, and to raise an efficient invading force. Yet because, as John C. Calhoun noted, the causes of the military failures of 1812 often lay "deep and coeval with the existence of Mr. Jefferson's administration," if not with

[8] Mitchill to Elizabeth Mitchill, November 24, 1812, Mitchill Papers, MCNY. See also William Burwell to Wilson Cary Nicholas, December 18, 1812, Wilson Cary Nicholas Papers, UVa.

[9] Hay to Monroe, September 22, 1812, and Dearborn to Monroe, December 13, 1812, James Monroe Papers, NYPL. See also *Natl Intelligencer*, November 26, 1812.

[10] Clay to Caesar A. Rodney, December 29, 1812, James F. Hopkins, ed., *The Papers of Henry Clay* (Lexington, 1959–   ), I, 750.

[11] Richard Rush to Charles Jared Ingersoll, November 17, December 1 and 28, 1812, Charles Jared Ingersoll Papers, HSP. See also Giles to Wilson Cary Nicholas, December 10, 1812, Nicholas Papers, UVa; George Maxwell to Samuel Southard, December 11, 1812, Samuel Southard Papers, Princeton University Library; Burwell to Elizabeth Burwell, December 20, 1812, Miscellaneous MSS, LC.

the very structure of the government itself, the administration's adjustment to this situation would necessarily be a difficult and, at best, a partial process.[12]

★

GIVEN THE SITUATION at the end of 1812, it was hardly surprising that Monroe should have privately admitted that the United States was "sincerely desirous of an accommodation with Great Britain."[13] But because of the very weakness of the American position, the administration could scarcely afford to make an accommodation—without virtually conceding defeat—on any terms other than those defined by itself. By releasing with his annual message on November 4 the diplomatic exchanges that had taken place with Great Britain since the declaration of war, Madison attempted to demonstrate that he had indeed sought an honorable peace for the United States, but in truth, there was little prospect for a settlement so long as the enemy occupied Michigan Territory, used the northwestern Indians as allies, and refused to make concessions on impressment. There was, therefore, no alternative to continuing the war, even if it seemed, as John Taylor of Caroline told Monroe, that the nation was condemned to the "droll policy" of "pursuing an object from which we are daily removed by the vehicle in which we ride. . . ."[14] Madison, too, had felt the "perplexity" involved in trying to coerce a victorious opponent, and his annual message invited Congress to prepare for a war of indefinite length.[15] For this purpose, the President requested his supporters to provide him with laws to raise the pay and fill up the ranks of the army, to provide for local defense, to reform the staff departments of the army, to revise the militia and volunteer laws, to enlarge the navy, providing especially for forces on the Great Lakes, and to prevent a "corrupt and perfidious intercourse with the enemy not amounting to treason nor yet embraced by any statutory provisions."[16]

The last of these requests seemed to be the most amenable to prompt action, and, on November 6, John Harper of the House committee on foreign relations and Thomas Newton of the Committee on Commerce and Manufactures offered resolutions to prohibit the export of flour

[12] Calhoun to James MacBride, December 25, 1812, Robert L. Meriwether, ed., *The Papers of John Calhoun* (Columbia, 1959–), I, 146.

[13] Monroe to Jefferson, November 11, 1812, James Monroe Papers, LC.

[14] Taylor to Monroe, March 18, 1813, ibid. See also Burwell Bassett to Josiah Bartlett, January 13, 1813, Josiah Bartlett Papers, LC.

[15] Madison to Jefferson, October 14, 1812, Madison Papers, LC.

[16] For the text of the message see James D. Richardson, comp., *A Compilation of the Messages and Papers of the Presidents* (New York, 1897-1914), II, 499-506.

and breadstuffs. The move suggested that the administration was troubled by the continuing ability of Great Britain to draw supplies, mainly through New England, for its armies in Canada and the Iberian Peninsula as well as for its colonies in the West Indies. The adoption of the resolutions would have instituted an embargo intended to exhaust the enemy's resources, but they were, for that very reason, voted down by a large majority of Congressmen.[17] Although the subject was never even debated in the House, most Representatives felt that the war had become so unpopular that they were not prepared to add to its difficulties by denying their constituents the profits of agriculture, even if it meant feeding the enemy. That the Senate also shared these sentiments was revealed later in the session when its members failed to act on measures that would have substantially realized the purpose of Harper and Newton's resolutions, specifically two bills to prevent trade under special licenses issued by British authorities and to ban the export of food and raw materials in foreign bottoms.[18] Events were now making war and commercial restriction conflicting rather than complementary policies, and the Congress that had voted for war thus served notice on the administration that the conquest of Canada would indeed have to be the principal means of bringing Britain to terms.

For the continuation of the war, however, the remnants of the military establishment—in a truly wretched condition by the end of 1812—required substantial reform[19] By November, Eustis and Gallatin were already advocating measures to reorganize the army and the militias along uniform lines, and the latter further insisted that greater heed be paid both to the defenses of the nation and to economy in army expenditure.[20] Moreover, all members of the cabinet, as well as Dearborn at the head of the army, were agreed on one point concerning the organization of the armed forces. Regardless of their reaction earlier in the year to the attempt to legislate an army of 35,000 men, they were now convinced of the need to raise as quickly as possible a large regular force, adequately trained and staffed and under the exclusive

[17] AC, 12th Cong., 2d sess., 142-143.

[18] Ibid., 118-121, 212-217, 1115-1116, 1134-1142, 1153-1164.

[19] The problems of the army over the winter of 1812-1813 were basically those which had plagued it throughout the campaigns of 1812: poor supply and inadequate organization, compounded by the effects of illness; bad weather; and the fragmentation of regiments. See Ebenezer Beebe to Adjutant General (AG), February 11, 1813; David Brown to Armstrong, February 10, 1813; David Campbell to AG, January 11, 1813; Isaac Coles to AG, January 6, 1813; Timothy Dix to AG, January 20, 1813; Edmund Gaines to AG, January 20, 1813; George Hight to AG, February 6, 1813, all in LRAG.

[20] Eustis, "Notes," Madison Papers, LC; Gallatin, "Memoranda" to Madison, November 1812, *Gallatin Papers*; Rush to Ingersoll, December 1, 1812, Ingersoll Papers, HSP.

control of the War Department. Only this could free the administration from the difficulties that had resulted from relying too heavily on militia and volunteers organized by the state governments. Dearborn believed the war could last as long as five years, and he argued that a future invasion of Canada ought not to be attempted with fewer than 30,000 men. To raise these quickly for service in 1813, he suggested that the administration impose enlistment quotas on the states nearest the theaters of war.[21]

While it had been impossible—thanks mainly to Congress—to raise a large number of men in peacetime, by the end of 1812 the situation looked rather more promising. By then nearly 19,000 men were enlisted into the three regular establishments, although there had not been time to organize them all to participate in the war.[22] The Adjutant General also reported that the figures would have been higher had it not been for the low rates of army pay, the long term of service for five years, and the tactics employed by Federalists to harass recruiting officers.[23] The President, too, agreed that shorter enlistment periods and greater financial encouragements might fill the ranks, and Eustis accordingly advocated a pay raise to $8.00 per month for enlisted men to the House committee on military affairs on November 11. He recommended as well that Federalist obstruction could be countered by the passage of laws exempting soldiers from civil suits and depriving parents, masters, and guardians of the right to demand the discharge of minors once they had been legally enlisted.[24] The committee, however, disagreed. Some of its members may have rejected the notion implied in the request for the pay raise—that the profession of arms be made financially and socially respectable—and all had probably expected a more intensive discussion of the failures of the campaigns, which Eustis's brief letter seemed to ignore. Indeed, most Congressmen felt that Eustis should resign his office to make way for a man who could inspire greater confidence, both as an administrator and as a military strategist.

Consequently, the committee chairman, David R. Williams of South

[21] See note 20. In his message to Congress, Madison conceded that the administration would have to rely on regulars in the future, since the alternatives of militia and volunteers were too unreliable and too costly. See also Dearborn to Thomas Cushing, December 24, 1812, Henry Dearborn Papers, MeHS. Dearborn wrote several similar letters to Madison, Monroe, Eustis, and Gallatin advocating the raising of a large regular army.

[22] The figure of 19,000 is from "Strength of the U.S. Army at the End of Each Campaign," Daniel Parker Papers, HSP. See also AG to Eustis, November 13, 1812, LSAG.

[23] AG to Eustis, November 17, 1812, LSAG.

[24] Madison to Monroe, September 21, 1812, Monroe Papers, LC; Eustis to David R. Williams, November 11, 1812, RCSW.

Carolina, replied that further information about the state of the army and the War Department was required before any bills could be reported to the House.[25] The Secretary's response gave them little satisfaction. Eustis provided some additional information about the difficulties of recruiting but then simply repeated his earlier requests, adding to them the demand for the creation of six more major generals and six brigadier generals.[26] Not wishing to defy openly the expressed wishes of the administration, the committee reported the measures to the House, where the Federalists strongly opposed the restrictions on the rights of parents, masters, and guardians over minors.[27] Congressional Republicans defended the measures but did not intend that their support for the administration be understood as acquiescing in Eustis's remaining in office. As soon as Madison's re-election had been placed beyond doubt in the first week in December, congressional deputations waited on both the Secretary and the President in order, as Jonathan Roberts of Pennsylvania put it, to urge "the appointing power to an exercize of its functions."[28] Eustis resigned immediately and retired to Boston.

His withdrawal compelled Madison to find a new Secretary of War. Many candidates were rumored to be in contention—including Monroe, Armstrong, James Wilkinson, William Crawford, and Dearborn—though none, as the *National Intelligencer* commented on December 10, seemed entirely suited for the position.[29] Monroe assumed that he was the logical choice, having already indicated to the President his wish for a military appointment where he could make a greater reputation for himself. Ideally, Monroe wanted to place Dearborn in the War Department while he assumed command of the whole army, preferably with the rank of lieutenant general, yet when Madison offered him the War Department after Eustis's resignation he was more than willing to accept.[30] However, his son-in-law, George Hay, pointed out that the formidable difficulties of successfully administering the department would probably do little to enhance his presidential prospects

[25] Williams to Eustis, November 14, 1812, LRRS. William Lowndes to Thomas Pinckney, December 13, 1812, Harriet H. Ravenal, *The Life and Times of William Lowndes of South Carolina, 1782-1822* (Boston, 1901), 118.

[26] Eustis to Williams, November 18, 1812, RCSW.

[27] Lowndes to Pinckney, December 13, 1812, and January 16, 1813, Ravenal, *Lowndes*, 118, 119. AC, 12th Cong., 2d sess., 156-193.

[28] Jonathan Roberts to William Jones, December 28, 1812, Uselma Clarke Smith Collection of William Jones Papers, HSP.

[29] *Natl Intelligencer*, December 10, 1812. See also *Baltimore Whig*, December 7, 1812; Thomas Leiper to Madison, December 17, 1812, Madison Papers, LC.

[30] Monroe to William H. Crawford, December 3, 1812, Monroe Papers, LC.

for 1816. Hay accordingly argued that Monroe should only involve himself in military affairs as lieutenant general and not organize the army to enable someone else to claim the credit for victory.[31] Monroe, always ambitious but cautious not to appear too much so, accepted this argument. He told Madison that he would take the War Department on a temporary basis only.[32] The President, no doubt irritated by these self-serving vacillations, had to look for another candidate, while Monroe made full use of his temporary tenure to plan the next campaign, very probably with the hope of taking command of the forces he had created in the spring of 1813.

In his dealings with Congress, Monroe was rather more tactful than Eustis had been. Recognizing that there was a widespread desire for better defense preparations, he accepted suggestions made to him by Gallatin that the United States be divided into military districts, each with a body of regular troops and a fully staffed commander who would be responsible for organizing local defense with the state governors and their militias. The possibility of a British attack on the coast could no longer be as easily disregarded as it had been earlier in the year, and the scheme was, as Gallatin saw it, a compromise between not defending the coast at all and raising the regular army to a level necessary to do so. The former alternative, he pointed out, risked making the administration "odious" to the public, while the latter would result in "oppressive taxes, high loans, and ruinous paper emissions."[33] Furthermore, both Gallatin and Monroe realized that recruiting for a successful offensive against Canada required a certain degree of local confidence in the administration's ability to defend the people.[34] The establishment of such confidence also promised to relieve the War Department of the increasing number of complaints that the defense of the nation was being neglected, a problem which if attended to in detail would exhaust the time and resources of the War Department.

Monroe and Gallatin estimated that the creation of the military districts would withdraw about 10,000 regular troops from the service. Theoretically, this left 25,000 men available for offensive operations, but since barely 40 percent of that number had been recruited by then, there was clearly a shortfall. Furthermore, Monroe doubted whether even 25,000 men would be sufficient for his purposes, since, on assuming the duties of the War Department, he had conceived the am-

[31] Hay to Monroe, November 1 and 23, December 13, 1812, Monroe Papers, NYPL.
[32] *Natl Intelligencer*, December 15, 1812.
[33] Monroe to George Washington Campbell and Williams, December 23, 1812, RCSW. Gallatin to Monroe, December 26, 1812, *Gallatin Papers*.
[34] Gallatin to Madison, December 12, 1812, Madison Papers, LC.

bitious scheme of occupying both East Florida and all British North
America from Malden to Halifax by the end of 1813. For these goals,
Monroe wanted another 35,000 men, including a reserve force of 10,000,
although he realized it was highly unlikely that either Gallatin or
Congress would tolerate the expenditure necessary to raise forces totaling 70,000 men.[35] To avoid this difficulty, he modified a plan sent
to him by Dearborn and proposed that the volunteer laws of 1812 be
replaced with an act enabling the President to raise 20,000 troops in
the states adjacent to Canada for one year's service. This scheme was
also intended to remedy the lack of coordination and central direction
which had undermined the operation of the volunteer laws, for it would
allow the President to nominate the colonels for the new force and, in
turn, empower them to select their own regimental officers without
the need for confirmation by the Senate. The plan represented not so
much an attempt to raise a national army as it was a device to encourage
the most patriotic units of the militia to join whatever regulars could
be obtained for a year's service. But to maintain for the regular service
a competitive position against the new volunteers, Monroe also suggested that the bounties to enlisted men and the premiums to recruiting
officers be more than doubled.[36]

The acting Secretary of War had outlined this scheme to Congress,
and the House military affairs committee, whose members admitted
that it had "an appearance of system," had reported a bill to enact it
when Gallatin belatedly grasped its financial implications. The Treasury Secretary had been engaged in drafting bills both to remedy the
disorder created by Eustis in the staff departments in 1812 and to
provide the military districts with their own staffs of officers, and he
was at all times concerned to limit expenditures where possible. To
reconcile the needs of stronger offensive and defensive forces with the
balancing of his budget, Gallatin had, in fact, begun to think in terms
of a smaller, more efficient regular army, and he approved his colleague's plan under the misapprehension that the 20,000 new troops
would be used to fill the ranks in the existing 35,000-man army. When
he realized that Monroe's bill was intended to raise an additional 20,000
men, and thereby create an establishment totaling 55,000 men, he
vetoed it. There were, he wrote, "natural limits" which could not be
passed, and the sum required to finance Monroe's plans, which he

[35] See note 33 and also John Harper to William Plumer, December 1, 1812, William
Plumer Papers, LC; Rush to Ingersoll, December 28, 1812, Ingersoll Papers, HSP.

[36] Dearborn to Madison, December 16, 1812, Monroe Papers, NYPL; Monroe to Campbell and Williams, December 23, 1812, RCSW; Monroe to Dearborn, January 31, 1813,
Monroe Papers, LC. See also *Daily Natl Intelligencer*, January 28, 1813.

estimated at $24 million only "proclaim[ed] the wants of the govern-
ment and [would] tend to destroy confidence and public credit." Even
a Federalist "having the confidence of moneylenders," he added, could
hardly succeed in financing Monroe's ambitions.[37]

Gallatin's objections here were reinforced by the practical and financial difficulties of organizing supplies for Monroe's plans. The army
contractors, Elbert Anderson and James Byers, pointed out that a
large number of troops moving toward Montreal and Quebec could
not be adequately provisioned from New England, which was, after
all, a grain-importing region. The supplies for the campaign would
therefore have to be purchased in western New York or from states
farther south and would not, in any case, be ready before October
1813.[38] Their cost threatened to be prohibitive as well, and for this
reason, to say nothing of the problems of trying to organize offensive
operations against Lower Canada in states where opposition to the war
was strong, Gallatin called for several modifications in Monroe's bill.
He believed that 15,000 was the maximum number of additional troops
that could be raised for offensive operations but was fully aware that
this would be insufficient to attempt the complete expulsion of British
power from the continent, as Monroe had wished. Accordingly, he
stated that the occupation of the Canadas between Lake Erie and
Montreal was the most the United States could realistically hope to
achieve in 1813. Moreover, to avoid the heavy expenses incurred in
assembling and supplying large forces on land, Gallatin wanted military operations postponed until the United States had gained naval

[37] Lowndes to Pinckney, December 23, 1812, William Lowndes Papers, LC; Gallatin to
Monroe, December 26, 1812 and January 4, 1813, Monroe Papers, LC. On the reorganization of the army staff see the twenty-two-page memorandum, "Notes on the General Staff
of the U. States," *Gallatin Papers*. Here Gallatin defined the duties of various staff officers,
trying as he did so to remove some of the duplication of functions that had arisen in 1812
with the creation of the Quartermaster's and Ordnance departments along with the Commissary General of Purchases. After the establishment of the military districts Gallatin sought
to achieve this goal by confining the duties of the quartermasters to the districts, while
limiting the functions of the Commissary General of Purchases to the procurement of clothing
and camp equipage. The office of Superintendent of Military Stores was to be suppressed
to allow for the creation of a new Superintendent of Military Supplies, who was to be based
in Washington for the purpose of keeping track of all accounts relating to army supply. All
these changes were embodied in two laws, passed at the end of the second session of the
Twelfth Congress, to increase the general staff and to provide for accountability in army
supply. The drafts for these laws are also in *Gallatin Papers*, and, after their passage,
Madison's kinsman, Richard Cutts, was appointed the first Superintendent of Military Supplies.
[38] James Byers to Eustis, December 20, 1812; Elbert Anderson to Monroe, January 6,
1813, LRRS. Anderson to Madison, January 6, 1813, Madison Papers, LC.

control of the Great Lakes, after which, he pointed out, it would be possible to move smaller bodies of troops rapidly on water and thus avoid the difficulties of coordinating separate invasions on land, which had been so difficult in 1812.[39]

Monroe might have defended his plans on the grounds that there were strong reasons for avoiding the dangers of a "lingering war," while stressing the importance of administering a crushing defeat to the enemy, but instead he accepted Gallatin's criticisms. He claimed, less than convincingly, that it was "more by accident than otherwise" that the bill had been reported from the committee in the form it had been, and he instructed Williams, without revealing the real reasons for doing so, to amend it to empower the President to raise only that number of troops, not exceeding 20,000, which would be necessary to complete the existing establishment.[40] The Republican majority in Congress then passed the bill into law by January 25, 1813, though the Senate insisted on its right to confirm all officer appointments and many legislators questioned whether the twelve-month term of service was sufficiently long.[41] But, as Monroe informed Dearborn, it had become "not a question of what species of force [was] best, but a question of what we [could] get to take the field with early next spring."[42] Possibly, too, Monroe may have realized by the end of January that it would be difficult, if not impossible, for him to realize his desire to command an American army anyway. The extent of his military ambitions had become public knowledge in Washington by the middle of the month and had led some Congressmen to question whether the Secretary of State had not succumbed to "the braggadocio style of William Hull and Alexander Smyth about the facility of conquering Canada." Such suspicions were eventually voiced publicly by Josiah Quincy of Massachusetts, who accused the Secretary of planning a

[39] Gallatin to Monroe, January 4, 1813, Monroe Papers, LC.

[40] Monroe to Gallatin, January 5, 1813, *Gallatin Papers*. AC, 12th Cong., 2d sess., 618.

[41] AC, 12th Cong., 2d sess., 58-63, 460-644, 649-772, 774-843. The bill passed the House by seventy-seven to forty-two. All votes in favor were cast by Republicans. Of the votes against, thirty-three were cast by Federalists, five came from the "Old Republican" faction, and three were antiwar Republicans from New York and New Jersey who had supported DeWitt Clinton in 1812. The remaining vote against the bill came from William Lowndes of South Carolina, who had not been very impressed by Monroe's plans and may have thought them inadequate for the occasion. The pattern on the final House vote was roughly the same as it had been on the various amendments to the bill that came up during the debate. In the Senate the final vote in favor was twenty to fourteen, with the six Federalists being joined by eight "malcontent" Republicans drawn largely from the Middle Atlantic states.

[42] Monroe to Dearborn, January 31, 1813, Monroe Papers, LC.

military dictatorship to ensure the political ascendancy of Virginia according to "the fundamental prescripts of the Montecellian dynasty," and Monroe, who had become very sensitive about sectional resentments against the "Old Dominion," would hardly have wanted to appear to have been verifying such partisan charges.[43] In addition, Gallatin's arguments had ruled out the possibility of operations against Lower Canada before the summer of 1813 at the earliest, thus leaving the Niagara frontier as the only alternative theater of action in the meantime. Monroe, however, seems to have had no interest in attacking Upper Canada from western New York, probably because it would not be a decisive action but only a diversion against the enemy.[44]

Having thus defined the range of operations that were militarily and financially feasible for the coming year, Gallatin then pressed the President to settle the appointment of the Secretary of War. The absence of a permanent head was impairing the work of the department, since Monroe had most of the army correspondence transferred to the State Department while he considered his options.[45] In the interim, Madison had offered the position to Crawford and Dearborn, only to see them both refuse.[46] The thrust of Gallatin's thinking about the campaign in 1813, however, had been to suggest that the approach to Canada should be through New York rather than New England, and this led him to point out to the President that the new Secretary of War should have the correct "geographical connections." This reduced the number of candidates to two—John Armstrong and Governor Daniel Tompkins. Gallatin favored Armstrong, partly because he had doubts about Tompkins's ability and partly because removing him from the governorship might tempt Clinton to seek the office in the spring elections

[43] John Randolph to Taylor, January 4, 1813, Randolph Papers, UVa; Samuel Taggart to John Taylor, January 17, 1813, George Haynes, ed., "Letters of Samuel Taggart, Representative in Congress, 1803-1814," *Proceedings of the American Antiquarian Society* 40 (1931), 419-420. AC, 12th Cong., 2d sess., 540-570.

[44] Monroe, of course, could not contemplate operations in any other parts of Upper Canada, since Harrison was still commander of the northwestern army. See also "General Plan of Campaign for the Year 1813," which isolated five points of entry into Canada without making any choice between them. This document, located in the Parker Papers, HSP, was probably written in December 1812 or January 1813. Stanislaus M. Hamilton, in his edition of *The Writings of James Monroe* (New York, 1898-1903), V, 237-241, has gathered some loose "war papers" at the end of 1812, one of which rejected a campaign plan on the Niagara Peninsula as being a "defensive" movement only. Internal evidence, however, suggests that these papers date from the middle of 1814 or even later, though Monroe may well have felt this way in early 1813 too.

[45] Parker to Eustis, January 16, 1813, Parker Papers, HSP.

[46] Gallatin to Madison, January 4, 1813, and Crawford to Madison, January 6, 1813, Madison Papers, LC.

in New York. And since "the fate of the Republican party and the nation" depended on the War Department, the Treasury Secretary argued, there were advantages in appointing Armstrong. He had a reputation as an authority on the art of war—enhanced by the publication in August 1812 of a treatise entitled *Hints to Young Generals from an Old Soldier*—and this reputation, combined with his abilities as a polemicist, would shield the administration from attacks such as those which had been made on Eustis.[47]

Madison and Monroe were, no doubt, more immediately impressed by the disadvantages of appointing Armstrong.[48] The "Old Soldier" was known to have presidential ambitions, and unquestionably he held Monroe in low esteem; even Gallatin conceded he might not bring "that entire unity of feeling, that disinterested zeal" to the cabinet which would be "so useful in producing hearty co-operation and unity of action."[49] Armstrong also had a bad temper, which was probably not improved by attacks of gout and rheumatism, and John Adams even believed that his eyesight was defective. Some Republicans also objected to him on the grounds that he was lazy, while others regarded the author of the Newburgh Letters as far too dangerous a man ever to be put at the head of a military establishment.[50] After much reflection, however, Madison decided that the advantages of having administrative energy and political influence in New York outweighed the possible disadvantages of Armstrong's appointment, and, in any case, the New Yorker could hardly realize any of the ambitions imputed to him without bringing military success to the administration as a whole. Believing, therefore, that he could control Armstrong's "objectionable" qualities, Madison offered him the War Department on January 14 and received an immediate acceptance.[51]

Armstrong and Ambrose Spencer thus finally achieved what they had sought since April 1812. But the new Secretary's acceptance of office was, in fact, tempered with many misgivings, and these stemmed

---

[47] Gallatin to Madison, January 7, 1813, ibid. Armstrong's *Hints to Young Generals* was published in Kingston, New York.

[48] Louis Sérurier to duc de Basano, January 8, 1813, Archives du Ministère des Affaires Étrangères, Correspondance Politique, États Unis, vol. LXX (photostats in LC).

[49] See note 47.

[50] John Adams to Benjamin Waterhouse, January 16, 1813, Adams Family Papers, MHS. John Nicholas to Wilson Cary Nicholas, January 18, 1813, Nicholas Papers, UVa.

[51] Madison to Armstrong, January 14, 1813; Armstrong to Madison, January 17, 1813, Madison Papers, LC. See also Madison's "Review of a Statement Attributed to General John Armstrong," in 1824, where Madison recalled that "a proper mixture of conciliating confidence and interposing controul would render Armstrong's objectionable peculiarities less in practice than in prospect." Ibid. See also *Albany Register*, February 2, 1813.

only partly from his doubts about Virginia politicians. He fully appreciated the difficulties of heading the War Department, knowing that under existing circumstances it was hardly a promising road to the reputation he so greatly wanted to establish. He had, too, already heard unwelcome rumors that Monroe wished to become lieutenant general of the army, and he knew that the administration had been planning army reorganization and a campaign without consulting him. And from conferences in Albany with Dearborn and the army contractors before leaving for Washington, he also knew that the strategic approach to Canada in 1813 was likely to be through New York rather than through New England. Armstrong thus entered the cabinet suspecting, as he told Spencer, that he was "to execute other men's plans and fight with other men's weapons."[52]

Armstrong arrived in Washington on February 4 and, in contrast with his predecessor, gave an immediate appearance of energy. He seized control of army patronage from Congress, talked of reorganizing all the staff offices and the War Department itself, and within four days took direction of the war away from Monroe by presenting a note to the cabinet on the campaign for 1813. In this outline, Armstrong doubted whether the army could make an effective move toward Montreal in the immediate future, which left the administration with the choice of appearing to do nothing for a long period or of attempting a more limited goal. Since he personally preferred the latter alternative, he called for a combined army and navy attack on the British base at Kingston sometime in April 1813, to be followed by the reduction of the enemy positions at York and Fort George. Such a campaign, the Secretary argued, would give the United States naval control of Lake Ontario by the spring of 1813 and would thereafter allow for greater flexibility in designing a strategy to approach Montreal. The success of the campaign was dependent on the assumptions that Lake Ontario would be free of ice shortly after April 1 and that it would be possible to assemble and train 6,000 men for action within a six-week period.[53] Madison approved the plan, and, on February 10, Armstrong instructed Dearborn—who was retained in command largely for lack of

[52] Armstrong to Spencer, January 25, 1813, William A. Chanler Collection of John Armstrong Photostats, NYHS. See also Anderson to Parker, January 26 and 27, 1813, Parker Papers, HSP; Armstrong to Dearborn, January 27, 1813, LSMA. Presumably Armstrong wrote this last letter to Dearborn while still in Albany and had it recorded in the War Department Letterbook after his arrival in Washington.

[53] Winfield Scott to Charles K. Gardner, February 6, 1813; Gardner to his parents, February 10, 1813; Gardner to Wade Hampton, February 17, 1813, Charles Kitchell Gardner Papers, NYSL. [Armstrong] "Note Presented to Cabinet," February 8, 1813, LSMA.

an alternative—to gather 4,000 men at Sacketts Harbor for the attack on Kingston and 3,000 at Buffalo for the subsequent operations at York and on the Niagara Peninsula.[54] In choosing to take the offensive in this manner rather than waiting for better weather and more extensive preparations, Armstrong was probably governed by two motives: a desire to vindicate American honor speedily and the need to influence the outcome of the spring elections in New York.

The Clintonians, who had won New York's vote in the presidential election in alliance with the Federalists, were assumed to be unreconciled to Madison's victory and the continuation of the war.[55] The proof of their opposition, in the eyes of most administration supporters, was the election in Albany on February 5 of the Federalist Rufus King to the United States Senate to replace John Smith, though this event may have owed as much to accident as it did to political management.[56] But if the same combination of forces could deliver the New York governorship to a Federalist in the state elections of April 1813, the opposition would be in a powerful position to obstruct the war and possibly even to form a New York–New England confederacy, an event that had been much discussed in 1812.[57] Most Republicans in Washington probably therefore shared William Burwell's observation that "a little success" in the war "would incline many who are clamerous to support the administration" while also helping to overcome the "great obstacles" to victory that had been created by "the violent state of parties in this country and the contest for the Presidency."[58] For this reason, the pro-administration Republicans in New York attempted to ensure Tompkins's renomination for the governorship and Clinton's exclusion from any statewide office by removing the nominating process from the Clintonian-controlled legislative caucus to a state convention, where anti-Clintonians would have a stronger voice.[59] The tactic was successful, and this may have induced the New York Federalists to abandon their alliance with Clinton in favor of an attempt to elect their own Stephen Van Rensselaer to the governorship. In any

[54] Armstrong to Dearborn, February 10, 1813, LSMA. Dearborn to Madison, February 14, 1813, Madison Papers, LC.

[55] Benjamin Romaine to Gallatin, December 13, 1812, *Gallatin Papers.*

[56] See Robert Ernst, *Rufus King: American Federalist* (Chapel Hill, 1968), 320-322.

[57] *Albany Argus*, March 2, 1813; (New York) *National Advocate*, April 13 and 22, 1813. See also Samuel E. Morison, *The Life and Letters of Harrison Gray Otis, Federalist, 1765-1848* (Boston, 1913), II, 84-85.

[58] Burwell to Nicholas, February 1, 1813, Nicholas Papers, UVa.

[59] Maturin Livingston to Gallatin, January 8, 1813, *Gallatin Papers. Albany Argus*, February 5 and 16, 1813; *Albany Register*, January 12 and February 12, 1813; *National Advocate*, January 6, 8, 11, and 19, 1813.

event, Clinton, after February 1813, fairly quickly receded as a threat to the administration, with John Smith remarking that "his popularity [had] quite gone in New York as well as everywhere else, and he [was] now despised and detested by both federalists and republicans alike."[60]

Still, the best campaign issue after the events of 1812 on the Niagara frontier was military victory, and Armstrong's efforts were devoted to obtaining such a victory by April 27, when the polls opened in New York for three days. Indeed, it was only in this context of New York politics that Armstrong's military policies between February and May 1813 made any sense. As his campaign plan of February 8 conceded, any American invasion directed west of Montreal did not greatly weaken British military power in Canada, but to influence an election in New York it probably made little difference how or where the British possessions on the state frontier and the lakeshore were attacked.[61] The Secretary doubtless would have preferred to have trapped the enemy in Kingston, but after the British reinforced that place in March 1813 he altered his strategy by consenting to the suggestions made by Dearborn and Commodore Isaac Chauncey that they attack York and then Forts George and Erie before attempting Kingston.[62] Dearborn tried to argue that the fall of York would give the United States naval control of Lake Ontario, but Armstrong made it clear to him that in his opinion the political and psychological consequences of a victory were more immediately important than the pursuit of any strategic objective. He further strengthened Dearborn's army and advised him to deliver a concentrated blow against the enemy's western posts, asking merely that the first service of the troops "should be a successful one . . . the good effects [of which would] be felt throughout the campaign."[63]

In completing their arrangements, the New York Republicans and Armstrong desired to leave nothing to chance. Over the winter, the local Republicans had established two new journals, the *National Advocate* and the *Albany Argus*, to support the administration's cause, and their editors, probably at the suggestion of Ambrose Spencer, proceeded to praise Armstrong as a military genius and promised their readers a "brilliant campaign" in Canada before May 1.[64] The Secretary

[60] John Smith to Nicholas, February 28, 1813, Nicholas Papers, UVa.

[61] See George Palmer to John Taylor, January 5, 1813, John Taylor Papers, NYHS.

[62] Armstrong to William Duane, March 16, 1813, "Selections from the Duane Papers," *Historical Magazine* 2d Ser., 4 (1868), 61-62. See also Dearborn's "Changes in Campaign Plan, 1813," LRUS; Dearborn to Armstrong, March 3, 14, and 16, E. A. Cruikshank, ed., *Documentary History of the Campaign on the Niagara Frontier* (Welland, Ont., 1898-1902), V, 87, 102, 103. Armstrong to Dearborn, February 24 and March 29, 1813, LSMA.

[63] Armstrong to Dearborn, March 29, 1813, LSMA.

[64] *Albany Argus*, March 2, 1813; *National Advocate*, April 17, 1813.

of War, rather than draw voters away from New York, decided to conduct the campaign with troop detachments drawn from New England, Pennsylvania, and Maryland.[65] When Congress, in early March, authorized the appointment of additional quartermasters for the army to complete Gallatin's reorganization of the staff departments, Armstrong moved rapidly to implement these changes in the Ninth Military District in upstate New York, and he made that area the most important center of War Department activity.[66] The sizable purchases of farm produce made by the quartermasters and army contractors no doubt strengthened the disposition of the Republican majority in the critical region of western New York to support Tompkins and the war, since the presence of the army greatly raised farm prices, thus compensating for the disruption of the trade with Canada. The price of wheat at Albany in 1813, in fact, rose some 16 percent over the level of the previous year, and the army contractor himself produced handbills and newspaper articles under the pseudonym of "The Spirit of Montgomery" to remind the voters that war and prosperity were not incompatible.[67] Armstrong, much to Monroe's alarm, even briefly considered, then rejected, the idea of joining the army at Sacketts Harbor to assist with the operations, but when Dearborn showed signs of immersing himself in his staff work, as he had done in 1812, the Secretary, wishing to prevent disputes between army and navy officers if nothing else, issued the general a clear directive to command the American forces in person.[68]

Only one problem threatened to undermine the campaign, and that was the failure of the ice to clear from Lake Ontario according to Armstrong's timetable. The troops were ready by April 5, and Dearborn declared that he hoped to be able to commence the campaign

[65] Armstrong to Dearborn, March 4, 1813, LSMA. See also AG to George Izard, February 15, 1813, LSAG.

[66] The staff of the Ninth Military District in western New York in 1813 constituted 35% of the entire army staff. The Register of the Army for 1813 is in *ASP: Military Affairs*, I, 385-388. In the critical position of Quartermaster General, Armstrong replaced Morgan Lewis with Robert Swartwout and gave him, in April 1813, $100,000 to spend. See Armstrong to Swartwout, April 25, 1813, Robert Swartwout Papers, NYPL

[67] *Ontario Repository*, March 16, 1813; *Albany Argus*, April 23, 1813; and David M. Ellis, *Landlords and Tenants in the Hudson-Mohawk Region, 1790-1850* (Ithaca,1946), 123. Elbert Anderson's letter to Daniel Parker on May 27, 1813, strongly suggests that the contractor was the "Spirit of Montgomery." See Parker Papers, HSP.

[68] Armstrong to Spencer, March 15, 1813, Chanler Collection, NYHS; Armstrong to Dearborn, April 8, 1813, Henry Dearborn Papers, MHS. Dearborn to Armstrong, April 14, 1813, LRRS; Armstrong to Dearborn, April 19, 1813, LSMA. Navy Secretary William Jones had warned Madison of the dangers of rivalry between army and naval officers; see Jones to Madison, April 26, 1813, Madison Papers, LC.

within the week, but Sacketts Harbor was not, in fact, free from ice until April 19.[69] Even as late as April 22, parts of the lake were still reported to be icebound, though the invading force decided to depart for York the next day, only four days before the polls opened and probably far later than Armstrong would have liked.[70] Still, John Canfield Spencer had already prepared electioneering handbills for the announcement of an American victory at York, and both Peter B. Porter and Martin Van Buren reported that the "Republican party was better united and exhibited more zeal than on any former occasion."[71] The election prospects thus seemed promising, and Armstrong had set the stage for the first American victory of the war.

★

THE DETAILS of military policy absorbed most of the energies of Congress and the administration during the winter of 1812-1813, but of equal importance were the problems of the navy, war finance, and diplomacy. These aspects of the war effort constituted as significant a test for the administration and its supporters as did the raising of an army, since military operations alone could not succeed without financial and naval support, and even victory itself would require a diplomatic strategy to bring Great Britain to agree to a satisfactory peace. The relationship between these matters and the campaigns against Canada, however, were not perceived equally clearly or even in the same way by all Republicans. The recognition of the strategic importance of the Great Lakes in the war, for example, made it difficult for the governing party to relegate the navy to a minor role in the conflict, but many of its members failed to appreciate that this required them to support both an increase in the navy and the measures necessary to finance it. The problems of relating military and naval spending to the political economy of Republicanism, of course, were hardly new, but by the end of the winter in 1813 they had finally overwhelmed the ability of Gallatin to cope with them to his satisfaction, and they also seriously weakened the cohesion of the congressional Republican party, which had so laboriously agreed on the declaration of war only a few months earlier. Here it became apparent that the repeal of the Orders

[69] Dearborn to Armstrong, April 5 and 19, 1813, LRRS; Dearborn to H.A.S. Dearborn, April 2, 1813, Dearborn papers, MeHS.

[70] Morgan Lewis to Armstrong, April 17, 18, and 22, 1813, LRRS. *Albany Argus*, April 30, 1813.

[71] John C. Spencer to Peter B. Porter, May 2, 1813; Porter to Armstrong, April 25, 1813, Peter B. Porter Papers, BEHS. John Taylor to Martin Van Buren, April 25, 1813, Martin Van Buren Papers, LC. See also Solomon to Stephen Van Rensselaer, May 11, 1813, Dearborn Papers, MHS. *Albany Register*, April 6, May 4 and 28, 1813, and (New York) *The Shamrock*, June 5, 1813.

in Council by the British government in June 1812 had removed an important grievance uniting most Republicans, and they found it very difficult thereafter to redefine the purposes of the war in ways which could assist the formulation of the domestic and diplomatic policies that were necessary for its triumphant conclusion. Of necessity, the efforts to do so were made, but their results were far from being wholly successful.

The first attempt to deal with this series of problems was provoked by the continuing presence in the administration of Paul Hamilton, the Secretary of the Navy. Although the navy had been the most fortunate of the nation's fighting services in 1812 with its unexpected victories over H.M.S. *Guerrière*, H.M.S. *Macedonian*, H.M.S. *Java*, and H.M.S. *Frolic*, it was not really possible for the Secretary to claim any personal credit for these results. Even more than Eustis, Hamilton was despised for his incompetence, and he was, moreover, an alcoholic; he was invariably asleep at his desk by noon, largely because, as Congressman Mitchill noted, of "the too free use of stimulant potation."[72] His behavior was, in fact, regarded as scandalous, and even the congressional delegation from his home state of South Carolina was keen to see him resign. But in this case, the tactics which had compelled the resignation of Eustis were less successful. The Navy Secretary depended on his office as a source of income, and congressional deputations, much to the annoyance of their members, could not persuade him to step down in the national interest.[73] And Hamilton not only clung to his position but tried, as he had done in the previous year, to persuade Congress to adopt naval policies that most Republicans considered to be unsupportable.

In this matter the Secretary revealed that he had paid even less attention to the lessons of military defeat in 1812 than had Eustis.

[72] Mitchill to Elizabeth Mitchill, December 22, 1812, Mitchill Papers, MCNY. Hamilton's condition and reputation raises the question of how a department so poorly run, could perform so creditably in the war. The problems of naval administration in this period have been neither properly defined nor adequately researched, but it seems not implausible to suggest that the successes of the navy in 1812 were, in some degree, related to the inability of the department in Washington to control officers, navy agents, and other personnel in the naval yards very closely. Because of the weakness of naval administration in this respect, commanders appear to have had a good deal of latitude in fitting out their vessels and determining their operations. This might have allowed greater play for the professionalism of many naval officers, thus making possible some outstanding individual performances. See Edward K. Eckert, *The Navy Department in the War of 1812* (Gainesville, 1973), 42, 43, 73-76.

[73] Harper to Plumer, December 1, 1812, Plumer Papers, LC; Nathaniel Macon to Joseph H. Nicholson, December 23, 1812, Joseph H. Nicholson Papers, LC. (Richmond) *The Enquirer*, December 24, 1812.

Relying, as always, on the views of his career naval officers, he ignored the question of naval control of the Great Lakes in relation to the war effort and called for a large increase in the oceangoing fleet with a mixed force of 74-, 38-, and 16-gun ships, arguing that such vessels would provide effective protection for both commerce and coastal defense.[74] The Senate reduced Hamilton's plans considerably, passing on December 15 a bill for a force of four 74's and six 44's, together with an appropriation of $2.5 million, but even this was too much for most House Republicans. The representatives from inland areas stated angrily that they were not prepared to be taxed to pay for the protection of the commerce of the coastal regions, and many did not believe that it was yet possible for the United States to challenge Great Britain for control of the seas. The bill, nevertheless, passed the House on December 23, when a minority of thirty-eight Republicans joined a solid bloc of Federalists to carry it against the wishes of the majority of their fellow partisans.[75] Future naval policy was thus settled in a manner that most Republicans felt the United States neither needed nor could afford, and several Congressmen complained to the President at a reception a few days later about Hamilton's role in this development, deploring his drinking as well as his extravagant spending. Whether anything else was said is not clear, but the President took the hint and summoned the Secretary for an interview.[76] The wretched man guessed its purpose but tried to defend himself, and thus compelled Madison to state explicitly that Congress might refuse future appropriations unless he resigned. Reluctantly Hamilton agreed to do so, but he remained in Washington for some time afterward, complaining bitterly that the President had betrayed him.[77]

Replacing Hamilton proved to be easier than replacing Eustis. Only two candidates were seriously considered for the position, William Jones of Pennsylvania and Langdon Cheves of South Carolina. The opinions of Cheves on financial and naval affairs were far too extreme for Gallatin to tolerate in the cabinet, and Madison undoubtedly preferred Jones anyway, to whom he had offered appointments in the past. Previously, Jones had always declined office because of his fi-

[74] Hamilton to Burwell Bassett, November 13, 1812, *ASP: Naval Affairs*, I, 276-280.

[75] AC, 12th Cong., 2d sess., 201-203, 404-428, 429-437, 443-450. The division in Republican ranks in the House cannot be easily explained in sectional or factional terms, though antinaval sentiment does seem to have been stronger in inland than in coastal regions.

[76] Harper to Plumer, January 5, 1813, Plumer Papers, LC; Roberts to Ingersoll, January 10, 1813, Ingersoll Papers, HSP.

[77] James A. Bayard to Caesar A. Rodney, January 31, 1813, "James Ashton Bayard Letters, 1802-1814," in *Bulletin of the New York Public Library* 4 (1900), 239.

nancial problems, but, on this occasion, he was persuaded to accept with the promise of an increase in salary.[78] As a Philadelphia merchant, the new Secretary could claim to have some familiarity with naval problems, while his appointment was also acceptable to all the factions within the badly divided Pennsylvania Republican party, including Gallatin, who was hoping to get some support in the cabinet in his struggle to hold the line on expenditures.[79] Yet Jones, no doubt to Gallatin's disappointment, proved to be just as much an advocate in doing away with the "Jeffersonian" naval establishment as were Hamilton, Cheves, and the naval officers. He, too, desired a fleet of 74's for the protection of commerce, the abolition of the gunboat division of the navy—which he felt properly belonged to the army for local defense—and a total reform of departmental administrative practices.[80]

On taking up his duties, Jones could only describe the state of naval affairs as "chaos," and he promptly fired the chief departmental clerk, Charles W. Goldsborough, as an indication of his desire for change. He believed that a radical reform of his department could save the administration over $1 million annually, but all his plans in this direction had to be subordinated to organizing short-term operations within the confines of Gallatin's budget. The first estimates the Treasury had made for this purpose in December 1812 allowed for no growth at all in the naval and military establishments above their existing levels, yet still left the administration with the task of finding nearly $20 million more than the anticipated receipts for 1813.[81] As always, Gallatin suggested more cost-cutting to his cabinet colleagues and hinted that the Navy Department might dispense with gunboats, frigates, and the ships of the line that were in the course of construction.[82] Jones was more than willing to comply with respect to the gunboats, dis-

[78] Roberts to Jones, December 28, 1812, Jones Papers, HSP. Philip S. Klein, ed., "Memoirs of a Senator from Pennsylvania, Jonathan Roberts, 1771-1854," *Pennsylvania Magazine of History and Biography* 42 (1938), 244, 248, 361. A bill was introduced in the House to raise Jones's salary to that of the level of other cabinet officers, but it failed to pass. AC, 12th Cong., 2d sess., 956-957.

[79] There is no biography of Jones, but for a brief outline of his life see Edward K. Eckert, "William Jones: Mr. Madison's Secretary of the Navy," *Pennsylvania Magazine of History and Biography* 96 (1972), 167-182.

[80] Jones to Langdon Cheves, January 9, 1813, Jones Papers, HSP; to Alexander James Dallas, March 10, 1813, George Mifflin Dallas Collection, HSP. See also the two drafts made in January 1813 entitled "Draft of an Act for the Better Organization of the Navy" and "Draft Notes in Reply to Senate Resolution on the Organization of the Navy." Both in Jones Papers, HSP.

[81] Eckert, "Early Reform in the Navy Department," *American Neptune* 33 (1973), 233-238; "State of the Finances," December 7, 1812, *ASP: Finance*, II, 580-581.

[82] Gallatin to Jones, February 12, 1813, Jones Papers, HSP.

missing them, in terms that would have bewildered Jefferson, as "recepticles of idleness and objects of waste and extravagance without utility."[83] Yet he could hardly accept the remaining suggestions without defeating the very purpose for which he took office, and the predicament revealed that there were limits to mere economy which could not be enforced without ending the war itself.

Furthermore, the financial embarrassments of the administration were becoming inexorably linked with the broader issue of the goals of the war and the very real problem of how to justify continuing so difficult a conflict. The close relationship between these matters was first exposed in the complicated question of whether to remit the penalties that many merchants had incurred in importing British merchandise after the repeal of the Orders in Council. Technically, the imports were forfeit under the terms of the 1811 Nonintercourse Law, though the importers argued, in the lengthy petitions they submitted to Congress on the subject, that they had acted in good faith and, sometimes, on the advice of the American chargé d'affaires in London, Jonathan Russell, as well.[84] The enforcement of the law, in effect, would confer an enormous windfall benefit on the customs collectors—thereby greatly alienating mercantile and banking circles against the administration and the war—while the relaxation of the penalties would similarly allow the importers to make great profits—to the annoyance of the supporters of the war—in a market starved of British goods. The problem was a difficult one, but Gallatin saw in it a partial solution for his troubles. Since he did not wish to press Congress toward imposing internal taxes—the members having already rejected his suggestions on that subject in the previous session—he reckoned he could raise nearly $10 million by levying double duties on the imports and requiring the importers to make a loan of one-third their value to the Treasury in return for the remission of the penalties.[85] This would then require him to find a balance of approximately $9.5 million from more conventional forms of borrowing and the issuing of Treasury notes, a task roughly comparable with that which he had just accomplished in his budget for 1812.

Gallatin might have attempted to execute this plan by employing

[83] Jones to Lloyd Jones, February 27, 1813, ibid.

[84] The petitions are contained thirty folders in LRHR, HR 12A-F10.3.

[85] Gallatin to Madison, November 1, 1812, Madison Papers, LC; Gallatin to Roberts, November 28, 1812, Roberts Papers; HSP; Gallatin to Monroe, December 26, 1812, *Gallatin Papers*. See also Klein, "Memoirs of Roberts," 244. Roberts was on the House Ways and Means Committee during the session and clearly acted as a spokesman for Gallatin's views.

discretionary executive powers, but the difficulties in doing so on such a vast scale led him instead to request Congress to sanction his intentions by providing for a temporary relaxation of the Nonintercourse Law. The administration's decision to proceed in this way, however, almost inevitably raised the question of whether nonintercourse, the only remaining part of the Republican "restrictive system," was to be enforced in conjunction with the war or whether the war was an alternative to it. The Republicans had been quarreling for some years over this point and the consequences flowing from it, and Gallatin, without question, made a serious tactical error in raising in so contentious a form the very issue that the declaration of war had been intended to transcend.[86] His apparently cynical manipulation of the technicalities of remission was more than enough to excite William B. Giles and the "malcontent" Republicans in the Senate—who were still as ready as ever to argue that Gallatin's methods of finance were an obstacle to defending the nation's honor—to an apoplectic outburst of indignation, and the administration was perhaps doubly unfortunate in that the chairman of the House Ways and Means Committee, Langdon Cheves, was also a strong supporter of the war as well as an outspoken opponent of the entire policy of commercial restriction.[87] Cheves—who along with Calhoun and William R. Lowndes represented the views of those South Carolina planters who had become convinced that the developing cotton economy of their state depended on absolute freedom of trade—refused to report Gallatin's plans to the House, then led both Federalists and Republicans against them when they did eventually come up for debate.[88] Ironically, almost all Republicans, despite their pledge to deal with the issue in this session of Congress, were united in a determination to avoid internal taxation for as long as possible, but they quarreled bitterly over the expediency and morality of Gallatin's proposal as a way of doing so.[89] The case of the opponents of the administration rested on the assumptions that the importers had acted in good faith, that the "restrictive system" hurt the United States

[86] See above, Chapter II.

[87] Giles described Gallatin's plan as a "miserable, impracticable attempt to plunder merchants . . . destitute of principle and of policy. . . . The notion of conducting a war upon the accidental results of fines, penalties, and forfeitures is a new thing under the sun, utterly unworthy of a great financier." Giles to Wilson Cary Nicholas, December 10, 1812, Nicholas Papers, UVa.

[88] On Cheves, whom Jonathan Roberts described as "outrageously independent" in his views and not really a Republican at all, see Archie V. Huff, *Langdon Cheves of South Carolina* (Columbia, 1977), 70-73, and also Margaret K. Latimer, "South Carolina: A Protagonist of the War of 1812," *American Historical Review* 61 (1956), 914-929.

[89] Mitchill to Elizabeth Mitchill, December 6, 1812, Mitchill Papers, MCNY.

far more than it did the enemy, and that the remission of the penalties would conciliate merchant groups opposed to the war and thus enable the Treasury to raise a loan by honest means.[90] The supporters of the administration argued the reverse, and the House debate in the committee of the whole was inconclusive, there being no majority to report a bill either for or against remission.[91]

The deadlock was broken only by the introduction on December 15 of a bill from the Senate, where the administration's supporters on the issue numbered only five, in favor of an unconditional remission of the penalties. This bill narrowly passed the House one week later, with a majority of the Republicans against it, but, as was the case with the navy bill, nearly thirty supporters of the war joined with the Federalists to frustrate the Treasury.[92] The administration was appalled at this outcome, and both the *National Intelligencer* and Speaker Henry Clay later severely criticized Cheves for his role in it.[93] More immediately, the remission of the penalties compelled Gallatin to try to raise nearly twice as much of the revenue, $21 million, through loans and Treasury notes as he would have liked, though Cheves in both cases guided the bills for these purposes through the House on almost straight party votes.[94] In the longer term, however, this increasing reliance on borrowing required still more ordinary revenue simply to maintain the government's credit, and Gallatin here could see no other source but customs duties, the imports for which again required some relaxation of the Nonintercourse Law. With considerable irritation, the Treasury Secretary at the end of January 1813 drafted the necessary bill and requested the legislative authorization, only to find that on this occasion he was supported by his former Republican opponents but still suffered defeat, now at the hands of the earlier administration supporters to whom the Federalists had thrown their votes.[95] By this behavior, the

[90] Jonathan to Matthew Roberts, November 15 and 25, 1812, Roberts Papers, HSP; Cheves to Gallatin, November 20, 1812, and Gallatin to Cheves, November 23, 1812, *Gallatin Papers*; Plumer to Harper, November 28, 1812, Plumer Papers, LC. AC, 12th Cong., 2d sess., 215-257, 267-348, 355-361.

[91] AC, 12th Cong., 2d sess., 364-368.

[92] Ibid., 394-404, 441, 442, 450-451. The five administration supporters in the Senate were Richard Brent (Va.), Jesse Franklin (N.C.), William Crawford (Ga.), George Washington Campbell (Tenn.) and Thomas Worthington (Ohio). Twenty Republican Senators voted against the administration. In the House those Republicans in favor of remission were drawn mainly from South Carolina and the New England and Middle Atlantic regions.

[93] *Daily Natl Intelligencer*, March 6, 1813.

[94] AC, 12th Cong., 2d sess., 869-882, 884-907, 908-919.

[95] Gallatin's draft of the bill is in HR 12A-B1 47, LRHR. Cheves to Gallatin, February 3, 1813, and Gallatin to Cheves, February 9, 11, and 12, 1813, *Gallatin Papers*.

Republicans tacitly admitted that after the repeal of the Orders in Council they were unable to form a majority over how to relate the war effort to their commercial policies, which the war had originally been declared to defend, and an early session of the Thirteenth Congress to impose taxation thus became unavoidable.[96]

This embarrassing situation focused attention on the issue of impressment, which, although a very serious grievance, had not been the subject of major negotiations between the United States and Great Britain since 1808. American repugnance for the British claim of the "right" to search neutral vessels for the King's subjects, however, had necessarily become the justification for continuing the war, and, to enable it to serve this function more effectively, Madison produced at the end of January 1813 the so-called Seamen's Bill. At first sight, the measure seemed an attractively simple solution for a difficult problem, being basically an American offer to exclude foreigners from employment in the merchant marine of the United States in return for a British renunciation of the "right to search" neutral vessels on the high seas. Madison had suggested a similar scheme—that Great Britain and the United States mutually renounce the employment of each other's citizens—in 1807 in a previous attempt to settle the impressment dispute, but had dropped it when Gallatin calculated that the American merchant marine could not afford to discharge the number of British seamen he estimated to be involved.[97] The implementation of the 1813 measure could therefore have been regarded as a real concession to Great Britain inasmuch as its workings would have considerably slowed the growth of American navigation, but it seems unlikely that Madison raised the idea again with that purpose in mind. Indeed, the British government had already rejected three times between July and November 1812 the American suggestion that the essence of the Seamen's Bill serve as a basis for discussions on impressment, and the President had no reason to believe that their attitude was about to change.[98]

The fact that Madison was calling for the proposal to be written into American law before the enemy had agreed to accept it in ne-

[96] Jonathan Roberts apparently tried to persuade the House Ways and Means Committee to call a Republican caucus in order to restore party unity on the problem of repealing the Nonintercourse Law. Cheves, however, refused to agree. See Roberts to Dallas, December 19, 1813, Dallas Collection, HSP.

[97] See Gallatin to Jefferson, April 13 and 16, 1807, Jefferson Papers, LC; Notes by Gallatin, April 13, 1807, and Jefferson to Madison, April 27, 1807, Madison Papers, LC; Madison to Jefferson, April 17 and 20, 1807, and Jefferson to Gallatin, April 21, 1807, Jefferson Papers, LC.

[98] Frank A. Updyke, *The Diplomacy of the War of 1812* (Baltimore, 1915), 141-142. *Baltimore Whig*, January 8, 1813.

gotiations suggested that the administration was more immediately concerned with domestic politics than with international diplomacy. The debates on the legislation during the first two weeks of February 1813 revealed that its supporters, in the words of Israel Pickens of North Carolina, regarded it as an attempt to "define the grounds of the contest and present them in such a view that we may stand justified in our own eyes, and in the eyes of the world."[99] In this respect, the Seamen's Bill posed an awkward dilemma for the opponents of the administration who had always contended that the impressment issue was not a sufficient reason for war. If Great Britain should reject the terms of the bill, which no one seriously doubted would be the case, then the opposition would be deprived of one of its strongest arguments.[100] As Gallatin informed Monroe as he drafted the bill for the House foreign relations committee, its main advantage would be to "take from England and from our domestic enemies any pretext to cavil" over the legitimacy of the war.[101] The Republican majority would presumably re-form round the bill, while the Federalists could either unite in its rejection or divide over the dilemmas it raised for them.

The bill certainly placed the Federalists in a difficult situation, and they resented it for that very reason. Senator James A. Bayard of Delaware denounced it to his cousin as "an artful and deceitful measure," adding that "if we are to continue to fight till the point is conceded to us, you and I at least will grow grey in the war," since "the explicit abandonment of the right of search is never to be expected from Great Britain."[102] Eventually, a majority of Federalists present in the House decided to vote for the bill, but they were outnumbered by the supporters of the war who opposed it. The Republican members on the foreign relations committee, in fact, failed to agree on whether to report the bill to the House, and, as Jonathan Roberts of Pennsylvania rightly pointed out, the measure would arouse the anger of every Irish newspaper editor in the country for its tacit concession to the British doctrine of inalienable allegiance that was at the root of the impressment dis-

---

[99] AC, 12th Cong., 2d sess., 1006.

[100] Mitchill to Elizabeth Mitchill, January 30, 1813, Mitchill Papers, MCNY; Monroe to John Adams, February 15, 1813, Monroe Papers, LC. See also *Daily Natl Intelligencer*, January 13 and February 13, 1813; *The Enquirer*, January 14 and 16, 1813.

[101] Gallatin to Monroe, January 4, 1813, Monroe Papers, LC.

[102] Bayard to Andrew Bayard, February 14, 1813, Elizabeth Donnan, ed., *The Papers of James A. Bayard, 1796-1815* (Washington, D.C., 1913), 203. Taggart to Taylor, February 4, 1813, Haynes, "Letters of Taggart," 424. See also John Adams to Monroe, February 23, 1813, Monroe Papers, LC.

pute.[103] The bill passed the House on February 12, but by dividing both parties and annoying some of the strongest advocates of the war, who attacked it as a needlessly weak concession to the enemy, it failed to provide what the administration needed most—a stable base of political support for the war effort.[104] The alarming practice that had developed in mid-December 1812 of the House Republican majority dividing on critical war measures and giving the Federalists a potential balance of power thus went unchecked, as did the longstanding Republican factionalism in the Senate.[105] In fact, the Federalists and the "malcontent" Republicans in that body, aided by the absence of some key administration supporters, even succeeded in having the Seamen's Bill postponed until the next session of Congress before the matter was reconsidered, and the bill passed on February 27 with margins no larger than those which had been obtained for the declaration of war eight months earlier.[106]

This failure to consolidate or rally further support for the adminis-

---

[103] Jonathan to Matthew Roberts, January 31, 1813, Roberts Papers, HSP. The bill was objectionable to naturalized Americans, since it could be regarded as an admission that the United States had no right to naturalize people born in Great Britain. See *Baltimore Whig*, January 8 and 14, February 4, 1813; (New York) *The Shamrock*, February 20, 1813; *The Enquirer*, February 3, 1813.

[104] AC, 12th Cong., 2d sess., 932-941, 960-1055. In the House nineteen Federalists voted for the Seamen's Bill, but twenty-three Republicans opposed it. In only nine cases, however, were these Republicans among those who had opposed the party majority on the navy bill and the plan to remit merchant forfeitures. See also Mitchill to Elizabeth Mitchill, February 6, 1813, Mitchill Papers, MCNY; Harper to Plumer, February 6, 1813, Plumer Papers, LC; Rush to John Binns, February 3, 1813, Simon Gratz Autograph Collection, HSP; Edward Fox to Roberts, February 4, 1813, Roberts Papers, HSP; Burwell to Nicholas, February 1, 1813, Nicholas Papers, UVa; Taylor to Monroe, March 18, 1813, Monroe Papers, LC.

[105] In his study of House voting behavior Harry W. Fritz notes that Republican unity scores—as measured by the Rice index of cohesion and the relative index of cohesion—were generally lower in the second session of the Twelfth Congress than in the first. It would be an exaggeration to assert that the Republican majority in the House became consistently factionalized over the winter of 1812-1813, though there was a tendency on naval and some financial issues for Republicans from South Carolina and those from coastal northern and Middle Atlantic districts to vote against the party majority. Rather, it would seem that the Republicans were experiencing increasing difficulty in putting together successive majority coalitions. Fritz estimates that the party could afford to lose the support of up to 20% of its members and still carry a measure, but the defection rates on the naval and financial issues discussed above were higher than that. See Fritz, "The Collapse of Party: President, Congress and the Decline of Party Action, 1807-1817," (Ph.D. diss., Washington University, 1971), 275-278, 283, 289.

[106] AC, 12th Cong., 2d sess., 108, 111. The Senate vote for the Seamen's Bill was eighteen to twelve and reflected the longstanding division between administration supporters and "malcontent" Republicans. See also *Daily Natl Intelligencer*, February 26 and 28, 1813.

tration was reflected in the poor response to the loan that Gallatin opened on February 24, 1813 to finance the war expenditures for the year. Seeking $16 million, the Treasury after one month of subscriptions had received only some $3,756,000, barely two-thirds of the sum borrowed in 1812.[107] The situation was so desperate that by the first week in March Gallatin had to inform the President that there were scarcely enough funds left to carry on the government for a month, let alone a year, and he raised the possibility of having to postpone all military operations until the finances were on a firmer footing. "It is better," he argued, "in case of [financial] failure, to limit ourselves to what is strictly necessary than to be compelled to take retrograde steps."[108] Early in February the Treasury had been hoping to borrow, from a group of financiers headed by John Jacob Astor, the $10 million it had sought to raise from the remission of the forfeitures of the Non-intercourse Law, but Astor pointed out that, as in 1812, the government interest rate of 6 percent was simply not competitive and that few of the prospective money-lenders regarded a loan as good business when the chances for American success in the war were so bad. And for one of these financiers, David Parish, who had invested extensively in lands along the New York–Canadian border, the war so far had only been harmful to his business interests. Astor could therefore suggest to Gallatin only that the administration try to charter another Bank of the United States, then borrow from it $30 million to finance the war.[109]

Astor's correspondence with the Treasury further emphasized that the most important cause of the administration's difficulties was a lack of widespread support for its war policies. He believed that there was enough money in the nation's commercial cities to lend the government $15 million at 5 percent had the financiers really been disposed to do so, and it was only the fortuitous intervention of Russia in the Anglo-American war with an offer of mediation that enabled the Treasury to tap any of these funds. The interest of Alexander I in acting as mediator stemmed from his desire to maintain friendship both with Great Britain as an ally against France and with the United States as an important carrier of neutral trade. His offer, first conveyed to the American minister in St. Petersburg, John Quincy Adams, in September 1812, did

---

[107] Gallatin to Stephen Girard et al., February 24, 1813; Gallatin to Dallas, March 19, 1813, *Gallatin Papers.*

[108] Gallatin to Madison, March 5, 1813, ibid.

[109] Astor to Gallatin, February 6 and 14, March 20, 1813, ibid. On Parish's activities in New York see Chapter V, above, and see also John Lovett to Joseph Alexander, May 18, 1813, Catherine V. Bonney, *A Legacy of Historical Gleanings* (Albany, 1875), I, 298.

not reach Washington until the end of February, and the administration, after confirming the details with the Russian minister to the United States, Andrei Dashkov, and despite its previous coolness toward Russia's triumph over France, did not hesitate long before accepting it.[110] There was later some criticism of the administration's apparent haste in taking this decision, but Madison must have felt that he had nothing to lose by it.[111] Given the longstanding interest of Russia in trying to compel Great Britain to accept liberal definitions of neutral rights as well as the fact that both Jefferson and Madison had long admired the Anglo-Russian Convention of 1801, which realized, albeit temporarily, this goal, the President assumed that the Emperor would not contemplate any basis for peace that was harmful to the maritime interests of the United States.[112] And, with the lack of precise information in Washington about the origins of the mediation offer, it is not entirely impossible that Madison may have believed it was prompted by Great Britain as an honorable way of escaping the inconveniences of the war with America.[113] Even if the British government should reject the offer, American acceptance could still lead to improved commercial relationships with Russia, while preserving the possibility of using Russian friendship as a diplomatic lever in the struggle against the enemy.[114]

The Russian mediation thus promised the administration the chance of making a better peace than its performance in the war would otherwise have justified. Gallatin certainly viewed the development in this light, and he traveled to Philadelphia to try to raise further loans for his budget on this basis. Offering to raise the interest rate to 7.5 percent, he was this time successful, persuading Astor to lend $2.5 million while Parish, with the banker Stephen Girard, undertook to raise

[110] Dashkov formally transmitted the offer of Russian mediation on March 8, 1813, and Monroe conveyed the administration's acceptance on March 11. However, Dashkov did not formally make the offer until discussions with Monroe before March 8 had revealed that Madison would respond to the Russian initiative. These background details can be most conveniently followed in Nikolai N. Bolkhovitinov, *The Beginnings of Russian-American Relations, 1775-1815*, Elena Levin, trans. (Cambridge, Mass., 1975), 304-314. See also Monroe to John Quincy Adams, April 26, 1813, Adams Family Papers, MHS.

[111] See, for example (Philadelphia) *Democratic Press*, March 20 and 30, 1813. But see also Madison to John Nicholas, April 2, 1813, Madison Papers, LC; and Rush to Ingersoll, March 29, 1813, Ingersoll Papers, HSP.

[112] For Madison's approval of the 1801 Anglo-Russian Convention see Madison to Monroe, December 26, 1803, Madison Papers, LC. See also Madison's 1805 pamphlet *Examination of the British Doctrine which subjects to capture a Neutral Trade Not Open in Time of Peace.*

[113] Jones to Dallas, March 10, 1813, Dallas Collection, HSP; Elbridge Gerry to Mercy Warren, April 4, 1813, Elbridge Gerry Papers, MHS.

[114] Monroe to James Barbour, March 21, 1813, Monroe Papers, LC.

nearly $8 million. The war could thus continue for another year at least.[115] There began circulating at the same time, though, rumors that the mediation would lead to an immediate armistice, which increased when Dashkov sent his legation counselor Aleksei Sverchkov, to the British admiral on the American coast, Sir John Borlase Warren, to obtain diplomatic passports for the American negotiators. On his own initiative, Dashkov did, in fact, propose on April 3 an armistice to Warren, who seemed disposed to discuss it, but the administration preferred to refer all negotiations to St. Petersburg and entrust them to the friendly influence of the Emperor.[116] The rumors, nonetheless, persisted, and the belief that the fighting in America would be terminated in favor of distant negotiations in a foreign capital led some Republican newspaper editors to criticize, and even abuse, Russia most severely for intervening in the quarrel with Great Britain.[117] Dashkov, understandably enough, took offense at some of these attacks, and John Armstrong eventually had to write to the worst of the offending editors, William Duane of the *Aurora*, to suggest that he subdue his anti-Slavic sentiments.[118]

The choice of commissioners to present the American case in Russia was a delicate matter. The American minister in Russia would clearly have to participate in the negotiations, and, to convince the administration's opponents that its policies were not governed by narrow party views, it seemed a good move to include one of their leaders in the delegation. For this purpose, Madison chose Senator James A. Bayard of Delaware, a Federalist who opposed the expediency of the war but

[115] Gallatin to Dallas, March 19, 1813, *Gallatin Papers*. See also Astor to Gallatin, April 5, 1813; Parish and Girard to Gallatin, April 5, 1813; Gallatin to Parish and Girard, April 7, 1813, ibid. For the details of the loan see Donald R. Adams, Jr., *Finance and Enterprise in Early America: A Study of Stephen Girard's Bank, 1812-1831* (Philadelphia, 1978), 30-34.

[116] Dashkov to Rumiantsev, April 10, 1813, and also the enclosed letters between Warren and Dashkov of March 24, April 3 and 4, 1813, Russian Archives. See also N. N. Bolkhovitinov and S. I. Divil'kovskii, "Russian Diplomacy and the Anglo-American War of 1812-1814," *Soviet Studies in History* 1 (1962), 23.

[117] William Barraud to John Hartwell Cocke, March 23, 1813, Cocke Family Papers, UVa. See also *The Enquirer*, March 26, 1813; *National Advocate*, March 5 and 29, May 7, 1813; *Baltimore Whig*, March 10, 1813; (Philadelphia) *Aurora General Advertiser*, April 10 and 22, 1813.

[118] Armstrong to Duane, April 29, 1813, "Selections for the Duane Papers," 62. Dashkov complained that Duane's anti-Russian editorials were "indecent," but he turned them to his advantage by using the issue to prevent the administration from instructing John Quincy Adams to complain about the participation of the Russian consul in Boston, Alexei Evstaf'ev, in the Federalists' celebrations of Napoleon's recent defeat. See Dashkov to Rumiantsev, July 1, 1813, Russian Archives.

who was also less favorably disposed toward Great Britain than many members of his party.[119] To balance Bayard's presence, Madison may have thought of nominating Henry Clay to represent the views of the majority of congressional Republicans who supported the war, but, according to Rufus King, Clay was passed over in favor of Gallatin.[120] Dashkov appears to have urged the appointment of the President's closest adviser in the cabinet as a mark of respect that would please Alexander I, and the Treasury Secretary himself, Madison's own reluctance notwithstanding, was more than willing to accept the assignment. It allowed him to state to the money-lenders that the administration was virtually pledged to ending the war honorably within the year, and, after twelve years of service in Washington, he also desperately wanted to escape from the increasing personal and political difficulties involved in financing the war.[121] In this way, the American delegation to St. Petersburg came to be composed of men who, in one form or another, had all been critical of the war; and this fact did not escape unfavorable comment about the administration's appearing to be too eager for peace.[122] If this was a disadvantage, however, the President very probably hoped that it would persuade Alexander I of American sincerity and thus leave the decision for the continuation of the war entirely with Great Britain.[123]

The instructions for the delegation to Russia were a less difficult issue than was its selection. The American terms for peace had already been defined in the Seamen's Bill, and above all else the commissioners had to get its provisions written into a treaty. The administration hoped that whatever progress the United States might make toward conquering Canada in the summer of 1813 would persuade the British government to concede the point, and on that basis Monroe issued the

[119] According to Ingersoll, Madison at first considered Rufus King and Harrison Gray Otis as the Federalists who might be sent to Russia before deciding on Bayard. See Ingersoll's *Historical Sketch of the Second War Between the United States of America and Great Britain* (Philadelphia, 1845), II, 248, 289.

[120] Madison to Gallatin, April 5, 1813, *Gallatin Papers*. See also King's observations in Charles R. King, *The Life and Correspondence of Rufus King* (New York, 1894-1900), V, 320.

[121] Gallatin to James W. Nicholson, May 5, 1813, and to William Few, May 9, 1813, *Gallatin Papers*. See also the diary entry for October 21, 1813, Donnan, *Bayard Papers*, 476. At the outset Dashkov was hostile toward Gallatin, whom he suspected of being too favorable toward France in his outlook, but gradually the Russian diplomat realized that the Treasury Secretary desperately wanted peace and had the most influence with the President. Dashkov to Rumiantsev, March 16, 1813, Russian Archives.

[122] See, for example (Lexington) *Kentucky Gazette*, April 20 and 27, 1813; *Democratic Press*, March 20 and 30, 1813.

[123] Dashkov to Rumiantsev, April 7, 1813, Russian Archives.

commissioners a series of instructions designed to cover the most likely contingencies. On the assumption that the American armies would actually succeed in occupying parts of Canada, Monroe explained that the administration did not wish the possession of such territory to be an obstacle to peace if Great Britain should insist on its restoration. Nevertheless, the administration also revealed its reluctance to have to renounce such a tangible proof of victory, and Monroe urged the commissioners to try to persuade Great Britain to cede to the United States at least Upper Canada, if not more. Great Britain's retention of Canada, he wrote, would only "hereafter prove a fruitful source of controversy which its transfer to the U.S. would remove. . . ." Since the Constitution forbade the taxing of exports, Great Britain could continue, Monroe pointed out, to draw on Canada after its annexation "as a source of supplies (presumably for the West Indies) as if it were her own," provided that she remained at peace with the United States.[124] Most of the remaining instructions were concerned with the provisions of commercial treaties which the United States might make with Great Britain and Russia, though at one point Monroe did add his wish that the mediation might induce the British government to accept the American position on East Florida. Gallatin, however, protested this as an irrelevant intrusion, adding that the prolongation of the war for the sake of East Florida would "disgust every man north of Washington."[125]

The commissioners left for Russia shortly after Dearborn opened the campaign of 1813 against York in Upper Canada. At this point, thanks largely to Armstrong's determination to seize personal control of the war and to the intervention of Alexander I, the administration seemed to have made a fair recovery from the difficulties that had beset it during the winter of 1812-1813. The composition of the administration had been changed, and this had resulted in a personally, if not yet politically, stronger cabinet than the one that had so badly mismanaged the war in 1812. Also, the war had been funded for another year, and its prospects, both militarily and diplomatically, were far better than anyone might have predicted at the end of 1812. Yet these prospects

[124] Copies of the instructions and papers relating to the Russian mediation can be found in the personal papers of all the commissioners, but see particularly Monroe to Gallatin, April 27, May 5 and 6, 1813, *Gallatin Papers*; Monroe to Commissioners, April 15 and 30, 1813; and Monroe to Gallatin and Bayard, June 23, 1813, Donnan, *Bayard Papers*, 204-206, 219, 226-229. On the future value of Canada to Great Britain either as an American state or as a British colony, Madison made an argument similar to Monroe's after the war. See Madison to Monroe, November 28, 1818, Madison Papers, LC.

[125] Gallatin to Monroe, May 2, 1813, Monroe Papers, LC.

rested on slender bases indeed. The administration, in fact, had solid political support for no more than an attempt to raise an army to defend the nation and to invade Canada; on almost all other issues related to these two policies, opinions were too opposed, and the Republican party too divided, for the administration to proceed with confidence. And even if the war had been more popular, its success as a measure of coercion against Great Britain was now partly dependent on the outcome of events in Europe over which the United States had no control. It was, in short, a difficult and unpredictable situation, and one which allowed little further margin for error or failure.

CHAPTER VII

★

POLITICS AND WAR, 1813

ON MAY 24, 1813, the Thirteenth Congress assembled in Washington for an early first session. The President had summoned the meeting as long ago as February 23, principally to raise additional revenue for the Treasury Department, which, as a result of the failure of the twelfth Congress either to impose taxes or to exact a revenue from the remission of the penalties of the Nonintercourse Law, faced a serious deficit after the end of the year. Extra sessions, however, were never popular, least of all in the hot, humid conditions of the Washington summer, and both Congressmen and the administration hoped that the Republican party could organize its almost two-to-one majority in both branches of the legislature and dispose quickly of the nation's business.[1] Since the only items on the agenda were the tax laws and the Senate confirmation of the nominations of the three commissioners recently dispatched by Madison to St. Petersburg, the session promised to be a short one—provided, as William Lowndes of South Carolina remarked to his wife, that nobody bothered to discuss the origins of the war or the question of whether it was "moral treason" to oppose it.[2] Instead, Congress sat for nearly ten weeks, almost as long as a regular session, with its proceedings more than realizing Lowndes's worst fears. By the first week in August, Madison's administration had sustained some serious political defeats, while the legitimacy of the war with Great

---

[1] John Wayles Eppes to Thomas Jefferson, May 25, 1813, Edgehill-Randolph Papers, UVa. *Daily Natl Intelligencer*, May 20 and 26, 1813. The strength of parties in the thirteenth Congress is usually given as 114 Republicans to 68 Federalists in the House, and 27 Republicans to 9 Federalists in the Senate. See (Baltimore) *The Weekly Register*, June 16, 1813.

[2] William Lowndes to Elizabeth Lowndes, June 23, 1813, William Lowndes Papers, UNC. See also Charles Cutts to William Plumer, June 8, 1813, William Plumer Papers, LC.

Britain was no more clearly established than it had ever been. The Republicans were neither sufficiently adroit nor unified enough to avert these setbacks.

As always, the President's message, delivered on May 25, defined the themes for political debate. Madison reviewed the events of the past few months, concentrating on the tragic death in Poland of Joel Barlow, the American minister to France, the state of the Treasury, and the Russian mediation. On this last subject, he announced his presumption that Great Britain had accepted the Russian offer, since he could see no motive for the enemy to continue the war for the possibility of obtaining better peace terms than those which the United States had already offered in the Seamen's Bill of February 1813. The President's language here, however, perhaps hinted at a suspicion that Great Britain might continue fighting for terms that Americans could not accept at all, and to deal with this contingency he promised a vigorous prosecution of the war "to demonstrate to the world the public energy of our political institutions."[3] Then, on May 31, Madison sent to the Senate the nominations of Adams, Bayard, and Gallatin, and added to them the nomination of Jonathan Russell as minister to Sweden. Three days later, acting Treasury Secretary Jones forwarded to the House a report on the nation's finances, including a list of nine direct and indirect taxes which Gallatin had considered necessary to balance the budget and maintain the government's credit in 1814.[4] The House Ways and Means Committee began to consider the necessary bills for its report, but, in the interim, the opponents of the war seized the initiative, which they held for the remainder of the session.

Here the Federalists were the first to take the offensive. Their numbers had been considerably strengthened by their electoral victories in the last months of 1812, and, led by Daniel Webster of New Hampshire in the House and Robert Goldsborough of Maryland in the Senate, they decided to re-examine the grounds on which Madison had justified the diplomacy which had led to the declaration of war. Their pretext was the publication in the United States of the so-called Decree of St.

[3] James D. Richardson, comp., *A Compilation of the Messages and Papers of the Presidents* (New York, 1897-1914), II, 515-516. The Russian minister, Dashkov, was still uncertain about how sincerely the administration was committed to Alexander I's mediation as a way of bringing peace. The minister's views on the subject were colored by his conversations with Federalists, and he reported his belief that most cabinet members would have preferred continuing the war to making peace. The President, Dashkov felt, favored peace, but governed his views in accordance with party sentiments in order to end the war without disgrace. Andrei Dashkov to Count Nikolai P. Rumiantsev, June 15, 1813, Archives of the Russian Foreign Ministry (microfilm of Arkhiv vneshnei politiki Rossii for 1809-1816, held in LC).

[4] AC, 13th Cong., 1st sess., 84, 91, 127-131.

Cloud bearing the date of April 28, 1811, in which Napoleon had announced the "definitive" repeal of the Berlin and Milan decrees, and which the French Foreign Minister, the duc de Bassano, claimed to have presented to the American chargé d'affaires, Jonathan Russell in Paris, at the time of its issue. The appearance of this decree caused Madison, and to a lesser extent John Armstrong and Russell, considerable embarrassment. The President, it will be recalled, had accepted the Cadore letter of August 5, 1810, as evidence of the repeal of the Berlin and Milan decrees, and had based his campaign against the Orders in Council on the strength of that document. The Decree of St. Cloud, on the other hand, was obviously a postdated fraud which had not existed before May 1812, but its publication as an official document of the French government seemed to call into question both the legitimacy and the necessity of the war against Great Britain, the more so since the Orders in Council had been lifted within six weeks of the "definitive" repeal of the French decrees.[5]

Webster and Goldsborough presented the Federalist attack in five resolutions requiring the administration to make known to Congress— by releasing all its diplomatic correspondence—the precise circumstances in which it had learned of the Decree of St. Cloud and whether it had ever demanded an explanation from France of its conduct toward the United States since August 1810. If either branch of the legislature voted to request the information, Madison could scarcely reply without incriminating both himself and the French Emperor, while, by refusing the information, he would expose himself to the dishonorable imputation that he did indeed have something to hide. Regardless of the outcome, therefore, the Federalists seemed bound to gain a tactical victory over the administration. The Senate referred the resolution to a select committee of two Federalists—Goldsborough and Rufus King of New York—and one Republican, Joseph Anderson of Tennessee, while Goldsborough then moved to postpone consideration of Russell's nomination to Sweden until his role in the French transaction had been clarified.[6] In subsequent meetings and correspondence with the Secretary of State, the committee learned from Monroe that his department had no official correspondence on the alleged transmission of the Decree of St. Cloud in April 1811, and Monroe added that Russell's private correspondence "unequivocally denied" that any such document had

---

[5] See above, Chapter II. When the Decree of St. Cloud was released in May 1812, Russell, then chargé d'affaires in London, reported that its origins were "equivocal" and that it looked like a "fraud." Jonathan Russell to James Monroe, June 30, 1812, Dispatches from American Ministers to Great Britain (M-30), Records of the Department of State (RG 59), NA.

[6] AC, 13th Cong., 1st sess., 91, 149-150.

been given to him at that time.[7] Since private correspondence could not be made public for examination, the Federalist Senators lost interest in the Decree of St. Cloud and decided instead to continue the attack on the administration through the nominations of Gallatin and Russell. This decision left the House Federalists to pursue their party's inquiry into the origins of the spurious French decree.

Webster's resolutions occupied the House for five days, although the immediate reaction of the Republicans was to reject them. The chairman of the House foreign relations committee, John C. Calhoun of South Carolina, denounced the resolutions as "novel" and "objectionable," arguing that he could see no good reason why the information was necessary to the House. Yet as the Republicans debated the matter with their opponents, they lost control of both their tempers and their grasp on the complexity of the issues involved. More than one prominent Republican attempted to talk his way out of the problem by asserting that the matter of French repeal had nothing to do with the justice or the expediency of Madison's decision to insist on an end to the Orders in Council, and some even went so far as to claim that war would have been declared over the impressment issue alone. The Federalists had little difficulty in refuting both arguments. Thomas Grosvenor of New York easily demonstrated that it was not possible either to regard the Cadore letter and the Decree of St. Cloud as equally valid proofs of the repeal of the French decrees or to assert that French diplomacy had not been without bearing on the coming of the war. He also pointed out that the impressment issue had never been presented to Great Britain as a sufficient cause of war in the years before 1812, thus leaving his fellow partisan, Thomas Oakley of New York, to draw the conclusion that the war had "its very foundation in the duplicity and fraud of the French government and in the blind and willful folly of our own."[8]

Forced back on the defensive, the Republican ranks divided. A small minority of about thirty administration supporters voted against requiring the President to respond to Webster's resolutions, while the remaining Republicans, about seventy in all, voted with the Federalists

[7] Ibid., 94.

[8] Ibid., 169-301, for the House debate. For an extremely derogatory Federalist opinion on the quality of Republican arguments on Webster's resolutions see John Lovett's notes of June 7, 1813, on a speech by Robert Wright of Maryland: "I say as the honest German did of the smell of the Polecat: 'ven I was kood vays off I smell'd em mighde strong: then I comps up glose py em, and py der divils kile, he sdankt so dat I could zmell noding unter Cot's heavens.'" Catherine V. Bonney, *A Legacy of Historical Gleanings* (Albany, 1875), I, 299.

to invite him to remove the suspicions and confusion they had both created about the grounds for war. Very possibly, many of the Republicans voted for the resolutions in order to move more quickly to a consideration of the tax bills, but they still left the Secretary of State with a difficult task.[9] Monroe, though, did not bother to trouble the French minister for an explanation of the Decree of St. Cloud, for he freely admitted that "in truth, we know, as I presume, all that we shall know on [that] subject. . . ." Instead, he simply sat on the resolutions for as long as possible, until the House foreign relations committee told him that further delay was impossible. Then, on July 12, 1813, he returned to Congress a lengthy report, complete with extracts from official State Department correspondence.[10]

Monroe decided not to answer seriatim the five resolutions that had been submitted by the House and chose instead to make some general observations about relations between Great Britain, France, and the United States as they affected the declaration of war. Given the difficulties of his task, this was probably as good a tactic as it was possible to adopt, but the report was, nonetheless, a tortuous and confusing document. It attempted to prove not only that the British refusal to repeal the Orders in Council—considered independently of the question of whether France had ever repealed its decrees in any form before May 1812—was a sufficient cause for war but also that the United States had been justified in declaring war over the Orders because the French decrees had, in fact, been repealed by November 1810. Similarly, Monroe attempted, too, to argue both that the eventual British repeal of the Orders in Council in June 1812 was not made in response to the appearance of the Decree of St. Cloud and that the British acceptance of that decree for that same purpose was proof that Great Britain was tacitly admitting that it should have repealed its Orders as long ago as November 1810. This last argument was only tenable on the assumption, which Monroe avowed, that there was, in fact, no difference between the two statements of French repeal, even though Monroe himself also admitted that the second of these had been "definitive" and the first only "conditional." The Secretary then went on to attack Great Britain for doubting the word of the French government

[9] *Daily Natl Intelligencer*, June 22, 1813. AC, 13th Cong., 1st sess., 302-310. On each of the five votes the Republican minority was composed of roughly the same members, but they exhibited no distinctively regional distribution. See also Lovett to John Alexander, June 17, 1813, Bonney, *Gleanings*, I, 300.

[10] Monroe to William H. Crawford, June 12, 1813, William H. Crawford Papers, LC; Felix Grundy to Monroe, July 8, 1813, James Monroe Papers, LC. The report, with accompanying documents, is in *ASP: Foreign Relations*, III, 608-618.

over the "conditional" repeal of its decrees announced in the Cadore letter. To have requested proof of repeal in addition to that letter, Monroe wrote, was "a demand without example in the intercourse between nations." If France had intended a fraud in the Cadore letter, he added, "might it not likewise commit a fraud in any other communication which it might make?"

Presumably, this question was meant to be purely rhetorical, but, under the circumstances, it perhaps should not have been asked at all. Even more awkward, though, was Monroe's claim that, while Great Britain had "maintained in full force its unlawful edicts" against the United States, France had made, in the Cadore letter, "a considerable advance at least . . . towards a complete accommodation." These last qualifications came close to conceding the thrust of Webster's resolutions—that American policy toward Great Britain after November 1810 was based on something of a misconception, willful or otherwise, about the true nature of French policy toward neutrals. The report eventually concluded with Monroe's observations that the war had been necessary, that the people had "not submitted to privations in vain," and that the problem of impressment was still a legitimate reason for its continuation.[11] The House foreign affairs committee then moved a resolution to approve the conduct of the executive as revealed in the report, but by mid-July many Republicans had already had more than enough of the interminable aridity of the debate. Among them, William Lowndes had been privately lobbying for some weeks on both sides of the House for an agreement that the matter would be considered no further, and the motion of the committee was first postponed, then finally voted down on July 20. A majority of Congressmen, no doubt, wanted no more than to conclude the session, even if they continued to disagree, as Rufus King put it, over whether the avowed objects of the war were the real ones.[12]

While the House had been debating Webster's resolutions to discredit the origins of the war, the Senate developed an attack on the administration's attempt to end it through the Russian mediation. On June 2, Rufus King presented two resolutions for the Senate to request the administration to lay before it the documents and diplomatic commissions relating to the American acceptance of the mediation of Alexander I. King also inquired whether Gallatin remained Secretary of

[11] *ASP: Foreign Relations*, III, 609-613.

[12] AC, 13th Cong., 1st sess., 435-439, 470. For Lowndes's role see Lowndes to Elizabeth Lowndes, June 7 and July 6, 1813, Lowndes Papers, UNC. See also King's notes on "Gallatin," Charles R. King, *The Life and Correspondence of Rufus King* (New York, 1894-1900), V, 337.

the Treasury, and, if so, how the departmental duties were being performed during the absence of its head for a long period in Russia. The New Yorker failed to gain sufficient support for his first two resolutions, but the Senators readily agreed to investigate Gallatin's status at the Treasury.[13] The Secretary had never been popular with the "malcontent" Republican Senators, and right from the outset of the session it was apparent that the manner of his departure for Russia had done nothing to improve his standing within the party. Almost all Republicans, including Monroe in the cabinet itself, believed that Gallatin had deliberately deserted the administration at a difficult time in order to evade the responsibility for the taxes which he had said Congress must now impose. Even Anderson of Tennessee—who had defended Gallatin strongly against the Federalists and the "malcontents" throughout the Twelfth Congress—decided he could support the Secretary no longer, and he had doubts about the Russell mission as well. He accordingly gained Federalist and "malcontent" support for a Senate investigation of the circumstances surrounding Russell's nomination to the court of Sweden.[14]

To these difficulties were added some unmistakable signs of serious differences of opinion between Gallatin and the new Secretary of War, Armstrong. These involved not so much matters of policy as they did conflicts of personality. Armstrong had begun to use the patronage of the War Department, which now more than rivaled that of the Treasury in its extent, to build up his political strength within the Republican party, and many of his appointments revealed a disposition to favor men or factions who had quarreled with Gallatin. This was particularly the case in Pennsylvania, where the highly vocal anti-Snyderite "Old School" Republicans of Philadelphia, led by William Duane of the *Aurora*, gained many important posts in the expanding military establishment.[15] Duane himself, much to Gallatin's horror, became Adjutant General of the Fourth Military District, and his military treatise, *A*

[13] See King's notes on Gallatin's mission, *King*, V, 318-327. *AC*, 13th Cong., 1st sess. 84-85. In the archives of the Senate there is a bundle of resolutions drafted by several Federalist Senators, including King, Gore, and Goldsborough, on Gallatin's nomination. See Sen 13B-D.2, Legislative Records of the United States Senate (RG 46), NA.

[14] *AC*, 13th Cong., 1st sess., 92. See Monroe to Jefferson, June 16, 1813, Monroe Papers, LC; Lowndes to Elizabeth Lowndes, June 7, 1813, and to Joseph Alston, June 23, 1813, Lowndes Papers, UNC; Cutts to Plumer, June 8, 1813, Plumer Papers, LC; Jonathan Roberts to Matthew Roberts, June 16, 1813, Jonathan Roberts Papers, HSP.

[15] See Richard Rush to Charles Jared Ingersoll, March 20, 1813; John Binns to Ingersoll, May 31, June 9 and 19, July 11 and 13, 1813, Charles Jared Ingersoll Papers, HSP. Madison's private secretary also warned that Armstrong thought "too highly of Duane and his friend" (i.e. Michael Leib), Edward Coles to Madison, May 22, 1813, "Abstracts of Letters of Edward Coles," James Madison Papers, LC.

Handbook for Infantry, became the prescribed manual for army drill instruction, replacing those written by Baron Steuben and Alexander Smyth.[16] Armstrong, moreover, employed as his private secretary John Spear Smith of Baltimore, a former diplomat whose career had seemingly been cut short by Madison's dismissal of his uncle from the State Department in March 1811, and, collectively, such appointments suggested, as William Jones humorously remarked, that the "Old Soldier" was "no legitimate son of Mars."[17] The war effort was clearly being organized with a view to the presidential election of 1816 as well as to the conquest of Canada, and this situation, more than likely, made Monroe, who could command only the limited resources of the State Department, resentful toward Gallatin for leaving him to oppose Armstrong unsupported in the cabinet.[18]

The President could hardly have been blind to the dangers of a revival of serious conflicts within the cabinet, but personal loyalty to Gallatin and an apparent lack of alternatives led him to underestimate the capacity of the Senate to exploit the situation to his disadvantage. His tactics, however, did nothing to placate the Senators, who if not spoiling for a fight were at least concerned about the difficulties the administration had created for itself by claiming that the President's closest adviser could be both Treasury Secretary and a diplomat in Russia at the same time. Yet this was exactly what Madison did claim on June 3, when he informed the Senate that Gallatin was indeed still Secretary of the Treasury and that his duties would be performed in his absence by Navy Secretary Jones.[19] Four days later, the President attempted to justify the nomination of a minister to Sweden by sending

[16] Gallatin to James W. Nicholson, May 5, 1813; to William Few, May 9, 1813, Carl Prince and Helen Fineman, eds., *The Papers of Albert Gallatin* (microfilm ed.). For the adoption of Duane's *Handbook* see Adjutant General (AG) to Callender Irvine, March 19, 1813, LSAG.

[17] Joseph H. Nicholson to William Jones, August 24, 1813, Uselma Clarke Smith Collection of William Jones Papers, HSP; Jones to Alexander James Dallas, July 19, 1813, George Mifflin Dallas Collection, HSP. Samuel Smith welcomed Armstrong as an ally against Gallatin; see Smith to Armstrong, April 2, 1813, Samuel Smith Papers, LC. See also *Baltimore Whig*, January 22, February 10, April 8, June 18 and 25, 1813.

[18] Dallas claimed that Armstrong was responsible for influencing the Senate vote on July 19, 1813, to reject Gallatin's nomination to Russia as a way of expelling the Treasury Secretary from the cabinet. See Dallas to Hannah Nicholson Gallatin, July 22, 1813, *Gallatin Papers*; Dallas to Jones, August 2, 1813, Jones Papers, HSP. While this is possible, there is no other evidence to support the claim that Armstrong was so openly hostile to Gallatin, nor would it have been necessary for him to have acted so to bring about Gallatin's rejection. Given Madison's behavior throughout the summer of 1813, Gallatin's nomination would have almost certainly failed in any case.

[19] Madison to Samuel Otis, June 3, 1813, *Gallatin Papers*; AC, 13th Cong., 1st sess., 85.

the Senate two old letters—one from Reuben Beasley, the commissioner for American prisoners of war in London, and the other from John Speyer, American consul in Stockholm—which confirmed the fact that agents of the Swedish government had suggested an exchange of ministers.[20] The administration, it might be surmised, was interested in having diplomatic representation in Sweden to strengthen Russian pressure on Great Britain during the course of the anticipated mediation, but the presidential communication did not explain these motives.[21] Nor did many of the Senators, who had specifically requested Madison's correspondence with the Swedish monarch, find the documents before them sufficiently authoritative sources to warrent Russell's nomination. There had, in fact, been no correspondence with the Swedish court, while the letter from Beasley actually contained evidence that Sweden was somewhat annoyed with the United States for maintaining a minister at the rival court of Denmark, and it even implied that future Swedish policy toward the Republic would be unfriendly if a minister were not sent. As William B. Giles of Virginia later observed, the administration had failed to show a clear cause for the nomination of Russell, and, in such a situation, the Senators were entitled to speculate freely, and unfavorably, as to what might be its real cause.[22]

The Senate debated the nominations of Gallatin and Russell for several days before referring them both by mid-June to select committees for further discussion and reports. These committees, though, contained few friends of the administration and were dominated by Giles and King. The committees sought interviews with Madison to discuss the nominations, only to be told that the President was willing to meet with the Senators as individuals but could not acknowledge that the committees had any official standing. The committee on Gallatin's nomination responded to this check by declaring that the duties of Treasury Secretary and commissioner to Russia could not be compatibly united in one person and by seeking a resolution to instruct

[20] AC, 13th Cong., 1st sess., 92-94. Monroe to Senate, June 7, 1813, Sen 13B-B.2, Legislative Records of the Senate, NA.

[21] On the strength of Speyer's letter, Monroe believed that the Swedish government, disapproving of the British practices of impressment and blockade, was disposed to use its good offices to bring about peace between Great Britain and the United States. See Monroe to Gallatin, Adams, and Bayard, April 15, 1813, Elizabeth Donnan, ed., *The Papers of James A. Bayard, 1796-1815* (Washington, D.C., 1913), 205-206.

[22] Giles's remarks on Russell's nomination were printed in the *Daily Natl Intelligencer*, November 16, 1813. Madison admitted that his attempts to justify the nomination had been unfortunate, since they enabled the Senate to misconstrue his views. Madison to Monroe, August 19, 1813, Monroe Papers, LC.

its members to discuss the matter further with the President.[23] The committee on Russell's nomination was about to embark on a similar course, even being on the threshold of the President's house on June 15, when it was informed that Madison had fallen ill and could not receive them.[24] The illness, though, was not a diplomatic one, for the President had suffered a serious attack of "bilious fever," probably brought on by the combined effects of advancing age, incessant overwork, and the unhealthy summer environment of Washington. He was unable to attend to any official duties for nearly a month, while reports circulated during that period that he was near death.[25]

In these circumstances, the Senate challenge to the President began to assume ominous overtones, the more so since Vice President Elbridge Gerry also fell ill shortly afterward.[26] Monroe feared that the "malcontents" had wider goals than the mere defeat of Gallatin's nomination; he believed that they were plotting in anticipation of the death of both Madison and Gerry to elect Giles, first as president pro tem of the Senate and then to elevate him to the Presidency itself.[27] The Secretary of State had been fretting about his own presidential prospects in 1816, realizing that he could possibly be excluded from the prize by a New Yorker with a western running mate, but to be thwarted prematurely by Giles through purely accidental circumstances was far more than he could bear to contemplate.[28] To relieve the pressure on the harassed President and to confront his adversaries, Monroe offered to meet with the committees to discuss the nominations. The Senators, however, declined the offer, stating that they preferred to wait for Madison's recovery before taking the matter any further.[29] The com-

[23] AC, 13th Cong., 1st sess., 85, 86, 95. Joseph Anderson to Madison, June 11, 1813, Madison Papers, LC.
[24] "Papers on Russell's Nomination," Sen 13B-D.2, Legislative Records of the Senate, NA. William Wells to Madison, June 15, 1813, James Madison Papers, NYPL.
[25] For some details of Madison's illness see Irving Brant, *James Madison: Commander in Chief, 1812-1836* (Indianapolis, 1961), 184, 187-188.
[26] Elbridge Gerry to Ann Gerry, July 5, 1813, Elbridge Gerry Papers, MHS.
[27] Monroe to Jefferson, June 28, 1813, Thomas Jefferson Papers, LC. It was for this reason that Gerry, at the end of the session, refused to observe the custom of retiring from the Senate to allow it to elect a president pro tem. If there was no president pro tem of the Senate, the Presidency of the United States, in the event of Madison's and Gerry's deaths, would have fallen to the Speaker of the House, Henry Clay—a more reliable supporter of the war. See Henry B. Larned, "Gerry and the Presidential Succession in 1813," *American Historical Review* 22 (1916), 95-97.
[28] Monroe to George Hay, October 17, 1813, James Monroe Papers, NYPL. Monroe worried greatly that anti-Virginian sentiment would deny him the Presidency, and he complained that "all the enemies of the Administration, of the war . . . will be enemies to me."
[29] Monroe to Jefferson, June 28, 1813, Jefferson Papers, LC. Anderson to Madison, July 12, 1813, Madison Papers, LC.

mittee on Russell's nomination did not, in fact, wait this long, the Senate voting on July 9 to declare that it was "inexpedient" to send a minister to Sweden, and thereafter the attack was concentrated on the nomination of Gallatin.[30]

Gallatin and his policies continued to dominate the proceedings of Congress during the period of Madison's illness as both houses moved to consider the list of taxes the Treasury required for 1814. There was little disagreement among Republican Congressmen at the beginning of the session that taxes would have to be imposed, but formidable problems arose from the selection of the objects to be taxed and their apportionment throughout the Union. The Republican acceptance of the need for taxation, moreover, was balanced by a fear of the political consequences of the policy, and this fear, combined with the requirement of devising a variety of taxes to distribute the burden evenly among the regions of the nation, encouraged inter- and intraparty conflict of the most complicated kinds as Congressmen tried to exempt their states from particular levies. This problem was compounded not so much by the lack of leadership from the administration during the President's illness—for there was no doubt what the Treasury wanted— but by the fact that congressional procedures themselves for handling legislation could not contain any prolonged controversy. Nor could the Republican party, as events were to prove, arrive at a consensus that wholly remedied this deficiency. In due course, the necessary taxes were passed, but the series of conflicts between Republicans and Federalists, between regional groups of Republicans, between House and Senate, and between executive and legislature only served to emphasize the lack of Republican unity that had already been exposed over foreign policy issues.

The first important Republican to desert the administration here was the chairman of the House Ways and Means Committee, John Wayles Eppes of Virginia. Admittedly, he had reported to the House early in the session the Treasury's recommendations for direct and indirect taxes totaling $6,365,000, but shortly thereafter he suffered a severe attack of gout, during which he began to rethink his principles of political economy.[31] The taxes suggested by Gallatin and the method of apportioning them differed little from those imposed by the Federalists between 1798 and 1800, and they did not, furthermore, apportion the levies among the people of the states according to the requirements of the Constitution—largely because no means had yet

[30] AC, 13th Cong., 1st sess., 98.
[31] Ibid., 148. See also Jonathan to Matthew Roberts, June 21, 1813, Roberts Papers, HSP.

314

been devised to administer such a system. Yet even had the taxes been strictly constitutional, Eppes declared that he would still have opposed them, since he came to believe that this method itself was inherently unjust. Taxation, he argued, should be levied only according to the ability to pay, and to achieve this he desired indirect taxation alone, which would avoid "oppression of the people."[32] He therefore declined to support the legislation in debate, while neither of the other two prominent Republicans on the committee, William Bibb of Georgia and Jonathan Roberts of Pennsylvania, showed any greater willingness to assume the lead. The duty of opening the House debate on June 26 accordingly fell on the freshman Republican committee member, Thomas Montgomery of Kentucky.

Montgomery was unequal to the assignment and clearly resented it. After suggesting a series of amendments on the methods of apportionment and collection of the taxes which the Treasury could not have implemented, he damned the tax bills as impolitic, unconstitutional, and unjust, but concluded with the remark that he would very likely have to vote for them anyway.[33] Republicans in both houses followed this lead, introducing amendments to modify or strike out those sections of the bills which bore most heavily on their constituents, while isolated appeals for party unity and equal sacrifice by all Republicans, such as that made by Charles Jared Ingersoll of Pennsylvania, went largely unheeded.[34] Eventually, the disagreements over the duty on imported salt became so serious that in mid-July Jonathan Roberts called a Republican caucus to try to restore some degree of unity to the "unmanageable monster" that the party had become.[35] The caucus does not appear to have produced a consensus among the Republicans to support the administration's program positively, but after its meeting most of the party members began to vote reluctantly for the taxes in

[32] Eppes to Jefferson, July 21, 1813, Jefferson Papers, LC.

[33] AC, 13th Cong., 1st sess., 319-328.

[34] Ibid., 47, 53, 56, 58, 59, 61, 62, 65-67, 68-69, 71, 73-74, 330-347, 351-383, 387-399, 405-412, 421-431. The taxes on domestic distilled spirits and distilling licenses provided good examples of how taxation could create sectional rivalries within the Republican party. The Treasury sought to tax the capacity of the still rather than the volume of spirits produced as a way of extending the tax system into the newer western states. Western Congressmen argued that this tax, combined with heavy license fees for distillers, discriminated against western farmers who were required to distill their surplus grain to get it to market. They accordingly sought to tax the quantity of spirits produced, which would have enabled producers to pass the tax on to consumers.

[35] Ibid., 439-440, 449-455. For the calling of the Republican caucus see Roberts to Dallas, December 19, 1813, Dallas Collection, HSP.

the spirit that Montgomery had predicted. In this manner, about three-quarters of the Republicans in both houses eventually voted for the taxes that they could accept while abstaining on those that they could not. Only small random groups, seldom larger than half a dozen, joined the Federalists in opposition, and the sole Republican against all the taxes was Richard Stanford of North Carolina.[36]

One result of this prolonged and divisive debate over taxation was, inevitably, to depress Gallatin's standing within the Republican party to the lowest point ever in the Secretary's twelve years of cabinet service. Yet it was precisely when the debate on taxes was at its height, on July 16, that the President chose to announce that he had sufficiently recovered to meet with the Senators on Gallatin's nomination to Russia. Ever since the Senate had declared Gallatin's two appointments to be incompatible, there had been an implied bargain in its communications with the President—that the nomination to Russia might be confirmed in return for a permanent change in the Treasury Department. The President, however, was unwilling to reduce his powers in such a way, and he told the Senators so by stating bluntly that he regretted they were declining to assist him on Gallatin's nomination.[37] He seemed to believe that if he stood firm he could still command a majority, while suspecting that the Senate might not confirm Gallatin's nomination for Russia even if he were replaced in the Treasury.[38] Sensing that Madison was not prepared to discuss the matter any further, the committee members also remained silent, apparently being reluctant to carry their opposition as far as dictating to the President on nominations in his presence. After an embarrassing silence, the Senators withdrew, and three days later they rejected the nomination of Gallatin, while confirming those of Adams and Bayard.[39]

The contest, nonetheless, was a very close one, and Gallatin's nomination failed by only one vote. The Federalists, with the exception of one absentee, and the "malcontent" Republicans voted solidly against the nomination, and they were joined by two Republicans—Elejius

[36] AC, 13th Cong., 1st sess., 457-469. On the final votes on tax bills in the House, Republican abstentions ranged from fifteen to thirty-three, with the number rising as the session drew to a close, as more and more members of both parties left Washington to go home early.

[37] Ibid., 87-88.

[38] Eppes to Madison, June 29, 1813; Madison to Gallatin, August 2, 1813, Madison Papers, LC.

[39] AC, 13th Cong., 1st sess., 89-90. The Republican Senators who voted against Gallatin's nomination were Nicholas Gilman (N.H.), Obadiah German (N.Y.), John Lambert (N.J.), Michael Leib (Pa.), Samuel Smith (Md.), William Giles (Va.), David Stone (N.C.), John Gaillard (S.C.), Joseph Anderson (Tenn.), and Elejius Fromentin (La.).

Fromentin of Louisiana and John Gaillard of South Carolina—whose support the administration believed it was fairly entitled to expect. The critical Senator in the outcome was Richard Brent of Virginia, normally a consistent supporter of the administration, who abstained from casting a vote. His defection, which was probably not caused by his well-known drinking problem, was an indication of how far the administration had overplayed its hand by trying to force the Senate, a fractious body at best, to accept the questionable nomination of a man whose popularity within the Republican party had been almost completely destroyed.[40] As William Lowndes noted, even those Senators who supported Gallatin "expressed very openly their disapprobation" of his selection.[41] For the Senate, of course, the triumph over Gallatin was the climax of opposition to the Secretary and his alleged influence on Madison's foreign and financial policies, a long campaign that stretched back to 1809. Yet despite these circumstances, it is impossible to avoid the conclusion that the whole episode, in a very real sense, was quite unnecessary, for Gallatin, in truth, did not intend to return to the cabinet position that Madison had fought so stubbornly to keep open for him. Right from the outset, the Secretary had predicted that the "malcontents" in the Senate would probably declare his two positions to be incompatible, and, by failing to make his personal wish not to return to the Treasury sufficiently clear to Madison, he gave his opponents a pointless victory over him, while also delaying his necessary replacement with a permanent head of the Treasury.[42]

[40] Crawford, who was not in Washington at the time, attributed Gallatin's defeat to Brent's "mobility or his thirst." See Crawford to Gallatin, April 20, 1814, *Gallatin Papers*. But Brent, in fact, seldom missed votes because of his alcoholism, and his abstention on Gallatin's confirmation was his only absence in twenty-four consecutive votes in the session. He later missed all the votes on taxes but resumed his seat at the end of the session. See also Monroe to Jefferson, June 28, 1813, Jefferson Papers, LC; and Madison to Gallatin, August 2, 1813, Madison Papers, LC.

[41] Lowndes to Elizabeth Lowndes, July 20, 1813, Lowndes Papers, UNC. George Hay also tried to point out to Monroe that Madison, by nominating Gallatin, was "playing the game of his enemies for them." "Is the peace of this nation," he asked, "to be jeopardized that Mr. G. may continue Secretary of the Treasury. We are playing at pushpin when we ought to be moving rocks and mountains." Hay to Monroe, July 6, 1813, Monroe Papers, NYPL.

[42] Gallatin to James W. Nicholson, May 5, 1813; to Thomas Worthington, May 8, 1813, *Gallatin Papers*. See also Astor to Gallatin, August 9, 1813, *Gallatin Papers*. Dashkov was greatly upset by Gallatin's rejection in the Senate, realizing that it would jeopardize the mediation as well as being construed in Russia as an insult to the Emperor. He wrote to Monroe to suggest that Madison should salvage the mediation by replacing Gallatin in the Treasury, and he was greatly offended when the President failed to do so. Dashkov to Rumiantsev, August 7, 1813, Russian Archives.

By the third week in July, therefore, the Republicans in both the executive and the legislature were physically and emotionally exhausted by the events of the session. Many, like Madison, had become unwell, and all were looking forward to escaping the oppressive climate of the capital, but the President had not yet finished trying the loyalty of his supporters.[43] The day after the Senate rejected Gallatin's nomination to Russia, Madison requested a temporary embargo on American exports. There had been many complaints that American vessels were openly trading with the enemy's fleet on the Atlantic coast, and the President doubtless wished to end this embarrassing spectacle as well as make the Royal Navy and Great Britain's colonies feel the effects of a shortage of American supplies.[44] The embargo would counter the British policies, pursued since October 1812, of making Bermuda a place of deposit for the importation of American produce into the West Indies and of granting licenses to American vessels to bring supplies to other islands.[45] Possibly, too, since it now seemed unlikely that the Russian mediation would produce peace in the near future, Madison was expressing his wish to exert as many forms of pressure on the enemy as possible, but for some of his supporters, already burdened with unpopular taxes and confused by the complexities of international politics, the request for the embargo promised to be the final straw. As Senator Thomas Worthington recorded in his diary at the time, Madison, in his pursuit of unpopular measures, seemed intent on giving "the finishing stroke to himself and [his] party."[46]

Much to the delight of the Federalists, Calhoun, who had always opposed the "restrictive system," persuaded the House foreign relations committee to report against an embargo.[47] The Republican majority in the committee of the whole, however, unexpectedly rallied to the President by amending the report in favor of the measure. The members were perhaps worried about the consequences of Gallatin's rejection on the chances for peace, and more probably they wished to drive away the Royal Navy, which, during its search for provisions over the

[43] Lovett to Alexander, July 17, 1813, Bonney, *Gleanings*, I, 303. Nicholas Gilman to Pierre Van Cortlandt, Jr., July 4, 1813, Pierre Van Cortlandt, Jr., Papers, NYPL.

[44] (Philadelphia) *Aurora General Advertiser*, July 20, 1813 (henceforth *Aurora*). Cushing Eels to Madison, May 17, 1813, Madison Papers, LC; Felix Grundy to Andrew Jackson, July 26, 1813, Andrew Jackson Papers, LC.

[45] See *ASP: Foreign Relations*, III, 606-608; and F. Lee Benns, *The American Struggle for the British West India Carrying Trade, 1815-1830* (Bloomington, 1923), 27.

[46] Diary of Thomas Worthington, LC, entry for July 26, 1813.

[47] AC, 13th Cong., 1st sess., 500. This event, as John Lovett reported, "was the d—l. Mr. Speaker stared and expressed his astonishment." Lovett to Alexander, July 27, 1813, Bonney, *Gleanings*, I, 306.

summer, had come close to threatening the defenseless capital itself. The House accordingly voted for an embargo on July 22, with only about a dozen Republicans, mainly South Carolinians and Clintonians, in opposition, but the Senate rejected the bill one week later, with the President being defied by the Federalists, the "malcontents," and five other Republican Senators.[48] This defeat was the climax to a session of failures and embarrassments for the administration. Almost every episode throughout June and July, including even the successful passage of the taxes, had further narrowed the extent of agreement among Republicans over the policies required to wage the war. The legitimacy of the conflict could still be made to seem questionable, and its supporters were increasingly losing confidence in those entrusted with its prosecution. Indeed, the divisions within the party, including those among the cabinet members themselves, suggested to many Republicans as well as to Federalists that the administration had no coherent plan to bring the war to a satisfactory conclusion and that the Republic was being cast at the mercy of events by men bent largely on gaining purely personal goals. As Senator Jesse Bledsoe of Kentucky sadly remarked: "The friends of this administration will put it down faster than its enemies."[49]

The immediate influence of these developments on the course of the war, however, was probably slight. The Secretary of the Navy, on July 29, issued instructions to all his available vessels to intercept American trade with the enemy, and he hoped to achieve at least some of the effects of the embargo by these means.[50] Also, after the rejection of that measure in the Senate, it had become known unofficially in Washington that Great Britain would not accept the mediation of Russia, and it was now unclear whether Alexander I would still be in as favorable a position to influence his British ally as he had seemed to be in March 1813.[51] The power of their mutual enemy, France, was clearly on the decline—as could be seen in the results of the battles of Bautzen, Lützen, and Vittoria—and even Republican newspapers in the United States were speculating by August on the prospects of peace in Europe. Napoleon himself, by proposing an armistice after

[48] AC, 13th Cong., 1st sess., 99-101, 501-503. The five Republican Senators other than the "malcontents" who refused to support the embargo were Joseph Varnum (Mass.), George Bibb (Ky.), Joseph Anderson (Tenn.), and James Brown and Elejius Fromentin (La.).

[49] Jesse Bledsoe to Isaac Shelby, July 21, 1813, Simon Gratz Autograph Collection, HSP. See also Jeremiah Mason to Jesse Appleton, July 20, 1813, G. S. Hillard, *Memoir and Correspondence of Jeremiah Mason* (Cambridge, Mass., 1873), 63.

[50] Jones to Dallas, July 29, 1813, Dallas Collection, HSP.

[51] Monroe to Adams and Bayard, August 5, 1813, Donnan, *Bayard Papers*, 241.

the battle of Lützen as a preliminary to a congress of the belligerent powers at Prague, at last seemed to be ready to negotiate a general settlement in Europe. And although most Republicans professed to believe that any settlement on terms agreeable to France and Russia would probably favor American efforts to obtain international recognition of their maritime rights, no one could deny that a European peace would probably leave Great Britain and the United States at war a while longer.[52] A year after the declaration of war, therefore, the successful occupation of Canada remained as essential to the United States as ever.

★

THE OUTLINES of the campaign against Upper Canada to be mounted from the American Northwest were fairly clearly defined by the administration well before the summer of 1813. Most thoughtful Republicans in the eastern states, including the members of the cabinet, had been dismayed, if not appalled, by the actions of William Henry Harrison throughout the fall and winter of 1812-1813. After six months of ceaseless activity and almost unlimited access to men, money, and supplies, Harrison had failed either to retake Detroit or to attack the British post at Malden. By the end of February 1813, his army had withdrawn to the hastily erected Fort Meigs at the head of the Maumee rapids, where it had dissolved as the volunteers from Virginia, Pennsylvania, and Kentucky returned home after their terms of service had expired.[53] The western mode of warfare, no matter how congenial to its practitioners, had proved to be wasteful, inefficient, and ineffective, and many Republicans felt that the nation could not afford to let Harrison and his Kentucky supporters repeat the experiment. The editor of the *Aurora* deplored the cost of Harrison's campaigns, while the *Virginia Argus* likened the general to an incompetent watchmaker, "always *winding* up, but . . . never striking."[54]

[52] *Daily Natl Intelligencer*, August 2, 1813. This editorial was written by Monroe and the draft is in the James Monroe Papers, NYHS. For other newspaper opinion, see *The Weekly Register*, July 31, 1813; (New York) *National Advocate*, July 31, August 3 and 6, 1813; *Albany Argus*, July 16, 1813; (Richmond) *The Enquirer*, August 27, 1813; (Boston) *Independent Chronicle*, August 12, 1813. See also Jones to Dallas, July 26, 1813, Dallas Collection, HSP.

[53] See above, Chapter IV.

[54] Duane to Jefferson, February 14, 1813, Worthington C. Ford, ed., "Letters of William Duane," *Proceedings of the Massachusetts Historical Society* 20 (1906-1907), 360. The *Aurora*, on March 20, 1813, criticized Harrison and called on Armstrong to "resist the artifice of those *speculators* upon the public, who, destitute of qualifications, build their pretensions to eminent stations upon their intrigues, and the interests they represent themselves to hold in their several states." See also (Richmond) *Virginia Argus*, March 29, 1813.

The new Secretary of War was fully in sympathy with these sentiments. Although never really a career soldier himself, General Armstrong, as he was always addressed, greatly prided himself on his
expertise and professionalism in military affairs. He disliked the American reliance on volunteer troops and militia, dismissing such forces as
"the *press* of valour under *popular* leaders."[55] Harrison, his years in the
regular army notwithstanding, Armstrong described as an "artificial
general," elevated to his rank by public opinion in Kentucky and the
western territories rather than by merit.[56] Despite these prejudices,
though, Armstrong was far from being completely blind to the needs
of the Northwest, nor did he intend to act in total disregard of the
political realities there. The region round and below the western Great
Lakes was of undeniable strategic and economic significance, and Harrison was still its most important military leader. Armstrong simply
wanted to subordinate this particular aspect of the war effort to the
administration's broader definitions of the national interest, and, to do
so, he offered Harrison, on March 3, one of the six major generalships
that had been created with the new army of 20,000 men over the
winter.[57] Acceptance of the offer would give Harrison fairly low seniority in the army's rankings, while finally making him accountable to
priorities other than those defined by the political leadership of Kentucky.

Here Armstrong's military decisions were reinforced by Gallatin's
financial policy. The budget drawn up by the Secretary of the Treasury
for the period from March to December 1813 required the strictest
economy and maximum efficiency in War Department expenditures.
These, Gallatin had stipulated, could not exceed $1.4 million per month,
and Armstrong had accepted the limitation, even though he realized
it would require "some generalship" on his part in keeping his department in order.[58] But after going through the accounts of the northwestern army for 1812, the Secretary of War quickly realized that
Harrison's operations presented the easiest target for retrenchment. As
he told Duane: "I have sent back all the western militia accounts and
have limited Harrison's drawers of bills to a very small sum per month.

[55] Charles Jared Ingersoll, *Historical Sketch of the Second War with Great Britain* (Philadelphia, 1845), I, 133.
[56] Armstrong to Duane, March 16, 1813, "Selections from the Duane Papers," *Historical
Magazine*, 2d Ser., 4 (1868), 62.
[57] Armstrong to Harrison, March 3, 1813, LSMA. Harrison accepted the commission on
March 13, 1813.
[58] Gallatin to Armstrong, April 17, 1813, LRUS. Armstrong to Robert Swartwout, May
4, 1813, Robert Swartwout Papers, NYPL.

Had I let them go as I found them (with every man's hand among them in the public coffers) the game would have been up for want of means. . . ."[59] Armstrong also decided to limit Kentucky's quota of the new 20,000-man army to merely one regiment, and, to pre-empt the outburst of western protest that these decisions would almost inevitably provoke, he encouraged Duane to concoct for publication in the *Aurora* a series of "letters from the West" attacking the wastefulness of Harrison's campaigns in 1812.[60]

Out of such circumstances, the War Department's strategy for the Northwest duly evolved. In the first week of March, Armstrong abruptly ordered Harrison to hold fast at Fort Meigs pending the building of an army base at Cleveland and the construction of a fleet at Presque Isle on Lake Erie in order to attack Malden by water. To supervise the construction of transports for the troops on Lake Erie, he sent to Cleveland Captain Thomas Jessup, and he predicted that the naval forces would be ready for operations after the middle of May.[61] Overland offensive operations in the style conducted by Harrison in 1812 were thus ruled out. Also ruled out was any reliance on volunteers and militia, and Harrison, along with Colonels Lewis Cass and Duncan McArthur, was ordered to devote his efforts to recruiting a regular army in Ohio and Kentucky. Only in the event of the failure of regular recruiting, Armstrong added, could there by any recourse to other types of forces.

Harrison did not like these orders at all. He could not altogether deny the logic behind the desire to secure naval control on Lake Erie to assist the operations of the campaign; indeed, both he and Governor Shelby of Kentucky had already pointed out to the War Department how such naval control would be of benefit to the Americans.[62] Instead, Harrison chose to assume that the United States might not achieve naval supremacy on Lake Erie and that this failure would eventually require a large army to advance round the head of the lake to attack Malden. The facilities and experience for such an expedition had, of

[59] Armstrong to Duane, March 21, 1813, "Selections from the Duane Papers," 61. Armstrong limited the expenditures of the northwestern army to $20,000 per month and advised all contractors in the Northwest accordingly. See the copy of Armstrong's letter to Harrison of March 15, 1813, in the Letterbook of John Piatt, LC. See also Armstrong to Harrison, March 17, 1813, LSMA; and Armstrong to Henry Clay, June 9, 1813, James F. Hopkins, ed., *The Papers of Henry Clay* (Lexington, 1959–), I, 801.

[60] Armstrong to Duane, April 29, 1813, "Selections from the Duane Papers," 62.

[61] Armstrong to Harrison, March 5 and 7, 1813; to Thomas Jessup, March 9, 1813, LSMA.

[62] Harrison to Armstrong, February 18, 1813; Shelby to Armstrong, February 21, 1813, LRRS.

course, been acquired in the previous campaign, and Harrison assured Armstrong that he would succeed on a second attempt.[63] The self-serving nature of such arguments was hardly to be concealed, but Harrison was justified in his objections on at least one point. Armstrong's orders, probably unintentionally, were not sufficiently clear about the future of Harrison's main base at the headwaters of the Maumee. Was this to be abandoned in favor of Cleveland—as parts of Armstrong's orders seemed to suggest—or was it to remain the principal base, with Cleveland serving only as a depot for transports, supplies, and artillery?

The matter was important, for if Cleveland should be given preference as the base over Fort Meigs and the headwaters of the Maumee, not only would all of Harrison's preparatory efforts of the previous year be slighted, but large areas of the western states and territories would also be exposed to attack by the British and the Indians in the spring. This possibility, as Harrison well knew, would carry most weight with the citizens and governments of Ohio and Kentucky.[64] The governors of these two states were, in fact, already protesting that the War Department was not doing enough to protect the frontiers against spring raids, and Shelby declared that he had no intention of cooperating with "half measures such as have been too often experienced. . . ." To convey this alarm to the administration, the Kentucky governor also wrote to Armstrong, informing him that the impression existed that the views of the War Department were "too limited" and that it was "not disposed to call an adequate force" for the region's needs.[65] Harrison developed this last point into a claim that the War Department could never successfully recruit an army in the Northwest. Large corps of "auxiliaries" as well as regulars, he argued, were essential for operations, both to guarantee military success and to stimulate public confidence in the areas most affected by the administration's policies.[66]

Clearly Armstrong had misjudged Harrison's tenacity of purpose if not his approach to the problems of the war. And, indeed, the general,

[63] Harrison to Armstrong, March 17, 1813, Logan Esarey, ed., *Messages and Letters of William Henry Harrison* (Indianapolis, 1922), II, 387-388.

[64] See Jessup N. Couch to Thomas Worthington, May 10, 1813, Thomas Worthington Papers, OSL; David Purviance to Return J. Meigs, March 19, 1813, Return Jonathan Meigs Papers, OSL.

[65] Shelby to Armstrong, March 20, 1813, LRRS. Meigs to——, April 5, 1813, Meigs Papers, OSL; Meigs to John Gano, March 2, 1813, L. B. Hamlin, ed., "Selections from the Gano Papers IV," *Quarterly Publication of the Historical and Philosophical Society of Ohio* 16 (1921), 55.

[66] Harrison to Armstrong, March 27 and 28, 1813, Esarey, *Messages of Harrison*, II, 401, 404-405.

though now under War Department authority, continued to act very much as if he were still a major general in the Kentucky militia. He lost little time in conveying to the governor of Kentucky his objections to Armstrong's orders, while other western political leaders soon realized that the attacks in eastern newspapers had the backing of the administration and represented an attempt to redirect the war in ways that they thought prejudicial to their interests.[67] Already the campaign of 1813 was assuming some of the characteristics of that of the previous year—a struggle between Republican leaders on the state and federal levels of government over how to identify the priorities of the war and allocate best the limited resources available for its prosecution. Consequently, Armstrong found himself listening to and reading endless versions of Harrison's objections to his plans from the general's supporters in the Northwest, including a plea from Shelby for an army of not less than 15,000 men to crush the British and the Indians, thus avenging the massacre on the river Raisin.[68] In this manner, the governor stated the terms for Kentucky's cooperation in the war effort.

Armstrong decided to stand firm. He minimized the dangers of attack by the British and Indians, claiming that the former had too few men at Malden to take the offensive and that the latter would be too busy seeking food in the spring to do anything else.[69] Shelby's call for 15,000 men, "mounted like Asiatics," simply infuriated him. Why, he fumed, were so many men needed "to take a work [Malden] defended on three sides by pickets [and] to fight an enemy not more than two thousand of all colors and kinds?"[70] The Secretary angrily lectured Harrison on the advantages of naval supremacy on Lake Erie, the superiority of regular soldiers, and the limits of the Treasury, as well as reprimanding him for not sending in the returns of his army to the Adjutant General's office.[71] So intent was Armstrong on putting down insubordination in the Northwest that he failed to deal with Harrison's queries about whether Cleveland or the headwaters of the

[67] Shelby to Harrison, March 20 and 27, 1813, ibid., 393-394. James Morrison to Harrison, April 25, 1813, William Henry Harrison Papers, LC; Joseph Kerr to Armstrong, May 8, 1813, LRRS. See also Robert B. McAfee, *History of the Late War in the Western Country* (Lexington, 1816), 254.

[68] McArthur to Armstrong, March 30, 1813; Worthington to Armstrong, March 31 and April 16, 1813; Richard M. Johnson to Armstrong, March 31, 1813; Lewis Cass and McArthur to Armstrong, March 31, 1813; Shelby to Armstrong, March 20, 1813, all in LRRS.

[69] See Armstrong's "Extract of a letter of March 19 from a Person just returned from Canada," Harrison Papers, LC.

[70] Armstrong to Duane, April 29, 1813, "Selections from the Duane Papers," 62.

[71] Armstrong to Harrison, April 3, 1813, LSMA. See also Armstrong to Meigs, March 28, 1813, in Armstrong's *Notices of the War of 1812* (New York, 1836), I, 248-250.

Maumee were to be the point of embarkation for the campaign. Not until May 8 did the Secretary realize that he had to explain to the general that he never meant that the army "now collected at Fort Meigs should be brought back to Cleveland" but instead that the troop transports were to follow the American fleet to Sandusky or the foot of the Maumee rapids to pick up the men.[72]

Harrison acquiesced in these arrangements, remarking somewhat ambiguously that Armstrong's plans were "the best that could have been devised in the event of the promised naval success and a prosperous issue to the recruiting business."[73] But the assembling of the American fleet at Presque Isle under Captain Oliver Hazard Perry and the building of the transports at Cleveland did proceed smoothly enough after April 1813, with Navy Secretary Jones being confident that the United States would control Lake Erie by the middle of the summer.[74] The other aspects of Armstrong's plans, though, were not so easy to execute, and the recruiting of the regular army failed miserably. Harrison, as well as Cass and McArthur, followed their orders here, visiting the townships of Ohio and issuing handbills and addresses to arouse the local patriots, but their hearts were not really in it. They found, as had been the case in 1812, that most communities in the Northwest were unable to spare their male population from agricultural labor in the spring and early summer and that the rates of army pay, the recent increases notwithstanding, were still far from competitive.[75] With laborers being able to make up to $16.00 per month, the pay of a soldier, as McArthur noted, was "no object in the lower end of the state of Ohio."[76]

Moreover, the attempts of army recruiters to establish a more efficient ratio of officers to men by drafting the rank and file of the local militias while ignoring their officers were unpopular and socially disruptive.[77] The problem was not so much that men were unwilling to serve—in fact, they were usually quite prepared to serve for short terms at their own convenience and in their own way—but that they would not join a regular establishment at the bidding of the government. As Cass had tried to point out to Armstrong, "names are often things,"

[72] Armstrong to Harrison, May 8, 1813, Esarey, *Messages of Harrison*, II, 434-435.

[73] Harrison to Armstrong, April 21, 1813, ibid., 422.

[74] Alfred T. Mahan, *Sea Power in its Relations to the War of 1812* (Boston, 1905), II, 63-69. See also Jones to (Chandler Price?), April 5, 1813, Jones Papers, HSP; Jessup to Armstrong, March 27 and April 3, 1813. Thomas Jessup Papers, LC.

[75] (Chillicothe) *Supporter*, April 7, 1813, Cass to AG, March 14 and 24, April 12, 1813; and McArthur to Armstrong, June 2, 1813, LRAG. See also David Preston et al. to Meigs, April 26, 1813, and Benjamin Hough to Meigs, May 7, 1813, Meigs Papers, OSL.

[76] McArthur to Worthington, June 9, 1813, Worthington Papers, OSL.

[77] Same to same, May 22, 1813; Couch to Worthington, July 5, 1813, ibid.

and the attempt to change from a volunteer to a regular force in the Northwest had unfortunate consequences which prevented the War Department from realizing its goals. Nobody in the Northwest believed that a compact regular force could serve the military needs of widely scattered farming communities, and the attempt to create one simply spread mistrust and a lack of confidence in the administration.[78] Almost inevitably, a decline in public confidence affected other aspects of war organization too, and local banks and business houses were only prepared to accept bills of credit passed by army officers and contractors at a considerable discount. The cost of the unsuccessful policies thus began to rise in proportion to their degree of failure, and, by the end of June, Henry Clay warned the War Department that it was becoming difficult to negotiate a government bill in Kentucky at all.[79]

Harrison's objections to Armstrong's plans were thus realized, as were western fears about enemy attacks when the British and Indians twice tried to drive the northwestern army out of Fort Meigs. The first of these unsuccessful assaults occurred in the first week of May and the second at the end of July, but Harrison had more or less anticipated them and dealt with them in his own way, usually disregarding the restraints of the War Department as he did so.[80] Throughout the summer of 1813, the general continued to negotiate his own troop requirements with the governors of Ohio and Kentucky, and he became heavily dependent on his relationship with Governor Shelby to provide the forces he needed.[81] Repeated experience here demonstrated that it was usually easier to obtain large bodies of volunteers from the more heavily settled counties of northern Kentucky than it was from the more isolated communities of central and western Ohio, especially when companies of troops from the latter state were often found to be only half the strength of those from the former. As the two crises at Fort Meigs subsided, Harrison tended to retain or to pay off as many of the Kentucky troops as he could while dismissing the more slowly mobilizing Ohio forces, sometimes without even using them in service at all.[82] This practice alienated many Ohio citizens still

[78] Cass to Armstrong, March 31, 1813, LRRS. See also John McCoy to Worthington, July 3, 1813, Worthington Papers, OSL.
[79] Martin Baum to Armstrong, March 25, 1813, LRRS. Clay to Armstrong, June 25, 1813, *Clay Papers*, I, 806.
[80] See McAfee, *History of the Late War*, 261-277, 316-321.
[81] Harrison to Shelby, April 9, 1813; Harrison to Armstrong, April 17 and 21, 1813, Esarey, *Messages of Harrison*, II, 416-417, 418, 423. Harrison to Meigs, April 1813, Harrison Papers, LC.
[82] See Harrison's General Orders, May 16, 1813; Harrison to Armstrong, April 17 and

further from the idea of serving in the northwestern army, and Ohio troops consequently took little part in the defense of their own state and none at all in the subsequent invasion of Upper Canada in the fall.[83]

By the end of July 1813, therefore—when Perry was ready to embark his fleet on Lake Erie—Armstrong's plans had not led to the creation of a better-organized military force in the Northwest. Harrison had only about 2,500 effective regulars at his disposal, and it was clearly going to be necessary to rely on the volunteer troops that Armstrong disliked so much to complete the forces being assembled for the invasion of enemy territory. Here the 1,200 mounted Kentucky riflemen raised in the spring by Representative Richard M. Johnson— who, by his own admission, had no desire to spend the summer in Washington voting for unpopular taxes—declared that they constituted a logical supplementary force.[84] Armstrong, however, was quite unable to visualize a role for mounted men in the combined naval and military operations which he anticipated would lead to the reduction of Malden, and, under the misapprehension that Illinois Territory was in serious danger from Indians, he ordered Johnson's men to undertake a 400-mile march in fifty days for its relief.[85] Johnson, who was seeking glory against the enemy in Upper Canada, refused to go, regarding the order as unrealistic as well as insulting, and Armstrong, after admitting that he had been misinformed over the situation in Illinois, reluctantly conceded that Johnson's men could undertake less remote defensive operations on the frontiers while Harrison and Perry dealt with the British.[86] Even this was not good enough for Johnson, who finally resolved the dispute by taking his mounted men to Fort Meigs and simply attaching them to the northwestern army.[87]

At the end of July, Harrison finally called upon the governors of Kentucky and Ohio for the militia and volunteers he needed to complete his army to the 7,000 men allowed by the War Department.[88] After the experiences of the summer, Governor Meigs of Ohio agreed to raise 2,000 men, but only on the condition that Harrison undertake

May 18, 1813; and Meigs's General Orders, May 14, 1813, Esarey, *Messages of Harrison*, II, 419, 447-451.

[83] See *Supporter*, October 6, 1813; McAfee, *History of the Late War*, 290.

[84] Johnson to Armstrong, April 13, 1813, LRRS.

[85] Armstrong to Johnson, June 9, 1813, LSMA.

[86] Johnson to Armstrong, July 9, 1813, LRRS; Armstrong to Harrison, July 14, 1813, Esarey, *Messages of Harrison*, II, 491-492.

[87] Leland W. Meyer, *The Life and Times of Colonel Richard M. Johnson of Kentucky* (New York, 1932), 117-118.

[88] Harrison to Shelby, July 20, 1813; to Meigs, August 6, 1813, Esarey, *Messages of Harrison*, II, 492-493, 517. Harrison to Meigs, August 18, 1813, Meigs Papers, OSL.

to pay them for their services in advance. Lacking the authority to make such a commitment, Harrison declined to do so, and was thus left dependent on the outcome of Shelby's efforts.[89] From the Kentucky governor he had requested up to 2,000 men, and to popularize the call for volunteers he had suggested that Shelby, although sixty-three years of age, lead the volunteers in person. "Scipio, the conqueror of Carthage," Harrison declared, "did not disdain to act as the lieutenant of his younger and less experienced brother Lucius."[90] Shelby agreed, but in order not to "disgust" the spirit of Kentucky he concealed the fact that Harrison had asked for only 2,000 men; he offered to bring 4,000 to 5,000 volunteers to the headwaters of the Maumee River. He also promised all these prospective volunteers that the administration would fully reimburse them all for their expenses, though neither he nor Harrison actually had the right to give such a pledge.[91] The governor, however, was counting on being able to shame the War Department into paying up after the campaign.[92]

While he was making his call for Kentucky volunteers, Shelby was not, in fact, at all confident that the public response would be adequate for his understanding of the army's needs, and, indeed, in the southern counties of the state it proved necessary to resort to a draft of the militia to procure the men.[93] Still, as the harvesting season passed, men gradually declared themselves willing to undertake a short term of service, and, by the end of August, Shelby had gathered about 3,500 men, whom he marched northward at the pace of about twenty to thirty miles per day. These forces were scarcely organized as a disciplined, cohesive army, and many, having only swords and knives, were not even equipped properly for military service.[94] Shelby, however, assumed that any deficiencies in supplies and equipment could be made up from Harrison's quartermaster's department and on the march through Ohio, though he was later to complain bitterly that the citizens of that

[89] Meigs to Harrison, September 22, 1813; Meigs to J. Hunt, September 23, 1813, and Hunt to Meigs, September 24, 1813, Meigs Papers, OSL.

[90] Harrison to Shelby, July 20, 1813, Esarey, *Messages of Harrison*, II, 493.

[91] Shelby to Madison, July 18, 1813, Madison Papers, NYPL; Shelby to Harrison, August 8, 1813, Esarey, *Messages of Harrison*, II, 518-519. See also (Lexington) *Kentucky Gazette*, August 3, 1813.

[92] See Shelby to Armstrong, November 19, 1813, LRRS.

[93] Shelby to Harrison, August 11, 1813, Esarey, *Messages of Harrison*, II, 522. See also James W. Hammack, Jr., "Kentucky and Anglo-American Relations, 1803-1815" (Ph.D. diss., University of Kentucky, 1974), 302-305.

[94] For the progress of Shelby's army see Milo M. Quaife, ed., "Governor Shelby's Army in the River Thames Campaign," *The Filson Club Historical Quarterly* 10 (1936), 135-165; and Bennett H. Young, *The Battle of the Thames* (Louisville, 1903), 31, 37-43, 62.

state overcharged his troops for their services.[95] In this manner, an American army consisting of 2,500 regulars, 3,500 Kentucky militia volunteers, and 1,000 of Johnson's mounted riflemen was assembled at the Maumee rapids. The administration viewed these developments with some alarm, Madison fearing that the accumulation of militia, unless it won some striking success, would be the topic "of great animadversion as well as the source of great fiscal embarrassment."[96] The army, however, untroubled by such considerations, advanced to the head of Lake Erie to await the outcome of Perry's contest with the British fleet.

Perry duly won control of Lake Erie for the United States at the Battle of Put-in-Bay on September 10, and, just over two weeks later, he was able to employ his fleet in shifting Harrison's army to Upper Canada. The general had prepared for a siege and a pitched battle with the enemy, but the British commander, Sir Henry Proctor, decided that the naval victory had made his positions at Malden and Detroit untenable.[97] He therefore abandoned both places by September 27 and began to retreat eastward around the northern shore of Lake Erie. There appears to have been some division among the Americans about the advisability of pursuing the enemy, with Harrison doubting whether the British could be caught. The general also sensed that the War Department might want to order him on quite different duties, including an advance down the lake to the Niagara Peninsula or an expedition northward to regain the American post at Michilimackinac.[98] The decision here, however, was not really made by Harrison, whose regulars were not in a position to commence an immediate pursuit anyway. Half their number had left much of their equipment on Middle Sister, an island in Lake Erie, while the troops were being ferried to Upper Canada.[99] The American army on the spot in Malden consisted overwhelmingly of Kentucky volunteers and mounted riflemen, and Shelby was strongly in favor of following the enemy. The Kentuckians, accompanied by Harrison and a mere 120 regulars, accordingly pursued the British and Indians, while the bulk of the remaining regulars stayed on garrison duty or ready for assignment

[95] Shelby to Ephraim McDowell, September 10, 1813, Shelby Family Papers, LC.

[96] Madison to Monroe, August 19, 1813, Monroe Papers, LC.

[97] See Harrison's General Orders, September 7, 1813, Esarey, *Messages of Harrison*, II, 546-550.

[98] Isaac to Susan Shelby, September 8, 1813, Shelby Family Papers, LC. Harrison to Armstrong, September 15, 1813, copy in Lewis Cass Papers, University of Michigan; Harrison to Armstrong, September 27, 1813, Esarey, *Messages of Harrison*, II, 551.

[99] Harrison to Armstrong, October 9, 1813, Esarey, *Messages of Harrison*, II, 558.

elsewhere. Shelby's forces eventually caught the enemy on the river Thames, where, on October 5, they won a decisive, if unorthodox, victory. After another apparent difference of opinion between Harrison and the Kentuckians over tactics, the mounted riflemen charged through the British lines, dismounted, and began firing from the rear, while the Kentucky and United States infantry attacked from the front.[100] The British surrendered after a short fight, during which the Indian leader Tecumseh was killed.

The Battle of the Thames was the most important American victory in the war to date, though its outcome was largely determined by Perry's earlier victory on Lake Erie. Without the naval triumph, it is not difficult to imagine Harrison, Armstrong, and Shelby engaging in disputes over strategy similar to those that were to take place shortly afterward between Wilkinson, Armstrong, and Hampton. The administration, of course, was understandably elated, though the victories must have been rather more gratifying for the navy and the state of Kentucky than they were for the War Department and the regular army. The force that triumphed at the Thames was organized into eleven regiments, commanded by seven generals and one state governor, and its very success negated many of the principles that Armstrong was laboring to impose on the organization of the war. For the Kentuckians, the defeat of the British and the death of Tecumseh seemed to end the war in the Northwest, promising security for the frontier as well as opening to American settlers the lands of Upper Canada, which many now confidently assumed would be annexed to the United States.[101] Yet the successes, though real, were perhaps still too partial to be completely satisfying. The rapid disbanding of the Kentucky army at the end of the campaign left the area around the western Great Lakes so poorly garrisoned as to tempt the British to consider regaining that region the next year. Throughout 1814, the American commanders at Detroit, Cass and McArthur, felt anything

---

[100] For brief discussions of the Battle of the Thames which emphasize the differing approaches of Harrison and Johnson see Beverly W. Bond, Jr., "William Henry Harrison in the War of 1813," *MVHR* 13 (1927), 513-515; and Meyer, *Johnson*, 123-127, 131, 132. The subject was much debated in political battles after the war, especially in the 1830's, but evidence after the event sheds little light on the problems, since all the participants attempted to claim responsibility for the victory. Eventually, the Battle of the Thames produced one President of the United States, one Vice President, three governors of Kentucky, three lieutenant governors, four United States Senators, and a score of Congressmen.

[101] See *Kentucky Gazette*, November 1, 8, and 22, 1813. See also George Washington Campbell to Jones, November 8, 1813, and Thomas Newton to Jones, October 14, 1813, Jones Papers, HSP. Even the *Daily Natl Intelligencer*, on November 9, 1813, declared that Canada, once taken, should never be handed back to Great Britain.

but secure there, and the latter, as late as February 1815, was even advocating employing an army to turn Upper Canada into a "desert" in order to seal off the American Northwest from the British.[102] Only with the end of the war itself could the illusion of a complete triumph in 1813 be allowed to flourish in safety.

★

IN EARLY MARCH 1813, while waiting for the weather to improve to allow Dearborn to attack the capital of Upper Canada at York, the Secretary of War began to think about the larger goals of the campaign. On March 12 he ordered his comrade in arms from the days of the Revolution, Brigadier General James Wilkinson, then based at New Orleans, to "hasten to the north," and suggested that together they could win great glory there. Wilkinson was not popular in the southern states—indeed, the two Senators from Louisiana had recently demanded that the President move him out of their area altogether—and Armstrong declared that the "*patriotism* and *ambition*" of the general immediately required his services in the "land of the laurel" rather than that of the "cypress." The Secretary further hinted that it might be possible for them, "if our cards be well played . . . *to renew the scene of Saratoga.*"[103] The imagery employed in this invitation was not altogether appropriate for the occasion, but Armstrong no doubt realized that in Wilkinson he was addressing a man who could be moved at least by extravagant flattery if not by a sense of patriotism or an overriding desire to expel the British from North America. And to nurse his vanity a little further, Armstrong offered Wilkinson a major general's commission in the army, which was duly and eagerly accepted.

The strategy whereby Armstrong hoped to obtain the surrender of a British army was not then revealed to Wilkinson, but by April the Secretary had formed some conclusions which were to govern his thinking for the remainder of the year. These he first conveyed to Dearborn for his consideration, before the general commenced operations against York and Forts George and Erie. Armstrong assumed that Great Britain, losing control of all Upper Canada above the Niagara Peninsula, would sooner or later be confronted with a choice between defending the naval base at Kingston or of abandoning it altogether in favor of withdrawing to the stronger position of Montreal. In the former case, Armstrong believed that the United States should

---

[102] McArthur to Monroe, February 6, 1815, Duncan McArthur Papers, LC.

[103] Armstrong to Wilkinson, March 12, 1813, James Wilkinson, *Memoirs of My Own Times* (Philadelphia, 1816), III, 342. See also Crawford to Madison, March 3, 1813, Madison Papers, LC.

sever communications between Kingston and Montreal, put an army across the St. Lawrence at some point between the eastern end of Lake Ontario and Ogdensburg, and then storm the enemy base from the rear in conjunction with the United States naval forces. The latter case raised the more difficult question of approaching Montreal by the route from Lake Champlain or, as Jeffrey Amherst had done in 1760, by moving down the St. Lawrence to attack the right flank of the army defending the city. Here the Secretary's preferences were decidedly for the St. Lawrence route, partly because he felt that the defenses of Montreal were at their strongest for resisting an attack from the south and partly because of the greater ease of traveling by water.[104] The alternatives were thus clearly defined, and they rested on the assumption, strongly implied rather than explicitly stated, that the United States, one way or another, had to take Kingston before advancing into Lower Canada.

How far Armstrong expected Dearborn to be able to commence or complete these plans is uncertain, just as it is not wholly clear how large a role Armstrong himself expected to play in them. Some years after the war, the former Secretary rejected the charge that his February announcement of the wish to oversee army operations in person in 1813, combined with his March order to Wilkinson, revealed a deliberate plan to replace Dearborn as commander of the American army, and it cannot be denied that, for as long as Dearborn exercised his command, Armstrong gave him every assistance and took no actions that prejudiced his prospects for success.[105] Yet, as Armstrong well knew, Dearborn certainly needed advice and assistance in directing an army, having demonstrated in 1812 a marked tendency to bury himself in the details of staff work, which suggested an aversion to leading troops into combat. The general had been retained in service in 1813 only for want of a clearly better replacement and because Madison had a personal attachment to him which Dearborn could do almost nothing to shake. Should Dearborn need supervision or assistance in the campaign, Armstrong was entitled to consider himself well able to provide these, and should he need replacement, Wilkinson, his past record notwithstanding, was the most reasonable choice then available as his successor. As Wilkinson himself pointed out, he had, if nothing else, served with the United States Army for twenty-three years.[106]

If Armstrong was looking for pretexts to remove Dearborn, however, the general did not fail to provide them. His management of the spring

[104] Armstrong to Dearborn, April 19, 1813, LSMA.
[105] Armstrong, *Notices of the War of 1812*, II, 23.
[106] Wilkinson to Armstrong, May 23, 1813, LRAG.

campaign on Lake Ontario, while by no means wholly unsuccessful, failed to establish the foundation for an attack on the strategically important point of Kingston in the manner that Armstrong had wished. The combined army and navy forces left Sacketts Harbor on April 23 and, after some delay caused by the lack of suitable winds, easily captured York four days later. Then, after a longer delay caused by bad weather, outbreaks of mumps, measles, and fevers among the troops as well as poor coordination between Dearborn and Commodore Isaac Chauncey, the Americans captured Fort George, the British post on the northern end of the Niagara Peninsula, at the end of May.[107] These victories, which owed far more to Colonels Zebulon Pike and Winfield Scott than they did to Dearborn, were hailed by the Republican press as the first successes of the war, but they were, in fact, far from decisive.[108] On both occasions, Dearborn failed to press home the advantage by pursuing and capturing the British forces as they retreated into Upper Canada, and each time he earned an increasingly severe reprimand from Armstrong. "Battles are not gained," the Secretary wrote, "when an inferior and broken enemy is not destroyed."[109]

Furthermore, after the British army escaped from Fort George on May 27, Dearborn fell ill, and his depressed and often irritable moods began to annoy intensely his fellow officers, some of whom began to agitate for his removal.[110] Effective command of the army then devolved on Brigadier General John Boyd at Fort George and Brigadier General Morgan Lewis at Niagara, the latter officer having been brought into the line by Armstrong at the insistence of Ambrose Spencer, who had become tired of Lewis's "political stupidity" in the New York state Senate.[111] In an attempt to remedy his neglect to pursue the enemy, Dearborn, however, on June 1 dispatched Brigadier Generals John Chandler and William Winder to round up the remaining British forces

[107] Dearborn to Armstrong, May 3 and 13, 1813, E. A. Cruikshank, ed., *Documentary History of the Campaign on the Niagara Frontier* (Welland, Ont., 1898-1902), V, 185, 229. See also Rufus McIntire to John Holmes, May 11, 1813, John Holmes Papers, NYPL.

[108] *Daily Natl Intelligencer*, May 21, 1813; *The Enquirer*, May 18, 1813; *The Shamrock*, May 22, 1813.

[109] Dearborn to Armstrong, May 29, 1813, *Documentary History*, V, 267; Dearborn to H.A.S. Dearborn, May 30, 1813, Henry Dearborn Papers, MeHS. Armstrong to Dearborn, May 15, 1813, *Documentary History*, VI, 3-4; same to same, June 19, 1813, LSMA.

[110] Dearborn to Armstrong, June 8, 1813, *Documentary History*, VI, 35; Alexander Macomb to Samuel Smith, June 24, 1813, Smith Papers, LC; Winfield Scott to Charles K. Gardiner, July 6, 1813, Charles Kitchell Gardner Papers, NYSL.

[111] Ambrose Spencer to Armstrong, February 20, 1813, William A. Chanler Collection of John Armstrong Photostats, NYHS. Samuel Conner to Armstrong, June 12, 1812, LRRS.

on the northern shore of Lake Ontario. They succeeded five days later in driving the enemy from the field in a disorderly conflict at Stony Creek, during the course of which both American generals became separated from their troops. Seeking to rally the nearest body of men to them, Chandler and Winder then inadvertantly stumbled into the British lines, where they were promptly captured.[112] The fiasco threw the army into confusion and the advantage of the victory was lost.

This third failure reduced the American forces in Upper Canada to a critical state. The inability to capture the enemy, of course, led to a loss of morale, but even more serious was the fact that the number of effective troops at Fort George began to decline from the combined effects of disease and exposure. The regiments were composed largely of raw recruits raised during the winter of 1812-1813 whose induction into the army had been invariably accompanied by severe outbreaks of diarrhea, sometimes complicated by typhus and pneumonia, from which they had barely begun to recover when they were exposed to the wet spring weather in overcrowded transport boats. Cooped up in Fort George and consuming bread made from fermenting or adulterated flour washed down with cheap spirits, their condition became increasingly unhealthy, while the everpresent prospect of British raids on their lines compelled the commanding officer to maintain large detachments of pickets constantly through the heat of the day and the chilly fog arising from Lake Ontario at night.[113] Most of the officers, moreover, were too inexperienced to care for their men properly in such circumstances, and they, too, had their own grievances. As the War Department reorganized the regiments in 1813, the Secretary frequently promoted promising officers from one regiment to another, thereby frustrating the hopes of many of their subordinates who had expected to rise through the workings of seniority. In protest, large numbers of officers at Fort George, especially those in the lower grades, resigned their commissions. Thus the invading army rapidly began to disintegrate.[114]

[112] Morgan Lewis to Armstrong, June 14, 1813, LRRS.

[113] For a description of army life in Fort George see James Mann, *Medical Sketches of the Campaigns of 1812, 13, 14* (Dedham, 1816), 58-68.

[114] The evidence on this point is voluminous, but see the letters from the following to the AG: John Campbell, May 24, 1813; Thomas Carr, June 2, 1813; Isaac Coles, June 18, 1813; Francis Cummins, June 20, 1813; John Sevier, July 4, 1813; Charles Gee, April 24, 1813; Moses Hall, June 26, 1813; Morgan Lewis, April 25 and May 18, 1813; John Martin, June 12, 1813; N. McLaughlin, June 10, 1813; D. Milliken, June 18, 1813; Isaac Meyers, June 18, 1813; Officers of the 12th Infantry, April 6, 1813; Charles Proctor, July 14, 1813; Samuel Tappan, June 22, 1813; John Wise, June 17, 1813, all in LRAG. The number of officer resignations in 1813 was twice that in 1812, and most of them occurred

In an attempt to break out of these deteriorating conditions at the end of June, Boyd ordered Lieutenant Colonel Charles G. Boerstler to drive the enemy raiding parties away from the Niagara Peninsula altogether.[115] Boerstler, however, had the misfortune to be ambushed with nearly 600 men at Beaver Dams on June 24, and he had to surrender when he ran out of ammunition. Throughout these melancholy proceedings, Dearborn, writing from his sickbed, had continued to plead the difficulties of his circumstances—the sickness, the weather, and the resignation of the officers—as an explanation for his lack of decisive results, but the news of Beaver Dams was more than even most of his supporters could bear.[116] Deputations of angry army officers and Congressmen in Washington began to wait on Armstrong to demand that Dearborn be relieved of his command, and, given the state of the general's own health if nothing else, Madison was scarcely in a position to resist the pressure. He consented to Armstrong's ordering Dearborn into retirement on July 6, while the Secretary, who had hoped that the army might advance toward Kingston, instructed Lewis to remain on the defensive and risk no further humiliating defeats. The only exception he allowed here was in the event of Chauncey's winning a decisive naval victory over his British counterpart, Sir James Yeo, on Lake Ontario.[117]

Thus ended Dearborn's campaign. It had started with promise, but by the end of June the army was clearly in no condition to risk continuing it. The preparations made for the campaign and the initial success at York had also undeniably assisted the Republican party in re-electing Governor Daniel Tompkins in May, and that victory was essential to any further American attempt to invade Canada.[118] But

in the forces serving on the New York frontier. The 12th, 16th, and 20th Infantry were particularly hard hit by resignations and were almost completely without officers by the middle of 1813. The promotion causing the most difficulty was that of Isaac Coles from major in the 20th Infantry to colonel of the 12th Infantry. The previous colonel of the 12th Infantry, James P. Preston, was removed to the 23rd Infantry to make room for Coles, but Preston and his fellow officers petitioned Congress for Coles's removal; see Thomas Sawyer et al. to Armstrong, August 21, 1813, and Preston's petition of December 26, 1813, both in Sen 13B-D.2, Legislative Records of the Senate, NA. Since Coles was the nephew of Dolley Madison, his promotion was widely resented as the case of "pettycoat government." See John to David Campbell, June 18, 1813, Campbell Family Papers, Duke University Library.

[115] John Christie to Dearborn, June 24, 1813, LRAG; Dearborn to Armstrong, June 25, 1813, LRRS.

[116] Dearborn to Armstrong, June 20, 1813, LRRS.

[117] Ingersoll to Dallas, July 6, 1813, Ingersoll Papers, HSP; Armstrong to Dearborn, July 6, 1813, LSMA; Armstrong to Lewis, July 2 and 8, 1813, LSMA.

[118] Tompkins won re-election with a majority of 3,506 votes, his smallest margin of victory

against this necessary political achievement had to be balanced the failure to destroy the British army or to attack Fort Erie, which left the New York frontier no more secure than in 1812. The army at Fort George could extend no protection to the frontier beyond the territory it immediately controlled, and the resulting sense of insecurity in many New York communities led first to petty guerrilla raids against the British and then to demands on the War Department for protection against any British retaliation. As Peter B. Porter angrily pointed out, a great many people at Niagara had become "tired of the games (disgraceful as respects the military character of the country and ruinous as regards their property) that have been playing upon this river for the year past," and he threatened that unless some more efficient commanders took over, the local inhabitants would have to conduct the war in their own way, as best they could.[119] This was bad enough, but considerably more serious for the administration was the fact that while the American forces had been engaged in fruitless operations in Upper Canada in May and June a British fleet had appeared on Lake Ontario that was sufficiently powerful to threaten the American naval base at Sacketts Harbor. Armstrong was greatly upset by this development, realizing all too well that it created serious difficulties for his plans to seize Kingston, and he began, quite maliciously and rather unfairly, to blame Dearborn publicly for not trying to take that place at the opening of the campaign.[120]

There was little, though, that the Secretary could immediately do about the situation. His March invitation to Wilkinson to come northward had been mislaid in the mails, and the general did not receive a copy of the letter until May 9. Even then, his journey to Washington was being made at a fairly leisurely pace, as the veteran of Saratoga paused en route to attend numerous public dinners given in his honor,

---

in his three terms as governor. Virtually all of these votes came from the Western District of the state, where Tompkin's majority was 3,274. Since Federalists and Republicans were evenly balanced in the Southern, Middle, and Eastern districts of the State and since the Republicans had lost the western counties in the presidential election of 1812, it seems not unreasonable to suppose that the effects of the army's presence in the Western District contributed to the party's recovery. The Federalists, however, retained a slight majority in the New York House of Assembly. For the election figures see the appendix to *The Weekly Register* IV (1813).

[119] See Lewis to Armstrong, June 24, 1813, LRRS; Porter to Augustus Porter, August 6, 1813, Peter B. Porter Papers, BEHS. The Porter Papers for this period contain much material on the inability of the U.S. Army to influence events beyond Fort George, particularly in the area around Fort Erie and Buffalo.

[120] Dearborn to Armstrong, June 20, 1813, LRRS; Armstrong to Dearborn, July 1, 1813, LSMA. See also the enclosure in Lewis to Dearborn, July 6, 1813, Henry Dearborn Papers, MHS; and *National Advocate*, August 18, 1813.

and, in truth, Wilkinson did not display much enthusiasm for a Canadian campaign, preferring instead to warn of the dangers to the southern states of the impending civil war in the Creek Nation.[121] In the interim, Armstrong announced again his intention to go to the frontier to "superintend" the operations of the armies, and some Republican newspapers in New York, no doubt to remove any misgivings their readers might have on the subject, declared in the most positive terms that the Secretary of War was a military genius who would not force the nation to endure a repetition of the events of 1812.[122] Before commencing military operations again, though, the army badly needed an infusion of new officers to restore the chain of command, and trained recruits to fill the ranks. As in the past, the officers were obtained more easily than the men, and some of the subalterns who had withdrawn their resignations after registering their protest on the promotions issue were eventually reinstated. In most cases, however, new and even more inexperienced candidates had to be nominated to the regiments, and these earned from one sergeant at Sacketts Harbor the description of "ignorant, willfull, ugly, ill-natured puppies."[123] The recruiting of privates in midsummer, on the other hand, was considerably less successful, especially in the Middle Atlantic states, where weary officers scoured the rural townships vainly trying to entice laboring men—who in some places could earn up to $20.00 per month at harvest time—into the ranks.[124]

While the War Department grappled with these difficulties, Armstrong considered again the possible strategies for a campaign. These he presented to the cabinet, along with a review of the military situation, on July 23. His first two suggestions differed little from those he had put forward earlier in the year, and involved completing Dearborn's campaign either by destroying British power opposite the Niagara Peninsula or by attacking Kingston in joint military and naval

[121] Wilkinson to Armstrong, July 6, 1813, LRRS; same to same, April 26 and May 22, 1813, LRAG.

[122] *Albany Argus*, June 29, July 13 and 20, 1813; *National Advocate*, July 7, 16, and 17, August 18 and 31, 1813; *Daily Natl Intelligencer*, August 7, 1813.

[123] Armstrong to Dearborn, July 1, 1813, LSMA; Rufus McIntire to Holmes, July 5, 1813, Holmes Papers, NYPL; A. S. Cogswell to J. Whitney, June 19, 1813, Wilmond W. Parker, ed., "Letters of the War of 1812 in the Champlain Valley," *Vermont Quarterly* 12 (1944), 107.

[124] See in particular the letters to Duane, in LRAG, of John Arrison, August 4 and 10, 1813; George Brent, September 4, 1813; Dominick Cornyn, who wrote twenty-seven letters on this subject between June and August 1813; Samuel Dewey, July 4, 1813; William Downey, September 3, 1813; Frederick Evans, June 28, 1813; Patrick Forde, July 13, 1813; and Robert Hall, June 9, 1813.

operations. The first Armstrong dismissed as more or less irrelevant—the more so if Harrison should succeed in taking Malden—since it would do little to give the campaign the appearance of a decided victory, while the second, he declared, was of vital importance, and, to encourage the enemy to weaken the naval base, he suggested that an army could move toward Montreal from Lake Champlain. The Secretary, however, also put forward a new plan which required an army to move down and cross the St. Lawrence at Madrid in order to fortify a position there, then advance toward Montreal by river in conjunction with an army approaching that city from the south. This last scheme was considerably more ambitious than anything that Armstrong had yet suggested, and it was his first serious statement of the idea that the United States might attack Montreal as the climax of the campaign. Previously, he had only hinted at this possibility in the event of the enemy's voluntarily evacuating Kingston, and to state at this stage that the United States might move on Montreal without first reducing the naval base indicated a rather desperate awareness that the administration needed a spectacular achievement to redeem itself. The idea was all the more risky since its success would clearly depend on the ability of the United States Navy to control the entire length of the St. Lawrence from Lake Ontario to Madrid, and Armstrong was not actually prepared to assume that he could count on having such naval control, at least not more than temporarily. Possibly for that reason, he declined to make an absolute choice between the attack on Kingston and the approach to Montreal, arguing that this decision should be left to the commanding general.[125]

The cabinet approved Armstrong's recommendations, apparently without comment or opposition, and waited for Wilkinson to arrive in Washington. This long-delayed event finally occurred on July 31, and the general immediately commenced discussions of the campaign with the administration. On the grounds that the United States lacked naval superiority on Lake Ontario, Wilkinson disapproved of attacking either Kingston or Montreal. Instead, he preferred to complete Dearborn's campaign across the Niagara Peninsula, declaring that it would be necessary to do this "to *popularize* the war" and, in the event of Harrison's failing to take Malden, to enable him to march westward round Lake Erie to remedy that situation. Only after all that had been accomplished, along with the razing of all the British positions in Upper Canada, was he prepared to consider going eastward to attack Lower Canada. He then proceeded to hedge the acceptance of his command

[125] Armstrong to Madison, July 25, 1813, Madison Papers, LC.

with stipulations limiting the Secretary of War's right to correspond with subordinate officers, while also requiring that official to remove from the army "all persons who may manifest a temper or disposition to excite discontents."[126] Wilkinson usually imposed conditions when he undertook assignments, and on this occasion his terms were inspired partly by suspicions about how Armstrong might interpret his role in "superintending" the army, and partly by the knowledge that the Secretary had chosen Major General Wade Hampton of South Carolina as the commander of the American forces at Lake Champlain. The two generals had long hated each other, and they had no desire either to work together in the same military district or to be equally subordinate to the Secretary of War.

Armstrong responded to these remarks on August 8 and 9 with a mixture of firmness and conciliation. He tried to finesse the problem of the relationship between Wilkinson and Hampton by telling the former that Hampton was to "operate cotemporarily with him and under his orders in the prosecution of the plan of the campaign," while to the latter he always gave the impression that his command was an independent one. This studied ambiguity, however, was insufficient to deal with the matter; Hampton promptly offered his resignation, to take effect at the end of the campaign, and remarked that he had not been satisfied with Armstrong's arguments on the subject.[127] But on the objects of the campaign, the Secretary was more adamant. He ruled out any operations west of Kingston, which, he declared, presented "the *first* and *great* object of the campaign," and he gave Wilkinson the choice of attacking it "directly" or "indirectly." This distinction between the modes of attack, Armstrong claimed, could be derived from the third plan he had presented to the cabinet on July 23, but, in fact, what the Secretary proceeded to describe was a rather different type of operation altogether. He suggested that the army go down the river to Hamilton in Madrid County, fortify that place, and then move

[126] Wilkinson to Armstrong, August 6, 1813, Daniel Parker Papers, HSP; Wilkinson to Thomas Cushing, August 4, 1813, James Wilkinson Papers, LC. In describing his intentions to Cushing, Wilkinson spoke only of his desire for "active and decisive operations . . . on the shores of Lake Ontario."

[127] Armstrong to Wilkinson, August 9, 1813, Parker Papers, HSP; same to same, September 6, 1813, *Documentary History*, VII, 106. Armstrong to Hampton, August 21, 1813, copy in Madison Papers, LC; Hampton to Armstrong, August 22 and 31, LRUS. The *Albany Argus*, on August 17, 1813, quoted Hampton as stating that he would serve with Wilkinson and that the present was no time "to quarrel about straws." It is, however, almost inconceivable that Hampton should have said this, and the expression sounds more like Armstrong's than Hampton's.

"to take a position which will enable you to secure what you gain." The vagueness of this expression could only have been designed to conceal a strong suspicion that the American armies would conclude their advances short of Montreal, and what Armstrong perhaps hoped to achieve by taking such a position was to create an extended pincer movement of naval and armed forces that would compel the British at Kingston either to surrender their position for want of subsistence or to try to fight their way back to Montreal.[128] As such, it was an ill-conceived scheme, with little apparent thought having been given to the final destination of Wilkinson's army or to the problems of how to maintain it there over the winter of 1813-1814.

At this point, Armstrong and Wilkinson left Washington and made their ways separately to the New York frontier. The general arrived at Sacketts Harbor on August 20, exuding considerable confidence as he gathered the troops and made arrangements for inspecting the American position at Fort George. He also swore, with oaths, that within the week he would have taken Kingston or commenced an advance down the St. Lawrence, but by August 26 he had done no more than call a council of his senior officers—including Lewis, Swartwout, Chauncey, and Jacob Brown—to seek their advice.[129] To the council Wilkinson confessed that the American forces were not really strong enough to deliver a decisive blow against the British, but he went on to outline four courses of action anyway. These included waiting until the American and British naval forces had conclusively settled the question of the control of Lake Ontario, shifting the offensive back to the Niagara Peninsula, risking an all-out assault on Kingston, or bypassing that place for an advance on Montreal. The council, with Brown and Lewis in the lead, rejected the first two choices as unnecessary time-wasting, doubted their strength to accomplish the third, and therefore decided on the fourth.[130]

This advice probably reflected a considered choice between the need for action and the desire for prudence, but the message proved to be too much for Wilkinson. After the council he wrote to Armstrong emphasizing "the necessity of settling the point of *naval superiority* before we commit ourselves," and four days later he vaingloriously promised either that he could take Kingston if he had 3,000 more men or that he would "winter in Montreal" if Chauncey would defeat Yeo.[131] The Secretary, who was reporting to the President by letter, did not

[128] Armstrong to Wilkinson, August 8, 1813, LSMA.
[129] Wilkinson to Armstrong, August 21, 1813, Parker Papers, HSP.
[130] For the council see *Documentary History*, VII, 72-74.
[131] Wilkinson to Armstrong, August 26 and 30, 1813, ibid., 75, 88.

expose these fluctuations in Wilkinson's mood, but he did not conceal the fact that by the end of August the army had not yet decided on its destination. Madison, still recovering from his summer illness, had no advice to offer, beyond warning against any harmful consequences of Wilkinson's and Hampton's mutual hatreds and declaring that in the event of failing to gain a better result he wanted at least "an intermediate establishment" between Kingston and Montreal from which to launch the next campaign.[132] Armstrong, for his part, chose not to reprimand Wilkinson for his vacillations, and, like the general, he too wished for a decisive naval victory on the lake, which would obviate the need to choose between difficult strategic goals.[133] In the interim, he tried to encourage Wilkinson by telling him that Hampton would resign at the end of the campaign, while also strengthening the latter's army at Burlington in an attempt to persuade the British to concentrate their forces at either Montreal or Kingston and thus make it easier for the Americans to decide which to attack.[134]

Throughout September, the two navies, increasingly hampered by adverse winds and weather, continued to maneuver inconclusively on Lake Ontario, while the morale of the American armies gradually declined.[135] Hampton reported that not only was he outnumbered by enemy forces to his north but also the British fleet on Lake Champlain restricted his movements, thus limiting his ability to make diversions in Wilkinson's favor.[136] Rather more ominously, the health of the army at Sacketts Harbor began to deteriorate, largely because the army bakers had been sufficiently thoughtless as to draw their water supplies from streams that flowed through the men's latrines.[137] The effects of consuming bread made from poor flour and polluted water took a predictable toll, and even Wilkinson himself, who had already been feeling the effects of the climatic change upon his health, took to his bed "with a giddy head and a trembling hand." By September 18, the general declared that he was "feeble to childhood" and revealed that he was on the point of giving up completely by asking Armstrong what he should do in the event of the navy's failing to obtain any sort of control on the lake. The Secretary, with remarkable forbearance,

---

[132] Armstrong to Madison, August 28, 1813; Madison to Armstrong, September 8 and October 30, 1813, Madison Papers, LC; Madison to Armstrong, September 24, 1813, Parker Papers, HSP.

[133] *Natl Advocate*, August 27 and October 1, 1813.

[134] Armstrong to Wilkinson, September 6, 1813, *Documentary History*, VII, 106.

[135] See Mahan, *Sea Power*, II, 51-56.

[136] Hampton to Wilkinson, September 7, 1813, *Documentary History*, VII, 108.

[137] Harrison Ellery, *The Memoirs of General Joseph Gardner Swift* (Worcester, 1890), 113.

advised him to forget the issue of naval control and simply to cooperate with Chauncey in making some sort of movement on Kingston to obtain the objectives of the campaign.[138]

The encouragement may not have been entirely without effect, for within two days Wilkinson declared that he had recovered. He responded to the call for a movement toward Kingston, though, with the announcement that he was ready to "step into the St. Lawrence" for an advance on Montreal, and for that purpose he gathered up his staff and brought down from Fort George to Sacketts Harbor another 3,000 troops.[139] At the naval base, on October 4, he met Armstrong for the first time since the beginning of August, and the two veterans of the Revolution then proceeded to embarrass the army by quarreling openly about the goals of the campaign. Wilkinson advocated bypassing Kingston altogether for an attack on Montreal, while Armstrong preferred a direct attack on the former place before any attempt was made on the latter. During the council of the officers to discuss the problem, it seems that Wilkinson's main objections to attacking Kingston were that it would be too difficult, would cost too many casualties, and would thus prevent an attempt to get Montreal. This last place, he declared, was the "chief object of the campaign," and he implied, if not actually promised, that he could take it. These arguments must have stunned Armstrong, for only briefly in July had the Secretary of War thought that Montreal might be an object in the campaign, and his orders of August 8 had never instructed Wilkinson to regard it as such at all. This sudden concern by Wilkinson for Montreal must have struck Armstrong as an elaborate piece of bluff, designed to evade the responsibility for accomplishing anything at all in the campaign, and to avoid this possibility he flatly insisted on the importance of obtaining Kingston. After making this point, though, Armstrong declared that the army and navy were free to chose whatever means they thought best to accomplish the goal.[140]

---

[138] Wilkinson to Armstrong, September 11 and 18, 1813, *Documentary History*, VII, 115-119, 135. See also Charles Bull to Duane, October 16, 1813, LRAG; Armstrong to Wilkinson, September 18 and 22, 1813, *Documentary History*, VII, 146, 157, 163-164.

[139] Wilkinson to Armstrong, September 29, 1813, LRUS. Wilkinson's behavior by now had thoroughly baffled many of his officers, one of whom remarked that the point of the campaign had become an "impenetrable" mystery. He defined the problem correctly, though, by observing that while Wilkinson did not consider control of Lake Ontario as necessarily connected with the movements of the army, he always argued that particular movements of the army were dependent on the navy. McIntire to Holmes, September 11, 1813, Holmes Papers, NYPL.

[140] For the council see *Documentary History*, VII, 197-198. Swift recorded that Wilkinson greatly resented Armstrong's presence with the army, since it confused the command and undermined his authority. Swift, *Memoirs*, 114.

While the Americans quarreled, the British reinforced Kingston on October 14 with 1,500 men drawn from Montreal. This development undermined Armstrong's insistence that the enemy base was a feasible goal, and the Secretary of War, on October 16 or shortly thereafter, decided, for reasons he had just ruled out, that the army would have to go down the St. Lawrence.[141] He did not indicate his change of mind to Wilkinson, however, until well after the boats and troop transports had commenced loading; then, on October 19, he urged the general to attack "the safer and greater object below (i.e. Montreal)."[142] Wilkinson was, no doubt, relieved that he would not have to attack Kingston, but he must also have realized that he was trapped by Armstrong's order, the more so since it was quite clear that the Secretary had never strongly favored the move down the St. Lawrence, regardless of its precise purpose. To the general, his new orders could have appeared only as an invitation to undertake and advance that was likely to have no useful result and could quite possibly lead to failure and humiliation.

The campaign of 1813 was now, to all intents and purposes, finished, and both Armstrong and Wilkinson knew it. Armstrong admitted as much when he ordered the quartermaster of Hampton's army, on October 16, to prepare winter quarters for his troops.[143] But neither Wilkinson nor Armstrong could admit this fact to themselves, nor could they admit it to the public, especially when there would have inevitably been embarrassing questions asked about the abandonment of a campaign before it had ever started, and in weather that did not absolutely preclude an American advance. The campaign was therefore continued, not with any real expectation of victory but in order to enable Wilkinson and Armstrong to try to arrange for its termination under circumstances least awkward to themselves. Wilkinson accordingly responded to Armstrong's order of October 19 by stating that he would now prefer to attack Kingston, but before he abandoned that goal for Montreal he felt it was "*necessary for* [his] *justification* that [Armstrong] should, by the *authority of the president*, direct the op-

[141] Armstrong to Hampton, October 16, 1813, *Documentary History*, VIII, 70; Lewis to his wife, October 16, 1813, *Documentary History*, VIII, 71; Armstrong to Madison, October 17, 1813, Madison Papers, LC.

[142] Armstrong to Wilkinson, October 19, 1813, *Documentary History*, VIII, 81-82. Wilkinson began embarking the army on October 17. He claimed later that when he talked with Armstrong on that day they were still agreed that Kingston was to be the object of the campaign, though the Secretary's letters of October 16 and 17 suggest that he was already thinking of abandoning it. See Wilkinson, *Memoirs*, III, 355.

[143] See Armstrong, *Notices of the War of 1812*, II, 63-64. Armstrong rationalized this order as an attempt to establish a base for a winter campaign against Montreal, which, he claimed, Madison later overruled. See also Wilkinson, *Memoirs*, III, 70-71, 356-357.

[Armstrong] should, by the *authority of the president*, direct the operations of the army under [his] command, *particularly against Montreal*."[144] The Secretary, though, declined to be drawn out in this manner, simply referring the general to his orders of August, which allowed him to choose between a "direct" and "indirect" approach to Kingston. "These are," he concluded, "the best thoughts I can offer, and it only remains to add to them my best wishes for your army and for yourself."[145]

Wilkinson swore to his officers that he had been trapped and betrayed, while Chauncey was appalled both at the manner in which the campaign had been decided and at the prospect of being reduced to no more than a transport service for the army.[146] But they had no choice but to complete the loading of the troops, and, on October 21, they headed for Grenadier Island at the entrance to the St. Lawrence. The movement was not finally completed until November 3, with many of the vessels and transports being dispersed by gale-force winds. This alone, Wilkinson reported, "very nearly blasted . . . all our hopes."[147] After resting and reorganizing the army on Grenadier Island, Wilkinson entered the St. Lawrence on November 5 with 6,000 men. As soon as he had done so, Armstrong departed for Albany, leaving the two American generals to arrange their affairs as best they could.[148] He continued, nonetheless, to correspond with both of them, assuming that their advances were proceeding well and that they had both "seized on all the advantages that the errors of an enemy may have given. . . ."[149] And, in the center of Albany on November 15, the Secretary of War pulled out his watch and announced to the bystanders his belief that the army was by now in Montreal.[150]

Wilkinson advanced steadily along the St. Lawrence, reaching Ogdensburg on November 7, where his officers, for want of a better idea, voted to continue toward Montreal. Their situation, however, was fraught with danger.[151] Chauncey had failed to blockade the British fleet in Kingston after the army had entered the St. Lawrence, and British gunboats in quick pursuit began to harass Wilkinson's rear. The general himself then succumbed again to fever and diarrhea brought

[144] Wilkinson to Armstrong, October 19, 1813, LRUS.
[145] Armstrong to Wilkinson, October 20, 1813, *Documentary History*, VIII, 85-86.
[146] Arthur Sinclair to John Hartwell Cocke, November 30, 1813, Cocke Family Papers, UVa. See also Chauncey to Jones, October 30, 1813, Jones Papers, HSP.
[147] Wilkinson to Armstrong, November 3, 1813, LRUS.
[148] Armstrong to Madison, November 11 and 19, 1813, Madison Papers, LC.
[149] Armstrong to Wilkinson, November 12, 1813, LSMA.
[150] *Albany Register*, March 29, 1814.
[151] For the council see *Documentary History*, VIII, 144-145.

on by eating bad bread and compounded his problems by consuming large quantities of whiskey and laudanum. Thus drugged out of his mind and causing much embarrassment to his officers and doctors, who eventually appealed to Armstrong to relieve him of his command, Wilkinson became "very merry, and sung, and repeated stories" as he progressed toward Montreal.[152] Furthermore, all attempts to cooperate with Hampton's army proved to be unsuccessful. First, Wilkinson had tried at the beginning of November to arrange with Hampton, through Armstrong, a juncture of their forces; then, in desperation, he ordered the South Carolinian on November 6 to meet him within three days at St. Regis as a preliminary to an attack on Montreal. Armstrong endorsed these orders, although he was fairly certain that Hampton would not obey them.[153]

And indeed, Hampton had his own difficulties which quite precluded a union of the two armies. In compliance with Armstrong's wishes that he advance in order to divide the British forces near Montreal, Hampton, after moving his army from Burlington to Cumberland Head, had marched westward to Four Corners, then northward along the Chateaugay River into Lower Canada, where he fought a minor battle with British forces. While still in enemy territory, on October 25, he saw a copy of Armstrong's order to his quartermaster to prepare winter quarters for his army, and this led him to assume that his own operations would receive no support at all from Wilkinson's army.[154] With some difficulty, Hampton withdrew his army back into northern New York and went into winter quarters at Four Corners, only to receive there Wilkinson's order of November 6 calling for a juncture of their forces. He regarded its contents as an utter impossibility, informing Wilkinson that he could neither supply his army nor meet him at St. Regis, for his own force, like that of his colleague, was sick and declining in numbers.[155] Hampton's response to Wilkinson, therefore, clearly implied that if the latter wished to advance beyond St. Regis, he would have to do so alone and at his own risk.

In the interval, Wilkinson had advanced to Chrysler's Point in Williamsburg County, Upper Canada, where he decided to give battle to the British forces that had been troubling his rear. The action, on

---

[152] Swift, *Memoirs*, 116. See also Charles Bull to Armstrong, November 17, 1813, LRRS.

[153] Wilkinson to Armstrong, November 1 and 3, 1813; Wilkinson to Hampton, November 6, 1813, LRUS. Armstrong to Madison, November 11, 1813, Madison Papers, LC.

[154] Hampton to Armstrong, November 1, 1813, LRUS.

[155] Hampton to Wilkinson, November 8 and 12, 1813; Hampton to Armstrong, November 12, 1813, ibid. For a recent account of Hampton's campaign see Allen S. Everest, *The War of 1812 in the Champlain Valley* (Syracuse, 1981), 126-133.

numerically superior Americans had failed to destroy the small enemy force of 800 that had been causing them so much difficulty. Wilkinson thought his recruits fought bravely, but not even he had the nerve to claim the affair as an American victory.[156] The day after the conflict, he received Hampton's refusal to advance to St. Regis, and, with the consent of his officers, he called off the campaign. Wilkinson then transferred his army to winter quarters at French Mills on the New York frontier with Lower Canada, and there he began the inevitable recriminations.[157] Claiming that had Hampton obeyed his orders he could have been in Montreal within ten days, Wilkinson accused the South Carolinian of "beastly drunkenness" and demanded his arrest and court-martial.[158]

Thus ended the campaign of 1813, a military enterprise which had often lacked a specific goal and had only been assigned one when it was virtually impossible to achieve it. It is difficult to decide who was most responsible for this state of affairs. Hampton, despite his refusal to join Wilkinson, was probably less accountable for the outcome than his colleagues, while the roles of Wilkinson and Armstrong can scarcely be considered apart. Wilkinson, nonetheless, was always reluctant to commit himself to decisive action, and the only strategy for which he ever showed any enthusiasm was on the Niagara Peninsula, despite the fact that the administration had already ruled out that area as insufficiently consequential for its larger goals. The general frequently boasted that he was prepared to die for his country, but, in reality, he had always preferred longevity to immortality, and in this respect the campaign of 1813 was no different from many other episodes in his checkered career.[159] Armstrong, on the other hand, was fairly insistent throughout the year about the importance of capturing Kingston, but he ultimately failed to pursue the goal consistently enough because of the need to placate and persuade Wilkinson. It was the Secretary's misfortune to be dependent on a general who refused to make a critical decision. Almost as reprehensible, though, was Armstrong's own refusal to decide to end the campaign when he believed that the chance of taking Kingston had gone, for his role in events after mid-October

[156] Wilkinson to Armstrong, November 17, 1813, copy in Swift, *Memoirs*, 120.

[157] Wilkinson to Hampton, November 12, 1813, LRUS.

[158] Wilkinson to Armstrong, November 24, 1813, LRRS; same to same, November 26, 1813, LRUS; and Wilkinson to Cushing, December 4, 1813, Dearborn Papers, MHS. The charge of "beastly drunkenness" probably arose from the fact that Hampton was in bed when the messenger bearing Wilkinson's orders arrived. See Swift to Wilkinson, November 20, 1813, Swift, *Memoirs*, 119.

[159] See Thomas R. Hay, "Some Reflections on the Career of General James Wilkinson," *MVHR* 21 (1935), 473-489.

was no more than a device to transfer to others the responsibility for the failures.

Here a curious parallel emerged in the careers of Wilkinson and Armstrong. Both men had risen to the top of their respective military hierarchies on the basis of very little practical military experience. Armstrong reputedly had a vast knowledge of strategy, tactics, and organization, but neither he nor Wilkinson had ever actually commanded an army in battle. For them to have done so in the difficult circumstances of the summer and fall of 1813 would have certainly been to have risked failure, possibly at the cost of shattering the illusions on which their public lives were based. Both men therefore shrank from the ultimate challenge and avoided responsibility for decisions until it was possible to try to place the blame on somebody else as well as on circumstances beyond their control. After all, they could always argue that in the next campaign they would do far better.

CHAPTER VIII

★

A WINTER OF DISCONTENT, 1813-1814

On July 27, 1813, shortly before James Wilkinson arrived in Washington to make arrangements for his abortive campaign, a group of American settlers in Mississippi Territory led by Colonel James Caller attacked a party of Creek Indians who were returning to their homes after visiting Pensacola in West Florida. The Americans, knowing that the Indians had been in Pensacola to obtain arms and ammunition from the Spanish governor there, suspected the Creeks of planning to wipe out their settlements, and they accordingly made the attack in order to prevent that misfortune. The Indians, however, had sought the arms and ammunition in the course of continuing a bitter feud that had broken out among the towns of the Creek confederation, and they were as yet far from contemplating the actions attributed to them. The American assault, known as the Battle of Burnt Corn Creek, was unsuccessful, but its failure led to the very event its success was supposed to forestall. The Indians demanded revenge for the unprovoked aggression, transforming as they did so a dispute within the Creek confederation into a war with the United States.[1] They thus added a second Indian conflict to the War of 1812.

In many respects, the origins of this second conflict were very similar to those which had led to the war in the Northwest, and the actions of the hostile Creeks can be understood as an attempt to resist the pressures of Americanization.[2] The Creek confederation had enjoyed

[1] For an account of the Creeks' visit to Pensacola see Elizabeth H. West, "A Prelude to the Creek War of 1813-1814," *Florida Historical Quarterly* 18 (1940), 248-257. For the Battle of Burnt Corn Creek see Henry S. Halbert and Timothy H. Ball, *The Creek War of 1813 and 1814* (ed. Frank L. Owsley, Jr., University, Ala., 1969), 125-142; and Albert J. Pickett, *History of Alabama and Incidentally of Georgia and Mississippi from the Earliest Period* (Charleston, 1851), II, 255-263.

[2] See Chapter IV above, and particularly Anthony F. C. Wallace, "Revitalization Movements," *American Anthropologist* 58 (1956), 264-281.

a long record of maintaining its independence against British, French, and Spanish encroachments in the American Southwest, but after 1783 it had become increasingly difficult for its peoples to resist the influence of the United States. The Creeks were forced to sign treaties which recognized American sovereignty over their lands as well as giving the United States greater control over their trade, and, of necessity, they had accepted the appointment of an agent to regulate their contacts with Americans.[3] The agent, Benjamin Hawkins of North Carolina, was a fair and just man, but his best efforts were devoted to "civilizing" the clans and townships of the Creeks by imposing on them American methods of agriculture and household manufacturing as well as a more formal and centralized system of government.[4] Since the Creeks were already more familiar than the northwestern Indians with sedentary forms of agriculture and the idea of a confederated form of government, many of Hawkins's schemes took root, especially among the lower Creek towns on the Chattahoochee and Flint rivers that were most directly exposed to his influence.[5] There was, though, always some opposition to Hawkins's efforts, which eventually came to be centered in the upper towns of the Alabama people along the Coosa and Tallapoosa rivers. These upper towns were at once more isolated from Hawkins's personal influence and more directly exposed to pressure from Tennessee, where both the settlers and the United States government wished to cut roads to connect the interior settlements with the Gulf Coast.[6] The cutting of these roads led to incidents between Americans and Indians, which, in turn, usually led to American demands for land cessions, and the decision of the United States in July 1811 to open a road from the Tennessee River to Mobile against the wishes of the Creeks was only the last in a long series of resented encroachments.[7]

[3] Ralph S. Cotterill, *The Southern Indians: The Story of the Civilized Tribes Before Removal* (Norman, 1954), 8-178; Angie Debo, *The Road to Disappearance* (Norman, 1941), 3-71; Frank H. Akers, Jr., "The Unexpected Challenge: The Creek War of 1813-1814" (Ph.D. diss., Duke University, 1975), 26-49.

[4] See Benjamin Hawkins, *A Sketch of the Creek Country in the Years 1798 and 1799* (Savannah, 1848), 51-79. For the full life of Hawkins see Merritt B. Pound, *Benjamin Hawkins—Indian Agent* (Athens, 1951), esp. 155-173; and Frank L. Owsley, Jr., "Benjamin Hawkins: The First Modern Indian Agent," *Alabama Historical Review* 30 (1968), 7-12.

[5] For developments during Hawkins's agency see Akers, "The Unexpected Challenge," 116-118; Debo, *Road to Disappearance*, 50, 68-69; and particularly James F. Doster, *The Creek Indians and their Florida Lands, 1740-1823* (New York, 1974), I, 216-218, and II, 4, 10. See also Arthur H. Hall, "The Red Stick War: Creek Indian Affairs During the War of 1812," *Chronicles of Oklahoma* 12 (1934), 265-266, 268.

[6] See Akers, "The Unexpected Challenge," 120-125, and Hall, "The Red Stick War," 277.

[7] Akers, "The Unexpected Challenge," 129-130; Doster, *Creek Indians*, II, 10; Hall, "The

By 1812, therefore, the Creek townships were being outnumbered and surrounded by the rapidly expanding American settlements, though their response to these developments was by no means a uniform one. The most hostile Indians were usually to be found in the upper "red" townships, as opposed to the "white" towns, and the "red" towns had always taken the lead in representing the confederation in diplomacy and war-making. Collectively, the townships could conduct their business in a general council, though recourse to this method appears to have been sporadic rather than regular, and the confederation rarely acted as a totally unified entity, least of all in matters of war and peace.[8] The United States, however, usually preferred to deal with Indian peoples as single entities, and since 1790 it had tried to manipulate the Creeks by paying their chiefs (*miccos*) special annuities so they would uphold the treaties between the two peoples. The policy was successful, but it heightened sectional and social differences within the confederation as American encroachments increased.[9] Here Creek dissatisfaction, as in the Northwest, took the traditional Indian form of religious revivalism, especially after Tecumseh visited the Creeks in the fall of 1811.[10] His preaching found a receptive audience among

Red Stick War," 269. For the decision to cut the road of 1811 see William Eustis to Wade Hampton, July 20, 1811, LSMA.

[8] The relationship between Creek social and political structure and the factionalism which led to the Creek war was extremely complicated, and it has never been explained wholly satisfactorily. The essential works on Creek social and political structure are by John R. Swanton, principally his *Early History of the Creek Indians and their Neighbors* (Washington, D.C., 1922), see 199-200, 215, and his *Social Organization and Social Usages of the Indians of the Creek Confederacy* (Washington, D.C., 1928), see 110, 113, 120-121, 165, 323, 324, 328. The most comprehensive discussion of Creek factionalism is Ross Hassig, "Internal Conflict in the Creek War of 1813-1814," *Ethnohistory* 21 (1974), 251-271, in which twenty-one definitely hostile Creek towns are identified and analyzed in relation to their location, their "red/white" affiliations, and their age structure. Hassig's tentative conclusion that "the most that can be said . . . is that among upper towns and among the young, there was a tendency to become Red Sticks" seems sound as far as it goes, though unfortunately his analysis fails to include any discussion of the prophets and the religious revivalism which were so influential in provoking the factionalism.

[9] This method of manipulating the Creeks was embodied in the secret provisions of the 1790 Treaty of New York whereby half a dozen important chiefs received special payments, medals, and educational privileges. See Akers, "The Unexpected Challenge," 108-109. See also Doster, *Creek Indians*, II, 4, 6; and George Stiggins, "A Historical Narration of the Genealogy, Traditions, and Downfall of the Ispocoga or Creek Tribe of Indians, written by one of the tribe," Lyman C. Draper Manuscript Collection, Georgia, Alabama, and South Carolina MSS, V 66ff, SHSW.

[10] Theron A. Nunez, Jr., "Creek Nativism and the Creek War of 1813-1814," *Ethnohistory* 5 (1958), 1-17. For a discussion of Tecumseh's role see Mary Jane McDaniel, "Tecumseh's Visits to the Creeks," *Alabama Review* 33 (1980), 3-14.

both the younger men of the townships and the class of priests or doctors in Creek society known as the *hilis-hoya*, or men of learning, who had some knowledge of medicine and clairvoyance and whose status and influence had possibly been declining as that of the *miccos* increased.[11] Tecumseh's standing as a gifted prophet was considerably enhanced by his prediction of the appearance of a comet in late 1811 and by the widely felt earthquakes in the South and the Midwest in early 1812, with the result that by the end of the latter year his example had produced a host of imitators throughout the Creek towns, of whom the best known were Josiah Francis, Paddy Walsh, Peter McQueen, and High-Headed Jim.[12]

The emergence of the prophets in the Creek townships inevitably constituted a serious threat to the authority of the *miccos* and the system of Indian-American relations which they upheld. The more enthusiastic followers of the prophets embarked on a campaign against all aspects of American "civilization" by destroying tools and livestock, and occasionally they murdered isolated American settlers as well.[13] The state government of Tennessee became particularly alarmed at this development, though at first neither Hawkins nor the administration in Washington seems to have felt that it would necessarily lead to war with the United States.[14] Hawkins, in fact, was able to prevail on the pro-American *miccos*, notably Big Warrior of Tuckaubatchee, to execute the murderers, but his very success here only worsened the divisions within the confederation.[15] And it was to punish Big Warrior and the other *miccos* who had obeyed Hawkins's wishes that the followers of Peter McQueen and Josiah Francis visited Pensacola in July 1813 to request arms from the Spanish governor. Rather belatedly, Hawkins realized that the anti-American factions among the Creeks— or the "Red Sticks," as they became known—were far stronger than

[11] See Hassig, "Internal Conflict," 258-59, 265, and also Swanton, "Religious Beliefs and Medical Practices of the Creek Indians," *Bureau of American Ethnology, 42d Annual Report* (1928), 615-617.

[12] Halbert and Ball, *Creek War*, 58-84; Hall, "Red Stick War," 277; and Pickett, *Alabama*, II, 240-254. See also Alexander Cornells to Benjamin Hawkins, June 22, 1813, *ASP: Indian Affairs*, I, 846. According to Stiggins, Paddy Walsh was anti-American because he was the son of "a despicable murdering swamp tory," James Walsh of South Carolina. See Stiggins, "Narration," Draper Collection, V 82, SHSW.

[13] See Akers, "The Unexpected Challenge," 134; Doster, *Creek Indians*, II, 40-41; Hall, "Red Stick War," 274; and Hassig, "Internal Conflict," 266.

[14] Elizabeth H. Peeler, "The Policies of Willie Blount as Governor of Tennessee, 1809-1815," *Tennessee Historical Quarterly* 1 (1942), 317-318; and Pound, *Hawkins*, 214-224.

[15] Hawkins to Cornells, March 25, 1813; Hawkins to Tustunneggee Thlucco (Big Warrior) et al., March 29, 1813; Big Warrior et al. to Hawkins, April 26, 1813; and Nimrod Doyell to Hawkins, May 3, 1813, all in *ASP: Indian Affairs*, I, 839-844.

he had allowed for and that events were rapidly outrunning his control. After the middle of June, he began to suggest to the War Department that a "military corrective" to the problem might be necessary, especially if Tecumseh should increase his influence among the Creek townships.[16]

The administration immediately responded to this news with a decision to intervene in the Creek disputes, and it did so, moreover, fully two weeks *before* the Battle of Burnt Corn Creek. The motives for the decision, however, were complex. There had long existed in most of the southern states a desire to expand the boundaries of the Republic to the Gulf of Mexico at the expense of the Indians and the Spanish, and both Madison and Monroe were fully in sympathy with it. The United States had claimed, and had forcibly occupied in August 1810, parts of Spanish West Florida on the grounds that it belonged to the Louisiana Purchase, and it also claimed the right to East Florida as an indemnity for Spanish spoliations against American commerce during the Quasi-War of the late 1790's. In 1812 and 1813, the administration had attempted to acquire parts of East Florida by fomenting revolution against Spanish rule and by the military occupation of Pensacola.[17] The attempts were not successful, thanks largely to the opposition of the United States Senate, but they had the enthusiastic support of the settlers of the southwestern states, who resented having to pay high tolls on the transportation of their produce through Spanish territory to reach a coastal port.[18] The realization of American territorial ambitions against Spain, which was assumed to be only a matter of time, would, in turn, require land cessions from the southwestern Indians, and, in this manner, Indian affairs and foreign policy became inextricably linked. As Monroe remarked on the problem posed by the Creek Indians in 1813, "our wavering policy respecting E. Florida has brought it on," and he clearly hoped that the United States would settle the two issues simultaneously.[19]

Of equal significance, however, in the American decision to intervene

[16] Hawkins to John Armstrong, June 22, 27, and 28, July 6, 13 and 28, 1813, ibid., 847-849.

[17] For the background here see Isaac J. Cox, *The West Florida Controversy, 1798-1813: A Study in American Diplomacy* (Baltimore, 1918); and Rembert W. Patrick, *Florida Fiasco: Rampant Rebels on the Florida Border, 1810-1815* (Athens, Ga., 1954).

[18] Willie Blount to Thomas Flournoy, October 15, 1813, *ASP: Indian Affairs*, I, 856-857. See also Robert V. Haynes, "The Southwest and the War of 1812," *Louisiana History* 5 (1964), 43.

[19] James Monroe to George Washington Campbell, October 16, 1813, Curtis W. Garrison, ed., *James Monroe Papers in Virginia Repositories* (microfilm ed.). See also (Washington, D.C.) *Daily Natl Intelligencer*, October 5, 1813.

in Creek affairs were considerations arising from the course of the war against Great Britain. On the optimistic assumption that the United States would occupy a good deal of Canadian territory during the campaigns of 1813, the administration believed that Great Britain would be tempted to regain lost ground by using the Royal Navy to launch attacks against the weakly defended American Southwest during the coming winter. Great Britain was already allied to the Spanish monarchy and could thus easily obtain entry to Spanish ports in the Floridas, and if she should extend her alliances to include the anti-American Creek townships in the interior, the position of the United States could become perilous in the extreme.[20] To forestall these possibilities, the Secretary of War, on July 13, ordered the governors of Georgia and Tennessee each to raise 1,500 troops to suppress the hostile Creek townships.[21] Once this had been accomplished, the United States would then be in a strong position to exact further land cessions from the Indians. And, if events should reveal that Spain and Great Britain had given military aid to the Creeks, the administration would also have the justification to seize and occupy Spanish territory itself.[22]

In acting on these considerations, though, the administration did not adopt any coherent strategy for a war against the Creek Indians, largely because it lacked a sufficient number of regular troops in the southern states for such a purpose. Moreover, in late July 1813, the administration was still more preoccupied with the campaigns against Canada, while, after the first week in August, its members, having departed from Washington, were too scattered to coordinate measures for a southern war effectively. Major General Thomas Pinckney in South Carolina was the highest-ranking army officer near the theater of war, and, as such, Madison felt he was entitled to command the operations against the Creeks, but the President realized that the general was also too remote from the scene to take the necessary immediate action. For this reason, Madison was prepared to leave the organization of the Creek war to the states nearest at hand, confident that their governors and citizens would fully understand the dangers to the Southwest from any alliance of Great Britain, Spain, and the Indians.[23]

[20] James Madison to Armstrong, September 8 and October 11, 1813, James Madison Papers, LC. Hawkins, too, had raised this possibility in his letters to the War Department in June and July 1813.

[21] Armstrong to Governors David B. Mitchell and Willie Blount, July 13, 1813, LSMA.

[22] Armstrong to Thomas Pinckney, July 24, 1813, ibid.; Armstrong to Daniel Parker, August 21, 1813, Daniel Parker Papers, HSP; Madison to Armstrong, October 8, 1813, Madison Papers, LC.

[23] Madison to Monroe, September 1 and 2, 1813, James Monroe Papers, LC; Monroe to Blount, October 19, 1813, copy in Andrew Jackson Papers, LC.

The President did assume, however, that the war in the South would be more effective, and less costly, if Georgia and Tennessee coordinated their actions rather than attacking the Indians in isolation. He further believed that Georgia would carry most of the burden of the war and, accordingly, suggested that its governor, David B. Mitchell, be entrusted with its overall direction.[24] Tennessee, particularly its western section, was thus relegated in the administration's thinking to a relatively minor role in the war, and Madison, instead, thought that its troops could be more usefully employed in strengthening the defenses of New Orleans against a possible British attack.[25]

The implementation of this conception of the war, though, was thwarted by both the behavior of the Creeks and the reactions of the Americans most affected by it. The news of the Indian conflicts had already encouraged many isolated settlers to take refuge in American forts throughout the Southwest, and this led the Red Sticks, in seeking their revenge for the affair at Burnt Corn Creek, to single out these positions for attack.[26] Warfare among the Creeks often amounted to virtual extermination, since it was considered a mark of bravery for warriors to penetrate enemy settlements in order to kill as many of their inhabitants as possible, and a party of Creeks, led by Josiah Francis and William Weatherford, largely succeeded in doing just that in their attack on Fort Mims in southeastern Mississippi Territory on August 30, 1813.[27] The commander of the fort had more than ample warning of the attack, but he neglected to take proper precautions, such as closing the gate of the fort, with the result that the Americans suffered extremely heavy losses. Recent estimates have lowered the death toll to about 250, but contemporary rumor, by contrast, placed it between 400 and 600. Furthermore, the news of the "massacre" of

---

[24] Parker to Hawkins, September 30, 1813, LSIA.

[25] See Madison's letters cited in note 20 and also Madison to Armstrong, October 30, 1813, Madison Papers, LC. See also Parker to Blount, October 30, 1813, LSMA. The governor of Louisiana believed that Great Britain had fomented the Creek war in order to draw American troops away from New Orleans as a means of facilitating an attack on the city. William C. C. Claiborne to Monroe, August 11, 1813, MLDS; and Claiborne to Flournoy, September 17, 1813, Dunbar Rowland, ed., *Official Letterbooks of W.C.C. Claiborne, 1801-1816* (Jackson, Miss., 1917), VI, 268.

[26] Akers, "The Unexpected Challenge," 145-146.

[27] See Swanton, *The Indians of the South Eastern United States* (Washington, D.C., 1946), 695; and Swanton's *Social Organization and Social Usages*, 434. William Weatherford's role in the war has usually been described by historians as one characterized by reluctance and ambiguity. See Thomas S. Woodward, *Woodward's Reminiscences of the Creek or Muscogee Indians Contained in Letters to Friends in Georgia and Alabama* (ed. Peter Brannon, Tuscaloosa, 1939), 37, 92, 98-99.

Fort Mims profoundly shocked and alarmed all the American settlements in the western sections of Mississippi Territory and Tennessee.[28]

In response to requests sent from Mobile to Nashville for aid in defending the frontiers, the leading citizens of Davidson County, Tennessee, held a meeting on September 18 where they decided to launch "a hurried campaign" against the upper Creek towns to draw their attention away from the Mobile frontier.[29] This plan won the approval of both the commander of the West Tennessee militia, Andrew Jackson—who was at the time still recovering from serious wounds received in a duel with Thomas Hart Benton—and the state governor, Willie Blount, who was trying to organize the 1,500 men requested by the War Department in mid-July. In fact, most Tennesseans felt that the administration's call for 1,500 men from the state was insufficient to deal with the crisis, and they quickly agreed to raise the number to 5,000.[30] The Tennessee legislature, which met on September 24, sanctioned these arrangements, and authorized the governor to negotiate loans of up to $300,000 to cover the costs of the campaign.[31] The first detachments of Tennessee troops—consisting largely of Jackson's militia, which had been called out earlier in the year for a projected attack on Pensacola, and a mounted brigade commanded by Jackson's kinsman, John Coffee—then assembled at Fayetteville in the first week in October.[32] This army, as Coffee put it, hoped to "drive the Creek nation like a flock of bullocks," and it entered the Indian country on October 12 with about 2,500 men.[33] It stopped briefly at Huntsville, then advanced farther to build a supply depot at Fort Deposit on October 24.

Jackson was eager to engage the Creeks, partly because he feared that they might invade Mississippi Territory or even Tennessee itself, and he accordingly fought two battles with them, at Tallushatchee on November 2 and at Talladega on November 9. On both occasions the

[28] For a detailed discussion of the Fort Mims "massacre" see Frank L. Owsley, Jr., "The Fort Mims Massacre," *Alabama Review* 24 (1971), 192-204.

[29] This meeting was described in detail by William Martin to Lyman Draper, September 12, 1844, Draper Collection, Tennessee Papers XX 3, SHSW.

[30] Akers, "The Unexpected Challenge," 206. Blount to Armstrong, July 30, 1813, LRRS. See also Blount to Jackson, August 14 and September 24, 1813; Blount to John Cocke, September 25, 1813; Jackson to David Holmes, September 26, 1813, all in Jackson Papers, LC.

[31] See Blount to Judge White et al., November 3, 1813, copy in LRUS.

[32] See Jackson's General Orders of September 24, 1813, Jackson Papers, LC.

[33] John Coffee to Mary Coffee (undated, but written between October 4 and 13, 1813), "Letters of John Coffee to his Wife, 1813-1815," *Tennessee Historical Magazine* 2 (1916), 274; John Reid to Elizabeth Reid, October 11, 1813, John Reid Papers, LC.

Creeks were defeated with heavy losses, but since over 700 of them escaped and withdrew farther south from Talladega, it was necessary for the Tennesseans to continue their advance in order to obtain a complete victory.[34] Jackson, too, had his own views on how to deal with the Creeks. He had long favored penetrating as far and as rapidly as possible toward the heart of the Creek confederation at the junction of the Coosa and Tallapoosa rivers, and, as he did so, he wished to inflict military defeats wherever he could, as well as build a chain of forts which would enable the United States to control the Creek country thoroughly for its own purposes. If he found evidence of Spanish involvement in the war, he intended to advance to Pensacola and end the war there, regardless of whether the United States and Spain had formally declared hostilities. Jackson did not believe, however, that he could accomplish all these feats single-handed, and, after constructing Fort Strother at the Ten Islands of the Coosa in the first week in November, he decided to rest his weary army and wait for supplies and assistance from the troops from East Tennessee, Georgia, and Mississippi Territory.[35]

This cooperation of the American forces in the Southwest never materialized, largely because it was never planned for in any systematic way and because the means for realizing it simply did not exist. The commanders of the various forces and the state and territorial governors constantly exchanged letters in which they declared their intentions to cooperate with one another, either by coordinating attacks against different towns or by advancing simultaneously to meet at the heart of the Creek confederation, but it always proved to be impossible for them to agree on more precise objects or to organize their forces to attain them.[36] Some troops from Mississippi Territory led by Ferdinand Claiborne did, in fact, penetrate by Christmas 1813 to the Holy Ground at the center of the Creek confederation, but their numbers were simply

[34] Coffee's estimate of the casualties for the Creeks and the Tennesseans in the two battles was 600 and 30 respectively. Coffee to Mary Coffee, October 13, November 4 and 13, 1813, "Letters of John Coffee," 275, 277. See also John Reid to Nathan Reid, December 24, 1813, Reid Papers, LC.

[35] Jackson to Coffee, September 29, 1813, Jackson Papers, LC; and Reid to Elizabeth Reid, October 24, 1813, Reid Papers, LC. See also Coffee to Mary Coffee, October 13 and 25, 1813, "Letters of John Coffee," 275-276; Blount to Cocke, September 25, 1813, Jackson Papers, LC; and Reid to Sophia Reid, October 4, 1813, Reid Papers, LC.

[36] Akers, "The Unexpected Challenge," 210-211. Blount to Cocke and Jackson, October 4, 1813; Jackson to Peter A. Early, October 10, 1813; Mitchell to Jackson, October 19, 1813; Blount to Jackson, November 9 and 17, 1813; John Floyd to Jackson, December 8, 1813, January 2 and February 4, 1814; and Jackson to Floyd, January 30, 1814, all in Jackson Papers, LC. See also Reid to Elizabeth Reid, November 1, 1813, Reid Papers, LC.

too few to affect the result of the war at the stage.[37] Cooperation between the forces from East and West Tennessee was always bedeviled by the longstanding personal and political rivalries between the two sections of the state, and the East Tennessee generals, particularly John Cocke, were all associates of John Sevier, Jackson's oldest and most bitter enemy.[38] Cocke's actions, both intentionally and unintentionally, hampered Jackson's movements; he attacked on November 20, 1813, the Hillabee towns of the upper Creeks, which, shortly before, had opened peace negotiations with Jackson, and he supported the rank and file of Jackson's army in disputes with their commander over the terms of their enlistment.[39] This last action eventually drove Jackson into demanding Cocke's arrest, which Blount finally agreed to in March 1814, but before that date the governor did nothing to bring about a more effective coordination of the state's forces. He simply wished to remain on good terms with all parties and assumed that the War Department would direct the armies during the campaign.[40]

Madison's hope that Georgia would take the lead in the Creek campaigns was undermined first by Governor Mitchell's belief that cooperation with Tennessee was not very practicable and then by his decision not to seek re-election in October 1813.[41] Furthermore, Georgia did not put a great deal of effort into the Creek war, and the state legislature, in sharp contrast with its Tennessee counterpart, authorized the governor to borrow only a mere $20,000 to finance its operations.[42] Consequently, both Mitchell and his successor, Peter A. Early, were always short of money, and they were, moreover, inclined to postpone action until they had made more thorough preparations.[43]

[37] Akers "The Unexpected Challenge," 168-174; John Francis Hamtramck Claiborne, *Mississippi as a Province, Territory, and State* (Jackson, Miss., 1880), 329-332.

[38] For the political background in Tennessee see William A. Walker, Jr., "Tennessee, 1796-1821" (Ph.D. diss., University of Texas, 1959), especially 89-90.

[39] See Akers, "The Unexpected Challenge," 217; Robert V. Remini, *Andrew Jackson and the Course of American Empire, 1767-1821* (New York, 1977), 202-203; and James W. Holland, "Andrew Jackson and the Creek War," *Alabama Review* 21 (1968), 253.

[40] Blount to Armstrong, August 1, 1813, LRRS; and Blount to Jackson, November 24, 1813, Jackson Papers, LC. See also Peeler, "Policies of Willie Blount," 324; and Walker, "Tennessee," 295.

[41] Mitchell to Armstrong, July 27, 1813, LRRS; and Mitchell to Monroe, October 26, 1813, MLDS.

[42] Peter A. Early to Armstrong, November 18, 1813, LRUS.

[43] Mitchell to Monroe, September 25, 1813, MLDS; Mitchell to Armstrong, August 9 and September 14, 1813, October 5, 1813, LRRS; Pinckney to Armstrong, December 2, 1813, and Early to Armstrong, January 12, 1814, LRRS. See also Akers, "The Unexpected Challenge," 183-184, 189, 190-193; and Hugh M. Thomason, "Governor Peter Early and the Creek Indian Frontier, 1813-1815," *Georgia Historical Quarterly* 45 (1961), 223-237.

They experienced particular difficulty in obtaining supplies in the western regions of Georgia, through which the forces would have to advance before reaching the Creek country, and the general orders for such a movement were not issued before November 12.[44] To replace Mitchell as the coordinator of the Creek campaigns, Madison eventually fell back on Pinckney in Charleston, and the administration extended his command to cover the Seventh Military District for that purpose.[45] Pinckney, though, was not able to come to Georgia before December, and he initially confined his role in the war to writing letters of advice to the commanders in the field.[46] His objectives in the war were, in fact, no different from Jackson's, but his only positive contribution to the war effort was to arrange for the dispatch of a brigade of troops in December 1813 from North and South Carolina, and even these arrived too late in the Creek country to see active service.[47]

The burden of carrying on the war then fell, by default and contrary to Madison's intentions, on Jackson's West Tennessee militia. The administration had previously tried to avoid giving Jackson an active role in the war for a number of reasons, not the least of which was a dislike for his notoriously ungovernable temper and some lingering suspicions about his involvement with Aaron Burr in his conspiracy of 1807. Jackson had resented the neglect, and he was resolutely determined to use the opportunities presented by the Creek war to vindicate his reputation. After his initial successes, however, he found himself stranded in the Creek country with an army for which the supply arrangements were totally inadequate and whose members were beginning to dispute the conditions of their service. The root of the latter problem was that Jackson's militia volunteers had been embodied for one year's service as long ago as December 1812 and that by November 1813 they were accordingly anticipating their discharge.

[44] The problem of supply in western Georgia was compounded by the reaction of the settlers to the war. Many inhabitants panicked, fled from their lands, and demanded the erection of fortifications, this last response being one which the state governor felt was both unnecessary and excessively costly. See David Blackshear to Mitchell, August 13, 1813, and Mitchell to Blackshear, August 14, 1813, both in Stephen F. Miller, *Memoir of Gen. David Blackshear including Letters from Governors Irwin, Jackson, Mitchell, Early and Rabun* (Philadelphia, 1858), 412-413.

[45] Monroe to Madison, October 18, 1813, Madison Papers, LC; Parker to Pinckney and Blount, November 7, 1813, LSMA.

[46] Pinckney to Armstrong, November 16, 1813, LRRS; and Pinckney to Jackson, November 16 and 29, December 2, 12, and 24, 1813, January 26, February 5, 17, and 26, March 8, 11, 20, and 23, 1814, all in Jackson Papers, LC.

[47] Pinckney to governors of North and South Carolina, December 27, 1813, copy in LRUS. See also John K. Mahon, "The Carolina Brigade Sent against the Creek Indians in 1814," *North Carolina Historical Review* 28 (1951), 421-425.

They were the more inclined to this point of view after a brief experience of the hardship caused by the failure of the contractor to deliver supplies and the inability of the army to live off the country. No one could agree with Jackson's claim, which probably owed much to his own peculiar digestive problems, that parched corn was "a most excellent substitute for bread and meat," and many of the men needed to return home to plant their own spring crops.[48]

By December 1813, therefore, Jackson's campaign against the Creeks had stalled for want of supplies and a series of disputes within the army which Jackson chose to regard as mutiny.[49] He refused to give his men their discharge and asserted that no one had the right to abandon an army in the country of the enemy. There then followed throughout the winter some tense and ugly incidents in which Jackson, together with some of his officers, threatened to shoot any man who attempted to return to Tennessee, but, by the end of January 1814, the general held his position at Fort Strother with barely 130 men.[50] Jackson's behavior throughout this period was characterized by a grimly intense personal commitment to success that was not matched by any other American commander in the war, and the considerable discomfort he undeniably suffered from his various pains and fevers probably made him quite unsympathetic to the complaints of his men, whose problems could always be seen as less severe.[51] But, regardless of his motives,

[48] Reid to Elizabeth Reid, October 29 and November 7, 1813, Reid Papers, LC. See also Mary H. McCowan, "The 'J. Hartsell Memora': The Journal of a Tennessee Captain in the War of 1812," *East Tennessee Historical Society Publications* 11 (1939), 96; and 12 (1940), 135.

[49] After the Battle of Talladega, Coffee predicted that the war would be over in three weeks, provided the army received supplies. Coffee to Mary Coffee, November 12, 1813, "Letters of John Coffee," 278.

[50] These disputes are described at length in almost any biography of Jackson. See, for example, Remini, *Jackson*, 197-205; and they are narrated extensively in the letters of Reid and Coffee, especially Reid to Abraham Maury, November 21 and December 9, 1813, Reid Papers, LC, and Coffee to Mary Coffee, December 19 and 27, 1813, and January 3, 1814, "Letters of John Coffee," 278-279.

[51] John Reid, Jackson's aide-de-camp, noted that the general seemed "to derive additional animation from the difficulties he [had] to encounter." To Nathan Reid, November 6, 1813, Reid Papers, LC. The problem of Jackson's personality and its effect on his career can be most interestingly approached in Michael P. Rogin, *Fathers and Children: Andrew Jackson and the Subjugation of the American Indian* (New York, 1975), 3-159. Rogin's arguments, resting as they do on the psychoanalytic theories of Melanie Klein, require the acceptance of some large and unprovable assumptions, and it is possible to reject the work as methodologically flawed. See William Gilmore, "The Individual and the Group in Psychohistory: Rogin's *Fathers and Children* and the Problem of Jackson's Health," *Psychohistory Review* 6 (1977-1978), 112-126. Nonetheless, Rogin does illuminate aspects of Jackson's extremely authoritarian behavior which historians had previously tended to disregard.

the general was not widely supported for his stand. Most Tennesseans, including the governor, no matter how much they might have deplored the consequences of disbanding the army, felt that the men were within their rights, and Blount, on December 22, 1813, suggested that Jackson abandon the campaign in order to make a fresh start later.[52] The general retorted by roundly ordering the governor to arouse himself from his lethargy, since he feared that while the Tennessee forces were immobilized the Creeks would regroup to attack the Georgia forces, who would be advancing into enemy country unsupported.[53] To prevent this development, Jackson even risked two diversionary actions in January 1814 at Emuckfau and Enotachopco, but he was unable to sustain an advance and had to withdraw to Fort Strother to await further supplies and reinforcements.[54]

The War Department, however, early in January 1814 gave Governor Blount the authority to raise more volunteers for Jackson's army and added to them as well the regulars of the 39th Infantry.[55] Jackson thus began to rebuild his army at Fort Strother until it was about 3,500 strong, but he was still far from ideally situated for taking the offensive. Many of his new Tennessee troops were only sixty-day volunteers, and the army lost one-third of their period of service in waiting for supplies to come through.[56] Also, in the interval, the Creeks had, as Jackson had feared, driven off the invading Georgia army at Calabee Creek and were concentrating their strength in the towns about sixty miles to the south of Fort Strother.[57] Infuriated by these developments, Jackson decided he had nothing to gain by further delay, and, relying on the strength of his regulars, he dealt with his discipline problems by taking the unprecedented step on March 14, 1814, of executing a

[52] John Sevier and his supporters blamed the difficulties of the army entirely on Jackson. Sevier claimed that Jackson's campaign was "badly planned" and that there "never was a finer set of men who . . . had they been properly led on into the midst of the Creek country before they became half starved . . . would have performed every desired [duty]." Sevier to Isaac Shelby, February 5, 1814, *Gulf States Historical Magazine* 1 (1903), 358. See also Blount to Jackson, December 10 and 22, 1813, Jackson Papers, LC; and Blount to Armstrong, January 5, 1814, LRRS.

[53] Jackson to Blount, December 26 and 29, 1813, Jackson Papers, LC.

[54] Akers, "The Unexpected Challenge," 231. Jackson to Pinckney, January 24, 1814, enclosed in Pinckney to Armstrong, February 16, 1814, LRRS.

[55] Armstrong to Blount, January 3 and 11, 1814, LSMA; Pinckney to Jackson, January 10, 1814, Jackson Papers, LC.

[56] Reid to Nathan Reid, February 14, 1814, Reid Papers, LC.

[57] Akers, "The Unexpected Challenge," 200-201; Hall, "The Red Stick War," 283. For a detailed description of the Georgia campaign see Frank L. Owsley, Jr., *Struggle for the Gulf Borderlands: The Creek War and the Battle of New Orleans, 1812-1815* (Gainesville, Fla., 1981), 51-60.

militiaman for disobedience of orders and mutiny. He then immediately resumed his advance toward the heart of the Creek confederation to prevent the Indians from consolidating their position any further.[58]

After building Fort Williams some fifty miles to the south of Fort Strother, Jackson then engaged the remaining Creek forces in their strongly defended position in a horseshoe-shaped bend on the Tallapoosa River. The battle that followed, on March 27, 1814, was the most costly of the entire campaign, but it resulted in a decisive victory for the Americans.[59] Before it took place, Jackson had, in fact, anticipated that it would be necessary to fight a further battle with the Creeks as they retreated toward Pensacola, but the defeat of March 27 finally broke the Creek capacity to resist.[60] The few remaining Red Sticks simply chose to flee to Spanish territory rather than risk another loss, which, by now, they could ill afford to sustain. Their casualties throughout the war had been very great, partly because of the Creek custom of drawing all their relatives into one place during wartime, which exposed not only the warriors but also large numbers of women and children to the risk of death. The American casualties, on the other hand, were relatively light, largely because the Creeks, under the influence of their prophets and possibly short of ammunition, often favored using traditional Indian weapons rather than muskets and rifles.[61] In the last analysis, the Creek Indians proved to be a desperate and brave enemy for the American forces, rather than a truly dangerous one.

Below the site of the battlefield of March 27, at the juncture of the Coosa and Tallapoosa rivers, Jackson proceeded to construct a fort which bore his name and from which, four months later, he dictated

[58] Reid to Elizabeth Reid, March 14, 1813, Reid Papers, LC. The execution of militiaman John Woods was one of the most controversial acts of Jackson's career, and by the disciplinary standards of the day as applied to militia it was a drastic punishment for a minor offense. But Jackson doubtless felt that had he allowed his newly recruited army to dissolve around him—as his first army had—his reputation as a military leader in Tennessee would have been ruined. There would also have been considerable discontent throughout Tennessee at the failure to settle the Creek problem conclusively.

[59] For an account of the battle of Horseshoe Bend see Remini, *Jackson*, 213-220. See also Reid to Elizabeth Reid, April 1, 1814, Reid Papers, LC.

[60] Reid to Elizabeth Reid, April 6, 1814, Reid Papers, LC.

[61] The Creeks lost between 1,900 and 2,500 warriors in the war, which represented over 40% of the total number of warriors in the Creek and Seminole nations. See Swanton, *Early History of the Creeks*, 443. The Americans probably lost no more than 600 lives in the entire war—if the losses at Fort Mims were no more than 250. For comments on the different methods of Indian and American warfare see Akers, "The Unexpected Challenge," 195; Woodward, *Reminiscences*, 101-102; Stiggins, "Narration," Draper Collection, V, 77, SHSW; and Reid to Nathan Reid, November 6 and December 24, 1813, Reid Papers, LC.

a treaty of peace that broke forever the power of the prophets within the townships and eliminated the Creek confederation as an obstacle to American expansion toward the Gulf Coast. As Jackson himself boasted, he seized the "cream of the Creek country, opening a communication from Georgia to Mobile. . . ."[62] With this result, the Creek war could be fairly described as the most decisive and most significant victory won by the United States in the entire War of 1812. Admittedly, as was the case in the Northwest in 1813, success had not come exactly in the manner in which the administration would have liked, and the war progressed more by a series of isolated raids than through the implementation of a coherent strategy. Very possibly, too, the administration might have felt at the time that the victory was slight compensation for the failure to take Canada, but, as later events were to prove, it also made it far more difficult for Great Britain to invade the American Southwest. And it was this possibility, after all, that had prompted the decision to intervene in the Creek disputes in the first place.

★

As JACKSON began his struggle with his army in the Creek country, Madison, in Washington, prepared to meet the second session of the Thirteenth Congress. The failure of Wilkinson's campaign to weaken the British in Canada, as Henry Clay pointed out, deprived the President as he wrote his message to Congress in early December of that "finishing stroke" so necessary for his complete success, while any hopes that Great Britain would be otherwise disposed to negotiate were undermined by the news of Napoleon's defeat in October at the Battle of Leipzig.[63] Consequently, the administration's position at the end of 1813, despite the successes of the year, was not greatly stronger than it had been at the end of 1812. The war had not become notably more popular throughout the nation, with the Republican party's success in New York in April being balanced by the continuing opposition of the Federalists in Massachusetts and New Hampshire. In the fall of 1813 the Republicans did win victories in the elections for the lower house in Maryland and Vermont, but in both states the Federalists, by challenging and invalidating crucial Republican votes, won control of the state senates and elected Federalist governors with narrow ma-

[62] For the treaty of Fort Jackson of August 9, 1814, see Owsley, *Struggle for the Gulf Borderlands*, 86-94. For the influence of the Creek war on later events see below, Chapter XI. For Jackson's remark see his letter to John Overton, August 10, 1814, John Overton Papers, UNC.

[63] Henry Clay to Caesar A. Rodney, December 11, 1813, Rodney Family Papers, LC; (Richmond, Va.) *The Enquirer*, November 2, 1813.

jorities on joint ballots. The new governor of Vermont, Martin Chittenden, then promptly celebrated his election by withdrawing the state militia from United States service on the frontier with Canada.[64]

In his message to Congress, Madison chose to ignore these difficulties, concentrating instead on the military and naval victories of the year.[65] The Russian mediation, however, Madison's hopes that peace "might grow out of it" notwithstanding, had to be admitted to have failed, and this left the President no choice but to promise a more successful war effort in 1814.[66] Apart from hinting at the need for reform of the militia, though, Madison did not make any suggestions about future American policies in the war. These would have to come, as in the past, from subsequent reports and recommendations by departmental heads, but even here there was still an element of uncertainty, since Armstrong, in the aftermath of Wilkinson's failure, had not returned to Washington to meet the inevitable request for explanations. Instead, the Secretary remained in upstate New York, his movements and motives unclear, and his absence was, as Jonathan Roberts of Pennsylvania complained, "all things considered a little singular."[67] In this situation, few Congressmen could have been moved by the superficial optimism of the President's message, and most of them probably shared the gloomy verdict of John Clopton of Virginia that the American position in the war was "very discouraging."[68]

While waiting for Armstrong's return from New York, the President recommended on December 9 that Congress pass a total embargo on American exports and a ban on all imports known to be of British origin. Madison's advocacy of a more stringent policy here than the one that had been rejected by the same Congress only four months earlier was proof both of his stubbornness and his desperation. The request to Congress clearly reflected Madison's belief that commercial restriction could still modify British hostility toward the United States, but his desire to persevere with the old Republican policies was also

[64] For the Maryland election see *Daily Natl Intelligencer*, October 13 and December 18, 1813; for Vermont see ibid., October 28 and November 29, 1813, and (Baltimore) *The Weekly Register*, October 30 and November 13, 1813.

[65] James D. Richardson, comp., *A Compilation of the Messages and Papers of the Presidents* (New York, 1897-1914), II, 519-525.

[66] See Madison to Monroe, November 22 and 27, 1813, Monroe Papers, LC.

[67] Jonathan Roberts to Alexander James Dallas, December 12, 1813, George Mifflin Dallas Collection, HSP. See also Joseph Desha to Shelby, December 11, 1813, Draper Collection, 3 X 49, SHSW.

[68] John Clopton to J. B. Clopton, January 12, 1814, John Clopton Papers, Duke University Library. Nathaniel Macon to Joseph H. Nicholson, January 12, 1814, Joseph H. Nicholson Papers, LC.

prompted by the need to maintain some sort of pressure on the enemy and to cut off the considerable traffic in supplies across the Canadian border.[69] Trading with the enemy in Canada had, in fact, reached enormous proportions, and, according to the collector at Boston, many American customs officials were in collusion with the smugglers. It was even reported in late November 1813 that a group of Boston merchants was able to arrange for the shipment of 30,000 barrels of flour to Canada.[70] The existence of such trade clearly made a mockery of American law and suggested, much to Madison's irritation, that not even a formal state of war could prevent Great Britain from continuing its traditional policies of exploiting American commerce to its advantage.[71]

Despite the unpopularity of similar measures in the past and widespread skepticism about their effectiveness, Madison's call for an embargo was acted on with surprising speed. The House passed the necessary bill after two days, and the Senate did likewise one week later. The congressional response was thus a victory for the President, though not one that could have been entirely pleasing to him. The chairman of the House foreign relations committee, John Calhoun of South Carolina, as had become his custom with all measures of commercial restriction, did not report the bill to the floor, nor did he make any case for it in debate. With the failure of the party's leading congressional spokesman on foreign affairs to give a lead, few other Republicans attempted to justify the embargo. Most simply voted for it, leaving the Federalists free to attack it in debate, while a small, disorganized group of Republicans, seldom more than a dozen strong, vainly joined them in attempts to amend or defeat it.[72]

In the Senate, five of the "malcontent" Republicans—Gilman, German, Lambert, Leib, and Smith—continued their longstanding opposition to the administration, but those Republicans whose votes or abstentions had been responsible for the defeat of the embargo in July now reversed their position and voted in favor. During the fall of 1813,

[69] See Richardson, *Messages and Papers*, II, 525-526; see also *The Enquirer*, December 21, 1813.

[70] Henry A. S. Dearborn to William Jones, November 30, 1813, MLDS; Elbridge Gerry to Madison, December 21, 1813, Elbridge Gerry Papers, MHS; Anon to Armstrong, undated, LRUS; (Portland, Me.) *Eastern Argus*, December 2, 1813; [William Bentley], *The Diary of William Bentley* (Salem, 1905-1914), IV, 238.

[71] Madison to Monroe, August 22, 1813, Monroe Papers, LC.

[72] See AC, 13th Cong., 2d sess., 2032-2053. In the House, the Republicans most consistently against the embargo were Langdon Cheves (S.C.), William Duvall (Ky.), Jacob Hufty (N.J.), John Hungerford (Va.), Nathaniel Ruggles (Mass.), and Richard Stanford (N.C.).

four of these Republicans—Giles, Stone, Turner, and Anderson—had been criticized or censured in their state legislatures for their obstruction of the administration, and their changed conduct, as Joseph Desha of Kentucky pointed out, was proof that public "switching" of opponents of the war sometimes had its advantages.[73] The passage of the embargo, in fact, signified the beginning of the disintegration of that amorphous group of Senate "malcontents" whose tactics had so embarrassed Madison since 1809.[74] Thereafter Smith, Giles, and Leib cast their votes for rather than against administration policy, and Leib eventually resigned from the Senate in February 1814 to accept— briefly as it proved—the appointment of postmaster in Philadelphia.[75] This development left only a hard core of "Clintonian" Senators— Gilman, German, and Lambert—consistently opposing the administration from within the Republican party, and death was shortly to remove Gilman from the scene as well.[76] In these ways, the administration's political position in Congress promised to be stronger than it had been in the past, but much would still depend on the Secretary of War and the policies that he proposed to carry on the conflict for the coming year.

Armstrong had not been altogether idle in his absence from Washington after the end of Wilkinson's campaign, though he had not appeared much in public and was obviously deeply embarrassed about the inconclusive operations on the St. Lawrence.[77] Almost inevitably, his thoughts soon turned to the campaign for 1814, since military

[73] Ibid., 550-561. Desha to Shelby, December 18, 1813, Miscellaneous MSS, NYHS. See also *Daily Natl Intelligencer*, September 20, 1813; and (Albany, N.Y.) *Albany Register*, March 25, 1814. Giles confessed to Senator Mason that although he expected no good from the embargo, he voted for it to "stem the torrent" of the demand for the measure in the southern states. See Jeremiah Mason to Jesse Appleton, December 21, 1813, G. S. Hillard, ed., *Memoir and Correspondence of Jeremiah Mason* (Cambridge, Mass., 1873), 70-71.

[74] John Smith to Thomas Worthington, March 20, 1814, Thomas Worthington Papers, OSL.

[75] Postmaster General Gideon Granger, long a covert opponent of the administration and supporter of the Clinton family, appointed Leib postmaster in Philadelphia, which caused such an outcry that Madison dismissed Granger. See Granger to John Todd, February 7, 1814, Simon Gratz Autograph Collection, HSP; and Chandler Price to Jones, February 14 and 28, 1814, Uselma Clarke Smith Collection of William Jones Papers, HSP. Leib was replaced in the Senate by Jonathan Roberts, normally a supporter of the administration, but he was in the early months of 1814 too busy paying court to his landlady's daughter to pay much attention to politics. See Roberts to Matthew Roberts, February 28, 1814, Jonathan Roberts Papers, HSP. Eventually, Leib was removed from the Philadelphia postmastership in early 1815 for his attacks on Madison.

[76] Gilman died in Philadelphia on May 2, 1814.

[77] See Harrison Ellery, *The Memoirs of General Joseph Gardner Swift* (Worcester, Mass., 1890), 121.

success, as the French minister in Washington observed, was absolutely essential for his presidential ambitions, while failure could only add "a bad odor to the sins of his youth."[78] Indeed, some of the political consequences of Wilkinson's failure were already becoming apparent. The Clintonian Republicans in New York were depicting the mismanagement of the campaign as part of a an extensive plot of Virginian intrigue, in which Armstrong was cast as a hapless Duke of York, to depress the political influence of the northern states by *not* conquering Canada. The Snyderite Republicans of Pennsylvania, outraged by Armstrong's patronage policies throughout the year, were less subtle in their attack. The *Democratic Press* criticized the Secretary of War as a "mere theoretical man," unfit for the real business of winning the war, while Charles Jared Ingersoll suggested that Madison should have sent Armstrong instead of Gallatin to Siberia.[79]

Armstrong's response and his prescription for military victory in 1814 were basically simple. American military and naval forces for the conquest of Canada would have to be vastly increased. To the President in November, Armstrong had already suggested that the United States should expand its fleets on Lakes Ontario and Champlain as well as build galleys on the St. Lawrence to control Lake St. Francis. Hampton and Wilkinson, he added, should be replaced by George Izard and Thomas Flournoy.[80] But the full scope of the Secretary's thinking did not become apparent until the *Albany Argus*, on December 3, published under the signature of "An Officer of the Army" a call for a regular army of 55,000 men to be raised by classification of the militia and commanded by a lieutenant general of "deep and comprehensive views." The editorial letter declared that army recruitment by voluntary enlistment had been a failure, and it assumed that both Congress and the nation had been sufficiently humbled by recent events to accept the need for more thorough measures. What the editorial failed to mention in this context, however, was the unpleasant fact that the army was approaching a state of crisis, since the enlistments of the five-year men from 1808 and 1809 as well as those of the twelve- and eighteen-month men from 1812 and 1813 were all due to expire within the next few months. An effective response to these developments was clearly needed, though the *Argus*, possibly for prudent reasons, did

[78] Louis Sérurier to duc de Bassano, November 20, 1813, Archives du Ministère des Affaires Étrangères: Correspondance Politique, États Unis, vol. LXX (photostats in LC).

[79] *Albany Register*, November 12 and 29, 1813; (Philadelphia) *Democratic Press*, December 29, 1813. Also see Charles Jared Ingersoll to Dallas, December 11, 1813, Charles Jared Ingersoll Papers, HSP.

[80] Armstrong to Madison, November 24 and December 5, 1813, Madison Papers, LC.

not urge classification on those grounds. Instead, the expense and effort of the reform were justified with the promise of the complete conquest of Canada in one campaign. In its conclusion the editorial then asserted that the architect of the flawlessly conceived (though badly executed) campaign of 1813 would be the best possible choice for lieutenant general.[81]

The "Officer of the Army" was universally recognized to be Armstrong, and the reactions to his proposals were mixed. Few Republicans questioned the notion that Hampton and Wilkinson might be replaced by a more competent and unified system of command, but that extensive military powers should be conferred upon the present Secretary of War was another matter altogether.[82] Many men continued to be deeply suspicious of his motives, and even Armstrong's advocacy of replacing old generals with young officers was sometimes regarded not so much as a necessary reform as an attempt to clear the field of rivals so that the Secretary could step forward with the claim that only he had the proper knowledge to command an army.[83] To the cheers of a dinner given by the Snyderite Republicans in Philadelphia on December 9, William Henry Harrison offered a toast to Armstrong's bête noire, volunteer militia, and observed that some very "unrepublican thoughts" dangerous to liberty had been circulating recently. Then both the *Albany Register* and the *Democratic Press* evoked scenes of the first American dictator marching into the Presidency at the head of a "praetorian band." The policy of classifying the militia, despite the desperate need for manpower, was similarly greeted with cries of "slavery" and "conscription," the last term by this period having become closely associated with the Grand Army and Napoleonic methods of warfare.[84] In response, the *Albany Argus* and the *National Advocate* dismissed these objections as imaginary, remarking that the Republic was neither sufficiently corrupt nor yet old enough to be vulnerable to the threat of despotism, and, in Washington, the Adjutant and

---

[81] (Albany, N.Y.) *Albany Argus*, December 3, 1814. For the state of the army at this time see J. Mackay Hitsman, *The Incredible War of 1812: A Military History* (Toronto, 1965), 183; and Murray A. McLauchlan, "The Army, Society, and the War of 1812" (M.A. research essay, University of Auckland, 1980), 34.

[82] *Albany Register*, December 17, 1813; *The Enquirer*, December 7 and 9, 1813.

[83] See Roberts to Dallas, December 19, 1813, Dallas Collection, HSP; Mason to Appleton, January 29, 1814, Hillard, *Mason*, 82; and Hosea Moffitt to Charles R. Webster, March 1, 1814, *Historical Magazine* 2d Ser., 8 (1870), 111-112.

[84] See Harrison's "Toast to the Militia," December 9, 1813, Logan Esarey, ed., *Messages and Letters of William Henry Harrison* (Indianapolis, 1922), II, 610. *Albany Register*, December 17, 1813.

Inspector General, Charles K. Gardner, prepared a classification bill for submission to Congress.[85]

Armstrong's ideas, however, gathered little positive support. Not even William Duane could bring himself to endorse in the *Aurora* any of the schemes that issued from New York in December, and the papers in the western states were openly hostile.[86] Congress, too, was reluctant to consider any form of militia classification, and the House signaled its opinion here on December 15 by instructing the military affairs committee to consider a motion made by William Lowndes of South Carolina that the present army should be maintained simply by persuading the existing short-term recruits to re-enlist for longer service in return for higher wages and bounties.[87] The opposition increased when Armstrong himself finally returned to Washington on December 24 and began lobbying immediately for a classification bill. His actions here finally roused Monroe to protest. The attempt to raise regulars by classification, Monroe argued to Madison, was unconstitutional, and trying to do so would bring the administration into disrepute. Yet the Secretary of State then went further and tried to eliminate his rival altogether by claiming that Armstrong was both disloyal to the administration and personally corrupt in the distribution of army patronage. The Republican party, Monroe concluded, could no longer afford Armstrong's stewardship in the War Department, and he urged the President to dismiss the Secretary for his role in the 1813 campaign, pointing as he did so to several specific incidents which could serve as pretexts.[88]

Monroe's protests and arguments were so transparently self-serving that Madison ignored them. The President did not actually oppose militia classification, though whether his general endorsement of it in his earlier message to Congress on December 7 was intended as support for Armstrong's views is uncertain. As evidence of Armstrong's disloyalty, Monroe had stated that the Secretary of War had asked Representative Jonathan Fisk of New York to move for an inquiry on the failure of the 1813 campaign, which Monroe claimed was to be turned into an attack on the administration. This argument was barely credible. Madison may have felt that an inquiry could serve no useful

[85] *Albany Argus*, December 21 and 24, 1813; and (New York) *National Advocate*, December 31, 1813. See also Gardner's "Estimate for Mr. Troup," December 10, 1813, LRUS.

[86] The (Philadelphia) *Aurora General Advertiser*, January 11, 1814, criticized Congress for not reforming the army but avoided any discussion of Armstrong's proposals. Cf (Lexington) *Kentucky Gazette*, January 10, 1814.

[87] AC, 13th Cong., 2d sess., 791.

[88] Monroe to Madison, December 27, 1813, Madison Papers, LC.

purpose, but some sort of congressional investigation was almost unavoidable, and the President could have had no real objection to Armstrong's trying to arrange it in a manner favorable to himself.[89] Besides, Armstrong could hardly have used the inquiry to attack the administration without making himself look ridiculous as well. Finally, Monroe's advice on how Armstrong might be dismissed was not only presumptuous but stupid, since it could only have reminded Madison that the motives and methods which the Secretary of State had used to acquire a detailed knowledge of the campaign of 1813 did not themselves bear a close examination.[90]

In declining to support Monroe against Armstrong, however, Madison failed to make any significant gesture of support for the Secretary of War or his policies, and Armstrong was quick to note and resent the omission. The Secretary had continued to advocate his militia classification scheme, though in his communications with congressional committees he began making concessions to the extent of asking the legislature to choose between classification and the established method of recruiting by premiums and bounties.[91] By presenting Congress with a choice, Armstrong, in effect, invited the rejection of his scheme for a large, drafted army in 1814, but, before Congress could do this, the developments of the last week of December 1813 completely undermined the Secretary's hopes for the conquest of Canada in the next campaign. On December 24, the British army, after reoccupying the positions taken by the United States on the Niagara Peninsula in the spring of 1813, invaded upstate New York, laying waste the towns of Buffalo, Black Rock, Lewiston, and Niagara.[92] One week

[89] The inquiry was actually proposed by Representative William C. Bradley of Vermont, and later the *Daily National Intelligencer*, on May 16, 1814, questioned its value by pointing out that it only encouraged quarrels within the army and allowed the enemy to receive information it otherwise would not have seen.

[90] When he returned to Washington at the end of October 1813, Madison found that Monroe had removed, during Armstrong's absence, all the correspondence relating to the campaigns of 1813 to the Department of State. The chief clerk of the War Department, Daniel Parker, recalled that the President was "more in a passion than [he] ever saw him at any other period of his life, and gave it very distinctly to be understood that he thought Mr. Monroe had been meddling with affairs of the War Department more than was proper." See Charles Francis Adams, ed., *The Memoirs of John Quincy Adams* (Philadelphia, 1874-1877), VI, 5, entry for June 2, 1822. Monroe may have corresponded with Hampton throughout the campaign of 1813, and he certainly made summaries for his own purposes of Hampton's correspondence between August 21 and November 20, 1813. These can be found in James Monroe Papers, NYPL.

[91] Armstrong to George Troup, December 29, 1813, Parker Papers, HSP.

[92] See Daniel D. Tompkins to Armstrong, December 24, 1813, LRRS; and (Canandaigua, N.Y.) *Ontario Repository*, December 28, 1813.

later, the administration received the official news of Great Britain's rejection of the Russian mediation and of Lord Castlereagh's subsequent offer of direct peace talks to be held at either London or at Gothenburg, Sweden, on the basis of "the maritime rights of Great Britain."[93] The cabinet met to discuss the offer on January 8, 1814, with Madison quickly deciding to accept it. He chose Gothenburg, and the public announcement of the decision was made on January 10.

Both these events were setbacks to Armstrong's plans. The British raids in New York starkly exposed the defenseless condition of the American frontier, and Armstrong was immediately overwhelmed with delegations and petitions from New York Republicans demanding protection and retaliation—in most cases by means of an American invasion of Canada from the Niagara Peninsula.[94] On January 12, 1814, Representative John Taylor of New York called at the War Department to repeat these requests on behalf of Governor Tompkins, who too wanted a campaign in February against the British positions on the peninsula. For this purpose, he had already decided to ask the New York legislature to raise 5,000 state troops, and he also wanted Armstrong to restore Dearborn to the command of the army and order him to attack either Kingston or Prescott.[95] As a New Yorker, Armstrong could hardly have been insensitive to these demands, and he must also have realized that failure to respond to the British raids would injure the Republican party in the May elections for the state legislature as well as in the later elections for Congress. Even worse was the possibility that Great Britain might be tempted to regain lost ground in Upper Canada and to re-establish contact with the northwestern Indians if it were allowed to consolidate its position on the Niagara Peninsula.[96] Yet to anticipate these developments by concentrating the War Department's limited resources in another Niagara campaign also risked the premature foreclosure of any opportunity to reduce the enemy positions in Lower Canada. As the new year opened, then, all that the future seemed to hold for Armstrong was another year of campaigning for very limited strategic gains.

[93] Jones to Dallas, January 4, 1813, Dallas Collection, HSP.

[94] Tompkins to Armstrong, January 2 and 9, 1814, LRRS; Tompkins to Madison, January 3, 1814, Madison Papers, LC; Tompkins to Isaac Chauncey, January 4, 1814, Jones Papers, HSP. Winfield Scott, *Memoirs of Lieutenant General Scott Written by Himself* (New York, 1864), 115.

[95] Tompkins to John W. Taylor, January 5, 1814, John W. Taylor Papers, NYHS; Tompkins to Armstrong, January 16, 1814, LRRS.

[96] Armstrong to Harrison, December 29, 1813, LSMA; and "Note by Armstrong," January 1, 1814, MLDS.

Reluctantly, Armstrong tried to make the best of the situation. He promised Taylor he would promote Izard to Hampton's old command at Plattsburg and assign Jacob Brown to command the regulars at Sacketts Harbor. Izard, if nothing else, always gave the appearance of competence, while Brown was trusted by both Armstrong and Spencer and promised to be a more vigorous campaigner than Dearborn.[97] Any British attempt to regain a position in the American Northwest, the Secretary had already suggested, could be dealt with by sending Harrison back to Malden to organize the Indians for a series of raids on the British settlements up to the Niagara Peninsula in the spring 1814.[98] On January 20, Armstrong ordered the right wing of the northern army to concentrate its forces at Plattsburg, and ten days later he authorized preparations for a campaign to drive the British from the Niagara, endorsing as he did so Tompkins's plans to raise state forces for this purpose.[99] Madison, however, overruled most of these suggestions; he disapproved of the idea of employing Indian methods of warfare, preferring instead to deal with the threat in the Northwest by naval expeditions against the remaining British positions there, and he wanted to remain on the defensive while he considered the chances for peace resulting from the recent British offer of negotiations.[100]

·In accepting this offer, Madison appears to have believed that it would still be possible to request Russia to exert some diplomatic pressure on the enemy but the President's decision here, unfortunately, also had the effect of dividing the cabinet.[101] Both Monroe and Jones favored negotiations with Great Britain, but Armstrong, most emphatically, did not.[102] The Secretary of War may have felt that no peace

[97] "Memo of a Conversation with General Armstrong," January 12, 1814, Taylor Papers, NYHS. See also Jacob Brown to Ambrose Spencer, December 17, 1813, Gratz Autograph Collection, HSP. Thomas Flournoy, whom Armstrong had earlier considered as a replacement for Hampton, resigned his commission at the end of 1813.

[98] See sources cited in note 96.

[99] Armstrong to Wilkinson, January 20 and 30, 1814; Armstrong to Tompkins, February 3, 1814, LSMA.

[100] See Armstrong to Harrison, January 1, 1814, LSMA, and Charles Jared Ingersoll, *Historical Sketch of the Second War between the United States and Great Britain* (Philadelphia, 1845), II, 80. Even after the Battle of the Thames, the British still occupied forts on Lake Huron at Mackinaw and St. Joseph's. For Madison's decision to attack these positions in 1814 see below, Chapter IX.

[101] Jones to Dallas, January 4, 1814, Dallas Collection, HSP; Monroe to Henry Clay and Jonathan Russell, February 14, 1814, Adams Family Papers, MHS.

[102] "Memo of a Conversation with General Armstrong," January 12, 1814, Taylor Papers, NYHS; Rufus King, "Notes, February 25, 1814," Charles R. King, ed., *The Life and Correspondence of Rufus King* (New York, 1894-1900), V, 371. Daniel Webster also noted

could result from negotiations on the basis of Great Britain's "maritime rights," since the very wording of the British offer implied that the Americans would have to concede at least the practice, if not the principle, of impressment. This possibility at best suggested a re-enactment of the negotiations that had led to the abortive Monroe-Pinkney treaty of 1806, and Armstrong could have opposed this as either too dishonorable to the nation or as too favorable to the reputation of the Secretary of State. Admittedly, Madison had stated that the negotiations with the British would have to be on the reciprocal basis of the rights of both powers "as sovereign and independent nations," but if this language had any meaning, it suggested that the talks would ultimately fail over the question of impressment.[103] In the interval, Armstrong felt that the hope for peace would prevent Congress and the nation from adopting the measures he felt were necessary for the conquest of Canada, but if the President really did desire peace from the negotiations, then Armstrong also believed that there was no justification for continuing with the war and its difficulties.[104]

With the announcement that the United States would send negotiators to Gothenburg, Madison had declared that the war would be continued in the meantime, but his attempt to position himself between the divisions in the cabinet did not satisfy Armstrong, least of all after Madison had started to overrule the measures that the Secretary had proposed for dealing with the British on the Niagara.[105] So upset was the Secretary of War by the accumulating setbacks to his plans that on January 9 he contacted, through the agency of Colonel Joseph Swift, Senator Jeremiah Mason of New Hampshire to discuss the formation of an alliance with the Federalists that would cast the Virginia Dynasty from power in 1816. Ironically, he was now following the same course for which he had so vigorously condemned DeWitt Clinton in 1812, and, in his conversations with the Federalists, he

---

that there were "evident symptoms of schism in the Cabinet. . . . Monroe will have it that the [British] dispatches are pacific; whence it is inferred that his thoughts are turned on peace. In truth, his thoughts are turned principally on the next election. Armstrong can see nothing in the dispatches which looks like sentiments of returning justice in the British Ministry. He is still for trying the tug of war." Webster to Isaac P. Davis, January 6, 1814, Charles M. Wiltse, ed., *The Papers of Daniel Webster: Correspondence, 1798-1824* (Hanover, N.H., 1974), I, 160.

[103] Dallas to Jones, February 4, 1814, Jones Papers, HSP. King, "Notes, February 25, 1814," King, *Life and Correspondence*, V, 371.

[104] "Memo of a Conversation with General Armstrong," January 12, 1814, Taylor Papers, NYHS.

[105] Sérurier to Bassano, January 14, 1814, Correspondance Politique, vol. LXXI. See also Webster to——, February 11, 1814, Wiltse, *Webster Papers*, I, 165.

bitterly complained that the President did not heed his advice and was about to sacrifice the American cause in the war for the sake of peace. This news could hardly have been unwelcome to the Federalists, and, with the exception of Timothy Pickering of Massachusetts, they displayed no great interest in Armstrong's plight.[106] The same complaints repeated before Republicans, though, were likely to meet a rather different reception. To John Taylor of New York, Armstrong began to talk of resignation if his views were not followed, and he hinted that Congress should adopt a declaration in favor of the American annexation of Canada. Such a step, Armstrong believed, would give purpose to the war, vindicate American rights, and justify the sacrifice that complete victory would require.[107]

Taylor did not act on Armstrong's suggestion, but, in spreading the rumor that the administration might sacrifice the conquest of Canada for the uncertain prospect of peace, the Secretary had, in fact, raised a difficult issue. Although the administration had never formally committed itself to acquiring Canadian territory, the retention of whatever conquests that might be made had become an increasingly important justification for the war with many of its supporters, and there was also some sense to Armstrong's view that the war should be given a distinct purpose which could be readily grasped by the public. On this subject, Armstrong's views were shared by most Republicans from the western states, for whom the expulsion of British power from North America was an essential guarantee against Indian hostilities as well as the source of an endless supply of fresh land, while in New England the former Republican governor of New Hampshire, William Plumer, noted at the same time that it was necessary for the United States to possess Canada to keep the British empire in a proper state of economic dependence on American supplies.[108] Madison, although perhaps not familiar with the extent to which Armstrong was opposing his policies, was well aware of these Republican sensibilities about the future of Canada, and he revealed as much in his selection of the negotiators for the Gothenburg talks with Great Britain. Here the most obvious course was to reissue the instructions and commissions of Adams, Bayard,

---

[106] King, "Notes, January 1814," King, *Life and Correspondence*, V, 370-371. For Pickering's interest see his letter to Robert Goodloe Harper, March 7, 1814, copy in William Astor Chanler Collection of John Armstrong Photostats, NYHS.

[107] "Memo of a Conversation with General Armstrong," Taylor Papers, NYHS.

[108] See Chapter VII above. See also Shelby to Sevier, January 26, 1814, Draper Collection, 9 DD 90, SHSW; William Crawford to Madison, February 18, 1814, Madison Papers, LC; and William Plumer to John Quincy Adams, January 24, 1814, Adams Family Papers, MHS.

and Gallatin—who were all still in Europe—and to add to them the nomination of Jonathan Russell on the grounds that now more than ever the United States needed diplomatic representation in Sweden. However, such a negotiating team could hardly be said to be representative of all shades of opinion in the Republican party, and the omission of any spokesman from the southern and western states, where support for the war had been most consistent, would only have given credibility to Armstrong's claims that Madison was eager for peace at almost any price, including the sacrifice of American hopes for Canada. The President, therefore, decided to protect himself from any criticism by nominating Speaker Henry Clay as a fifth peace commissioner. The instructions issued for this enlarged diplomatic delegation were virtually the same as those for the Russian mediation, and they included provision for the Americans to obtain, if possible, the cession of Canada.[109]

The addition of Clay to the negotiating delegation appears to have satisfied most Republicans in Washington. It was widely assumed that the Kentuckian would not sign any peace treaty that did not vindicate American honor or gratify any western ambitions for Canada.[110] Yet the departure of the diplomats for Gothenburg, as Armstrong had predicted, did undoubtedly weaken the war effort. The Federalists, both in Congress and in New England, became more aggressive in their opposition to the war and the embargo, and they increasingly came to dominate congressional proceedings. They argued that the administration could not consistently negotiate for peace and continue the war for the conquest of Canada at the same time, while they also introduced endless resolutions to stop the war or to confine its operations to the defense of the frontiers, and to repeal or modify the embargo.[111] The Republicans voted down all these motions easily enough, but they did not introduce any new measures to carry on the war with vigor. The House tabled a resolution to create the rank of lieutenant general, and its military affairs committee, on January 13, 1814, also declined to report Armstrong's proposals for militia classification. Instead, both House and Senate two weeks later voted on straight party lines for bills to re-enlist the existing troops and to continue recruiting

[109] Monroe to Commissioners, January 28, 1814, Adams Family Papers, MHS.

[110] Sérurier to Bassano, January 24, 1814, Correspondance Politique, vol. LXXI; Joseph Kerr to Worthington, February 11, 1814, Worthington Papers, OSL; William Short to Thomas Jefferson, January 18, 1814, Thomas Jefferson Papers, LC. Clay was actually less committed to the annexation of Canada than many assumed, and he believed that the question would be decided by circumstances. See Clay to Thomas Bodley, December 18, 1813, James F. Hopkins, ed., *The Papers of Henry Clay* (Lexington, 1959–), I, 841-842.

[111] AC 13th Cong., 2d sess., 1048-1052, 1054-1056, 1115-1122, 1265-1269.

by the established methods, allowing only for a sizable increase in bounty payments to $100 for men willing to enlist for either five years or the duration of the war.[112] Armstrong, however, expected nothing from these measures, and, in desperation, he declared to John Taylor his opinion that there would be no army if it became widely believed that peace was at hand.[113]

★

EVEN MORE SERIOUS than the failure of Congress to follow Armstrong's lead in the matter of military policy was its inability to provide money for continuing the war. Acting Treasury Secretary Jones presented a gloomy budget to the legislature on January 10, 1814, in which he estimated the total costs of the war establishments for the coming year at $45,350,000, an increase of over one-half the amount that had been required in 1813. For the army alone Armstrong needed $24,550,000, while for the navy Jones called for nearly $7,000,000. Yet the revenue for 1814, according to Jones's calculations, would cover little more than the ordinary costs of the civil list and debt financing. The taxes voted by Congress in the summer of 1813 were only just beginning to be collected, and Jones believed that they would produce barely two-thirds of their estimated yield of $6,350,000.[114] In some parts of the country, notably New England and Louisiana, the Treasury had been unable to find suitable men to accept the unpopular appointments of tax collectors and revenue inspectors, while the tax laws allowed state governments to assume quotas of the federal taxes at a discount of 15 percent.[115] This last provision was designed to facilitate payment and collection of the taxes, but it also cost revenue and tended to undermine very basic principles of federal authority.

The Indian wars in the South and the Northwest had also seriously reduced federal income from public land sales, while the customs as a source of revenue under the embargo and nonimportation laws had almost ceased to exist. From this last source, Jones could, in fact, only hope to glean a doubtful $5,500,000 still outstanding from the double duties that had been imposed in 1812. Consequently, almost the entire cost of the war for 1814 would have to come from another loan, which

[112] Ibid., 856-858, 928-979, 981-1008, 1012-1046, 1060-1093, 1099-1114. For the Senate see ibid., 574-595. See also Troup to Armstrong, January 24, 1814, LRRS.

[113] "Memo of a Conversation with General Armstrong," Taylor Papers, NYHS.

[114] Jones, "Estimate, 1814," and "Ways and Means for 1814," Jones Papers, HSP. See also Jones's report of January 10, 1814, *ASP: Finance*, II, 651-653.

[115] Madison to Jones, October 11 and 17, 1813, Madison Papers, LC; Tristam Dalton to Dolley Madison, May 14, 1814, Cutts Collection of the Papers of James and Dolley Madison, University of Chicago (microfilm in LC).

Jones believed would have to raise the unprecedented sum of $29,350,000. The House debated the enormity of this loan for nearly three weeks before authorizing on March 3, 1814, the borrowing of $25,000,000, but many Congressmen doubted whether the money could ever be raised, since a government without revenue would clearly lack the credit to borrow in competitive markets.[116] Moreover, Jones was rebelling under the burden of his two cabinet positions. While daily praying for Gallatin's return, he pointed out that his tasks at the Treasury prevented him from introducing necessary reforms in the Navy Department and that his duties in Washington generally were ruining his personal finances. Unwilling to abandon the President, who was still in poor health, Jones agonized over the problem of how to resign decently and reluctantly yielded to Madison's pleas that he serve a little longer.[117]

One way for the administration to borrow money was to charter another Bank of the United States to replace the one that had ceased operations in 1811. Gallatin had suggested this shortly before he left for Russia but did not dare recommend it in the financial program that he had drawn up for the first session of the Thirteenth Congress. But by the beginning of 1814, many Republicans, despite their constitutional scruples, were becoming convinced of the need for a national bank to enable the government to raise and handle its own revenues. The proliferation of state and local banks after the dissolution of the first Bank of the United States threatened to disperse government funds and other capital throughout a large number of small financial institutions of varying degrees of reliability, and these local banks, furthermore, negotiated Treasury bills at widely differing rates of discount.[118] Many of them throughout 1813 had also become increasingly short of specie as their reserves had been drained away to New England, while that region had continued to export and import goods during the period of its exemption from the Royal Navy blockade.[119] This development had, by the beginning of 1814, given the Federalist-controlled banks of New England an unprecedented control over the nation's money supply. As part of their growing opposition to the war,

[116] See sources cited in note 114, and AC, 13th Cong., 2d sess., 1269-1586, 1590-1609, 1628-1694, 1770-1798.

[117] Jones to Dallas, December 21, 1813, Dallas Collection, HSP.

[118] For the background see Robert W. Keyes, "The Formation of the Second Bank of the United States, 1811-1817" (Ph.D. diss., University of Delaware, 1975), 8-12. In 1812 the number of state banks in existence was 112; in 1814 it was 202, with 41 being created in Pennsylvania alone in 1814. See also Manuel Eyre to Jones, January 5, 1814, Jones Papers, HSP; and *Daily Natl Intelligencer*, March 26, 1814.

[119] John Hoff to Madison, January 28, 1814, Madison Papers, LC.

376

Boston bankers were exerting pressure on the Manhattan Company, a leading Republican bank and government depository in New York, to prevent it from subscribing to any government loans in 1814, and these bankers also hoped that their moves would coerce the repeal of the embargo. To relieve the administration from this myriad of local political and financial pressures, a national bank was clearly essential.[120]

Nonetheless, the establishment of a second national bank was a politically difficult task. Differences of opinion over the constitutionality of the measure were bound to divide Republicans, and it would be almost impossible for the administration to establish a bank that would inspire the confidence of potential money-lenders without giving offense to some Republican factions as well as to a host of local financial interests.[121] Some of these problems immediately became apparent when Madison sought a permanent replacement for Gallatin in the Treasury. The President's first choices were the Pennsylvanians Alexander James Dallas and Richard Rush. Both men declined the position in early February 1814 because they were reluctant to take on its difficulties before a national bank had been established, and both knew they risked being rejected for the nomination in the Senate by the Pennsylvania Senators, Abner Lacock and Michael Leib.[122] Madison then offered the vacancy to Senator George Washington Campbell of Tennessee, whose acceptance virtually guaranteed his confirmation in the Senate but whose lack of financial experience did nothing to create the impression that the Treasury was in capable hands.[123] Joseph H. Nicholson, kinsman of Gallatin and president of the Commercial and Farmers Bank of Baltimore, observed that Campbell lacked the confidence of the "monied men," while Congressman Samuel Taggart of Massachusetts jeered that the appointment of "*GWC*" openly proclaimed that the "*Government Wants Cash!*"[124] Indeed, the only real advantage that resulted from Campbell's appointment was not of a

[120] Jesse Bledsoe to William Worsley, February 12, 1814, Draper Collection, 6 CC 3, SHSW. See also E. T. Winter to Lewis Ransome, March 25, 1814, LRRS.

[121] Macon to Nicholson, March 26, 1814, Nicholson Papers, LC.

[122] Jones to Dallas, February 1, 1814; Dallas to Jones, February 3, 1814, Dallas Collection, HSP; Dallas to Jones, April 3, 1814, Jones Papers, HSP. See also John H. Powell, *Richard Rush: Republican Diplomat, 1780-1859* (Philadelphia, 1942), 48.

[123] For Campbell's career see Weymouth T. Jordan, *George Washington Campbell of Tennessee: Western Statesman* (Tallahassee, 1955), esp. 110-136.

[124] Jones to Dallas, (February 1814), Dallas Collection, HSP; Mason to Mary Mason, February 10, 1814, Hillard, *Mason*, 83; Nicholson to Macon, February 17, 1814, Nicholson Papers, LC; and Samuel Taggart to John Taylor, February 15, 1814, George H. Haynes, ed., "Letters of Samuel Taggart, Representative in Congress, 1803-1814," *Proceedings of the American Antiquarian Society* 33 (1923), 428.

financial nature at all, but political; since he was a firm supporter of the war, his presence in the cabinet somewhat mollified the disgruntled Armstrong, and the friendship between the two men reduced the Secretary of War's sense of isolation within the administration.[125]

To get round the constitutional problem, Madison's kinsman, James G. Jackson of Virginia, had introduced in the House on January 28 a constitutional amendment to authorize the establishment of a bank, but the House postponed consideration of the matter while it debated the loan and a variety of other issues.[126] This delay provoked the *National Intelligencer* on February 18 into sharply criticizing Congress for wasting its own time and the public's money, and the next day, John Taylor of New York reported from the House Ways and Means Committee a bill to create a national bank in the District of Columbia.[127] This measure avoided many of the constitutional problems in establishing a bank, but as a compromise measure it highlighted a conflict of opinion among the Republicans. The chairman of the Ways and Means Committee, John Wayles Eppes of Virginia, refused to support a national bank in any form, and many Congressmen from the commercial cities between Baltimore and New York who might have accepted a bank had it been established in their localities showed little interest in supporting a bank for the District of Columbia. The *National Intelligencer* appealed to the congressional Republicans on at least three occasions to vote for this measure, but Congress continued to postpone it, debating it again only briefly on March 10, 1814. The matter then lapsed till April 4, near the end of the session, when it was again referred to another committee, which failed to produce a report at all.[128]

During the course of these inconclusive proceedings, Campbell had decided to open, on April 2, a short-term loan of $10 million to enable the government to carry on pending a more comprehensive solution of its financial problems. As had been the case in 1813, the financiers John Jacob Astor and David Parish showed some interest in taking up this loan, but they hung back when they learned that Campbell had also been approached by Jacob Barker of New York, who was

[125] Webster to Benjamin J. Gilbert, February 8, 1814, Wiltse, *Webster Papers*, I, 163. Here Webster described Campbell as "the mere creature of Armstrong and [he] is a great zealot for the war and the conquest of Canada." See also Webster to——, February 11, 1814, Wiltse, *Webster Papers*, I, 165.

[126] AC, 13th Cong., 2d sess., 1191-1194.

[127] *Daily Natl Intelligencer*, February 18, 1814.

[128] Ibid., February 22, March 28, and April 4, 1814. AC, 13th Cong., 2d sess., 1860-1862, 1941, 1954.

offering to subscribe $5 million.[129] Barker, in truth, did not have this much capital, and he was really acting as an agent for a number of state and local banks who were prepared to lend money in return for the Treasury transferring its business to them. Campbell desperately wanted Barker's $5 million, but he could not give any undertakings about transferring Treasury business without violating agreements made with the government's existing creditors, while Barker's rivals in banking circles informed Monroe and Jones that the New York banker was unlikely to be able to deliver on his promises anyway.[130] The chief clerk of the Treasury, Daniel Sheldon, who undoubtedly understood more about these problems than the Secretary, was also adamantly opposed to doing business with Barker, and, at one point in the discussions, Barker tried to expedite matters by telling Campbell to dismiss Sheldon. The Secretary confessed that he could not do so, since he "knew nothing about the details of the office and was too unwell to conduct its business with strangers."[131] Eventually, at the beginning of May, Barker agreed to make a loan of $5 million to the Treasury in return for some unwritten promises that Campbell would do what he could about transferring some government business to other banks, and Campbell was able to fill the remainder of the $10 million loan from some forty individuals and institutions in Boston, New York, and Philadelphia.[132]

The government thus tottered on, but even as Campbell began his difficult duties its position was deteriorating rapidly on all fronts, and soon the course of events far outran the ability of both Congress and the administration to understand, let alone control. The first member of the administration to realize that the war was becoming not merely difficult to manage but absolutely impossible was Jones, who, though now freed from the duties of the Treasury, still had many contacts in

[129] John Jacob Astor to Monroe, April 30 and June 1, 1814, Monroe Papers, LC. Stephen Girard, an important contributor to the 1813 loan, had subsequently quarreled with Astor and Parish and was no longer willing to enter a syndicate to lend money to the United States. See Donald R. Adams, Jr., *Finance and Enterprise in Early America: A Study of Stephen Girard's Bank, 1812-1831* (Philadelphia, 1978), 36, 37, 44.

[130] For Barker's activities see Jacob Barker, *Incidents in the Life of Jacob Barker of New Orleans, Louisiana; with Historical Facts, His Financial Transactions with the Government, and His Course on Important Political Questions* (Washington, D.C., 1855), 45-51. See also Dallas to Monroe, May 3, 1814, Monroe Papers, LC; and E. Fox to Jones, May 9, 1814, Jones Papers, HSP. Monroe seems to have favored trying to raise loans in Europe rather than in the United States. See his "Notes on Loans," May 14, 1814, Madison Papers, LC.

[131] Barker, *Incidents*, 51.

[132] Ibid., 52-53. Campbell to Madison, May 4, 1814, and Madison to Campbell, May 7, 1814, Madison Papers, LC. The list of subscribers to the loan is in *ASP: Finance*, II, 846.

the merchant community and was thus in a rather better position than Campbell to assess the situation of the country. On March 9, he informed Madison that no matter what Campbell did the loan was likely to fail and that the administration would sooner or later face a severe financial crisis. The basis for his opinion was the general lack of confidence among financiers in both the administration and the future of the war, while many merchants, he reported, were saving their money for trade after the restoration of peace rather than risking it in loans to the administration. Above all else, Jones argued that the administration had to be able to raise money to continue governing, and the only reliable prospect for this lay in the immediate repeal of the embargo. With the revival of trade, the Treasury could raise revenue from double customs duties, and, with the revenue thus assured, financiers might be willing to contribute to government loans.

Jones realized that the total abandonment of the "restrictive system" would not be an easy step for Madison to take. It would not only require the acknowledgment of a personal failure, with the discarding of a cardinal tenet of the President's diplomacy, but it also entailed allowing American merchants and farmers to trade with the enemy again, including feeding its armies in Canada. This, the Navy Secretary pointed out, was simply unavoidable but still preferable to enforcing unpopular laws which discredited the administration, encouraged smuggling and the corruption of officials, and could never completely stop the drain of specie into New England banks anyway. Rather than wanting to involve the administration in the palpable absurdity of supplying the British while trying to defeat them in Canada, Jones argued that the United States should give up its attempts to seize enemy territory. It was better, he added, to raise money, go on the defensive on the frontiers, and let the navy take the offensive on the oceans.[133] No doubt, Jones had been brought to this argument by his gradual realization that the United States, despite a considerable transfer of men and naval resources from the Atlantic coast to the Great Lakes, was unlikely to enjoy in 1814 a decisive superiority over the British on Lakes Ontario and Champlain.[134] And without such superiority, the success of future military operations against Lower Canada was, at best, problematical, whereas the navy on the Atlantic Ocean could still inflict some damage on British commerce.

---

[133] See "Thoughts on the Present State of Affairs," March 9, 1814, Jones Papers, HSP. See also Jones to Nicholson, March 12, 1814, Nicholson Papers, LC; and Jones to Madison, March 17, 1814, MLDS.

[134] Jones to Armstrong, March 20 and April 5, 1814, LRRS. Jones to Madison, May 25, 1814, Jones Papers, HSP.

Madison did not immediately respond to Jones's memorandum, but events increasingly lent force to the Secretary's opinions. The embargo was undeniably unpopular, especially with merchants and farmers who depended on the export trade, and its impact was probably heightened by the collection of the taxes and internal duties levied in 1813. Resistance to the embargo and war in New England, somewhat restrained throughout 1813, was now far greater, and was threatening to erupt into violence. Town meetings throughout the Connecticut Valley protested in apocalyptic tones, even calling for bloodshed, while the Massachusetts legislature, in an attempt to make the administration even more unpopular, had refused to assume the state's federal taxes at a discount.[135] The legislature also debated the calling of a state convention to protect the violated rights of the people, discussed the raising of a state army to enforce those rights, and even talked about secession and a separate peace with Great Britain. An overwhelming Federalist victory in the Massachusetts elections of April 1814 could conceivably encourage or compel the leaders of that party to take some decisive action in an attempt to end the hardships of the war.[136] And should such a Federalist victory be followed by a Republican defeat in New York in May, then the prospects for continuing the war against Canada would indeed be well nigh hopeless.[137]

This last development was by no means impossible. The Federalist-controlled lower house in the New York legislature had refused to cooperate with Tompkins's attempts to raise forces to retaliate for the British raids of December 1813, and the Federalist leaders in Albany had virtually demanded an end to the war.[138] Recruiting and fund-raising for Tompkins's forces therefore had to proceed largely on a voluntary basis, with the Republicans being able to offer only vague promises about state and federal reimbursement at a later date.[139] This recruiting did not go well. Peter B. Porter, by virtue of his reputation,

---

[135] (Boston) *Independent Chronicle*, February 17, 1814.

[136] See James M. Banner, Jr., *To the Hartford Convention: The Federalists and the Origins of Party Politics in Massachusetts, 1789-1815* (New York, 1970), 313-319; and also Samuel E. Morison, *The Life and Letters of Harrison Gray Otis, Federalist, 1765-1848* (Boston, 1913), II, 78-92.

[137] See *National Advocate*, March 29 and April 18, 1814.

[138] See the New York Assembly reply to Tompkins, February 4, 1814, Hugh Hastings, ed., *The Public Papers of Daniel D. Tompkins* (Albany, 1898-1902), III, 434-436. Tompkins remarked that the Assembly had "too much of the Massachusetts leaven in it." To Armstrong, March 30, 1814, *Papers of Tompkins*, III, 460.

[139] See Tompkins's appeal for volunteers, March 13, 1814, ibid., III, 478-479, and a similar appeal by Peter B. Porter, March 25, 1814, Peter B. Porter Papers, BEHS. See also *Albany Argus*, April 20, 1814.

was able to assemble about 1,000 men, but most of his associates working with him could report only failure.[140] Even in Virginia, the war had become quite unpopular. Here Tidewater planters felt exposed to the combined dangers of invasion and slave revolt, and Armstrong greatly offended their sensibilities by scornfully declaring that the construction of forts along Virginia's river systems was a total waste of money. Madison eventually felt compelled to overrule the Secretary, but, even so, Republicans in the "Old Dominion" feared that their Federalist opponents would greatly increase their strength in the forthcoming state elections.[141] This possibility, in turn, profoundly depressed Monroe, who felt sure that the war was failing for want of "proper" measures. His instinctive reaction was to resign from the administration in order to avoid being associated with the disgrace of defeat, which might harm his presidential prospects, but, on reflection, he decided that the political disadvantages of such a step outweighed the gains, and he remained complainingly at his position.[142]

If the domestic situation was becoming complicated for the administration, the news from overseas at the same time was little short of disastrous. In the early months of 1814 it became clear that the European campaigns of that year would not, as many Republicans believed, merely establish a balance of power between France and the Allies but were instead a prelude to the total defeat of Napoleon. Equilibrium among the powers of Europe, Republicans had felt, was not harmful to the interests of the United States, since Great Britain, in order to maintain the coalition against France, would eventually be required to pay some attention to the opinions of its eastern European

[140] Porter to Armstrong, March 27, 1814, LRRS; Porter to Tompkins, April 1814; and to Armstrong, May 3, 1814, E. A. Cruikshank, ed., *Documentary History of the Campaign on the Niagara Frontier* (Welland, Ont., 1898-1902), I, 7-8, and II, 390-391. See also the letters to Porter from the following: S. R. Jones, April 2, 1814; Joshua Hathaway, April 4 and 20, 1814; T. C. Chapin, April 14, 1814; John Campbell, April 18, 1814; William Rochester, April 22, 1814; and James McNair, May 15, 1814, all in Porter Papers, BEHS.

[141] James Barbour to Madison, February 17, 1814, and Madison to Barbour, February 26, 1814, Madison Papers, LC; Andrew Stevenson to Monroe, March 30, 1814, Monroe Papers, NYPL. See also Joseph Carrington Cabell to Hugh Nelson, February 17, 1814, Cabell Family Papers, UVa.; and James Garnett to John Randolph, May 9 and 25, 1814, Randolph-Garnett Letterbook, LC.

[142] Monroe to Hay, March 11, 1814, Monroe Papers, NYPL. Hay told Monroe to give Madison an ultimatum that he would resign unless his advice were followed. See Hay to Monroe, March 14, 1814. Monroe Papers, NYPL. Monroe lacked the nerve for this, but he did sketch a long private letter to William H. Crawford in Paris, complaining of how he had opposed every administration measure since the nomination of Gallatin to Russia. The letter was probably not sent; see Monroe Papers, LC.

allies on questions of maritime rights.[143] A decisive Allied victory over France, however, was a very different matter, since Russia, as it became more involved in European problems, might lose interest in the issue of maritime rights, thus leaving Great Britain's naval pretensions unchecked.[144] Yet even though many Republicans realized that Great Britain could no longer be forced into making concessions to the United States, they were still unprepared for the developments in Europe after March 1814. Expecting that the Allies would confine a humbled Napoleon within the boundaries of France as they had existed in 1792, all Americans, and Republicans in particular, were stunned to learn that the Allies had crossed both the Rhine and the Pyrenees and were advancing on Paris.[145] The deposition of Napoleon suddenly emerged as an unexpected development with quite unpredictable consequences.

The possiblity that France might suffer total defeat galvanized Madison into action. Learning at the end of March that the Allies had invaded France, the President called a cabinet meeting on March 30, at which the subject for discussion was the future of the embargo. No member of the administration appears to have opposed the end of the "restrictive system"; and all the arguments put forward earlier by Jones could only have been reinforced by the news from Europe.[146] Not only had the embargo become an unrealistic policy with the imminent defeat of France, but Madison must have realized that future American diplomacy would actually require its repeal as quickly as possible. If the President wished to obtain any European support at all for American positions on maritime rights, it was essential that the United States restore trade relations with neutral European nations at once. If Great Britain chose to disrupt this commerce as part of its war effort against the United States, Madison's views could gain a fresh hearing in the courts of Europe.[147] In fact, the recently liberated Kingdom of Holland had already dispatched a minister to the United States, and an addi-

---

[143] See *Daily Natl Intelligencer*, February 17, 1814; *National Advocate*, January 29 and February 25, 1814; and *Boston Patriot*, February 12, 1814.

[144] William Lee to Monroe, January 29, 1814, Monroe Papers, NYPL; Monroe to Dallas, January 30, 1814, Garrison, ed., *James Monroe Papers in Virginia Repositories* (microfilm ed.).

[145] Israel Pickens to William Lenoir, February 20, 1814, Lenoir Family Papers, UNC; J. G. Jackson to Return Jonathan Meigs, January 20, 1814, Return Jonathan Meigs Papers, OSL; William T. Barry to Thomas D. Owings, February 3, 1814, Draper Collection 6 CC 2, SHSW. See also *The Enquirer*, February 19, April 2 and 6, 1814; *Independent Chronicle*, January 20 and April 28, 1814; and *National Advocate*, May 25, 1814.

[146] Jones to Dallas, March 30, 1814, Dallas Collection, HSP.

[147] Monroe to Commissioners, April, 4, 1814, Adams Family Papers, MHS; and Monroe to Ingersoll, May 16, 1814, Ingersoll Papers, HSP.

tional advantage of the resumption of diplomatic relations with the Dutch was the prospect of raising loans in Amsterdam.[148]

Madison thus proved to be sufficiently flexible to abandon his long-cherished diplomacy of commercial restriction, but most of his supporters turned out to be less so. Many Republicans were shocked by the President's request, made on April 1, 1814, to repeal the measure they had been defending throughout the session against attacks by the Federalists. As William Lowndes complained, congressional Republicans felt that Madison had given them neither adequate warning nor sufficient reason for his move, and the justifications printed in the *National Intelligencer*—the need for revenue, the problems of enforcement, and the desirability of restoring trade with Europe—clearly did not carry much weight.[149] Instead, congressional Republicans worried about the appearance of inconsistency, the problems of American trade being used to supply the enemy in Canada, and the possibility that the lifting of the embargo was too important a concession to make before the commencement of peace negotiations in Gothenburg. Consequently, the President's call for repeal further divided a congressional party that was already badly split over the war and the question of the bank. Calhoun, who had never defended the embargo, now came forward to lead the debate for repeal, but a solid core of some twenty-five to thirty-five Republicans in the House and six to nine Senators, all of them previously regular supporters of the war, resisted the change to the very end.[150] In fact, Representatives John Wayles Eppes and Samuel Ringgold even called at the State Department and pointedly inquired if the administration had decided to sue for peace.[151] The Republican "malcontents" in the Senate, however, enjoyed a final moment of vindication in supporting the President to end the embargo,

[148] S. Bourne to Madison, February 20, 1814, Monroe Papers, LC; and Monroe's "Notes on Loans," May 14, 1814, Madison Papers, LC. The Russian minister in Washington, Andrei Dashkov, also hoped that the repeal of the embargo would lead to an increase in neutral trade with the United States. To encourage this, he asked Rear Admiral Sir George Cockburn of the British blockading force for permission to dispatch a vessel to Russia and Great Britain to carry news of the repeal of the embargo. Cockburn refused. See Dashkov to Cockburn, April 16, 1814, Cochrane Papers, folio 2333, NLS.

[149] Lowndes to Pinckney, April 16, 1814, William Lowndes Papers, LC; Macon to Nicholson, April 6, 1814, Nicholson Papers, LC. See also *Daily Natl Intelligencer*, April 1, 1814. As he reported the "funeral" of the restrictive system, James M. Garnett wrote: "You have no adequate idea of the sheepish looks exhibited on the occasion by the devoted victims of Executive fatuity and incapacity." To John Randolph, April 8, 1814, Randolph-Garnett Letterbook, LC.

[150] AC, 13th Cong., 2d sess., 731-741, 1946, 1962-1977, 1986-2001. See also *Kentucky Gazette*, April 18 and 25, May 2, 1814.

[151] Monroe to Madison, April 10, 1814, Madison Papers, LC.

with David Stone of North Carolina exulting that this measure as well as the war, products of an "insanity" in government both, were now finally doomed.[152]

The end of the embargo was a crucial episode, for it required all Americans to reassess their attitudes to the war and its future. For the Federalists, the news from Europe, combined with the domestic difficulties of the administration, seemed to vindicate their view that Madison's hostility to Great Britain was dependent on the power of France to give it effect, and it thus confirmed them in their opposition to continuing the war. Yet the repeal of the embargo and Napoleon's difficulties in Europe also suggested that the war would shortly come to an end, a possibility which may have persuaded the Massachusetts Federalists from taking any dramatic action, such as the raising of state troops or the calling of a state convention.[153] The Republicans, however, could not indulge any feelings that events were on their side. With the repeal of the embargo, there now seemed, as Jones had predicted, little chance of bringing the war in Canada to a successful conclusion, and Madison apparently conceded the force of the argument by allowing Brigadier General William Winder to negotiate for an armistice during his meeting with British officials in Lower Canada on the problems of exchanging prisoners of war. The President stipulated, though, that any armistice had to include the cessation of hostilities on both land and sea, for he was not prepared yet to renounce the possibility of invading Canada if the Royal Navy could continue raiding at will on the Atlantic coast.[154]

The news of the armistice talks became commonplace during April 1814, and it raised hopes for an end to the fighting, which would be followed by a negotiated peace at Gothenburg.[155] Yet the chances for an armistice were, in reality, slight. The British had little reason to concede anything to the United States at this stage in the war, nor

[152] David Stone to John Haywood, April 1, 1814, John Haywood Papers, UNC; Nicholas Gilman to Pierre Van Cortlandt, Jr., April 3, 1814, Pierre Van Cortlandt, Jr., Papers, NYPL.

[153] See Morison, *Otis*, II, 95.

[154] For the armistice see Richard Rush to John Adams, April 20, 1814, Adams Family Papers, MHS; "Notes on Armistice," April 1814, Monroe Papers, LC; Daniel Brent to Monroe, April 30, 1814, Monroe Papers, LC; Jones to William Young, May 5, 1814, Jones Papers, HSP; Monroe to Winder, May 7, 1814; and Monroe to Madison, May 14, 1814, Madison Papers, LC. See also *The Enquirer*, April 30, 1814.

[155] Obadiah German to R. Rathburn, March 9, 1814, Gratz Autograph Collection, HSP. Rufus King believed, more cynically, that the armistice rumors were floated to help the Treasury raise a loan. See King to Gouverneur Morris, April 10, 1814, King, *Life and Correspondence*, V, 394.

did Lieutenant General Prevost in Montreal and Vice Admiral Sir Alexander Cochrane on the Atlantic coast have the power to commit each other's forces to a truce. Prevost, much to Madison's annoyance, dragged out the talks, then added insult to injury by asking for proof of the United States' good intentions.[156] The talks duly stalled on the failure to include the Atlantic coast in the armistice, and Vice Admiral Cochrane, in the first week in May, underlined the superiority of British naval power by proclaiming the entire American coast to be under blockade. The administration promptly declared the blockade to be illegal, instructing American diplomats in Europe to point this out to all neutral governments, but Cochrane's action, highlighting as it did the vulnerability of the Atlantic coast, left Madison with little choice but to continue with some sort of campaign against Canada.[157] Yet this campaign would now be a very different one from those that had been attempted in 1812 and 1813. There was, in truth, very little chance that a Canadian invasion could force Great Britain to respect American maritime rights, and the settlement of these matters, if they could be settled at all, would now depend largely on events in Europe and the peace talks at Gothenburg. In the interim, the administration would simply have to defend the Republic as best it could, but just how desperate that defense might have to be remained to be seen.

[156] Rush to Ingersoll, May 24, 1814, Ingersoll Papers, HSP; Madison to Monroe, May 19 and 21, 1814, Monroe Papers, LC.

[157] Monroe to John Quincy Adams, May 2, 1814, Adams Family Papers, MHS. Madison's protest against the British blockade received only perfunctory notice in Europe. In St. Petersburg, the American consul, Levitt Harris, transmitted the protest to the Russian government and received the reply that the matter would be referred to the Emperor, who ignored it. See Harris to Ivan Weydemeyer, September 14, 1814 and Weydemeyer to Harris, September 21, 1814, Archives of the Russian Foreign Ministry (microfilm of Archiv vneshnei politiki Rossii for 1809-1816 held in LC).

CHAPTER IX

★

THE CAMPAIGNS OF 1814 AND THE FALL OF WASHINGTON

ON JUNE 3, 1814, Madison summoned his cabinet for an emergency meeting in four days time. The President gave as his reason for the meeting the need to plan the campaign for the coming summer, but, in truth, there was far more to discuss than simply the strategies for the occupation of Canada.[1] Developments in Europe by the last week in May had led Madison to doubt whether the negotiations with the British due to commence at Gothenburg would produce a peace settlement, while the difficulties of securing the New York frontier against an enemy invasion, combined with the lamentably disorganized state of the army itself, severely limited the possibilities for taking the offensive in the war.[2] Indeed, Armstrong as well as Jacob Brown and

[1] Madison to Armstrong, Campbell, Jones, Monroe, and Rush, June 3, 1814, James Madison Papers, LC.

[2] Madison to Monroe, May 23, 1814, James Monroe Papers, LC. The problems of the army after the failure of Wilkinson's 1813 campaign were formidable. At French Mills the troops endured a difficult winter during which both food and clothing were in short supply, and the health and morale of the army suffered accordingly. Wilkinson, after going down the St. Lawrence, apparently neglected the fact that his army could no longer draw on western New York for supply, and he had failed to make alternative arrangements. See Elbert Anderson to Wilkinson, December 16, 1813, Northern Army Provision Papers, NYHS. The uniforms of the army were described by one observer as "scandalously and infamously bad," and he added that "so long as such clothing is palmed upon the army . . . the troops will feel no pride. . . . Police will be destroyed and consequently discipline impaired and the soldier . . . will consider himself a forlorn being in the world. . . ." John O'Conner to Alexander Macomb, May 23, 1814, LRAG. The hardships of the troops were exacerbated by the inability of young, inexperienced officers to cope with basic matters of camp administration and hygiene. Under the impact of spotty recruiting and sickness, many regiments were reduced to mere skeletons of their full strength and few had more than six complete companies. Correspondence on the state of the army for this period can be found throughout the records of the Adjutant General's office, but the most valuable sources of information are the inspection reports written by John R. Bell and Robert Jones in December 1813 and January 1814. With only a few exceptions, these reports present a picture of unrelieved

George Izard—whom the Secretary of War had recently promoted as replacements for Major Generals Wilkinson and Hampton—had already agreed before the cabinet meeting that another Niagara campaign was the only realistic way of carrying the war to the enemy in the immediate future. This decision was reached more by accident than design, but, given the lack of alternatives to opening the campaign along lines similar to those attempted in 1813, it was unlikely that the cabinet would reject the War Department's sense of what was militarily possible—unless, of course, it wished to change entirely its strategy in the war from an offensive effort against Canada to the mere defense of American territory.[3]

The real issue of the cabinet meeting, therefore, was the future of the war itself. Madison admitted as much when he advised the departmental heads to attend the meeting armed with as much information on the relative strengths of the British and American forces as they could accumulate as well as their assessments of the British position in the European war. The reports submitted by the Navy and War Secretaries in response to this request told a rather sorry story, though they scarcely indicated the extent of the crisis. Despite the fears expressed by Armstrong earlier in the year, the army had, more or less, survived the threat posed to its existence by the expiry of many enlistments in the first months of 1814, and, according to the Adjutant General, it had by the end of April recruited another 9,588 men willing to serve for five years or for the war. The total strength of the army in all military districts was now over 31,000, though only 27,000 of these, Armstrong noted, could be described as "effectives."[4] Jones

squalor in the army, with inadequately clothed men existing in filthy conditions. All the regiments, too, were six to eight months behind in their pay.

[3] Armstrong had originally wanted a quick campaign across the ice against Kingston in late winter, but he had also suggested to Brown, probably as a ruse to deceive the British, that he assemble a further 2,000 troops at Niagara. Brown doubted the expediency of Armstrong's original suggestion and therefore concentrated on taking troops to the peninsula. By the time the misunderstanding was sorted out, it was too late to attack Kingston, and this left Armstrong as summer approached with little choice but to try to turn American strength at Niagara to some advantage. See Armstrong to Brown, February 28 and April 7, 1814, Jacob Brown Papers, MHS; Brown to Armstrong, March 4, 1814, LRRS; Brown to Armstrong, April 17, 1814, Brown Papers, MHS. See also Armstrong to George Izard, May 6, 1814, Izard, *Official Correspondence with the Department of War Relative to the Military Operations of the American Army under the Command of Major General Izard on the Northern Frontier of the United States in the Years 1814 and 1815* (Philadelphia, 1816), 9.

[4] Armstrong to Madison, June 4, 1814, Madison Papers, LC. This letter contained an enclosure entitled "Number of Recruits Enlisted," prepared by John R. Bell. Army recruiting, in fact, was more successful throughout 1814 than at any other time during the war. Between February and October 1814 the Registers of Enlistments recorded some 20,300

provided more detail about the Navy than Armstrong did about the army, but his resources were far smaller. On the Great Lakes and on Lake Champlain, he believed that the United States enjoyed a slight superiority in the number of vessels of all sizes, though it lacked the trained seamen to press the advantage. On the Atlantic coast the situation was reversed; there Jones reckoned that the Royal Navy held a clear advantage, especially in ships of the line and in frigates, though he was not sure of the exact size of the enemy's fleet.[5] And, as Secretary Campbell's difficulties with the finances had already revealed, the money to increase American military and naval power simply could not be raised.[6]

The effectiveness of these meager American forces, however, would depend on the strength and intentions of the enemy, and nobody could calculate these with any certainty. Armstrong estimated that Great Britain had 12,000 regular troops in Canada, and he believed that it would soon be increasing this number by an unknown amount according to its commitments in Europe.[7] The administration had already learned, on May 19, that the Allied armies had entered Paris, but the fate of Napoleon was still unknown, as were the chances for a general European peace.[8] Privately, most of the cabinet members were convinced that the fall of France was a disaster for the American cause, but in the absence of complete information it was still possible for a wide range of speculation to flourish.[9] The The National Intelligencer

---

names, and this total can be explained only by the attractiveness of the large recruiting bounties offered by the legislation of January 1814. See Murry A. McLauchlan, "The Army, Society, and the War of 1812" (M.A. research essay, University of Auckland, 1980), 35.

[5] Jones to Madison, June 6, 1814, Madison Papers, LC. There is an element of irony in Jones's complaints about the shortage of trained seamen for the navy, since seamen from the port towns enlisted in some number in the army, amounting in fact to 3.2% of the recruits whose occupations are known. The Registers of Enlistments for the war years contain over 2,000 soldiers who gave their previous occupation as seaman. Probably, these men were persuaded, at least in part, to enlist by the effects of the war and the policies of commercial restriction on maritime enterprise. (I am indebted to Mr. McLauchlan for this figure.)

[6] See Chapter VIII above.

[7] Armstrong to Madison, June 4, 1814, Madison Papers, LC.

[8] (Washington, D.C.) *Daily Natl Intelligencer*, May 19, 1814; Madison to Monroe, May 19, 1814, Monroe Papers, LC.

[9] Jones to Madison, May 18, 1814; Monroe to Madison, May 20, 1814, Madison Papers, LC. Dashkov reported that the Federalists had enthusiastically celebrated the fall of Napoleon, but he complained that not a single Republican in Washington had congratulated him on Russia's triumph over its enemy. Dashkov to Count Nikolai P. Rumianstev, June 28, 1814, Archives of the Russian Foreign Ministry (microfilm of Archiv vneshnei politiki Rossii for 1809-1816 held in LC). (Henceforth Russian Archives.) See also (Richmond) *The Enquirer*, May 21 and 18, 1814; (Albany, N.Y.) *Albany Argus*, May 27, 1814; *Boston*

struck the most optimistic note here on June 2 by printing some reports, quickly proved to be false, that Napoleon had recovered lost ground by defeating the Allies on French soil, but the drift of Republican opinion tended to be more pessimistic. The *National Advocate* in New York flatly contradicted the administration newspaper by asserting that the defeat of France would give Great Britain the freedom to attempt to "recolonize" America and that not even the influence of Russia could be relied on to restrain this intention.[10]

The administration doubtless realized there was now little reason to expect that Russia or any other neutral nation would actively take America's side against Great Britain, but it decided on June 7—probably on the assumption that the European situation would nonetheless require the enemy to retain large numbers of troops there for some time—to persevere with the strategy of invading Canada. A joint army-navy expedition on Lake Huron under Navy Commander Arthur Sinclair was to attempt to capture the British posts at Macadash and St. Josephs, while another, under Major General Brown, would invade Upper Canada from Lake Erie in an attempt to reduce all the enemy positions below Burlington Heights. If successful in this last objective, and depending on how far the American navy had won control of Lake Ontario, Brown would then advance on York and the other British positions around the northern shore of the lake. To assist these operations, the American forces under Brigadier General Edmund Gaines at Sacketts Harbor were ordered to build a fleet of armed vessels to control the entrance to the St. Lawrence—thus cutting the communications between Montreal and Kingston—while Izard, commanding the army at Plattsburg, was instructed to make "demonstrations" toward Montreal. This last tactic was intended to prevent the commander in Lower Canada, Lieutenant General Sir George Prevost, from reinforcing British positions farther to the west and, more optimistically, to provoke him into fighting "disadvantageously or [to] break up his connection with Lake Champlain."[11]

The cabinet accepted these policies, but the decision to do so concealed a good deal of disagreement and dissatisfaction with them. Armstrong had felt for some time that the proposed Huron expedition was a waste of men and ships that might have been better concentrated on

---

Patriot, May 18, 1814; (Lexington) *Kentucky Gazette*, June 27, 1814; and (Boston) *Independent Chronicle*, May 12, 1814.

[10] *Daily Natl Intelligencer*, June 2 and 6, 1814; cf. (New York) *National Advocate*, June 3, 1814.

[11] Cabinet Memorandum, June 7, 1814, Madison Papers, LC. See also *Daily Natl Intelligencer*, May 21 and 24, 1814.

operations on Lake Ontario, and he accepted the Lake Erie strategy only as a way of facilitating Brown's entry into Upper Canada. Jones initially favored the Huron expedition, possibly seeing in it the chance to gain fresh triumphs for the navy, but eventually he too came to regard it as unnecessary and reaffirmed his opinion that the war on the Great Lakes was too costly to be justified. Madison, however, remained attracted to the scheme, principally because he did not wish to allow Great Britain the chance to re-establish any links with the northwestern Indians.[12] Monroe, for his part, had some doubts about Brown's proposed expedition, claiming that it was "hazardous" and unlikely to weaken British power in Canada anyway, while Rush, for the sake of winning a victory, urged his colleagues to concentrate all their attention on Lake Ontario, even to the extent of diverting men and materials from the Atlantic fleet to build up Commodore Chauncey's forces.[13] The Secretary of the Navy, however, favored continuing and increasing the operations on the Atlantic, believing that the occasional victories they brought kept up the "national spirit" and thus had a value "infinitely beyond their intrinsic importance."[14] The cabinet decisions, however, made some concessions to almost everybody's views, thus enabling Madison to preserve the appearance of harmony in the administration, but subsequent events and quarrels suggested that nobody was particularly happy about the compromises they had made. The thrust of the American invasion pointed westward, which in itself was an admission of weakness, and Madison's colleagues probably all felt that the campaigns would have gone better had their individual views prevailed.

Moreover, as the cabinet reached its decisions, it was aware that a continuing war against Canada would be no more popular than it had ever been. Admittedly, the Republicans won the state and congressional elections in May in New York, though the victory there may

[12] Armstrong to Madison, May 1, 1814; Madison to Armstrong, May 2 and 4, 1814; Madison to Jones, May 4, 1814, Madison Papers, LC. Jones to Chauncey, April 1814; Jones to Madison, May 25, 1814, Uselma Clarke Smith Collection of William Jones Papers, HSP. The naval operations on the upper lakes in 1814 were unsuccessful. See Alfred T. Mahan, *Sea Power in its Relations to the War of 1812* (Boston, 1905), II, 324-328.

[13] In Stanislaus M. Hamilton's *The Writings of James Monroe* (New York, 1898-1903), V, 237-241, there are some loose papers dated late 1812 and entitled "War Papers—Notes—Certain Reports—Jessup, Graham etc." Much of this material, however, cannot date from the end of 1812, and the material on the Niagara campaign, including the objection that it was "rather a defensive than an offensive movement," would seem to belong more properly to 1814. See also Richard Rush to Charles Jared Ingersoll, June 12, 1814, Charles Jared Ingersoll Papers, HSP.

[14] Jones to Madison, May 10, 1814, Madison Papers, LC.

have owed as much to high farm prices supported by military spending as it did to a desire to drive the British away from the Niagara Peninsula.[15] The Federalist-dominated legislature of Massachusetts, however, called for peace and for an end to the futile attempts to conquer Canada, while Charles Jared Ingersoll informed Monroe that Pennsylvania Republicans were rapidly losing confidence in the administration. The problem, according to Ingersoll, was simply that administration policies were not sufficiently vigorous to arouse the public to support them, and he predicted that unless decisive actions were taken soon there would be a "torrent" of opinion against the war.[16] This lack of public support became all the more evident on June 9 when the *National Intelligencer* received and printed the full details of the Allied occupation of Paris and the abdication of Napoleon. These developments were the worst setback to the war effort since the abortive campaigns of 1812 and Napoleon's defeat in Russia, and they led William Short to remark, almost humorously, that Madison might as well send the whole House foreign relations committee to sue for peace as do anything else.[17] The Federalists openly and joyously celebrated the occasion, assuming that the President would now have no choice but to make peace, and, in the cabinet, Jones appears to have come to the same conclusion. On June 12 he submitted some "further thoughts" for the President's consideration, and, although the text of his remarks seems to have been lost, there is little reason to suppose that they were not in harmony with the Navy Secretary's views expressed earlier, in March 1814, that the continuation of the war could serve no purpose and that the United States must make peace, hoping that Great Britain would concede it on the basis of the "extreme moderation" of American demands.[18]

Madison could scarcely deny that Great Britain's capacity to harm the United States had greatly increased as a result of Napoleon's fall. He was, however, unwilling to be panicked into action without more

[15] *Daily Natl Intelligencer*, May 5 and 28, 1814. The Republicans won twenty-one seats in the New York congressional delegation to the Federalists' six. See also David M. Ellis, *Landlords and Farmers in the Hudson-Mohawk Region, 1790-1850* (Ithaca, 1946), 118-120.

[16] For the proceedings in Massachusetts see (Baltimore) *The Weekly Register*, June 11 and 25, 1814. Ingersoll to Monroe, June 8, 1814, Monroe Papers, LC; Alexander James Dallas to Jones, August 13, 1814, Jones Papers, HSP.

[17] William Short to Thomas Jefferson, June 9, 1814, Thomas Jefferson Papers, LC.

[18] For descriptions of the Federalist celebrations see *Independent Chronicle*, June 16, 1814; and Samuel E. Morison et al., *Dissent in Three American Wars* (Cambridge, Mass., 1970), 8-9. In the Jones Papers, HSP, there is a cover for a letter with "further thoughts" for the President's consideration, dated June 12, 1814. The letter itself, however, is not in that collection, nor is it in the Madison Papers.

detailed information from Europe. In response to a request for advice from Governor James Barbour of Virginia, he declared that the United States should certainly anticipate and prepare for the worst that Great Britain might do, but the President had, as his advice to Barbour revealed, additional reasons for delaying his response to the rapidly altering situation. It was already apparent that the mere possibility of Great Britain's increasing its forces in North America would precipitate a flood of demands from state and city governments that the administration employ the nation's forces in local defense. The city authorities of Boston, New York, and Philadelphia were already complaining that they were inadequately fortified against an invasion, while the governors of the southern states were requesting the federalization of large portions of their militias to guard against the combined threats of invasion and slave revolt. Should the administration yield to these rising demands, it would deprive itself of the means for independent action and exhaust the limited budgets of the War and Navy departments.[19]

For the remainder of June 1814, Madison considered the possibilities. From the American viewpoint, there was no reason to allow the abdication of Napoleon and his replacement by Louis XVIII to interrupt the President's attempts to cultivate good relations with France as a counterweight to British power. Indeed, with the fall of Napoleon, it was even possible to believe—assuming that the Bourbons had no interest in defending Napoleon's seizures of American vessels—that Franco-American relations would start to improve. Here the administration was probably heartened by the fact that the restored monarchy appeared to have accepted William Crawford's credentials as minister to France, and there was still the possibility that Russia and the Baltic powers might obtain a settlement of maritime issues in a general peace that would undercut British justifications for continuing the war with America.[20] Nonetheless, Madison must also have been mindful of Rush's remark that Louis XVIII's position was too dependent on British power for him to risk differing with Great Britain on its American policy, and that no matter how peace was eventually made in Europe the United States would have to endure a difficult campaign. Jones, too, was privately predicting "a bloody and devastating summer and autumn."[21]

---

[19] See Madison to James Barbour, June 16, 1814; and Elbridge Gerry to Madison, July 17, 1814, Madison Papers, LC. See also Joseph Bloomfield to Armstrong, June 14 and 25, 1814, LRRS.

[20] *Daily Natl Intelligencer*, June 16, 1814. Monroe to William H. Crawford, June 25, 1814, Monroe Papers, LC.

[21] Rush to John Adams, June 17, 1814, John H. Powell, ed., "Some Unpublished Cor-

Accordingly, at the end of the month, Madison again sounded out the cabinet on their understanding of the European situation and its effects on the United States. On June 23 and 24 he asked his colleagues to consider three possibilities—that the surrender of the British practice of impressment be made an ultimatum in a peace treaty to run for a limited period, that a peace treaty be signed without reference to the problem of impressment, and that impressment and other commercial disputes be referred to separate negotiations after the signing of a peace treaty. Only Rush favored the first proposal, being strongly committed to the view that after two years of war the United States should not settle for a mere armistice which would leave all the basic issues unresolved. Monroe, Campbell, Armstrong, and Jones all rejected this policy, probably arguing that such an ultimatum was unrealistic under existing circumstances. The second proposal amounted to abandoning the justification for the war, and it was supported only by Jones and Armstrong. Jones's position here was consistent with all his arguments to Madison since March 1814, but that he should have been joined by Armstrong was surprising, especially since the Secretary of War had previously opposed entering into negotiations at Gothenburg on the basis of Great Britain's "maritime rights." The motives for Armstrong's change of mind can only be conjectured, but possibly he too had simply become convinced that the war could not now be won, no matter what he did. All the cabinet except Rush, however, were prepared to accept a peace treaty on the basis of Madison's third proposal. Very likely they felt that the United States had upheld its honor by resisting impressment until the end of the European war had removed the need for Great Britain to practice it, and that peace should be made on that basis.[22]

This last decision probably reflected a general desire to end the war quickly while also trying to avoid the impression of conceding too much from fear of Great Britain's superior military and naval resources. But immediately after Monroe had conveyed the decision in fresh instructions to the American commissioners in Europe, the administration received from them, on June 26, their latest dispatches.[23] These

---

respondence of John Adams and Richard Rush, 1811-1822," *Pennsylvania Magazine of History and Biography* 61 (1937), 49; Jones to William Young, undated 1814, Jones Papers, HSP.

[22] Cabinet Memorandum, June 23 and 24, 1814, Madison Papers, LC. For Rush's views see Rush to Adams, April 20, 1814, Powell, "Unpublished Correspondence between Adams and Rush," 44-45.

[23] Monroe to Commissioners, June 23 and 25, 1814, Carl Prince and Helen Fineman, eds., *The Papers of Albert Gallatin* (microfilm ed.). See also Reuben Beasley to Monroe, May 9, 1814, Monroe Papers, LC.

covered events in Europe to the first week of May 1814, and their accounts were uniformly pessimistic. The opinions of Gallatin and Bayard, who had just paid a private visit to London, were of greatest interest to the administration, but they were also by far the most gloomy. Gallatin believed that a "general peace" was at hand in Europe, which would leave Great Britain free to divert "all its forces" against the United States. Great Britain, he reported, was in an angry mood; it desired to punish the United States, and its terms for peace would be harsh. The British government would never renounce the "right" of impressment, and there were rumors in London that the United States should be compelled to give up its fishing rights in the 1783 treaty, accept modifications in its boundaries with Canada, forgo the right to navigate the Great Lakes, and restore Louisiana to Spain. It was even rumored that Great Britain would be prepared to pursue these goals to the point of dissolving the Union itself.[24]

This news shocked the cabinet into meeting again on June 27 to reconsider its last decision. In view of the reported British intransigence on impressment, the cabinet unanimously agreed to instruct the commissioners in Europe as a last resort to negotiate a treaty without reference to that grievance, with the reservation that American silence here did not acknowledge the legitimacy of the British practice. Thus did the United States abandon its remaining justification for the war, admitting as it did so the prudent need to retreat before superior military force. This, however, was the limit to the concessions that the cabinet was prepared to make, and its members seem to have felt that they were sufficient to gain peace for the United States.[25] The French minister in Washington, Louis Sérurier, was probably exaggerating when he reported at the time that the recent news from Europe had terrified the administration, and Madison certainly did not believe some of the more extreme rumors that Great Britain was about to send 40,000 troops to America. Nor was he willing to prepare for this sort of contingency without having more definite proof, such as troop movements and ship sailings, of these intentions.[26]

The news from Gallatin and Bayard notwithstanding, Madison also continued to rely on diplomacy as much as military means to defend

[24] Albert Gallatin and James A. Bayard to Monroe, May 6, 1814, Monroe Papers, LC.

[25] Cabinet Memorandum, June 27, 1814, Madison Papers, LC; Monroe to Commissioners, June 27, 1814, Monroe Papers, LC.

[26] Louis Sérurier to Comte de la Forest, June 27, 1814, Archives du Ministère des Affaires Étrangères, Correspondance Politique: États-Unis, vol. LXXI (photostats in LC). Rush to Adams, July 11, 1814, Powell, "Unpublished Correspondence between Adams and Rush," 51.

the United States. On June 29 he issued a proclamation declaring Great Britain's recent blockade of the entire American coast to be illegal and invited the newly neutral nations of Europe to resume trade with the United States. Monroe sent copies of the proclamation to American diplomats in Europe and requested them particularly to bring it to the attention of Alexander I as a way of reminding him that Russia and the United States had some common grievances against Great Britain.[27] Madison's hopes here, however, were undermined in the first week of August by the receipt of further dispatches from Europe, this time covering events to the middle of June. As was the case with the May dispatches, the news was depressing, especially that from Gallatin. The former Treasury Secretary reported that Great Britain intended to inflict "very serious injury" on the United States and that it would probably land 15,000 to 20,000 troops on the Atlantic coast to do so. At the worst, Gallatin estimated the scope of British intentions to include attempts to sever the Union by occupying New York, assistance to the Federalists in regaining power, and a general chastisement of Americans on the battlefield before the imposition of a harsh peace. At the very least, he believed that Great Britain would engage in "predatory warfare" by attacking major coastal cities and destroying public property such as forts, arsenals, and navy yards. Moreover, Gallatin again pointed out that it was useless to expect other European nations to moderate British policy toward America, since no European power had a navy capable of resisting the Royal Navy and none was prepared to jeopardize its interests for the sake of restoring Anglo-American harmony.[28]

On reading these reports, Monroe complained bitterly to Sérurier that the United States had been abandoned by the nations of Europe, and even Madison added that Alexander I's neglect of the issue of maritime rights was "most unkind." The President then instructed Monroe to draft further instructions for the commissioners in Europe giving them complete discretion to handle the impressment issue as they saw fit. He also issued, on August 8, a proclamation calling Congress into session on September 19, partly to make further provision for the Treasury and partly to be able to respond promptly to any developments in the negotiations between the United States and

[27] *Daily Natl Intelligencer*, June 30, 1814. Monroe to Commissioners, June 25, 1814, and Monroe to Gallatin, June 29, 1814, *Gallatin Papers*. See also Dashkov to Rumianstev, July 10, 1814, Russian Archives.

[28] Gallatin to Monroe, June 13, 1814, *Gallatin Papers*.

Great Britain.[29] In concluding his June report from Europe, Gallatin had declared that the Republic could survive provided that the administration could "stand the shock of the campaign, and provided that the people will remain and show themselves united." This, however, was no small order. The people had never been united over the war and were becoming less so as peace returned to Europe. Nor was the administration itself fully agreed on strategies, and divisions within the cabinet were to influence profoundly the course of the 1814 campaign. Throughout July, Monroe and Campbell had conducted a private dispute over ways in which money for the war might be raised, while Brown's Niagara campaign was to be limited in its effectiveness by a growing quarrel between Armstrong, Jones, and Madison.[30] The President had hoped, very probably, to impose a degree of unity on his divided colleagues by trying to fix a short-term course at the cabinet meetings, where all could have an equal say, but his actions did not have the desired result. Even worse was the inability of the cabinet to agree on a defense policy for the District of Columbia, and their differences here ultimately enabled the British army to capture and burn Washington.

★

DISUNITY in Madison's cabinet, of course, was hardly a new phenomenon, but it became more serious in the summer of 1814 than it had been at any other time in the war. The most serious clash developed between Madison and Armstrong, whose relationship had never been comfortable at the best of times. The President was apprehensive about Armstrong's irritable personality and known ambition to succeed him in office, while the Secretary of War felt that Madison lacked competence in military matters and suspected that the Viriginia Republicans were only trying to exploit his (Armstrong's) skills without any

[29] Séurier to de la Forest, August 9, 1814, Correspondance Politique. Monroe to Commissioners, August 11, 1814, Adams Family Papers, MHS. *Daily Natl Intelligencer*, August 10, 1814. As Madison's hopes for Alexander I's intervention waned, he lamented the lack of unity among the Baltic powers that allowed British doctrines of maritime rights to prevail. A "purified" code of maritime law was essential for international harmony, and the United States, Madison believed, should still strive for its adoption. See Madison to Ingersoll, July 28, 1814, Madison Papers, LC.

[30] Monroe to [John Wayles Eppes?], July 3, 1814, Monroe Papers, LC; Campbell to Gallatin, July 30, 1814, *Gallatin Papers*. By July the Treasury was again short of funds, and Campbell wished to raise a further installment of the $25 million loan authorized for 1814. Monroe wanted to issue a strong public statement about the seriousness of the national crisis to arouse patriots to invest, while Campbell argued that this course would only create a lack of confidence in the administration among money-lenders. In deference to Campbell's wishes, Monroe suppressed his statement.

397

intention of acknowledging New York's claims to the Presidency in 1816. Several years after the war, Madison recalled that Armstrong's "defects" required on the President's part "a proper mixture of conciliating confidence and interposing control" so that the New Yorker's talents might be utilized for the national good.[31] This "mixture" Madison in his own way had tried to provide, but the fact was not readily apparent either to Armstrong or to others in the cabinet. Throughout 1813 Madison had approved most of Armstrong's policy suggestions, thus giving him a free hand in running the War Department. He had, moreover, resisted several attempts by Monroe to meddle in War Department affairs, and he had also rejected Monroe's demand that Armstrong be dismissed. All this notwithstanding, Armstrong never felt that he enjoyed the confidence of other members of the administration. He chafed under the budgetary restraints imposed on him by Gallatin and Jones, while the presence of Monroe in the cabinet as a rival for the 1816 presidential nomination was a constantly unsettling experience. Even Attorney General Rush belonged to a Pennsylvania Republican faction that was in conflict with the Secretary's supporters in that state, and his only friend in the cabinet during his tenure of office was Campbell, who was frequently ill and clearly unfit for his post.[32]

Armstrong's relations with his colleagues became increasingly strained after his failure to win a decisive victory in the 1813 campaign, and his opposition to negotiating with Great Britain at Gothenburg had heightened the tension still more. A more serious breach between the President and the Secretary, though, occurred at the end of May 1814 after the resignation of William Henry Harrison. Armstrong had never liked Harrison or his mode of warfare in the western states and territories, and he had struggled against both with limited success throughout 1813.[33] Nor was he by any means inclined to allow Harrison to claim vindication by virtue of the victory at the Thames. Early in 1814 the War Department began to examine the accounts of the northwestern army, and here Harrison seemed to be vulnerable. He frequently used troops and funds in excess of the limits stipulated by the War Department, purchased supplies at inflated prices, and employed his own private supply agents rather than the contractors designated for the army. To Armstrong, and to the congressional committees investigating the conduct of the war, Harrison's system was

[31] Madison, "Review of a Statement Attributed to Genl. John Armstrong," Congressional Edition, *The Letters and Writings of James Madison* (Philadelphia, 1865), III, 384.
[32] See Chapters VI-VIII above.
[33] See Chapter VII above.

not merely disorderly and irregular; it was patently self-serving and possibly corrupt as well.[34]

When Armstrong pressed Harrison to clarify his accounts, the hero of the Northwest resigned his commission in a huff on May 11, 1814.[35] Armstrong eagerly forwarded the resignation to Madison, who was vacationing in Virginia, but he also offered the vacant major generalship, without informing the President, to Andrew Jackson.[36] Madison was probably not greatly upset by the departure of Harrison—he too had reservations about the general's methods—but he expressly instructed Armstrong not to fill the vacancy before he returned to Washington in the first week of June. Since Madison had already agreed that "something had to be done for Jackson" and that the Tennessean should receive the next vacant major general's commission, Armstrong was at a loss to understand what he regarded as the President's "indecisive" conduct in the matter.[37] He therefore allowed his offer of promotion to Jackson to stand, no doubt hoping to gain an ally and some influence with the new major general for doing so. Madison, however, was annoyed to find that his authority had been defied and made use of in such a way.

Undoubtedly determined not to be placed in a similar position again, Madison began to scrutinize Armstrong's management of the War Department. He started by checking Armstrong's decisions on matters of routine administration, such as the consolidation of regiments, then extended his interest to cover Armstrong's actions in both the past and present campaigns, and ultimately he looked into the War Department accounting system as well.[38] In the cabinet meeting of June 7 neither Madison nor any other cabinet member had seriously opposed the plans for the Niagara campaign previously agreed upon by Armstrong and Brown, but their success would clearly depend upon Brown's ability to cooperate with Chauncey's fleet on Lake Ontario and, to a

[34] See William R. Barlow, "Congress during the War of 1812," (Ph.D. diss., Ohio State University, 1961), 84-85.

[35] Harrison to Armstrong, May 11, 1814, Logan Esarey, ed., *Messages and Letters of William Henry Harrison* (Indianapolis, 1922), II, 647.

[36] Armstrong to Madison, May 20, 1814; to Jackson, May 28, 1814, Madison Papers, LC.

[37] See the statement by Armstrong in *The Literary and Scientific Repository and Critical Review* 3 (1821), 502-503.

[38] Madison to Armstrong, May 24, June 15, and July 6, 1814, Madison Papers, LC. For the problems in the Accounting Office of the War Department see William Simmonds, *A Letter to the Senate and House of Representatives of the United States, Shewing the Profligacy and Corruption of General John Armstrong in his Administration of the War Department* (Georgetown, 1814).

lesser extent, with Izard's army at Plattsburg.[39] In the absence of a clear-cut system of command to cover combined army and navy operations, the President had the ultimate responsibility for mediating disputes between the branches of the armed services, and it was in this area that his relations with Armstrong deteriorated into an open quarrel. At the same time, a similar tension developed in the relationship between Izard and Brown. The former was a Federalist and a career officer, while the latter had risen from the New York militia through the patronage of Armstrong and Spencer. Izard, furthermore, disliked Armstrong, especially resenting the tone of "the pedagogue" in War Department orders, and early in June the general revealed his distaste for these orders to Monroe, even hinting that he was not prepared to accept the responsibility for mishaps resulting from their execution. If Monroe disagreed with his stand here, Izard declared that he would resign. It is difficult to imagine a more blatant invitation to the Secretary of State to intervene in War Department affairs, and, since Izard did not resign, the 1814 campaign was thus threatened by divisions in the American command similar to those that had occurred between Hampton and Wilkinson in the previous year.[40]

Brown, for his part, was eager, almost impatient, to seek out the enemy in Upper Canada. He had been waiting for action at Buffalo since March but was compelled to delay it while Winfield Scott gave the regulars some intensive and badly needed training and while Peter B. Porter gathered a volunteer force to bring his army up to the 5,000 men which would equal the enemy forces on the Niagara Peninsula.[41] Brown gratuitously assumed that the navy—in return for the army having protected it while it was being built at Sacketts Harbor—would be obligated to subordinate its movements to those of the army, and, as he waited for Porter, he announced to Armstrong at the beginning of June his desire to attack Fort Erie, then Fort George, after which he intended to take the remaining British positions round the lake-

[39] See Armstrong to Brown, June 9, 1814, Jacob Brown Papers, BEHS (microfilm in LC).

[40] Izard to Monroe, May 24, June 3 and 4, 1814 Monroe Papers, LC. See also Charles K. Gardner to Jonathan Fisk, November 20, 1814, Charles K. Gardner Papers, NYSL; Armstrong to Joseph Desha, March 16, 1816, Joseph Desha Papers, LC; Brown to Armstrong, November 2, 1814, and Armstrong to Brown, November 16, 1814, Brown Papers, MHS. Also "Spectator" [John Armstrong?], *An Inquiry Respecting the Capture of Washington by the British on the 24th August 1814; with an Examination of the Report of the Committee of Investigation Appointed by Congress* (Washington, D.C., 1816), 27-29.

[41] Brown to Armstrong, May 30, 1814, Brown Papers, BEHS. See also Winfield Scott to Armstrong, May 17, 1814, LRRS.

shore—Burlington Heights, York, and Kingston.[42] Jones had informed Armstrong that Chauncey's fleet would be out on Lake Ontario in force by July 15, and, on this assumption, Brown rather summarily told the naval commander to meet his army off Fort George on July 10.[43] Brown was confident that if both the army and the navy moved quickly he could trap the British fleet while it was still in Kingston, a claim that was reinforced by reports from Gaines at Sacketts Harbor that the enemy base was only lightly defended and could be easily captured.[44] Having thus announced his intentions, Brown entered Upper Canada on July 1, 1814.

The War Department was therefore hoping for some speedy victories, but its expectations were blasted by both the American navy and the British army. Brown's concept of warfare offended the professional vanity of Chauncey, who replied to the general's letters with the statement that naval movements would be governed solely by the conduct of the British fleet. He further announced that he would still be in Sacketts Harbor on July 10—not meeting Brown's army at Fort George—and he even doubted the United States could take the offensive at all that summer.[45] Brown, nonetheless, tried to proceed with his plans. On July 3 he easily overpowered the small British garrison at Fort Erie, then two days later he drove a superior British regular force under Major General Phineas Riall from the field at the Battle of Chippewa.[46] Elated by these victories, Brown advanced to Queenstown, then toward Fort George in the hope of meeting Chauncey, and on July 13 he repeated his invitation to the naval commander to join him in a campaign, which, the general claimed, could still culminate in the occupation of Kingston within two months.[47]

Unable to meet up with Chauncey, who was still in Sacketts Harbor, and deciding that he could not risk an assault on Fort George unassisted, Brown withdrew back toward Chippewa, where the British army, recently reinforced by Lieutenant General Gordon Drummond, followed him. Just above Chippewa, at Lundy's Lane on July 25, the two armies met again, with the result on the field once more being honorable to the Americans.[48] However, the cost in casualties was high,

---

[42] Brown to Armstrong, June 7, 1814, Brown Papers, BEHS. Brown to Armstrong, June 3, 12, 15, 17, and 22, 1814, LRRS.

[43] Brown to Chauncey, June 21 and 22, 1814, LRUS.

[44] Edmund P. Gaines to Armstrong, June 23, 1814, LRRS.

[45] Chauncey to Brown, June 25, 1814, Brown Papers, BEHS.

[46] Brown to Armstrong, July 6 and 7, 1814, LRRS.

[47] Brown to Armstrong, July 16, 1814, LRRS.

[48] Brown to Armstrong, July 25, 1814, E. A. Cruikshank, ed., *Documentary History of the Campaign on the Niagara Frontier* (Welland, Ont., 1898-1902), I, 87. The best account

including both Brown and Scott among the wounded, and the day after the battle Brigadier General Eleazar Ripley, on whom the command had devolved, withdrew the army in disorder to Fort Erie, where it remained on the defensive for the rest of the campaign. Ten days later, on August 5, the American naval squadron appeared off Fort George, but it was too late. The British general, Drummond, had decided to follow the American army and had besieged it in Fort Erie two days before.

Brown's performance throughout July 1814, though, was by no means disgraceful. Indeed, it marked the first occasion in the war when American regulars had met and beaten British regulars on anything like equal terms, and he no doubt also saved western New York from the possiblity of an invasion in 1814. Yet in terms of what the administration had hoped to achieve—a systematic advance by army and naval forces round Lake Ontario—the campaign was a failure. Perhaps Brown's hopes for Kingston were too sanguine, but it seems not unreasonable, as Armstrong had felt, that with naval aid Brown might have ended the campaign at least in possession of Fort George, York, and Burlington Heights instead of in what proved to be a rather desperate defense of Fort Erie. Armstrong surmised that Brown might have avoided the battle and the heavy losses at Lundy's Lane by outflanking the British army and advancing toward Burlington Heights, but Brown did not do so, probably because naval cannon were needed to reduce Burlington as much as they were to take Fort George. Possibly, too, such a move could have exposed New York to punitive raids by the unguarded British army, but Armstrong had no fundamental quarrel with Brown. He believed, as did the general himself, that the limited gains of the campaign could be blamed on the noncooperation of the navy.[49]

Throughout Brown's movements on the Niagara Peninsula, Chauncey had remained in Sacketts Harbor, content to build vessels in an attempt to gain a decisive superiority over the British fleet before risking battle. For much of the summer of 1814, Chauncey appears to have had an advantage over the enemy in terms of the ability to throw a greater weight of shot, but he lacked both the manpower and willpower to risk exploiting it.[50] Nor was he ever really disposed to

---

of the entire campaign was written by Thomas Jessup, "Memoirs of the Campaigns on the Niagara" (1814), Thomas Jessup Papers, LC.

[49] Armstrong to Brown, July 22, 1814, Brown Papers, BEHS.

[50] The *Ontario Repository*, August 2, 1814, claimed that the American naval force on Lake Ontario had 225 guns, while that of Great Britain had 219. American guns could throw a greater weight of shot, and Great Britain did not gain a clear supremacy on the

consider cooperating with Brown's army, especially after he fell ill in mid-July from a combination of fever and constipation. After Brown withdrew to Fort Erie, the two men engaged in an undignified public controversy, with Brown deploring Chauncey's refusal to aid the army and claiming that the commodore's treatment of the fleet as his private property was responsible for the failure of the United States to accomplish more in the campaign.[51] Chauncey, declining as he saw it to be made a scapegoat for the army's shortcomings, responded with the argument that Brown's goals, and by implication those of the administration as well, were unrealistic. His orders, he declared, imposed on him the "higher destiny" of capturing the enemy fleet, not acting as a transport service for the army, and he concluded the exchange by denouncing Brown as "political demagogue" and a dangerous "romantic."[52]

Such conflict over implementing a strategy agreed upon in the cabinet was largely the result of the absence of an adequate command structure to carry out the administration's decisions. This aspect of the military operations had always troubled Armstrong, though he was in no position to advocate as the solution that army generals be given supreme command over all American forces. Instead, he had no other recourse but to complain, first to Jones, then to Madison, about Chauncey's inaction at Sacketts Harbor.[53] These complaints he could document with reports that Gaines sent both to him and to Brown, which presented a most unflattering picture of the navy's performance.[54] Jones's sympathies, though, lay wholly with Chauncey. He told the commodore that he did not see how it was possible for the navy to cooperate with Brown's Niagara schemes—a point which he appears not to have raised in the cabinet meeting of June 7—nor would he attempt to define ways in which the army and navy might cooperate. Instead, he

---

lake until September 1814, with the launching of the 112-gun H.M.S. *St. Lawrence*. See J. Mackay Hitsman, *Safeguarding Canada, 1763-1871* (Toronto, 1968), 98, 103-104.

[51] Brown to Armstrong, August 25, 1814, LRRS; Brown to Moss Kent, September 24, 1814, Simon Gratz Autograph Collection, HSP; Brown to Chauncey, July 13 and September 4, 1814, and Brown to Monroe, October 10, 1814, Brown Papers, BEHS.

[52] Chauncey to Jones, August 10, 1814, Cruikshank, *Documentary History* I, 125-128; Chauncey to Brown, August 10, 1814, Brown Papers, BEHS; Chauncey to Jones, August 19, 1814, Jones Papers, HSP. The problem here was more than a conflict of personality between Brown and Chauncey. When Izard, some eight weeks later, was considering extending his operations in Upper Canada, he found he could not do so because Chauncey had retired with the fleet to Sacketts Harbor. See Izard to Monroe, October 16, 1814, LRRS.

[53] Armstrong to Madison, July 25, 1814, John Armstrong, *Notices of the War of 1812* (New York, 1836-1840), II, 237.

[54] Gaines to Brown, July 12 and 27, 1814, Brown Papers, BEHS.

simply instructed Chauncey to give priority to contesting control of Lake Ontario with the Royal Navy.[55]

Madison was clearly reluctant to press Jones on this issue. The Navy Secretary had submitted his resignation as long ago as April 25 and was only remaining at his duties as a personal favor to Madison, who was thus probably unwilling to do anything that might precipitate his departure from office. It was, in fact, not until the last week of July—by which time Chauncey's inactivity had become almost scandalous—that Madison felt the need to raise the matter with Jones. The Secretary reported that Chauncey had fallen ill and would be replaced by Captain Stephen Decatur, whom he ordered from New York to Sacketts Harbor on July 28.[56] However, Jones gave Decatur the same orders as he had given Chauncey, therefore making his first priority the attempt to gain naval control on Lake Ontario too. As a slight concession, Jones told Decatur to cooperate with the army on the Niagara if he could. For Armstrong, this was simply not good enough. He pointed out to the President that Brown could only win total victory with full naval cooperation and that Decatur's orders were not adequate to achieve this. He therefore asked Madison to alter those orders.[57]

Madison, however, did not do so, and he countered Armstrong's complaints with the suggestion that the main problem of the campaign was the lack of proper coordination between Brown and Izard. The two generals, he pointed out, were not "apprized" of each other's instructions, and attempts to bring about "a mutual understanding" between them "through Washington alone would lose its effects from delay."[58] Armstrong—who had actually sent Brown and Izard identical copies of the most important instructions for the campaign—could not have been wholly unaware of the problems of communication between Plattsburg and Niagara, but he doubtless regarded these as less important than obtaining better cooperation between the army and the navy.[59] But the President adhered to his views, especially after Izard, in mid-July, had become worried about enemy movements up the St.

---

[55] Jones to Chauncey, July 20, 1814, Area Files of the Naval Records Collection, Area 7 (M-625), vol. 71, Records of the Department of the Navy (RG 45), NA.

[56] Jones to Stephen Decatur, July 28, 1814, Jones Papers, HSP.

[57] Armstrong to Madison, July 28, 1814, *Notices of the War of 1812*, II, 242-244.

[58] Madison to Armstrong, July 18 and August 10, 1814, Madison Papers, LC; Madison to Armstrong, July 27, 1814, Daniel Parker Papers, HSP.

[59] See Armstrong to Izard and Brown, July 10, 1814, Parker Papers, HSP. Izard had, in fact, already tried to establish a regular communications link between Plattsburg and the St. Lawrence. Since he could not spare officers to act as messengers, he employed local men, but suspected that they were in the pay of both the United States and Great Britain. See Izard to Armstrong, May 24, 1814, Izard, *Official Correspondence*, 14.

Lawrence and had suggested to the War Department that he impede such movements by detaching some of his forces westward to menace Kingston.[60] Madison and Armstrong agreed, and the Secretary of War on July 27 and August 2, 1814, ordered Izard to march some 4,000 men westward for that purpose. Armstrong first suggested that these forces go to Ogdensburg to menace Kingston from the rear, but if that were not possible, the Secretary said that half of them should be sent to the Niagara Peninsula with the other half remaining to build fortified positions on the St. Lawrence. In the latter case, Izard himself, Armstrong felt, should go to the Niagara to take command of the American forces there and should then try to reduce the British positions on the peninsula.[61]

These orders irritated both Izard and Madison. The President crossly maintained that they did not meet his objections about the failure to provide for constant communication between the two generals, without which, he stressed, "no system of operations [could] take place." He also came to realize that a move westward by Izard would now not only be too late to prevent the movement of British troops and supplies to Lake Ontario but would also leave the American positions on Lake Champlain exposed to attack. Yet Madison did not directly overrule Armstrong's orders; instead he suggested that if Izard were to move westward he should coordinate his movements with navy officers in order to protect Sacketts Harbor, and that alternative defensive arrangements should be provided around Lake Champlain.[62] Izard fully supported Madison's last point, having changed his mind since mid-July on the desirability of moving troops westward, and for that reason he announced that he would take his time in executing the movement toward Niagara and make "no excuse for the delay." The dangers of exposing Plattsburg to an attack by "greatly superior" British forces, he added, were very great.[63] Armstrong, however, had actually provided for militia reinforcements for Plattsburg from both New York and Vermont, and he was very probably perplexed, if not angered, by the shifting arguments of Madison and Izard. He followed the President's orders to the extent of arranging for an express mail service between Plattsburg and Sacketts Harbor to improve communications

[60] Izard to Armstrong, July 19 and August 7, 1814, Izard, *Official Correspondence*, 54, 55, 60.

[61] Armstrong to Izard, July 27 and August 2, 1814, ibid., 61, 65. Armstrong's first letter appears to have gone astray in the mails, and Izard did not receive a copy of it until August 11.

[62] Madison to Armstrong, August 12 and 16, 1814, Madison Papers, LC.

[63] Izard to Armstrong, August 11 and 20, 1814, LRRS.

between the two divisions of the army, though as he did so he did not conceal his opinion that the reports and rumors of British troop movements and reinforcements in Canada which troubled Madison and Izard so greatly had been "much exaggerated." He therefore simply repeated on August 12 his earlier orders for Izard to go to the assistance of Brown, and he did not encourage the generals to correspond with each other as strongly as the President would have wished.[64]

In so acting, Armstrong's main concern was to enable Brown to leave Fort Erie as soon as possible—before Great Britain could put more vessels on the lake—and to resume the campaign to occupy enemy positions on the peninsula and around the lakeshore. The union of any British forces in the area to obstruct this advance could still doubtless be prevented by dividing the detachments from Izard's army and dispatching the divisions to both ends of Lake Ontario.[65] Under such circumstances, Armstrong probably saw no very great need for Izard and Brown to communicate frequently, the more so since such a practice would have been contrary to War Department procedures and would have deprived the Secretary of much of his influence in determining important military movements. Unfortunately for Armstrong, Izard—as he declared he would, and much to Armstrong's distress—moved westward too slowly to prevent Brown's army from being besieged by Drummond in Fort Erie, though Brown eventually counterattacked on September 16 and drove the British away. By that time, though, Izard had barely reached Sacketts Harbor, and he did not arrive on the Niagara Peninsula itself until the end of the month. When he did so, he immediately concluded that it was too late to resume the offensive in Upper Canada, and he sent the army into winter quarters while Brown destroyed the works at Fort Erie.[66]

In refusing to give Armstrong the fullest support which the Secretary felt was necessary for the success of Brown's campaign, Madison struck not only at the administrative workings of the War Department but also at Armstrong's self-esteem and his few remaining hopes to accomplish some military advantage in 1814. Admittedly, the ultimate success of Brown's campaign was supposed to be dependent on Chauncey's

[64] Armstrong to Izard, August 10 and 11, 1814, Izard, *Official Correspondence*, 67, 68; Armstrong to Izard, August 12, 1814, LSMA. Armstrong agreed that Izard's movement to the west risked exposing Lake Champlain, but he weighed the problem "seriously and scrupulously" and concluded that the British valued their westward lines of communication more than they did the chance to attack Plattsburg. See Armstrong to Brown, August 16, 1814, Brown Papers, BEHS.

[65] Armstrong to Brown, August 16, 1814, Brown Papers, BEHS.

[66] Izard to War Department, August 23, September 1 and 7, October 16, 1814, Izard, *Official Correspondence*, 73-76, 100-103.

gaining control of Lake Ontario, but at no time had Madison positively told Armstrong to order his general to remain inactive while waiting for the commodore's victory, and once Brown had commenced his campaign his position could not really be improved by better communications with Izard, as the President seemed to suggest. The implementation of the cabinet decisions of June 7 thus served only to expose the full extent of the misunderstandings, born of personal animosities, that existed within the administration, and by August the Secretary of War seems to have been convinced that his rival, Monroe, had been encouraging both Jones and Izard to frustrate his military plans. Madison's increasing intervention in War Department affairs over the summer, moreover, only reinforced Armstrong's suspicion that he lacked adequate support and that his usefulness in office was now limited.[67] These conclusions could only have been confirmed by the President's massive reprimand to Armstrong on August 13 over the way he had been running his department. On this occasion Madison accused the Secretary of failing to consult him properly on significant areas of military policy, and he also made it clear that he still resented Armstrong's conduct over the promotion of Jackson. In the future, the President stipulated, Armstrong would have to consult him on *all* matters of policy, and he outlined ten areas, covering virtually every aspect of military administration, in which the Secretary could issue no orders without the President's prior consent.[68] To all intents and purposes, therefore, Madison had decided to take over the duties of the War Department himself. Unfortunately for him, he did so at a time when the threat of a British invasion of the United States was at its greatest.

★

ALTHOUGH it was probably not until the first week in August 1814 that Madison fully realized that the United States was facing a long and costly war for survival, he had always believed that British forces would try to harass largely defenseless coastal communities throughout the summer. As early as May the President had noted with alarm that the enemy might concentrate its attacks on the southern states, inciting the slave population to desert to its ranks and possibly even to rebel. He also pointed out to Armstrong that, among the likely targets for attack, "the seat of government cannot fail to be a favorite one."[69] Despite this apprehension, though, the President did not raise the

[67] See the sources cited in note 40.
[68] Madison to Armstrong, August 13, 1814, Madison Papers, LC.
[69] Madison to Armstrong, May 20, 1814, ibid.; to Jones, May 26, 1814, Jones Papers, HSP.

407

problem of how to defend the capital during the June cabinet meetings. The subject was, in fact, according to Rush, "excluded" from discussion, which suggests that Madison felt that British activities would be neither sufficiently serious nor sustained long enough to warrant any extraordinary exertions on the part of the federal government.

Yet as rumors reached Washington throughout June of Great Britain's increasingly hostile attitude toward the United States, Madison's concern for the safety of the capital grew. Accordingly, he summoned a cabinet meeting for July 1 to discuss the adequacy of the defense arrangements in the Fifth Military District, which included Annapolis, Baltimore, Washington, and Norfolk. So impressed was Madison with the danger to the capital that he decided shortly before the cabinet meeting to create a special Tenth Military District to include both Baltimore and Washington and to place it under the command of Brigadier General William Winder of Maryland. The cabinet appears to have accepted the decision without much discussion, authorizing the establishment of a special military force of 3,140 men as well as providing for equipping and holding in reserve 10,000 militia.[70] Armstrong may have preferred Brigadier General Moses Porter, then in charge of the defense of Norfolk, for commander, but he accepted Madison's argument that Winder, being the nephew of the Federalist governor of Maryland, Levin Winder, was more likely to inspire the confidence of the state government providing most of the essential military forces.[71]

Nonetheless, Madison was alone in the cabinet in his concern for the capital. Armstrong was openly skeptical that Washington was of sufficient strategic importance to attract the enemy, and the other cabinet members appear to have agreed with him.[72] After all, the Royal Navy had moved freely around the Chesapeake area in the summer of 1813 without attempting to assault the defenseless capital, and, if the enemy were intent on making punitive raids, the leading coastal cities from Boston to New Orleans presented far more tempting targets than did Washington. Even if the British should decide to come to Washington, Armstrong believed they could be easily stopped. The approach by the Potomac, he pointed out, was "long and sinuous" and presented problems of navigation for larger vessels, while that by the Patuxent, though more direct, required a considerable march by troops over

[70] Cabinet Memorandum, July 1, 1814, Madison Papers, LC.

[71] See Kosciuszko Armstrong, *Examination of Thomas L. McKenney's Reply to the Review of his Narrative* (New York, 1847), 5.

[72] Jones to Richard M. Johnson, October 31, 1814, "Report on the Capture of the City of Washington," *ASP: Military Affairs*, I, 540.

difficult terrain which could be strongly defended. Great Britain would attempt neither approach, Armstrong argued, without a decisive superiority in numbers, which, according to his information, it simply lacked. For these reasons, Armstrong had always felt that it was unnecessary to fortify extensively the approaches to the capital, claiming in addition that the expense of building up "the several points to be defended" would have "exhausted the treasury."[73]

Madison considered these opinions, and the next day, July 2, decided that the entire American coastline as well as the capital needed a systematic plan of defense. This he instructed Armstrong to prepare, with special reference to the cities of Boston, New York, Wilmington, Norfolk, Charleston, Savannah, and New Orleans. The state governors, the President noted, should also be advised of the need for defense preparations by gettng quotas of their militias "in the best readiness for actual service."[74] Armstrong responded promptly enough, issuing on July 4 a circular inviting all the governors to organize militia or volunteer forces totaling 93,500.[75] Madison criticized this circular on the grounds that it failed either to designate to the governors specific points for the concentration of forces or to instruct them to decide on such points in consultation with the commander of the appropriate military district.[76] These matters notwithstanding, Madison accepted Armstrong's circular and assumed that the Secretary of War would implement it, as well as give special assistance to Winder in defending the Tenth Military District.

Armstrong, however, did not share the President's understanding of his duties, convincing himself instead that Madison had virtually freed him from responsibility for defending the District of Columbia. He gave Winder little assistance, and not before August 10 did he offer the general any staff resources—and even then he provided only an assistant adjutant and a chaplain.[77] Indeed, throughout July and August, Armstrong continued to assume that Washington would not be attacked, and he simply instructed Winder to implement the outlines of the policy already agreed on.[78] The Secretary of War instead devoted

[73] Armstrong to Johnson, October 17, 1814, ibid., 538.

[74] Madison to Armstrong, July 2, 1814, Madison Papers, LC.

[75] Armstrong to all Governors, July 4, 1814, LSMA.

[76] Madison to Armstrong, July 6, 1814, Madison Papers, LC.

[77] Adjutant General to N. G. Hite, August 9, 1814, and same to Reverend R. Elliott, August 17, 1814, LSAG. See also Edward D. Ingraham, *A Sketch of the Events which Preceded the Capture of Washington by the British on the Twenty-Fourth of August, 1814* (Philadelphia, 1849), 9.

[78] Armstrong to Winder, July 2 and 18, LSMA. This point continued to be the subject of controversy long after the war. See the pamphlets by John and Kosciuszko Armstrong

all his energies to Brown's peninsula campaign and, to a lesser extent, struggled with the administrative details of carrying out his defense circular of July 4. And even here, Armstrong felt no great sense of urgency. Admittedly, the task of defending the entire American coastline was extremely difficult, and, perhaps because of its difficulty, Armstrong tried to convince others that the dangers were not very great. Excessive "bustle" over local defense, he told Senator Samuel Smith of Maryland, would only indicate to the enemy that the people were afraid, which was to be avoided at all costs. Otherwise, he declared, British forces were still too weak to inflict serious damage on the coast and could be easily driven off.[79] Not even the British occupation of Eastport in the District of Maine on July 18, without serious local resistance, altered these beliefs.[80]

All along the Atlantic coast, on the other hand, local concern about enemy attacks increased. Samuel Smith, amazed at the Secretary of War's apparent calm, implored Armstrong to make more militia and regulars available for the defense of Baltimore and Washington.[81] Farmers and planters in the Tidewater regions of Maryland and Virginia too became more and more upset over Great Britain's "ruffian system of warfare"—coastal raids to steal water and supplies and to encourage slaves to desert for enlistment in the British ranks—and they demanded more War Department expenditure on troops and fortifications.[82] The city councils of New York, Philadelphia, and Baltimore formed special associations and committees for local defense, which, together with the state governments, began to subject the administration by letter and by delegations to a barrage of demands for greater defensive preparations. The Corporation of Philadelphia, in particular, was most insistent that army engineers construct an elaborate and costly system of fortifications along the shores of the Delaware River and in an area known as the Pea Patch. Their determination was reinforced by po-

and Ingraham cited in notes 40, 71, and 77 above. See also John Armstrong, *Notice of Mr. Adams' Eulogium on the Life and Character of James Monroe* (Washington, D.C., 1832), 3-4, 7-9, 13; Thomas L. McKenney, *Reply to Kosciuszko Armstrong's Assault upon Colonel McKenney's Narrative of the Causes that Led to General Armstrong's Resignation of the Office of Secretary of War in 1814* (New York, 1847), 5-7; and [Rider H. Winder], *Remarks on a Pamphlet Entitled "An Inquiry Respecting the Capture of Washington by the British on the 24 August 1814 etc. etc.* (Baltimore, 1816), 24.

[79] Armstrong to Moses Porter, July 16, 1814, LSMA. Armstrong to Samuel Smith, July 15, 1814, Samuel Smith Papers, LC.

[80] See *Boston Patriot*, July 20, 1814; *Independent Chronicle*, July 25, 1814.

[81] Smith to Armstrong, July 14 and 20, 1814, Smith Papers, LC.

[82] Philip Stuart to Madison, July 29, 1814, Madison Papers, LC; Thomas Bayly to James Barbour, April 14, 1814, Monroe Papers, LC.

litical animosities, since both Governor Simon Snyder and Corporation chairman Thomas Leiper were intensely suspicious of the War Department officials in the region. The commander of the Fourth Military District was Brigadier General Joseph Bloomfield from New Jersey, while Armstrong had given many of the army staff appointments to Duane's "Old Republican" faction, which had been locked in bitter conflict with the "Snyderites" for years.[83] In truth, Snyder and Leiper wanted not just their "share of the *Public Protection*," as they claimed, but also insurance against the consequences of neglect by their political opponents.[84]

Most alarmed of all about the prospects of an attack were the inhabitants of Washington, who were also almost completely powerless to take steps for their own protection. On July 18, the mayor and the Washington City Council memorialized Madison and the War Department about the lack of defense arrangements for the city.[85] Two days later, according to the French minister, they demanded, in response to rumors that the Duke of Wellington was en route to America, an immediate session of Congress to deal with the emergency.[86] Delegations of the capital's residents, usually led by the prominent banker John P. Van Ness, repeatedly tried to obtain commitments from the War Department to mobilize the local militia, but without any success. Armstrong simply brushed aside their fears with easy assurances, combined with contemptuous asides, that the British, whatever their goals, were not bound for Washington.[87] On July 28, however, the British fleet entered the Patuxent River, then carried its "ruffian system of warfare" to within twenty miles of Washington. An angry crowd formed outside the President's house and threatened to prevent Madison and his family from leaving the area should they try do so.[88]

Armstrong dealt with these demands in various ways. He continued to ignore the residents of Washington but could not take quite the same course with respect to the cities and the states of the nation. Here, though, his response was necessarily determined by the administration's limited resources and the law governing the federalization of the militias in a time of emergency. Given the decision to continue the offensive against Canada, there were few regular troops available for

[83] Simon Snyder to Armstrong, July 20, 1814; Liberty Brown and Thomas Leiper to Armstrong, July 29, 1814; William Duane to Armstrong, July 29, 1814, all in LRRS.
[84] John Binns to Madison, July 11, 1814, Madison Papers, LC.
[85] ——to Madison, July 18, 1814, ibid.
[86] Sérurier to de la Forest, July 20, 1814, Correspondance Politique, vol. LXXI.
[87] John P. Van Ness to Madison, July 28, 1814, Madison Papers, LC.
[88] Dolley Madison to Hannah N. Gallatin, July 28, 1814, *Gallatin Papers*.

local defense, and neither Armstrong nor Madison wanted to embarrass the Treasury by prematurely calling out detachments of militia for national service. The War Department therefore had to try to persuade state governors to hold their militias "in readiness" for service at state expense, intending to call them out only for "actual service" in the event of a real emergency, after which the United States would assume the costs.

The state governors were often unwilling to bear such costs and were unhappy with such a diminished definition of federal responsibility for national defense. Not infrequently they tried to argue that the War Department should pay the costs of all state troops called out against the British. The foremost advocate of this position was Governor Barbour of Virginia, who further irritated Armstrong by insisting that state officers should retain control of the militia while it was being held in readiness, thus complicating future cooperation between state and federal troops in the event of action against the enemy.[89] Armstrong was the less willing to tolerate such restrictions since he suspected that the Virginians were more interested in mobilizing large numbers of troops to patrol their slaves than they were in repelling the enemy.[90] The additional demands from the cities and local defense committees, however, were quite beyond the capacity of the War Department to meet, and Armstrong did not seriously attempt to do it. In the case of Philadelphia, which Madison had not designated as a city requiring a systematic plan of defense, Armstrong simply informed Governor Snyder that his ideas for the Delaware were excessively costly, quite unrealistic, and of no possible use in the present situation.[91]

Armstrong's preoccupation with other matters, of course, greatly increased the vulnerability of Washington to attack. Yet the capital might not have fallen had others, notably Winder and to a lesser extent Madison, concentrated their energies on that concern. They did not do so, with the result that the District of Columbia was never made ready to meet an attack in accordance with Madison's belief that the British would single out the capital for a predatory raid. Shortly after the establishment of the Tenth Military District, a War Department cartographer, William Tatham, surveyed the area and reported to Arm-

[89] Barbour to Armstrong, March 20, 1814, LRUS; same to same, July 19 and 25, 1814; Moses Porter to Armstrong, July 12, 1814, LRRS.
[90] Armstrong to Barbour, July 18, 1814, LSMA. For the concern of Virginians about slave unrest see R. E. Barker to Barbour, June 11, 1814, and John P. Hungerford to Claiborne Gooch, August 5, 1814, H. W. Flournoy, ed., *Calendar of Virginia State Papers and Other Manuscripts, 1808-1835* (Richmond, Va., 1875-1892), X, 338, 367, 368.
[91] Armstrong to Snyder, August 6, 1814, LSMA.

strong on the most likely course of events in a British attack on the capital. The city of Washington itself, Tatham believed, was not defensible, mainly because Congress had repeatedly declined to vote funds for that purpose. This meant, therefore, that an invading force would have to be stopped long before it reached the city, and Tatham suggested that the town of Bladensburg was the best place to attempt this. Tatham also predicted that if his advice were not followed, Washington would fall, and that Armstrong would get the blame "for being less than omnipotent."[92] Armstrong, however, disregarded the advice, and left the problem to Winder and the President.[93]

Madison had chosen Winder as commander of the Tenth District largely for political reasons. Yet both he and Armstrong knew that there was good reason to suspect Winder's competence as an officer. The general had allowed himself to be captured by the enemy in 1813 in quite embarrassing circumstances, while in his subsequent negotiations with the British over the exchange of prisoners of war he had also failed to follow the President's instructions satisfactorily.[94] And in July and August 1814 he again showed that he was incapable of fulfilling the responsibilities assigned to him. Ultimately, Washington fell to the British because Winder, like Armstrong, was never wholly convinced that the British would attack it. Only Madison had insisted that Washington had to be defended, but throughout July and August he failed to check on how far his orders were being followed. More concerned with developments in Europe and in Canada, then increasingly preoccupied with Armstrong's past record in the War Department, Madison tended to lose sight of the problem of the capital. The President's wife, on hearing that the enemy was only twenty miles away at the end of July, doubted that they would come on to Washington, and Madison, learning on August 20 that British forces had again entered the Patuxent and had landed at Benedict, also expressed his surprise that they should be venturing so close.[95]

---

[92] William Tatham to Armstrong, July 2, 10, and 13, 1814, LRRS.

[93] See Winder to Armstrong, July 7, 1814, LRRS.

[94] See Chapter VII above. Also Daniel Brent to Monroe, April 30, 1814; Madison to Monroe, May 1 and 19, 1814, Monroe Papers, LC.

[95] Dolley Madison to Hannah Gallatin, July 28, 1814, *Gallatin Papers*; Madison to Monroe, August 21, 1814, Madison Papers, LC. Even as late as August 23, Dolley Madison told her sister, Anna Cutts, that the British army was stronger than expected and *might* advance on Washington to destroy it. See Dolley Madison Papers, LC. Throughout July and August, the *Daily Natl Intelligencer*—July 12, 15 and 27, August 6 and 9—also downgraded the threat to the capital, and Winder consequently criticized this policy as tending to "paralyze the public zeal." Winder to Armstrong, July 15, 1814, William Henry Winder Papers, Transcripts in Peter Force Papers, Series VII-E, LC (henceforth Force Transcripts).

Winder, like Armstrong, believed that the city of Washington itself could not be defended. He was, moreover, dissatisfied with the plans and the forces provided for his district in the cabinet meeting of July 1. The general, accordingly, pleaded with Armstrong to modify those plans to allow him to call out bodies of militia long before there was any likelihood of an attack. Waiting until the enemy arrived, he argued, would be too late to "disseminate through the intricate and winding channels the various orders to the militia," and, above all, he wanted to avoid being left dependent in the moment of crisis on "a disorderly crowd without arms, ammunition or organization."[96] Here Winder anticipated one of his major problems—defending a large area with untrained troops under a divided command—and his position was made even more difficult by circumstances quite beyond his control. The administration on July 1 had designated Pennsylvania as a source of militia for the Tenth District, apparently unaware that the state had in 1813 passed legislation to reorganize its militia which was about to go into effect on October 1, 1814. All of Winder's calls on Governor Snyder for aid thus fell into an administrative void, because the officers' commissions under the old law had expired, while the new commissions had not yet come into effect.[97] Winder, therefore, had far fewer troops to call on than he needed, and this compelled him to increase his demands on the militia from Maryland and the District of Columbia. The militia of the latter, however, had not been fully mobilized because of Armstrong's strained relations with its commander, John P. Van Ness, over the question of whether Washington would be attacked at all. Van Ness eventually came to feel that his services were being so neglected by the War Department that he resigned his commission in protest shortly before the British attack.[98]

Yet despite these very real organizational difficulties, Winder's defense of the Tenth District was more seriously flawed by his failure to

[96] Winder to Armstrong, June 30, July 9 and 16, 1814, LRRS.

[97] Winder to Snyder, August 8, 1814, Force Transcripts, LC. N. Boileau to Armstrong, June 25, 1814; and same to Winder, August 11, 1814, John B. Linn and William H. Egle, eds., *Pennsylvania Archives* (2d Series, Harrisburg, 1880), XII, 699, 705. The Pennsylvania militia law of 1813 was extremely complex, totaling eighty-eight printed pages in length. See (Philadelphia) *Democratic Press*, February 13, 1813.

[98] Van Ness to Johnson, November 23, 1814; same to Armstrong, August 20, 1814, *ASP: Military Affairs*, I, 580-583. Winder's problems were by no means confined to the local militia. He invited a detachment of Colonel William King's 3d Rifle Regiment, then based at Easton, Maryland, to join his forces for the defense of the capital, only to see King refuse on the grounds that "voluntarily [he] would never enter the field with a corps of militia." King asked for a transfer to Plattsburg instead. See William King to Armstrong, August 4, 1814, LRAG.

visualize the ways in which the British might attack and to allocate his meager resources accordingly. Throughout July and August, he constantly toured around his command, receiving and making reports on the defense needs of all the towns and cities, and calling for troops and supplies to meet them. Indeed, his movements were so rapid and frequent that the mail service was unable to keep up with him, and seldom was he in effective communication with his superiors in Washington or his subordinates throughout the district.[99] By moving so incessantly, he subjected himself to considerable local pressure to disperse his resources throughout the district, and he consequently found himself unable to concentrate them for effective defense. He also tried to raise special companies for the defense of the President's house, a pointless exercise which scarcely harmonized with his belief that the capital itself could not be defended.[100] Yet if the enemy approached by the Patuxent, Winder—and here Armstrong agreed with him—was uncertain whether it would mean that the British were heading for Baltimore or for Washington. This uncertainty led him to hesitate about where to concentrate his forces, since he was reluctant to commit his troops in ways that might leave Baltimore exposed. And the pressures on Winder to defend Baltimore were greater than those on him to defend Washington, especially after the governor of Maryland, on August 19, appointed Senator Samuel Smith commander of the state militia for the defense of Baltimore, a move which looked very like a vote of no confidence in Winder's conduct.[101] Consequently, Winder failed to make any special effort to defend the Bladensburg route to Washington, and, even as the British began their advance on August 20 from Nottingham on the Washington side of the Patuxent, he appalled a group of District residents by remarking that it was "very probable that the enemy would suddenly turn about and make a blow at Baltimore."[102]

The result of Winder's efforts was that Washington was far less prepared, both psychologically and militarily, for an attack than it might have been. Future dangers were anticipated, but few were provided for in the present, and the root of the problem was the widespread disinclination to believe that the capital really would be attacked. In the final days of the crisis, only Monroe voiced any concern about the fate of the city. Lending a ready ear to Van Ness's complaints about Armstrong's indifference, Monroe—who confessed that he had "a hor-

[99] See Johnson's report on the capture of Washington, *ASP: Military Affairs*, I, 525.
[100] Winder to Henry Carberry, August 21, 1814, Charles E. French Collection, MHS.
[101] See Samuel Smith to Levin Winder, August 19, 1814, Smith Papers, LC.
[102] Van Ness to Johnson, November 23, 1814, *ASP: Military Affairs*, I, 582.

ror at remaining inactive . . . to be involved indiscriminately in the censure which . . . so eminently belonged to the Secretary of War"— began pointing out to both Armstrong and Madison after August 16 that the capital was in real danger.[103] He offered his services to Winder as a scout, though his frenetic activities on horseback along the banks of the Patuxent failed to shed much light on the intentions of the invading British force, and, at times, he also exposed himself to capture by advancing into areas that left the British army between him and his route back to the capital.[104] Madison, rather belatedly, did not become fully aware again of the danger to Washington until August 20 and 21. By that time, however, he realized he had no alternative but to continue to leave matters in Winder's hands and hope for the best. On August 22, the President informed Monroe that nothing more could be done to assist Winder and that he was making arrangements for the government to evacuate Washington. "The crisis," he concluded, "will be of short duration."[105]

Even as late as August 22, two days before the British attack, the French minister reported that there was still skepticism in the administration about an assault on Washington.[106] Armstrong was firmly convinced that Baltimore was the target of the British forces, while Winder, becoming ever more confused, believed that they would head for Annapolis before making a final decision between Baltimore and the capital. On August 23 the advancing enemy forces paused in their march, and by evening there was little doubt that the British commanders had chosen to attack Washington. Before August 20, Winder had made no serious attempts to obstruct the gradual British advance by felling trees, destroying bridges, or harassing the enemy's flanks, and he was now accordingly compelled to improvise a desperate last-minute defense—the very thing that in early July he had declared he should avoid.[107] He issued some final calls for volunteers, and, by the morning of August 24, he had been able to assemble a mixed force of

[103] Ibid., 527. Monroe to Armstrong, August 18, 1814, Monroe Papers, LC; Monroe to George Hay, September 7, 1814, Monroe Papers, NYPL. The navy took little part in preparing the defenses of Washington. On August 22, two days before the British attack, Secretary Jones ordered a gig from the navy yard in Washington to reconnoiter to learn the size and intentions of the enemy fleet. See Jones to John Creighton, August 22, 1814, HR 13A-D15.3, LRHR. On August 24, Jones ordered Creighton to destroy the bridge over the eastern branch of the Potomac.

[104] Monroe to Armstrong, August 20, 1814, LRRS. Monroe to Winder, August 21, 1814, Force Transcripts, LC.

[105] Madison to Monroe, August 22, 1814, Madison Papers, LC.

[106] Sérurier to duc de Talleyrand, August 22, 1814, Correspondance Politique, vol. LXXI.

[107] See Winder to T. Tilghman, August 20, 1814, Force Transcripts, LC.

regulars, volunteers, navy yard workers, artillerists, and militia from the District and Maryland.[108] Altogether his forces totaled nearly 7,000 men, which numerically gave him an advantage over the British commanders, whose troops amounted to 4,500.

These forces were arranged haphazardly on the field at Bladensburg by their commanders as they arrived. Winder himself seemed to be incapable of exercising any overall direction, and on the morning of August 24 he made a last-minute appeal to Armstrong for assistance. Madison intercepted the note bearing this request and sent Monroe off to do what he could while he gathered the other members of the cabinet in order to ride out to Bladensburg to survey the proceedings. As they did so, Treasury Secretary Campbell suggested to Madison that he make greater use of Armstrong's military knowledge in the crisis. Madison agreed, informing Armstrong that his reprimand of August 13 by no means meant that he should cease to exercise any initiative in office, and that he would see that Winder obeyed any orders Armstrong cared to give. To Armstrong this remark must have seemed nonsensical, and he had no desire to become too closely involved in what he had already predicted would be a defeat for American arms. He agreed that he would see what he could do but added that under the circumstances there seemed to be little that could be done. By now, however, the Battle of Bladensburg, as Madison later recalled, had "decidedly commenced," and he ordered the cabinet members to withdraw to the rear, remarking that they should leave the "military movements to the military functionaries who were responsible for them."[109] The President probably anticipated a lengthy pitched battle, but the ensuing clash was a fiasco, with the undisciplined and ill-organized American forces being driven from the field in only three hours fighting by a smaller army that was in unfamiliar surroundings and exhausted by a long sea voyage and the uncomfortable climate.[110]

In the event of the administration being forced to abandon Washington, Madison had given instructions to its members to reassemble in Frederick, Maryland. All notions of an orderly withdrawal and return, however, were lost in the confusion of the American retreat from Bladensburg to Washington. The President and his family, together with Jones and Rush, left for Loudon County, Virginia, hoping later to recross the Potomac River and meet the American forces again.

[108] *ASP: Military Affairs*, I, 547.

[109] Madison, "Memorandum, August 24, 1814," Madison Papers, LC. See also Armstrong to Desha, October 4, 1814, and January 16, 1815, Desha Papers, LC; and Campbell to Johnson, November 27, 1814, George Washington Campbell Papers, LC.

[110] For a brief account of the battle of Bladensburg see *ASP: Military Affairs*, I, 529-530.

Monroe, Winder, and Armstrong paused in Washington, debating whether to make a last-ditch defense in the Capitol or to withdraw to make a stand above Georgetown, only to find that both possibilities were ruled out by the disorderly retreat of the American forces through the city to Tenleytown beyond. Monroe then went in search of the President, while Winder marched toward Baltimore.[111] Armstrong and Campbell alone made their way to Frederick to wait in vain for their colleagues.[112] The British army entered Washington unopposed, burning the public buildings on August 25 and 26 and withdrawing immediately afterward. The flames lit up the night sky for miles around until doused by a storm. Madison, receiving the news in a tavern at Montgomery Courthouse in Maryland, decided to return to the capital as soon as possible.[113] On the evening of August 27 he re-entered the destroyed city to attempt the difficult tasks of reuniting his administration and restoring the government of the nation.

[111] Ibid., 530.

[112] Winder to John Stricker, August 25, 1814, Force Transcripts, LC; Madison to Monroe, August 26, 1814, Madison Papers, LC.

[113] Madison to Dolley Madison, August 27, 1814, Madison Papers, LC; Madison to Jones, August 27, 1814, Jones Papers, HSP.

★

CHAPTER X

THE ADMINISTRATION AND CONGRESS, 1814-1815

MADISON DECIDED to return to Washington on the evening of August 27, after receiving from Monroe a note stating that the British had left the capital and were returning to their ships. Scarcely had the President re-entered the city, however, when he heard a thunderous cannonade from the Potomac, followed by a "dreadful explosion" and concussion. The British had attacked Fort Washington, which had been promptly blown up by its commanding officer, and were advancing on Alexandria. In short, the enemy had *not* left the District of Columbia at all, and Madison realized that they could remain in the area for some time, raiding and looting at will. A second attack on Washington itself was by no means impossible.[1] The administration, though, was in no condition to deal with another military crisis so soon after its return to the capital, with only Madison, Rush, and Monroe so far being on the spot. Jones was in Virginia searching for Mrs. Madison and her family, Campbell and Armstrong were in Frederick, Maryland, while Winder, the commander of the Tenth Military District, was in Baltimore.

The personal and political consequences of being driven from the capital twice within four days were, as Madison told his wife, too "disagreeable" to be considered, though the inhabitants of the city, according to Mrs. Anna Thornton, were also "violently irritated" at the prospect of the administration's attempting any more "futile resistance" to the enemy.[2] The popular mood was reflected on August 28 in the decision of the mayor of Alexandria to request and accept terms of capitulation from the British, and Madison and Monroe spent

[1] The Diaries of Anna Thornton, entries for August 27 and 28, 1814, LC. Monroe to Winder, August 28, 1814, James Monroe Papers, LC.

[2] Madison to Dolley Madison, August 28, 1814, James Madison Papers, LC; Thornton Diaries, entry for August 28, 1814, LC.

most of that day trying to dissuade the citizens of Georgetown and Washington from following his example. The President declared that the people "must all arm" to resist, and he asked Monroe, in Armstrong's absence, to take temporary command of the defense. The popular inclination to surrender, however, could not so easily be controlled, and Monroe felt he could master the situation only by threatening to stop with the bayonet any deputation to the British.[3] The determination of Madison and Monroe on this point ensured that the administration would continue to operate from Washington, but the decision to confer military powers on the Secretary of State created for the President a difficult political problem that required an immediate solution.

That problem was the position of Armstrong, and to a lesser degree that of Winder, since Monroe, in agreeing to take temporary command, insisted that Madison settle the status of the Secretary of War in order to avoid a conflict of authority. Here Monroe had the support of the citizens of Washington and the fragmented militia units of the Tenth District, who had been extremely critical of Armstrong's failure to exert himself in the defense of the capital.[4] Even in Frederick, some distance from Washington, where Armstrong had retired after the Battle of Bladensburg, the people were annoyed with the Secretary. According to one observer, they were "disposed to hang him."[5] On August 29, officers of the militia in the Tenth District, headed by John Williams and Thomas McKenney, made it known to the President that they were not prepared to serve under Armstrong but added that they had no objection to taking orders from other members of the administration. They dramatized their opinions by refusing to greet Armstrong when he returned to Washington and visited the militia at Windmill Point shortly after noon on the same day. Since Madison felt that the militia still might be required to defend the capital against another attack, he promised Williams and McKenney that he would not allow Armstrong to issue any further orders to them.[6]

That evening Madison, probably with no very clear idea about what to do, called on Armstrong to explain why Monroe was exercising

[3] Documents relating to the capitulation of Alexandria can be found in the Cochrane Papers, folio 2329, NLS. See also Thornton Diaries, entry for August 28, 1814, LC; and Monroe to George Hay, September 7, 1814, James Monroe Papers, NYPL.

[4] Thornton Diaries, entry for August 31, 1814, LC.

[5] William C. Williams to James Barbour, August 28, 1814, in H. W. Flournoy, ed., *Calendar of Virginia State Papers and Other Manuscripts, 1808-1835* (Richmond, 1875-1892), X, 378.

[6] John S. Williams, *History of the Invasion and Capture of Washington, and of the Events which Preceded and Followed* (New York, 1857), 104-108.

some of the functions of the office of Secretary of War. He did not, however, want Armstrong to resign, and rejected the Secretary's suggestion that he do so. Despite mounting personal doubts about the Secretary, Madison realized that he needed to retain Armstrong as a representative of the pro-war Republicans of New York, and to have found a suitable replacement for him would have been extremely difficult anyway. Moreover, the President would not have wanted to resolve the problem in a way that reinforced Armstrong's suspicions that Monroe was constantly intriguing to force him out of the administration. In fact, Madison almost implored Armstrong to remain in the cabinet, declaring that he wished above all "to preserve harmony and avoid change" in his administration so that he could retire honorably from public life at the end of his second term. Had he wished to do so, Armstrong could have regarded this statement as a thinly disguised appeal to his presidential ambitions in the form of an implied promise that Madison would remain neutral in any further conflicts between the Secretaries of War and State.

As an alternative to resignation, Armstrong suggested that he briefly withdraw from Washington to pay his family a visit in New York. Madison finally accepted this offer as the most suitable course, one which would minimize embarrassment while restoring the administration in Washington without necessarily prejudicing a later solution to the longstanding personal and political differences that divided the cabinet. Armstrong, though, must have realized that his situation was precarious, and he insisted on vindicating himself against the charges he suspected had been made against him. This led to a quarrel over who was responsible for the fall of Washington, a subject which Madison would probably preferred to have avoided but which, once raised, could hardly be allowed to pass. The President therefore declared that he had been dissatisfied with Armstrong's performance, but he ended the argument by stating that he still respected the Secretary's abilities and by urging him to pay a brief visit to New York. Armstrong agreed to do so, and the two men parted, as Madison recalled without any apparent sense of irony, "in a friendly manner."[7]

Armstrong traveled to Baltimore, where he spent six days with Samuel Smith reviewing his situation. At first, according to Joseph H. Nicholson, he seemed to expect to be recalled to the capital, but eventually, as he realized he was being blamed in Washington not simply for the fiasco at Bladensburg but also for the destruction of the capital, the navy yard, and Fort Washington, the difficulties of his

[7] "Memorandum," August 29, 1814, Madison Papers, LC.

position became fully apparent to him.[8] Even less did Armstrong like hearing reports of the deputations of militia and citizens waiting on the President to complain about the War Department, nor could he endure accounts of how Madison had bowed to these pressures by placing Monroe in charge of the defenses.[9] Feeling threatened by "military usurpation" and "political faction," Armstrong concluded that his position was intolerable and that Madison's assurances to him before he left Washington were worthless. Armstrong had always wanted rather more than Madison's neutrality in his contest with Monroe for the succession anyway, and, accordingly, he sent the President his resignation on September 4, publishing it in the *Baltimore Patriot* on the preceding day with an angry letter in which he accused Madison of succumbing to the demands of a "village mob stimulated by faction."[10] Madison, as Treasury Secretary Campbell recalled, received the resignation "without comment," while Armstrong departed for New York, telling Joseph H. Nicholson that he was "glad to be out of it all" and that he felt no bitterness.[11]

This last statement was simply untrue. Armstrong felt extremely bitter at the conduct of the militia, and he was furious at the "imbecility" of his colleagues in agreeing to its demands. Nor did he intend to withdraw completely from politics. Once back in New York, he resumed his former correspondence with Rufus King and the Federalists about displacing the "Virginia Dynasty" in 1816, while his ally, Justice Ambrose Spencer, lobbied in the state legislature to have him elected to the United States Senate to succeed the retiring Obadiah German, a Clintonian Republican.[12] Neither the Clintonians nor the supporters of the administration in New York, however, would agree to embarrass Madison in a period of crisis by sending Armstrong to the Senate, and the former Secretary was thus compelled to remain in retirement.[13] He

[8] Joseph H. Nicholson to Albert Gallatin, September 4, 1814, in Carl Prince and Helen Fineman, eds., *The Papers of Albert Gallatin* (microfilm ed.).

[9] Armstrong to Ambrose Spencer, September 3, 1814, William Astor Chanler Collection of John Armstrong Photostats, NYHS; Armstrong to Joseph Desha, October 4, 1814, Joseph Desha Papers, LC.

[10] Armstrong to Madison, September 4, 1814, Madison Papers, LC. A copy of Armstrong's letter to the *Baltimore Patriot* may be found in the Chanler Collection, NYHS.

[11] George Washington Campbell to Armstrong, January 2, 1815, George Washington Campbell Papers, LC; Nicholson to Gallatin, September 4, 1814, *Gallatin Papers*.

[12] John Jacob Astor to Monroe, September 22, 1814, James Monroe Papers, NYHS; Spencer to Armstrong, January 17, 1815, Chanler Collection, NYHS. See also John C. Fitzpatrick, ed., *The Autobiography of Martin Van Buren* (Washington, D.C., 1920), 66.

[13] (New York City) *National Advocate*, September 10, 1814; (Albany, N.Y.) *Albany Register*, September 27, 1814.

never ceased to believe that he had been the victim of a "dirty business," and he was not entirely alone in this feeling.[14] Some Republicans and not a few army officers, who now feared that their careers would suffer from their previous association with the Secretary of War, felt that Armstrong had been unfairly made the scapegoat for the failures of the administration as a whole, and it was always difficult to remove the suspicion that he had been sacrificed to make way for Monroe.[15]

In Washington, though, Armstrong's colleagues did not regret his departure.[16] Since their return to the capital they had been preoccupied with reorganizing the government to continue the war and to enable the administration to meet the third session of the Thirteenth Congress, which was due to assemble on September 20. The first task, as Rush and Jones pointed out, was to demonstrate that the government was in possession of the capital and that it would continue to exercise its functions. To bear witness to these facts, both Rush and Jones urged Madison to issue a proclamation. The fall of the capital, Rush declared, required an explanation "to the whole nation, which might serve to inform, to balm and to rouse" the patriotism of the people. It would also be necessary to send the proclamation to Europe to minimize the embarrassment to American diplomats and to demonstrate to the governments of Europe that the fall of Washington did not signify "the reduction of the country."[17]

After consulting Monroe, Rush accordingly drew up a draft proclamation for the President which at once condemned the British for conducting the war in an "uncivilized" manner and yet minimized the damage inflicted during the brief occupation of Washington. To the nation at large, Rush suggested that the President declare that administration efforts to combat the British mode of warfare were of little

[14] Armstrong to Desha, January 16, 1815, Desha Papers, LC; and Armstrong to Daniel Parker, December 19, 1814, Chanler Collection NYHS.

[15] Jacob Brown to Armstrong, November 2, 1814, Jacob Brown Papers, MHS; Brown to Spencer, November 27, 1814, Simon Gratz Autograph Collection, HSP. See also Robert Swartwout to Brown, November 20, 1814; Peter B. Porter to Brown, December 13, 1814, Brown Papers, MHS. On Monroe's role see Armstrong to Brown, November 16, 1814; Armstrong to Spencer, January 27, 1815, both in Chanler Collection, NYHS. Monroe was deeply troubled by the charge that he had sought Armstrong's removal, and he protested his innocence until his death in 1831. See Thomas L. McKenney, *Reply to Kosciuszko Armstrong's Assault upon Colonel McKenney's Narrative of the Causes that led to General Armstrong's Resignation of the Office of Secretary of War in 1814* (New York, 1847), 5.

[16] William Jones to Alexander James Dallas, September 15, 1814, George Mifflin Dallas Collection, HSP.

[17] Richard Rush to Monroe, August 28, 1814, Letters of Richard Rush, HSP; [Jones], "Thoughts for the President," September 1, 1814, Uselma Clarke Smith Collection of William Jones Papers, HSP; Jones to Madison, September 5, 1814, Monroe Papers, LC.

use unless "seconded or anticipated by the spontaneous efforts and sacrifices of the people themselves. . . ." Madison issued the proclamation on September 1, though he probably felt that some of Rush's suggested remarks exposed too starkly the weaknesses of the federal government. In their place, he substituted an injunction to all civil and military officeholders, especially the generals commanding the various military districts, to be "vigilant and alert" in providing for the defense.[18] Even so, this final form of the proclamation tacitly admitted that the effective defense of the nation in the immediate future would be determined more by local efforts than by administration policy.

The effect of the proclamation was almost the reverse of that intended by Madison. Confidence in the ability of the administration to defend the nation, never high at any time, had been declining throughout 1814 and was permanently shattered by the fall of Washington. Madison's condemnation of the British policy of negotiating for peace by giving the war "a character of extended devastation and barbarism" only heightened fears along the Atlantic coast that the events at Washington would be repeated elsewhere. Indeed, it was taken for granted by the administration as well as by state and local governments that the enemy would strike at one or more of the major coastal cities between Boston and New Orleans, and the ability of the British to attack anywhere almost at will was again highlighted by the surrender of Castine in the District of Maine to an enemy force from Halifax on September 3.[19] Fortifications, of course, had been built in the major coastal cities, but the War Department had tended to use them as recruiting depots rather than build them up for strictly defensive purposes. The number of regular troops in these positions usually fluctuated according to the needs of the war in Canada, and, even before the fall of Washington, several coastal towns and cities had signaled a lack of confidence in their adequacy, as well as in the resources of the federal military districts, by establishing committees of vigilance and public safety to organize their local defense.[20]

The leadership of these local defense committees consisted of a cross-section of the most prominent bankers, lawyers, and merchants in the

[18] There is a draft of the proclamation in the Rush letters, HSP, and it may be compared with the final version printed in the *Daily Natl Intelligencer*, September 3, 1814.

[19] See Paul Woehrmann, "National Response to the Sack of Washington," *Maryland Historical Magazine* 66 (1971), esp. 240-245. For the fall of Castine see Robert Barrie to Edward Griffith, September 3, 1814 Cochrane Papers, NLS; and *Boston Patriot*, September 7, 1814.

[20] See, for example, Robert Sterry to Armstrong, July 10, 1814, LRAG. See also Arthur P. Wade, "Artillerists and Engineers: The Beginnings of American Seacoast Fortifications, 1794-1815," (Ph.D. diss., Kansas State University, 1977), 302-303.

community, and their members were usually chosen without reference to party politics.[21] According to one resident of Philadelphia, the committee in that city tried "to mix characters so as to keep politics out of the question" in order to enable it to mobilize the resources of the entire community, but, as Brigadier General Joseph Bloomfield pointed out, the city's action also added to the structure of government an "imperium in imperio," whose actions were to cause administration officials no end of difficulties.[22] Almost invariably these local defense committees demanded that any nearby regular troops and army engineers be placed at their disposal and that the War Department agree to assume the costs of calling out the local militia. Throughout the war the administration had fought against such attempts to use federal authority and resources for purely local purposes, but after the fall of Washington it could no longer easily resist such pressures. For moving Commodore John Rodgers's squadron to Philadelphia from Baltimore at the end of August, Navy Secretary Jones found his life being threatened in the latter city, and none of the local authorities in the cities most at risk would cooperate with officers in the federal military districts on any terms other than their own.[23] Brigadier General Thomas Cushing was heartily disliked throughout the First District in New England, the Common Council of New York demanded that Brigadier General Morgan Lewis be removed from the command of the Third District, and in the Fourth District Governor Simon Snyder of Pennsylvania simply refused to place the militia at the disposal of General Bloomfield.[24] In Maryland the command of the militia had been con-

[21] This section is based on the extensive records of local defense committees in the major coastal cities and correspondence in the War Department. The Proceedings of the Committee of Defense of New York City can be found in the NYHS; those of the General Committee of Defense for Philadelphia are in the HSP. See also William D. Hoyt, Jr., ed., "Civilian Defense in Baltimore, 1814-1815: Minutes of the Committee of Vigilance and Safety," in *Maryland Historical Magazine* 39 (1944), 199-224, 293-309, and ibid. 40 (1945), 7-23, 137-153; W. K. Watkins, "The Defense of Boston in the War of 1812," *Proceedings of the Bostonian Society* 4 (1899), 35-74; and "The Vigilance Committee: Richmond during the War of 1812,".*Virginia Magazine of History and Biography* 7 (1900), 225-241, 406-418. For relevant War Department correspondence see Morgan Lewis to Armstrong, August 31, 1814; Manuel Eyre and Thomas Cadwallader to Armstrong, August 30, 1814; and James Barbour to Monroe, September 13, 1814, LRRS.

[22] Chandler Price to Jones, October 1814, Jones Papers, HSP; Joseph Bloomfield to Armstrong, August 29, 1814, LRRS.

[23] Jones to Eleanor Jones, September 20 and 21, 1814, Jones Papers, HSP.

[24] For the unpopularity of the military commanders respectively see Donald R. Hickey, "New England's Defence Problem and the Genesis of the Hartford Convention," *New England Quarterly* 50 (1977), 592-594; Peter Mercier to Madison, September 3, 1814, and Corporation of New York to Madison, October 10, 1814, both in LRRS; and Simon Snyder to Monroe, September 10, 1814, LRRS.

ferred on Samuel Smith, despite the fact that General Winder was not only commander of the Tenth District but also the governor's nephew, while the governor of Virginia repeatedly argued that both the state finances and the militia had been exhausted by frequent calls on their service and would now have to be replaced by regular troops at administration expense.[25]

Monroe, as temporary Secretary of War, had neither energy nor resources to deal with these complaints.[26] While trying to defend Washington himself, he tolerated the Maryland government's elevation of Samuel Smith over Winder, and he had no wish to see Winder back in the capital, where a similar conflict of authority between the general and himself might occur.[27] Elsewhere, it was equally in vain that Monroe tried to uphold federal authority. The Secretary feared that the enemy would continue to concentrate on the Chesapeake area, selecting either Baltimore or again Washington as its target, but he could not convince other state and local authorities that their communities were in any less danger. To defend the Chesapeake, Monroe tried to create a force at Snowdens, Maryland, consisting of troops from Maryland, Pennsylvania, and Virginia, which, he believed, could defend both Baltimore and Washington and, if necessary, be marched northward to the Delaware.[28] However, the governor of Pennsylvania demanded the withdrawal of all his state's forces in Baltimore to Philadelphia, only to see Samuel Smith refuse to heed the demand, while the latter declined at the same time to release any of his Baltimore troops for location nearer to Washington. The governor of Virginia likewise rejected Monroe's scheme, and, to help defend the approaches to Richmond, Monroe eventually had to order the militia of North Carolina to Norfolk and Hampton.[29]

The political incapacity of the administration was further undermined by its financial weakness. After the fall of Washington, many of the banks south of New England, already short of specie and in

[25] Monroe to Samuel Smith, September 2, 1814, LSMA; Winder to Monroe, September 4, 1814 LRRS. See also Barbour to Monroe, September 30, 1814, LRRS.

[26] Monroe to Snyder, September 25, 1814, LSMA.

[27] See Ralph Robinson, "Controversy over the Command at Baltimore During the War of 1812," *Maryland Historical Magazine* 39 (1944), 177-198. See also the letters sent by Winder and Smith to Monroe between August 27 and September 7, 1814, LRRS, and also Monroe to Winder, September 8, 1814, LSMA.

[28] Monroe to Smith, September 19, 1814, LSMA; and same to same, September 21, 1814, Samuel Smith Papers, LC.

[29] Smith to Monroe, September 20, 1814, Smith Papers, LC; Monroe to Snyder, September 20, 1814, LSMA. Monroe to William Hawkins, September 6 and October 25, 1814, LSMA.

some cases overly dependent on War Department drafts, suspended all specie payments. As they did so, the nation's rudimentary banking structure collapsed, and the federal government was left without the means to remit or withdraw money.[30] Most of the banks, however, were prepared to lend what money they could spare to their state governments or to their local committees of defense. This development placed the War Department almost completely at the mercy of these authorities, since the banks refused to lend funds to the administration unless they were specifically pledged to local defense. Monroe thus had no choice but to make the best deals he could. He borrowed money from the local banks to enable the coastal cities to provide for defense against a British attack; only the fiction of federal supremacy was preserved, by allowing the local troops to be called into national service and by the banks lending the money to the state governments and local committees in the name of the United States. The precise details of reckoning the respective claims of federal and state authorities were left until after the war.[31]

With the administration thus preoccupied it was hardly surprising that Madison and Monroe lost sight of the larger course of the war. Quite forgotten in Washington in the first weeks of September was the campaign of Brown and Izard on the Niagara Peninsula, and the fact that Izard's march from Plattsburg to Sacketts Harbor had exposed Vermont and upstate New York to invasion by a British force under the command of Sir George Prevost. Events were to demonstrate that the local militias, aided by Captain Thomas Macdonough's naval victory on Lake Champlain, were adequate for the crisis, but it was not until four days after the British withdrew from the area, following the Battle of Plattsburg on September 11, that Monroe thought to order the state governments of New York and Vermont to replace the troops left by Izard's departure.[32] The unsuccessful British attempt to capture Baltimore between September 12 and 14 told a similar story. The city

[30] *Daily Natl Intelligencer*, September 4, 1814.

[31] Monroe to Bloomfield, September 5, 1814; Monroe to Joseph Norris, September 6, 1814; Monroe to Messrs. Brackett and King, September 13, 1814; Monroe to Joseph Petonis, October 3, 1814; Monroe to the Public Committee of Baltimore, October 7, 1814; Monroe to the Corporation of Wilmington, December 23, 1814, all in LSMA. See also New York Committee of Defense to Monroe, September 11, 1814; and Joseph Norris to Monroe, September 17, 1814, both in LRRS.

[32] For the Battle of Plattsburg see Alexander Macomb to Monroe, September 15, 1814, LRRS; George H. Richards, *Memoirs of Alexander Macomb* (New York, 1832), 83-98; and Allan S. Everest, *The War of 1812 in the Champlain Valley* (Syracuse, 1981), 179-192. For Monroe's delayed response see his letters to the governors of Vermont and New York, September 15, 1814, LSMA.

was defended not through the efforts of the federal government but by the mobilization of the local community under the leadership of Samuel Smith, who, more often than not, defied rather than followed Monroe's directives.[33]

Nevertheless, the repulse of the British at Plattsburg and Baltimore did promise to strengthen the administration's position in dealing with Congress after it met on September 20. Well before that date it was clear there would be considerable pressure to remove the government from the District of Columbia and to persuade Madison to change his cabinet to broaden support for the war, possibly by appointing some Federalists to high office.[34] As the Congressmen gathered in Washington, they were disheartened and alarmed by what they saw. The burning of the public buildings in the capital had made the physical conditions of living and working there even more unpleasant than usual. Congress was compelled to meet in the Patent Office and the Post Office, which, Senator Jesse Bledsoe of Kentucky complained, were "far too small" and subjected the legislators to "enormous privations."[35] There was even greater concern at the possibility of a further British attack, and little confidence in Monroe's ability to organize the defense. Observing the Secretary's constant round of activities, Senator Worthington remarked, "Mr. Monroe seems to have so much to do that I suppose (from my knowledge of the man) that he has time to do little or nothing."[36] Acting on this fear, deputations of Congressmen waited on Monroe to insist that the capital be better defended, and they compelled him to summon Winfield Scott from Philadelphia for this purpose.[37] The administration, though, aided by offers of loans from the local banks, had decided to remain firm. Madison stressed in his message to Congress that the enemy entrance into Washington had "interrupted for a moment only the ordinary public business. . . ."[38]

Congressmen, however, were not so easily convinced. The House

[33] On the defense of Baltimore see Frank A. Cassell, "Response to Crisis: Baltimore in 1814," *Maryland Historical Magazine* 66 (1971), 261-287.

[34] Thomas Leiper to Madison, August 29, 1814; Mathew Carey to same, September 30, 1814, Madison Papers, LC. Lewis to Monroe, September 11, 1814, Monroe Papers, LC; Nicholson to same, September 19, 1814, Monroe Papers, NYHS.

[35] Jesse Bledsoe to William Worsely, September 26, 1814, Lyman C. Draper Manuscript Collection, 6 CC 14, SHSW.

[36] Thomas Worthington to Duncan McArthur, September 21, 1814, Duncan McArthur Papers, LC.

[37] Monroe to Winfield Scott, September 19, 1814, LSMA.

[38] John P. Van Ness to Monroe, September 20, 1814, LRRS; Monroe to William B. Giles, September 24, 1814, RCSW. For Madison's message see James D. Richardson, comp., *A Compilation of the Messages and Papers of the Presidents* (New York, 1897-1914), II, 533.

organized for business by electing as Speaker Langdon Cheves of South Carolina, a Republican suspected of "quiddism" for his opposition to many key administration policies since 1813. His election was regarded as a vote of no confidence in the administration, which was known to have preferred Felix Grundy of Tennessee.[39] Then, on September 22 and 23, both branches of the legislature established committees of inquiry into the fall of Washington. The main burden of investigation here fell on the House committee chaired by Richard M. Johnson of Kentucky, who declared that he would attempt to apportion blame for the deplorable incident.[40] Johnson obtained written statements from all civilian and military officials involved in the affair with the exception of Madison, who indirectly expressed his opinions through Attorney General Rush. Rush may also have suggested to the committee that recriminations at this time would not promote national unity, and eventually the committee issued at the end of November 1814 a lengthy but bland report which carefully avoided blaming any individual for the loss of the capital.[41] Instead, the report implied that all involved were in some way at fault, and even Armstrong could accept this verdict as "not unfavorable" to himself, though he wished that the committee had not so deliberately avoided showing "more discrimination" in its views.[42]

While Johnson was gathering evidence, the Common Council of Philadelphia, no doubt hoping to improve the defenses of the Delaware, sent a memorial to Congress on September 28 offering to act as host should the legislature decide to shift from the District of Columbia. Over the strong objections of the *National Intelligencer*, the House had already decided to establish a committee to consider removing the capital to "a safer place," though it also seems probable that the President, right from the outset, had resolved to veto any bill requiring

---

[39] Charles Jared Ingersoll, *Historical Sketch of the Second War between the United States of America and Great Britain* (Philadelphia, 1845), II, 67, 260.

[40] *AC*, 13th Cong., 3d sess., 17-18, 305, 308.

[41] The testimony on the fall of Washington in the legislative records of Congress contains a letter from Rush to Johnson, dated October 27, 1814, in which Rush requested a private conversation in the executive buildings region of the capital, where there would be little danger of interruption. Possibly Rush prevailed upon Johnson to produce a neutral report, in which, as John S. Williams later complained, the responsibility for the Bladensburg fiasco was placed on the militiamen themselves and not on their superiors. See HR 13A-D.15 3, LRHR; and Williams, *History of the Invasion and Capture of Washington*, 240-241. Rush furthermore took pains to obtain neutral testimony from former Treasury Secretary Campbell, who was, at the time, the cabinet member most likely to support Armstrong's version of events. See Rush to Campbell, November 2, 1814, Campbell Papers, LC.

[42] For the report see *ASP: Military Affairs*, II, 524-599. See also Armstrong to Desha, January 16, 1815, Desha Papers, LC.

removal.[43] Madison, however, was always reluctant to impose his opinion on the legislature, and he withheld his views, thus allowing debate on the issue to proceed over the following month. The advocates of removal usually stressed that the District of Columbia was not safe against the enemy and that the financial needs of the administration would be better served by relocation in a northern commercial city. Removal, Representative Jonathan Fisk of New York argued, would make for a closer relationship between the government and the "monied interests," thus enabling the administration to mobilize the nation's resources for the war. The opponents of removal replied that Washington was adequately defended, and that the effect of putting the capital "on wheels" would rouse "local feelings" which could destroy the Union.[44]

The committee on removal had a majority of members from districts north of the Potomac, but on October 3 it reported to the House that removal was inexpedient. The committee asked, however, that the whole House express its view on the issue, and the vote revealed that opinions were equally divided. In exercising his casting vote, Speaker Cheves then shocked his fellow southerners by voting for removal, on the grounds that the expense of defending Washington was so great that it hampered prosecution of the war elsewhere.[45] A new committee, with a majority favoring removal, was then appointed to bring in a bill requiring removal within twenty days of its passage, but this bill, on October 15, failed to pass to a third reading. Throughout the debate, the influence of section on both the rhetoric and the voting of the Representatives was generally stronger than that of party. Southern Federalists joined with southern and western Republicans to keep the capital in Washington against the removal campaign led by the middle-state Republicans, who were supported by the northern Federalists. On successive votes, however, the numbers against removal rose, until enough northern and middle-state Republicans changed position or abstained to prevent the further progress of the bill.[46]

---

[43] *Daily Natl Intelligencer*, September 2 and 28, 1814; AC, 13th Cong., 3d sess., 19, 312. On October 18 the administration newspaper hinted that Madison would have vetoed any bill requiring the removal of the goverment. See also Louis Sérurier to duc de Talleyrand, October 7, 1814, Archives du Ministère des Affaires Étrangères, Correspondance Politique: États-Unis, vol. LXXI (photostats in LC).

[44] AC, 13th Cong., 3d. sess., 314, 357. See also Ingersoll to Dallas, September 30, 1814, Charles Jared Ingersoll Papers, HSP.

[45] AC, 13th Cong., 3d sess., 341, 342. Cheves's argument was untrue; the loans offered by the banks and citizens of Washington had relieved Congress of much of the financial burden of defending the capital.

[46] Ibid., 376-395. See also *Daily Natl Intelligencer*, October 18, 1814.

While fighting to keep the government in Washington, Madison also had to struggle to retain a cabinet to his liking. Monroe, after taking over the War Department, began to press the President to clarify his status in the administration.[47] At first, the Secretary was anxious mainly to counter the impression that he had intrigued to bring about Armstrong's departure, and he may have told some Congressmen from Virginia and Pennsylvania that he was not seeking the Presidency in 1816 and asked them to spread this information among their colleagues.[48] Gradually, though, Monroe became more confident, and he convinced himself that he could carry out the duties of both the War and State departments. Toward the end of September, Monroe may also have asked the President to appoint him to the two offices, claiming that he could cope with State Department duties on the basis of two days work each week. The War Department was now the most important cabinet post, and Monroe, though he did not say so openly, seems to have felt that Madison owed him the office for having put up with Armstrong for so long. Furthermore, the Secretary wished to plan and manage the 1815 campaign himself; he still retained grandiose visions, formed in the winter of 1812-1813, of ending the war in one successful campaign, and to do so he needed immediate confirmation of his authority over the War Department.[49] Throughout September 1814, Worthington watched the Virginian's conduct with alarm, recording in his diary that Monroe seemed "determined on his own views." "I am persuaded," Worthington added, that "his object is to be the next president and he is so blinded as not to see the dangerous means he uses to attain his ends."[50]

Madison clearly resented this pressure and did not want Monroe to control two important executive departments. Yet Monroe pressed his case precisely when the President was least able to resist and, indeed,

[47] Monroe to Madison, September 3, 1814, Monroe Papers, LC.

[48] Later Monroe claimed he told Hugh Nelson of Virginia "at a most critical period of the war" that he would not be a presidential candidate in 1816, but it is not clear how widely this information was disseminated. See Monroe to John Taylor, December 23, 1815, Worthington C. Ford, ed., "Letters of James Monroe, 1790-1827," *Proceedings of the Massachusetts Historical Society* 42 (1909), 373; and also Charles F. Adams, ed., *Memoirs of John Quincy Adams* (Philadelphia, 1874-1877), V, 475, entry for January 2, 1821.

[49] Monroe to Madison, September 25, 1814, Monroe Papers, LC. There are good reasons to suspect that Monroe drafted this letter some time after the fact, but its contents, nevertheless, are probably still indicative of his attitude. See Irving Brant, *James Madison: Commander in Chief, 1812-1836* (Indianapolis, 1961), 330-332.

[50] Thomas Worthington Diary, entry for September 26, 1814, LC. Navy Secretary Jones shared Worthington's views, noting that Monroe was "governed by reputation" and had "a strong military passion, but without the requisite qualifications." Jones to Dallas, September 15, 1814, Dallas Collection, HSP.

was in danger of losing his entire cabinet. On September 11, Navy Secretary Jones, after agonizing over the problem since April, finally communicated to the President his decision to leave office by December 1, 1814. Barely a fortnight later, Treasury Secretary Campbell, whose brief tenure of office had been plagued by ill-health, also resigned, declaring that he had been completely "humbled" by the complexities of the finances.[51] The President was being abandoned on all sides, and to find competent replacements with acceptable political connections promised to be extremely difficult. In the interim, newspapers and interested individuals, such as John Jacob Astor, seized the opportunity to air their views on the subject. The changing nature of the war, together with its mounting financial problems, led to calls for Madison to abandon the practice of partisan appointments and to create a broadly based coalition of national unity by bringing prominent Federalists into his administration. The Federalist leader most frequently mentioned in this context was Senator Rufus King of New York, who was widely suggested as Secretary of State or Secretary of the Treasury. Even in far-distant Ohio, a Republican newspaper named an ideal cabinet in which three of the four leading positions would be held by Federalists.[52]

For Madison these suggestions were no more useful than Monroe's pressure. Federalists could not easily be brought into the administration without alienating Republican supporters of the war, and the Federalist leaders themselves would be unlikely to accept appointment unless Madison abandoned his policy of continuing the war until a peace treaty was made.[53] Gradually, though, the President attempted to maneuver his way through his difficulties. He decided, on September 27, to nominate Monroe as Secretary of War, but at the same time sent

[51] Jones to Madison, September 11, 1814; Campbell to Madison, September 28, 1814, Madison Papers, LC. See also Jones to Eleanor Jones, September 30, 1814, Jones Papers, HSP.

[52] Astor to Monroe, September 2, 1814, Monroe Papers, LC; Marinus Willett to same, September 2, 1814, Monroe Papers, NYPL. Elkanah Watson to Madison, September 8, 1814, and Mathew Carey to same, September 30, 1814, Madison Papers, LC. See also (Chillicothe, Ohio) *The Supporter*, September 24, 1814; and Andrei Dashkov to Count Nikolai P. Rumiamstev, September 30, 1814, Archives of the Russian Foreign Ministry (microfilm of Arkhiv vneshnei politiki Rossii for 1809-1816, held in LC).

[53] According to Sérurier, Madison was never keen on the idea of taking Federalists into the administration. To Talleyrand, October 7, 1814, Correspondance Politique, vol. LXXI. Congressional Federalists met in early October at Crawford's boarding house to consider their strategy for the session. They resolved to defend the "soil and sovereignty" of the nation but had little expectation the administration could obtain peace if it continued its past policies. See the paper dated October 1814 and endorsed by Rufus King in Charles R. King, ed., *The Life and Correspondence of Rufus King* (New York, 1894-1900), V, 422-424.

his private secretary, Edward Coles, to sound out the Republican members of the New York congressional delegation on the possibility of governor Daniel D. Tompkins's accepting appointment to either the State Department or to the Treasury. Speaking for the delegation, Jonathan Fisk declared that Tompkins would not be suitable for the Treasury, and he doubted the governor would want to come to Washington anyway.[54] Nonetheless, Madison wrote to Tompkins the next day, asking him to accept the State Department.[55]

For the Treasury, Madison had, since Gallatin's resignation, favored Alexander James Dallas of Pennsylvania, but Dallas on several occasions had expressed reluctance to live in Washington, and he had no desire to put up with Armstrong as a colleague. Also Dallas—who was frequently described as "aristocratic" in his bearing and disliked by many for his foreign birth—was unpopular with the Pennsylvania congressional delegation, and Senators Michael Leib and Abner Lacock had always made it clear they would never vote to confirm Dallas in office.[56] The replacement of Leib by Jonathan Roberts earlier in the year, then the retirement of Armstrong, seemed to remove some of these obstacles, and Madison was tempted to sound out Dallas again through the agency of Secretary Jones to see if he would accept nomination.[57] This time, the President's argument, that the urgent state of the finances should override any doubts about accepting, was not without effect; even Senator Lacock, with very bad grace, let it be known on October 1 that he would not object to Dallas in office, and the President accordingly made the nomination five days later.[58] Until Dallas accepted and took up his duties, Madison named Revenue Commissioner Samuel Harrison Smith as acting Treasury Secretary.

Unfortunately for Madison, Tompkins refused to accept the State Department. The governor declined on the grounds that personal and political considerations forbade his leaving New York and that he could better serve the Republic by remaining in his present position. By this Tompkins meant that his personal finances, to the extent of $100,000,

[54] Jonathan Fisk to Tompkins, October 5, 1814, Daniel D. Tompkins Papers, NYSL.

[55] Madison to Tompkins, September 28, 1814, Madison Papers, LC.

[56] See Chapter VIII above. Also Dallas to Jones, August 13, 1814, Jones Papers, HSP. The opposition of Pennsylvania's Senators to Dallas was rooted in factional state politics. Since 1805, Dallas had opposed the majority Republican faction in Pennsylvania, especially the Snyderites, and had, on occasion, sided with the Federalists. See Kim T. Phillips, "William Duane, Philadelphia's Democratic Republicans, and the Origins of Modern Politics," *Pennsylvania Magazine of History and Biography* 101 (1977), 365-387.

[57] Dallas to Jones, August 28, 1814, Jones Papers, HSP; Dallas to Monroe, September 8, 1814, Monroe Papers, NYPL.

[58] Ingersoll, *Historical Sketch*, II, 253.

had become so entangled with the state's finances relating to the prosecution of the war that he could not afford to resign the governorship for fear that his political enemies, the Clintonians, would take over the state government and ruin him both politically and financially. Madison, however, was bitterly disappointed, and angrily reminded Tompkins that the President should be considered the best judge of how the Republic might be served.[59] He safeguarded Tompkins's personal interests by nominating him on October 14 to replace Morgan Lewis as commander of the Third Military District, though the governor, in refusing the President's offer, probably lost an opportunity to position himself favorably for the Republican presidential nomination in 1816.[60] Several New York newspapers declared that either DeWitt Clinton or Ambrose Spencer should be nominated to the State Department, but Madison was tired of ambitious and calculating New York politicians whose motives he could never understand.[61] The President therefore left the State Department vacant, possibly thinking that he could nominate Gallatin or one of the other American diplomats in Europe to the position should they return in the near future, after negotiating with the British.[62] This decision in the meantime left Monroe filling the duties of the State Department on a temporary basis, which he continued to do until the end of the war.

On this basis the administration struggled for a month before facing another crisis with the death of Vice President Elbridge Gerry on November 23. Since it was widely rumored that the Senators would elect a Federalist as Gerry's successor to the position of president pro tem of the Senate, the event again raised the problem of the relationship of the opponents of the war to the administration and its policies. The election of John Gaillard of South Carolina to preside over the Senate, however, ensured a Republican succession, and this left Madison with the task of finding a replacement only for the departing Secretary of the Navy.[63] Jones had promised to stay on until Madison had found

[59] Tompkins to Madison, October 6 and 8, 1814; Madison to Tompkins, October 18, 1814, Madison Papers, LC.

[60] Speculating on the 1816 election, Matthew L. Davis remarked that if Tompkins did not have some "warm, open, and active friends [in Washington], he [would] be *led off the course as a distanced poney [sic]; or not in a condition to run the heats.*" To William P. Van Ness, January 17, 1815,. Van Ness Family Papers, NYHS.

[61] *Albany Register*, October 14, 1814; *National Advocate*, October 24, 1814.

[62] Dolley Madison to Hannah Nicholson Gallatin, December 1814, *Gallatin Papers*; Campbell to Armstrong, January 2, 1815, Campbell Papers, LC.

[63] George Walker to Worsley, November 24, 1814, Draper Manuscript Collection, 6 CC 19, SHSW; Jeremiah Mason to Jesse Appleton, November 24, 1814, in George S. Hillard, ed., *Memoir and Correspondence of Jeremiah Mason* (Cambridge, Mass., 1873), 106.

a successor, but, in truth, he was no more able to suggest a suitable nomination than was Madison. The engineer Robert Fulton offered the President his services, but Fulton lacked strong political connections, and his bold ideas about naval warfare were not sufficiently proven for him to inspire the confidence of the senior naval officers.[64] The only alternative, therefore, seemed to be to nominate a navy officer to the cabinet, and Gerry, before his death, had frequently mentioned to Madison the name of Commodore John Rodgers for this reason. In desperation, Madison offered the position to Rodgers on November 24, only to see the Attorney General oppose the move by stating that it would be illegal for a commissioned officer to hold a civilian position. Since Rodgers was reluctant to serve and did not want to resign his commission anyway, the nomination lapsed, and the Navy Department remained vacant for nearly one month after Jones's departure on December 1.[65] Madison then fell ill for some time, but his kinsman Richard Cutts finally prevailed upon a Republican merchant from Massachusetts, Benjamin W. Crowninshield, to accept the Navy Department. Crowninshield, too, hesitated to serve, not taking up his duties until the end of January 1815, when he slowly began to introduce some reforms in naval administration that had been suggested by Jones.[66] No significant progress was made here, however, before the war ended in February 1815.[67]

In this halting fashion Madison held together the elements of a cabinet in Washington while trying to restore the federal government

[64] For Fulton's offer see Wallace S. Hutcheon, Jr., "Robert Fulton and Naval Warfare" (Ph.D. diss., George Washington University, 1975), 174-176.

[65] Elbridge Gerry to Ann Gerry, November 15, 1814, Elbridge Gerry Papers, MHS; Madison to John Rodgers, November 24, 1814, and Rush to Madison, December 4, 1814, Madison Papers, LC.

[66] Mason mentioned that Madison was "now sick, though not dangerously." To Appleton, November 24, 1814, Hillard, *Memoir and Correspondence*, 106. See also Richard Cutts to Benjamin W. Crowninshield, December 14 and 20, 1814, Crowninshield Family Papers, Essex Institute. Madison to Crowninshield, December 15, 1814; Crowninshield to Madison, December 26 and 28, 1814, Madison Papers, LC.

[67] The war had exposed serious problems in naval administration. Rising costs highlighted the need for the Navy Department to exert greater control over the building and fitting of vessels in the navy yards, and these duties, combined with the problems of being chief naval strategist, were proving to be too much for one Secretary and a small number of clerks. Jones's solution was to create additional naval administrators such as a paymaster and a naval constructor, and, most importantly, to transfer much of the Navy Secretary's work to a board of naval commissioners. This board would bring about uniformity in naval construction, equipment, and repairs, which previously had been carried out very much at the discretion of individual naval officers. Jones made these recommendations to Congress on November 16, 1814, but Congress did not begin considering them before February 1815. See *ASP: Naval Affairs*, I, 320-324, 354-359.

to its functions in the national political system. The President, for a variety of reasons, was not as successful as he would have wished; he was often frustrated in his choice of administrators, and his cabinet as a whole was weaker, less competent, and far less representative of Republican interests throughout the nation than it had been at any time throughout the war. Politically, too, the federal government immediately after the fall of Washington was less effective than it had ever been before, lacking the means and the confidence to carry out its policies against the will of state and local officials who were determined to rely on their own resources and authority for survival. But that government should have survived in Washington at all after August 1814 was itself no mean achievement, and for this Madison was largely responsible. By persisting in his duty and refusing to admit defeat, even under the most difficult circumstances, he ensured that his administration could survive the war and enjoy the benefits of peace when it came.

★

No LESS DIFFICULT for the administration than restoring the federal government to Washington was the problem of dealing with Congress. That body, Jones predicted, would be "sulky," its members would resent the hardships of the session, and they would make demands the administration could not easily meet. The result, he prophesied to his wife, would be an unproductive session.[68] These anticipated difficulties were compounded by the fact that the administration, while preoccupied with restoring the government in Washington, had given little thought to what measures Congress should be asked to pass. Madison appears to have begun drafting his message to Congress only on September 20 the day it assembled, and none of his colleagues had yet prepared specific recommendations for the legislative committees to consider.

On September 21, Madison released his annual message to Congress. In it he tried to convince the legislators of the wisdom and necessity of his actions since 1812, while at the same time preparing them to make greater efforts on behalf of the war. He admitted that the grievances justifying war in 1812 were becoming less relevant with the restoration of peace in Europe but added that this development could not have been reasonably predicted. The President, however, did not encourage the thought that peace would come in the near future; Britain had showed no disposition to negotiate, and, he warned, its future conduct could be governed by "extravagant views and unwar-

---

[68] Jones to Eleanor Jones, September 20, 1814, Jones Papers, HSP.

rantable passions" which could lead the ministry to attempt "a deadly blow at our growing prosperity, perhaps at our national existence." To underline the threat to the Republic, Madison stressed the "barbarous" and "unrighteous" methods of British warfare, reminding the Congressmen that they were dealing with a nation which could not be expected to conform to "the usages of civilized warfare." To inspire Congress to resist, the President invoked the memory of the Revolution, pointing out that the nation should now be better fitted to maintain its independence than it had been to acquire it thirty years earlier. The repulse of the enemy at Baltimore and Plattsburg, as well as the victories on the Niagara Peninsula, against the Creeks, and on the oceans, were all evidence, he argued, that Britain would fail in the war. To ensure this result, Madison recommended that the ranks of the regular army should be filled, that the militia should be disciplined and classified, that special corps should be provided for local defense, and that to realize these goals "large sums" would have to be voted for the Treasury.[69]

Following this announcement, the Treasury was the first department to have material to submit to Congress. Secretary Campbell prepared a financial statement which he forwarded to the Senate on September 26, the day of his resignation. The report stated the Treasury would require $23,327,586.00 in additional revenue to meet its estimated expenditures for 1814. Campbell pointed out, however, that previous sources of revenue—taxes, loans, customs, land sales, and Treasury notes—would yield little more than half the sum required and that these same sources would also be inadequate to meet future needs. These Campbell declined to predict, but he added that the recent suspension of specie payments by banks south of New England had placed the nation's finances on a "new and uncertain footing." He also declined to make any recommendations for these problems, contenting himself with the remark that the "powers of Congress, so far as they extend, will be required to be exerted in providing a remedy . . . and in placing, if practicable, the currency of the country on a more uniform, certain, and stable footing."[70]

[69] See Richardson, *Messages and Papers*, II, 532-536.

[70] *ASP: Finance*, II, 840-843. The banking crisis was most severe in the Middle Atlantic states, where there had been the greatest expansion of the banks during the war. These banks, unlike those in New England, had little specie coming into their vaults from foreign trade, and, once the middle-state banks had drained institutions farther south and west of their specie while redeeming their notes, the system collapsed. New England banks received specie from foreign trade while also purchasing British government bills in Canada. See J. Van Fenstermaker, *The Development of American Commercial Banking, 1782-1837* (Kent, Ohio, 1965), 8-13.

This last observation was deliberately ambiguous. Campbell did not believe that the Treasury could raise any more money in the United States, and, as he had suggested earlier, the only solution he could see for the nation's financial problems was the establishment of a Bank of the United States. His eventual successor, Dallas, furthermore, was known to be of the same opinion. Yet Congress, in April 1814, had failed to establish a national bank, partly because the Republican party was divided over its constitutionality and partly because those Republicans who did favor a bank differed over the details of its organization.[71] Campbell's silence here probably reflected an unwillingness to commit either himself or his successor on such a controversial issue. The incoming Treasury Secretary, Dallas, for his part had no quarrel with Campbell's analysis of the nation's financial weaknesses, but since Jones had informed him that he thought Congress would now accept a national bank, Dallas regretted that Campbell had not told Congress a national bank was essential and thus compelled it to face the problem squarely.[72]

The chairman of the House Ways and Means Committee, John Wayles Eppes of Virginia, on the other hand, was opposed to a national bank for constitutional reasons. Wishing to forestall debate on the issue, Eppes, a son-in-law of Thomas Jefferson, recalled that Jefferson in 1813 had sent him several lengthy letters on methods of war finance that relied on neither bank loans nor a national bank, and so he asked his father-in-law for advice. Jefferson—who was alarmed at the possible consequences of a sudden collapse of the banking system but who also wished to prevent a restoration of that same system—responded quickly.[73] He forwarded to Monroe the outlines of a paper-money scheme whereby Congress would issue Treasury notes to the extent of the government's needs, make them legal tender, and pledge all taxes and duties for their eventual redemption. The advantages of such a scheme, according to Jefferson, would allow Congress not only to avoid repeating Alexander Hamilton's funding and banking policies of the 1790's but would also free the Treasury from dependence upon state-chartered, private banks as sources of loans and from having to use their bills as a circulating

[71] See Chapter VIII above. Also Campbell to Gallatin, August 1, 1814, *Gallatin Papers*; Dallas to Monroe, September 7, 1814, Monroe Papers, LC; and Dallas to Jones, September 18, 1814, Jones Papers, HSP.

[72] Jones to Dallas, September 15 and 25, 1814, Dallas Collection, HSP; Dallas to Jones, September 30, 1814, Jones Papers, HSP.

[73] Raymond Walters, *Alexander James Dallas* (Philadelphia, 1943), 189. See also John Wayles Eppes to Jefferson, July 21, 1813; Jefferson to Eppes, September 11, 1813; Eppes to Jefferson, September 7, 1814; Jefferson to Eppes, September 9, 1814, Thomas Jefferson Papers, LC.

medium.[74] At the former President's request, Monroe publicized the scheme in Congress, and he and Eppes prevailed upon the Ways and Means Committee to report it to the House on October 10. Eppes called for an increase in taxes to the amount of $22,435,000 to support the issue of an equivalent volume of Treasury notes, claiming that this would provide a national circulating medium as well.[75]

Monroe also gave the details of Jefferson's scheme to Dallas, and, when he read them, the new Secretary, though polite, was appalled.[76] All his correspondence with Jones prior to his accepting office was based on the premise that he would be free to work out in conjunction with bankers and government stockholders the details for establishing a new Bank of the United States, from which the Treasury would then borrow considerable sums of money to finance the war. Now Monroe had pre-empted this plan with a scheme that conflicted with Dallas's own views, and one that would do nothing to inspire the confidence of bankers in the administration.[77] The new Treasury Secretary apparently expressed his concern to Madison, and on October 14 Eppes withdrew his earlier recommendation to the House in order to allow Dallas to present his own policies. The President also wrote to Jefferson, rejecting his financial theories with the argument that the revenue they might bring to the government could not be increased without eventual recourse "to loans of the usual sort, or an augmentation of taxes according to the public exigencies."[78]

This episode, though brief, was unfortunate. On the vital matter of war finance the administration had revealed it was divided and slow to formulate policy. Divisions within the administration would, in turn, encourage divisions within the Republican ranks in Congress, and those who wished to oppose Dallas's policies could now do so on the grounds that they were upholding pure Republican principles while the Treasury was deviating from them. Moreover, the Federalists would be free to embarrass and obstruct the administration by casting their votes to defeat measures intended to assist the war effort, while pro-

[74] Jefferson to Monroe, September 24, 1814, Jefferson Papers, LC. See also same to same, October 15, 1814, Monroe Papers, NYPL.

[75] *ASP: Finance*, II, 854-855; AC, 13th Cong., 3d sess., 378-381.

[76] Monroe to Jefferson, October 10, 1814, Jefferson Papers, LC.

[77] Jones, too, was furious with Monroe, remarking that the Virginian's views on finance were "the most crude and visionary that can be conceived." Jones to Dallas, September 15, 1814, Dallas Collection, HSP. See also Kenneth L. Brown, "Stephen Girard, Promoter of the Second Bank of the United States," *Journal of Economic History* 2 (1942), 128-131; and Raymond Walters, "The Origins of the Second Bank of the United States," *Journal of Political Economy* 53 (1945), 120-123.

[78] Madison to Jefferson, October 10 and 23, 1814, Madison Papers, LC.

moting those that would not. Under these circumstances, it was hardly surprising that finance and banking, in the words of John Clopton of Virginia, became the "apple of discord" in the Republican party for the entire session of Congress.[79] Madison may have sensed this possibility too, when, according to Charles Jared Ingersoll, he took Dallas aside shortly after his arrival in Washington and advised him not to offend congressional sensibilities by taking a "high tone" in his dealings with the legislators.[80]

Dallas, however, proceeded to do just that. Convinced that he alone could bring order to the nation's finances, he sent on October 17 a long letter to the House Ways and Means Committee. Its recommendations were inevitably controversial, but the justifications the Secretary provided for his policies were scarcely designed to win him friends in Congress. No doubt wishing to impress upon the committee the seriousness of the financial crisis, Dallas implied that Congress in the past had acted without "wisdom, patriotism, and fortitude" and in ways that had "cast an inauspicious shade" over the nation's credit. The recent report by Eppes calling for the emission of Treasury notes he dismissed as a "pernicious palliative," producing "no countervailing profit" and exposing the government's credit "to every breath of popular prejudice or alarm." Eppes's suggestion that the notes be made legal tender he denounced as a "desperate expedient" which no "honest and enlightened statesman" could approve. The finances, he argued, could still be restored, but only with "prompt and resolute" action.[81]

To cover expenses for the remainder of 1814, Dallas admitted he would have to borrow more money, both at home and abroad, and issue Treasury notes to make up any shortfall. His main concern, though, was for the following year and the problem of financing a "protracted war." The needs of the government, he declared, were now far greater than could be reasonably or safely met by the "constant imposition of taxes," and there would therefore have to be "a resort to credit." In future years Dallas suggested that the ordinary sources of revenue be devoted to meeting the costs of administration and to paying the interest on existing loans and issues of Treasury notes; and, to supply the credit for 1815, the Secretary called for the establishment of a national bank for twenty years at Philadelphia, with branch offices of discount and deposit throughout the Union. This bank should have

[79] John Clopton to Thomas Ritchie, February 4, 1815, John Clopton Papers, Duke University Library.

[80] Ingersoll, *Historical Sketch*, II, 254.

[81] Dallas to Eppes, October 17, 1814, George Mifflin Dallas, *Life and Writings of Alexander James Dallas* (Philadelphia, 1871), 234-243.

a capital of $50 million to be subscribed by both individuals and corporations, partly in gold and silver coin but mostly in government 6 percent stock, which had been issued to subscribers of earlier government loans. The bank would be authorized to lend the United States up to $30 million at 6 percent, and Dallas planned to borrow that amount almost immediately, since he estimated the cost of the war for 1815 would be $28 million. Finally, the President was empowered to nominate the president of the bank and one-third of its directors; otherwise the bank was to be in private hands, exempt from taxation by the United States or the individual states.[82]

In short, Dallas had asked a Republican Congress to restore Alexander Hamilton's bank and had declared his intention to save the nation's finances by emulating Hamilton's methods. Anticipating opposition on the question of constitutionality, Dallas stated his opinion that the passage of time had settled the issue forever and that a national bank was "necessary and proper for carrying into execution some of the most important powers constitutionally invested in the government." Even if Congressmen should disagree, Dallas asked them to suppress their doubts, support his measures, and leave the question of constitutionality to the judiciary. The *National Intelligencer* supported the Secretary's position and called on Congress to vote quickly the full range of his recommendations.[83]

On October 18, Eppes presented Dallas's report to the House, which began discussing it in a committee of the whole three days later. For a week the House debated the taxes needed to balance that part of Dallas's budget dealing with the costs of administration and the repayment of interest on loans and Treasury notes. Here Dallas had accepted many of the tax increases called for by Eppes to finance his Treasury note scheme, though in some cases, notably those of the direct tax and the spirit duty, he called for even greater increases. His policy, he declared, was to spread "the general amount of the taxes over a wide surface, with a hand as light and equal as is consistent with convenience in the process and certainly in the result."[84] Most Republicans seemed to accept the inevitability of tax increases; few rose either to defend or attack the measures, and the debates were dominated by Federalists who constantly moved amendments to specific taxes, particularly the direct tax and the spirit duty, in order to exploit sectional differences among their opponents by encouraging Republicans from one region to lighten their tax burden at the expense of another.

[82] Ibid.
[83] Ibid. See also *Daily Natl Intelligencer*, October 19, 1814.
[84] Dallas, *Life of Dallas*, 241.

As they did so, the Federalists attacked the administration for prosecuting an offensive war, announced they would only support taxes for a defensive war, and occasionally called upon the President to change his cabinet by bringing Federalists into office. Many of the taxes, though, such as those on letters, papers, harnesses, and wine, were agreed to without debate, and all had been sent to the Senate by October 27.[85]

The next day the House began debate on that part of Dallas's report calling for a national bank. Several Republicans from the southern states—principally Clopton, Burwell, and Eppes of Virginia—immediately declared the measure to be unconstitutional, while others, including Robert Wright of Maryland and Richard Stanford of North Carolina, moved amendments confining its operations to the District of Columbia, a stratagem that would have frustrated the Treasury's desire to use the bank and its branches as an instrument of national policy.[86] The *National Intelligencer* repeated its arguments about the necessity of a national bank, but the House postponed discussion of the issue for two weeks in favor of debating the loans Dallas sought in order to carry on the government for the remainder of 1814.[87] In the interval, the House Ways and Means Committee considered Dallas's bank scheme more closely, and Eppes appears to have tried to use his position as chairman to influence the committee to bring in a report against the Secretary's proposals. Dallas, on receiving word of this development, sought a conference with the committee on November 7 to persuade it to report his plans to the House. He was successful, but only at the cost of permanently dividing the committee and driving chairman Eppes into open opposition against the administration.[88]

When the House reconsidered the finances for 1815 on November 12, evidence of divisions within the Republican party was all too clear. Bolling Hall of Georgia moved that the Ways and Means Committee be instructed to report a scheme similar to that proposed earlier by Eppes to issue Treasury notes and to make them legal tender. The House rejected the motion, but the vote revealed that a solid minority of thirty-nine Republicans was still opposed to accepting a bank; the remaining Republicans, fifty in all, united with an almost equal number of Federalists to defeat Hall's motion, but should the Federalists decide to change their votes, Dallas's schemes would obviously fail to pass

[85] AC, 13th Cong., 3d sess., 401, 419, 420-437, 438-452, 454-458, 465-478, 479-480.
[86] Ibid., 496-499.
[87] *Daily Natl Intelligencer*, October 29 and November 15, 1814.
[88] Ingersoll, *Historical Sketch*, II, 255.

the House.[89] Two days later, on November 14, Fisk of New York, the second-ranking member on the divided Ways and Means Committee, reported to the House a bank bill in conformity with Dallas's wishes. It was immediately attacked by the Federalists, who, under William Gaston of North Carolina, moved to thwart Dallas by reducing the bank's capital to $20 million and requiring that an unrealistically high percentage of that sum be subscribed in specie.[90]

To John Caldwell Calhoun of South Carolina, who had already expressed concern that excessive delay in debating bills would seriously hamper the war preparations for 1815, the bank bill was clearly destined to defeat. Accordingly, on November 16 he moved that Congress consider a different bill, one which created a bank with $50 million in capital, but with 95 percent of that sum consisting of a fresh issue of Treasury notes, most of which were to be put into circulation immediately. Financially, Calhoun's bill made little sense; it was, in fact, a paper-money scheme which Calhoun tried to disguise as an indirect loan to the bank, and the bank would have no regulatory powers over the notes as a circulating medium. Admittedly, Calhoun's plan might provide the nation with a currency more quickly than would Dallas's bank, but it would also be inflationary and would not absorb the existing government stock in the financial markets.[91] Politically, however, Calhoun's bill was defensible as an attempt to compromise the widely divergent views within the Republican party as represented by the stands of Dallas and Eppes. The Treasury Secretary, though, was horrified by Calhoun's bill and tried to stop debate on it, but he was powerless to do so, since the divisions in the Ways and Means Committee itself made it impossible for him to get any suitable proposal onto the floor of the House. Sadly, Senator Jonathan Roberts of Pennsylvania reported that the Republican party was now hopelessly "distracted" by internal quarrels.[92]

The *National Intelligencer* implored the House not to debate Calhoun's bill, pointing out that it would be passed by Federalist votes in the House and then rejected by the votes of the same party in

[89] AC, 13th Cong., 3d sess., 557-559.

[90] Ibid., 561-562, 564, 566-586. See also Daniel Webster to Ezekiel Webster, November 21, 1814, Charles M. Wiltse, ed., *The Papers of Daniel Webster* (Hanover, N.H., 1974–), I, 176-177.

[91] AC, 13th Cong., 3d sess., 587. See also Thomas Law to Madison, December 10, 1814, Madison Papers, LC; Mason to Appleton, November 24, 1814, Hillard, *Memoir and Correspondence*, 105.

[92] See Walters, "Origins of the Second Bank of the United States," 124-125; and Ingersoll, *Historical Sketch*, II, 256. See also Jonathan Roberts to Matthew Roberts, November 17, 1814, Jonathan Roberts Papers, HSP.

the Senate.[93] The House, however, decided by over sixty votes to consider Calhoun's bill. For the next ten days its opponents denounced it as ruinous to the nation's credit and unfair to the government's creditors, who would see their stock holdings depreciate in value, while Calhoun defended it on the grounds that the "monied class" was too exhausted to provide further credit to the administration, which would now have to induce the "farming interest" to accept government paper as a means of creating a circulating medium.[94] By November 25 it was clear that the differences between the administration, the House Ways and Means Committee, and the Republicans in Congress were irreconcilable. Accordingly, William Lowndes of South Carolina suggested that a new select committee be created to report another scheme to the House. The committee was duly appointed, but its membership was weighted against Dallas's bank plans. Four of the members—Calhoun, Lowndes, Gaston, and Thomas Oakley of New York—had all opposed the Secretary, while only Fisk, John Forsyth of Georgia, and Samuel Ingham of Pennsylvania had supported him.[95]

Dallas was by now beside himself with rage. He wrote an angry letter to Eppes declaring "the public credit no longer existed" and blaming Congress for the nation's plight. Eppes replied in a similar vein, deploring the Secretary's outburst and claiming that the letter had "mortified and astonished" the friends of the administration. Eppes further pointed out that Dallas's remarks about the finances were irresponsible, and their effect would "blast our hopes . . . and damn the public credit." Carried away by his own temper, Eppes then accused the Secretary of being overwhelmed by despair and wantonly plunging "a dagger in the breast of [his] friends." The exchange painfully illustrated the limits of executive influence over Congress and revealed the extent to which the administration had to rely on congressional tolerance and compliance to get a hearing for its plans. As Eppes pointed out to Dallas, it was a chairman's duty to "unite" with every measure he could approve, but the bank, he added, "was unfortunately [not] one of those questions." "I have done," he continued, "what an honest man alone could do—closed my lips [and] to all your other measures I have given every aid in my power and there is no doubt they will be adopted." A few days later the two men apologized to

[93] *Daily Natl Intelligencer*, November 15 and 18, 1814. For the accuracy of this prediction see Samuel Taggart to John Taylor, November 22, 1814, George Haynes, ed., "Letters of Samuel Taggart," in *Proceedings of the American Antiquarian Society* 33 (1923), 434.

[94] AC, 13th Cong., 3d sess., 613-634.

[95] Ibid., 642-644; Ingersoll, *Historical Sketch*, II, 256-257.

each other for their letters, regretting that they had been written "on the impulse of the moment," but the differences between them remained.[96]

During this quarrel, Lowndes, as chairman of the select committee on banking, requested the Secretary to give his opinion on the effects of Calhoun's bill on the national credit. Dallas was irritated by this request to repeat his views, since he had no intention of modifying them to suit Congress. Indeed, he had already received letters and memorials from bankers in Philadelphia stating that they would not support a bank created by Calhoun's bill. These he laid before Congress, and, in his reply to Lowndes, he amplified the case he had made for establishing a national bank—that the administration of the Treasury had become impossible and that nobody was willing to accept issues of Treasury notes, since they would cause depreciation, thus undermining all confidence in the public credit. Dallas therefore hoped that the committee would have "the intelligence and candor" to realize the "injurious" and "dangerous" consequences of Calhoun's bill.[97]

This time the Secretary's bluntness was partly rewarded. Lowndes's committee, despite its majority in favor of Calhoun's scheme, reported to the House on November 28 that it was unable to reconcile conflicting opinions on the bank and that it could therefore do no more than bring Calhoun's bill forward for a vote. Lowndes had the clerk read to the House his correspondence with Dallas and, during the debate, tried to meet what he understood to be the Secretary's objections by moving that the capital of the bank, and hence the volume of Treasury notes it could issue, be reduced to $30 million. The majority of House Republicans, sixty-five, voted against this motion, but it was passed by the minority of antibank Republicans in alliance with the Federalists.[98] In financial terms, however, this halfhearted compromise was quite indefensible, and even its supporters admitted as much. The Maryland Federalist Alexander Hanson, after voting for it, described the amended bill as "deformed," "absurd," and "visionary." The House then voted on November 29 to end the debate, and a majority of both Federalist and Republican members decided against letting the bill pass to a third reading.[99]

[96] Eppes to Dallas, November 26 and 30, November 1814, John Wayles Eppes Letters, Duke University Library.

[97] Dallas to Lowndes, November 27, 1814, *ASP: Finance*, II, 872-873. AC, 13th Cong., 3d sess., 651. See also S. Clarke to Jones, November 23, 1814, Jones Papers, HSP; and William Davy to Dallas, December 5, 1814, Dallas Collection, HSP.

[98] AC, 13th Cong., 3d sess., 651, 655.

[99] Ibid., 656, 685-686.

The House thus rejected the attempt to establish a national bank, and the *National Intelligencer*, again calling for Republican unity, lamented the decision.[100] Many Republicans, in Congress and throughout the nation, also bewailed the confusion in their party. According to Representative Samuel Dana of Massachusetts, all Republicans in Congress realized the need for a national bank, but he believed only about one-third of their number could bring themselves to support Dallas's schemes.[101] Indeed, most congressional Republicans, in their speeches, their correspondence, and in their voting, revealed that they were willing to go along with almost any temporary expedient to continue financing the war, even if that expedient assumed the form of a bank.[102] Dallas, however, flatly rejected temporary expedients, regarding these as insufficient for the nation's needs and unworthy of the role he had conceived for himself in accepting Madison's offer of the Treasury. He insisted repeatedly that it was his duty to introduce "a permanent plan for reviving the public credit," and at the heart of that plan was a national bank.[103] Unfortunately, Dallas's method of organizing the bank and the nation's financial system was too openly "Hamiltonian" for a majority of Republicans to accept it.

The defeat of the bank, of course, intensified the ever pressing need to provide money for the government. On December 2, Monroe informed Eppes that the War Department had exhausted its funds and would require an emergency appropriation of $3 million at once.[104] Eppes himself realized that the state of the finances was still critical, and, on the same day, he wrote to Dallas asking how the Treasury intended to meet the interest charges on its loans as well as continue paying the cost of government operations for the remainder of the year. Dallas replied by requesting discretionary authority to issue Treasury notes, raise loans, and to transfer bank credits where necessary "to meet the public arrangements."[105] These proposals caused no controversy in the House when Eppes reported them on December 7, but Dallas had by no means yet given up his attempt to persuade Congress to establish a national bank. A bank bill, substantially along the lines that Dallas had earlier recommended to the House, was reported in

[100] *Daily Natl Intelligencer*, November 29, 1814.

[101] Samuel Dana to William King, November 26, 1814, William King Papers, MeHS.

[102] See, for example, John W. Taylor to Mrs. Taylor, November 29, 1814, John W. Taylor Papers, NYHS.

[103] See, for example, Dallas's letter to Lowndes cited in note 97 above. Also Monroe to Jefferson, December 21, 1814, Jefferson Papers, LC.

[104] Monroe to Eppes, December 2 and 6, 1814. RCSW.

[105] Eppes to Dallas, December 2, 1814; Dallas to Eppes, December 2, 1814, Dallas, *Life of Dallas*, 248-256.

the Senate in the first week of December, and the Secretary still believed that the pressure of circumstances would compel Congress to accept it.[106]

In contrast to the House, the Senate spent little time in debating the bank bill. The Federalists, led by Jeremiah Mason of New Hampshire and Rufus King of New York, along with "malcontent" Republican Obadiah German of New York, all moved amendments to reduce the bank's capital and to give Congress the right to legislate on the bank's operations, but they failed to have them adopted. All nine of the Federalist Senators present voted for the amendments, but they could never get more than four or five Republicans—usually German, John Lambert of New Jersey, and James Brown and Elejuis Fromentin of Louisiana—to support them. The Republican majority voted for the bill in its original form, and passed it on December 9.[107] Dallas's supporters in the House realized that on this occasion considerable caution and skill would be required in mediating between Republican factions to ensure the bill's passage. The key to success, John Taylor of New York believed, was to get the antibank Republicans to abstain so that the Federalists would not be able to create a majority against any bill that satisfied the administration's wishes.[108]

It proved difficult, however, to obtain favorable circumstances for the introduction of the new bank bill. By his very action of reporting it to the House on December 23, Fisk of New York revealed that the Ways and Means Committee was still divided over the bank and that chairman Eppes would withhold his support.[109] Republicans immediately rose to denounce the measure as unconstitutional, while Federalists attacked several details of the bill as unsound. The House then spent most of December 24 in this fashion before adjourning without making any progress. In order to prevent the bill being defeated by the slow process of amendment, Ingersoll of Pennsylvania, on December 27, moved to cut off debate, and he was supported by a seemingly solid Republican vote of seventy-two. All fifty-one Federalists present voted against Ingersoll's motion, but for the first time in the debates on the bank issue they were unable to obtain a sufficient number of Republicans to defeat the administration. This sudden change owed much to the abstention of the antibank Republicans, and, on the fol-

---

[106] AC, 13th Cong., 3d sess., 118, 761. Dallas to Monroe, December 7, 1814, Monroe Papers, LC.

[107] AC, 13th Cong., 3d sess., 120-126.

[108] John Taylor to Martin Van Buren, December 10, 1814, Martin Van Buren Papers, LC; George Walker to Dallas, December 20, 1814, LRRS [misfiled?].

[109] AC, 13th Cong., 3d sess., 976.

lowing roll call to pass the bill for a third reading, the Republican majority in favor rose to eighty-one, while the Federalists were left with little more than a dozen Republican allies, mostly from Virginia and North Carolina.[110] The administration must have been encouraged by these two votes, but its hopes were dashed the next day when the antibank Republicans, led by Calhoun, returned to the House to support a Federalist motion to recommit the bill to require that 40 percent of the bank's capital be subscribed in either gold and silver or in government stock that was circulating at its face value.[111] Both these conditions were generally regarded as impossible to fulfill.

The debate on recommittal on December 29 was, as Joseph Gales recorded, "long and animated" before the Republicans agreed to terminate it and pass the bank bill to a third reading. The Federalists, this time led by Daniel Webster of Massachusetts, tried to repeat their earlier tactics of dividing the barely solidified majority by moving a series of amendments, but without success. Webster led another lengthy attack on the bill on January 2, 1815, to have it tabled or recommitted, only to meet with failure again. All the Federalists present supported Webster, but only nine Republicans appeared in opposition, while the supporters of the bank now numbered eighty-nine. The bank at last seemed certain to pass the House, but on the final vote the Republican majority again eroded. A small group of ten antibank Republicans, predictably led by Calhoun, changed their votes and produced a tie. Then Speaker Cheves, as he had done previously on the vote to remove the capital to a safer place, took an obvious pleasure in using his casting vote against the bill and against the administration. The bank proposed by the bill, Cheves declared with "more than his usual eloquence and impressiveness," was "a dangerous, unexampled . . . and almost desperate resort. Neither the safety nor the credit of the nation," he argued, required the passage of the bill, and he concluded that it was impossible to frame a bank bill to answer the "avowed objects" of the administration. This last remark must have galled the cabinet. Cheves had implicitly questioned the integrity of Dallas and his Republicanism and had warned him, in effect, that Treasury notes were the only way to finance the war.[112]

The National Intelligencer was appalled at these Republican defections, which had defeated the bank for the second time.[113] Even the

[110] Ibid., 977-988, 989, 990, 994-995.
[111] Ibid., 996-997.
[112] Ibid., 996, 998-1004, 1022-1026.
[113] Daily Natl Intelligencer, January 3, 1815.

Federalists were surprised at the outcome, with Cyrus King of Massachusetts remarking that the voting on the bank had been inconsistent and impossible to understand.[114] Many House Republicans were stunned by their failure to carry their point, with Hugh Nelson of Virginia expressing the fear that the Republic could not survive if Congress could not govern.[115] Accordingly, Bolling Hall of Georgia, who had consistently opposed a bank, moved on January 3 that the House reconsider the Speaker's vote. After a long debate, the Republican majority reformed in favor of reconsideration and was even joined by six Federalists from New York and Virginia. Only six Republicans—including, perversely enough, Hall himself—voted to uphold Cheves's decision. The Republican majority, however, did not hold sufficiently firm to prevent some of its members, led by Samuel McKee of Kentucky, from moving the recommittal of the bill to consider further amendments. The Federalists quickly seized the opportunity to embarrass the administration further by reuniting to carry McKee's motion. A new select committee, with a majority favoring recommittal, was appointed, and the House was condemned once again to repeat the debate on the bank bill.[116]

On January 6, McKee reported an amended version of the bank bill. Its contents suggested that the committee's decisions had been prompted by a desire to concede something to all factions in the House so as to guarantee passage of the bill. To please the Federalists, the capital of the bank was reduced to $30 million, and its directors were no longer required to make loans to the United States. To please antibank Republicans, the amount of stock needed to capitalize the bank was reduced to $10 million, and the bank was stripped of the power to suspend specie payments. To provide for a circulating medium, the bank was authorized to issue $15 million in Treasury notes. In truth, however, McKee's bill did not represent a compromise between the desires of the administration and the divided opinions in the House; instead, it was essentially a compromise between the Federalists and the antibank Republicans, and both groups were intent on denying the administration a bank bill that met Dallas's wishes. McKee's bill did not absorb enough United States stock to satisfy the government's

[114] Cyrus King to William King, January 3, 1815, King Papers, MeHS.

[115] Hugh Nelson to Charles Everett, January 3, 1815, Hugh Nelson Papers, LC. Nelson also remarked that the standing of the administration in Congress was so low that most committee chairmen were distancing themselves from legislative proposals coming from executive departments.

[116] AC, 13th Cong., 3d sess., 1027-1032.

creditors, while Dallas had repeatedly rejected Treasury notes as a method of war finance.[117]

Speaking for the administration's supporters in the House, Fisk of New York pointed out that the bill would not meet the needs of the Treasury, but a majority of the Republicans were clearly disposed to vote for any compromise measure simply to get the bank established. The Federalists were willing to support them here, obviously content to see the passage of a bill which would embarrass rather than aid the administration. Consequently, McKee's bill quickly passed the House through all stages by large bipartisan majorities on January 7. Only about thirty members voted against the bill, all of them being Republicans who either felt that the administration should have been allowed to have its way or believed, for constitutional reasons, that Congress could not establish any sort of bank at all.[118]

The administration disliked McKee's bill, but, apart from noting its passage by an "amalgamation of parties" in the House, the *National Intelligencer* withheld any comments or criticisms.[119] The Senate began consideration of the bill on January 13 by reporting it with amendments to increase the capital of the bank as well as to empower it to suspend specie payments and to allow Congress the right to inspect its books. The amendments passed easily enough, with only the Federalists together with German, Lambert, Fromentin, and Brown consistently in opposition, but the Senate as a whole later declined to insist on them when they were rejected by the House.[120] By this stage, the Senate, too, wished to compromise to pass a bill, and it did not even insist that the bank be authorized to suspend specie payments, despite

[117] Ibid., 1039-1042. Also see Jesse Wharton to John Overton, January 15, 1815, John Overton Papers, UNC. How far McKee was responsible for the details of this bill is uncertain. Ironically, McKee had supported the recharter of the first Bank of the United States in 1811, which suggests that his motives, whatever they were, did not include opposition to banks on constitutional grounds. Bray Hammond has distinguished between "agrarian" Republicans, who disliked all banks, and "business" Republicans, who were often connected with state banks and who feared a national bank as a regulator and competitor. Possibly, McKee, in 1814, fell into the latter category. See Hammond, *Banks and Politics in America from the Revolution to the Civil War* (Princeton, 1957), 217-219. Of McKee's bank bill, Webster, speaking for the Federalists, wrote: "It will now be harmless, as we think. We had a hard task to prevent its passing in its worst shape." To Ezekiel Webster, January 9, 1815, Wiltse, *Webster Papers*, I, 179.

[118] *AC*, 13th Cong., 3d sess., 1043-1045. Even Monroe could not accept McKee's bill, pointing out that the bank it would establish would "be turned against the govt. Our friends," he added, "want harmony and concert." Monroe to Hay, January 12, 1815, Monroe Papers, NYPL.

[119] *Daily Natl Intelligencer*, January 7 and 9, 1815.

[120] AC, 13th Cong., 3d sess., 166-169, 173-174.

the *National Intelligencer*'s warning that the failure to do so would allow the bank to be drained completely of its own specie holdings.[121] Senator Roberts then asked Dallas if the bill was acceptable to him. The Secretary's reply was probably stronger than Roberts had anticipated, since Dallas declared he was quite indifferent to all the equally bad pieces of banking legislation that had emerged from Congress during the session. As he could not carry his policies, Dallas informed Roberts of his intention to resign, and he sent to Congress an estimate of the costs of the war for the coming year.[122] These now amounted to some $56 million, of which little more than $15 million could be met from existing sources of revenue; the deficit of nearly $41 million might be made up from an almost endless multiplication of taxes, issues of Treasury notes, and appeals for loans, none of which Dallas believed would be successful, and none of which would guarantee the restoration of a circulating medium.[123]

It was clear that McKee's bill was of no use to the administration, but the President carefully considered his response for several days.[124] To sign the bill, as Monroe pointed out, would not only be a humiliating admission of weakness, but it would also seem to sanction the conduct of those Republicans who had consistently voted with the Federalists to thwart the administration. Monroe therefore argued for a veto, which would serve to draw the line between the parties again and would give those who were disposed to support the administration an opportunity to re-form a majority.[125] Dallas endorsed this line of reasoning insofar as he refused to accept any bank bill other than the one he had recommended. He informed both Madison and Monroe of his wish to resign, promising only to remain in Washington until the end of the session of Congress and to help the President choose a successor.[126] Madison could hardly have been surprised by this move, having long since recognized that the Secretary's usefulness in the Treasury had become limited, and he kept Dallas busy with the drafting of a pamphlet justifying the war in anticipation of a breakdown of

[121] *Daily Natl Intelligencer*, January 19, 1815.

[122] Roberts to Dallas, January 19, 1815, with an endorsement by Dallas, Dallas Collection, HSP.

[123] Dallas to Eppes, January 17, 1815, Dallas, *Life of Dallas*, 262-271.

[124] James Caldwell to Worthington, January 21, 1815, Thomas Worthington Papers, OSL. Possibly Madison hesitated before taking the step, unusual for the time, of vetoing a bill for reasons of policy rather than for constitutional reasons.

[125] Monroe to Madison, January 26, 1815, Madison Papers, LC.

[126] Dallas to Jones, January 29, 1815, Jones Papers, HSP; Dallas to [Madison], February 2, 1815, Dallas Collection, HSP. See also Walters, "Origins of the Second Bank of the United States," 126.

the peace negotiations at Ghent.[127] On January 30, Madison vetoed the bank bill, sending to Congress a lengthy message summarizing the outlines of the debate on the issue and emphasizing the bill's inadequacy for the Treasury's requirements. The President also asked Congress to "make haste" and pass a better bill.[128]

The Republicans in the Senate sustained the President by declining to repass the bank bill, and, on February 6, Senator James Barbour of Virginia introduced a new measure which met the main points raised in the veto message: the bank was to be capitalized to the extent of $50 million, it was to be required to lend to the government sums up to $30 million, and its directors were to control specie payments in conjunction with the Treasury.[129] The Senate passed the bill within the week, and it gave Dallas substantially what he had long wanted.[130] This success, though, did little to relieve the Secretary's pessimism; he remained firmly convinced that no useful legislation could emerge from Congress, remarking that that body could best serve the national interest only by adjourning.[131] The House began consideration of the bank bill on February 13, and its behavior justified all Dallas's suspicions. The antibank Republicans, led by Calhoun and Solomon Sharp of Kentucky, attempted to send the bill back to committee for amendment. A majority of the Republicans opposed this motion, but their margin of victory was extremely narrow, fewer than half a dozen votes, while a handful of Republicans, numbering between fourteen and sixteen, continued to join the Federalists in opposition. When the House resumed the debate on February 17, the news of the peace treaty made at Ghent on December 24, 1814, had reached Washington; this took the urgency out of the bank issue. The Republicans accordingly felt even freer to express their differences on the subject, and the bank bill was postponed indefinitely by a large bipartisan vote.[132]

[127] The pamphlet was published after the war under the title *An Exposition on the Causes and Character of the Late War Between the United States and Great Britain*. Its contents were as much the work of Madison as they were of Dallas. See the sketch notes, made at the end of 1814, in Madison Papers, LC.

[128] For the text of the bill and Madison's veto see *ASP: Finance*, II, 891-895.

[129] AC, 13th Cong., 3d sess., 214, 226. On February 4, 1815, the *National Intelligencer* reported there had been a Republican caucus meeting, at which it was decided to support the administration bill.

[130] Eppes to Worthington, February 10, 1815, Worthington Papers, OSL.

[131] Dallas to Jones, February 9, 1815, Jones Papers, HSP.

[132] AC, 13th Cong., 3d sess., 1149-1152, 1168. See also Walters, "Origins of the Second Bank of the United States," 127. By now, Calhoun's "little squad" had become quite unpopular in Congress for its ability to frustrate administration wishes by allying with Federalists. See J. Norvell to Campbell, February 10, 1815, Campbell Papers, LC; and Joseph Varnum to William Eustis, February 17, 1815, William Eustis Papers, LC.

As Jones had predicted in September 1814, the third session of the Thirteenth Congress was indeed unrewarding, and it produced no legislation to finance the war for another year. The development of this political impasse, which was far more serious than any previous difficulties encountered in organizing the war effort, might be attributed to a number of factors. By deciding that a national bank was the only solution to the problem of war finance, the administration espoused a position bound to divide its supporters in Congress, while also giving its opponents, including both the Federalists and Speaker Cheves, an opportunity to exploit those divisions to the full. But even if the administration had supported not the bank but the paper-money schemes of Eppes and Calhoun, it seems not unlikely that political factionalism in Congress would still have led to a similar legislative stalemate. Hostility to banks no longer united as many Republicans as it had done in the early 1790's, and the real root of the administration's difficulties lay not so much in the financial problems of the nation as it did in the inability to find a stable Republican majority either in Congress or in the cabinet to support any consistent policy.[133] For this state of affairs no individual or group could be held responsible, though it seems undeniable that Dallas might have cultivated better personal relations with the House Ways and Means Committee than he did. Jones believed that Madison complicated the Treasury's task by not wholly understanding its financial problems, but this view is neither true nor just.[134] Madison's preference for a national bank as a solution to the financial problem, his position of 1791 notwithstanding, was clearly understood by all in Washington, and even when he unambiguously proclaimed his stand in his veto message of January 30, 1815, it produced no change in the behavior of Congress. The establishment of the second Bank of the United States was thus delayed until the meeting of a less divided Republican Congress in 1816, which eventually carried the administration's wartime banking policies into effect.

★

EQUALLY AS URGENT and contentious an issue as war finance was the need for Congress to consider legislation to fill the ranks of the army and for the War Department to formulate plans for continuing the war.

---

[133] The politics of banking, particularly the development of Republican attitudes on the issue between 1791 and 1814, is still not sufficiently well understood. Hammond's survey provides some general explanations, but it is impossible to say whether his distinction between "agrarian" and "business" Republicans explains the factionalism of the winter of 1814-1815. See Hammond, *Banks and Politics*, 209-250; and Joseph Dorfman, *The Economic Mind in American Civilization* (New York, 1946-1959), I, 341-344, 352-359.

[134] Jones to Dallas, September 15, 1814, Dallas Collection, HSP.

Under Izard and Brown the army had performed honorably throughout the summer of 1814, but its efforts had not improved the American strategic position. The British army had not been driven from the Niagara Peninsula, the Royal Navy could still contest control of Lake Ontario, and it was unclear how, or even whether, the United States could continue its policy of trying to conquer Canada. Furthermore, the enemy attacks on Plattsburg, Washington, and Baltimore had led Congressmen and state governors to insist that the War Department devote more resources to local defense. Consequently, the combined burdens of the War Department were now more formidable than they had been at any time since 1811, and Monroe, though eager enough to assume them, had few ideas about how to proceed. This fact became all too apparent when a letter from William Branch Giles of the Senate military affairs committee on September 23 requesting a statement of the administration's military policies went unanswered for over three weeks.[135]

Monroe's first month in the War Department was devoted largely to organizing the defenses of the Chesapeake and the Atlantic coast cities, and, as he later pointed out, the destruction of the government buildings in Washington made it difficult for him to come to grips with the problems of military administration. The Adjutant General's office had lost some recruiting returns in the burning of the capital, and it was proving awkward to obtain such basic information as an accurate return of the regular army.[136] Some Republicans felt that the tasks of war organization were now so great that they should be given to a Board of War rather than to an individual, but Monroe, no doubt feeling that he could not afford to be unequal to the challenge he had criticized his predecessors for failing to meet, struggled on.[137] He did admit, though, that the "pressure of business" was very great, the more so since he was besieged almost daily by deputations of Congressmen and state legislators from Virginia demanding that he improve not only the defenses of the "Old Dominion" but also reimburse it for past claims for calling the state militia into national service. Finally Monroe had to tell the Virginians, many of whom were his personal and political friends, that he simply could not allow them at present to subject the administration to such extensive demands. The financial settlement of

[135] Giles to Monroe, September 23, 1814, LRRS.

[136] Adjutant General to Monroe, October 26, 1814, LSAG.

[137] Henry Dearborn to Monroe, September 5, 1814, Monroe Papers, NYPL; Jonathan Dayton to Madison, September 6, 1814, Madison Papers, LC. Also (Richmond, Va.) *The Enquirer*, September 21, 1814.

claims for all states, he added, would have to be postponed until after the war.[138]

Early in October, however, the administration began reconsidering the problem of conquering Canada. The President asked the Secretary of the Navy to prepare a plan for the United States to win naval supremacy on Lake Ontario in the spring of 1815, but Jones's response could hardly have been what Madison and Monroe expected to hear. After making an appraisal of the resources of the navy, Jones declared it would be difficult for the United States to obtain more than a "vacillating" superiority on the lake. The trouble was not so much doubt that the United States could build more vessels than Britain as it was the inability to man them with trained seamen, and Jones believed he could not supply a fleet on Lake Ontario without stripping the Atlantic fleet and ports of more men and guns than he thought advisable. For this reason he suggested that the administration abandon the strategy pursued since 1813 of trying to reduce Canada by joint naval and military operations and shift its offensive eastward by taking a strong position at St. Regis on Lake St. Francis. Here the United States could not only cut enemy communications along the St. Lawrence but could also mount a major campaign against Montreal. If the administration could not make this change in policy, the implication of Jones's arguments was clearly that the continuation of the war would be pointless.[139]

These statements certainly had an impact, and Madison later told Jones they had "corrected some erroneous impressions he had entertained."[140] Since there was still no question in the President's mind of abandoning the war before a peace treaty had been made, administration policy began to focus on the problems of invading Lower Canada, and Monroe, from this time onward, showed no interest in encouraging Izard to continue military operations on the Niagara Peninsula or in Upper Canada.[141] Unfortunately, providing for a new offensive strategy

[138] See Charles Everett to Barbour, October 6, 1814; Monroe to Everett, October 6, 1814, both in Curtis W. Garrison and David L. Thomas, eds., *James Monroe Papers in Virginia Repositories* (microfilm ed.). See also Monroe to Barbour, October 26, 1814, James Barbour Papers, NYPL.

[139] Jones to Madison, October 15 and 26, 1814, Madison Papers, LC; Jones to Monroe, November 7, 1814, LRRS. Also see Caleb Nichols to Monroe, November 24, 1814, LRUS. Sérurier also reported that the administration was considering abandoning the struggle for the lakes in favor of a land strategy. To Talleyrand, November 21, 1814, Correspondance Politique: États-Unis. vol. LXXI.

[140] Jones to Eleanor Jones, November 6, 1814, Jones Papers, HSP.

[141] Monroe to George Izard, October 24, 1814, George Izard, *Official Correspondence with the Department of War Relative to the Military Operations of the American Army under*

as well as meeting the increased needs of the nation for defense required the War Department to raise a far larger number of troops than it had so far been able to do, and this became Monroe's most difficult problem. On paper, the regular establishments allowed for the enlistment of 62,000 men, but the most optimistic return provided by the Adjutant General's office at this time could find no more than 34,000 men in the ranks, and it was also apparent that current recruiting practices were unlikely to furnish very many more.[142] As a result of the increases in wages and bounties for regulars under the legislation of January 1814, the costs of recruiting, successful or not, had become enormous, and this had also inflated wages paid to laborers and artisans. By midsummer 1814, the Adjutant General was receiving reports from officers that laborers could command wages of $18.00 to $20.00 per month, while regimental paymasters were accumulating sizable amounts of bounty money which was being put to no useful purpose.[143] Military service, in short, was still relatively unattractive, and the situation was not improved by the fact that brutal treatment of enlisted men by many of their officers was becoming, as Jonathan Fisk of New York informed Madison, a matter of "common report."[144] Clearly, different methods of military mobilization would have to be found and Congress persuaded to pass them into law.

To underline the seriousness of the military situation, Madison, on October 10 and 14, sent Congress selections from the correspondence between the State Department and the American peace commissioners in Europe. The negotiations with Britain had been shifted, at the

---

the command of Major General Izard on the Northern Frontier of the United States in the Years 1814 and 1815 (Philadelphia, 1816), 107-108.

[142] Several attempts were made between September and November 1814 to draw up a return of the regular army. Initially, the Inspector General tried to estimate the number of men enlisted since January 1814, and he produced three different totals of 8,340, 9,991, and 13,848. He then produced two estimates for a return of the whole army by August 1814, 29,107 and 34,029, but reckoned that only one-quarter of these could be considered as "effectives." Many of the more recent recruits had yet to join their regiments, while Brown's division of the army in the Ninth Military District had suffered a casualty rate of 48% in the summer campaign. See ASP: Military Affairs, I, 512-513, 518, 520-522; "Estimate Force of the U. States," September 24, 1814, LSAG, and "Abstract of the Army," November 5, 1814, Sen 13B-D.2, Legislative Records of the United States Senate (RG 46), NA.

[143] See, for example, the claim of the Adjutant General that it cost $50,000 to recruit only 300 men in one particular regiment. Adjutant General to H. Atkinson, August 15, 1814, LSAG. See also Jonas Simonds to Adjutant General, June 5, 1814; James Reed to same, July 1, 1814; A. Eustis to same, July 6, 1814, LRAG; and Thomas Cushing to Monroe, September 28, 1814, LRRS.

[144] Fisk to Madison, October 5, 1814, LRAG. For an example of a typical complaint by enlisted men against their officers see "Old Soldier" to Armstrong, June 7, 1814, LRAG.

initiative of the British government, from Gothenburg in Sweden to Ghent in the Austrian Netherlands, but had quickly reached a deadlock with a series of British demands for far-reaching American concessions on the Newfoundland fisheries, the problems of Canadian and Indian boundaries, as well as the American acceptance of the claim that other territorial issues involved in the war be settled on the basis of *uti possidetis*. The refusal of the American commissioners to negotiate on these terms suggested that the peace talks would soon rupture, and perhaps in anticipation of that development Madison included in the correspondence he released a lengthy justification of the administration's conduct since it had accepted the Russian offer of mediation in 1813. As he had done in the past, Madison stressed the willingness of the administration to negotiate for peace, while contrasting it with the hostility which governed the British refusal to reciprocate.[145] Within the week, on October 17, Monroe followed up the President's messages with his own proposals to improve and increase the military establishment. Like Madison, he alluded to the presumed object of the British government "to diminish the importance, if not to destroy the political existence, of the United States," and he emphasized the need for "firm and vigorous" resistance to end the war once and for all.[146]

Monroe's plans mentioned no radical changes in the organization of the army, but they did recommend that the ranks be filled and that a special force of 40,000 be created for defensive purposes. Since these two requests would require the War Department to mobilize in 1815 a further 70,000 men in addition to those already enlisted, the Secretary of War concentrated on explaining how this could be accomplished. He submitted to the Senate military affairs committee four different plans, making it clear as he did so that the administration regarded the first as the most "efficient." This plan departed significantly from the existing methods of recruitment; in it Monroe proposed to conscript an army by classifying the free male population between eighteen and forty-five years of age into groups of 100, compelling each group to furnish four men for service within thirty days. If a class failed to provide

---

[145] For the documents released see *ASP: Foreign Relations*, III, 695-703. See also *Daily Natl Intelligencer*, October 12, 1814; and Monroe to the American Commissioners, October 19, 1814, Adams Family Papers, MHS. Madison no longer expected that Russia could mediate in the war, but he retained some hope that Alexander I might lead European neutral nations in an attempt to restrain British maritime pretensions. The President later admitted that his motive for instructing Dallas to draw up his *Exposition on the Causes and Character of the . . . War* was to appeal to the "neutral public" (of Europe) in the event of the failure of the Ghent negotiations. See Madison to Jefferson, March 12, 1815, Madison Papers, LC.

[146] Monroe to Giles, October 17, 1814, *ASP: Military Affairs*, I, 514.

the men, they were to be raised by a draft on the whole class, and the bounties paid to these recruits charged against the taxable property of "all the inhabitants within the precinct of the class." The men thus raised were to be embodied into the existing regiments, there to mix and train with more experienced troops. "Courage in an army," Monroe declared, was, "in a great measure, mechanical," and within a few months it would be "difficult to distinguish between the new and the old levies."[147]

The second plan proposed an alternative method of classification by dividing the militias of the various states into three groups according to age—eighteen to twenty-five years, twenty-five to thirty-two years, and thirty-two to forty-five years. The President was to be given the power to call any portion of the troops from these classes into service and to detain them for up to two years. This plan was not dissimilar to militia reform schemes unsuccessfully advocated by Jefferson and Madison before the war. Had it been adopted in the circumstances of 1814, it would have required the War Department to abandon any attempt to recruit a regular army, since the classes created would have absorbed all the men potentially available for enlistment. Hence Monroe's warning that if this plan were accepted by Congress, it followed "that . . . the militia must be relied on principally, if not altogether, in the further prosecution of the war." It was for this reason, too, that Monroe insisted the militia be held in service for two years—to maintain the semblance of a trained, disciplined force rather than continually drafting bodies of "raw and inexperienced" men.[148]

The third plan reversed the methods proposed in the second. Monroe offered exemption from militia service to every five men who could provide one to serve for the war. He disliked this method, however, because he suspected it would hamper other ways of enlisting men into the regular army. Throughout the war many men had hung back from volunteering or enlisting, preferring to wait for a militia draft which would enable them to earn more money by selling themselves as substitutes for those wishing to avoid service. If Congress were to pass a law placing a premium on men exempting themselves from service, Monroe warned, the sums the wealthy might offer to substitutes could rise to the point where all forms of service other than militia would cease to be attractive. The fourth plan, presented on the assumption that Congress might reject all the others, was to continue the existing policy of enlisting men voluntarily in the regular army.

[147] Ibid., 514-516.
[148] Ibid., 516.

Should Congress choose this method, Monroe suggested that the land bounty, though not the money bounty, offered to recruits be increased.[149]

The response of Congress to these messages was not what Madison and Monroe had hoped for. The release of the diplomatic documents, intended to unify both Federalists and Republicans in a national effort to resist the enemy, failed to alter existing attitudes.[150] Alexander C. Hanson of Maryland, on October 13, did declare the Federalists would support the war now that the fate of the nation was at stake, but he was promptly repudiated by most of his fellow partisans.[151] Possibly the Federalists would have followed Hanson's lead had the administration renounced its intention to attack Canada, but Monroe had not only declared that the Canadian war was necessary to relieve enemy pressure on the Atlantic coast but also openly justified his military plans with the claim that they would enable him "to expel British forces from this continent" altogether. He had, in fact, already discussed with Winfield Scott the prospects for organizing some 50,000 to 60,000 troops to "carry the war to the walls of Quebec by the first of November 1815 and perhaps [dictating] a peace within that fortress."[152] Republicans usually did not require much convincing that the war had to be continued, but they now dreaded the measures they might be called on to vote for and questioned if radical changes in policy were really necessary. Even the most enthusiastic Republican supporters of the war were unhappy about policies which deranged the militia systems, and one of their number, William Lowndes of South Carolina, in dismissing all Monroe's plans as too "incongruous" to be useful, even wondered if the enemy's peace demands at Ghent were nothing but a game of bluff that need not be taken seriously.[153]

Monroe had reason to believe that the House would consider his plans favorably, but the Senate was far more hostile.[154] On October

[149] Ibid., 516-517.

[150] See William Lowndes to Elizabeth Lowndes, October 9 and 16, 1814, William Lowndes Papers, UNC; Desha to Isaac Shelby, October 12, 1814, Draper Manuscript Collection, 5 X 53, SHSW; Samuel Sherwood to Amasa Parker, October 26, 1814, J. D. Crocker, ed., *Letters and Journals of Samuel and Laura Sherwood* (Delhi, N.Y., 1967), 7.

[151] Samuel Dana to William Walker, October 13, 1814, Walker-Rockwell Family Papers, NYHS.

[152] Scott to Van Buren, October 22, 1814, Van Buren Papers, LC.

[153] David Campbell to J. G. Jackson, October 12, 1814 Campbell Family Papers, Duke University Library; Lowndes to Thomas Pinckney, October 20, 1814, Lowndes Papers, UNC.

[154] See George Troup to Monroe, October 19, 1814, LRUS; Nathaniel Macon to Nicholson, October 28, 1814, Nicholson Papers, LC.

19, Giles whose estimation of Monroe's abilities had never been high, requested an explanation of the defects in the existing recruiting laws, asking what plans the War Department had for remedying these. He also demanded to be given full details of the scheme to raise 40,000 troops for the defense of nation.[155] Monroe was taken aback by such disregard for his plans, and anxiety may have led him to date incorrectly his reply to Giles, in which he sought an interview with the Senate military affairs committee to explain his policies in person. With considerable relish, Giles then informed the Secretary that he appeared to be incapable of doing his correspondence correctly, while Senator German of New York persuaded the military affairs committee to consider an alternative scheme of militia classification. German's plan proposed dividing the militia into classes of ten, with each class to provide one man for service for one year. The adoption of this plan would have completely frustrated Monroe's goals, since it would have required all men raised in this way to serve in a local defense corps.[156] Suspecting that the Senate was going to be intolerably perverse, Monroe hastily arranged a joint meeting between the military affairs committees of both House and Senate for October 22, hoping no doubt to obtain a more sympathetic audience.[157]

This joint meeting appears to have gone badly for Monroe. The Senate committee ignored most of the War Department's proposals, discussing instead German's scheme, and Giles seemed to be interested only in remedying defects in the existing recruiting laws.[158] The House military affairs committee, on the other hand, agreed to report Monroe's plans to the floor on October 27, but debate on them was postponed while some tax and loan bills passed to a third reading.[159] The reaction of Congressmen against Monroe's plans in the interval, however, was considerable, because when the War Department report was reconsidered in the House on November 2, military committee chairman George Troup of Georgia replaced it with a bill which merely authorized the President to accept volunteers for up to nine months. There was only one objection to this summary dismissal of Monroe's plans, and Troup declared rather vaguely that the War Department's two main proposals, classification and the raising of defense forces,

---

[155] Giles to Monroe, October 19, 1814, LRRS.

[156] Monroe to Giles, October 21, 1814, RCSW. The letter should have been dated October 20—see Giles to Monroe, October 21, 1814, LRRS. See also AC, 13th Cong., 3d sess., 30.

[157] Monroe to Giles and Troup, October 21, 1814, RCSW.

[158] AC, 13th Cong., 3d sess., 32; Giles to Monroe, October 24, 1814, LRRS.

[159] AC, 13th Cong., 3d sess., 34-36, 482-484.

would have to be postponed while alternatives were being considered. Troup then amended his own bill to allow the President to call for volunteers for twelve months service and reported it again to a committee of the whole. The House began debating Troup's proposal on November 5 but two days later laid the bill aside to turn its attention again to financial legislation.[160]

At this point, the administration supporters in the Senate intervened, seeking a compromise position between the demands of the War Department and the formidable opposition that they were arousing in Congress. On November 1, Senator William Bibb of Georgia, who was also on the Senate military affairs committee, wrote to Monroe proposing three measures which, while ignoring Monroe's call for "efficient" conscription schemes, went some of the way toward implementing the less sweeping ideas that the Secretary had mentioned. For the regular army, Bibb suggested few changes in the recruiting laws beyond legalizing the enlistment of all adult males between eighteen and fifty years of age, repealing the law requiring the consent of parents and guardians for the recruiting of minors, and doubling the land bounty for military service to 320 acres. For the militia, he advocated that the President be authorized both to call on the states for quotas of 100,000 militia to serve for two years, and to accept any other forces organized by the states for the same period of service. To induce militiamen to enter the regular army, however, Bibb—on the assumption that the quotas totaling 100,000 represented approximately one-tenth of the combined militia forces of the states—suggested exempting classes of militiamen from national service in the quotas in proportion to the extent to which they furnished volunteers for the army. Regardless of how militiamen responded to these schemes, Bibb believed that the administration would be able to use them to raise larger numbers of men than before, either as militia in national service or as regulars.[161]

Monroe did not respond positively to any of Bibb's suggestions, and it seems unlikely that he thought they would do much good. However, the Secretary of War did not actively oppose Bibb's proposals either, and he retired to his plantation in Virginia for the next few weeks, leaving Congress free to adopt whatever military policies it chose. Bills embodying the essence of Bibb's ideas for both the regular army and the militia, with a change in the bill for the latter where the total militia force was reduced to 80,000, were introduced in the Senate on No-

[160] Ibid., 518-520.
[161] William Bibb to Monroe, November 1, 1814, LRRS.

vember 5, and the former bill passed easily within the week.[162] The militia bill, though, caused some contention. A motion by Senator Joseph Anderson of Tennessee, who privately believed that the War Department now needed a permanent army, to strike out the requirement of national militia service for two years was defeated by only one vote.[163] This and subsequent amendments to frustrate the purpose of the bill attracted support not only from Federalists and Republican "malcontents" but also from four other Republicans who usually supported the administration. The New England Republicans, particularly Joseph Varnum of Massachusetts, were incensed by the bill, partly because it disrupted the state militias and threatened to work undue hardship on the "respectable and useful" classes of farmers, laborers, and mechanics, and partly because they feared that an objectionable militia law would present the Federalists of New England with a pretext for continuing their opposition to the war, possibly even to the point of secession.[164] And the Federalists were indeed outraged by the militia bill. Mason of New Hampshire denounced it as the product of a "weak, violent, and wicked" administration, bent on destroying the ties of family and community in order to establish an American despotism. Monroe's "pompous" plan to conquer Canada, however, he simply mocked as "bold counsels" from men who had fled "in dismay and disgrace from their own capital." Nonetheless, the bill passed the Senate on November 22 and was sent to the House.[165]

Before the House began to consider the Senate's military legislation, Madison, on December 1, sent Congress another collection of documents relating to the peace negotiations at Ghent. These included Monroe's instructions to the commissioners, which thus made public the fact that the administration had abandoned all its previous conditions for the restoration of peace, including the renunciation of impressment by Britain. The dispatches from the commissioners showed that Britain was still unwilling to make peace on the basis of the status quo ante bellum, but they also recorded that the enemy had receded

[162] AC, 13th Cong., 3d sess., 45-47.

[163] Anderson to Campbell, November 1, 1814, Campbell Family Papers, Duke University Library. Anderson also disliked classification schemes because they bore unequally on the citizenry. See Anderson to Campbell, November 23, 1814, Campbell Papers, LC.

[164] AC, 13th Cong., 3d sess., 46-47. Varnum to Eustis, November 14, 1814, Eustis Papers, LC. For the fear that the Federalists might use the classification bill as a pretext for secession see James Pleasants to Joseph Carrington Cabell, December 10, 1814, Joseph Carrington Cabell Papers, UVa.; and Zebulon Shipherd to Charles Webster, December 12, 1814, Historical Magazine 2d Ser., 8 (1870), 113.

[165] AC, 13th Cong., 3d sess., 58, 91, 93, 94, 95, 102, 103, 109. See also Morris Miller to Jacobus Bruyn, November 30, 1814, Miscellaneous Papers, NYHS.

considerably from the claims made at the beginning of the negotiations. In fact, only the problem of making peace on the basis of the *uti possidetis* now seemed to divide the two nations, but the *National Intelligencer* still insisted that there was no chance of ending the war in the immediate future.[166] Most Republicans, however, thought otherwise, so much so that chairman Troup of the House military affairs committee feared that his colleagues would be induced by a premature sense of optimism "to relax the preparations necessary for a vigorous prosecution of the war."[167]

Against this background, Troup reported the Senate bills to the House on December 2, declaring as he did so that he disliked them both, since they would not enable the administration to raise a regular army for the invasion of Canada. The bill to fill the ranks of the regular army passed by a straight party vote on December 6, while the militia bill, as it had in the Senate, caused divisions in the Republican party over the course of a six-day debate.[168] Right at the outset of this debate, Eppes—who may have taken a hint from Monroe that the cost of implementing the bill might be considerable and who possibly feared that this would strengthen Dallas's case for a national bank—tried to emasculate it by reducing the period of service required from two years to one.[169] This motion passed, Joseph Gales reported, by about twenty votes, but it did not make the bill any more acceptable, and it seems likely that most Republicans were reluctant to support any measure they felt might be too unpopular. The debates revealed that few Republicans, in fact, approved of allowing the administration to call on the militia for any lengthy period, and they could oppose the bill either because it was too weak to be effective or because it was too drastic to be tolerated. Yet because the Federalists vehemently attacked the bill and constantly moved amendments to undermine it, the Republicans were reminded that the onus lay on them to produce some piece of military legislation for the coming year, even if only to defend the nation against future enemy offensives. Probably for this reason, most of the amendments to the bill were defeated by straight party votes

[166] AC, 13th Cong., 3d sess., 113. For the documents see *ASP: Foreign Relations*, III 703-707; and *Daily Natl Intelligencer*, December 2, 1814.

[167] For Troup's remarks see AC, 13th Cong., 3d sess., 706. See also Monroe to Jefferson, November 30, 1814, Jefferson Papers, LC; Lowndes to Elizabeth Lowndes, November 30, 1814, Lowndes Papers, UNC; John Lovett to Solomon Van Rensselaer, December 1, 1814, Simon Gratz Autograph Collection, HSP; Lewis Condit to Samuel Southard, December 4, 1814, Samuel Southard Papers, Princeton University Library; and Hugh Nelson to Charles Everett, December 2, 1814, Nelson Papers, LC.

[168] AC, 13th Cong., 3d sess., 705-710.

[169] See Monroe to Eppes, December 6, 1814, RCSW.

until the measure was finally passed on December 14, and only then did a dozen or so Republicans feel that it was safe to desert the majority.[170]

The militia bill then went to a conference committee on December 24, which duly produced the inevitable compromise of an eighteen-month term of service, although the conferees, it would seem, did not expect this to make the measure more acceptable to either branch of the legislature.[171] Neither the House nor the Senate would recede from the versions of the bill they had originally passed, and, once this was apparent, Senator Rufus King of New York succeeded on December 28 in having it postponed until March 1815. Here the Senate Federalists were joined by five Republicans who had consistently opposed the measure, while seven of its former supporters, by accident it would seem, abstained.[172] This development promised to kill what was left of Monroe's hopes of carrying the war into Canada in 1815, while it also left the nation inadequately defended against a British invasion. Monroe therefore was compelled to try again, and, in anticipation of the final defeat of the militia bill, he had already written on December 20 to the military affairs committees of both House and Senate to ask them if they thought that Bibb's remaining proposal, not yet considered, to authorize the President to call on troops organized by the states was any more acceptable.[173] Opponents of the administration had earlier predicted that it would be reduced to this necessity, and by December 1814 some eight states, with New York in the fore, had already begun to create special state forces for defense. Monroe still had no expectation that the regular army could be filled by voluntary enlistments, and he began to think of ways in which administration goals might be realized through the agency of these state armies.[174]

There were, nonetheless, problems with this approach. The state governments raising the troops would have to be in sympathy with

[170] AC, 13th Cong., 3d sess., 720-749, 772-830, 834-870, 876-897, 901, 904-929.

[171] See Jeremiah Morrow to Worthington, December 24, 1814, Worthington Papers, OSL.

[172] AC, 13th Cong., 3d sess., 135-141, 972-975, 992-993. Although the bill was unpopular, even among Republicans, King's success in postponing it was fortuitous. According to Daniel Webster, King simply decided to put the motion for postponement when "some members happened to be out," and "it was immediately . . . carried." To Ezekiel Webster, January 9, 1815, Wiltse, *Webster Papers*, I, 180.

[173] Monroe to Giles and Troup, December 20, 1814, RCSW.

[174] The states were New York, Maryland, Virginia, South Carolina, Kentucky, New Jersey, Pennsylvania, and Vermont. See also Webster's remark that "the people must look for protection to the *State Govts.* This Govt cannot aid them—or will not—or both." To Ezekiel Webster, December 22, 1814, Wiltse, *Webster Papers*, I, 178.

the aims of the administration and allow their forces to be employed for these purposes. The government of New York had already indicated its willingness to cooperate with the War Department during the passage in October 1814 of a bill to raise 20,000 state troops, but the New England states had already shown how easy it was for a resourceful governor to thwart the administration by exploiting differences and technicalities in conflicting state and federal laws.[175] More serious, though, was the fact that raising special state armies, as distinct from maintaining state militias, violated the spirit if not the letter of the Constitution, and it might also tempt state governments to use the weakness of the administration for their own ends. Indeed, this disposition already existed in many states, and it was further encouraged by the failure of Congress to pass any financial or military legislation for the coming year. Whenever state legislatures considered raising special wartime corps, it was generally assumed that the states could specify their terms of service while holding the Treasury liable for their costs, and the governments of Virginia and Ohio at the same time were even trying to persuade the Treasury to allow them to collect and deduct federal taxes against their existing claims on the United States.[176] That this development, in the words of the recently elected governor of Virginia, Wilson Cary Nicholas, threatened to bring the Republic "back to the disjointed state from which it was fondly hoped that the federal constitution had rescued us" was not lost on the states or the administration.[177] Its influence could be seen in the resolutions of the Hartford Convention as well, and the administration proved here to be no more sympathetic to the demands of its Republican supporters than it was to those of its Federalist opponents. Dallas deplored and rejected the initiatives of Ohio and Virginia, declaring they would "disorganize" the Treasury, reduce the fiscal powers of the federal government to an "idle ceremony," and effectively dissolve the Union.[178]

However, after the failure of Bibb's militia bill, there was no choice for the administration and its supporters but to try to proceed within these limitations, unsatisfactory though they were. Accordingly, on January 7, Bibb amended a Senate bill authorizing the President to

[175] For the New York bill see Fitzpatrick, ed., *Autobiography of Martin Van Buren*, 55-57.

[176] See John Brockenborough to Monroe, January 8, 9, and 10, 1815, Monroe Papers, NYPL; and the resolution of the Ohio Legislature, December 28, 1814, Governors' Papers, OHS. See also the Treasury memo on South Carolina loans, November 7, 1814, LRRS.

[177] Nicholas to Monroe, December 24, 1814, LRRS.

[178] Dallas to Monroe, January 14, 1815, LRRS; Dallas to Worthington, January 17, 1814, LRRS; and Monroe to McArthur, February 1, 1815, LSMA. For the Hartford Convention see below, Chapter XI.

call on the services of volunteers to include the acceptance of "state troops" as well, and Congress considered the measure during the second and third weeks of January. The *National Intelligencer* endorsed the bill on January 13, claiming it would provide troops both for local defense and for the invasion of Canada, but the house and Senate disagreed seriously over its provisions. The Senate wished to enable the President to call up to 70,000 state troops at his discretion, but the House wanted to limit the number to 40,000 as well as to include them in whatever quotas of the state militia the administration might want to mobilize for national service. After a conference committee on January 20 had failed to resolve these disagreements, the House simply insisted on its bill, and the measure of its victory could be seen in the version Madison finally signed on January 27. The number of state troops the President could call on for twelve months service was set at 40,000, and none could be employed outside their home state or an adjoining state without the consent of the governor of the state that had raised them. These terms reflected a deeply held suspicion that was occasionally articulated in Congress: that the War Department, in its present difficulties, was not to be entrusted with powers enabling it to "derange" the militias for its own purposes, and the conditions imposed by Congress, in effect, amounted to a rejection of the idea that a Canadian campaign was the best way of continuing the war. Should the administration, however, require additional troops for an invasion of Canada, the War Department, under the terms of the law signed on January 27, could obtain them only by accepting the services of privately organized volunteer companies, and these too were not to exceed 40,000 officers and men from all states.[179]

Monroe immediately sent copies of this bill to the state governors and began to plan his strategy within its restrictions.[180] Under the terms of the act, it was unlikely that the War Department would be offered a large enough number of state troops to assist the regular army in an invasion of Canada. The Federalist-controlled states of New England could be expected to do little more than provide forces for their own defense, and this would place the burden of offensive operations on the state troops of Vermont and New York, whose combined quotas were set by the act at a total of 7,251 men. For this reason, Monroe had to rely on the success of schemes to raise private volunteer companies, and he began writing to Republican leaders in

[179] AC, 13th Cong., 3d sess., 162, 166, 173, 177, 179, 1042, 1047, 1084, 1086, 1102-1103. The act was repealed on February 27, 1815.

[180] See Monroe's circular letter, February 1, 1815, LSMA. Also Monroe to Dearborn, January 31, 1815; Monroe to Swartwout, January 31, 1815, CULS.

New England and New York to encourage them to make "patriotic exertions" on behalf of the war. To broaden support for the war in these regions, Monroe realized that a greater effort would have to be made to win Federalist cooperation, and he urged Republican leaders to sound out for service "any meritorious, honorable men, who, jealous of the rights and honor of their country [were] willing to vindicate them in the present controversy."[181] The Secretary of War assumed that his willingness to commission Federalists as volunteer officers would be met by reciprocal offers of service, despite the fact that there had been little evidence to date to support such a belief. The need to win more support for the war in the northern states also dictated the choice of the army commander. Izard had resigned his commission in December 1814, and Monroe, very probably, had been thinking of advancing his fellow Virginian Winfield Scott as commander of all the northern forces, but, as Izard pointed out in his resignation, prudence suggested that Jacob Brown of New York would have to be the man. Brown had the advantages both of residence in a critically important state and extensive experience with regular and volunteer forces.[182]

Brown had been visiting Washington during January 1815, and he had several meetings with Monroe to discuss problems of strategy for the coming year. Despite some initial mutual distrust, the general and the Secretary soon found they were agreed on the broad outlines of the next campaign. After his recent indecisive efforts on the Niagara Peninsula, Brown, too, had become convinced of the need to invade Canada at some point east of Lake Ontario to break out of what Monroe described as the "lingering," "fish-pond" war of the past two years.[183] That point of entry was not specified, but Monroe told Brown it would be either at the head of Lake Champlain or somewhere between Kingston and Montreal.[184] The preliminary disposition of the troops in New York at Lake Champlain, Sacketts Harbor, and Greenbush would, in the meantime, create doubts for the British about the final American course of action, but ultimately Monroe envisaged about 15,000 regulars, aided by some 40,000 volunteers, carrying "the war into Canada and [breaking] the British power there to the utmost practicable ex-

[181] Monroe to the governors of Vermont and New York, February 4, 1815; to William King, February 5, 1815, CULS. See also Monroe to Dearborn, January 31, 1815, CULS.
[182] Izard to Monroe, November 20, 1814, Monroe Papers, LC; same to same, December 18, 1814, LRRS.
[183] See Monroe to John Holmes, April 3, 1815, Monroe Papers, NYPL.
[184] Monroe to Brown, February 10, 1815, CULS. For further discussion see C. P. Stacey, "An American Plan for a Canadian Campaign," *American Historical Review* 46 (1941), 348-356.

tent." Ideally, Monroe wanted to defeat an enemy army in the field near Montreal, then drive its remnants into Quebec. Throughout these operations, Brown was instructed to work in close cooperation with the governors and leading Republicans of New York and New England, and, while en route to the north, he was also ordered to sound out the governor of Pennsylvania about the possibility of his raising volunteer troops as well.[185]

This campaign plan was never carried out. News of the Treaty of Ghent ending the war reached Washington on February 13 and 14, and Monroe ordered all American army commanders to cease hostilities on February 16.[186] Whether the outlines of the campaign plan devised for Brown could ever have been implemented successfully is, at best, uncertain. It is not at all clear how far the invasion of Canada, as Monroe assumed, would have prevented the Royal Navy from attacking the Atlantic coast of the United States, while Monroe's offensive, in turn, depended for its success far more on the cooperation of state political leaders than it did on the efforts of the War Department. Moreover, Monroe's plans may have underestimated the capabilities of the British army in Canada, and the decision to bypass the enemy forces on Lake Ontario might still have compelled the government of New York to commit more state troops and volunteers to the defense of the lakeshore and the Niagara Peninsula than the Secretary might have liked. The hope of reaching Quebec by November 1815 was perhaps a little too optimistic, and it may have been as well for Monroe's reputation that the attempt was never made. Had it succeeded, of course, Monroe's stature would have been far greater than it ever became, but, had it failed, he probably would not have followed Madison as President in 1817.

[185] See Monroe to Snyder, February 10, 1815, CULS.
[186] Monroe to all District Commanders, February 16, 1815, LSMA.

468

CHAPTER XI

★

THE FINAL CRISES:
HARTFORD AND NEW ORLEANS

THE SERIES of British offensives against the United States in the summer of 1814 exacerbated one of the administration's recurrent problems: that of widespread Federalist opposition to the war throughout
New England. That opposition had always been strong, but the degree
of outright Federalist obstruction had fluctuated according to circumstances. Federalist outrage in Massachusetts at the declaration of war
in 1812 had fueled a brief, but abortive, drive for a convention of New
England states to redress, at least, the region's longstanding grievances
against Republican policies, if not to prepare the way for eventual
secession from the Union. Little more was heard of the convention
scheme in 1813 until the embargo of December of that year led the
hard-pressed yeomanry of the Connecticut Valley to urge Federalist
leaders to provide immediate relief for their problems. As in 1809, this
popular pressure was satisfied by the repeal of the embargo in April
1814, an administration retreat that was quickly followed by the fall
of Napoleon and the Allied liberation of France. The Federalists enthusiastically celebrated these developments as preludes to a general
peace, only to find that Britain, in intensifying the war against the
United States, carried it for the first time to New England. The Royal
Navy extended its blockade along the northeastern coastline, while
combined army and navy forces quickly and easily seized Eastport and
Castine, thereby allowing the British to occupy the District of Maine
as far south as the Penobscot River.[1]

These last developments caused hardship and provoked fears that
the British would eventually extend southward their occupation of
American territory, and the inhabitants of the coastal towns, especially

[1] See Samuel E. Morison, *The Life and Letters of Harrison Gray Otis, Federalist, 1765-
1848* (Boston, 1913), II, 52-92; James M. Banner, Jr., *To the Hartford Convention: The
Federalists and the Origins of Party Politics in Massachusetts, 1789-1815* (New York, 1970),
306-322.

Boston, felt vulnerable against a sudden attack from Halifax.[2] Vice President Gerry, fully expecting an attack on Boston, hastily arranged for the evacuation of his family.[3] Unlike their counterparts throughout the nation, the Federalist governors of the New England states had not extensively mobilized their militias, nor had they attempted very energetically to strengthen local defenses, relying instead on the forbearance of the enemy while they disputed with the administration the justice of the war. The recent turn of events, however, seemed to require an end once and for all to the prolonged constitutional debate between Washington and the northern state capitals over who was to arm, control, and pay for the militia. Indeed, the New England governors now expected the War Department to come to their rescue.[4]

The administration, having written off the New England states after 1812 as virtual noncombatants, may have derived some satisfaction from the sudden interest of many Federalists in the needs of national defense. It had not feared talk of secession from New England, since the balance of parties in the region was still very close, nor was it greatly concerned to defend Boston or other port towns, as Monroe believed that the British would be much more likely to attack New York City than to advance into New England.[5] Yet the administration was concerned that the enemy had seized part of the District of Maine. That area was one of the principal strongholds of Republican strength in New England, and the failure to expel the enemy there threatened to undermine the morale of the supporters of the administration; as it was, the inability of the settlers to resist the British attack and the ease with which the occupying forces exacted oaths of loyalty to George III was depressing enough.[6] Moreover, the occupation of Castine had greatly enhanced the ability of the British authorities in Canada to trade illegally with Americans along the border. Smuggling, by late

[2] Anna Gerry to Elbridge Gerry, October 24, 1814, Elbridge Gerry Papers, MHS; [William Bentley.] *The Diary of William Bentley* (Salem, Mass., 1905-1914), IV, 281, entry for September 3, 1814. See also the petition of the citizens of Nantucket to Vice Admiral Sir Alexander Cochrane, July 22, 1814, Charter Collection, Ch 946, NLS.

[3] Gerry to R. Cutler, September 23, 1814, Gerry Papers, MHS.

[4] Dearborn to Madison, September 6, 1814, James Madison Papers, LC; Caleb Strong to Monroe, September 7, 1814, LRRS; William Jones to Monroe, September 8 and 28, 1814, LRRS; Dearborn to Monroe, October 9, 1814, LRRS. See also Monroe to Jones and Strong, September 17, 1814, LSMA.

[5] See *Daily Natl Intelligencer*, April 17, 1813.

[6] See Edward Griffith to Cochrane, September 9, 1814; and the copy of the capitulation of U.S. forces in Washington County, Maine, September 13, 1814, both in the Cochrane Papers, folio 2335, NLS. Also George Ulmer to William King, September 13, 1814, William King Papers, MeHS; and Barry J. Lohnes, "A New Look at the Invasion of Eastern Maine, 1814," *Maine Historical Society Quarterly* 15 (1975), 5-29.

1814, was reported to have reached scandalous heights; the trade in livestock alone provisioned the British army, while the failure of customs and army officers to stem the traffic both undermined respect for American authority and drained the nation's specie supply northward, thus weakening the banking system.[7] Finally, enemy possession of American soil gave the British negotiators at Ghent a considerable advantage over their American counterparts; the British government could, at the very least, try to insist on a peace which would incorporate its gains into Canada or exact a concession for their return. Either result would humiliate the administration, and expose the weakness and the folly of its policies. As Richard Rush lamented to John Adams: "If New England would only *threaten* to invade Canada and make some bustle, it will go far towards altering the tone of Britain and scaring her into a peace."[8]

If, however, the administration felt that the British occupation of Maine would strengthen its hand with recalcitrant Federalist governors, the illusion was short-lived. The presence of the enemy in New England, far from stiffening their will to resist, only heightened the Federalists' desire for peace and furnished another opportunity for the calling of a New England convention for the redress of sectional grievances.[9] Interest in a convention, seemingly stilled in June, was quickly revived, and by October had been overwhelmingly endorsed by the Massachusetts General Court. On October 18 that body agreed to issue a call for a convention of the New England states to be held at Hartford, Connecticut, and decided to elect delegates for it.[10] The report accompanying this call for the convention did not mention the possibility of secession, but it did proclaim that the New England states should take the first step toward "a radical reform in the national compact." The goal of many of the leaders of Massachusetts Federalism had long been to obtain constitutional reform to prevent a recurrence of their present grievances, but they realized this could not be achieved

[7] C. P. Van Ness to William Cummings, July 29 and August 6, 1814, LRAG; King to Dearborn, July 26, 1814, Henry Dearborn Papers, MHS, and same to same, October 6, 1814, King Papers, MeHS. Also Dearborn to Monroe, November 10, 1814, LRRS; John Chandler to Monroe, November 21, 1814, LRRS; and James Byers to Daniel Parker, November 5, 1814, LRRS. Also Samuel Dana to Monroe, November 30, 1814, LRUS; and William Eustis to Richard Rush, December 10, 1814, Rush Family Papers, Princeton University Library.

[8] Rush to John Adams, October 23, 1814, in John H. Powell, ed., "Some Unpublished Correspondence of John Adams and Richard Rush, 1811-1822," *Pennsylvania Magazine of History and Biography* 61 (1937), 138.

[9] Mark S. Hill to King, October 7, 1814, King Papers, MeHS.

[10] *Boston Patriot*, October 19, 1814. See also Morison, *Otis*, II, 104.

immediately; instead, they approached their aims piecemeal by calling a convention to deal with the urgently pressing issues of the war, notably local defense and the control of tax monies to pay for it. Only secondarily would the convention deal with the larger grievances of New England, such as embargoes, slave representation, and the admission of new states.[11]

Most Republicans, though, were not inclined to accept at face value these professions of Federalist interest in mere constitutional reform. In their eyes, the calling of the Hartford Convention was not simply another act in opposition to the war but an event fraught with uncertainty, since there could be no knowing how far the Federalist leaders—who were assumed to be desperate men aching for power—would go. From resisting the war it seemed only a short step to neutrality, then to making a separate peace with the enemy, and ultimately to seceding from the Union.[12] From Boston, Major General Henry Dearborn reported that it *was* the purpose of the Federalist leaders to create a separate northern confederacy, though he admitted that some Federalists doubted whether they had the strength to go so far.[13] When Madison received the news that the Hartford Convention would meet, William Wirt reported him to be "miserably shattered and woe-begone." The New England "sedition," Wirt added, preoccupied him constantly, and his "heart and mind were painfully full of the subject."[14] The President's anxiety, no doubt, would have been all the greater had he known that, while the arrangements for the Hartford Convention were advancing, Governor Caleb Strong of Massachusetts had

[11] The resolutions and report of the Massachusetts General Court were printed in (Baltimore) *The Weekly Register*, November 12, 1814. See also Donald R. Hickey, "New England's Defense Problem and the Genesis of the Hartford Convention," *New England Quarterly* 50 (1977), 587-604.

[12] Republicans in the General Court, led by Levi Lincoln and John Holmes, opposed the convention, arguing that "more is designed than is distinctly avowed" and that the real purpose of the meeting was "to prepare the way for a separation and division of the union." See also Francis Gilmer to Peter Minor, November 1814, Gilmer Family Papers, UVa; William Plumer to John Quincy Adams, November 25, 1814, Adams Family Papers, MHS; Wilson Cary Nicholas to Madison, November 11, 1814, Madison Papers, LC; Isaac Shelby to George Walker, December 25, 1814, LRRS; Plumer to Jeremiah Mason, December 29, 1814, William Plumer Papers, LC. For newspaper opinion see (Philadelphia) *Aurora General Advertiser*, November 14 and December 15, 1814; (New York) *National Advocate*, October 14, 21, and 24, December 28, 1814; and (Boston) *Independent Chronicle*, December 12, 1814.

[13] Dearborn to Monroe, October 15, 1814, LRRS. Also Dana to Eustis, November 2, 1814, Eustis Papers, LC.

[14] William Wirt to Mrs. Wirt, October 14, 1814, William Wirt Papers, Maryland Historical Society.

sent an agent to the British commander at Halifax, Sir John Coape Sherbrooke, to sound him out on the chances for a separate peace. And this agent's proposals to the British did not rule out the possibility of secession if Strong and the Massachusetts Federalist leadership could not compel Madison to end the war quickly and to their own satisfaction.[15] Outwardly, though, the administration put on a bold front. The French minister was told that the New England states would not secede, while the *National Intelligencer* warned that Congress, in the event of any attempts at secession, would immediately tax all New England produce in order to encourage the migration of its inhabitants to other parts of the Union.[16]

To deal with the New England sedition, Madison felt that above all he needed accurate information about the Federalists and their intentions. Having briefly visited the region only once, in 1791, the President was unfamiliar with New England society and not very sympathetic to its concerns. He had always assumed that the yeomanry of New England was basically republican in outlook and that its true political sentiments were, to a greater or lesser degree, misrepresented by the Federalists, who claimed to be their natural leaders. By the end of 1814, however, Madison seems to have concluded that this analysis of New England Federalism was inadequate; the Federalist leaders and their ambitions were certainly still a problem, but the President sensed that their hold over the yeomanry, aided and abetted by the preaching of the Congregationalist clergy, was very strong. Indeed, so strong did it seem to Madison that he described the region as suffering from a "delusion" he could only liken to "the reign of witchcraft."[17] The problem of New England then was not simply to guard against the potentially treasonous activities of its malcontent leaders but also to ensure that they did not plunge their society, and the nation as a whole, into civil war.

Madison sought information about New England from the region's Republican leadership of his acquaintance, principally from his kinsman Richard Cutts, from his former cabinet colleagues Eustis and Dearborn, and, above all, from Vice President Gerry. For the first time

[15] Strong may have decided to send the agent at a time when he feared that British forces would shortly attack Boston. See Morison, *Otis*, II, 96-97, and also the documents assembled by J. S. Martell, "A Side Light on Federalist Strategy During the War of 1812," *American Historical Review* 43 (1938), 553-566. See also Griffith to Cochrane, November 30, 1814, Cochrane Papers, folio 2574, NLS.

[16] Sérurier to duc de Talleyrand, November 20, 1814, Archives du Ministère des Affaires Étrangères, Correspondance Politique: États Unis, vol. LXXI (photostats in LC). *Daily Natl Intelligencer*, October 21, November 21, and December 15, 1814.

[17] Madison to Wilson Cary Nicholas, November 25, 1814, Madison Papers, LC.

in his second term, Madison appears to have regularly asked Gerry's advice and, throughout October, held several consultations with him.[18] Gerry was always ready to assume the worst about his Federalist opponents, and he constantly stressed that the safety of the Union required greater organization and vigilance on the part of the New England Republicans. Here his thinking had, in fact, changed little from the schemes he had outlined shortly after the declaration of war in 1812: encourage the local Republicans to organize vigilance committees; arouse the populace with patriotic addresses and appeals; and earmark potential traitors for observation and denunciation. The Vice President also argued for the creation of a special force of up to 15,000 men to drive the British out of the District of Maine. The raising of such a force in New England would also serve to overawe the Hartford Convention by conveying the message that the federal government would be prepared to vindicate its authority forcibly if necessary.[19]

On the need to organize the New England Republicans to prevent rebellion, Madison was at this time receiving similar advice from Mathew Carey and Wilson Cary Nicholas, governor-elect of Virginia. Carey, who was busily gathering material for his pamphlet *The Olive Branch*, wished to appeal to both Federalists and Republicans to ignore their differences in order to preserve the Union against invasion, and he urged the administration to take the lead in organizing vigilance committees rather than rely on local initiative alone.[20] Neither Madison nor the cabinet gave Carey personally the attention and assistance he felt he deserved, but the administration, in fact, accepted his advice and that of Gerry as well. Attorney General Rush approved of the contents of *The Olive Branch*, suggesting that 20,000 copies be distributed in New England, while Madison made a point at dinner parties of asking the Vice President to repeat his thoughts on the problem of New England to members of Congress and the cabinet. Usually the President remarked that he could see no objection to what Gerry was proposing.[21]

By the middle of November 1814, Madison had decided to attempt

---

[18] Gerry to Ann Gerry, October 25, 1814, Gerry Papers, MHS.

[19] Same to same, November 9, 1814, ibid.; Gerry to Madison, November 17, 1814, LRRS. Also see above, Chapter V.

[20] Carey to Madison, November 16, 1814, Madison Papers, LC. On the *Olive Branch*, which ultimately went through ten editions selling more than 10,000 copies, see Edward C. Carter II, "Mathew Carey and 'The Olive Branch,' 1814-1818," *Pennsylvania Magazine of History and Biography* 84 (1965), 399-415.

[21] Rush to Carey, November 17, 1814, Rush Family Papers, Princeton University Library. In the preface to the second edition of the *Olive Branch* Carey complained of the neglect of his schemes by public officials. See also Gerry to Ann Gerry, November 9 and 15, 1814, Gerry Papers, MHS.

the expulsion of the British from Maine. He turned the responsibility for this over to Monroe, who then asked Dearborn to begin raising volunteer troops. But Monroe also intended to challenge the New England governors over the control of the militia, since he ordered Dearborn to call out as well the militia under the 1795 law by issuing commands directly to its officers and thus bypassing the governors. For obvious military reasons, these activities were to be kept as secret as possible, and to finance them Monroe promised Dearborn that he would send him $100,000 in Treasury notes to be used to obtain credit from the local banks. The command of the expedition to recover Maine, however, was to be given not to Dearborn but to a regular army officer, Colonel James Miller.[22]

These orders threw Dearborn into spasms of doubt and confusion. He pointed out, not unreasonably, that the raising of large numbers of men could hardly be kept a secret and that the recruitment of those men might be made easier if the reasons for it were made known. Yet he also doubted if the attempt to expel the British from Castine, a strongly defended position, would succeed. Moreover, he was reluctant to challenge the New England governors again over the militia issue, and he was unable to persuade local banks to issue him credit on the basis of Treasury notes.[23] A few days later, on November 27, he reported that Colonel Miller was too ill to take command of the expedition.[24] After some hesitation, Monroe accordingly decided to transfer the command to William King, a leading Republican in the District of Maine, no doubt hoping that his appointment would stimulate his supporters to volunteer for service.[25] To improve the military capabilities of the force, the Secretary of War also determined to assign to it all the regular troops stationed in the First Military District, and he set the militia component of the force at 6,000 men. For finance and additional support, he finally gambled on informing Governor Strong of the planned expedition, specifically requesting him to get Massachusetts to provide the funds.[26]

[22] Monroe to Dearborn, November 14, 1814, James Monroe Papers, LC; Monroe to Tompkins, November 25, 1814; and Monroe to Strong, December 1, 1814, both in LSMA.

[23] Dearborn to Monroe, November 21, 1814, LRRS.

[24] Same to same, November 27, 1814, LRRS.

[25] Dearborn to King, December 7 and 22, 1814, King Papers, MeHS; Monroe to Dearborn, December 1, 1814, LSMA. Monroe was hesitant about King, partly because he did not know him personally and partly because he suspected the loyalty of a man related to Cyrus King, a strident critic of the war in Congress. Republican Congressmen from Massachusetts, however, assured Monroe that King was the most influential and energetic Republican in Maine. See Dana to Monroe, November 30, 1814, LRUS.

[26] Monroe to Dearborn, December 1, 1814, James Monroe Papers, NYHS; Monroe to Strong, December 1, 1814, LSMA.

In the first week of December, General Dearborn visited Strong to repeat Monroe's requests in person. As the general feared, Strong was cool about the proposals; he too doubted whether the seizure of Castine would be easy, but even more troubling was his apparent lack of concern about whether the British were expelled from Maine or not.[27] And in truth, many Federalists were more interested in finding ways of compelling the administration to make peace than in trying to continue the war. Governor Strong himself may have had a tacit understanding with the enemy that neither side would do anything to expand the war in New England, while the idea that the District of Maine might actually be separated from Old Massachusetts rather than restored to it was by no means new.[28] Many Federalists, who held sizable tracts of land in the district, had long felt that their investments would prosper better under British than under American rule.[29] For some, if not all, of these reasons, Strong refused to provide funds for the expedition, and, after their meeting, Dearborn suspected that he informed the Boston *Centinel* of the administration's plans, since that paper promptly published them for all, including the British, to read.[30]

This sudden publicity for the Castine expedition led to its postponement. Monroe, Dearborn, and King all agreed that to make the attempt and fail would be worse than not trying at all.[31] Dearborn, King, and Miller, however, were ordered to continue raising volunteers, largely to arouse the people, to strengthen the hand of the administration in dealing with the Federalists, and to try to check smuggling with the enemy. The quartermaster general of the northern army, Elisha Jenkins, pointed out to Monroe that something had to be done

[27] Dearborn to Monroe, December 8, 1814; Strong to Monroe, December 9, 1814, both in LRRS. For Strong's reservations about operations against Castine see Samuel E. Morison, "Dissent in the War of 1812," in Morison et al., *Dissent in Three American Wars* (Cambridge, Mass., 1970), 13-14.

[28] See Griffith to Cochrane, November 30, 1814, Cochrane Papers, NLS. Also Ronald F. Banks, *Maine Becomes a State: The Movement to Separate Maine from Massachusetts, 1785-1820* (Middletown, Conn., 1970), passim. For its part, Britain had long been interested in obtaining part of Maine to connect Halifax more directly with Quebec. See J. Leitch Wright, Jr., *Britain and the American Frontier, 1783-1815* (Athens, Ga., 1975), 168.

[29] Samuel Taggart to John Taylor, November 2, 1814, George Haynes, ed., "Letters of Samuel Taggart," in *Proceedings of the American Antiquarian Society* 33 (1923), 431; Matthew Cobb to King, November 24, 1814, King Papers, MeHS; David Cobb to Charles Willing Hare, August 7, 1814, and March 30, 1815, David Cobb Papers, MHS. See also Lohnes, "The Invasion of Eastern Maine," 16-17.

[30] Dearborn to Monroe, December 20, 1814, LRRS.

[31] Dearborn to Monroe, November 19, 1814; King to Monroe, December 27, 1814, both in LRRS. Monroe to Dearborn, December 19, 1814; Monroe to King, January 2, 1815, both in LSMA.

about this last problem, since it had become so serious that it would jeopardize preparations for the 1815 campaign. The United States could hardly invade Canada, he argued, if the northern country had been previously stripped and exhausted of supplies necessary to support the army.[32] Monroe, too, was still anxious to find ways of carrying through the plans for an attack on Castine. As temporary Secretary of State, he was only too well aware that the continuing British occupation of Maine could be a major obstacle in the peace negotiations at Ghent.

With the postponement of the Castine expedition, the problem of the Hartford Convention, due to meet on December 15, became more urgent. Dealing with the convention was also complicated by the fact that both state and city governments in Connecticut were pursuing their own brand of opposition to the war by trying to prevent the army from recruiting and playing martial music within city limits.[33] To be defied by the cities as well as the states of New England was more than the administration could endure. To assert federal authority in both cases, Monroe ordered the 23d and the 25th Infantry regiments into Connecticut for recruiting over the winter.[34] Both these regiments consisted largely of New Englanders who had fought creditably in the last campaign on the Niagara Peninsula. As he did this, Monroe, on November 26, also withdrew part of Izard's army from Plattsburg back to Greenbush in New York. Greenbush was an established army camp, but its location was conveniently close to the western boundaries of both Connecticut and Massachusetts. If the administration should need to intervene in New England or to dissolve the Hartford Convention, the forces were thus near at hand.[35]

To the commander of the 25th Infantry regiment, Colonel Thomas Jessup, Monroe gave special instructions. The Secretary feared that while the Hartford Convention was meeting, the British forces might attack New York on two fronts—one at Buffalo and the other at Long Island.[36] Such an attack could also be part of a prearranged campaign with the New England Federalists, whose part in it would be to raise the standard of rebellion against the United States. Jessup was there-

[32] Monroe to King, December 26, 1814, CULS; Dearborn to King, December 24, 1814, King Papers, MeHS. On the problem of smuggling see Elisha Jenkins to Monroe, December 3, 1814, and Samuel Whitney et al. to Madison, December 8, 1814, both in LRRS.

[33] Joseph Smith to Monroe, December 26, 1814; Thomas Jessup to same, January 21 and 23, 1815, LRRS. For an example of local authorities in Connecticut bringing nuisance charges against U.S. troops to obstruct recruiting see Enoch Perkins to David Daggett, October 12, 1814, LRAG.

[34] Adjutant General to Jessup, December 1, 1814, LSAG.

[35] Monroe to Izard; to Tompkins, November 26, 1814, CULS.

[36] For this possibility see Swift to Monroe, October 12, 1814, LRRS.

fore ordered to observe closely both the activities of the convention and the British fleet presumed to be hovering off Long Island Sound. If he suspected the slightest intention to disrupt or to invade the Union, he was to seize the federal armory at Springfield, Massachusetts, and to call on General Brown and Governor Tompkins of New York for assistance. Should it be necessary to use force, Monroe advised Jessup to employ it, if possible, only against the enemy and not against American citizens. He was also to keep in constant touch with the Republican leaders of New England, both to assure them that the administration would not allow treason to prosper and to protect them against attack.[37]

It is possible too that Monroe wished to rely on more than the threat of force in his dealings with the Hartford Convention. According to Charles Jared Ingersoll, whose recollections cannot now be verified, the Secretary of War gave Jessup oral instructions to inform the convention delegates that the United States intended to drive the British off the North American continent in 1815 and that this strategy could entail a campaign against Nova Scotia to seize the Royal Navy base at Halifax. The idea of a campaign against Nova Scotia at a time when Congress was resisting the approval of laws required to raise men to take Montreal and Quebec seems hopelessly ambitious, but Monroe perhaps intended the mere knowledge that such a move might be attempted to cause headaches for the convention delegates. If they were contemplating secession, they would have to reckon with the possibility that the administration was also considering military activity on a sizable scale in New England in the coming year, not only to regain the District of Maine but also to push on through New Brunswick to Halifax. Alternatively, the prospect of the occupation of Nova Scotia might lead the disaffected Federalists to reconsider the value of the Union.[38] The addition of the British Maritime Provinces to the United States would enhance greatly the economic and political power of New England, the decline of which was a root cause of the meeting of the convention in the first place.[39]

The delegates to the Hartford Convention duly assembled on December 15. Their meeting was universally deplored by Republicans

[37] Monroe to Jessup, November 26, 1814, CULS.

[38] Charles Jared Ingersoll, *Historical Sketch of the Second War between the United States of America and Great Britain* (Philadelphia, 1845), II, 236-237. There is no discussion of a campaign against Nova Scotia in 1815 in any of Monroe's letters at the time, but such a campaign would have been a logical sequel to his hopes to drive the British out of Quebec in 1815. It is also possible that Jessup himself was the advocate of the campaign. See Chester L. Kieffer, *Maligned General: A Biography of Thomas S. Jesup* (San Rafael, Calif., 1979), 45, 328.

[39] On this point see Banner, *To the Hartford Convention*, 12-22.

as an unwarranted challenge to the administration, including those Republicans who had no great liking for Madison. Even John Randolph of Roanoke wrote an open letter to James Lloyd of Massachusetts criticizing the convention as untimely, unwise, and unnecessary.[40] There still existed among Republicans considerable apprehension about the prospects for secession, which was largely the result of their inability to obtain reliable information about the delegates' intentions. From December 15 to January 5 the convention met behind closed doors, and no one, either then or since, ever obtained a complete record of its deliberations.[41] The little information that the administration did receive from those observing the convention, however, was generally encouraging. Jessup's predecessor in Connecticut, Colonel Joseph Smith, for example, reported to the War Department that he doubted whether the convention would attempt "open rebellion"; it would try instead to give "tone, confidence, and *system* to an opposition which shall *continue* its *equivocal* course, possessing *all* the moral qualities of treason and rebellion and at the same time avoiding a liability to their penalties."[42]

Jessup, while en route to Hartford, met with Governor Tompkins in early December and learned that the New Yorker likewise questioned whether the convention would do much more than complain, issue an address to the people, and then go home.[43] The leaders of the Republican party in Connecticut shared this view, informing both Jessup and Monroe that the thin attendance at Hartford—Vermont and New Hampshire were not officially represented at all—was hardly representative of New England opinion as a whole, and that many of the delegates, especially those from Connecticut itself, were not advocates of secession.[44] Connecticut had accepted the call for the convention only with the reservation that its activities would be consistent

[40] *Daily Natl Intelligencer*, December 15, 1814. Randolph's letter to Lloyd, dated December 15, 1814, appeared in (Richmond) *The Enquirer*, December 31, 1814.

[41] Theodore Dwight's *A History of the Hartford Convention: With a Review of the Policy of the United States Government, which led to the War of 1812* (New York, 1833) is a remarkably uninformative source, consisting of lengthy justifications of Federalist opposition to the war, and copies of the report and journal of the convention. The journal is little more than the outline of the formal proceedings of the convention, for which Dwight was the secretary.

[42] Smith to Monroe, December 26, 1814, LRRS. See also Smith to Jessup, December 26, 1814, Thomas Jessup Papers, LC.

[43] Jessup to Monroe, December 31, 1814, LRRS.

[44] For a discussion of Vermont's absence from the convention see Edward Brynn, "Patterns of Dissent: Vermont's Opposition to the War of 1812," *Vermont History* 40 (1972), 24; and for New Hampshire's absence see Lynn W. Turner, *William Plumer of New Hampshire, 1759-1850* (Chapel Hill, 1962), 231.

with the state's obligations as a member "of the national union," and much of the Connecticut debt was invested in lands in New York and Ohio to provide money for the state school fund.[45] Furthermore, it was not difficult for Republican newspaper editors to provide other examples of New England's very considerable dependence on trade and investments with other parts of the Union and to make the point that disunion would cost the states involved far more than it would cost the United States itself.[46] Nonetheless, the Connecticut Republicans urged Monroe to appear to take a very hard line; they wanted the public appointment of a brigadier general, possibly even a "loyal" Federalist, to dissolve the convention, and Congress to pass a law to encourage local Republicans to form committees of "public safety."[47]

Jessup, though, quickly threw himself into his assignment. Because of the War Department's dispute with the city of Hartford over recruiting, he had reason to seek regular meetings with one of the convention delegates, Chauncey Goodrich, who was also the mayor of Hartford. Goodrich never divulged to Jessup the daily proceedings of the convention, but he made it plain there was little enthusiasm in that body for disunion.[48] Jessup, in turn, cultivated that sentiment by flying a British flag at half-mast under an American flag, by ostentatiously parading recruiting parties beating drums through the streets of Hartford, and by taking his officers to balls where they displayed both their uniforms and their recently acquired wounds in Brown's Niagara campaign. The risks of violent rebellion were thus made perfectly explicit.[49] Occasionally, the city and state authorities ventured to protest to Jessup about "this insolence of military power"; the state legislature considered a bill to outlaw the enlistment of minors, while the Hartford town council once waited on him to discuss a regulation limiting recruiting activities on the grounds that the playing of martial music disturbed

[45] For Connecticut's reservations see the reports in *The Weekly Register*, November 19 and 26, 1814.

[46] See particularly Hezekiah Niles's articles in *The Weekly Register*, November 12 and 26, December 3 and 24, 1814, January 21 and 28, 1815. Here Niles drew heavily for statistical material in support of his argument from Carey's *The Olive Branch*. See also *Independent Chronicle*, December 8 and 22, 1814; *Aurora*, November 26, 1814; and John B. Cutting to Eustis, November 20, 1814, Eustis Papers, LC. For a more recent treatment stressing the same points see Robert A. East, "Economic Development and New England Federalism, 1803-1814," *New England Quarterly* 10 (1937), 430-446.

[47] Samuel Huntington to Monroe, December 22, 1814, LRUS: Smith to Monroe, December 26, 1814, LRRS.

[48] Jessup to Monroe, January 21 and 23, 1815, LRRS.

[49] Jessup to Monroe, January 2, 1815, LRRS. See also Ingersoll, *Historical Sketch*, II, 232-233; and Simeon E. Baldwin, "The Hartford Convention," *Papers of the New Haven Colony Historical Society* 9 (1918), 19.

the citizens. Though enraged by their presumption, the colonel actually seems to have been more impressed by the caution, almost bordering on pusillanimity, with which the New Englanders pursued their case.[50] The town council apologetically informed Jessup that their restrictions on recruiting were not aimed at him personally but at one of his predecessors, Colonel Cutting, whose practices had greatly annoyed the citizenry. Jessup bluntly dismissed their appeals, reminding them that he could not enter into any arrangements which compromised the authority of the United States.[51]

Also, according to Ingersoll, Jessup informed Goodrich of the idea of attacking Nova Scotia. The mayor was initially skeptical, pointing out that the administration was inherently incapable of being so generous to New Englanders and that any such conquests were likely to be returned to Britain in a peace treaty. Jessup, however—and with what authority here is uncertain—spoke of the annexation of conquests, and he ultimately seems to have touched Goodrich's "Eastern pride." The vision of an extended coastline, with good harbors, new states, and thus greater political power, must indeed have been appealing to all but the most insular of Federalists, though whether Goodrich ever discussed the question of Nova Scotia with his fellow delegates is unclear, and whether it actually influenced the decisions of the convention is perhaps unlikely. Both Jessup and Ingersoll, however, believed that the scheme had a positive effect on the resolution of the sectional crisis.[52]

For the administration, the most tense period came between the adjournment of the Hartford Convention on January 5 and the publication of its report one week later. Not even Jessup could entirely rule out the possibility that secession might be the result of the convention's deliberations, and he warned Monroe it would have to be crushed immediately. If the rebellious New England states were given time to organize an effective government, he believed they could, by virtue of their large populations and well-equipped militias, successfully "bid defiance" to the Union, seize all the property of the federal government, and perhaps enter into an alliance with Britain. Monroe took the advice to heart. He increased the guard on the Springfield armory and on January 10 authorized New York Republican leaders, including Robert Swartwout and Peter B. Porter, to draw on more

---

[50] Jessup to Monroe, January 31, 1815, LRRS; same to same, February 4, 1815, Jessup Papers, LC.

[51] Jessup to Monroe, April 15, 1815, Jessup Papers, LC; same to same, May 2, 1815, LRRS. See also Kieffer, *Maligned General*, 48, 49.

[52] Ingersoll, *Historical Sketch*, II, 237.

money and volunteers to crush a rebellion or an invasion. All would depend, the Secretary felt, on the report of the convention. If it did not call for disunion, he informed Swartwout, little would happen; if, on the other hand, it threatened violence, force would have to be used. He urged Swartwout to do what he could to organize opposition to the convention within New England, among both Federalists and Republicans.[53] By an odd coincidence, Madison, on November 16, 1814, had also proclaimed January 12, 1815, as a day of national humiliation and fasting, and the President may have hoped that its observance by administration supporters would help neutralize any dangerous actions advocated by their opponents.[54]

After all the fear and all the preparations, the report of the Hartford Convention, released on January 12, was something of an anticlimax. It condemned the administration for failing to defend New England but did no more than recommend that the states negotiate arrangements with the federal government to ensure they could earmark their share of the nation's taxes for their own defense and also raise local forces. Otherwise, the delegates decided to content themselves with yet another recitation of New England's grievances against the rule of Virginia—embargoes, slave representation, expansionism, the admission of new states—and to ask the other states to consider seven constitutional amendments to outlaw these problems in the future. Far from calling for secession, the delegates were, in fact, pleading for a sectional truce in national politics. The convention also adjourned itself indefinitely—which could be taken to mean that the delegates might reassemble later to reconsider their course—but Massachusetts immediately appointed three commissioners to go to Washington to negotiate on the problems of defense and taxation.[55] Yet even this action resulted as much from weakness as it did from any desire to confront the administration; like the federal government, the state of Massachusetts was short of money because the banks would not lend to it either.[56]

---

[53] Jessup to Monroe, December 31, 1814, LRRS. Also Tench Ringgold's "Notes of a Conversation between J. Monroe and R. Swartwout on January 10, 1815," James Monroe Papers, NYPL; and Monroe to Swartwout, January 11, 1815, Robert Swartwout Papers, NYPL.

[54] A resolution calling for a day of humiliation and fasting was introduced in the House by John Clopton of Virginia on October 29, 1814, and had passed both branches of Congress by November 9. See AC, 13th Cong., 3d sess., 35, 40, 500, 513, 516. Madison issued the proclamation one week later. Also see *Daily Natl Intelligencer*, January 11, 1815.

[55] For the text of the report see Dwight, *History of the Hartford Convention*, 352-379.

[56] See Eustis to Madison, undated but written late 1814, Eustis Papers, LC.

Republicans everywhere were audibly relieved.[57] Senator Jeremiah Morrow of Ohio, whose state legislature was pressing for a similar arrangement on taxes and defense, described the Hartford report as "very moderate" and "not at all objectionable."[58] The *National Intelligencer*, while still deploring that the convention had met at all, agreed with Morrow's verdict.[59] Indeed, as the event receded into the past, Monroe came to feel irritated at having spent so much energy in watching over such a pointless event. He continued to keep an eye on the opposition in New England but now felt free to concentrate his attention on problems related to Maine and the invasion of Canada. He wanted to organize the army along the St. Lawrence in readiness for action in the spring of 1815, and, on January 31, he ordered both Dearborn and Swartwout to resume the drive to raise 15,000 volunteers, commanded by both Federalist and Republican officers, to expel the British from Castine.[60] Jessup remained involved in his dispute with the Hartford city council over recruiting, and for a brief period he feared that the New England states might thwart him by raising the legal age of consent for enlistment to twenty-five or thirty years. But Monroe, especially with the news of peace, was not inclined to press the matter, and Jessup quickly came to share the Secretary's attitude. That there were extremists in New England who would have welcomed secession Jessup never doubted, but in retrospect it seemed clear to him that they had controlled neither the Federalist party nor the Hartford Convention. The whole affair had been a piece of bluff to intimidate the administration, and the delegates had been cautious "almost to timidity." "Power," he concluded, "and not revolution was their object," a verdict later echoed by Ingersoll when he graphically dismissed the Hartford Convention as "the abortion of an enigma."[61]

The threat to the integrity of the Republic, if the Hartford Convention could be so described, had passed. The Treaty of Ghent made the Federalist mission to Washington to discuss the defense of Mas-

---

[57] (Pittsfield, Mass.) *The Sun*, January 12, 1815; *National Advocate*, January 12, 1815; *Independent Chronicle*, January 19, 1815.

[58] Morrow to Thomas Worthington, January 12, 1815, Thomas Worthington Papers, OSL.

[59] *Daily Natl Intelligencer*, January 13, 1815.

[60] Monroe to Dearborn and Swartwout, January 31, 1815, CULS.

[61] Jessup to Monroe, January 31, February 1, and May 2, 1815, LRRS; Ingersoll, *Historical Sketch*, II, 216. For more recent scholarship confirming the "moderation" of the Hartford Convention see Morison, *Otis*, II, 110-159; and Banner, *To the Hartford Convention*, 323-350.

sachusetts look both unnecessary and ridiculous, and it supported as well the administration's claim that it had triumphed over the narrow forces of sectionalism and localism. But the episode had revealed, too, that the bonds of union were still far from strong. Over the winter of 1814-1815, the administration had been compelled to make the uncomfortable admission that force alone might be all that could hold the nation together. The New England Republicans, whom Madison had initially regarded as the foundation of the Union in the region, played a comparatively minor, almost ineffectual, part in the crisis. Admittedly they were numerous, and their numbers alone would have posed severe problems of military and political control for the Federalists, even to the point of causing civil war, had secession been seriously attempted.[62] But, as Jessup very quickly realized, the New England Republicans were often timid in spirit, completely without adequate organization above the township or county level, and badly lacking in competent leadership. In fact, it became all too apparent that in the event of a crisis the administration would have to save the local Republicans, and not they save the nation.[63]

Consequently, nowhere in New England did there appear a regional, or even statewide, organized movement to resist Federalist scheming. Instead, there appeared a series of isolated, localized movements where handfuls of Republicans got together to consider the possibility that in response to Federalist secession they should secede from the jurisdictions claimed by their opponents. Only in northwestern Maine did these efforts really come to anything, when, on December 28 in Oxford County, a small Republican convention met to call for the secession of the District of Maine from Old Massachusetts.[64] Local Republican newspapers applauded their actions, but the administration, significantly, did not.[65] There was little point in encouraging the fragmentation of New England, if for no other reason than the fact that the British actually controlled much of the area the Republican leaders wanted to detach from Old Massachusetts. Unfortunately for the

[62] See James M. Banner, Jr., "The Problem of South Carolina," in Stanley Elkins and Eric McKitrick, eds., *The Hofstadter Aegis: A Memorial* (New York, 1974), 85-87.

[63] Jessup to Monroe, December 31, 1814, LRRS. See also Isaac Monroe to King, November 21, 1814, King Papers, MeHS; John Holmes to Monroe, January 28, 1815, Monroe Papers, NYPL.

[64] [Bentley], *Diary of William Bentley*, IV, 297; *Boston Patriot*, November 16 and 23, December 21, 24, and 28, 1814, January 4, 21, and 25, 1815; *The Sun*, January 26, February 2 and 16, 1815. See also Jonathan Hunt to William Walker, January 30, 1815, Walker-Rockwell Family Papers, NYHS; and Banks, *Maine Becomes a State*, 60-66.

[65] The *Daily National Intelligencer*, February 3, 1815, simply reported developments in Oxford County, Maine, without comment.

administration, the War of 1812 had dealt the rapidly growing Republican parties of New England an almost fatal blow, while giving their Federalist opponents, at the same time, a new lease on life. This state of affairs was not immediately altered by the restoration of peace in 1815. Not until 1823 were the Republicans of Massachusetts able to recover and reorganize to elect William Eustis as governor over Harrison Gray Otis, one of the leaders of the Hartford Convention. Only then did Madison feel that the "factious ascendancy" of Federalism, "so long forming a cloud over the state of Massachusetts," had been given "the coup de grâce" it so richly deserved for its opposition to the War of 1812.[66]

The repulse of the British forces at Baltimore and Plattsburg in September 1814 by no means ended the direct military threat to the United States. Although the approach of winter would rule out further operations on the northern frontier, it was generally assumed in Washington that the Royal Navy would gradually shift its attention southward and harass the weakly defended coasts of South Carolina, Georgia, and Louisiana. The prospect of British raids in areas where slaves, more often than not, outnumbered the white population greatly alarmed the War Department and the governors of the states concerned, but the administration had reason to suspect that the enemy was contemplating far more than merely attacking coastal cities.[67] Throughout the summer of 1814 both Madison and Monroe had been receiving reports that the British government would send from Europe a sizable force to attack the Gulf Coast. This force—at first reported to be under the command of Lord Rowland Hill and then Major General Robert Ross—would rally to its standard rebellious slaves, disgruntled tribes of southwestern Indians, the disaffected French and Spanish communities of Louisiana, and the pirates of Barataria, and then seize some strategic point in the American Southwest.[68]

The administration feared New Orleans would be the object of this attack. The British government had not objected to the United States purchasing the Louisiana Territory in 1803, but, at the same time, it had not accepted the Treaty of San Ildefonso whereby Napoleon had acquired the territory to sell to the Jefferson administration in the first

---

[66] Madison to Eustis, June 14, 1823, Madison Papers, LC.

[67] William Hawkins to Monroe, September 11, 1814, LRRS; Thomas Pinckney to Monroe, October 6, November 19 and 30, 1814, LRRS; Joseph Alston to Monroe, September 4, 1814, LRRS; and David R. Williams to Monroe, December 22, 1814, LRUS.

[68] See "Notes" in Monroe's hand, September 1814, LRRS; B. B. Mumford to R. J. Meigs, June 25, 1814, Madison Papers, LC; and Albert Gallatin to Monroe, August 20, 1814, in Carl Prince and Helen Fineman, eds., *The Papers of Albert Gallatin* (microfilm ed.).

place. Nor had Britain accepted without protest Madison's occupation of parts of West Florida in 1810, and, if the ministry of Lord Liverpool decided to insist that both areas still belonged to Spain, it might try to end the 1814 campaign, and the war as well, by occupying the Mississippi Valley, perhaps even detaching it from the United States.[69] Indeed, substantial revision of the 1783 treaty establishing American independence—if the British negotiating position at Ghent was any indication—seemed by no means impossible, and Madison, in his more pessimistic moments, feared that the enemy would continually raise the terms for peace. The French minister, Louis Sérurier, reported to Talleyrand over the winter of 1814-1815 that the President had contemplated with alarm the prospect that Spain would cede to Britain both the Floridas and the claim to Louisiana and that the ministry would press these claims to the utmost while also trying to shift the boundary with Canada farther south. If such a situation ever developed, the Republic, as Sérurier remarked, would be in "a difficult position."[70]

There seems little doubt now, though, that many Americans, including the administration, misunderstood British intentions in the final months of the war. There was, to be sure, much discussion in Britain over the winter of 1814-1815 of how far the treaty of 1783 might be revised, but these discussions ultimately did not determine the decisions of the ministry, which, at all times, were concerned principally with the defense of Canada.[71] Lord Liverpool and his colleagues supported military operations farther south only to the extent that they promoted their policies regarding Canada, and Britain at this time could still hardly afford to devote men and money to embark on ambitious schemes of conquest in America. After the defeat at Plattsburg had ruled out prospects for immediately improving its position on the northern frontier, Britain, in fact, quickly withdrew its territorial demands at Ghent, and eventually settled for a peace treaty based on the status quo ante bellum. The time lost in this process, however, as well as unusually bad weather in the Atlantic Ocean, delayed the arrival of the news of peace in the United States until February 1815, and in the interim the administration was left to contend with the actions of the British forces that had been sent to America in the summer of

[69] In this context it is significant that Dallas, in his *Exposition on the Causes and the Character of the . . . War*, took pains to defend American claims to both Louisiana and the Floridas against challenges from Britain.

[70] Sérurier to Talleyrand, January 5, 1815, Correspondance Politique, vol. LXXI.

[71] The most convenient treatment of British thinking on the possibility of revising the 1783 treaty is Wright, *Britain and the American Frontier*, esp. 151-185.

1814.[72] The behavior of these forces, particularly the Royal Navy, continued to provide substance for American fears that Britain might yet attempt to "recolonize" parts of the United States.[73]

By September 1814 the British government had provided its commander on the North American station, Vice Admiral Sir Alexander Cochrane, with a fleet and 10,000 men for an expedition against New Orleans. Cochrane was attracted to the city by both its strategic importance and its very considerable wealth as a source of prizes, but he planned initially to approach it indirectly rather than directly. His plan was first to seize Mobile, which would provide the British with access to the river systems of Georgia and Mississippi Territory, and then to advance on New Orleans, either through the Mississippi Sound and Lake Pontchartrain or overland by isolating the city through the capture of Baton Rouge. This main strategy was to be supplemented with a series of attacks on American positions in the interior from a base on the Apalachicola River, and for these purposes the British had already dispatched agents inland earlier in the year. Cochrane also envisaged that these secondary attacks could be coordinated with the activities of Rear Admiral Sir George Cockburn on the Atlantic coast, thus dividing the American forces in the south while facilitating British operations against New Orleans.[74] What exactly the British intended to do with New Orleans once they had taken it was unclear, but the Liverpool ministry probably contemplated little more than a temporary

[72] See, for example, Lord Liverpool to Earl Bathurst, September 15, 1814, in Francis Bickley, ed., *Report on the Manuscripts of Earl Bathurst* (London, 1923), 288-289. There has been much controversy over British intentions in the final months of the war, particularly over the possibility that Britain intended to disavow the Treaty of Ghent after seizing New Orleans in order to begin new imperialistic policies in America. For a thorough discussion see James A. Carr, "The Battle of New Orleans and the Treaty of Ghent," *Diplomatic History* 3 (1979), 273-282. Carr convincingly argues that by the end of 1814 Britain, above all else, wanted peace and did *not* intend to disavow the peace treaty with the United States. See also Wilbur D. Jones, "A British View of the War of 1812 and the Peace Negotiations," *MVHR* 45 (1958), 486.

[73] It is important to remember that Royal Navy officers had a reputation for acting on their own initiative, often taking actions which the British government later could not condone. Madison was familiar with Sir Home Popham's unauthorized capture of Buenos Aires in 1806, while the commander on the North American station in the summer of 1814, Vice Admiral Sir Alexander Cochrane, had improperly assisted Francisco de Miranda in his rebellions against Spain. See Wright, *Britain and the American Frontier*, 142.

[74] Frank L. Owsley, Jr., *Struggle for the Gulf Borderlands: The Creek War and the Battle of New Orleans, 1812-1815* (Gainesville, Fla., 1981), 95-105, 133-136. See also Owsley, "The Role of the South in British Grand Strategy in the War of 1812," *Tennessee Historical Quarterly* 31 (1972), 22-35; and John K. Mahon, "British Strategy and Southern Indians, War of 1812," *Florida Historical Quarterly*, 44 (1966), 287-302.

occupation depending on the progress of the peace talks at Ghent and, perhaps, the reaction of the Spanish to the British success.[75]

The prospects for Cochrane's success were greatly enhanced by the vulnerability of New Orleans itself. Its remoteness from the East Coast had always been a problem, which had led Thomas Jefferson as long ago as 1806 to advocate military colonization of the Southwest in order to support the forces necessary for its defense. Nothing had come of this idea, nor had much progress been made in building military roads to bridge the distances between Georgia and the Mississippi River or Tennessee and the Gulf Coast.[76] Consequently, letters usually took over three weeks to travel from Washington to New Orleans, while the movement of men and supplies through the difficult terrain took far longer. The reports of the army inspectors made in June 1814 on the defenses of the New Orleans region thus revealed considerable disorder: there existed some ruined or half-completed fortifications that were inadequately garrisoned, while nobody seemed to have any idea of how many regular troops were available in the 39th and 44th Infantry regiments based in the Seventh Military District.[77] The administration, being in no condition itself after the fall of Washington to respond rapidly to a crisis on the farthest extremity of the nation, had therefore no alternative but to place its trust in the irascible and temperamental Andrew Jackson, who had just been promoted to the Seventh District after his victory over the Creek Indians in March 1814. By virtue of this victory, Jackson had suddenly become a military hero in the South, and as such he enjoyed the confidence of the governors and the militias of the region. Yet Jackson, the southern governors, and the administration interpreted the developing threat to the Gulf Coast very differently, and these differences were to influence the

[75] Carr, "The Battle of New Orleans and the Treaty of Ghent," 278.

[76] Everett S. Brown, "Jefferson's Plan for a Military Colony in Orleans Territory," *MVHR* 8 (1922), 373-376.

[77] [Philander Hughes], "Inspector's Report on the State of the Barracks . . . in New Orleans," June 20, 1814, Inspection Reports of the Office of the Inspector General (M-624), Records of the Office of the Inspector General (RG 159), NA. According to an analysis of the Registers of Enlistments in the United States Army, 1798-1815, the 39th Infantry had recruited about 800 men by the end of 1814, though possibly the strength of the regiment in the middle of the year might not have been much more than 500, especially after allowance is made for the expiry of the terms of men enlisted for twelve months only. The strength of the 44th Infantry does not seem to have been any greater, and it also suffered from a high desertion rate. (I am indebted to Mr. Murray McLauchlan for these estimates). See also A. La Carrière Latour, *Historical Memoir of the War in West Florida and Louisiana in 1814-1815* (Philadelphia, 1816), 6, 62.

American response in ways that at times seriously hampered the preparations for the defense of New Orleans.

By the time Monroe took over the duties of the War Department in early September, he was convinced that the goal of the British was to possess New Orleans and that the city should be the focal point of Jackson's defensive efforts. Throughout September and October he therefore urged the general to concentrate on New Orleans, and he ordered the governors of Georgia, Tennessee, and Kentucky to organize some 12,500 troops in all to be marched immediately to the city to strengthen its defenses. To finance these operations Monroe also forwarded to Jackson and the govenors about $200,000 in Treasury notes.[78] In taking this stand, the Secretary of War was supported by the increasingly worried governor of Louisiana, William C. C. Claiborne, and the state congressional delegation. These state leaders, not unnaturally, feared for the safety of New Orleans, and they stressed to both Jackson and Monroe that Louisiana's military resources were too few and her political loyalties too divided for the governor to deal with an invasion without outside help. As Claiborne told Jackson, "I have a difficult people to manage." He wished the general would finish his business in the Indian country and hasten to New Orleans.[79]

Jackson, on the other hand, regarded the British approach not as a campaign specifically directed at New Orleans but as a continuation of the earlier Creek war for control of the Indian territory of the southwest. He had spent much of the summer at Fort Jackson in Mississippi Territory, where, on August 9, he eventually compelled the Creek Indians to sign away most of their lands in a harsh peace treaty. Yet the treaty did not entirely remove the Indian threat, since the most disaffected Creek leaders had not been at Fort Jackson at all but had fled to the town of Pensacola in Spanish West Florida, where, Jackson suspected, the British would re-arm them and encourage them to continue their resistance.[80] His belief that the British were not principally concerned with New Orleans was confirmed by their attack on Fort

[78] Monroe to Jackson, September 5, 1814, Monroe Papers, LC; Monroe to the governors of Georgia, Kentucky, and Tennessee, September 25, 1814, LSMA; Monroe to Jackson, September 27, 1814, LSMA; Monroe to governors of Kentucky and Tennessee, October 3 and 10, 1814, Monroe Papers, LC.

[79] William C. C. Claiborne to Jackson, August 8, 12 and 24, September 20, 1814, Andrew Jackson Papers, LC. See also Claiborne to Madison, September 22, 1814; Madison Papers, LC; Alan B. Magruder to the Secretary of War, August 30, 1814, LRRS; Elejuis Fromentin and James Brown to Monroe, September 23, 1814, LRRS; and Claiborne to Fromentin, October 24, 1814, in Dunbar Rowland, ed., Official Letterbooks of W.C.C. Claiborne, 1801-1816 (Jackson, Miss., 1917), VI, 285.

[80] Wright, Britain and the American Frontier, 171.

Bowyer at the entrance to Mobile Bay on September 16—which was beaten off by the defending American troops—and by the reports of American spies who had visited Pensacola.[81] Jackson therefore resolved to concentrate on the emerging alliance of Indians, British forces, and slaves which was being formed on neutral Spanish territory. Once this threat was removed, Jackson assumed that the entire Gulf Coast would be secure, after which he looked forward not to going to New Orleans but to returning home to Tennessee.[82] The general accordingly concentrated on gathering his regular forces, together with the Tennessee militia, at Mobile. Indeed, at times Jackson spoke as if he would have to withdraw troops from Louisiana to defend Mobile rather than march them all to New Orleans.[83]

The governor of Tennessee, Willie Blount, and the political leaders of that state shared Jackson's understanding of the situation. They, too, had little expectation of making a sustained defense of New Orleans, and they regarded the concentration at Mobile as a necessary and inevitable move to consolidate Tennessee's earlier victories in the Creek war.[84] On several occasions Jackson sent bombastic, insulting letters to the Spanish governor of Pensacola, Gonzales Manrique, warning him not to violate the neutrality existing between the United States and Spain, and threatening him with violence to ensure that this neutrality was preserved.[85] Manrique, who had neither the means nor the desire to expel the British, replied sharply that in the past the United States had not hesitated to ignore Spanish neutrality when it suited them. Enraged, Jackson decided to settle the issue once and for all by storming Pensacola on November 7. The attempt was successful and accomplished with little cost to the Americans, but the British forces

[81] For the attack on Fort Bowyer see Wilburt S. Brown, *The Amphibious Campaign for West Florida and Louisiana, 1814-1815: A Critical Review of Strategy and Tactics at New Orleans* (University, Ala., 1969), 44-45. For Jackson's agents in Pensacola see John S. Bassett, *The Life of Andrew Jackson* (New York, 1931), 129.

[82] Jackson to Rachel Jackson, August 5, 1814, in Avery O. Craven, "Letters of Andrew Jackson," *The Huntington Library Bulletin* 3 (1933), 116-117. See also Jackson to Armstrong, August 10, 25, and 30, 1814, and same to James Winchester, November 22, 1814, Jackson Papers, LC.

[83] Jackson to Claiborne, August 22, 1814; Jackson to Monroe, October 10, 1814, Jackson Papers, LC.

[84] Jesse Bledsoe to William Worsley, September 26, 1814, Lyman C. Draper Manuscript Collection, 6 CC 14, SHSW; Willie Blount to David Holmes, November 14, 1814, Draper Collection, 5 X 56, SHSW; Blount to Monroe, November 8 and 18, 1814, LRUS; Blount to Jackson, November 26, 1814, Jackson Papers, LC; and Shelby to Monroe, November 30, 1814, LRRS.

[85] Jackson to Monroe, October 27 and 31, 1814; same to the governor of Pensacola, November 6 and 7, 1814, Jackson papers, LC.

at Pensacola eluded Jackson in his moment of victory. Realizing they were outnumbered, the British withdrew to their ships, destroying as they did so their stronghold at Fort Barrancas.[86] Jackson, however, felt vindicated, as he could claim that he had deprived the enemy of an important base providing easy access to the American interior, and indeed he had thwarted, albeit unwittingly, Cochrane's first move.[87]

The administration observed Jackson's behavior with considerable unease. Monroe could sympathize with the general's anger, believing too that the Spanish were unfairly aiding the British. Nonetheless, the Secretary genuinely felt that Mobile was less at risk than New Orleans, and he feared that Jackson's actions could lead to an unwelcome and unnecessary war with Spain. And the military and diplomatic consequences of a formal alliance between Britain and Spain against the United States at this time were, in fact, quite unthinkable. Above all, Monroe was concerned that Jackson's preoccupation with Mobile had already left New Orleans fatally unprepared, since the general had placed most of his best troops—including the 3d Infantry, parts of the 2d Infantry, and about 1,000 Tennessee militia—well to the east of New Orleans. Monroe therefore ordered Jackson to leave Mobile, warned him of the diplomatic consequences of his actions, and urged him to hasten to New Orleans.[88] To reinforce these orders, Monroe dispatched another regular army general, James Winchester of Tennessee, to take over at Mobile, while he sent to New Orleans Brigadier General Edmund P. Gaines to assist both Claiborne and Jackson in the defense of the city.[89]

When Winchester reached Mobile on November 21, Jackson finally decided to leave for New Orleans. His actions, along with the unanticipated publicity given to the supposedly secret British intention to attack New Orleans, had, in fact, induced Cochrane to abandon the capture of Mobile in favor of making a more direct approach to the city by sea, and the campaign now became something of a race to see which army could get there first to assume the best positions for offense

[86] See Frank L. Owsley, Jr., "Jackson's Capture of Pensacola," *Alabama Review* 19 (1966), esp. 176-177. For a discussion of relations between the Spanish and the British see Owsley, *Struggle for the Gulf Borderlands*, 106-107, 114-119.

[87] Jackson to the governor of Pensacola, November 9, 1814; same to Monroe, November 14, 1814, Jackson Papers, LC.

[88] Monroe to Jackson, October 21, 1814, Madison Papers, LC; same to same, December 7, 1814, Jackson Papers, LC. On the troops Jackson diverted to Mobile see Owsley, "The Role of the South . . . in the War of 1812," 33.

[89] Monroe to Jackson, December 10, 1814, LSMA; same to Gaines, December 17, 1814, LSMA.

and defense.[90] Throughout his stay at Mobile, Jackson had been kept informed of the situation in New Orleans by both Governor Claiborne and the army engineers, and he had urged them to organize what defenses they could, including the controversial measure of accepting a troop of free colored volunteers.[91] Neither Jackson nor Claiborne particularly relished this last action, but they both realized that the free colored people of the city were simply too numerous not to be included, as Claiborne put it, "in the bosom of Louisiana," at least for the crisis of an invasion.[92] Jackson also sent addresses and proclamations to the governor for him to read to the local troops in order to reinforce their morale. Nevertheless, Claiborne experienced difficulties in organizing the defense of New Orleans and badly needed, as he had always maintained, outside help to overcome them.

These difficulties were rooted in the complex political and social problems of early Louisiana. Although Claiborne—whose family and marriage ties linked him with the planters of both Virginia and Tennessee as well as some of the most prominent Spanish families of New Orleans—had survived for nearly a decade as the executive of Louisiana, he had never been wholly accepted by the *ancienne population* of the state.[93] This group, consisting of French and Spanish people who had settled prior to the American annexation of 1803, felt uneasy about the increasing "Americanization" of their homeland with the steady influx of American settlers, both into New Orleans itself and, above all, into the parishes of the hinterland. The Americans, for their part, suspected the *ancienne population* of disloyalty, fearing that the old ties to Spain and France would dispose this group to support Britain in the event of an invasion. These deep-seated rivalries were overlaid and complicated by the more recent arrival of large numbers of French refugees from Santo Domingo—the so-called "Foreign French"—and the presence of the large community of free blacks.[94] In this context, as one American settler observed, political differences in Louisiana

[90] Owsley, "The Role of the South . . . in the War of 1812," 35.

[91] New Orleans Committee of Safety to Jackson, September 18, 1814; Jackson to Claiborne, September 21, 1814, Jackson Papers, LC. See also Bassett, *Life of Jackson*, 148-149.

[92] Claiborne to Jackson, October 17, 1814, Jackson Papers, LC.

[93] On Claiborne's background see Joseph T. Hatfield, *William Claiborne: Jeffersonian Centurion in the American Southwest* (La Fayette, La., 1976), esp. 266.

[94] Lewis W. Newton, "Creoles and Anglo-Americans in Old Louisiana: A Study in Cultural Conflicts," *Southwestern Social Science Quarterly* 14 (1933), 31-48; Joseph G. Tregle, Jr., "Early New Orleans Society: A Reappraisal," *Journal of Southern History* 18 (1952), 20-36; and George Dargo, *Jefferson's Louisiana: Politics and the Clash of Legal Traditions* (Cambridge, Mass., 1975), 6-11.

were not comparable to those in other parts of the Union. Federalism and Republicanism meant the same thing to most people, while "the *American party*," this observer continued, "differ[ed] as to the policy of the war, the *French party* as to the right of our government to the country, [and] the *Spanish* party [cursed] everything." On top of all this, the "*Creoles* [were] discontented, the *Negroes* insolent, [and] the Indians sulky." "What political chemist," he despaired, "will ever unite us?"[95]

In 1813, Claiborne had already had trouble trying to weld these disparate elements into a united force. His attempt in December of that year to call out the militia had met with such a mixed response that it could only be described as a failure. The Americans in the inland parishes were willing enough to organize and serve in the militia, but, with memories of the slave revolt of 1811 still fresh in their minds, they were reluctant to be marched very far from their homes. The population of New Orleans had not responded to the call for service at all, while the legislature, dominated by planters of French background, had refused to allow Claiborne to act as commander in chief of the militia.[96] Despite the broad powers of his office, the governor was, in the words of an American lawyer, a "mere cypher."[97] And as Claiborne himself put it to Jackson, "from the *great mixture of persons and characters in this city*, we have much to apprehend from *within* as well as from *without*." He continually begged the general to bring outside forces into the city to control the factionalism that he could not.[98]

These fears of the British turning Louisiana's divided loyalties to their advantage were largely unjustified. The *ancienne population* and other minorities, no doubt, failed to manifest a sense of patriotism that satisfied the Americans, but they were not so discontented with American rule as to want to exchange it willingly for occupation by the British.[99] The Americans had not during the territorial stage of Louisiana's history, Thomas Jefferson's inclinations notwithstanding, con-

---

[95] John W. Windship to William Plumer, Jr., November 1, 1813, in Everett S. Brown, "Letters from Louisiana, 1813-1814," *MVHR* 11 (1925), 571.

[96] Claiborne to James Brown, December 11, 1813, Rowland, *Claiborne Letterbooks*, VI, 281-282; Windship to Plumer, March 20, 1814, "Letters from Louisiana," 574. See also Reed McB. Adams, "New Orleans and the War of 1812," *Louisiana Historical Quarterly* 17 (1934), 169-170; Powell A. Casey, *Louisiana in the War of 1812* (New Orleans, 1963), 31-37; and Charles Gayarré, *History of Louisiana* (3d ed., New Orleans, 1885), IV, 320-321.

[97] Windship to Plumer, April 2, 1814, "Letters from Louisiana," 575.

[98] Claiborne to Jackson, September 8, 1814, Jackson Papers, LC.

[99] See same to same, November 5, 1814, Rowland, *Claiborne Letterbooks*, VI, 310-311.

sistently overridden all local laws and customs in a determined effort to remake Louisiana and its people into a wholly "American" society. The Louisiana Civil Law Digest of 1808, for example, had provided the territory with a body of law that preserved much of the French and Spanish-based civil law with only minimal concessions to the American preference for the common law.[100] Furthermore, the Louisiana constitution of 1812—by virtue of its high property and residence requirements for voting and officeholding, along with its deliberately weighted system of legislative apportionment—provided the *ancienne population* with the political means to defend their interests, even if these also contributed to the factionalism Claiborne feared so much.[101] Nor were the French settlers, by far the largest single group in the *ancienne population*, for all their distaste for Americans, likely to welcome British forces which had recently triumphed over the French empire in Europe. And possibly, all the inhabitants of New Orleans feared that their property and commercial interests would be seriously endangered by a successful British assault.[102] In short, the *ancienne population* was not so much likely to commit treason as its leaders would be prone to question the means whereby the Americans would defend Louisiana, but this situation in no way lessened the need for leadership and unity within the state.[103]

That leadership and unity was eventually provided by Jackson, who exploited his position as an outsider, together with his military resources and overbearing personality, to the utmost. Arriving in New Orleans on December 1, he immediately set about organizing its defenses to withstand a major assault from the British forces, and there was no longer much doubt in his mind that the city would be their target.[104] Although he had previously underestimated the threat to New Orleans, Jackson was by no means unaware of the problems involved in its defense. As early as September 1814, the local defense committees and the army engineers had pointed out to him that the

[100] Dargo, *Jefferson's Louisiana*, 105-174.

[101] Joseph G. Tregle, Jr., "Political Reinforcement of Ethnic Dominance in Louisiana, 1812-1845," in Lucius F. Ellsworth et al., *The Americanization of the Gulf Coast, 1803-1850* (Pensacola, Fla., 1972), 80-82; Perry Howard, *Political Tendencies in Louisiana* (Baton Rouge, La., 1971), 20-22.

[102] See Owsley, "The Role of the South . . . in the War of 1812," 32. The arrival of a consul in New Orleans representing the restored Bourbon monarch, Louis XVIII, was greeted with much hostility. See Gayarré, *History of Louisiana*, IV, 373.

[103] Gayarré, *History of Louisiana*, IV, 566.

[104] Jackson to Monroe, December 2, 1814, LRRS. See also Bassett, *Life of Jackson*, 144-147; New Orleans Committee of Safety to Jackson, September 18, 1814; and Edward Livingston to Jackson, November 21, 1814, both in Jackson Papers, LC.

geography of the Mississippi delta dictated that the enemy would have to approach the city by one of six routes. These included two southern routes, one up the Mississippi River from its mouth and the other overland after entering Lake Barataria; two eastern approaches in the area between the Bayou Terre aux Boeufs and the Plains of Gentilly; one western approach through the Bayou La Fourche; and a descent from the north through Lake Pontchartrain and the Bayou St. John.[105] No one could be certain which route the enemy would take, though Jackson was inclined to believe that their approach would still be from the direction of Mobile in the east and might be supplemented by naval operations on Lakes Borgne and Pontchartrain.[106]

In any event, Jackson decided to cut off as far as possible all these avenues to New Orleans, both by positioning men and guns in the six approaches and by obstructing the waterways. This decision caused little dissent within the city, and it enabled Jackson to employ the governor and the leaders of New Orleans' diverse and quarrelsome interest groups in a wide variety of tasks. The general's real difficulty here was whether he would have sufficient men and weapons to support so comprehensive a defense. The city militia itself, even when augmented with the controversial troops of free coloreds, was inadequate for the task, and Jackson was again compelled to look beyond the state for assistance. He called on volunteers from the militia of Mississippi Territory, recalled to his command many of the Tennessee troops left at Mobile under his kinsman John Coffee, and anxiously awaited the detachments and supplies from Kentucky that had been promised by the War Department.[107] Eventually, he even made an alliance with the pirates of Barataria under the leadership of the notorious Jean Laffite. As was the case with the free coloreds, Jackson would have preferred to have avoided this last measure, but the familiarity of the pirates with the Delta region, coupled with their skills in gunnery and their supplies of powder, was essential to the Americans and could not be allowed to fall to the enemy by default.[108]

In most of these arrangements Jackson's orders were accepted, though, from time to time, there were conflicts of interest and opinion. Neither

[105] See Robert V. Remini, *Andrew Jackson and the Course of American Empire, 1767-1821* (New York, 1977), 246, 250.

[106] Jackson to Monroe, December 10, 1814, Jackson Papers, LC. See also Brown, *Amphibious Campaign*, 68; and Charles B. Brooks, *The Siege of New Orleans* (Seattle, 1961), 87-88.

[107] Jackson to John Coffee, December 11 and 16, 1814, Jackson Papers, LC. Brown, *Amphibious Campaign*, 83.

[108] Jane Lucas de Grummond, *The Baratarians and the Battle of New Orleans* (Baton Rouge, La., 1961), 43, 54, 55, 81; Brown, *Amphibious Campaign*, 86.

the governor nor the state legislature wished Jackson's authoritarian ways to deprive them of playing a conspicuous role in the city's defense. Claiborne was privately torn between his desire to serve as Jackson's second in command, which would improve his standing in the city, and an unwillingness to interfere too openly in the general's business.[109] The governor was troubled too by Jackson's tendency to rely on some of his most prominent political opponents—most notably Edward Livingston—for advice and assistance, and he may have suspected that Jackson was gratifying an old resentment, incurred when Jefferson had preferred him over the general as governor of Louisiana Territory back in 1805. Claiborne on one occasion sought a private interview with Jackson to discuss their relationship—which the general appears not to have granted—but for most of the time the governor had to keep his sense of grievance to himself.[110] Some of the French leaders, however, were more openly suspicious of both Jackson and Claiborne, and their spokesmen in the legislature refused the governor's requests, made on December 14, that they suspend *habeas corpus* and adjourn their sessions for the duration of the crisis. Jackson and the chief naval officer at New Orleans, Master Commander Daniel Patterson, had sought the suspension of *habeas corpus* to enable them to press men into service more easily and to control access to and from the city, while Claiborne had suggested the adjournment to scotch rumors that the French leaders were contemplating some sort of capitulation to the British. Jackson dealt with the first problem by simply declaring martial law on December 16, and he reacted to the second, when it occurred again two weeks later, by threatening to blow up the legislature.[111]

These last two episodes were closely connected with the approach of the British forces to New Orleans and the tension this development inevitably created. On December 14 the Royal Navy defeated the small American gunboat fleet on Lake Borgne, which enabled Cochrane, without Jackson's knowledge, to transfer all the British forces to the Isle aux Pois as a preliminary to crossing over to the mainland.[112] Jackson's military resources here were strengthened within the week by the arrival on December 21 of some 4,000 Tennessee and Missis-

[109] Claiborne to Monroe, December 9, 1814, LRRS.

[110] Garrayé, *History of Louisiana*, IV, 346. Livingston, who was Jackson's aide-de-camp, had offered his services to the general the day after Claiborne tried to remove him from the New Orleans Committee of Safety. Livingston to Jackson, September 21, 1814; and Claiborne to Jackson, September 20, 1814, both in Jackson Papers, LC. See also Remini, *Jackson*, 128; and Claiborne to Jackson, December 20, 1814, Jackson Papers, LC.

[111] For these episodes see Garrayé, *History of Louisiana*, IV, 392, 540-576; Brooks, *Siege of New Orleans*, 118, 190; and Brown, *Amphibious Campaign*, 118.

[112] Brown, *Amphibious Campaign*, 77-82.

sippi militia under Coffee and William Carroll, but the general was again caught by surprise on December 23 when the enemy advanced through the Villeré Canal, which contrary to his orders had not been blocked, and camped nine miles outside New Orleans.[113] These gains by the enemy greatly reduced Jackson's chances of dealing with the invasion short of repelling an outright British assault on the city itself, and to do this he concentrated on turning New Orleans into an armed camp. Martial law was rigorously enforced, and Jackson reviewed and addressed the troops—praising them for forgetting "the differences of language and the prejudices of national pride"—on December 18 in order to stir up patriotism.[114] These preparations and the proximity of the British notwithstanding, Jackson could still not be certain about where and when the British would approach. He decided to risk a night attack on December 23 on the forces camped at Villeré's plantation to see if he could drive them back to their ships, but even as he carried out this operation he could not be sure whether he had been tricked into committing himself to battle while another enemy force launched a major attack from the north of New Orleans.[115] The night engagement failed to dislodge the British, though it did demonstrate that Jackson could successfully employ his forces under difficult conditions and inflict serious casualties.[116]

On Christmas Day the British army commander, Lieutenant General Sir Edward Packenham, arrived to join Cochrane in the assault on New Orleans. How far Packenham actually relished the position Cochrane had chosen for the army is uncertain, but both of the British commanders seem to have decided to continue the advance, if for no other reason than that they might as well attempt to defeat the Americans where they were before considering alternative approaches.[117] They accordingly spent the next two weeks in exploring various ways

[113] William Carroll to Jackson, December 20, 1814, Jackson Papers, LC. Why the Villeré Canal was not blocked is not clear. There are a variety of explanations, ranging from simple neglect to the desire of prominent French planters not to let the war restrict their smuggling activities. See Carson I. A. Ritchie, "The Louisiana Campaign," *Louisiana Historical Quarterly* 44 (1961), 41.

[114] Brooks, *Siege of New Orleans*, 106, 112. Jackson's address on December 18, 1814, is in Jackson Papers, LC.

[115] One of Jackson's aides, John Reid, mentioned that the general was hourly expecting, on December 23, a British attack on the fort at Petites Coquilles near the Rigolets, the pass entering into Lake Pontchartrain. See Reid to Abraham Maury, December 23, 1814, John Reid Papers, LC.

[116] For the engagement of December 23 see Latour, *Historical Memoir*, 84-112.

[117] See J. W. Fortescue, *A History of the British Army* (London, 1899-1930), X, 161-162, but cf. Brown, *Amphibious Campaign*, 109-112.

to penetrate the American defenses. Jackson by now had decided to make his main stand on the east bank of the Mississippi at the Rodriguez Canal, where he was busily building lines of mud fortifications behind which he placed most of his artillery and riflemen.[118] On December 28, Packenham made a reconnaissance in force to test the strength of the Americans and to see if they would retreat at the sight of a British army, as had been the case at Bladensburg. Jackson, however, thwarted this hope with some well-placed artillery fire, both from the American lines and the schooner *Louisiana* on the river, which led Packenham to withdraw in favor of attempting a more sustained artillery attack in order to breach the American earthworks. This effort, made on January 1, 1815, was also unsuccessful, and Packenham therefore decided to risk heavy casualties in a frontal assault on the American positions. In the interim, Jackson considerably strengthened his earthworks and his artillery, and the result of the attack on January 8 was an unexpected and dreadful slaughter of the British troops. Packenham and two of his generals were killed, while some 2,000 of their men were reported as casualties.[119]

In this last engagement Jackson won a great victory. He did so not so much because he had anticipated his enemy's every move—indeed, he had twice failed to do so, and the defensive preparations on the west bank of the Mississippi revealed that he had also failed to predict events there correctly—but he ultimately triumphed because his major efforts, particularly with the placing of the American artillery, were more than adequate to deal with events as they developed.[120] The

[118] Latour, *Historical Memoir*, 113, 121; Bassett, *Life of Jackson*, 184-185.

[119] Jackson to Monroe, January 9 and 13, 1815, Jackson Papers, LC. See also Latour, *Historical Memoir*, 119-178; and Bassett, *Life of Jackson*, 186-202. There are many, perhaps too many, accounts of the Battle of New Orleans. Most recent works agree on the broad outlines of the campaign, especially praising Jackson for the energy and thoroughness of his defense, while differing on points of detail. These disagreements usually reflect the different sources consulted by their authors, especially the rather colored memoirs of the battle written up to forty years after the event by participants from both sides. The best recent accounts are Brown's *Amphibious Campaign*, esp. 112-151; Brooks, *Siege of New Orleans*, 183-252; Owsley, *Struggle for the Gulf Borderlands*, 144-168; and Robin Reilly, *The British at the Gates: The New Orleans Campaign in the War of 1812* (New York, 1974), 263-299.

[120] Bassett, *Life of Jackson*, 197, 205. That the American artillery rather than the riflemen were responsible for the heavy British casualties seems to be generally accepted in most recent accounts of the battle. See Ritchie, "The Louisiana Campaign," 56, 72-74, 118; and Reilly, *The British at the Gates*, 297-298. But cf. Brown, *Amphibious Campaign*, 149-150, for a statement of the case for the importance of riflemen. However, Brown concedes—see p. 208—that cannon loaded with musket balls were likely to have inflicted most of the casualties caused by musket balls.

British, in fact, overwhelmed the defenses on the west bank, but this advantage was quite nullified by the heavy casualties they suffered on the east.[121] On January 18, the British army, now under the command of Major General John Lambert, began a retreat to the Royal Navy vessels on Lake Borgne, where together they attempted to revive Cochrane's earlier strategy of advancing on New Orleans overland after the seizure of Mobile. The British were successful here to the extent of capturing the American position at Fort Bowyer on Mobile Point on February 11, but three days later Lambert suspended all military operations after learning by sloop of the news that a peace treaty had been signed.[122] Jackson, however, did not receive official confirmation of the news of peace until March 13, and in the period that followed the British withdrawal from New Orleans he insisted on maintaining martial law within the city. This decision cost him much of the good will earned by his previous efforts and provided a convenient pretext for the reappearance of factionalism in Louisiana politics.[123] Claiborne declared the return of peace in a proclamation that criticized Jackson for the "violence of his character," while the state legislature, no doubt irritated by Jackson's suspicions about the loyalty of its members, omitted the general's name from a vote of thanks to the army officers for their defense of New Orleans.[124] Consequently, many French-speaking citizens impatiently sought their discharge from militia service, some even obtaining certificates of French nationality from the French consul in order to do so, while Jackson responded by expelling his critics, and the French militia, from the city. With the return of peace, however, he had ultimately to submit to the rule of law by appearing in court and paying a $1,000 fine for his refusal to obey a writ of *habeas corpus* brought by one of his opponents.[125]

[121] On the west bank of the Mississippi, the defense was entrusted to Major General David Morgan with some Louisiana militia, to Master Commander Patterson with some naval gunners, and to the Kentucky militia under Colonel John Adair. The earthworks on the west bank, by contrast with those on the east, were only half completed, the artillery was positioned to enfilade the British advance on the east bank and could not stop a frontal assault, and the Kentuckians, arriving in New Orleans only on January 4, 1815, were inadequately armed and equipped. Moreover, the American commanders had difficulty in maintaining lines of communication across the river. See Latour, *Historical Memoir*, 164-177; Brooks, *Siege of New Orleans*, 230, 242, 282; and Brown, *Amphibious Campaign*, 151-158.

[122] Latour, *Historical Memoir*, 207-216; Brown, *Amphibious Campaign*, 158-162.

[123] Claiborne to Monroe, February 10, 1815, Rowland, *Claiborne Letterbooks*, VI, 345; same to same, February 24, 1815, LRRS.

[124] See Rowland, *Claiborne Letterbooks*, VI, 347, for the governor's proclamation. Also Latour, *Historical Memoir*, 205.

[125] For these events see Remini, *Jackson*, 308-315.

The administration in Washington viewed Jackson's conduct after the Battle of New Orleans with some distaste, but there could be no mistaking their pleasure at the news of the victory itself. This reached the capital on February 4, and it was followed ten days later by copies of the Treaty of Ghent, which the Prince Regent had ratified as long ago as December 28, 1814.[126] This prompt British ratification reflected not only the desire of the British government to be "released from the millstone of the American war" but also Lord Liverpool's wish to discourage Madison from playing "some trick in the ratification" by quibbling over a treaty which made no concessions to American views on maritime rights.[127] After the tense and tumultuous events of the last six months, however, neither Madison nor his colleagues in Washington had any intention of prolonging the war, and the news of Jackson's victory and the peace produced in the capital, as Senator Jonathan Roberts recalled, a sense of relief and exultation that was almost "childish" in its nature.[128] The President accordingly sent the Treaty of Ghent to the Senate on February 15, where it was ratified in little more than twenty-four hours.[129] Rufus King, speaking for the Federalists, pointed out with sarcasm and bitterness that the administration had obtained none of its stated war objectives in the peace, and his views here may have been shared by those Republican Senators, such as Giles and Samuel Smith, who were disposed to be critical of the President.[130] Most Republicans, though, felt that the treaty was none the worse for its omissions, since, as William Lowndes observed, "the time of making it [was] more fortunate than the peace itself."[131] As the administration completed the formalities of ratification, it also ceased hostilities against Britain, and, on February 17, Madison was able to proclaim formally that the War of 1812 was at last at an end.[132]

[126] *Daily Natl Intelligencer*, February 6 and 15, 1815.

[127] Carr, "The Battle of New Orleans and the Treaty of Ghent," 277, 281. See also Frank A. Updyke, *The Diplomacy of the War of 1812* (Baltimore, 1915), 360-361.

[128] Philip S. Klein, ed., "Memoirs of a Senator from Pennsylvania: Jonathan Roberts, 1771-1854," *Pennsylvania Magazine of History and Biography* 62 (1938), 377-378.

[129] Updyke, *Diplomacy of the War of 1812*, 362.

[130] Klein, "Memoirs of . . . Jonathan Roberts," 379. The New York *Evening Post* reported that King, in a speech on the treaty, "pointed out the great blessings of the present war in a style of biting satire scarcely ever equalled." See Charles R. King, ed., *The Life and Correspondence of Rufus King* (New York, 1894-1900), V, 470.

[131] William Lowndes to Elizabeth Lowndes, February 17, 1815, William Lowndes Papers, UNC.

[132] *Daily Natl Intelligencer*, February 18, 1815.

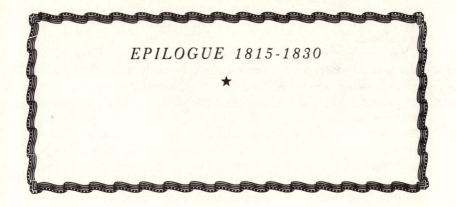

EPILOGUE 1815-1830

★

THE ACHIEVEMENTS of the War of 1812 have always been difficult to assess. Generally, Americans raised the estimate of their accomplishments the further the war receded into the past, and, even as early as 1816, British visitors to the United States were complaining they had to endure such boastful claims that Andrew Jackson was a better general than the Duke of Wellington and that the abilities of Lord Nelson paled beside those of Commodore Rodgers.[1] The realities of the war, of course, had been very different, and by 1815 the United States had done little more than survive some of the most dangerous threats that had yet been posed to its existence as a nation. That in itself was no mean achievement, and the outcome of the war might have been far worse, especially if the American negotiators at Ghent had been panicked into making concessions or into rupturing the discussions that finally led to peace.[2] But mere survival, whatever its psychological satisfactions for Americans at the time, was far less than the United States had hoped to accomplish in the months after June 1812. The purpose of the war was to relieve the Republic from the burdens of British maritime policies, and specifically Madison sought, as Monroe told the British minister, Augustus Foster, on the day hostilities were declared, a settlement of the impressment problem—presumably by an agreement that each nation forgo the use of each other's seamen—and a definition of naval blockades to preclude widespread seizures of neutral shipping under Orders in Council.[3] The

---

[1] Bradford Perkins, *Castlereagh and Adams: England and the United States, 1812-1823* (Berkeley and Los Angeles, 1964), 147.

[2] Ibid., 131.

[3] Monroe's words, according to Foster, were that Madison wanted "an act of Parliament about impressment on [the British] side, on [the American] an act of Congress," as well as "a definition of blockades according to the Russian treaty [of 1801]." Augustus Foster, Journal entry, June 18, 1812, Augustus Foster Papers, LC.

invasion of Canada was to be the means whereby these goals were to be realized.

Yet throughout the war, and afterward too, observers often felt that Madison failed to pursue realistic or coherently defined policies to accomplish his broader purpose.[4] This impression arose as much from the practical difficulties of waging a Canadian war as it did from any errors of judgment on the part of the President. Madison's actions throughout the war, given the premises on which they were based, were always logical, and he usually tried to pursue them in the best ways that circumstances permitted. The requirements of a successful Canadian war, though, were not always compatible with the considerations that had led Madison into adopting that policy in the first place. Between 1812 and 1814, the United States tried to gain control of Upper Canada and the area around Montreal, adopting for that purpose strategies shaped by the interplay of a variety of factors, most notably the limited military resources available to the administration, some political considerations arising from the sectional nature of the support for the war, and an awareness that the part of Canada under attack was of some importance to Britain in its quest for resources to maintain its navigation system. Working against the success of this American war, however, was the fact that the strategically important centers of British power in Canada were the fortress at Quebec and the naval base at Halifax, and the American campaigns were never successful enough to obtain control of the St. Lawrence at Montreal, much let alone move on from there to attempt the capture of the strongest enemy positions in North America. Yet both goals had to be accomplished if Britain was ever to be deprived of its Canadian possessions and thereby coerced into respecting American rights.[5]

The effects of this dilemma were constantly felt, especially in 1813 and 1814, and it led the United States to concentrate on lesser strategic goals rather than incur the costs and risks of attempting larger ones.[6] For this reason the war did not exert as much pressure on the enemy

[4] See, for example, the verdicts of Perkins, *Castlereagh and Adams*, 54, 154; Reginald Horsman, *The War of 1812* (New York, 1969), 264; and Russell F. Weigley, *History of the United States Army* (New York, 1967), 117.

[5] See the works by J. Mackay Hitsman, *The Incredible War of 1812: A Military History* (Toronto, 1965), 39-41, and *Safeguarding Canada, 1763-1871* (Toronto, 1968), 79-110. As Madison recalled later, the difficulties of invading Canada were caused by "the forests to be penetrated, the savages to be encountered, and the Lakes and other waters to be passed in order to reach a distant theatre, where the adversary was at home in the midst of all his resources for defence." To Henry Lee, February—1827, James Madison Papers, LC.

[6] Russell F. Weigley, *The American Way of War: A History of United States Military Strategy and Policy* (New York, 1973), 47-48.

as Madison would have liked, and this, in turn, contributed to the increasing sense of frustration experienced by both its supporters and its opponents during its course. As the Canadian war failed to accomplish its purpose, Madison began to place greater reliance on European diplomacy as an alternative method of pressuring the enemy, hoping in particular that Alexander I of Russia could extract either by mediation or by even more direct pressure on Britain the concessions on neutral rights that he desired. This resource, too by 1814 had clearly failed, and in its last year the war underwent a profound change in nature. From being an offensive measure designed to coerce Britain, the Canadian war, in effect, became a more desperate measure of self-defense, designed to spare the Republic the full weight of British military and naval power after the fall of Napoleonic France. The variety of problems Canada posed for the United States in its relations with Britain thus went largely unsolved, and only in the final months of the war did the administration seriously consider striking at the centers of British military power in Lower Canada rather than concentrating on Montreal and the Great Lakes. The Treaty of Ghent made the attempt unnecessary, but the circumstances at the time hardly favored its success. The third session of the Thirteenth Congress, by refusing to charter a national bank or to reform methods of army recruiting, had, in effect, declared it could no longer endorse a Canadian war, and the administration would have experienced increasing difficulty in waging war in the face of waning public support for its policies.

But no matter what strategic goal the administration attempted, its efforts were always handicapped by its inability to mobilize fully the resources of the nation for war. This failure became manifest in a number of ways, the most serious of them being the difficulty of raising an army. The army had, of course, long been a problem in the political economy of Republicanism, and one reason why the Madison administration was so troubled by the lack of regular forces was the failure of previous administrations to obtain the militia reform that was deemed necessary to enable the federal government to tap the nation's reserves of manpower. It had never been Madison's, or any President's, wish to prepare for or to wage war by relying heavily on a regular army, but the attempt had to be made between 1812 and 1815 because of the refusal of all Congresses after 1789 to limit the powers of the states over the militia. The militia clauses of the 1787 Constitution, framed initially as a compromise measure which Madison and others had hoped might be improved over time, thus became a permanent obstacle to an effective military policy for the Republic. The conflict between the administration and the New England states over the control of the militia during the war was only the most extreme manifestation of this more deeply rooted problem, but as early as 1788 in the *Federalist* papers Madison had ruled out coercion of the states as its solution. Neither prudence nor the circumstances confronting Madison after 1812 suggested a departure from this position of restraint, but the fact only confirmed Madison's suspicion, expressed as early as 1787, that the Constitution might not "effectually answer its national object."[7]

Moreover, the regular army was not a popular institution in the early Republic, and neither the army itself, at least not before the summer of 1814, nor the administration could do very much to alter the situation. The army's inefficiency and poor reputation in the society it served was most graphically measured by the way in which soldiers' wages were never even remotely competitive with the returns that could be made in any other occupation, including those of the most lowly paid laborer. This fact, no doubt, underlay Jefferson's observation, made at the nadir of the war in October 1814, that it "was nonsense to talk of regulars," since they were "not to be had in a people so easy and happy at home as ours," but the problem, in truth, was rather more complex.[8] It is possible to exaggerate the degree of "happiness" of the American people, especially at a time when their government was pursuing foreign policies that contributed materially to depressing the nation's prosperity, and the army, despite the formidable obstacles it encountered, appears to have recruited more men than it either realized or knew what to do with. By the end of 1814 the extent to which the administration underestimated the forces available to it might have been as much as 10,000 men, but neither then, when the army was at its most efficient, nor at any other period of the war was the number of men ready for active service any more than a fraction of what it might have been.[9] The difficulties of the years 1812 to 1815 involved more than the problems of mobilizing an "unmilitary" society for war; the administration could not even organize efficiently the resources that were available.

The roots of administrative inefficiency are often difficult to trace,

[7] Madison to Jefferson, September 6, 1787, in William T. Hutchinson, William M. E. Rachal, and Robert A. Rutland, eds., *The Papers of James Madison* (Chicago and Charlottesville, 1962–), X, 163-164.

[8] Jefferson to Monroe, October 16, 1814, Thomas Jefferson Papers, LC.

[9] According to an analysis of the "Records of Men Enlisted in the U.S. Army prior to the Peace Establishment, May 17, 1815," the number of regulars enlisted by January 1815, after allowing for men whose terms of service had expired, could have been as high as 45,000. See Murray A. McLauchlan, "The Army, Society, and the War of 1812" (M.A. research essay, University of Auckland, 1980), 106. Yet Jacob Brown could assemble for his peninsula campaign in the summer of 1814 an army of barely 4,000 regulars.

but the main one in this context was undoubtedly the small size of the government establishments of the time. Ironically, a reduction in the scale of government operations had been pursued by Treasury Secretary Gallatin after 1801 as a way of increasing their overall efficiency, but during the War of 1812, if not in fact some time before it, the strain administrators experienced in carrying out ambitious policy goals with limited means became all too apparent. In struggling with this impossible situation, the Treasury probably continued to be the best-run government department, even after Gallatin was replaced by Jones and Campbell. Certainly the Treasury was increasingly embarrassed by the lack of funds to finance the war, but the reasons for this were more broadly political in nature and were not really the fault of the department itself.[10] The same, however, could not be said for the departments most directly concerned with the prosecution of the war. The War Department had always suffered from inadequate staff arrangements, and the reforms attempted by Eustis in 1812 only compounded an already bad situation, the more so since the overlap of functions he created in many branches of the service helped drive up the costs of the war. Gallatin removed these overlapping functions in army administration early in 1813, but thereafter neither Armstrong nor Monroe, despite the claims sometimes made for their infusing "energy" into the army, contributed anything to the efficiency of the military bureaucracy.[11] Similarly, many critical elements in the management of naval affairs often eluded the control of the Secretary of the Navy, mainly because of the difficulty of supervising adequately the activities of navy agents and officers in the navy yards. Only by extraordinary exertions could the Secretary cope with this problem as well as deal with his other duties, such as corresponding with officers and devising war strategies.[12] The burdens of administration here did not unduly trouble Secretary Hamilton, but his successor, Jones, constantly complained of them, and they were clearly instrumental in driving him into retirement in 1814.

As a result of the administrative problems experienced during the war, both the War and Navy departments underwent significant reform

[10] See Dall W. Forsythe, *Taxation and Political Change in the Young Nation, 1781-1833* (New York, 1977), 57-61. Most students of the early Republic would probably accept this claim, although the empirical research to verify it has yet to be done.

[11] Leonard White, *The Jeffersonians: A Study in Administrative History* (Chicago, 1951), 211-239. For a fuller discussion of Armstrong's role see C. Edward Skeen, "John Armstrong and the Role of the Secretary of War in the War of 1812," (Ph.D. diss., Ohio State University, 1966), 269-272, 285-292, 307-313.

[12] Edward Eckert, *The Navy Department in the War of 1812* (Gainesville, Fla., 1973), 41, 52, 53, 74.

in the years immediately after 1815, but the absence of such reform during the conflict itself, together with the lack of any broader Republican theory of administration to guide officials in such critical areas as establishing effective cooperation between the army and the navy, left the war effort greatly dependent on the degree of personal harmony that existed among the members of Madison's cabinet.[13] Unfortunately, Madison's administrations were characterized by anything but harmony and cooperation, and the war undeniably suffered because of this. The President held cabinet meetings regularly enough to discuss and define policy, but Madison was often at odds with at least one of his colleagues—who were also at odds with each other—and he had developed as a consequence the habit of tolerating, usually by recourse to ambiguity, personal differences of opinion rather than trying to settle them. This practice stemmed not so much from uncertainty in the President's mind about what actions might be required but rather from his awareness that the advantages of settling disputes decisively could be outweighed by the disadvantages. Given the difficulties which the President had in persuading men to serve in office, there was nothing to be gained by not at least appearing to make concessions to opposing points of view, even though the resulting misunderstanding usually had harmful effects on the execution of policies. Consequently, the President dealt with many serious problems only when he could no longer avoid the difficulties his own methods had created, and this was the context in which most of his many cabinet changes took place, with Robert Smith, Eustis, Hamilton, Armstrong, and even Gallatin all leaving the administration in circumstances which had become absolutely intolerable. The President thus appeared to react to events instead of anticipating them, and the prestige of his administrations suffered accordingly. Possibly, too, Madison kept a rather looser control over the daily business of government than had Jefferson, and his correspondence with Armstrong in the summer of 1814 suggests that he had become badly out of touch with the implementation of military policy.[14] He was, there can be no doubt, an inept manager of men,

[13] On postwar administrative reforms see White, *The Jeffersonians*, 240-250, 272-280; and Weigley, *History of the United States Army*, 134-153. On the navy see David F. Long, "The Navy Under the Board of Navy Commissioners," in Kenneth J. Hagan, ed., *In Peace and War: Interpretations of American Naval History, 1775-1978* (Westport, Conn., 1978), 63-77; and Craig L. Symonds, *Navalists and Anti-Navalists: The Naval Policy Debate in the United States, 1785-1827* (Newark, Del., 1980), 213-216.

[14] To obtain an overview of his administration, Jefferson required from his cabinet members summaries and the forwarding of the most important departmental papers and letters as well as some of the outgoing letters in reply. See Noble E. Cunningham, Jr., *The Process of Government Under Jefferson* (Princeton, 1978), 27-31. Madison seems to have been much

unable, as Jonathan Roberts of Pennsylvania wrote, to "hook men to his heart as his predecessor could."[15]

This being said, though, it must also be pointed out that Madison's colleagues themselves were not the easiest of people to deal with. Gallatin, the ablest cabinet member, had become embittered by too many frustrations in his long years of service, and he often used his superior administrative skills, coupled with the power of the purse, to encroach on the activities of his colleagues, sometimes causing resentment as he did so. Monroe, by contrast, appeared to be more congenial, but his amiability barely concealed a nervous anxiety about his presidential prospects, and he constantly lived in fear of being thwarted by his enemies and too many unfavorable events. His emotions often betrayed him and invariably provoked Armstrong, himself a scheming malcontent, into actions that were governed by even deeper fears and resentments.[16] He, too, desired the succession, so much so that he eventually convinced himself that the war was being deliberately mismanaged in order to deprive him of his just rewards, and he resigned. Dallas was regarded as an able financier, but his period of wartime service, brief as it was, was limited in its effectiveness because he was completely inflexible and gave offense as easily as he took it. Those colleagues who did not present personal problems for the President, such as Eustis or Campbell, were invariably incompetent or unequal for some other reason, such as health, to the demands of office. Only Jones approached the ideal of a good colleague, being useful and fairly well respected by most of those with whom he worked, and his influence with the President seems to have risen steadily throughout the war. But even he eventually felt driven to quit and left Madison stranded at the most difficult period of the entire conflict.[17]

There was, of course, far more to the problems of Madison's administrations than differences of opinion, and many of these personal conflicts themselves only reflected the almost chronic factionalism that prevailed in the unwieldy Republican coalition after 1809.[18] Despite the impression of chaos that this factionalism imparted to the politics

---

less systematic, and the increasing volume of paperwork generated by the war would have made it difficult to keep track of everything, with the result that his cabinet members had a good deal of latitude in managing their departments.

[15] Jonathan Roberts to Matthew Roberts, January 12, 1813, Jonathan Roberts Papers, HSP.

[16] C. Edward Skeen, "Monroe and Armstrong: A Study in Political Rivalry," *New York Historical Society Quarterly* 57 (1973), 121-146.

[17] See Madison to Henry Lee, February—1827, Madison Papers, LC.

[18] For a general discussion of Republican factionalism and its effects see James Sterling Young, *The Washington Community, 1800-1828* (New York, 1966), 179-210.

of the period, Republican divisions, especially in Congress, fell into fairly clear, if not always consistent, patterns, and their effects on policy-making were quite predictable. In the Senate, the schism created by the Republican "malcontents" was a longstanding one, with the "malcontents," when joined by the Federalists, usually enjoying a veto power over administration wishes. This situation lasted into 1814, if not slightly longer. In the House, Republican divisions were of a less permanent nature, but when they occurred, especially during the war years, they invariably gave the Federalists an ability to influence legislation far beyond that which their numbers would have otherwise entitled them. In this respect, it was to prove to be Madison's greatest misfortune that Britain withdrew the Orders in Council on the eve of the conflict, since those Orders had been the single most important factor in creating the Republican unity that led to the congressional vote for war. Once the Orders in Council had gone, Madison and his fellow Republicans experienced considerable difficulty in justifying the war to which they were committed, and they could never do so in way that created a sufficiently broad basis of support to enable the administration to pursue its goals with any degree of real confidence. Instead, the Republicans frequently divided over the justification for continuing the war as well as over the measures necessary to do so, and such divisions undermined the war effort.

Furthermore, the administration had few resources to deal with a Congress thus divided. The role of the legislature in policy-making, despite the prominence allowed to it in Republican theory, was either a passive or, worse, a negative one. Legislators, regardless of their personal views, always looked to the executive for the lead in framing legislation; individual Congressmen seldom took the initiative here, and even when they did—as Giles did on the 25,000-man army or Calhoun did on the bank bill—they invariably complicated matters rather than otherwise. The President's powers of leadership and persuasion, though, were limited largely to messages and proclamations.[19] Other potential sources of executive power, such as patronage and vetoes, were used far less systematically in this period than they would be later, and to obtain a hearing for its policies the administration was heavily dependent on the cooperation of congressional committees. If the cabinet members could persuade the committees to endorse the administration's wishes in their reports, the President stood a reasonable chance of gaining the necessary legislative assent. If not, the com-

---

[19] See ibid., 229-249; and Robert M. Johnstone, Jr., *Jefferson and the Presidency: Leadership in the Young Republic* (Ithaca, 1978), esp. 23-27.

mittee system simply became a barrier to executive influence, there being few means available to the President to overcome it. When this occurred, policy-making was usually left at the mercy of circumstances, and no one could safely predict the final result.

For all these reasons, then, the war policies of the Madison administration were often very different from those the President thought were the most appropriate for the occasion. Nonetheless, Madison knew that it was his duty to execute the laws as much as it was his practice to suggest informally what they should be, and when all else failed the President stoically persevered in doing his duty. The obstacles to coherent policy-making and enforcement in the early Republic, though, were formidable, and when it is remembered that in waging war the administration was often dependent on the cooperation of state and territorial governments—where barriers to effective action comparable to those already operating in Washington also existed—it is hardly surprising that the attempt to conquer Canada should have proved so difficult. The trials of waging war through the cooperation of state governments, moreover were complicated by inadequate communications, coupled with marked regional differences within the nation.[20] As a consequence, those Americans most closely affected by the conduct of the war often had a very different perception of its needs than that held by the administration and Congress in Washington. In fact, the entire course of the war was characterized by the inability of the administration, either in victory or in defeat, to conduct the conflict in accordance with its own definition of its priorities. Madison's hopes in 1788 that it might be possible to establish a government that could define and communicate a concept of the national interest that would generate adequate popular support for its realization proved to be largely illusory. Despite the reforms of the Founding Fathers and the progress made in nation-building since independence, the government of the United States was simply too small and too weak for such an ambitious task as the conquest of Canada, and Americans therefore had to derive their sense of gratification in the peace from the fact that their republican experiment had at least survived for the future.

★

THAT THE CLAIMS that many Americans made for their accomplishments in the war were somewhat inflated could be seen in the ways in which the issues at stake in the conflict were finally laid to rest in the years after 1815. With the exception of the influence which Britain

[20] For a discussion of federal-state relations during the war see Edward J. Wagner II, "State-Federal Relations during the War of 1812," (Ph.D. diss., Ohio State University, 1963).

had sometimes exercised over the Indians on the American frontiers, the peace of Christmas Eve, 1814, as has often been noted, settled none of the questions that had disturbed Anglo-American relations before or during the War of 1812.[21] Certainly, it can be argued that most of the American grievances against Britain, such as impressment and blockades, had become irrelevant with the ending of the Napoleonic wars in Europe, but this view needs to be qualified in some respects. Madison had objected to many British maritime practices precisely because he believed that they could *not* be justified as legitimate belligerent measures but were instead part of a larger British design to protect the commercial and navigation systems of the empire from American competition. This rivalry for commerce and power would continue regardless of the existence of peace or war in Europe, and nowhere was this more likely to be true than in the tangled web of commercial relationships between Britain, Canada, the United States, and the West Indies that had contributed so much to the outbreak of war. Thirty months of fighting had placed these issues no nearer solution than before, and this, too, was another reason why the Treaty of Ghent was such an empty document. With the return of peace, the Orders in Council and the "rule of '56" were placed in abeyance, but the ports of the British empire, in the Western Hemisphere anyway, remained as tightly closed to American commerce as they had ever been.

Consequently, much of the postwar diplomacy between Britain and the United States was strongly conditioned by the legacies of the previous years of conflict. Both Americans and Britons assumed that a future war was as likely to occur between their nations as was the continuation of peace, and both governments pursued policies to meet that contingency. During the war the British government had become only too well aware of the vulnerability of Canada, and, as Foreign Secretary Lord Castlereagh wrote while traveling to the Congress of Vienna in 1814, it had also "acquired a very increased notion of the value of our North American possessions to us as a naval power." And it was determined, Castlereagh added, never again to "commit the egregious folly of spoiling America by acts signally unjust to our own

---

[21] The British negotiators at Ghent abandoned their initial demand for the creation of an Indian buffer state in the Northwest and substituted for it the ninth article in the peace treaty, whereby both Britain and the United States agreed to restore the Indians to the status and privileges they had enjoyed in 1811. Given the defeats sustained by the Indians in the war, this article was virtually meaningless, and Britain never used it as the basis for any future claim against the United States.

subjects."[22] After 1815, therefore, Britain embarked on policies of maintaining stronger garrisons in Canada, encouraging more immigrants to settle there, improving communication between the Great Lakes and the Atlantic, and further fortifying the approaches to Montreal. For their part, Americans still feared that Britain, by virtue of controlling the Great Lakes and the St. Lawrence, would attempt to dominate the commerce of the region for the benefit of British navigation, and this concern provided much of the impetus behind the construction of the Erie and Champlain canals. To cope with a recurrence of Prevost's invasion of September 1814, the United States Army fortified Rouse's Point on Lake Champlain, while the threat posed to the Atlantic cities by the Royal Navy led similarly to the adoption of an extensive program of coastal fortifications.[23]

That all these plans were not fully realized owed less to the rise of Anglo-American friendship than it did to more pragmatic considerations, especially the need for financial retrenchment that was forced on both nations after 1817. Such expedient motives underlay the signing of the Rush-Bagot agreement of 1818 whereby Britain and the United States undertook not to engage in a costly competition for naval su-

---

[22] Lord Castlereagh to Earl Bathurst, October 4, 1814, in Francis Bickley, ed., *Report on the Manuscripts of Earl Bathurst* (London, 1923), 295-296. At this time, Canadian lobbyists were pressuring the British government to impose a harsh peace on the United States in order to further the growth of Canada. See Nathaniel Atcheson, *A Compressed View of the Points to be Discussed in a Treaty with the United States of America; A.D. 1814* (London, 1814).

[23] The best general discussions of these issues are Kenneth Bourne, *Britain and the Balance of Power in North America, 1815-1908* (London, 1967), esp. 3-71; Hitsman, *Safeguarding Canada*, 117-129; and C. P. Stacey, "The Myth of the Unguarded Frontier, 1815-1871," *American Historical Review* 56 (1950), 2-12. On canal-building in the United States as a response to commercial and military threats posed by the British in Canada see the material in David Hosack, *Memoir of DeWitt Clinton* (New York, 1829), esp. 406-439. The wartime governor of New York, Daniel D. Tompkins, who became Vice President in 1817, disapproved of the Erie Canal on the grounds that the Treaty of Ghent was no more than a truce; instead, he argued that for the next war the United States should prepare properly for the conquest of Canada. See Jonas Platt to Hosack, May 3, 1828, Hosack, *Memoir of Clinton*, 387. See also the debates on the so-called Bonus Bill of 1817 in AC, 14th Cong., 2d sess., 260-262, 772, 783, 786-842, 851, 860-870, 877-879, 881-915. In his last official act, Madison, on March 3, 1817, vetoed the Bonus Bill—which provided funds for an Erie canal—on constitutional grounds. However, Madison very probably shared Gallatin's view, expressed in his 1808 report on internal improvements, that a canal to Lake Erie was also impracticable, and he would, moreover, have resented DeWitt Clinton's lobbying for it in Washington over the winter of 1816-1817, just as he had resented the New Yorker's actions on a similar occasion in 1811-1812. See Ronald E. Shaw, *Erie Water West: A History of the Erie Canal, 1792-1854* (Lexington, Ky., 1966), 34, 67, 68, 79; and also George R. Taylor, *The Transportation Revolution, 1815-1860* (New York, 1951), 163.

premacy on the Great Lakes. The agreement seemed to favor the United States more than Britain because it tacitly acknowledged that all the advantages for naval construction in the area really lay with the former. Such a concession promised to enhance the ability of Americans to conquer Canada in a future war, but for Britain the agreement, at the most, represented little more than a change of tactics in defending its North American possessions. The British defense of Canada had always been based on a firm control of positions to the east of the Great Lakes, and one reason why the Admiralty consented to abandoning the rivalry on Lake Erie, if not on Ontario, was the fact that Lake Erie, Commodore Perry's victory there in 1813 notwithstanding, was a poor location for naval operations anyway. After 1819 the British government, following the recommendations of the Dukes of Wellington and Richmond, concentrated on strengthening the land defenses of the key positions for its control of Canada—Halifax, Quebec, Montreal, Kingston, and also the Niagara frontier. In the event of war the strongest positions would be defended at the risk of sacrificing more exposed areas farther west, while pressure would be brought to bear on the United States by occupying Long Island and Staten Island with a strong force, and from there blockading the American coast.[24]

The most serious source of friction between the United States and Britain after 1815, however, was still the old and vexed question of American access to the colonial trades. A commercial convention, negotiated by Albert Gallatin and Frederick Robinson of the Board of Trade in July 1815, provided for reciprocity in the trade between the United States and the British Isles but excluded Americans from the West Indies, while also failing to make any arrangements about Canadian-American trade.[25] The British government declined, albeit more courteously than in the past, to negotiate on these colonial issues, thus prompting Madison, then John Quincy Adams, who became Secretary of State under President Monroe, to resort to commercial restrictions by way of retaliation. In 1817 and 1818 Congress passed two navigation acts, the first excluding imports from British colonies unless carried in American bottoms and the second prohibiting both exports to and imports from all colonial possessions closed to American shipping. As in the past, Britain met the challenge by opening free ports in Canada to encourage their development as entrepôts for commodities needed in the West Indies, and this move, in turn, prompted the United States in 1820 to exclude both the produce and the vessels of Canada

[24] Bourne, *Britain and the Balance of Power*, 9-26, 33-43; Stacey, "The Myth of the Unguarded Frontier," 9-12.
[25] Perkins, *Castlereagh and Adams*, 168-170.

and the West Indies from American ports.[26] These measures, as well as the debates on them, were heavily reminiscent of the policies advocated by Madison in the 1780's and 1790's, and the views of Lord Sheffield, William Knox, and George Chalmers were also given a similar revival as the explanation of the motives behind the British behavior.[27] Madison retired from public life in 1817 at the end of his second term, but his preference for commercial restriction as a diplomatic weapon was inherited by John Quincy Adams, who added to it an inveterate Anglophobia.

Yet as British and American diplomats seemed bent on re-enacting the past, events were also occurring that led to a very different future in their relations. The West Indian trades, which had been so important to the economies of both Britain and the United States before 1812, steadily declined in significance after 1815, and were superseded by new patterns of commerce. The most important development for Americans here was their domination of the rapidly expanding cotton trade across the Atlantic to meet the demands of Britain's industrial revolution, and no American diplomat ever considered applying policies of commercial restriction to this vastly profitable traffic.[28] On the British side, the West Indies lost their pre-eminent position as the nation's most valued colonies as the planters there struggled with rising costs and falling returns and with competition from newer areas in the East Indies and Latin America, and then finally had to endure the abolition of slavery itself. The difficulties of the islands were reflected in the actions of Joseph Marryat—whose influence had been so important in shaping Britain's anti-American policies before 1812—who now ignored the United States in order to concentrate on the threat posed to the Caribbean economies by competition from sugar and coffee grown in the East India possessions of the empire.[29] Accompanying these developments was Britain's interest in creating a new commercial empire, as distinct from a territorial one, in its trade with the newly

[26] F. Lee Benns, *The American Struggle for the British West India Carrying Trade, 1815-1830* (Bloomington, Ind., 1923), 29-70.

[27] AC, 14th Cong., 1st sess., 878, 883, 977; 14th Cong., 2d sess., 783-786; 15th Cong., 1st sess., 311, 335. It was also pointed out during these debates that commercial restriction, having been unsuccessful before 1812, was not likely to succeed now, and John Randolph of Roanoke accused the advocates of restriction of laying the groundwork for another Anglo-American war.

[28] Douglass C. North, *The Economic Growth of the United States, 1790-1860* (New York, 1966), 17-74; Perkins, *Castlereagh and Adams*, 222-227; and Taylor, *The Transportation Revolution*, 176, 185-190.

[29] Lowell J. Ragatz, *The Fall of the Planter Class in the British Caribbean, 1763-1833* (New York, 1928), 331-383, 408-457.

independent Latin American nations.[30] The United States, too, sought commercial expansion in Latin America, but the rivalry between the two nations there was necessarily conducted in a more restrained manner than it was in the West Indian dispute. It expressed itself on the American side not so much in trade war as in the grander, though less effective, gesture of the Monroe Doctrine of December 1823.[31]

With the declining importance of the West Indies, the British government became less rigid in its defense of the old colonial system. This change coincided with the death in 1821 of Lord Sheffield, the ideologue of the navigation system, and the gradual acceptance of more flexible commercial policies by the Board of Trade, which, in 1822, came under the control of the liberal William Huskisson.[32] In that year, too, Britain suggested a solution to the West Indian problem by offering to open the island ports to American trade in certain enumerated products, which, in fact, constituted most of the items American merchants had always sought to carry to and from the Caribbean.[33] In taking this step, Britain wished in addition to give a degree of imperial preference, as Frederick Robinson put it, to the "more extended use of corn, flour and lumber from Canada . . . [in] the British West Indies," but since Congress, in 1821, had passed a bill authorizing the President to negotiate on a reciprocal basis any relaxations in the British navigation system, the prospects for a final settlement of the dispute seemed promising.[34] President Monroe, however, in proclaiming the resumption of the West Indian trade in response, omitted to provide for the removal of the heavy discriminatory duties that American law still imposed on British vessels engaged in the colonial trades. When the British government protested that the United States had met neither the letter nor the spirit of its offer on the West Indian trade, John Quincy Adams replied that the discriminatory duties would remain in

[30] See William W. Kaufmann, *British Policy and the Independence of Latin America, 1804-1828* (New Haven, Conn., 1951), passim; D.C.M. Platt, *Latin America and British Trade, 1806-1914* (London, 1972), 3-61; C. K. Webster, ed., *Britain and the Independence of Latin America, 1812-1830* (Oxford, 1938), I, 1-79; and H.W.V. Temperley, *The Foreign Policy of Canning, 1822-1827* (2d ed., London, 1966), 157-162.

[31] For the background see James F. Rippy, *Rivalry of the United States and Great Britain Over Latin America* (Baltimore, 1929). Both Rippy—pp. 117-118—and Dexter Perkins, *The Monroe Doctrine, 1823-1826* (Cambridge, Mass., 1927), 16-19, stress John Quincy Adams's desire for commercial equality with Britain in his advocacy of the doctrine of noncolonization.

[32] See Robert L. Schuyler, *The Fall of the Old Colonial System: A Study in British Free Trade, 1770-1870* (New York, 1945), 97-131.

[33] Benns, *Struggle For the West India Carrying Trade*, 82-86.

[34] For Robinson's remarks see George Dangerfield, *The Era of Good Feelings* (New York, 1952), 260.

force until Britain not only removed the restrictions on American trade but also gave up the preference that it wished to give other parts of the empire, principally Canada, in trade with the West Indies.[35]

Adams made this demand, it would seem, from the desire to wrest a symbol of American equality from the British, and perhaps he was attempting to remove the cause of a future war as well, but it soon became clear that the normally cautious diplomat had badly over-reached himself. The claim that American vessels be admitted to the trade of the empire on the same terms as British ones was unprece-dented, and it proved too much for even the most generous British government to concede. Negotiations on the issue between 1823 and 1825 produced no solution, and Britain, after first imposing retaliatory duties on American produce entering the West Indies, finally closed the islands altogether to American trade by Order in Council in 1826. John Quincy Adams, now President himself after Monroe's retirement in 1825, correspondingly proclaimed the American restrictions of 1818 and 1820 to be once more in force, and the British government, pre-dictably enough, resorted in 1827 to the old tactic of opening free ports in Canada to encourage an indirect trade.[36] Throughout this tiresome replay of past maneuvers, the United States proceeded on the assumption that the West Indies were still dependent on the United States for supply and that Britain would eventually be compelled to accept American demands for that reason. This assumption, however, was no longer true, though the United States, on this occasion, was slow to realize it and adapt accordingly.

The true picture was not finally revealed until Adams, in July 1827, dispatched the American consul at St. Bartholemew, Robert Monroe Harrison, as a special agent to report on the state of affairs in the West Indies after the Order in Council of 1826.[37] Harrison's mission lasted for nearly a year and his reports were long and complex, but their message was clear. Harrison conceded that it was certainly true West Indian planters preferred American supplies, largely because they were cheaper and their availability was more regular than supplies from anywhere else, but he also found that they could draw on a number of alternative sources. He reported that many of the islands did, in fact, receive substantial quantities of timber, flour, oats, beef, and pork from

[35] Benns, *Struggle For the West India Carrying Trade*, 87-95.

[36] Ibid., 95-162.

[37] Shortly after the Order in Council of 1826 came into effect, Harrison, then consul at Antigua, reported on British attempts to organize alternative sources of supply. See Harrison to Henry Clay, August 17, 1826, in James F. Hopkins et al., *The Papers of Henry Clay* (Lexington, Ky., 1959–   ), V, 625.

Canada and that it was also possible to obtain some of these items from places as far distant as Danzig, Brazil, and Colombia. Reporting from Barbados, Harrison further noted, with some sense of surprise, that "the inhabitants of this island, as well as the others, have less regard for Mr. Jefferson than any of our Presidents (not excepting Mr. Madison who manfully declared war against their nation) yet they say he nevertheless, though not intentionally, rendered them a great service by laying on the Embargo which taught them to find resources within themselves, that is to say, by cultivating ground provisions, which they never did before, and were entirely dependent on the United States." "This they tell you," he concluded, "is not now the case and never will be so again."[38] In short, the highly structured colonial world created by the navigation system was collapsing, and the diplomacy that tried to manipulate the weaknesses of that system for American advantage was no longer, if indeed it ever had been, a viable course of action.

By 1828 it had also become apparent to many Americans and Britons that any advantages to be derived from dominating the navigation to the West Indies no longer outweighed the disadvantages that American producers, West Indian planters, and Anglo-American relations generally had to suffer from the diplomacy of commercial restriction.[39] The deadlock between the two nations, though, seemed to be complete, the more so because neither George Canning nor John Quincy Adams appeared to be willing to make the mutual concessions required to resolve it. Any personal barriers to a settlement, however, were removed by the death of Canning in 1827 and the failure of Adams, in 1828, to gain re-election, and the uncompromising stand of the latter may have contributed to the alienation of the American electorate with his administration.[40] His successor, Andrew Jackson, was determined

[38] Robert Monroe Harrison to Clay, August 9 and 16, November 17, 1827, March 2 and April 2, 1828, all in "An Account of a Mission or Tour of Observation and Inquiry throughout the British West Indies. By Command of the President of the United States," Communications from Special Agents (M-37), Records of the Department of State (RG 59), NA.

[39] See, for example, Littleton W. Tazewell, *A Review of the Negotiations between the United States of America and Great Britain Respecting the Commerce of the Two Countries, and More Especially Concerning the Trade of the Former with the West Indies* (London, 1829). Tazewell was severely critical of the commercial restrictions advocated by Madison before 1812, dismissing them (p. 16) as the product of a "vain, reckless, speculative politician, fancying himself to be a statesman and more solicitous to obtain ephemeral popularity by the exhibition of some specious, glittering scheme than to vest his hopes for future fame upon the solid basis of his country's real and permanent interest. . . ."

[40] Benns, *Struggle For the West India Carrying Trade*, 158-162.

to end the dispute, and did so by 1830. The basis of the settlement was the British offer of 1822, though as well as sanctioning a direct trade with the islands Britain also removed all duties on the importation of American produce into Canada in order to continue encouraging an indirect trade through that region.[41] Nonetheless, with the "reciprocity of 1830" one of the most important sources of the commercial rivalry that had divided the United States and Britain since 1783 and contributed so greatly to the war in 1812 was finally removed.

With this settlement Lord Sheffield's vision of the second British empire, which had troubled American diplomats for so long, was effectively banished, and few contemporaries, with the exception of those Canadians who had glimpsed in Sheffield's arguments a mirage of future greatness, seemed to have any regrets.[42] Madison, who still followed events in retirement, thus became more optimistic about the future. A settlement of the West India dispute, he declared in 1829, would remove the most serious obstacle to "commercial harmony" between the United States and Britain, and thereafter time would be on the side of the former. Confronted with the vast natural resources and flourishing commerce of America, Britain could "no longer hope to continue mistress of the seas." "The Trident," the former President observed shortly before his death in 1836, "must pass to this hemisphere, where it may be hoped it will be less abused than it has been on the other."[43] Events in the fullness of time bore out his prediction.

[41] Ibid., 163-188.

[42] John Bartlett Brebner, *North Atlantic Triangle: The Interplay of Canada, the United States and Great Britain* (New Haven, Conn., 1945), 93, 104, 109, 111; D. G. Creighton, *The Commercial Empire of the St. Lawrence, 1760-1850* (Toronto, 1937), 190, 207, 208; and W. S. McNutt, *The Atlantic Provinces: The Emergence of Colonial Society, 1712-1857* (Toronto, 1965), 169-173.

[43] Madison to James Barbour, February 6, 1829; to Charles Jared Ingersoll, May 14, 1836, Madison Papers, LC.

THREE *National Intelligencer* EDITORIALS ON CANADA

THE CANADAS

The following article on the subject of the British provinces on our Northern frontier is from the pen of a valuable Correspondent whose sources of information are unquestionably correct, and whose statements may therefore be relied on.

FOR THE *National Intelligencer*

Mr Editor,

In the present state of our foreign relations, I presume some account of these important colonies will be acceptable to your readers. This information has become the more necessary in consequence of the erroneous opinions which are too generally entertained on that subject, and which errors the British party strive to perpetuate.

Most of the ideas which prevail relative to Canada have been drawn from former times, without allowing for the rapid changes which have been effected by settlements, by commerce, and by war—whereas no country furnishes an example where those causes have operated so powerfully in raising colonies in wealth and importance as in the Canadas. I do not hesitate to say that in the present situation of the world these provinces are of more vital importance to Great Britain than one half of her West India colonies. Till lately, the inhabitants of the Canadas were few in number, and those without energy or enterprise. The American settlements had not been pushed forward to the northern and western frontier of the Union—into those vast and fertile regions which border on the Lakes of Canada. The British possessions in the West Indies, much smaller than at present, were amply supplied from the United States and the Baltic furnished her with lumber and naval stores in abundance. The principal settlements of Canada were begun in a northern and sterile part, and by a people not fitted to prosecute them with success; but for some years past, the settlements have been progressing south-westerly along the St Lawrence and spreading into one of the most desirable countries of the globe. The colonists have not only increased in number by emigration from Europe, but have been roused to action and enterprise by the newcomers. The American settlements have been extended to the fertile frontier of the state of New York, embracing the five hundred miles of navigable water, and even beyond the shores of Lake Erie.

Here let me correct an impression of superficial observers, already prejudiced against the government of their own country. It is this: that the rapid increase of the trade of Montreal and Quebec has been promoted by our embargo and other restrictive laws: I do not deny that they have had some effect in producing that effect, but the principal causes are to be found in the increase of British possessions in the West Indies; in the exclusion of Great Britain from the North of Europe; and, above all, in the extension of the American settlements to those places which naturally communicate with Canada. These settlements have not only furnished much for the markets of Montreal and Quebec, but have facilitated the making of roads and other establishments for those who had previously settled further from the water. It is but to cast one's eye on the map of the state of New York, and to perceive by the roads and names of the towns, that the settlements did not lately extend so far as to open a trade with Canada. These causes (the opening of roads, and the growth of settlements) will continue to increase the trade down the St Lawrence till it will be equalled only by that of the Mississippi.

In the next, I shall give an account of the water, soil, and productions of the Canadas—the population and the character of the inhabitants—their military strength, and their *importance to the United States*. A.B.

National Intelligencer, November 23, 1811

THE CANADAS—NO. II.

The human mind, not content with knowledge of the present, and of the past, longs to penetrate the gloom which shrouds futurity; but in the incident pursuit often outstrips the feeble rays reflected from experience and in the visionary chase of objects far beyond her power. In her attempts to seize on forms which must forever elude her grasp, she stumbles over the most useful knowledge, and loses possession of the most valuable objects. A new time shews her the folly of that particular pursuit, but she goes on to repeat the same process, though with other objects. This reflection has been forced upon me by the idle speculation of a French domination over these states after the fall of Britain, and the contemptuous inattention with which now many turn from a treasure of infinite importance, and lying at our doors.

But to return to my subject:— The Canadas have as great an extent of coast washed by navigable waters, as the whole shore of the Baltic, with a better climate and more productive soil than surrounds that sea. There is a fine ship navigation from the ocean to Montreal, a distance of more than five hundred miles—from there to Oswegatchee (above one hundred miles) the river is ascended by large boats and descended by vast rafts, and boats or arks of any shape. From Oswegatchee into Ontario, to Niagara and every part of the lake is a fine ship navigation. At the falls of Niagara there is a short portage, and then commences an uninterrupted navigation throughout Lake Erie, lake Huron, and lake Michigan, extending to more than 3000 miles of coast. From Lake Huron to lake Superior, the navigation is interrupted by a fall, which may be easily locked, and two thousand five hundred miles more of coast be added to the sloop navigation. There are many canals in Europe which have cost twice as much money as would be necessary to open a complete navigation for large vessels from the remotest part of lake Superior to the ocean.

The present price of transportation is, for a barrel of flour from any part of lake Erie to Montreal about one dollar seventy-four cents, from any part of lake Ontario to Montreal, one dollar, and other articles in like proportion. So easy is the descent from Ontario that immense rafts of staves, ship timber and spars are annually sent down to Montreal. The inhabitants of the county of Jefferson alone have received from these articles one hundred thousand dollars in a single year. The price of fine oak timber has sometimes been so high at Quebec as would fully justify bringing it from the shores of Lake Erie, where that species of timber abounds much more than in any of the Atlantic parts of the United States.

From the vast extent of the Canadas they must be expected to embrace a great diversity of soils as well as of climates. The north-easterly part, as has been already remarked, is cold and unproductive. Between Quebec and Montreal the land improves as you ascend the river becoming very fine in the neighborhood of the latter place. From Montreal to Kingston (at the outlet of Lake Ontario) the land is generally good, producing all the crops and vegetables which are common to New York and Pennsylvania in abundance. The country round Lake Ontario is almost everywhere extremely fertile, particularly that part which lies at the western end, and on the Niagara river. Perhaps this is exceeded by no part of the world. For besides all the more important productions of the garden and of the field, the peach, cherry, nectarine and many other delicious fruits thrive in perfection. The soil along lake Erie is excellent, and that of Huron and Superior is understood to be in general good. Perhaps no country on the globe could furnish such inexhaustible stores of the finest ship timber as that which surrounds lake Erie and Ontario.

From the view I have presented of the subject, it will readily be perceived that inhabitants alone are wanting to raise this country to the first importance. By natural increase—by emigrations, and by the rapid extensions of the American settlements, that deficiency will soon be supplied, and when once supplied, should Great Britain be allowed to retain possession of the Canadas she may laugh at any attempts to distress her West Indies or to exclude from the Baltic; for she will have more than a Baltic of her own. A.B.

National Intelligencer, November 28, 1811

THE CANADAS, No. III.

In my last I presented a general view of the soil, climate and waters of the Canadas, and stated that inhabitants only were wanting to raise them to the first commercial importance. As no recent enumeration has been made, and as the settlements are extended over a vast region, it is not to be expected that an accurate estimate of the population can be made. My opinion is that Lower Canada contains about 160,000, and Upper Canada contains 150,000, being together 310,000. The population, except the cities of Quebec and Montreal (containing about 10,000 souls each) forms a narrow but almost continual settlement from Quebec along the St Lawrence, round lake Ontario and along the Niagara river; thence westward, settlements are scattered throughout the whole peninsula formed by lakes Erie, Huron, Ontario etc and are rapidly increasing. The residue of inhabitants are chiefly in the neighborhood of small trading establishments. The French population may be estimated at 80,000 or 90,000. These are a simple, inoffensive people—disaffected toward Great Britain, partly from an hereditary national antipathy; and partly from viewing her in the light of a conqueror. They are generally well disposed towards the United States. Of the remainder about 20,000 or 30,000 may be considered as European and American Tories—the latter most incorrigible. The residue are a mixed multitude having few predilections, except those created by interest, and consequently leaning on the side of America.

I have thought this account of the Canadians the more necessary as it is intimately connected with their reduction and affiliation with the United States.

522

The commerce of Canada till lately consisted chiefly of furs and peltries, of which they exported about [$]1,300,000 worth annually, and of all other fur articles, perhaps to the amount of 200,000 dollars. The fur trade employs 150 clerks, interpreters, and agents; and about 1200 boatmen etc. Of the amount of capital employed, the writer of these essays has no data from whence to judge—and it is unnecessary to inform the reader that the fur trade has always been considered extremely profitable to the company as well as to Great Britain. But from the causes I have before explained the exports of the Canadas have wonderfully increased within a few years. It is believed they do not now fall short of 5,600,000 of dollars per annum—and this in articles of the utmost importance to Great Britain. They are either precisely fitted for the support of her fleets, armies, and colonies or are to employ her merchants and mechanics in such a way as to give the greatest scope to their capital and ingenuity.

I have now to give some account of the military strength of the Canadas. And while on this subject the reader must bear in mind that it may be greatly increased or diminished according to the exertions G.B. may think best to make for the preservation of the country. The best course will be to expect that she will make every effort which can be attended with the hope of success. Pursuing this principle, I take it for certain that she will not attempt to defend the country above Quebec if rigorously assailed, but she will defend that city to the last. The whole country above Quebec is in the power of the United States, because it consists of a long and slender chain of settlers unable to succour or protect each other, and separated only by a narrow water from a populous and powerful part of the Union. The distance of Great Britain—the ice of the St Lawrence—the difficulty of supporting and recruiting an army—the ease with which it might be outnumbered from the U. States and the impossibility of retreat in case of disaster will prevent Great Britain from sending any considerable army into the interior. It has doubtless been from these considerations that she has not erected any strong fortifications or stationed any large numbers of troops above Quebec. To that city she has directed her whole attention. It was strongly fortified by the French when in their possession—the works were considerably strengthened after its transfer to the British and have been greatly extended and improved within the last four years. At present though not regularly, it is strongly and systematically fortified, and fitted for a garrison of about 5000 or 10,000 men. It is well known to those versed in the military art that any place may be reduced by a regular siege, provided the besieging army be sufficiently powerful to protect its works, and provided there be a necessary extent of ground on which to construct those works. But a siege ought never to be attempted by other than regular troops accustomed to the tented field and directed by skillful engineers. There is great reason to believe that Great Britain has not more than 7000 or 8000 men in both Canadas, four or five thousand of which are at Quebec. Should war with Great Britain come, it would be the duty of the government of the United States to lose no time in reducing the whole country above Quebec. For this service about 20,000 men would be proper, two thirds of whom might be volunteers and one third regulars. They should be directed principally to the region of Montreal—the outlet of Ontario—and across the Niagara river. This force would probably reduce the country with little bloodshed—delay would make it more difficult: and would subject our western frontier to murderous and predatory warfare carried on by Indians, British and Tories. After the reduction of the country, a station might be chosen and fortified above Quebec which would prevent inroads from the garrison and at the same time cut off its supplies. Thus situated, the city would be of no service to Great Britain but would be kept by her at enormous expense till a proper time should present for us to reduce it by a regular siege. A.B.

National Intelligencer, December 3, 1811

INDEX

★

Adams, Henry, x, xi
Adams, John, 92, 123, 130, 148, 176, 283, 471
Adams, John Quincy, 47, 56, 58, 164, 298, 300, 305, 316, 373, 512-16
additional army (of 1812), 86-89, 101-2, 147, 153-54, 164, 168-69, 175
Additional Military Force (of 1808), 23, 137-39, 164, 168
Address to the People of the United States (1811), *see* Smith, Robert, quarrels with Madison
Adjutant General, xii, 161-62, 168-71, 324, 388, 454, 456
Alabama Indians, 349
Albany *Argus*, 286, 366-67
Albany *Register*, 81, 104, 238-39, 367
Alexander I (of Russia), 22n, 298, 300-302, 309, 319, 368n, 396, 397n, 457n, 503
Alexandria, Va., 419
Allen, James, 10n, 32n, 33n
Alley, Jerome, 37n
Allies (vs. France), 382-83, 389, 392, 469
Amelia Island, 26
Amherst, Jeffrey, 332
Amherstburg, 190
ancienne population (La.), 492-96, 499
Anderson, 177
Anderson, Adam, 13n, 15n
Anderson, David, 46n
Anderson, Elbert, 156, 280, 287
Anderson, Joseph, 86, 147, 227, 306, 310, 316n, 319n, 366, 462
Anglo-Russian Convention (1801), 299, 501n
Anti-Federalists, 125-26, 129
armistice talks: in 1812, 245; in 1813, 300; in 1814, 385-86
Armstrong, John: commander in New York City, 240-41, 272, 277, 282; criti-

cal of Madison administration, 58-60, 63, 66, 72, 75, 81, 85, 104, 372-73; and fall of Washington, 408-9, 411-19, 429; feud with Monroe, 63, 70, 72, 283, 287, 311, 368-69, 398, 400, 407, 415-16, 421, 423, 431, 507; minister to France, 51-61, 306; plans 1813 campaign, 284, 286, 331-32, 337-40; resigns, 422; as Secretary of War, 283-84, 286-87, 300, 310, 320-23, 325, 330-33, 335-37, 339-44, 346-47, 353, 363, 365-75, 378, 387-89, 394, 397, 399-403, 405-8, 420-21, 423, 505-7; supports war, 103-4, 116, 240-41, 248, 252
Army (U.S.): 25, 122, 127, 130n, 131-32, 137-38, 140, 145, 153-54, 156, 162, 164, 167-69, 172-73, 175-76, 230-31, 249-52, 268, 271-72, 274-76, 279, 281, 287, 321, 333-34, 341, 345, 360, 366-68, 374-75, 387-89, 401-2, 404, 425, 437, 453-54, 456-59, 461, 463, 477, 488, 491, 503-4, 524; clothing for, 156-57, 159, 173, 175; costs of, 127, 130, 132, 321, 322n, 375; health of, 174, 250-52, 268, 333-34, 341, 387n; pay in, 137, 170, 173, 274, 276, 325, 368, 375, 388, 456, 504; supply, 155-56, 173, 217-18, 221, 223, 275n, 280, 287, 387n; in war in Northwest, 184, 187, 189, 193, 197, 200, 215, 220, 321-22, 327, 329-30. *See also* additional army; Additional Military Force; Armstrong, John; Dearborn, Henry; Eustis, William; Monroe, James; Peace Establishment; recruiting; War Department
Army Register, for 1812, 167; for 1813, 287n
Articles of Confederation, 9, 120-21
Astor, John Jacob, 44, 228, 298-99, 378-79, 432
Atcheson, Nathaniel, 37n

Attwater, Reuben, 191
Auglaize River, 196
Aurora (Philadelphia), 44, 52, 65-68, 74-75, 90, 300, 310, 320, 322, 368

Bacon, Ezekiel, 90, 98
Badollet, John, 183
Baltic Sea, 8, 16, 22n, 39, 46-47, 84, 99, 271, 519, 521-22
Baltimore, defense of (1814), 427-28, 437
Baltimore Whig, 67, 74-75, 81, 85
Bank of America (New York), 103, 237
Bank of the United States: first BUS, 61, 151-52, 376, 450n; debate on second BUS, 298, 376-78, 438-42, 444, 446-47, 452-53, 503
Barataria: pirates of, 485, 495
Barbour, James, 207, 393, 412, 426, 452
Baring, Alexander, 19n, 29n
Barker, Jacob, 378-79
Barlow, Joel, 58n, 68n, 73, 75, 104, 107-8, 305
Bartlett, Josiah, 111-12
Bassano, duc de, 306
Bathurst, Earl, 19n, 42
Bautzen, battle of (1813), 319
Bayard, James A., 91, 95, 98, 113, 296, 300-301, 305, 316, 373, 395
Beasley, Reuben, 312
Beaver Dams, battle of (1813), 335
Bentley, William, 261, 265, 268
Berlin Decree, 22, 29, 38-39, 55-57, 64, 72, 75-77, 99-101, 108, 141, 306, 308. *See also* Milan Decree
Bibb, George, 85, 319n
Bibb, William, 315, 461, 464-65
Bidwell, Barnabas, 133
Big Warrior (of Tuckaubatchee), 351
Bingham, William, 10n, 32n
Black Swamp (Ohio), 197, 221
Bladensburg, 413, 415; battle of (1814), 417, 420-21, 429n, 498
Bledsoe, Jesse, 312, 428
blockades, 5, 312n, 386, 396, 501. *See also* Orders in Council
Bloomfield, Joseph, 166, 169, 239, 241, 267-68, 411, 425
Blount, Willie, 355, 357, 360, 490
Blue Jacket, 180
Boerstler, Charles G., 335

Bonus Bill (of 1817), 511n
bounties, 170, 279, 368, 375, 456, 459, 461. *See also* Army (U.S.), pay in; recruiting
Boyd, Adam, 111n
Boyd, John, 184, 187, 333, 335
Bradley, Stephen, 86, 105
Brent, Richard, 97, 294n, 317
Brock, Isaac, 205n
Brown, Jacob, 340, 371, 387, 388, 390-91, 399, 400; in campaign of 1814, 400-404, 406, 410, 427, 454, 456n, 467-68, 478, 504n
Brown, James, 319n, 447, 450
Brush, Elijah, 204
Burlington Heights, 390, 401-2
Burnt Corn Creek, battle of (1813), 348, 352, 354
Burwell, William A., 80, 86, 285, 442
Byers, James, 156, 280

cabinet, disunity in, 146, 283, 310-11, 369, 371-73, 390-91, 397-98, 407-8, 439, 506-7
Cadore letter, 29, 55-58, 61, 64, 71, 77-78, 306-7, 309
Calabee Creek, battle of (1814), 360
Calhoun, John C., 97, 101-2, 273, 293, 307, 318, 364, 384, 443-45, 448, 452-53, 508
Caller, James, 348
Campbell, George Washington: resigns from Treasury, 432; as Treasury Secretary, 377-80, 389, 394, 397-98, 417-18, 422, 429n, 437-38, 504, 507; in U.S. Senate, 86, 147, 227, 294n
Campbell, John, 220
Canada, ix, 4-7, 9, 23, 26, 34-35, 40, 45-46, 93, 136, 147, 330, 519-24; defense of, 181, 228-29, 343, 403n, 486, 502, 510-12, 523-24; economic development of, 32, 34, 38-44, 46n, 47, 84-85, 94, 229, 302, 502, 512-13, 515-16, 519, 521, 523; U.S. policy toward, 4-7, 46-47, 94, 136, 279-81, 284, 301-2, 330, 373-74, 385-86, 388, 390-91, 454-55, 459, 464, 466, 478, 502-3, 523-24
Canning, George, 25-26, 516
Carey, Mathew, 474, 480n
Carroll, William, 497

Carsewell, Samuel, 158

Cass, Lewis, 196-98, 202-5, 207, 322, 325, 330

Castine, British occupation of, 424, 469-70, 475-77, 483

Castlereagh, Lord, 97, 370, 510

Chalmers, George, 8n, 513

Champion, Richard, 9-11, 32n, 33

Champlain Canal, 511

Chandler, John, 166, 333-34

Chattahoochee River, 349

Chauncey, Isaac, 286, 333, 335, 340-41, 344, 391, 399, 401-4, 406

Chesapeake affair (1807), 21-22, 75, 135-38, 230

Cheves, Langdon, 95, 150, 249n, 290, 293-95, 364n; as Speaker of the House, 429-30, 448-49, 453

Chippewa, battle of (1814), 401

Chittenden, Martin, 363

Chrysler's Farm, battle of (1813), 345-46

Claiborne, Ferdinand, 356

Claiborne, William C. C., 354n, 489, 491-94, 496, 499

Clay, Henry, 86-87, 95-96, 101, 106, 109, 147, 161, 164, 211-12, 214, 216, 218, 273, 294, 301, 313n, 326, 374

Clinton, DeWitt, 49, 66, 74, 81-84, 92, 103-4, 106, 111, 116-17, 234-36, 238-41, 248, 268n, 272, 282, 285-86, 373, 434, 511n

Clinton, George, 48-49, 53, 59-60, 62n, 74, 83, 95, 106-7

Clintonians, 49, 50, 52-53, 59-60, 66, 68, 81-82, 92-94, 99, 102-3, 111n, 113-14, 118n, 232, 235, 237-41, 252, 273, 285, 319, 365-66, 422, 434

Clopton, John, 98, 363, 440, 442, 482n

Cochrane, Sir Alexander, 386, 487-88, 491, 496-97, 499

Cock, Simon, 33n

Cockburn, Sir George, 384n, 487

Cocke, John, 357

Coffee, John, 355, 495, 497

Coles, Edward, 71, 94, 116, 310n, 433

Coles, Isaac, 80n, 335n

Columbia College riot (1811), 235

Colvin, John, 35n, 73

commercial restrictions, 4, 7, 12, 14-16, 17n, 20-21, 31, 34-35, 38, 46, 51, 57, 65, 102, 106, 126, 189, 293, 363-64, 380, 383-84, 512-13, 516, 520. *See also* embargo; Nonimportation Law; nonintercourse policy

Commissary General of Purchases, 158, 280n. *See also* Irvine, Callender

committees, congressional: House committee on foreign relations, 28n, 45, 84, 86, 89, 96-97, 101-2, 106, 111, 144-45, 147, 149, 153, 192, 275, 296, 307-9, 318, 364, 392; House committee on military affairs, 149, 158, 168, 276-77, 279, 281, 368, 374, 460, 463; Ways and Means Committee, 88, 90, 150-51, 154, 293, 295n, 305, 314, 378, 438-40, 442-44, 447, 454

Connecticut, and the Hartford Convention, 477, 479-81

Congress, 3, 4, 14-15, 21, 23-24, 28, 31, 45, 54, 508-9; declares war, 111-15; 11th Cong., 56, 62, 139-43; 12th Cong., 1st sess., 79-80, 84, 86-89, 110, 144-45, 147-48, 150-51, 227; 12th Cong., 2d sess., 274-77, 279, 281, 290, 293-94, 296-97; 13th Cong., 1st sess., 304, 306-8, 315-16, 318; 13th Cong., 2d sess., 362, 364, 368, 374, 376, 378, 384; 13th Cong., 3d sess., 396, 423, 428-30, 436, 440-50, 452-53, 459-61, 463-64, 466, 503

Congressional Caucus (1812), 83, 92, 106, 107n, 111n

Constitution (U.S.), xi, 96, 125, 129, 314, 465, 503

Constitutional Convention (1787), 121, 124

Continental Army, 121

Continental Congress, 4, 11-12, 120-21

Continental System, 47. *See also* Berlin Decree; Milan Decree; Napoleon Bonaparte

convention movement, in New England: 260-61, 381, 385, 469, 471-72. *See also* disunion, threat of; Hartford Convention

Coosa River, 349, 356, 361

Corporation of Philadelphia, 410-11

Council of State (Va.), 64

Coxe, Tench, 9-11, 32n, 34, 157-59

Crawford, William H., 62, 113, 155, 277, 282, 294n, 317n, 393

Creek Indians, 348-50, 354, 361-62, 485
Creek prophets, 350-51, 354, 361
Creek war, 337, 348-62, 437, 490
Crillon, Eduoard, 97. *See also* Henry, John
Crowninshield, Benjamin W., 435
Crowninshield, Jacob, 35n
Cushing, Thomas, 425
Cutts, Richard, 21, 280n, 435, 473

Daliba, James, 205
Dallas, Alexander James, 311n, 377, 433; as Treasury Secretary, 438-48, 451-52, 457n, 463, 465, 486n, 507
Dana, Samuel, 446
Dashkov, Andrei, 271n, 299-301, 305n, 317n, 384n, 389n
Daviess, Joseph Hamilton, 186-87
Dayton, Jonathan, 98
Dearborn, Henry: on Hartford Convention, 472-73, 475-76, 483; major general in U.S. Army, 89, 129, 165, 167, 175n, 193, 202, 208-9, 228n, 230-32, 237, 239-42, 244-46, 248-49, 252, 255, 258-69, 275-77, 282, 284-87, 331-33, 336, 370; retires, 335; as Secretary of War, 23, 131-32, 137-39, 181
Decatur, Stephen, 404
Decree of Rambouillet, 54-55
Decree of St. Cloud, 305-8
defense, of coasts and frontiers, 135, 146, 188-90, 261, 272, 274-75, 278, 370, 393, 407-12, 424-25, 427, 437, 454, 460, 464, 469-70, 472, 482, 490, 494, 503, 511
Delaware Indians, 174, 206
Dennis, Richard, 172
Denny, Ebeneazar, 218
Desha, Joseph, 365
Detroit, 190-93, 195-96, 201-4, 206-7, 217, 220, 222-23, 320, 329-31; surrender of, 205
District of Columbia, 397, 411, 414, 419, 429-30. *See also* Washington, fall of
disunion, threat of, 258, 260, 285, 381, 395-96, 462, 469-74, 477, 479, 481, 483-84, 486. *See also* convention movement; Hartford Convention
Dorchester, Lord, 32
Drummond, Gordon, 401-2, 406

Duane, William, 44, 49-51, 53, 60-61, 66-69, 71, 74, 81, 90, 95, 100, 116-17, 161, 208-9, 300, 310, 320-22, 368, 411
Dutton, Warren, 260
Duvall, Gabriel, 67

Early, Peter A., 357
East Florida, 98, 279, 302, 352. *See also* Spain, U.S. relations with
Eastport, British occupation of, 410, 469
Edwards, Bryan, 9-11, 33
Edwards, Ninian, 206, 210
election of 1812, 59-60, 65, 67, 72-74, 83, 92n, 219, 252, 261, 267-68, 272-73
Ellicott, Joseph, 233, 243
embargo: of 1794, 15; of 1807-1809, 17-18, 22-25, 29, 41, 43, 46, 53-54, 136-37, 139-41, 181, 233, 253, 520; of 1812, 95-96, 101-2, 105-6, 109, 155, 232-34, 237, 256; of 1813-1814, 318-19, 363-65, 374-75, 377, 381, 383-85, 469
Emuckfau, battle of (1814), 360
Enotachopco, battle of (1814), 360
Eppes, John Wayles, 56, 67, 314-15, 378, 384, 438-39, 441-47, 453, 463
Erie Canal, 511
Erskine, David M., 17, 24-25, 27, 51, 71, 94, 139
Erving, George W., 60n
Essex Junto, 94
Eustis, Jacob, 255
Eustis, William: resigns from War Dept., 277; Secretary of War, 57, 66n, 72, 89-90, 96, 104, 108, 140, 142-44, 146, 153-61, 165, 167-69, 175, 181, 184, 186, 188-89, 191, 196, 198, 200, 207-10, 214, 218, 228, 237, 242, 244, 258, 260, 263-64, 267, 273, 275-76, 283, 289, 473, 485, 505-7

Fallen Timbers, battle of (1794), 174
fast days, 264, 482
Federalism, xi, 127-28, 253-55, 452. *See also* Federalist party
Federalist Papers, 125, 504
Federalist party, 28, 34, 53, 83, 90-91, 94, 97-98, 103, 105, 107, 112-14, 117, 121-24, 126-27, 129, 166-67, 209, 242, 246, 248, 252-55, 272-73, 277, 285-86,

290, 294, 296-97, 300n, 304n, 305-8, 316, 318-19, 364, 372, 374, 381, 385, 389n, 422, 430, 432, 439, 441-42, 445, 447-50, 453, 459, 462, 464, 469-71, 473, 476, 478, 481, 485, 500, 508; opposes war, 231, 252, 255-56, 258-65, 276-77, 362-63, 376-77, 381, 385, 392, 432n, 442-45, 463, 466, 469-71, 476, 484

Fenner, John, 265

Findlay, James, 197, 202-4

Fisk, Jonathan, 368, 430, 433-44, 450, 456

Flint River, 349

Flournoy, Thomas, 166, 366, 371n

Forsyth, John, 444

Fort Barrancas, 491

Fort Bowyer, 489-90, 499

Fort Defiance, 196, 220, 224

Fort Deposit, 355

Fort Erie, 242, 250, 286, 331, 336, 400-403, 406

Fort George, 284, 286, 331, 333-34, 336, 340, 342, 400-402

Fort Harrison, 185

Fort Malden, 182, 190, 200-203, 221, 223-26, 279, 322, 324, 327, 329, 338

Fort Meigs, 226, 320, 322-23, 325-27

Fort Mims, 354-55, 361n

Fort Strother, 356, 359-61

Fort Washington, 419, 421

Fort Wayne, 200, 210, 212-16, 220, 229n

Foster, Augustus J., 27n, 39, 42n, 68, 71-72, 75-79, 87, 94, 97, 99-100, 108-10, 115, 501

Founding Fathers, 120, 509

France, 5, 13, 20, 23, 26, 28-29, 38, 40, 46-47, 51-52, 54-56, 70, 76, 92, 98, 100-101, 104, 108, 129, 271, 298, 306-9, 319-20, 383, 389-90, 393, 469, 503. *See also* Napoleon Bonaparte

Francis, Josiah, 351, 354

Franklin, Benjamin, 13n, 15n

Franklin, Jesse, 6, 294n

free blacks (La.), 492-93

French Mills, 346, 387n

Fromentin, Elejius, 316, 319n, 447, 450

Fulton, Robert, 435

Gaillard, John, 316, 434

Gaines, Edmund P., 390, 401, 403, 491

Gales, Joseph, 57, 61, 68-69, 109, 265, 448, 464

Gallatin, Albert: commissioner in Europe, 305, 307, 310-12, 316, 318, 366, 374, 395-97, 434, 512; financial policies, 88-89, 127-31, 133-35, 137, 141-42, 146, 150-52, 154, 275, 278-80, 291-94, 298-99, 301, 305, 321, 376; offers resignation, 62-63; quarrel with the Smiths, 50, 52, 60, 62, 134-35, 140-41, 311; Treasury Secretary, 23, 26-27, 30, 44, 50-52, 58, 65-67, 86, 88, 94, 132, 150-52, 154, 161, 228, 301, 305, 310, 398, 505-7; views on war, 31, 79-80, 90, 108, 112, 129, 136, 145, 155, 161, 207-8, 222-23, 230, 259, 270, 275, 278, 280, 282, 297, 298-99, 301

Gansevoort, Peter, 241-42

Gardner, Charles K., 368

Garnett, James Mercer, 70

Gaston, William, 443-44

Gee, Joshua, 13n

general staff, 160, 173, 261, 274, 279-80, 287, 505

Genet, Edmund, 53, 82n

George III, 27, 64, 68

Georgia, role in Creek war: 353-54, 357-58, 360

German, Obadiah, 54n, 113-14, 316n, 364, 422, 447, 450, 460

Gerry, Elbridge: governor of Mass., 94, 97, 107, 254-58, 265n; Vice President, 107, 257, 261-62, 265-66, 268, 313, 434-35, 470, 473-74

gerrymander, 254, 256

Ghent, negotiations at, 452, 457, 459, 462, 471, 477, 486, 488, 501, 501n

Gibson, John, 220

Giles, William B., 49-50, 52-54, 74, 85-88, 95, 98, 101, 115-16, 147, 149n, 293, 312-13, 316n, 365-66, 454, 460, 500, 508

Gilman, Nicholas, 54n, 81, 87, 113-14, 316n, 364-65

Girard, Stephen, 299, 379n

Godfroy, François, 199

Goldsborough, Charles W., 291

Goldsborough, Robert, 305-6, 310n

Goodrich, Chauncey, 480-81

Graham, John, 111n, 208-9
Granger, Gideon, 365n
Gray, Nicholas, 245
Great Britain, ix, xii, 3-8, 10, 13, 15-16, 18, 20-21, 23, 25-28, 38, 52, 55, 69, 71, 76, 78, 84, 105, 119, 132, 228, 271, 275, 295, 299, 308-9, 319, 370, 382-83, 395-96, 457, 485-88, 503, 509-17, 519, 520, 522-24
Great Lakes, 23, 32, 41n, 43, 189, 192, 228, 274, 281, 288, 290, 321, 330, 380, 389, 391, 395, 435n, 467, 503, 511-12, 519. See also Lake Erie, Lake Huron, etc.
Greenbush, 232, 240, 244, 246, 260, 268, 467, 477
Gregg, Andrew, 86, 115
Grenadier Island, 344
Grosvenor, Thomas, 307
Grundy, Felix, 84, 102, 165, 429
gunboats, 134-35, 140, 144, 150, 291. See also Navy Dept.

habeas corpus, 172, 264, 496, 499
Halifax, N.S., 26, 30, 136, 230-31, 253, 261, 279, 470, 473, 478, 502, 512
Hall, Bolling, 442, 449
Hamilton, Alexander, 121-22, 126-29, 141, 438, 441
Hamilton, Paul: resigns from Navy Dept., 290; Secretary of the Navy, 57, 72, 96n, 140, 142, 144, 146, 150, 273, 289, 505-6
Hampton, Wade, 164, 330, 339, 341, 343, 345-46, 366-67, 371, 388, 400
Hanson, Alexander C., 445, 459
Harmar, Josiah, 187, 215
Harper, John A., 106, 274
Harrison, Robert Monroe, 515-16
Harrison, William Henry: governor of Indiana Territory, 177, 180-89, 208, 210-12; and northwestern army, 172, 213-26, 236, 282n, 320-30, 338, 367, 371; resigns, 398-99
Harrowby, Lord, 18
Hart, Nathaniel, 218
Hartford Convention, 465, 471-72, 474, 477-80, 482-83
Hawkesbury, Lord, 12n. See also Liverpool

Hawkins, Benjamin, 349, 351-52
Hawley, Jesse, 82n
Hay, George, 69, 273, 277, 317n
Henry, John, 93-94, 97-99, 256, 261
High-Headed Jim, 351
Hill, Lord Rowland, 485
Hillabee Indians, 357
Holland, Lord, 36n
Holland Land Company, 232-33, 242-43
Holroyd, John Baker, first Earl of Sheffield, 7-13, 32-34, 36-39, 42, 44, 513-14, 517
Hopkins, Samuel, 220
Horseshoe Bend, battle of (1814), 361
Howell, Jeremiah, 114
Hull, Abraham, 205n
Hull, William, 166, 190-93, 196-204, 207, 210, 213-14, 230, 244, 247, 281; surrenders Detroit, 205
Hume, David, 15n
Hunter, William, 105n
Huskisson, William, 514

impressment, 5, 18, 21, 69, 110, 271, 274, 295-97, 307, 309, 312n, 372, 393-96, 462, 501, 510. See also Seamen's Bill
Indiana, territory of, 182-84, 212, 215
Ingersoll, Charles Jared, 115, 268, 301n, 315, 366, 392, 440, 447, 478, 480, 483
Ingham, Samuel, 444
Inspector General, 169-70, 174, 456n
Irvine, Baptist, 67-68, 74
Irvine, Callender, 158-59
Izard, George, 166, 366, 371, 388, 390, 400, 404-7, 427, 454-55, 467, 477

Jackson, Andrew: and Creek war, 355-62, 399, 488-89; and defense of New Orleans, 488-90, 492, 494-99, 501; as President, 516-17
Jackson, Francis James, 25-27, 41, 44, 68
Jackson, James G., 378
Jay Treaty (1794), 17, 67
Jefferson, Thomas, 11, 17-18, 20, 22-23, 34, 36, 48, 51, 53, 61, 65, 67, 77, 91, 129-35, 137, 141, 162, 181, 208-9, 292, 438-39, 458, 488, 493, 496, 504, 506, 516
Jenkins, Elisha, 240, 476-77

Jennings, Jonathan, 183, 187
Jessup, Thomas, 164, 202, 322; and Hartford Convention, 477-81, 483-84
Johnson, Richard M., 327, 330n, 429
Johnston, John, 206, 220
Jones, William, 158; resigns from Navy Dept., 432; as Secretary of the Navy, 278n, 290-91, 311, 319, 325, 376, 379-81, 383, 388-94, 401, 403-4, 407, 416n, 417, 423, 425, 433-34, 436, 438-39, 453, 455, 505, 507; as acting Treasury Secretary, 305, 375-76, 379, 398, 504
Jordan, Gibbes W., 33n
Joy, George, 36n, 38n

Kentucky: role in 1812 campaign, 211-12, 214, 216-17, 219-20, 225, 320; role in 1813 campaign, 322-24, 326, 328, 330
Kentucky volunteers, 185-86, 213-14, 216-18, 220-21, 224-26, 320, 322, 326-30
Kerr, John, 219
Kickapoo Indians, 179, 186
King, Cyrus, 449
King, Rufus, 285, 301, 306, 309-10, 312, 385n, 422, 432, 447, 464, 500
King, William, 238, 263, 475-76
Kingsbury, Jacob, 193
Kingston, 228-29, 284-86, 331-33, 336-37, 339-43, 346, 370, 388n, 401-2, 405, 467, 512
Knox, William, 34, 41-42, 513

Lacock, Abner, 377, 433
La Cole Mill, battle at (1812), 268
Lafayette, Marquis of, 11
Laffite, Jean, 495
Lake Champlain, 29, 156, 228, 232, 266, 332, 338, 341, 366, 380, 389-90, 405, 467, 511
Lake Erie, 81-82, 178, 190, 192-93, 196, 219, 222, 226, 238, 280, 322, 324-25, 327, 329-30, 338, 390-91, 512, 520-22
Lake Huron, 201, 390-91, 521-22
Lake Michigan, 178, 521
Lake Ontario, 29, 40-41, 81, 232-33, 242, 284, 286-87, 332-36, 338, 340-42, 366, 380, 390-91, 399, 401-2, 404, 405-7, 455, 467-68, 512, 521-22, 524

Lake Pontchartrain, 487, 495, 497n
Lake Superior, 521-22
Lambert, John, 114, 316n, 364-65, 447, 450
Lambert, John (major general), 499
Langdon, John, 107
Laulewasikaw, 178. See also Prophet, the
Lee, William, 58n, 59, 73n
Leftwich, James, 220-21
Leib, Michael, 50-51, 54n, 67, 102-3, 105, 107, 113, 115, 117, 161, 310n, 316n, 364-65, 377, 433
Leiper, Thomas, 411
Leipzig, battle of (1813), 362
Le Maigouis, 178n
Lewis, Morgan, 66, 75, 236, 240, 252, 333, 335, 340, 425, 434; as Quartermaster General, 159-60, 287n
license trade, 26, 108, 275, 318
Linnard, William, 160
Little Belt affair (1811), 45, 70, 144
Little Turtle, 177, 199
Liverpool, Lord, 118, 295, 299, 437, 486-87, 500
Livingston, Edward, 496
Livingston, Robert, 75, 236
Lloyd, James, 479
Long, Edward, 9, 33n, 35n
Louis XVIII, 393, 494n
Louisiana, politics in, 489, 492-96, 499
Louisiana Purchase, 130, 352, 395, 485, 486n
Lovett, John, 307n, 318n
Lowe, Joseph, 33n
Lower Canada, see Canada
Lowndes, William, 281n, 293, 304, 309, 317, 368, 384, 444-45, 459, 500
Lundy's Lane, battle of (1814), 401-2
Lützen, battle of (1813), 319

McArthur, Duncan, 197-98, 201-5, 322, 325, 330
Macdonough, Thomas, 427
McKee, Samuel, 449-50
McKenney, Thomas, 420
Macomb, Alexander, 174
Macomb, Robert, 237
Macon, Nathaniel, 28n, 62, 165
Macon's Bill Number 1, 28, 52, 85

Macon's Bill Number 2, 28-29, 52, 55, 85, 142

Madison, Dolley, 335n, 413

Madison, James, ix-xi, xiii, 3-4, 6-7, 10-11, 14-15, 18; advocates embargo, 20-23, 27, 35; appoints Monroe to State Department, 63-65; attitude to armed forces, 121, 126, 133, 139, 141-44, 164-67, 176; cabinet problems in 1814, 431-36, 506-7; and Creek war, 352-54, 357; decides to prepare for war, 69, 71, 76, 78-79, 143-44; defends war policies, 274, 305, 363, 436-37, 451-52, 456-57, 462, 508; and fall of Washington, 416-20, 423-24, 428; and Hartford Convention, 472-75, 482, 485; influenced by Lord Sheffield, 10-12, 34; nationalism of in 1780's and 1790's, 48, 122, 125-27, 129, 504; nominated for Presidency, 106-7; preparedness policies of, 79-80, 87-89, 91-92, 96-97, 100, 102, 104, 109-10, 115-16, 144-45, 152, 155, 161; as President, 25-26, 28-31, 46, 49, 56, 86-87, 99, 516-17; proclamation of November 1810, 55-56, 76; relations with Armstrong, 397-400, 403-9, 413, 416-17, 420-22, 506; relations with 13th Cong., 305, 311n, 312-14, 316, 318-19, 362-63, 436-37, 451-53, 459, 466; and Republican disunity, 49, 52-54, 60, 62, 65-67, 71, 77, 79, 81, 93, 104, 116, 239, 311, 373, 397, 453, 506, 508-9; as Secretary of State, 16-22, 35, 38; theory of commercial restriction, 7-8, 11-14, 16, 27, 33n, 35, 46, 513, 516n, 517; views on Canada, 4, 6-7, 30-31, 34-39, 43-44, 46-47, 373; and war in Northwest, 184, 188-89, 192-93, 197-98, 209-10, 214-15, 222-23, 329, 391; 'war message' of, 110; wartime diplomacy of, 295-96, 299-301, 305, 318, 370-71, 380, 383, 386-87, 390, 392-97, 457n, 462, 503; war strategy of, in 1812, 227, 229-30, 234, 264-66, 269, 523-24

Maine, district of, 469-71, 474, 476, 478, 484

"malcontents," 50, 54, 59-61, 67-68, 71-72, 74-75, 78-81, 85-88, 90, 98-100, 102-3, 105, 107, 111-13, 115, 209,
281n, 293, 297, 310, 316-17, 319, 364-65, 462, 500, 508

Malthus, Thomas, 15n

Manhattan Company, 377

Manrique, Gonzales, 490

Marryat, Joseph, 19, 37-39, 513

Marshall, John, 259

Mason, Jeremiah, 372, 462

Mason, John, 207

Mathews, George, 99

Maumee River, 196, 220, 320, 323-24, 328-29

Medford, Macall, 33n, 35n

Mediterranean Fund, 133

Meigs, Return Jonathan, 189-90, 194-98, 204, 206, 213, 215, 217, 221-22, 225, 327

merchantmen, arming of, 80, 84, 145, 149

Merry, Anthony, 20

Miami Exporting Company, 218

Miami Indians, 177, 179-82, 187, 199, 206, 212, 215-16, 220. See also northwestern Indians

Miami of the Rapids, 196, 203-4, 220, 224-26

Michigan, territory of, 190, 192, 197, 274

Michilimackinac, 201, 329

Milan Decree, 22, 29, 38, 39, 55-57, 64, 72, 75-77, 99-101, 108, 141, 306, 308. See also Berlin Decree

military districts, 278, 287, 310, 358, 408-9, 411-14, 419-20, 424, 426, 434, 475, 488

militia: classification of, 121-24, 132-33, 135, 139, 143, 145, 149, 176, 363, 366-69, 374, 437, 457-60, 503; laws relating to, 124, 132, 136, 138, 163, 172, 259-60, 274, 411, 462-66, 475

militia, state, 87, 132-33, 138-39, 145, 148, 150, 153, 163, 172, 251, 393, 412, 461-66, 503; in Massachusetts, 258, 262-63, 470, 475; in New York, 239, 241-43, 245-47, 249, 266; in Pennsylvania, 251-52, 414

Miller, James, 203-4, 475-76

Mississinewa River, 187, 199, 220

Mississippi, territory of, 348, 354-56, 487

Mitchell, David B., 354, 357-58

Mitchill, Samuel L., 111n, 270, 272-73, 289

Mobile, 349, 355, 362, 487, 490-92, 495, 499

Monroe, James, 18, 21, 31, 49, 54, 63-65, 69, 252, 263; as President, 512, 514; presidential ambitions of, 278, 282, 313, 372n, 382, 431, 468, 507; as Secretary of State, 4, 47, 69, 70-72, 74-75, 78, 80, 84-85, 87-89, 96, 99-102, 105, 108, 112, 148, 153, 163-64, 207, 274, 277, 297, 302, 306, 308-10, 312n, 352, 379, 391, 394, 396-97, 431, 434, 477, 501; as Secretary of War, 223-24, 277-82, 420-22, 426-28, 431-32, 438-39, 446, 451, 454-55, 457-64, 466-68, 475-78, 481, 483, 485, 489, 491, 505; seeks military command, 208-10, 213-14, 222, 278, 281, 284

Monroe Doctrine (1823), 514

Monroe-Pinkney Treaty (1806), 49, 67, 372

Montgomery, Richard, 230, 242

Montgomery, Thomas, 315

Montreal, 30, 40-41, 81, 156, 191, 227-30, 233, 245-56, 266-68, 280, 284, 331-32, 338-40, 342-45, 390, 455, 467-68, 502-3, 511-12, 520-21, 524

Morier, John Philip, 57, 69n

Morris, Gouverneur, 81-83

Morrison, James, 218-19

Morrow, Jeremiah, 206-7, 483

Napoleon Bonaparte, 21-22, 26, 29, 39, 47, 54-58, 61n, 64, 76, 78n, 84, 271, 300n, 305, 319, 362, 383, 385, 389-90, 392-93, 469

Napoleonic wars, xi, 17, 382, 510

National Intelligencer (Washington, D. C.), 17n, 22, 27, 29, 38, 44-46, 68, 73, 76n, 77n, 79, 88, 90-91, 94, 96-97, 102, 105, 109, 144, 152, 154, 169, 207, 227, 257-58, 265, 277, 294, 378, 384, 389, 392, 429, 441, 443, 446, 448, 450-51, 466, 473, 483, 519-24

naval stores, 16, 39, 519, 521-22

navigation laws, of 1817 and 1818, 512, 515

navigation system, of Great Britain: 5, 6, 8, 13, 33-34, 45, 47, 502, 510, 514, 516

Navy (U.S.), 127, 133-36, 145, 150, 256, 288, 290-91, 330, 375, 389; on Great Lakes, 338, 341, 380, 389, 400, 402-4, 455

Navy, 4, 123, 130, 134, 289n, 291, 435, 505. *See also* Crowninshield, Benjamin; Hamilton, Paul; Jones, William

Nelson, Hugh, 83-84, 449

neutral rights, 18, 33n, 43, 47, 70, 76, 299, 320, 397n, 500, 502-3

New Brunswick, *see* Canada

Newburgh letters (1783), 60, 116, 283. *See also* Armstrong, John

New Orleans, battle of (1815), 498-99; defense of, 485, 487-89, 491-92, 494-95, 497-99

Newton, Thomas, 275

New York Council of Appointment, 240-41

New York State Canal Commission, 81-83

Niagara Peninsula, 231-32, 238, 242-46, 248, 251, 265-66, 268-69, 282, 285, 331, 333, 336-38, 340, 369-71, 388, 392, 400, 404-6, 427, 437, 454-55, 467-68, 512

Nicholas, Wilson Cary, 49, 51, 53, 116, 465, 474

Nicholson, Joseph H., 115, 377, 421-22

nonimportation, 15. *See also* commercial restrictions

Nonimportation Law (1806), 20-22, 24

Nonintercourse Law (1809), 24, 26, 30n, 54

nonintercourse policy, 24-27, 29, 41-42, 55, 69, 105, 189, 292-94, 298, 304. *See also* commercial restrictions

North, William, 167

northwestern army, 195-97, 199, 201, 204, 215-23, 225-26, 320-22, 326-27, 329-30, 398-99

northwestern Indians, 110, 114, 126, 177-81, 191, 195, 197, 199, 203, 206-7, 213, 220, 222, 224, 272, 274, 323-24, 326, 371, 510

Nova Scotia, *see* Canada; Halifax

Oakley, Thomas, 307, 444

Observations on the Commerce of the American States (1783), 7-10, 32. *See also* Holroyd, John Baker

officers, army, 166-67, 173-75, 334-35, 337, 387n

Ohio, in northwestern war, 194, 197, 206, 208, 213, 217, 219-20, 225, 323, 326-28, 465

"Old Republicans," 49, 54, 63, 70, 81, 91, 114, 129, 281n

Olive Branch, The, 474, 480n

Olmstead affair, 67

Orders in Council: of 1783, 7, 14, 34; of 1807 and 1809, 5, 18-19, 22, 24-25, 29, 35, 36n, 38-39, 52, 54-56, 65, 69-70, 75-79, 91, 94, 100, 108, 110, 118-19, 141, 259, 288-89, 292, 295, 306-8, 501, 508, 510; of 1811, 45; of 1826, 515

Ordnance Department, 140, 159, 161, 280n

Otis, Harrison Gray, 301n, 485

Ottawa Indians, 179

Pacanne, 177

Packenham, Sir Edward, 497-98

Parish, David, 234, 298-99, 378-79

Parke, Benjamin, 261

Parker, Daniel, 163

Patterson, Daniel, 496, 499n

Patuxent River, 408, 411, 413, 415-16

Paymaster, army, 171

Peace Establishment (1802), 130-32, 138, 160, 163, 168. *See also* Army (U.S.)

Peace of Paris (1783), xi, 4, 9, 395, 486

Pensacola, 348, 351-52, 355-56, 361, 489-90. *See also* Spain, U.S. relations with

Perceval, Spencer, 26, 47, 64, 71n, 77-78, 97, 118, 259

Perry, Oliver Hazard, 325, 327, 329-30, 512

Petty, William, 15n

"Philadelphia Junto," 50, 66, 75, 310, 411. *See also* Republican party in Pennsylvania

Piatt, John, 218

Piatt, William, 218

Pickens, Israel, 296

Pickering, Timothy, 256, 373

Pike, Zebulon, 174, 333

Pinckney, Thomas, 165, 353, 358

Pinkney, William, 21, 24, 38, 49, 64n, 68, 71n, 75, 259

Piqua, Council of (1812), 200-206

piracy, 126, 133-35

Plattsburg, battle of (1814), 427, 437, 486

Plumer, William, 257, 259, 373

Polk, William, 165

Pope, John, 85, 105, 107, 114

Porter, Moses, 408

Porter, Peter B., 82, 85n, 87, 89, 97, 101, 145, 147-49, 192, 227, 240, 242-43, 246-47, 250-51, 288, 336, 381, 400, 481

Potawatomi Indians, 179, 185-86, 206, 216

Potomac River, 408, 417, 419, 430

Prague, Congress of (1813), 320

Preston, James P., 335n

Prevost, Sir George, 386, 390, 427, 511

Prince Regent, 27, 64-65, 68, 78, 96-97, 500

Proctor, Henry, 329

Prophet, the (Shawnee), 178-79, 181-85, 187, 189, 199

Prophetstown, 178, 182, 184-85, 187

Purveyor of Public Supplies, 123, 157-58. *See also* Coxe, Tench

Put-in-Bay, battle of (1813), 329

Quartermaster General's Department, 140, 142, 157-61, 280n, 287n

Quasi-War (with France), 123-24, 127-39, 352

Quebec, 40-41, 43, 227-30, 242, 459, 468, 512, 520-24

Queenstown Heights, battle of (1812), 249

Quincy, Josiah, 281-82

Raisin, battle of (1813), 225, 324

Raisin River, 202-4, 217, 224-25

Randolph, John (of Roanoke), 5, 48, 62, 70, 81, 85, 88, 91, 95, 101, 108, 111-12, 142, 479, 513n

recruiting: for army, 162, 164, 169-75, 264, 276, 325, 337, 368, 374, 388-89,

456-59, 477; obstruction of, 172-73, 271, 276, 477, 480, 483
Reed, Philip, 114
Religious Freedom Act (Mass.), 254-55
remission of forfeitures, 292-95, 298, 304. *See also* Gallatin, Albert, financial policies
Republicanism, xi, 127-29. *See also* Republican party
Republican party, xi, 28, 48, 52, 61n, 64-65, 72, 80, 90, 106, 110-11, 127, 132, 134-35, 147, 150, 166, 168, 271-73, 277, 281, 283, 288, 290, 293-94, 296-97, 304, 307, 309-10, 315, 317-18, 362, 364, 374, 385, 430, 432, 436, 441, 459, 463, 472, 483; attitude to war finance, 90-91, 314, 377, 441; disunity in, 28, 48, 51, 53-54, 59-61, 63, 65, 69, 72, 77, 91-93, 97, 108, 142, 146, 270, 272, 288, 290, 294-97, 303, 305, 307, 314-16, 319, 377-78, 384, 438-39, 442-46, 448-49, 452-53, 463, 507-8; fear of debt, 127-30, 135, 141, 377; in Massachusetts, 253-55, 257, 260-62, 265-69, 467-68, 470, 472, 474-75, 478, 482, 484-85; in New York, 60, 66, 92-93, 103, 117, 167, 231, 234-41, 246, 250-52, 285-88, 335-36, 362, 370, 381, 391-92, 421-22, 433, 467-68; in Ohio, 188, 194-95, 213, 219; in Pennsylvania, 50-52, 67, 75, 92, 112, 118, 291, 310, 366-67, 377, 392, 398, 411, 433; in Vermont, 266
Richardville, 199
Ringgold, Samuel, 384
revival movements: in Northwest, 178-81; in Southwest, 350-51. *See also* Creek Indians; northwestern Indians
Riall, Phineas, 401
Richmond, Duke of, 512
Ripley, Eleazar, 402
Roberts, Jonathan, 83, 277, 292-93, 295-96, 315, 363, 365n, 433, 444, 451, 500, 507
Robinson, Frederick, 512, 514
Rodgers, John, 425, 435, 501
Rodman, William, 111-12
Rodney, Caesar A., 30
Rodriguez Canal, 498
Rose, George, 137

Ross, Robert, 485
Rouse's Point, 511
Royal Navy, 15-16, 24, 39-49, 54, 80, 126, 136, 144-45, 230, 318, 353, 376, 385-86, 389, 396, 408, 468-69, 478, 485, 487, 496, 499, 511; on Great Lakes, 336, 341, 406, 454
"rule of '56," 5, 18-20, 35, 510
Rush, Richard, 67, 91, 94, 102, 109-10, 161, 166-67, 207, 265, 273, 377, 391, 393-94, 408, 417, 423-24, 429, 435, 471, 474
Rush-Bagot agreement (1818), 511-12
Russell, Jonathan, 4, 108, 292, 305-7, 310, 312-14, 374
Russia, 39, 46-47, 271n, 298-302, 320, 383, 390, 393, 396, 457n; offer of mediation (1813), 298-99, 304-5, 310, 312, 316-19, 363, 370, 374, 457, 503

Sacketts Harbor, 231-32, 285, 287, 333, 336-37, 340-42, 371, 400-401, 403-6, 427, 467
Sailly, Peter, 30
St. Clair, Arthur, 124, 187
St. Joseph's River, 217
St. Lawrence River, 23, 32, 40-44, 46, 81, 227, 233, 237-38, 332, 338, 340, 342-44, 366, 390, 405, 455, 483, 502, 511, 522-23
St. Mary's River, 215, 217
salt annuities, 182, 184
Sammons, Thomas, 111n
Sandusky, 220, 224-25, 325
Savage, William, 43
Scott, Charles, 185, 212-13
Scott, Winfield, 333, 400, 402, 428, 459, 467
Seamen's Bill (1813), 295-97, 301, 305
Sedition Law (1798), 259
Sérurier, Louis, 57, 70, 97, 99-100, 106, 109, 366, 395-96, 411, 416, 432n, 435n, 473, 486
Sevier, John, 357, 360n
Sharp, Solomon, 452
Shaw, Samuel, 102
Shawnee Indians, 178-80, 182, 206
Sheffield, first earl of, *see* Holroyd, John Baker

Shelby, Isaac, 202n, 211-12, 215, 217, 220-21, 225, 322-24, 326-30
Sheldon, Daniel, 379
Sherbrooke, Sir John Coape, 473
Short, William, 392
Simcoe, John Graves, 32
Simmonds, Jonas, 176
Sinclair, Andrew, 390
slave revolt, fear of, 272, 382, 393, 410, 412, 485, 493
Smilie, John, 97, 147, 227
Smith, Adam, 13n
Smith, John, 54n, 285-86
Smith, John Spear, 71n, 311
Smith, Joseph, 479
Smith, Robert: quarrels with Madison, 56-57, 60-61, 65-66, 71-73, 79, 311; Secretary of State, 27n, 49-50, 52, 56-57, 63-64, 74, 77, 81, 117, 141, 146, 191n, 506
Smith, Samuel, 49-50, 52-54, 58, 61, 73-74, 81, 83, 85, 88n, 95, 99, 101-2, 113, 115, 117, 311n, 316n, 364-65, 410, 415, 421, 426, 428, 500
smuggling, into and from Canada, 23n, 29-31, 36, 42-43, 78, 81-82, 139, 264, 274, 364, 380, 470-71, 476
Smyth, Alexander, 169, 242, 244, 311; in Niagara campaign, 244-45, 249-52, 281
Snyder, Simon, 67, 83, 92, 244, 411-12, 414, 425-26, 468
Southwick, Solomon, 238
Spain, U.S. relations with, 17, 18, 21n, 98, 132, 141, 183, 302, 352-53, 486, 490-91
Spence, William, 33n
Spencer, Ambrose, 63, 66, 103-4, 116, 236, 239-40, 283, 286, 333, 371, 400, 422, 434
Spencer, John Canfield, 238, 246-47, 288
Speyer, John, 312
Stanford, Richard, 111-12, 316, 364n
state forces, 464-65, 482. See also militia, state; volunteering
Stephen, James, 19, 37, 44
Steuart, James, 15n
Steuben, Baron Frederick, 143, 311
Stevenson, John, 10n
Stickney, Benjamin F., 228-29
Stone, David, 316n, 365, 385

Stony Creek, battle of (1813), 334, 413
Story, Joseph, 259
Strong, Caleb, 258, 260-63, 472, 473n, 475-76
substitutes (militia), 172
Superintendent of Military Stores, 123, 158, 161, 280n. See also Irvine, Callender
Superintendent of Military Supplies, 280n
Sverchkov, Aleksei, 300
Swartwout, Robert, 287n, 340, 481-83
Sweden, U.S. relations with, 305-6, 310-12, 314, 374
Swift, Joseph, 372

Taggart, Samuel, 377
Talladega, battle of (1813), 355
Tallapoosa River, 349, 356, 361
Tallman, Peleg, 111-12
Tallushatchee, battle of (1813), 355
Tatham, William, 412-13
taxation, 88-90, 93, 151-52, 154, 292-93, 295, 304-5, 308, 310, 314-16, 319, 375, 437, 439-41, 465, 472, 482
Taylor, Creed, 81
Taylor, James, 204
Taylor, John (of Caroline), 93, 274
Taylor, John (of New York), 239, 370-71, 373, 375, 378, 447
Taylor, John (of South Carolina), 28n
Tazewell, Littleton W., 516n
Tecumseh, 179-80, 182-83, 185, 189, 199-200, 203, 212, 216, 220, 330, 350-52
Tennessee: in Creek war, 349, 351, 353-60; in New Orleans campaign, 490-91, 497
Thames, battle of (1813), 202n, 330, 398
Thorndike, Israel, 260
Thornton, Anna, 419
Tiffin, Edward, 196
Tippecanoe, battle of (1811), 185-89, 191, 193
Tompkins, Daniel D., 103-4, 167, 282; as war governor, 235-41, 243, 245, 247-48, 285, 287, 335-36, 370-71, 381, 433-34, 478-79, 511n
Treasury Department, 22, 30, 44, 90, 91, 105, 128, 130, 137, 154, 161, 219,

298, 304, 314, 316-17, 375, 377, 397n, 433, 437-39, 445, 465, 504. *See also* Campbell, George Washington; Gallatin, Albert; Jones, William
Treasury notes, 154, 292, 294, 437-43, 445-46, 448-50, 475, 489
Treaty of Fort Jackson (1814), 361-62, 489
Treaty of Fort Wayne (1809), 177, 179, 181-82
Treaty of Ghent (1814), xi, 452, 468, 483, 486, 499, 500, 503, 510
Treaty of Greenville (1795), 177-80, 197, 206
Treaty of San Ildefonso (1803), 485
Treaty of Tilsit (1807), 22n, 520
Trescott, Lemuel, 231, 263
Troup, George, 460, 461, 463
Tucker, Josiah, 13n
Turner, James, 165, 365
Turreau, Louis Marie, 57
Two Million Act (1806), 21

Uniform Militia Act (1792), 124, 132, 136, 143, 198
Upper Canada, *see* Canada
U.S.S. *Hornet*, 84-85, 91, 96, 101, 106-7, 109
U.S.S. *Louisiana*, 498

Van Buren, Martin, 116, 288
Van Cortlandt, Pierre, Jr., 111n, 234
Van Horne, Thomas, 203
Van Ness, John P., 411, 414
Van Rensselaer, Solomon, 247
Van Rensselaer, Stephen, 241-42, 244-49, 252, 268, 285
Varnum, Joseph, 133, 262, 319n, 462
Villeré Canal, 497
Vincennes, 178, 183-85, 187, 196
Virginia, attitudes to war in, 272, 382, 410, 412, 454, 465
Virginia Argus, 44, 92, 320
Virginia Port Bill (1784), 10, 12
Vittoria, battle of (1813), 319
volunteering, 121, 124, 133, 136-40, 145, 147-49, 163, 322, 460-61, 464-68, 475, 483, 524
Volunteer Law: of 1812, 87-88, 95, 147-

49, 153, 163, 194, 238, 258, 263-64, 274, 279; of 1815, 466

Wabash River, 178-80, 182-83, 185, 200, 212-13, 216, 220
Wadsworth, Decius, 159
Walbach, John B., 168
Walsh, Paddy, 351
Warden, David Baillie, 58n
War Department, xii, 4, 23, 123, 125, 128, 130, 136-40, 146, 154-56, 158, 161-64, 166, 169-71, 174-76, 183, 210, 236-37, 242, 244, 251, 271, 276-78, 282, 284, 310, 321, 330, 334, 398-99, 406-7, 411-12, 424, 427, 454, 456-58, 460, 466, 505. *See also* Armstrong, John; Eustis, William; Monroe, James
War in Disguise, 19, 37
war loans, 151, 294, 298, 375-80, 384-85, 397n, 437, 440-41, 446
Warren, Sir John Borlase, 300
Washington, fall of (1814): 408-9, 411-19, 421, 423, 436
Washington Benevolent Society, 256
Washington, George, 121, 123-24
Waterhouse, Benjamin, 198
Wayne, Anthony, 183, 187
Wea Indians, 185
Weatherford, William, 354
Webster, Daniel, 305-6, 448, 450n, 464n; resolutions of (1813), 307-9
Wellesley, Lord Richard, 68, 79, 97
Wellington, Duke of, 411, 500, 512
Wells, Samuel, 209
West Florida, 279, 348, 352, 486, 489. *See also* Spain, U.S. relations with
West India interest, 18-20, 25, 29, 33, 36-37, 39
West India Reciprocity Agreement (1830), xii, 514, 517
West India trade, xii, 7, 14, 18-20, 26-27, 34, 36-37, 42, 44, 76n, 275, 510, 512-15
West Indies, 11n, 14, 15, 18-20, 22-23, 27, 33, 36, 43, 45-46, 275, 302, 318, 513-16, 519-20, 522
Whiskey Rebellion (1794), 126-27
White, James, 218
Wilkinson, James, 25n, 131, 144, 164,

Wilkinson, James (*cont.*)
277, 330-31; in 1813 campaign, 331-
32, 336-48, 365-67, 387-88, 400
Williams, David R., 149, 276, 281
Williams, John, 420, 429n
Winchester, James, 166, 201, 208-11,
213-17, 220, 224-25, 491
Winder, Levin, 408, 415
Winder, William, 333-34, 385, 426; and
fall of Washington, 408-9, 412-20
Winnebago Indians, 179, 186

Wirt, William, 472
Witherell, William, 205n
Worthington, Thomas, 114, 163, 175,
188-89, 192, 194, 196, 198, 200-201,
206-7, 219, 223, 294n, 318, 428, 431
Wright, Robert, 307n
Wyandot Indians, 179, 206, 225

Yeo, Sir James Lucas, 335, 340
York, 284, 286, 331, 333, 390, 401-2
Young, Arthur, 10n

Library of Congress Cataloging in Publication Data

Stagg, J. C. A. (John Charles Anderson), 1945-
Mr. Madison's war.

Includes index.
1. United States—Politics and government—War of 1812.
2. United States—History—War of 1812—Causes.
3. Madison, James, 1751-1836. 4. United States—Politics
and government—1789-1815. I. Title.
E357.S79 1983   973.5   82-61386
ISBN 0-691-04702-2
ISBN 0-691-10150-7 (pbk.)